Contributions to Finance and Accounting

The book series 'Contributions to Finance and Accounting' features the latest research from research areas like financial management, investment, capital markets, financial institutions, FinTech and financial innovation, accounting methods and standards, reporting, and corporate governance, among others. Books published in this series are primarily monographs and edited volumes that present new research results, both theoretical and empirical, on a clearly defined topic. All books are published in print and digital formats and disseminated globally.

Duncan Smith

Fraud and Corruption

Cases and Materials

Duncan Smith
European Investment Bank
Luxembourg, Luxembourg

ISSN 2730-6038 ISSN 2730-6046 (electronic)
Contributions to Finance and Accounting
ISBN 978-3-031-10062-8 ISBN 978-3-031-10063-5 (eBook)
https://doi.org/10.1007/978-3-031-10063-5

© The Editor(s) (if applicable) and The Author(s), under exclusive license to Springer Nature Switzerland AG 2022

This work is subject to copyright. All rights are solely and exclusively licensed by the Publisher, whether the whole or part of the material is concerned, specifically the rights of translation, reprinting, reuse of illustrations, recitation, broadcasting, reproduction on microfilms or in any other physical way, and transmission or information storage and retrieval, electronic adaptation, computer software, or by similar or dissimilar methodology now known or hereafter developed.

The use of general descriptive names, registered names, trademarks, service marks, etc. in this publication does not imply, even in the absence of a specific statement, that such names are exempt from the relevant protective laws and regulations and therefore free for general use.

The publisher, the authors, and the editors are safe to assume that the advice and information in this book are believed to be true and accurate at the date of publication. Neither the publisher nor the authors or the editors give a warranty, expressed or implied, with respect to the material contained herein or for any errors or omissions that may have been made. The publisher remains neutral with regard to jurisdictional claims in published maps and institutional affiliations.

This Springer imprint is published by the registered company Springer Nature Switzerland AG
The registered company address is: Gewerbestrasse 11, 6330 Cham, Switzerland

Foreword

This collection of some 30 case studies compiled by Duncan Smith is impressive in terms of both its breadth and selection method chosen by the author. The collection consists of original texts with appropriate commentary by the author. Apart from detailing the examples of fraud and corruption, the contents of this work include international regulatory measures, official policies plus some key "local" legislation, such as the UK Bribery Act 2010.

The text places its focus on treatment of the complex issue of the incidence and regulation of fraud and corruption. "Fraud" is widely defined so as to include diverse aspects such as counterfeiting, identity theft, and investment fraud. It thus examines the phenomenon of fraud from a variety of operational perspectives and by reference to real cases. The author's examination of the modus operandi of fraud from a business sectoral context is helpful. Sectors under the microscope include construction, manufacturing, financial services, transport, communications, education, health, energy, retail, and the military arena sector. Smith eschews jurisdictional barriers and covers case studies from a wide range of contexts. In our modern globalized world where multinationals predominate, this methodology is entirely appropriate. The diverse case studies illuminate the extent of this problem of fraud and corruption in modern times. The usual suspects are included, alongside some less notorious incidences of fraud. The text concludes with an interesting "filmography" section listing movies where the fraud/corruption scenario has featured.

Readers of this collection will gain immensely from the insights offered by Duncan Smith. In my considered opinion, it provides an invaluable collection of source material which can be used to good effect by researchers and policymakers in the years to come.

Law School, University of Lancaster, David Milman
Lancaster, UK

Acknowledgments

This book demonstrates that there are many devious and deceitful people in the world today who seek to misuse their position, power, influence, and the trust of others to benefit themselves and their family and friends. However, there are also lots of good, decent people, and organizations working with honesty and integrity for the betterment of humanity.

I am wholeheartedly grateful to my family (Ella, Kirsty, Laura & Jo) for their love and support, especially since my serious cycling accident in 2018. My colleagues in the EIB and more broadly the MDBs (too many to name here but some of whom are identified in the Acknowledgments in my earlier book: *Promoting Integrity in the Work of International Organisations: Minimising Fraud and Corruption in Projects*) also deserve my gratitude for their support and assistance.

As a result of the UN Convention Against Corruption and the endeavours of the World Economic Forum PACI, OECD, B20, Transparency International, FCPA Blog, Basel Institute on Governance, law enforcement/ prosecutors/ judges, compliance teams and many others, there are many people promoting integrity in international development work and more generally in economies around the world. There is excellent progress but it remains a costly and time-consuming process.

The text is correct as of January 1, 2022 (please check the websites for recent updates and corrections). Although I work at EIB, I wrote the book in a personal capacity.

Quote:
Power tends to corrupt, and absolute power corrupts absolutely...
John Emerich Edward Dalberg-Acton, 1st Baron Acton, 13th Marquess of Groppoli, KCVO, DL (10 January 1834–19 June 1902) was an English Catholic historian, politician, and writer and is perhaps best known for this remark.

Contents

1 Introduction ... 1
   1.1 What Is Fraud and Corruption? ... 1

Part I Fraud and Corruption Cases

2 Construction/Manufacturing ... 15
   2.1 Siemens ... 15
      2.1.1 Text from the Website of the US Department of Justice ... 15
      2.1.2 Text from the US Department of Justice Website ... 17
      2.1.3 The Following Text is from the EIB Website (18/1/2020): ... 18
      2.1.4 The Following Text is from Siemens' Website ... 19
   2.2 Alstom ... 21
      2.2.1 Text from the US Department of Justice (DoJ) Website ... 21
      2.2.2 Text from the Website of the UK SFO ... 23
      2.2.3 Text from the Website of the UK SFO ... 24
      2.2.4 Text from EIB Website (8/1/22) ... 26
      2.2.5 Text from the EBRD's Website (3/12/2019) ... 27
      2.2.6 Text from the AfDB's Website ... 28
      2.2.7 Also, Text from the FCPA Blog (www.fcpablog.com) Article ... 29
   2.3 SNC Lavalin ... 31
      2.3.1 Text is an excerpt from Wikipedia (on 30/11/19) ... 31
      2.3.2 Text from the World Bank Website (14 January 2020) ... 33
   2.4 Wasim Tappuni ... 34
      2.4.1 Text from the UK's City of London Police Website ... 34
   2.5 Odebrecht/Braskem ... 36

		2.5.1	Text from BBC News Website	36
		2.5.2	Text from the US DoJ Website	36
		2.5.3	Text from the US DoJ Website	41
		2.5.4	From the US Department of Justice Website	43
		2.5.5	From IDB's Website	45
3	**Financial Services**			47
	3.1	Malaysia Development Berhad		47
		3.1.1	Text from Wikipedia (January 21, 2022)	47
		3.1.2	Text from US Department of Justice Website (January 21, 2022)	76
		3.1.3	Text from US Department of Justice Website (January 21, 2022)	79
	3.2	Goldman Sachs: 1MDB		81
		3.2.1	Text from US Department of Justice Website (11 February 2022)	81
	3.3	Bernard L Madoff		85
		3.3.1	Text from Wikipedia (January 21, 2022)	85
	3.4	Wells Fargo		130
		3.4.1	Text from Wikipedia (January 23, 2022)	130
	3.5	NatWest		139
		3.5.1	Text from the US Department of Justice	139
	3.6	Credit Suisse (Mozambique)		140
		3.6.1	Text from US DoJ Website (February 5, 2022)	140
	3.7	Deutsche Bank AG		144
		3.7.1	Text from Wikipedia (February 5, 2022)	144
	3.8	BCCI		147
		3.8.1	Text from Wikipedia (February 5, 2022)	147
4	**Transport**			157
	4.1	Airbus		157
		4.1.1	Text from the US DoJ Website Friday, January 31, 2020	157
	4.2	VW		161
		4.2.1	Text from US Department of Justice	163
		4.2.2	Text from US Department of Justice Website	165
		4.2.3	Text from US Department of Justice Website	168
		4.2.4	Text from EIB's Website	171
	4.3	Rolls Royce		172
		4.3.1	Text from UK SFO Website (February 11, 2022)	172
		4.3.2	Text from UK SFO Website (February 11, 2022):	173
		4.3.3	Text from UK SFO Website (February 11, 2022)	175
		4.3.4	Text from US DoJ Website (February 11, 2022)	176
5	**Communications**			179
	5.1	Ericsson		179

		5.1.1	Text from US Department of Justice Website (January 21, 2022)	179
	5.2	Telia		182
		5.2.1	Text from Wikipedia (22 January 2022)	182
		5.2.2	Text from US Department of Justice Website	185
	5.3	WorldCom		188
		5.3.1	Text from Wikipedia (26 January 2022)	188
6	**Education**			193
	6.1	US College Corruption		193
		6.1.1	Wikipedia Summary of US College Corruption (August 10, 2022)	193
	6.2	Oxford University Press		222
		6.2.1	Text from the Website of the UK SFO	222
7	**Health**			225
	7.1	Fresenius		225
		7.1.1	Text from US DoJ Website	225
		7.1.2	Text from US DoJ Website (February 10, 2022)	227
		7.1.3	Text from US DoJ Website	228
	7.2	HealthSouth		230
		7.2.1	From Wall Street to Prison: The HealthSouth Story	230
	7.3	Guralp		231
		7.3.1	Text from UK SFO Website (February 11, 2022)	231
	7.4	Theranos/Elisabeth Holmes		233
		7.4.1	Text from Wikipedia (February 11, 2022)	233
	References			241
8	**Energy**			249
	8.1	Petrofac Ltd		249
		8.1.1	Text from the UK SFO Website (January 14, 2022)	249
		8.1.2	Text from the SFO Website (14 Jan 2022)	250
		8.1.3	Text from the UK SFO Website (August 11, 2022)	251
	8.2	Enron		252
		8.2.1	Text from Wikipedia (August 11, 2022)	252
	References			275
9	**Retail**			283
	9.1	Walmart Inc.		283
		9.1.1	Text from US Department of Justice Website	283
	9.2	Tesco		286
		9.2.1	Text from UK SFO Website (February 10, 2022)	286
		9.2.2	Text from UK SFO Website (February 10, 2022)	287
		9.2.3	UK SFO Website (February 10, 2022)	288
		9.2.4	Extract from UK SFO Website (February 10, 2022)	289

10	**Military**		295
	10.1	Fat Leonard/US Navy	295
	References		301

Part II Fraud and Corruption Materials

11	**International Treaties/Documents**			309
	11.1	United Nations Convention Against Corruption (UN CAC)		309
12	**Integrity Materials of International Organisations**			381
	12.1	Multilateral Development Bank (MDB) Documents		381
		12.1.1	International Financial Institutions (IFI) Task Force on Anti-Corruption: Uniform Framework Agreement	381
		12.1.2	MDB Cross Debarment Agreement	381
		12.1.3	MDB Harmonised Guidelines	382
	12.2	European Investment Bank (EIB)		382
		12.2.1	Anti-Fraud Policy	382
		12.2.2	Exclusion Policy	383
		12.2.3	List of Settlements and Excluded Entities	383
		12.2.4	Whistleblower Policy	383
		12.2.5	Covenant of Integrity (Annex 5 of the EIB Guide to Procurement)	384
13	**National Legislation**			385
	13.1	UK Bribery Act 2010		385
	13.2	US Foreign and Corrupt Practices Act (FCPA)		400
14	**Other Integrity Materials**			419
	14.1	Corporate Anti-Corruption Policies: FCPA Blog Articles		419
		14.1.1	Benchmarking Alert: Here is 3M's Anti-bribery Policy, Harry Cassin, November 1, 2021	419
		14.1.2	Benchmarking Alert: Here's General Motor's Full Anti-corruption Policy, Harry Cassin, September 1, 2021	420
		14.1.3	Benchmarking Alert: Here's Coca-Cola's Full Anti-bribery Policy, Harry Cassin, July 20, 2021	422
		14.1.4	Benchmarking Alert: Here is Pfizer's Anti-bribery Policy, Harry Cassin, December 20, 2021	423
		14.1.5	Benchmarking Alert: Here's Walmart's Full Global Anti-corruption Policy, Harry Cassin, May 12, 2021	424
		14.1.6	Benchmarking Alert: Here's the Full Airbus Anti-corruption Policy, Harry Cassin, April 28, 2021	425
		14.1.7	Benchmarking Alert: Here's Volkswagen's Full Anti-corruption Policy, Harry Cassin April 8, 2021	427

	14.1.8	Benchmarking Alert: Here's the Full Microsoft Anti-corruption Policy, Harry Cassin, March 24, 2021	428
	14.1.9	Benchmarking Alert: Here's the Full Novartis Anti-bribery Policy, Harry Cassin, March 17, 2021	429
	14.1.10	Benchmarking Alert: Here's Tesla's Full Anti-corruption Policy, Harry Cassin, March 10, 2021	430
	14.1.11	Benchmarking Alert: Here's Apple's Full Anti-corruption Policy, Harry Cassin, March 1, 2021	431
14.2	Lists of Movies	433
	14.2.1	Movies About Fraud and Corruption	433
	14.2.2	Movies about Whistleblowers	436

Chapter 1
Introduction

Fraud and corruption are major problems affecting economies around the world. In some places, the preventive controls and likely regulatory and law enforcement/judicial involvement minimizes it; in others, this is less likely or consistent so fraud and corruption is more likely.

However, whatever the circumstances of each individual transaction, the risk of fraud or corruption can never be completely eradicated as noted by Alan Greenspan (the American economist who served as Chair of the United States Federal Reserve from 1987 to 2006):

> Corruption, embezzlement, fraud, these are all characteristics which exist everywhere. It is regrettably the way human nature functions, whether we like it or not. What successful economies do is keep it to a minimum. No one has ever eliminated any of that stuff.

This book provides cases and materials to facilitate the study of the risks of fraud and corruption, the problems and related issues that can arise as a result of such conduct, as well as a wider consideration of other possible ways to prevent and detect such issues.

1.1 What Is Fraud and Corruption?

In order to obtain a sense of the problem, we first look at two jurisdictions (UK and USA) to see the approach that is taken by domestic law enforcement agencies (UK's Serious Fraud Office or SFO and the National Crime Agency and USA's Department of Justice and Federal Investigation Bureau or US DoJ and FBI, respectively).

After that, we look to see how the major Multilateral Development Banks (MDBs—Asian Development Bank or ADB, African Development Bank or AfDB, European Bank of Reconstruction and Development or EBRD, European Investment Bank or EIB, Inter-American Development Bank or IDB, and the World Bank) define the issues.

(a) The **UK's National Crime Agency** website[1] notes (February 13, 2022) the following:

Fraud

Fraud is the most commonly experienced crime in the UK. Fraud costs the UK many billions of pounds every year. The impact of fraud and related offences such as market abuse and counterfeiting, can be devastating, ranging from unaffordable personal losses suffered by vulnerable victims to impacting the ability of organisations to stay in business.

Data breaches continue to be a key enabler of fraud. Personal and financial information obtained in a breach can be used to commit frauds affecting individuals, the private and public sectors alike. By harvesting personal and financial information through data breaches, criminals are able to commit fraud and damage people, businesses and services.

The most robust figures currently available from the Crime Survey of England and Wales reveal there were 3.4 million incidents of fraud in 2016–17. However we think that fewer than 20% of incidents of fraud are actually reported so the true figure may be much higher. This means that the scale of fraud is very significant, but that under-reporting also hampers our understanding of the threat.

Much of the proceeds will be laundered within the UK or moved overseas. To launder the proceeds of fraud, organised crime groups often use 'mule networks', with bank accounts owned by witting and unwitting members of the public being used to obscure the source and nature of the funds.

Victims of fraud range across vulnerable individuals, major corporations, smaller businesses, as well as the public sector. The 2017 Annual Fraud Indicator estimates fraud losses to the UK at around £190 billion every year, with the private sector hit hardest losing around £140 billion. The public sector may be losing more than £40 billion and individuals around £7 billion.

Businesses and high-net-worth individuals are now also being increasingly targeted due to their larger financial transactions and the greater potential profits for fraudsters. Aside from the financial costs, being a victim of fraud can cause serious reputational damage for businesses. Concern about adverse publicity probably contributes to under-reporting.

Fraud against individuals is typically targeted at elderly and other vulnerable people, for whom the consequences can often be devastating—psychologically as well as financially.

Fraud is increasingly being committed online. Where previously a fraud may have been committed by phone, post or in person, online access enables fraudsters to exploit victims remotely, often from another country. Some investment frauds, and most computer software service fraud, are known to be perpetrated from overseas.

---

[1] https://www.nationalcrimeagency.gov.uk/what-we-do/crime-threats/fraud-and-economic-crime

Crime groups attack the UK public sector and government departments, such as the NHS, and billions are estimated to be lost to tax and benefit fraud each year.

Counterfeit and Pirated Goods

Counterfeit or pirated goods results in lost profits and taxes, and put consumers at risk from poor quality, unsafe goods. Counterfeiting is attractive to organised criminals because it brings high financial return from low investment.

The market for counterfeit currency has changed over the last ten years. High quality counterfeit notes can be produced very quickly by skilled printers using traditional offset lithographic methods. However, organised crime groups are also producing digitally printed fakes, using the latest technology and laser or inkjet printing techniques. Offset lithographic printing remains the more serious threat; notes are of a high quality and can be produced quickly. UK crime groups continue to counterfeit £20 notes, but the problem has reduced with the new £1 coins and the polymer £5 and £10 notes, which have increased security features

Identity Theft

Identity theft occurs when criminals access enough personal information about an individual to commit fraud. They use various techniques to steal these details, from outright theft and social engineering to harvesting data through cybercrime. With this information, criminals can impersonate the victim in order to access bank accounts, fraudulently claim benefits or obtain genuine documents in the victim's name. Criminals are increasingly stealing identity data online, for example persuading individuals to disclose personal details and passwords through 'phishing' emails, and then trading the data.

Our Response to Fraud

We work with partners from across the public, private and third sectors to pursue serious and organised fraudsters, make individuals and businesses more resilient to fraud and other economic crimes, and, wherever possible, to return funds to victims. Our key partners include the Serious Fraud Office, City of London Police (lead police force for fraud), Metropolitan Police Service, Financial Conduct Authority and the National Cyber Security Centre.

The UK National Central Office for the Suppression of Counterfeit Currency and Protected Coins (UKNCO) provides advice and support to UK and international law enforcement about counterfeit currency....

(b) **UK SFO**

In a speech at the Royal United Services Institute in London entitled "Fighting fraud and corruption in a shrinking world"[2] (on April 3, 2019), Lisa Osofsky, Director of the SFO said: (February 13, 2022)

> I applaud the work that the Centre for Financial Crime and Security Studies is doing to address the challenges that financial crime poses to the UK and across the globe. The

---

[2] https://www.sfo.gov.uk/2019/04/03/fighting-fraud-and-corruption-in-a-shrinking-world/

Centre's focus on the public and private sectors to transform the ways we disrupt financial crime is key to tackling this threat.

... the damage that fraud, corruption and money laundering do, to society and its citizens, often in the poorest parts of the world, but also to our own people and markets, as well as to democracy and the rule of law. I know you understand not only the scale of the challenge law enforcement faces in combatting these crimes but also how quickly those challenges evolve and change in our globalized and digital world...

The SFO's Remit

The SFO's remit is to investigate and prosecute the most difficult kinds of fraud and corruption. We focus on cases with great harm and complexity, those that may undermine the integrity of our economy and markets. And unusually for UK law enforcement, we operate in multidisciplinary teams with investigators, accountants, prosecutors and other specialists working together through the lifetime of the case—from investigation through prosecution.

This last is crucial ... I have recently updated my Statement of Principle, which guides my decisions on which cases to investigate, to emphasise this: we take on those cases that require the SFO's unique multidisciplinary structure and approach...

The increasingly transnational nature of serious economic crime—including the ease and speed with which criminals transfer money across borders—means criminal funds can travel through more complex structures further and faster. This makes it harder to trace and harder to detect in our "shrinking world."

So there is a double challenge to law enforcement: we need to cooperate more effectively across jurisdictions while the quantity of data is increasing exponentially. We need technological solutions to address technological hurdles...

... in meeting these challenges, the collective hand of law enforcement, at least, has some strong cards. The people in our sector have a common mission. We are, or can become, natural allies, not competitors. We want the same thing—to make our shared world a better place by bringing to justice those who seek to profit through fraud and corruption. By any rational assessment, there's plenty of work to go around...

... (and) differences in the rules of engagement, national law and procedure can hinder or limit how we cooperate—if we let them.

We need to understand the differences embedded in different nations' legal systems. Cases are often reported to multiple law enforcement agencies and regulators simultaneously; at times, cases are reported publicly.

Corporate entities who wish to cooperate with law enforcement look for certainty about who they are dealing with and to whom they should be providing data and information. There can be—and there are—weighty differences in how different countries' laws protect their citizens. Countries deeply committed to human rights, the rule of law, and to expunging corruption can have very different rules as to how to do it....

There is a community—made up of the public, private, academic and civil society—that cares deeply about the damage that fraud and corruption inflicts. Organised criminals exploit international gaps; they react quickly to embrace new technologies; and they don't have to follow legal rules or norms when relentlessly pursuing their goals...

(c) **US Department of Justice (US DoJ)** website notes[3] (February 13, 2022):

About the Fraud Section

The Fraud Section plays a unique and essential role in the Department's fight against sophisticated economic crime. The Section investigates and prosecutes complex white collar crime cases throughout the country. The Section is uniquely qualified to act in that capacity, based on its vast experience with sophisticated fraud schemes; its expertise in managing complex and multi-district litigation; and its ability to deploy resources effectively to address law enforcement priorities and respond to geographically shifting crime problems.

These capabilities are an essential complement to the efforts of the United States Attorneys' Offices to combat white-collar crime. The Fraud Section also plays a critical role in the development of Department policy. The Section implements enforcement initiatives and advises the Department leadership on such matters as legislation, crime prevention, and public education. The Section frequently coordinates interagency and multi-district investigations and international enforcement efforts.

The Section assists prosecutors, regulators, law enforcement and the private sector by providing training, advice and other assistance. The Section, often in a leadership capacity, participates in numerous national, regional and international working groups.

To fulfill its mission, the Fraud Section seeks to build and enhance its most valuable resources by maximizing opportunities for its dedicated professionals. By providing direct supervision, training and mentoring for its attorneys and other professionals, the Section seeks effectively to develop the knowledge, skills and judgment required to fulfill its unique and important mission.

(d) The **US FBI** website[4] noted (February 13, 2022)

White-Collar Crime

Reportedly coined in 1939, the term white-collar crime is now synonymous with the full range of frauds committed by business and government professionals. These crimes are characterized by deceit, concealment, or violation of trust and are not dependent on the application or threat of physical force or violence. The motivation behind these crimes is financial—to obtain or avoid losing money, property, or services or to secure a personal or business advantage.

---

[3] https://www.justice.gov/criminal-fraud
[4] https://www.fbi.gov/investigate/white-collar-crime

These are not victimless crimes. A single scam can destroy a company, devastate families by wiping out their life savings, or cost investors billions of dollars (or even all three). Today's fraud schemes are more sophisticated than ever, and the FBI is dedicated to using its skills to track down the culprits and stop scams before they start.

The FBI's white-collar crime work integrates the analysis of intelligence with its investigations of criminal activities such as public corruption, money laundering, corporate fraud, securities and commodities fraud, mortgage fraud, financial institution fraud, bank fraud and embezzlement, fraud against the government, election law violations, mass marketing fraud, and health care fraud. The FBI generally focuses on complex investigations—often with a nexus to organized crime activities—that are international, national, or regional in scope and where the FBI can bring to bear unique expertise or capabilities that increase the likelihood of successful investigations.

FBI special agents work closely with partner law enforcement and regulatory agencies such as the Securities and Exchange Commission, the Internal Revenue Service, the U.S. Postal Inspection Service, the Commodity Futures Trading Commission, and the Treasury Department's Financial Crimes Enforcement Network, among others, targeting sophisticated, multi-layered fraud cases that harm the economy.

Major Threats & Programs
Corporate Fraud

Corporate fraud continues to be one of the FBI's highest criminal priorities—in addition to causing significant financial losses to investors, corporate fraud has the potential to cause immeasurable damage to the U.S. economy and investor confidence. As the lead agency investigating corporate fraud, the Bureau focuses its efforts on cases that involve accounting schemes, self-dealing by corporate executives, and obstruction of justice.

The majority of corporate fraud cases pursued by the FBI involve accounting schemes designed to deceive investors, auditors, and analysts about the true financial condition of a corporation or business entity. Through the manipulation of financial data, the share price, or other valuation measurements of a corporation, financial performance may remain artificially inflated based on fictitious performance indicators provided to the investing public.

The FBI's corporate fraud investigations primarily focus on the following activities:

- Falsification of financial information
- False accounting entries and/or misrepresentations of financial condition;
- Fraudulent trades designed to inflate profits or hide losses; and
- Illicit transactions designed to evade regulatory oversight.
- Self-dealing by corporate insiders
- Insider trading (trading based on material, non-public information);
- Kickbacks;
- Misuse of corporate property for personal gain; and

1.1 What Is Fraud and Corruption?

- Individual tax violations related to self-dealing.
- Fraud in connection with an otherwise legitimately operated mutual hedge fund
- Late trading;
- Certain market timing schemes; and
- Falsification of net asset values.

Obstruction of justice designed to conceal any of the above-noted types of criminal conduct, particularly when the obstruction impedes the inquiries of the U.S. Securities and Exchange Commission (SEC), Commodity Futures Trading Commission (CFTC), other regulatory agencies, and/or law enforcement agencies.

The FBI has formed partnerships with numerous agencies to capitalize on their experience in specific areas such as securities, taxes, pensions, energy, and commodities. The Bureau has placed greater emphasis on investigating allegations of these frauds by working closely with the SEC, CFTC, Financial Industry Regulatory Authority, Internal Revenue Service, Department of Labor, Federal Energy Regulatory Commission, and the U.S. Postal Inspection Service.

Asset Forfeiture

Asset forfeiture is a powerful tool used by law enforcement agencies, including the FBI, against criminals and criminal...

Financial Institution/Mortgage Fraud

The FBI is committed to aggressively pursuing those who endanger the stability of our banking system and the...

Health Care Fraud

Health care fraud is not a victimless crime. It affects everyone causes tens of billions of dollars in losses each...

Identity Theft

Identity theft occurs when someone assumes your identity to perform a fraud or other criminal act. Criminals can get the information they need to assume your identity from a variety...

Intellectual Property Theft/Piracy

Preventing intellectual property theft is a priority of the FBI's criminal investigative program. It specifically focuses on...

Election Crimes and Security

Fair elections are the foundation of our democracy, and the FBI is committed to protecting the rights of...

Money Laundering

Money laundering is the process by which criminals conceal or disguise their proceeds and Stock image of a glass globe atop a trail of money. make them appear to have come from legitimate sources.

Money laundering allows criminals to hide and accumulate wealth, avoid prosecution, evade taxes, increase profits through reinvestment, and fund further criminal activity.

While many definitions for money laundering exist, it can be defined very simply as turning "dirty" money into "clean" money. And it is a significant crime—money laundering can undermine the integrity and stability of financial institutions and systems, discourage foreign investment, and distort international capital flows.

The FBI focuses its efforts on money laundering facilitation, targeting professional money launderers, key facilitators, gatekeepers, and complicit financial institutions, among others.

Money laundering is usually associated with crimes that provide a financial gain, and criminals who engage in money laundering derive their proceeds in many ways. Some of their crimes include:

- Complex financial crimes
- Health care fraud
- Human trafficking
- International and domestic public corruption
- Narcotics trafficking
- Terrorism

The number and variety of methods used by criminals to launder money make it difficult to provide a complete listing, but here are a few of the ways through which criminals launder their illicit proceeds:

- Financial institutions
- International trade
- Precious metals
- Real estate
- Third-party service providers
- Virtual currency

There are three steps in the money laundering process—placement, layering, and integration. Placement represents the initial entry of the criminal's proceeds into the financial system. Layering is the most complex and often entails the international movement of funds. Layering separates the criminal's proceeds from their original source and creates a complex audit trail through a series of financial transactions. And integration occurs when the criminal's proceeds are returned to the criminal from what appear to be legitimate sources.

Detection and Deterrence

Money laundering is a massive and evolving challenge that requires collaboration on every level. The FBI regularly coordinates with:

- Other federal, state, and local law enforcement agencies to detect and deter the money laundering threat in the USA;
- Our international partners to help address the increasingly complex global financial system, the cross-border nature of many financial transactions, and the increased sophistication of many money laundering operations; and
- All aspects of industry touched by the money laundering efforts of criminals.

Securities and Commodities Fraud

The continuing integration of global capital markets has created unprecedented opportunities for U.S. businesses to access capital and investors to diversify their portfolios. Whether through individual brokerage accounts, college savings plans, or retirement accounts, more and more Americans are choosing to invest in the U.-S. securities and commodities markets. This growth has led to a corresponding rise in the amount of fraud and misconduct seen in these markets. The creation of complex investment vehicles and the tremendous increase in the amount of money being invested have created greater opportunities for individuals and businesses to perpetrate fraudulent investment schemes.

The following are the most prevalent types of securities and commodities fraud schemes:

- **Investment fraud**: These schemes—sometimes referred to as "high-yield investment fraud"—involve the illegal sale or purported sale of financial instruments. The typical investment fraud schemes are characterized by offers of low- or no-risk investments, guaranteed returns, overly consistent returns, complex strategies, or unregistered securities. These schemes often seek to victimize affinity groups—such as groups with a common religion or ethnicity—to utilize the common interests to build trust to effectively operate the investment fraud against them. The perpetrators range from professional investment advisers to persons trusted and interacted with daily, such as a neighbor or sports coach. The fraudster's ability to foster trust makes these schemes so successful. Investors should use scrutiny and gather as much information as possible before entering into any new investment opportunities. Here are some examples of the most common types of investment fraud schemes:
- **Ponzi schemes**: These schemes involve the payment of purported returns to existing investors from funds contributed by new investors. Ponzi schemes often share common Stock image characteristics, such as offering overly consistent returns, unregistered investments, high returns with little or no risk, or secretive or complex strategies.
- **Pyramid schemes**: In these schemes, as in Ponzi schemes, money collected from new participants is paid to earlier participants. In pyramid schemes, however, participants receive commissions for recruiting new participants into the scheme. Pyramid schemes are frequently disguised as multi-level marketing programs.
- **Prime bank investment fraud/trading program fraud**: In these schemes, perpetrators claim to have access to a secret trading program endorsed by large financial institutions such as the Federal Reserve Bank, Treasury Department, World Bank, International Monetary Fund, etc. Victims are often drawn into prime bank investment frauds because the criminals use sophisticated terms and legal-looking documents and also claim that the investments are insured against loss.
- **Advance fee fraud**: Advance fee schemes require victims to pay upfront fees in the hope of realizing much larger gains. Typically, victims are told that in order to participate in a lucrative investment program or receive the prize from a lottery/

sweepstakes, they must first send funds to cover a cost, often disguised as a tax or participation fee. After the first payment, the perpetrator will request additional funds for other "unanticipated" costs.
- **Promissory note fraud**: These are generally short-term debt instruments issued by little-known or nonexistent companies. The notes typically promise a high rate of return with little or no risk. Fraudsters may use promissory notes in an effort to avoid regulatory scrutiny; however, most promissory notes are securities and need to be registered with the Securities and Exchange Commission and the states in which they are being sold.
- **Commodities fraud**: Commodities fraud is the illegal sale or purported sale of raw materials or semi-finished goods that are relatively uniform in nature and are sold on an exchange (e.g., gold, pork bellies, orange juice, and coffee). The perpetrators of commodities fraud entice investors through false claims and high-pressure sales tactics. Often in these frauds, the perpetrators create artificial account statements that reflect purported investments when, in reality, no such investments have been made. Instead, the money has been diverted for the perpetrators' use. Additionally, they may trade excessively merely to generate commissions for themselves (known as "churning"). Two common types of commodities fraud include investments in the foreign currency exchange (Forex) and into precious metals (e.g., gold and silver).
- **Broker embezzlement**: These schemes involve illicit and unauthorized actions by brokers to steal directly from their clients. Such schemes may be facilitated by the forging of client documents, doctoring of account statements, unauthorized trading/funds transfer activities, or other conduct in breach of the broker's fiduciary responsibilities to the victim client.
- **Market manipulation**: These "pump and dump" schemes are based on the manipulation of lower-volume stocks on small over-the-counter markets. The basic goal of market manipulation frauds is to artificially inflate the price of the penny stocks so that the conspirators can sell their shares at a large profit. The "pump" involves recruiting unwitting investors through false or deceptive sales practices, public information, or corporate filings. Many of these schemes use boiler room methods where brokers—who are bribed by the conspirators—use high-pressure sale tactics to increase the number of investors and, as a result, raise the price of the stock. Once the target price is achieved, the perpetrators "dump" their shares at a huge profit and leave innocent investors to foot the bill.

The FBI anticipates that the variety of securities and commodities fraud schemes will continue to grow as investors remain susceptible to the uncertainty of the global economy. To investigate and help prevent fraudulent activity in the financial markets, the Bureau continues to work closely with various governmental and private entities. For example:

FBI field offices operate task forces and working groups with other law enforcement and regulatory agencies, including:

- the Securities and Exchange Commission,
- U.S. Attorney's Offices,

1.1 What Is Fraud and Corruption?

- Commodity Futures Trading Commission,
- Financial Industry Regulatory Authority,
- U.S. Postal Inspection Service, and
- the Internal Revenue Service;

And nationally, the FBI participates in several working groups and task forces such as the Financial Fraud Enforcement Task Force, which coordinates the efforts of the Department of Justice at all levels of government to disrupt and dismantle significant large-scale criminal enterprises.

(e) **International Impact**

A number of cases have a major international element (while others are almost entirely based in one legal jurisdiction). In international cases, fraud and corruption issues can be pursued by law enforcement organizations in the various affected jurisdictions. In addition, fraud and corruption may also be investigated and sanctioned by the MDBs (or other international organizations) if their financing or activities are involved.

The six major MDBs harmonized the definitions of fraud and corruption in the **IFI Anti-Corruption Task Force's Uniform Framework** agreement that was signed by the International Financial Institutions (or IFIs) presidents in September 2006[5] as reflected in the following text:

> Critical to the success of a harmonized approach is a common understanding of the practices prohibited. To this end, the Task Force has agreed in principle on the following standardized definitions of fraudulent and corrupt practices for investigating such practices in activities financed by the member institutions.
> - A **corrupt practice** is the offering, giving, receiving, or soliciting, directly or indirectly, anything of value to influence improperly the actions of another party.
> - A **fraudulent practice** is any act or omission, including a misrepresentation, that knowingly or recklessly misleads, or attempts to mislead, a party to obtain a financial or other benefit or to avoid an obligation.
> - A **coercive practice** is impairing or harming, or threatening to impair or harm, directly or indirectly, any party or the property of the party to influence improperly the actions of a party.
> - A **collusive practice** is an arrangement between two or more parties designed to achieve an improper purpose, including influencing improperly the actions of another party.
>
> Each of the member institutions will determine implementation within its relevant policies and procedures, and consistent with international conventions.

Since the Uniform Framework was agreed in 2006, the MDBs have also harmonized the definition of obstruction[6] (February 13, 2022) such as included by EIB in the Anti-Fraud Policy:

---

[5] https://www.eib.org/attachments/general/uniform_framework_en.pdf

[6] https://www.eib.org/attachments/publications/eib_group_anti-fraud_policy_en.pdf

An **obstructive practice** which means (a) destroying, falsifying, altering or concealing of evidence material to the investigation, or making false statements to investigators, with the intent to impede the investigation; (b) threatening, harassing or intimidating any party to prevent it from disclosing its knowledge of matters relevant to the investigation or from pursuing the investigation; or (c) acts intended to impede the exercise of the EIB Group's contractual rights of audit or inspection or access to information.

Involvement of Law Enforcement

Depending on the jurisdiction(s) affected and the law enforcement agency(ies) concerned, there may be certain distinct criminal law and/or regulatory provisions applying to the way in which an agency can conduct the investigation.

For example, UK Serious Fraud Office investigators can question (and request relevant documents from) witnesses and suspects about issues which are under investigation by using section 2 powers, which requires disclosure irrespective of sensitivity or commercial confidentiality.

In terms of case management and charging offenders, the USA's Department of Justice and FBI may take a "start at the bottom and work up as far as the criminality goes" approach which, if it works, can see senior managers and chief corporate officers implicated in corporate criminal wrongdoing.

Different Sectors

Fraud and corruption can impact a wide range of circumstances and situations. Consequently, there are a large number of sectors and industrial processes that have been affected, including transport, pharmaceuticals, construction, manufacturing, health/medical equipment, communications, education, and even the military as demonstrated by the cases included in this book.

Replication of Text

Please note that the text in this book is collected and reproduced from the publicly-accessible websites of a number of organisations', in fairness to all parties involved in the cases. The date at which the text has been transferred and the link to the website are both included.

If necessary, please check the website for updates.

Part I
Fraud and Corruption Cases

Chapter 2
Construction/Manufacturing

2.1 Siemens

2.1.1 Text from the Website of the US Department of Justice[1]

Siemens Aktiengesellschaft (Siemens AG), a German corporation, and three of its subsidiaries today pleaded guilty to violations of and charges related to the Foreign Corrupt Practices Act (FCPA), the US Department of Justice and US Securities and Exchange Commission announced.

At a hearing before US District Judge Richard J. Leon in the District of Columbia, Siemens AG pleaded guilty to a two-count information charging criminal violations of the FCPA's internal controls and books and records provisions. Siemens S.A.—Argentina (Siemens Argentina) pleaded guilty to a one-count information charging conspiracy to violate the books and records provisions of the FCPA. Siemens Bangladesh Limited (Siemens Bangladesh) and Siemens S.A.—Venezuela (Siemens Venezuela), each pleaded guilty to separate one-count informations charging conspiracy to violate the anti-bribery and books and records provisions of the FCPA. As part of the plea agreements, Siemens AG agreed to pay a $448.5 million fine; and Siemens Argentina, Bangladesh, and Venezuela each agreed to pay a $500,000 fine, for a combined total criminal fine of $450 million.

According to court documents, beginning in the mid-1990s, Siemens AG engaged in systematic efforts to falsify its corporate books and records and knowingly failed to implement and circumvent existing internal controls. As a result of Siemens AG's knowing failures in and circumvention of internal controls, from the time of its listing on the New York Stock Exchange on March 12, 2001, through approximately 2007, Siemens AG made payments totalling approximately $1.36 billion through various mechanisms. Of this amount, approximately $554.5 million was paid for unknown purposes, including approximately $341 million in direct

---

[1] https://www.justice.gov/archive/opa/pr/2008/December/08-crm-1105.html

© The Author(s), under exclusive license to Springer Nature Switzerland AG 2022
D. Smith, *Fraud and Corruption*, Contributions to Finance and Accounting,
https://doi.org/10.1007/978-3-031-10063-5_2

payments to business consultants for unknown purposes. The remaining $805.5 million of this amount was intended in whole or in part as corrupt payments to foreign officials through the payment mechanisms, which included cash desks and slush funds.

From 2000 to 2002, four Siemens AG subsidiaries—Siemens S.A.S. of France (Siemens France), Siemens Sanayi ve Ticaret A.S. of Turkey (Siemens Turkey), Osram Middle East FZE (Osram Middle East) and Gas Turbine Technologies S.p.A. (GTT)—each wholly owned by Siemens AG or one of its subsidiaries, were awarded 42 contracts with a combined value of more than $80 million with the Ministries of Electricity and Oil of the government of the Republic of Iraq under the United Nations Oil for Food Program. To obtain these contracts, Siemens France, Siemens Turkey, Osram Middle East and GTT paid a total of at least $1,736,076 in kickbacks to the Iraqi government, and they collectively earned more $38 million in profits on those 42 contracts. Siemens France, Siemens Turkey, Osram Middle East and GTT inflated the price of the contracts by approximately 10 percent before submitting them to the United Nations for approval and improperly characterised payments to purported business consultants, part of which were paid as kickbacks to the Iraqi government as "commissions" to the business consultants. For the relevant years, the books and records of Siemens France, Siemens Turkey, Osram Middle East and GTT, including those containing false characterisations of the kickbacks paid to the Iraqi government, were part of the books and records of Siemens AG.

As the charging and plea documents reflect, beginning around September 1998 and continuing until 2007, Siemens Argentina made and caused to be made significant payments to various Argentine officials, both directly and indirectly, in exchange for favourable business treatment in connection with a $1 billion national identity card project. From the date that Siemens AG became listed on the New York Stock Exchange on March 12, 2001, through approximately January 2007, Siemens Argentina made approximately $31,263,000 in corrupt payments to various Argentine officials through purported consultants and other conduit entities, and improperly characterised those corrupt payments in its books and records as legitimate payments for "consulting fees" or "legal fees." Siemens Argentina's books and records, including those containing the false characterisations of the corrupt payments, were part of the books and records of Siemens AG.

According to court documents, beginning around November 2001 and continuing until approximately May 2007, Siemens Venezuela admitted it made and caused to be made corrupt payments of at least $18,782,965 to various Venezuelan officials, indirectly through purported business consultants, in exchange for favourable business treatment in connection with two major metropolitan mass transit projects called Metro Valencia and Metro Maracaibo. Some of those payments were made using US bank accounts controlled by the purported business consultants.

In the charging and plea documents, Siemens Bangladesh admitted that from May 2001 to August 2006, it caused corrupt payments of at least $5,319,839 to be made through purported business consultants to various Bangladeshi officials in exchange for favourable treatment during the bidding process on a mobile telephone project.

At least one payment to each of these purported consultants was paid from a US bank account.

2.1.2 Text from the US Department of Justice Website[2]

The former Technical Manager of the Major Projects division of Siemens Business Services GmbH & Co. OGH (SBS), a wholly owned subsidiary of Siemens Aktiengesellschaft (Siemens AG), pleaded guilty today to conspiring to pay tens of millions of dollars in bribes to Argentine government officials to secure, implement and enforce a $1 billion contract to create national identity cards.

Acting Assistant Attorney General John P. Cronan of the Justice Department's Criminal Division, US Attorney Geoffrey S. Berman of the Southern District of New York and Assistant Director in Charge Andrew W. Vale of the FBI's Washington, DC Field Office made the announcement.

Eberhard Reichert, 78, of Munich, Germany, was employed by Siemens AG from 1964 until 2001. Beginning in approximately 1990, Reichert was the Technical Manager of the Major Projects division of SBS. Reichert pleaded guilty today in the Southern District of New York to one count of conspiring to violate the anti-bribery, internal controls and books and records provisions of the Foreign Corrupt Practices Act (FCPA) and to commit wire fraud. Reichert was arraigned last December on a three-count indictment filed in December 2011 charging him and seven other individuals. He will be sentenced by US District Judge Denise L. Cote of the Southern District of New York, who accepted his plea today.

"Far too often, companies pay bribes as part of their business plan, upsetting what should be a level playing field and harming companies that play by the rules," said Acting Assistant Attorney General Cronan. "In this case, one of the largest public companies in the world paid staggeringly large bribes to officials at the uppermost levels of the government of Argentina to secure a billion-dollar contract. Eberhard Reichert's conviction demonstrates the Criminal Division's commitment to bringing both companies and corrupt individuals to justice, wherever they may reside and regardless of how long they may attempt to avoid arrest."

"Eberhard Reichert tried to sidestep laws designed to root corruption out of the government contracting process," said US Attorney Berman. "As he admitted in Manhattan federal court today, Reichert helped to conceal tens of millions of dollars in bribes that were paid to unfairly secure a lucrative contract from the Argentine government. Today's plea should be a warning to others that our office is committed to bringing corrupt criminals to justice, no matter how long they run from the law."

In 1998, the government of Argentina awarded to a subsidiary of Siemens AG a contract worth approximately $1 billion to create state-of-the-art national identity

---

[2] https://www.justice.gov/opa/pr/former-siemens-executive-pleads-guilty-role-100-million-foreign-bribery-scheme

cards (the Documento Nacional de Identidad or DNI project). The Argentine government terminated the DNI project in 2001. In connection with his guilty plea, Reichert admitted that he engaged in a decade-long scheme to pay tens of millions of dollars in bribes to Argentine government officials in connection with the DNI project, which was worth more than $1 billion to Siemens. Reichert admitted that he and his co-conspirators concealed the illicit payments through various means, including using shell companies associated with intermediaries to disguise and launder the funds.

Reichert also admitted that he used a $27 million contract between a Siemens entity and a company called MFast Consulting AG that purported to be for consulting services to conceal bribes to Argentine officials.

In 2008, Siemens AG, a German entity, pleaded guilty to violating the books and records provisions of the FCPA; Siemens Argentina pleaded guilty to conspiracy to violate the books and records provisions of the FCPA; and Siemens Bangladesh Limited and Siemens S.A.—Venezuela each pleaded guilty to conspiracy to violate the anti-bribery and books and records provisions of the FCPA. As part of the plea agreements, the Siemens companies paid a total of $450 million in criminal fines. The US Securities and Exchange Commission (SEC) also brought a civil case against Siemens AG alleging that it violated the anti-bribery, books and records and internal controls provisions of the FCPA. In resolving the SEC case, Siemens AG paid $350 million in disgorgement of wrongful profits. The Munich Public Prosecutor's Office also resolved similar charges with Siemens AG that resulted in a fine of $800 million. In August 2009, following these corporate resolutions with US and German authorities, Siemens AG withdrew its claim to the more than $200 million arbitration award.[3]

2.1.3 The Following Text is from the EIB Website (18/1/2020)[4]:

EIB and Siemens Settlement Agreement 15 March 2013
The European Investment Bank (EIB) and Siemens have entered into a Settlement Agreement that addresses alleged past violations of the EIB Anti-Fraud Policy in connection with projects financed by the EIB. The Agreement follows an investigation carried by the EIB with the support of the Siemens Group and OLAF on the past conduct of a Siemens' business unit in relation to a tender process.

---

[3] In addition to other proceedings, in November 2019 (fourteen years after a judicial inquiry was first launched), a Greek court found 22 people guilty including the former Siemens Hellas CEO Michalis Christoforakos. The case related to an estimated EUR70 m bribes paid by the German electronics giant and its local subsidiary to clinch a contract with telecom provider OTE, which was owned by the Greek state at the time, see www.greece.greekreporter.com

[4] www.eib.org/en/press/news/eib-and-siemens-settlement-agreement

2.1 Siemens

The Settlement Agreement includes a commitment by Siemens that the concerned business unit will voluntarily refrain from bidding on EIB financed projects or enter into any relationship with the EIB as a tenderer, contractor, supplier, consultant or any other form, for a period of 18 months.

As part of this Settlement, Siemens also commits to provide funds, totaling EUR 13.5 million over five years, to international organizations, inter-governmental organizations, non-governmental organizations (NGO), business associations, and/or academic institutions that support projects or other initiatives that promote good governance and the fight against corruption. Details on the management of this fund, eligibility criteria and selection process will be published on Siemens and EIB's websites when available.

Furthermore, Siemens has agreed to closely cooperate and assist the EIB going forward in its efforts to investigate alleged prohibited conduct in any EIB-financed project. Both parties also agreed to exchange best practices in relation to compliance standards and the fight against fraud and corruption.

2.1.4 The Following Text is from Siemens' Website[5]

Siemens Integrity Initiative
Collective Action—building alliances against corruption

In the face of the widespread and deep-rooted corruption problem that affects society in general, governments, their procuring entities and the private sector in equal measure, it seems highly unlikely that individual activities alone will be sufficient to bring about significant ethical changes and improve the transparency of business processes.

This is precisely where Collective Action methods become important: Collective Action enables corruption to be fought collectively, with various interest groups, working together and building an alliance against corruption so that the problem can be approached and resolved from multiple angles.

The advantages of Collective Action:

- Collective Action describes various methods of combating corruption. It is a matter of acting collectively and forming alliances against corruption. Collective Action calls for cooperation on the part of participants from the worlds of politics, business and society at large.

---

[5] https://new.siemens.com/global/en/company/sustainability/compliance/collective-action.html

- The ultimate goal is thereby to create fair and equitable market conditions, that is a "Level Playing Field", for all marketplace participants and to eliminate the temptation of corruption for all those concerned.
- Collective Action helps to set up the conditions for fair competition within a corrupt environment.
- Collective Action promotes innovation, as the bidder is selected solely on the basis of price, quality and capacity to innovate.
- Observance of anti-trust law when collaborating with other companies must be ensured by a neutral monitor (e.g., in the form of a non-governmental organization).
- Collective Action can, if necessary, cover gaps in legislation or replace or augment inadequate local law.

Please also see the joint article by Siemens and EIB published[6] by the Basel Institute on Governance (December 2021) that raises awareness of EIB's exclusions and settlements of entities for engaging in fraud & corruption on the projects that EIB has financed and of the work that the Siemens Integrity Initiative is undertaking globally to promote good governance and collective action.

---

[6] https://baselgovernance.org/blog/siemens-eib-collective-action

2.2 Alstom[7]

2.2.1 Text from the US Department of Justice (DoJ) Website[8]

Alstom S.A. (Alstom), a French power and transportation company, pleaded guilty today and agreed to pay a $772,290,000 fine to resolve charges related to a widespread scheme involving tens of millions of dollars in bribes in countries around the world, including Indonesia, Saudi Arabia, Egypt and the Bahamas.

Deputy Attorney General James M. Cole, Assistant Attorney General Leslie R. Caldwell of the Justice Department's Criminal Division, First Assistant US Attorney Michael J. Gustafson of the District of Connecticut and FBI Executive Assistant Director Robert Anderson, Jr. made the announcement.

"Alstom's corruption scheme was sustained over more than a decade and across several continents," said Deputy Attorney General Cole. "It was astounding in its breadth, its brazenness and its worldwide consequences. And it is both my

---

[7] In addition to other proceedings, in November 2019, a jury in USA found Lawrence Hoskins, a former senior vice president of France-based Alstom SA guilty of helping orchestrate a bribery scheme in Indonesia, a verdict that reinforces the reach of the US law prohibiting bribes to foreign government officials. See also FCPA Blog article: "Jury convicts Hoskins of multiple FCPA and money laundering offenses" by Richard L. Cassin November on 8, 2019, in which he noted: "Alstom SA pleaded guilty in December 2014 to violating the Foreign Corrupt Practices Act by bribing officials in Indonesia, Saudi Arabia, Egypt, and the Bahamas." Three other Alstom executives pleaded guilty in the United States to bribing officials in Indonesia. After the company's FCPA resolution, General Electric bought Alstom's power business in 2015 … The DOJ indicted Hoskins in 2013. His trial was delayed while he challenged the reach of the FCPA through motions to the trial court and during government appeals … Prosecutors were able to convince the jury that Hoskins, who worked for the Alstom parent company in France, violated the FCPA by acting as an agent for the Connecticut subsidiary when he helped arrange the Indonesia bribes … Prosecutors said Hoskins helped hire two "consultants" who were supposed to bribe Indonesian officials, including a member of parliament. Alstom's Connecticut unit eventually won a $118 million contract from Indonesia's state-owned electricity company … After the verdict … the DOJ said it appreciated "significant cooperation" from "law enforcement colleagues in Indonesia, Switzerland's Office of the Attorney General and the United Kingdom, as well as authorities in France, Germany, Italy, Singapore, and Taiwan." See also reports at www.wsj.com . See also FCPA Blog article: "Here's the 'agent' instruction from US v. Hoskins" by Richard L. Cassin, December 20, 2019, about Hoskins' (who worked for Alstom SA, a French company, in Paris, he was a British national and said he never set foot in the United States) challenged whether the U.S.'s Foreign Corrupt Practices Act could apply to him.

Also in November 2019, a UK Judge imposed a fine for bribery in respect of a contract on the Tunis metro—the British division of Alstom was ordered to pay £16.4 m after being convicted of paying bribes to win a contract to supply trams to the metro system in Tunis. The Judge at Southwark crown court in London fined the French multinational's British subsidiary £15 m plus £1.4 m in costs. The company was convicted in April 2018 of conspiracy to corrupt after paying Construction et Gestion Nevco, an intermediary, €2.4 m to secure a contract (worth nearly €80 m with Transtu, the company that runs the metro system in the Tunisian capital). More info on this at www.thetimes.co.uk

[8] www.justice.gov/opa/pr/alstom-pleads-guilty-and-agrees-pay-772-million-criminal-penalty-resolve-foreign-bribery

expectation—and my intention—that the comprehensive resolution we are announcing today will send an unmistakable message to other companies around the world: that this Department of Justice will be relentless in rooting out and punishing corruption to the fullest extent of the law, no matter how sweeping its scale or how daunting its prosecution."

"This case is emblematic of how the Department of Justice will investigate and prosecute FCPA cases—and other corporate crimes," said Assistant Attorney General Caldwell. "We encourage companies to maintain robust compliance programs, to voluntarily disclose and eradicate misconduct when it is detected, and to cooperate in the government's investigation. But we will not wait for companies to act responsibly. With cooperation or without it, the department will identify criminal activity at corporations and investigate the conduct ourselves, using all of our resources, employing every law enforcement tool, and considering all possible actions, including charges against both corporations and individuals."

"Today's historic resolution is an important reminder that our moral and legal mandate to stamp out corruption does not stop at any border, whether city, state or national," said First Assistant US Attorney Gustafson. "A significant part of this illicit work was unfortunately carried out from Alstom Power's offices in Windsor, Connecticut. I am hopeful that this resolution, and in particular the deferred prosecution agreement with Alstom Power, will provide the company an opportunity to reshape its culture and restore its place as a respected corporate citizen."

"This investigation spanned years and crossed continents, as agents from the FBI Washington and New Haven field offices conducted interviews and collected evidence in every corner of the globe," said FBI Executive Assistant Director Anderson. "The record dollar amount of the fine is a clear deterrent to companies who would engage in foreign bribery, but an even better deterrent is that we are sending executives who commit these crimes to prison."

Alstom pleaded guilty to a two-count criminal information filed today in the US District Court for the District of Connecticut, charging the company with violating the Foreign Corrupt Practices Act (FCPA) by falsifying its books and records and failing to implement adequate internal controls. Alstom admitted its criminal conduct and agreed to pay a criminal penalty of $772,290,000. US District Judge Janet B. Arterton of the District of Connecticut scheduled a sentencing hearing for June 23, 2015, at 3pm.

In addition, Alstom Network Schweiz AG, formerly Alstom Prom (Alstom Prom), Alstom's Swiss subsidiary, pleaded guilty to a criminal information charging the company with conspiracy to violate the anti-bribery provisions of the FCPA. Alstom Power Inc. (Alstom Power) and Alstom Grid Inc. (Alstom Grid), two US subsidiaries, both entered into deferred prosecution agreements, admitting that they conspired to violate the anti-bribery provisions of the FCPA. Alstom Power is headquartered in Windsor, Connecticut, and Alstom Grid, formerly Alstom T&D, was headquartered in New Jersey.

According to the companies' admissions, Alstom, Alstom Prom, Alstom Power and Alstom Grid, through various executives and employees, paid bribes to government officials and falsified books and records in connection with power, grid and transportation projects for state-owned entities around the world, including in Indonesia, Egypt, Saudi Arabia, the Bahamas and Taiwan. In Indonesia, for example, Alstom, Alstom Prom, and Alstom Power paid bribes to government officials—including a high-ranking member of the Indonesian Parliament and high-ranking members of Perusahaan Listrik Negara, the state-owned electricity company in Indonesia—in exchange for assistance in securing several contracts to provide power-related services valued at approximately $375 million. In total, Alstom paid more than $75 million to secure $4 billion in projects around the world, with a profit to the company of approximately $300 million.

Alstom and its subsidiaries also attempted to conceal the bribery scheme by retaining consultants purportedly to provide consulting services on behalf of the companies, but who actually served as conduits for corrupt payments to the government officials. Internal Alstom documents refer to some of the consultants in code, including "Mr. Geneva," "Mr. Paris," "London," "Quiet Man" and "Old Friend."

The plea agreement cites many factors considered by the department in reaching the appropriate resolution, including: Alstom's failure to voluntarily disclose the misconduct even though it was aware of related misconduct at a US subsidiary that previously resolved corruption charges with the department in connection with a power project in Italy; Alstom's refusal to fully cooperate with the department's investigation for several years; the breadth of the companies' misconduct, which spanned many years, occurred in countries around the globe and in several business lines, and involved sophisticated schemes to bribe high-level government officials; Alstom's lack of an effective compliance and ethics program at the time of the conduct; and Alstom's prior criminal misconduct, including conduct that led to resolutions with various other governments and the World Bank.

2.2.2 Text from the Website of the UK SFO[9]

Former Alstom Power Global Sales Director sentenced to 4.5 years for corruption, 21 December 2018[10]

Today, Nicholas Reynolds received 4 years and 6 months imprisonment for his part in a conspiracy to bribe officials in Lithuania's Elektrenai power station and senior Lithuanian politicians in order to win two contracts worth €240 million.

He was also ordered to pay costs of £50,000.

In sentencing the former Global Sales Director for Alstom Power Ltd's Boiler Retrofits unit, HHJ Beddoe said:

---

[9] www.sfo.gov.uk/2018/12/21/former-alstom-power-global-sales-director-sentenced-to-4-5-years-for-corruption/

[10] See other reports including the FCPA Blog article on March 29, 2016, by Richard Cassin entitled: "SFO Charges another individual in Alstom corruption case"

This was sophisticated corruption, planned and executed under your direction over many years. This was a very serious example of the bribery and corruption that beleaguers the civilised commercial world and is a cancer upon it. Even if you do not create the disease but help it spread, you bear a very heavy responsibility, and the more senior your position, the more serious it obviously is.

Lisa Osofsky, Director of the Serious Fraud Office said:

The substantial prison sentences imposed in this case reflect the seriousness of the bribery and corruption. We can only hope that this may deter others tempted to resort to illicit means to win contracts.

We are grateful for the assistance provided by our international partners across more than 30 countries for helping us deliver these results.

Reynolds' sentencing follows the conviction and sentencing of Alstom Power Ltd, its former Business Development Manager John Venskus and former Regional Sales Director at Alstom Power Sweden AB Göran Wikström for their part in the conspiracy.

John Venskus was sentenced to 3 years and 6 months imprisonment on 4 May 2018. Göran Wikström was sentenced to 2 years and 7 months imprisonment on 9 July 2018, and was also ordered to pay £40,000 in costs.

Alstom Power Ltd was ordered to pay a total of £18,038,000 which included:
A fine of £6,375,000
Compensation to the Lithuanian government of £10,963,000
Prosecution costs of £700,000

2.2.3 Text from the Website of the UK SFO[11]

Five convictions in SFO's Alstom investigation into bribery & corruption to secure €325 million of contracts, 19 December, 2018

Nicholas Reynolds was found guilty of conspiracy to corrupt today at Blackfriars Crown Court following an extensive investigation and prosecution brought by the Serious Fraud Office.

The conviction brings to four the number of total convictions in relation to this conspiracy to bribe officials in a Lithuanian power station and senior Lithuanian politicians in order to win two contracts worth €240 million. These individuals falsified records to avoid checks in place to prevent bribery and between them, the Alstom companies paid more than €5 million in bribes to secure the contracts.

The conviction of Nicholas Reynolds who is a UK national and former Global Sales Director for Alstom Power Ltd's Boiler Retrofits unit followed a guilty plea from former Business Development Manager at Alstom Power Ltd John Venskus on

---

[11] www.sfo.gov.uk/2018/12/19/five-convictions-in-sfos-alstom-investigation-into-bribery-and-corruption-to-secure-e325-million-of-contracts/

2 October 2017 and former Regional Sales Director at Alstom Power Sweden AB Göran Wikström on 22 June 2018 on the same charge. Alstom Power Ltd entered a guilty plea to conspiracy to corrupt on 10 May 2016.

In sentencing Göran Wikström HHJ Martin Beddoe said:

> This was a very serious example of bribery and corruption that beleaguers the civilised, commercial world and is a cancer upon it

Venskus was sentenced to 3 years and 6 months imprisonment on 4 May 2018. Wikström was sentenced to 2 years and 7 months imprisonment on 9 July 2018. He was also ordered to pay £40,000 in costs.

Alstom Power Ltd was ordered to pay a total of £18,038,000 which included:
A fine of £6,375,000
Compensation to the Lithuanian government of £10,963,000
Prosecution costs of £700,000

Nicholas Reynolds is due to be sentenced at Blackfriars Crown Court on 21 December 2018.

Lisa Osofsky, Director of the Serious Fraud Office said:

> The culture of corruption evident within the Alstom Group was widespread. Their illicit activities to win lucrative contracts were calculated and sustained, undermining legitimate business and public trust.

> These convictions were a result of a truly global investigation and I thank our case team for their effort and persistence in bringing the individuals and companies involved to justice.

The SFO's investigation involved cooperation with more than 30 countries including France, Canada, Hungary, Denmark, Austria, Slovakia, Czech Republic, Lichtenstein, Cyprus, Singapore, the Seychelles, India, Sweden, Lithuania, Switzerland and Tunisia.

Due to the lifting of reporting restrictions, the conviction of Alstom Network UK Ltd in a linked case can also now be reported.

Alstom Network UK Ltd were found guilty of one count of conspiracy to corrupt on 10 April 2018 for making corrupt payments to win a tram and infrastructure contract in Tunisia.

In return for its work in securing the €85 million contract, Alstom Network UK Ltd paid €2.4 million to a company called Construction et Gestion Nevco Inc, which Alstom Network UK Ltd itself acknowledged was a front for corruption when it decided not to make a final payment of €240,000 in its contract.

Staff within the Alstom Group helped the consultants produce paperwork to satisfy internal compliance checks, cobbling together 'evidence' of the services provided, which at best were of a nominal nature because the company was, in reality, just a conduit for bribes.

Graham Hill, Robert Hallett and Alstom Network UK Ltd were acquitted of other charges in this case, relating to alleged corruption to win transport contracts in India and Poland, on 10 April 2018.

Alstom Network UK Ltd will be sentenced at Southwark Crown Court on a date to be determined.

Alstom Network UK Ltd along with Michael Anderson, Terence Watson and Jean-Daniel Lainé were acquitted of a charge in a linked investigation into alleged corruption relating to a Budapest Metro rolling stock contract.

2.2.4 Text from EIB Website (8/1/22)[12]

Agreement Between the EIB and GE Steam Power
Agreement between the European Investment Bank and GE Steam Power (in relation to prohibited conduct by Alstom Power Systems S.A, Alstom Power Systems GmbH and Alstom Hrvatska d.o.o in the Sostanj Power Project, Slovenia)

The European Investment Bank and GE Steam Power have reached agreement regarding historical cases of Prohibited Conduct by various Alstom Steam Power companies, in particular, Alstom Power Systems S.A (France), Alstom Power Systems GmbH (Germany) and Alstom Hrvatska d.o.o (Croatia) in the Šoštanj Power Project in Slovenia.

According to the Agreement, the European Investment Bank has concluded its investigation and the three Alstom Steam Power companies involved have voluntarily agreed not to participate in any European Investment Bank project during exclusion periods of varying lengths (being 12 months for Alstom Power Systems S. A, 12 months for Alstom Power Systems GmbH and 18 months for Alstom Hrvatska d.o.o.), which started running from November 15, 2021 when they voluntarily agreed to refrain from involvement in European Investment Bank funded projects.

GE Steam Power has implemented and will continue to maintain its rigorous compliance procedures in these Alstom Steam Power companies that it acquired in 2015, to mitigate the risk of any similar issues arising in the future.

Additionally, the three companies involved will finance anti-corruption, integrity, sustainability, climate change and/or environmental protection activities and, in this context, have agreed to provide EUR 7 million to fund such projects in the next 5 years.

Furthermore, the three companies involved will cooperate with the European Investment Bank in the exchange of best practices in relation to compliance standards and the fight against fraud and corruption.

In addition, the three companies involved have settled the civil case in Slovenia.

---

[12] https://www.eib.org/en/press/news/agreement-between-eib-and-ge-steam-power

2.2.5 Text from the EBRD's Website (3/12/2019)[13]

EBRD Debars GE Power of Sweden for Six Years By Anthony Williams@ebrdtony, 27 November 2019

The European Bank for Reconstruction and Development (EBRD) has imposed a six-year term of debarment on GE Power Sweden AB following an investigation in cooperation with the Serious Fraud Office of the UK.

The six-year debarment means that GE Power Sweden will not be eligible to be a Bank Counterparty from 27 November 2019 until 26 November 2025.

The EBRD's Office of the Chief Compliance Officer (OCCO) will also submit debarment of GE Power Sweden to the World Bank, the African Development Bank, the Asian Development Bank, and the Inter-American Development Bank, so that this entity is also debarred by these multilateral development banks.

The investigation relates to a project to install flue gas desulphurisation (FGD) units at the Lithuanian Power Plant, a project financed by donor funds administered by the EBRD.

The investigation found that, from as early as 2002, representatives of Alstom Power Sweden AB, a predecessor company to GE Power Sweden, had conspired with another Alstom entity to manipulate the technical specifications for the FGD contract in their favour by making payments to Lithuanian government officials.

The six-year debarment is the longest to have been imposed in the history of the Bank, and reflects the egregious nature of the misconduct involved. The action also reflects close collaboration with the European Commission and the International Ignalina Decommissioning Support Fund, the donor fund that provided financing for the project.

The EBRD's Chief Compliance Officer Lisa Rosen said:

> The EBRD's decisive response in this case underscores how seriously the EBRD takes corruption, especially when it involves donor funds.

The Bank's cooperation with UK's Serious Fraud Office also led to the successful prosecution in the UK of three individuals and one entity in relation to the misconduct.

* * *

In addition in 2019, another MDB (the AfDB) also imposed sanctions against Alstom power entities, now owned by GE Power.

---

[13] www.ebrd.com/news/2019/ebrd-debars-ge-power-of-sweden-for-six-years.html

2.2.6 Text from the AfDB's Website[14]

Integrity in Development Projects: The African Development Bank and GE Power Reach Settlement on Legacy Alstom Misconduct
The African Development Bank imposes debarments of 76 months and 12 months on former Alstom companies found to have engaged in bribery and fraud in 2006 and 2011 in relation to two Bank-financed Egyptian power generation projects. GE Power acquired the companies in 2015. 22-Mar-2019

The African Development Bank Group today announced the conclusion of a settlement agreement with GE Power, thus resolving sanctionable practices committed by former Alstom companies.

An investigation conducted by the Bank's Office of Integrity and Anti-Corruption established that in 2006 and 2011 the companies, then named Alstom Power Generation AG, Alstom Power GmbH and Alstom Egypt for Power & Transport Projects S.A.E., engaged in two instances of corrupt practices and in one instance of a fraudulent practice in the context of the Bank-financed Suez Thermal Power Plant Project and the El Kureimat III Power Project, both in Egypt.

GE Power assumed control over these three companies in 2015, after the misconduct had occurred, when it acquired Alstom's thermal power generation business. As part of the settlement, the Bank imposes on former Alstom Egypt for Power & Transport Projects S.A.E. (now known as Alstom Egypt for Power Projects S.A.E.), based in Cairo, Egypt, and on former Alstom Power Generation AG (now known as GE Power Systems GmbH), headquartered in Mannheim, Germany, a debarment of 76 months.

The debarment period may be reduced to 48 months if the companies comply with all conditions of the agreement early. This debarment may be enforced by other multilateral development banks under the Agreement for Mutual Enforcement of Debarment Decisions, including the Asian Development Bank, the European Bank for Reconstruction and Development, the Inter-American Development Bank and the World Bank Group. Further, pursuant to the settlement, former Alstom Power GmbH (now known as GE Power GmbH), equally based in Mannheim, Germany, is debarred for a period of 12 months.

Among other conditions for release from debarment, GE Power commits to collaborate with the Office of Integrity and Anti-Corruption in the fight against corruption in the power generation and transmission sector.

> Corrupt practices in the power generation sector directly undermine the African Development Bank's operational priority to light up and power Africa. This can never be accepted by the Bank,

says Bubacarr Sankareh, Manager of the Investigations Division within the Office of Integrity and Anti-Corruption.

---

[14] www.afdb.org/en/news-and-events/integrity-in-development-projects-the-african-development-bank-and-ge-power-reach-settlement-on-legacy-alstom-misconduct-19116

We are very pleased that GE Power is joining us today in our efforts to fight corruption and to ensure the delivery of value for money to the Bank's regional member countries.

In 2006, Alstom Egypt for Power & Transport Projects S.A.E. and Alstom Power Generation AG participated in a tender for steam turbine generators in the context of the Bank-financed El Kureimat III Power Project. The companies indirectly paid an amount of 963,477 EURO to their local agent.

The Office of Integrity and Anti-Corruption has concluded that one purpose of the payment was to ensure the support of public officials involved in the procurement process in order to gain an unfair competitive advantage in the tender. Further, the Office of Integrity and Anti-Corruption established that the companies had erroneously only declared 50,000 EURO in fees paid to its local agent.

In 2011, Alstom Egypt for Power & Transport Projects S.A.E., Alstom Power GmbH and Alstom Power Generation AG, by then renamed Alstom Power Systems GmbH, participated in a tender for a steam turbine generator and condensers for the Bank-financed Suez Thermal Power Plant. In the context of this tender, the companies indirectly offered 1.7 million EURO to their local agent. The Office of Integrity and Anti-Corruption has concluded that one objective of the offer was to ensure that public officials would assert undue influence on the procurement process in favour of the companies' bid.

In reaching this settlement, the African Development Bank took into account General Electric's substantial cooperation with the investigation of the legacy cases as well as the high quality of the company's comprehensive compliance programme, which now applies to the Alstom entities acquired by GE Power.

2.2.7 Also, Text from the FCPA Blog (www.fcpablog.com) Article[15]

ADB Debars GE Power Units Tied to Alstom Offenses, By Harry Cassin, March 25, 2019
The African Development Bank said Thursday it debarred several former Alstom companies now owned by GE Power for up to 76 months because of fraud and bribery committed on two bank-financed projects in Egypt.

The bank said the offenses occurred in 2006 and 2011.

GE Power acquired the former Alstom companies in 2015.

The bank said three former Alstom companies "engaged in two instances of corrupt practices and in one instance of a fraudulent practice" in connection with two bank-financed power projects in Egypt.

The bank imposed a 76-month debarment on two of the former Alstom units. Those units are now known as Alstom Egypt for Power Projects S.A.E. based in Cairo and GE Power Systems GmbH headquartered in Mannheim, Germany.

---

[15] https://fcpablog.com/2019/03/25/adb-debars-ge-power-units-tied-to-alstom-offenses/

And it debarred GE Power GmbH (formerly Alstom Power GmbH), also based in Mannheim, for 12 months.

The bank said GE Power entered into a voluntary settlement of the legacy offenses.

The 76-month debarment can be reduced to 48 months based on the companies' compliance with the settlement terms, the bank said.

Among other things, GE Power promised to collaborate with the African Development Bank's Office of Integrity and Anti-Corruption "in the fight against corruption in the power generation and transmission sector."

In 2015, an ex-Bechtel Corporation vice president was sentenced to 42 months in prison in the United States for taking $5.2 million in kickbacks to rig bids for state-run power contracts in Egypt.

Asem Elgawhary, 73, of Potomac, Maryland pleaded guilty to mail fraud, conspiracy to commit money laundering, obstruction, and interference with the administration of the tax laws.

The judge also ordered Elgawhary -- a dual US and Egyptian citizen -- to forfeit $5.2 million.

From 1996 to 2011, Bechtel assigned Elgawhary to be the general manager at a joint venture between Bechtel and Egypt's state-owned and state-controlled electricity company. Elgawhary took a total of $5.2 million from three power companies to rig bids for the project contracts.

One of the power companies that bribed Elgawhary was Paris-based Alstom S.A. Bechtel wasn't charged in the case.

In December 2014, Alstom paid $772 million in criminal penalties to resolve FCPA offenses, including bribing Elgawhary.

The African Development Bank's statement Thursday said in 2006 Alstom companies tendering for a bank-financed project paid their agent in Egypt about $1.1 million.

The African Development Bank said it took into account "General Electric's substantial cooperation with the investigation of the legacy cases as well as the high quality of the company's comprehensive compliance program, which now applies to the Alstom entities acquired by GE Power."

Thursday's 76-month debarment qualifies for cross debarment by other multilateral development banks under their mutual enforcement agreements. The other multilateral development banks include the Asian Development Bank, the European Bank for Reconstruction and Development, the Inter-American Development Bank, and the World Bank Group.

2.3 SNC Lavalin[16]

2.3.1 Text is an excerpt from Wikipedia (on 30/11/19)[17]

Legal Issues

SNC-Lavalin's management team have been investigated in a number of allegations under the Corruption of Foreign Public Officials Act regarding contracts beginning with SNC-Lavalin Kerala hydroelectric dam scandal (1995–2008) [49] through to the allegations involving the bribing of Libyan officials between 2001 and 2011... [50]

Libya (2011)

A 2012 CBC News report, said that the first reports of murky affairs surfaced against the company in 2010 in relation to contracts in Libya [6]. According to a CBC News article, a Libyan bribery and fraud scandal involving crimes that took place from 2001–2011 led to charges in "connection with payments of nearly $48 million" to Libyan public officials [58]. In the same article, it was reported that the company was also accused of "defrauding Libyan organizations of an estimated $130 million"[50, 58].

In 2015, SNC-Lavalin was charged with bribing Libyan officials in exchange for construction contracts between 2001 and 2011 [50]. In 2011, the RCMP began their investigation called Project Assistance which was triggered by a tip from Swiss authorities [59]. According to an August 8, 2013 Financial Post article, Michael Novak who, had been the head of SNC International, had signed "several of the contracts between SNC and "unknown commercial consultants to help win contracts" for "work in Africa"[60, 61]. This included a contract with former Libyan dictator Muammar Gaddafi's controversial government [62]. By the summer of 2013, police alleged that the "unknown commercial consultants" had never existed and that Ben Aissa had "set up shell companies so he could pocket the [$56 million]

---

[16] See also FCPA Blog article: Former SNC-Lavalin Chief Pleads Guilty in Bribery Case by Richard Cassin, February 4, 2019, noting "In 2012, the Royal Canadian Mounted Police filed an affidavit that tied former SNC-Lavalin executive Riadh Ben Aissa to more than $160 million in alleged bribes paid to Libyan officials in exchange for contracts." and "In 2013, the World Bank barred SNC-Lavalin from bank-funded projects for ten years because of alleged corruption in Bangladesh and Cambodia" and the FCPA Blog article: SNC-Lavalin Blowback: Reconsidering corporate criminal liability by Lincoln Caylor and Nathan Shaheen, May 8, 2019. In addition to other proceedings, in December 2019, a division of SNC-Lavalin Group Inc. pleaded guilty to fraud in relation to the company's activities in Libya. SNC-Lavalin Construction paid $127 million to two shell companies between 2001 and 2011, according to an agreed statement of facts presented in a Montreal court. Duvel Securities Inc. and Dinova International Inc. both listed as the sole beneficial owner Riadh Ben Aissa. He was a former top executive of the company who pleaded guilty in Switzerland to bribery and laundering funds to win SNC-Lavalin contracts in Libya. About $47 million of the money was then used to reward Saadi Gadhafi, son of the late dictator Moammar Gadhafi, for helping SNC-Lavalin secure lucrative construction projects. More info at www.cbc.ca

[17] www.en.wikipedia.org/wiki/SNC-Lavalin

himself" [61, 63]. By July 2014, Aissa was jailed in Switzerland for "suspicion of corruption, fraud and money-laundering in North Africa"[64, 65] [Notes 4]. When SNC-Lavalin pulled out of Libya in 2011, it left behind $22.9 million in Libyan banks [66]. In 2013, Roy filed a countersuit for wrongful dismissal, claiming lost wages and damages to his reputation, alleging that he had been framed and scapegoated by higher-level executives whose directives he was obliged to follow [67–70] [Notes 5].

By February 2012, SNC investors had found out that audited financial statements had been delayed to accommodate an internal review relating to SNC's operations. The internal review probed $35 million of unexplained payments in Libya. Prior to the launch of the investigation, there had been months-long media speculation about the company's work in Libya and its ties to the Muammar Gaddafi family [71–73]. In 2012, the Royal Canadian Mounted Police investigated the company on these charges in the Project Assistance investigation and [74], in 2015, they charged SNC-Lavalin with "fraud and corruption", which the company indicated they would contest in court [75].

McGill University; The Arthur Porter Kick-Back Scandal (2011–2014)
Charges were laid against senior executives from 2014 through 2019 in the bribery cases involving Arthur Porter at the McGill University Health Centre. According to a 2012 article in The Globe and Mail, these reports prompted calls for Canada to tighten bribery laws [76].

According to the National Post, SNC-Lavalin employees allegedly were involved in fraud and forgery in relation to a $22.5 million kick-back described as "consulting fees" to Arthur Porter [77] [Notes 6] on the contract to build the new $1.3 billion hospital at the McGill University Health Centre's CEO in violation of the Quebec Health Act. SNC-Lavalin were awarded the contract even though they were outbid by $60 million [36]. The case led to an investigation by the Charbonneau Commission. Porter resigned from the post on December 5, 2011 in light of substantial public pressure [78–80]. Porter was arrested in Panama on fraud charges on May 27, 2013, which alleged that he took part in the kick-back scheme [81]. The Canadian Broadcasting Corporation called it the biggest fraud investigation in Canadian history [82, 83]. SNC CEO, Pierre Duhaime in March 2012 [6, 84, 85], Duhaime was arrested on fraud charges by Quebec authorities on November 28, 2012 [86, 87] [Notes 7] [Notes 8] [88].

SNC-Lavalin sued Duhaime for millions of dollars in damages, claiming that he stained its goodwill by means of the McGill University Health Centre super hospital scandal. The company claims that Duhaime "facilitated the execution of the embezzlement" of $22.5 million of company funds. Duhaime was charged with several counts related to the bribe. In February 2019 he pleaded guilty to one count of breach of trust. The prosecution vacated some 15 further charges [89].

Padma Bridge (Since 2011)
An investigation into an alleged graft related to 2011 bids for the construction of the 6.51 kilometre (four-mile) USD$3 billion road—rail bridge crossing the Padma River in Bangladesh [90], resulted in the former SNC-Lavalin employees being

cleared of all charges by a Canadian court. In May 2011, two former SNC-Lavalin International Inc. (SLII) employees Ramesh Shah and Mohammad Ismail met government officials in Bangladesh to discuss a bid for the $50-million supervision contract to build the Padma Bridge, a project estimated to be worth USD$3 billion [49]. Part of the allegations were related to SLII common practice of list project consultancy costs (PCC), also known as project commercial cost, as a line item in internal budgets documents related to the bidding process [Notes 9] [49]. As a result of the original investigation by World Bank investigators who worked with RCMP officers, in September 2013, the World Bank blacklisted SNC-Lavalin and its affiliates from bidding on the World Bank's global projects [91]. The World Bank had originally offered to fund $1.5 billion of the $3 billion but pulled back following the allegations. However, on February 11, 2017, the Ontario Superior Court found no proof of the Padma bridge bribery conspiracy, dismissed the case, and acquitted the ex-SNC-Lavalin executives [92]. According to the Dhaka Tribune, Justice Ian Nordheimer rebuked the Canadian police, saying: "Reduced to its essentials, the information provided in the [wiretap applications] was nothing more than speculation, gossip, and rumor" [92].

2.3.2 Text from the World Bank Website[18] *(14 January 2020)*[19]

World Bank Debars SNC-Lavalin Inc. and Its Affiliates for 10 Years
This represents the longest debarment period that has ever been agreed to in a World Bank settlement.

WASHINGTON, April 17, 2013—The World Bank Group today announced the debarment of SNC-Lavalin Inc.—in addition to over 100 affiliates—for a period of 10 years following the company's misconduct in relation to the Padma Multipurpose Bridge Project in Bangladesh, as well as misconduct under another Bank-financed project. SNC-Lavalin Inc. is a subsidiary of SNC-Lavalin Group, a Canadian company, and represents more than 60% of its business.

The debarment is part of a Negotiated Resolution Agreement between the World Bank and SNC-Lavalin Group following a World Bank investigation into allegations of bribery schemes involving SNC-Lavalin Inc. and officials in Bangladesh.

---

[18] www.worldbank.org/en/news/press-release/2013/04/17/world-bank-debars-snc-lavalin-inc-and-its-affiliates-for-ten-years

[19] World Bank Sanctions Board decisions 54 (Bangladesh). https://www.worldbank.org/content/dam/documents/sanctions/sanctions-board/2018/nov/SanctionsBoardDecisionNo-54.pdf and 69 (Lebanon) https://www.worldbank.org/content/dam/documents/sanctions/sanctions-board/2018/nov/Sanctions-Board-Decision-No-69.pdf were discussed the FCPA Blog article "Is debarment for fraud 'fair and appropriate'?" by Giuliana Dunham Irving and Ryan Velandria McCarthy (January 31, 2022): https://fcpablog.com/2022/01/31/is-debarment-for-fraud-fair-and-appropriate/

While the investigation was ongoing, the World Bank's Integrity Vice Presidency also learned of misconduct by SNC-Lavalin Inc. in relation to the World Bank-financed Rural Electrification and Transmission project in Cambodia.

The debarment can be reduced to eight years if the companies comply with all conditions of the agreement. The remainder of the SNC-Lavalin Group has been conditionally non-debarred for the same period of time. Under this sanction, the remainder of SNC-Lavalin Group faces debarment if they fail to comply with the terms and conditions of the Agreement.

"This case is testimony to collective action against global corruption," **said Leonard McCarthy, World Bank Integrity Vice President.** "Once we had evidence of the company's misconduct, we referred the matter to the Royal Canadian Mounted Police whilst the World Bank finalized its investigation. Going forward, I hope that SNC-Lavalin's commitment under this agreement represents meaningful action in deterring the risks of fraud and corruption to development projects."

SNC-Lavalin's misconduct involved a conspiracy to pay bribes and misrepresentations when bidding for Bank-financed contracts in violation of the World Bank's procurement guidelines. Under the Agreement, the SNC-Lavalin Group and its affiliates commit to cooperating with the World Bank's Integrity Vice Presidency and continuing to improve their internal compliance program. The debarment of SNC-Lavalin Inc. qualifies for cross-debarment by other MDBs under the Agreement of Mutual Recognition of Debarments that was signed on April 9, 2010.

2.4 Wasim Tappuni

2.4.1 Text from the UK's City of London Police Website[20]

22 September 2017—Man sentenced for £1.7 million corruption involving the World Bank

Today (22 September 2017) a man has been sentenced to six years imprisonment at Southwark Crown Court after an investigation led by the City of London Police's Overseas Anti Corruption Unit (OACU) found that he had entered into corrupt agreements with 12 medical supply companies that had submitted tenders for projects mostly financed by the World Bank.

Wasim Tappuni, 64, of Coombe Neville in Kingston upon Thames, was sentenced to six years imprisonment following a six week trial. A 74 year old man who also stood trial was found not guilty of money laundering and false accounting.

Tappuni, who was an independent medical procurement consultant, was employed by the World Bank between August 2007 and October 2011. He acted

---

[20] http://news.cityoflondon.police.uk/r/914/man_sentenced_for__1_7_million_corruption_involvi

as an independent advisor on their medical procurement projects. Over the course of four years, Tappuni received payments from companies based in the Netherlands, Germany, France, Austria, and Kazakhstan, of approximately £1.7 million.

Following an anonymous tip in 2011, the World Bank began an internal investigation into a Dutch medical supply company and made a referral to the Dutch authorities. The Dutch investigation identified Tappuni as the 'insider' at the World Bank and led to a criminal investigation being carried out on the company in the Netherlands.

It was suspected that Tappuni provided these companies with confidential information held by the World Bank which was not in the public domain, including tender documents and competitors' bids, prior to the information becoming public. This information allowed these companies an unfair advantage in the tendering process. He also offered to amend the criteria to suit particular suppliers and unfairly reject competitors, allowing them to unfairly win the contract.

Tappuni would then benefit from the corrupt arrangement and receive a pre-arranged percentage of the contract value, should the company, with whom he had the corrupt arrangement, be successful.

In September 2011 the Dutch authorities made OACU aware of their investigation which resulted in a joint operation team being set up by Eurojust on 21 October 2011 to further investigate Tappuni and the Dutch medical supply company.

On 25 October 2011 coordinated searches took place in the Netherlands and at Tappuni's home address in Kingston where a large amount of documentation and material from his computer were recovered. Tappuni was arrested and interviewed on the same day.

As a result of this search and extensive international enquiries, it was discovered that Tappuni had received approximately £1.7 million in corrupt payments from 12 medical companies relating to 44 corrupted contracts totalling £42 million in value. For all but two of these contracts Tappuni was engaged by the World Bank as an independent advisor. For the remaining two, he was similarly engaged by the United Nations Development Programme (UNDP). Most of these corrupt monies had been paid into accounts, held in Switzerland that he controlled.

Acting Detective Superintendent Peter Ratcliffe, Head of the City of London Police's Overseas Anti Corruption Unit (OACU), said:

> This corrupt manipulation of the tendering process meant that the reputation of the World Bank would be tarnished and taxpayers money wasted, as the medical supply companies that won the contracts did so having been unfairly assisted in the process. This case and subsequent sentencing highlights the severity of this crime and demonstrates that such acts will not go unpunished.

> The Overseas Anti Corruption Unit and the World Bank have worked together on this case and by sharing information, we have been able to successfully uncover Tappuni's crimes and expose the sheer extent of his corruption. The investigation led to not only the identification of a large number of corrupt relationships, but also the 12 medical suppliers being investigated by and in most cases barred from bidding on World Bank contracts.

> This case should serve as a warning to those who engage in such crimes that justice will be served.

2.5 Odebrecht/Braskem

2.5.1 Text from BBC News Website[21]

17 April 2019

For years, Latin America's construction giant, Odebrecht, built some of the region's most crucial infrastructure projects.

But then it became well-known for another superlative: its involvement in one of the biggest corruption cases in history.

In 2016, the Brazilian-based group signed what has been described as the world's largest leniency deal with US and Swiss authorities, in which it confessed to corruption and paid $2.6bn (£2.1bn) in fines.

Seventy-seven company executives agreed to plea bargains with Brazilian authorities, and their statements to investigators were made public.

Their revelations had strong political and economic repercussions throughout Latin America...

2.5.2 Text from the US DoJ Website[22]

Wednesday, December 21, 2016

Odebrecht and Braskem Plead Guilty and Agree to Pay at Least $3.5 Billion in Global Penalties to Resolve Largest Foreign Bribery Case in History
Odebrecht S.A. (Odebrecht), a global construction conglomerate based in Brazil, and Braskem S.A. (Braskem), a Brazilian petrochemical company, pleaded guilty today and agreed to pay a combined total penalty of at least $3.5 billion to resolve charges with authorities in the United States, Brazil and Switzerland arising out of their schemes to pay hundreds of millions of dollars in bribes to government officials around the world.

Deputy Assistant Attorney General Sung-Hee Suh of the Justice Department's Criminal Division, U.S. Attorney Robert L. Capers of the Eastern District of New York, Assistant Director Stephen Richardson of the FBI's Criminal Investigative Division and Assistant Director in Charge William F. Sweeney of the FBI's New York Field Office made the announcement.

"Odebrecht and Braskem used a hidden but fully functioning Odebrecht business unit—a 'Department of Bribery,' so to speak—that systematically paid hundreds of millions of dollars to corrupt government officials in countries on three continents," said Deputy Assistant Attorney General Suh. "Such brazen wrongdoing calls for a

---

[21] www.bbc.com/news/amp/business-39194395

[22] www.justice.gov/opa/pr/odebrecht-and-braskem-plead-guilty-and-agree-pay-least-35-billion-global-penalties-resolve

strong response from law enforcement, and through a strong effort with our colleagues in Brazil and Switzerland, we have seen just that. I hope that today's action will serve as a model for future efforts."

"These resolutions are the result of an extraordinary multinational effort to identify, investigate and prosecute a highly complex and long-lasting corruption scheme that resulted in the payment by the defendant companies of close to a billion dollars in bribes to officials at all levels of government in many countries," said U.S. Attorney Capers. "In an attempt to conceal their crimes, the defendants used the global financial system—including the banking system in the United States—to disguise the source and disbursement of the bribe payments by passing funds through a series of shell companies. The message sent by this prosecution is that the United States, working with its law enforcement partners abroad, will not hesitate to hold responsible those corporations and individuals who seek to enrich themselves through the corruption of the legitimate functions of government, no matter how sophisticated the scheme."

"This case illustrates the importance of our partnerships and the dedicated personnel who work to bring to justice those who are motivated by greed and act in their own best interest," said Assistant Director Richardson. "The FBI will not stand by idly while corrupt individuals threaten a fair and competitive economic system or fuel criminal enterprises. Our commitment to work alongside our foreign partners to root out corruption across the globe is unwavering and we thank our Brazilian and Swiss partners for their tireless work in this effort."

"No matter what the reason, when foreign officials receive bribes, they threaten our national security and the international free market system in which we trade," said Assistant Director in Charge Sweeney. "Just because they're out of our sight, doesn't mean they're beyond our reach. The FBI will use all available resources to put an end to this type of corrupt behavior."

Odebrecht pleaded guilty to a one-count criminal information filed today by the Criminal Division's Fraud Section and the U.S. Attorney's Office in the U.S. District Court for the Eastern District of New York, charging the company with conspiracy to violate the anti-bribery provisions of the Foreign Corrupt Practices Act (FCPA). Odebrecht agreed that the appropriate criminal fine is $4.5 billion, subject to further analysis of the company's ability to pay the total global penalties. In related proceedings, Odebrecht also settled with the Ministerio Publico Federal in Brazil and the Office of the Attorney General in Switzerland.

Under the plea agreement, the United States will credit the amount that Odebrecht pays to Brazil and Switzerland over the full term of their respective agreements, with the United States and Switzerland receiving 10 percent each of the principal of the total criminal fine and Brazil receiving the remaining 80 percent. The fine is subject to an inability to pay analysis to be completed by the Department of Justice and Brazilian authorities on or before March 31, 2017, because Odebrecht has represented it is only able to pay approximately $2.6 billion over the course of the respective agreements. Sentencing has been scheduled for April 17, 2017.

Braskem, whose American Depositary Receipts (ADRs) are publicly traded on the New York Stock Exchange, separately pleaded guilty to a one-count criminal information filed in the Eastern District of New York charging it with conspiracy to violate the anti-bribery provisions of the FCPA. Braskem agreed to pay a total criminal penalty of $632 million. Sentencing has not yet been scheduled. In related proceedings, Braskem also settled with the U.S. Securities and Exchange Commission (SEC), the Ministerio Publico Federal in Brazil and the Office of the Attorney General in Switzerland. Under the terms of its resolution with the SEC, Braskem agreed to a total of $325 million in disgorgement of profits. Braskem agreed to pay Brazilian authorities 70 percent of the total criminal penalty and agreed to pay the Swiss authorities 15 percent. The department has agreed to credit the criminal penalties paid to Brazilian and Swiss authorities as part of its agreement with the company. The United States will receive $94.8 million, an amount equal to 15 percent of the total criminal fines paid by Braskem.

Under their respective plea agreements, Odebrecht and Braskem are required to continue their cooperation with law enforcement, including in connection with the investigations and prosecutions of individuals responsible for the criminal conduct. Odebrecht and Braskem also agreed to adopt enhanced compliance procedures and to retain independent compliance monitors for three years. The cases are assigned to U.S. District Judge Raymond J. Dearie of the Eastern District of New York.

The combined total amount of United States, Brazilian and Swiss criminal and regulatory penalties paid by Braskem will be approximately $957 million. The combined total amount of penalties imposed against Odebrecht will be at least $2.6 billion and up to $4.5 billion. With a combined total of at least $3.5 billion, today's resolutions with Odebrecht and Braskem are the largest-ever global foreign bribery resolution.

The Bribery Schemes

According to its admissions, Odebrecht engaged in a massive and unparalleled bribery and bid-rigging scheme for more than a decade, beginning as early as 2001. During that time, Odebrecht paid approximately $788 million in bribes to government officials, their representatives and political parties in a number of countries in order to win business in those countries. The criminal conduct was directed by the highest levels of the company, with the bribes paid through a complex network of shell companies, off-book transactions and off-shore bank accounts.

As part of the scheme, Odebrecht and its co-conspirators created and funded an elaborate, secret financial structure within the company that operated to account for and disburse bribe payments to foreign government officials and political parties. By 2006, the development and operation of this secret financial structure had evolved such that Odebrecht established the "Division of Structured Operations," which effectively functioned as a stand-alone bribe department within Odebrecht and its related entities. Until approximately 2009, the head of the Division of Structured Operations reported to the highest levels within Odebrecht, including to obtain authorization to approve bribe payments. After 2009, this responsibility was delegated to certain company business leaders in Brazil and the other jurisdictions. To conceal its activities, the Division of Structured Operations utilized an entirely separate and off-book communications system, which allowed members of the Division of Structured Operations to communicate with one another and with outside financial operators and other co-conspirators about the bribes via secure emails and instant messages, using codenames and passwords.

The Division of Structured Operations managed the "shadow" budget for the Odebrecht bribery operation via a separate computer system that was used to request and process bribe payments as well as to generate and populate spreadsheets that tracked and internally accounted for the shadow budget. These funds for the company's sophisticated bribery operation were generated by the Odebrecht Finance Department through a variety of methods, as well as by certain Odebrecht subsidiaries, including Braskem. The funds were then funneled by the Division of Structured Operations to a series of off-shore entities that were not included on Odebrecht's balance sheet as related entities. The Division of Structured Operations then directed the disbursement of the funds from the off-shore entities to the bribe recipient, through the use of wire transfers through one or more of the off-shore entities, as well as through cash payments both inside and outside Brazil, which were sometimes delivered using packages or suitcases left at predetermined locations.

Odebrecht, its employees and agents took a number of steps while in the United States to further the scheme. For instance, in 2014 and 2015, while located in Miami, two Odebrecht employees engaged in conduct related to certain projects in furtherance of the scheme, including meetings with other co-conspirators to plan actions to be taken in connection with the Division of Structured Operations, the movement of criminal proceeds and other criminal conduct. In addition, some of the off-shore entities used by the Division of Structured Operations to hold and disburse unrecorded funds were established, owned and/or operated by individuals located in the United States. In all, this conduct resulted in corrupt payments and/or profits totaling approximately $3.336 billion.

Braskem also admitted to engaging in a wide-ranging bribery scheme and acknowledged the pervasiveness of its conduct. Between 2006 and 2014, Braskem paid approximately $250 million into Odebrecht's secret, off-book bribe payment system. Using the Odebrecht system, Braskem authorized the payment of bribes to politicians and political parties in Brazil, as well as to an official at Petróleo Brasileiro S.A.—Petrobras (Petrobras), the state-controlled oil company of Brazil. In exchange, Braskem received various benefits, including: preferential rates from Petrobras for the purchase of raw materials used by the company; contracts with Petrobras; and favorable legislation and government programs that reduced the company's tax liabilities in Brazil. This conduct resulted in corrupt payments and/or profits totaling approximately $465 million.

The Corporate Resolutions
The department reached these resolutions with Odebrecht and Braskem based on a number of factors, including: the failure to voluntarily disclose the conduct that triggered the investigation; the nature and seriousness of the offense, which spanned many years, involved the highest levels of the companies, occurred in multiple countries and involved sophisticated schemes to bribe high-level government

officials; the lack of an effective compliance and ethics program at the time of the conduct; and credit for each company's respective cooperation. The companies also engaged in remedial measures, including terminating and disciplining individuals who participated in the misconduct, adopting heightened controls and anti-corruption compliance protocols and significantly increasing the resources devoted to compliance.

The criminal penalty for Odebrecht reflects a 25 percent reduction off the bottom of the U.S. Sentencing Guidelines fine range because of Odebrecht's full cooperation with the government's investigation, while the criminal penalty for Braskem reflects a 15 percent reduction off the bottom of the U.S. Sentencing Guidelines as a result of its partial cooperation.

Odebrecht has represented its ability to pay a maximum of $2.6 billion of the total fine amount. The department and Brazilian authorities are engaged in further analysis regarding the company's claimed inability to pay, which will be completed on or before March 31, 2017.

* * *

The FBI's New York Field Office is investigating the case. Chief Dan Kahn and Trial Attorneys Christopher Cestaro, Sarah Edwards, David Fuhr, Kevin R. Gingras, Lorinda Laryea and David Last of the Criminal Division's Fraud Section and Assistant U.S. Attorneys Julia Nestor and Alixandra Smith of the Eastern District of New York are prosecuting the case.

The Criminal Division's Office of International Affairs also provided substantial assistance. The SEC and the Ministerio Publico Federal in Brazil the Departamento de Polícia Federal and the Office of the Attorney General in Switzerland provided significant cooperation.[23]

The Criminal Division's Fraud Section is responsible for investigating and prosecuting all FCPA matters.[24]

---

[23] See also FCPA Blog article "Former Braskem CEO charged with FCPA and money laundering conspiracies" by Richard L. Cassin November 21, 2019, in which notes that the US DoJ charged: "... the former chief executive officer of Braskem S.A. with helping his company and Odebrecht S.A. amass a giant slush fund and use it to bribe officials and political parties in Brazil. Jose Carlos Grubisich, 62, a Brazil citizen, was charged in federal court in Brooklyn, New York. He faces one count of conspiracy to violate the anti-bribery provisions of the Foreign Corrupt Practices Act, one count of conspiracy to violate the FCPA's books and records provisions and falsely certifying financial reports, and one count of conspiracy to commit international money laundering ... Braskem's controlling shareholder is Odebrecht, a Brazilian construction firm, with nearly 40 percent ownership and just over 50 percent of the voting shares. Brazil's state energy company, Petroleo Brasileiro S.A. (Petrobras), owns about a third of Braskem ... In December 2016, Odebrecht and Braskem pleaded guilty to bribing officials around the world. The companies agreed to pay $3.5 billion for a global settlement with authorities in the United States, Brazil, and Switzerland..."

[24] Additional information about the Justice Department's Fraud Section FCPA enforcement efforts can be found at www.justice.gov/criminal/fraud/fcpa

2.5.3 Text from the US DoJ Website[25]

Wednesday, November 20, 2019

Former Chief Executive Officer of a Brazilian Petrochemical Company Charged for His Role in a Scheme to Pay Bribes to Brazilian Officials and to Falsify Company Books and Records
An indictment was unsealed today charging a former chief executive officer (CEO) of Braskem S.A. (Braskem), a publicly traded Brazilian petrochemical company, for his role in a massive bribery and money laundering scheme involving **Braskem and its parent company, Odebrecht S.A. (Odebrecht)**, that resulted in the diversion of hundreds of millions of dollars from Braskem into a secret slush fund that was used, in part, to pay bribes to government officials, political parties and others in Brazil to obtain and retain business.

Jose Carlos Grubisich, 62, a citizen of Brazil who served as the CEO and a member of the board of directors of Braskem, as well as in various capacities for Odebrecht, was charged with one count of conspiracy to violate the anti-bribery provision of the Foreign Corrupt Practices Act (FCPA), one count of conspiracy to violate the books and records provision of the FCPA and to fail as a corporate officer to certify financial reports and one count of conspiracy to commit international money laundering. Grubisich was arrested this morning, and is scheduled to be arraigned this afternoon before U.S. District Judge Raymond J. Dearie of the Eastern District of New York.

"Grubisich and other senior executives at Braskem and Odebrecht allegedly engaged in a massive and sophisticated international bribery and money laundering scheme, employing secret slush funds, shell companies, and false accounting," said Assistant Attorney General Brian A. Benczkowski of the Justice Department's Criminal Division. "As demonstrated by the charges unsealed today, the Department continues to work closely with our domestic and international partners to root out and prosecute corporate fraud and corruption at the highest levels."

"As alleged in the indictment, Jose Carlos Grubisich used his position as CEO of a major publicly traded petrochemical company to funnel hundreds of millions of dollars through offshore accounts to bribe power brokers and serve the interests of his company," said U.S. Attorney Richard P. Donoghue for the Eastern District of New York. "Today's indictment once again demonstrates the commitment of the U.S. Department of Justice to investigate and prosecute those who take advantage of the United States financial system to further their financial crimes."

As alleged in the indictment, between approximately 2002 and 2014, Grubisich, together with other co-conspirators, including certain former Braskem and Odebrecht employees, engaged in a widespread bribery and money laundering scheme that resulted in the diversion of approximately $250 million of Braskem's

---

[25] https://www.justice.gov/opa/pr/former-chief-executive-officer-brazilian-petrochemical-company-charged-his-role-scheme-pay

funds into a secret slush fund, which was used, in part, to pay bribes to government officials, political parties and others in Brazil to obtain and retain business and certain business advantages for Braskem. The slush fund was allegedly generated by payments from Braskem's bank accounts in Brazil, New York and Florida pursuant to fraudulent contracts with offshore shell companies that were secretly controlled by Braskem. These shell companies funneled the slush funds to a department within Odebrecht responsible for making bribe payments, which ultimately made corrupt payments on Braskem's behalf, the indictment alleges.

Additionally, as alleged in the indictment, while CEO of Braskem, Grubisich was involved in negotiating and approving bribes to government officials using money from the slush fund. These included alleged payments made to ensure that Braskem could retain a contract for a significant petrochemical project in Brazil, and to ensure that Braskem could obtain favorable pricing in contract negotiations with Petroleo Brasileiro S.A.—Petrobras, Brazil's state-owned and state-controlled oil company. Grubisich regularly discussed the bribe payments with other co-conspirators, and was kept informed about bribe payments made on behalf of Braskem, the indictment alleges. Certain of the bribe payments that were allegedly negotiated and authorized by Grubisich were ultimately paid after Grubisich left his position as CEO of Braskem in 2008, but while he continued to serve in other capacities at Odebrecht and Braskem, and while he was a stockholder of Braskem.

Furthermore, as alleged in the indictment, while CEO of Braskem, Grubisich agreed to falsify Braskem's books and records by causing Braskem to falsely record the payments to the offshore shell companies controlled by Braskem as "commissions." Grubisich also signed false certifications submitted to the SEC that, among other things, attested that Braskem's annual reports fairly and accurately represented Braskem's financial condition, and that Grubisich, as Braskem's principal officer, had disclosed all fraudulent conduct by Braskem's management and other employees with control over Braskem's financial reporting, the indictment alleges.

The charges in the indictment are allegations, and the defendant is presumed innocent unless and until proven guilty.

Braskem and Odebrecht have each pleaded guilty in the Eastern District of New York to one-count criminal informations separately charging each with conspiracy to violate the anti-bribery provisions of the FCPA for their involvement in the widespread bribery and money laundering scheme. The cases are also assigned to Judge Dearie.

The FBI's International Corruption squad in New York investigated this case. Assistant Chief Lorinda Laryea and Trial Attorney Leila Babaeva of the Criminal Division's Fraud Section and Assistant U.S. Attorneys Alixandra Smith and Julia Nestor of the Eastern District of New York are prosecuting the case.

The Criminal Division's Office of International Affairs also provided substantial assistance. The U.S. Securities and Exchange Commission, the Brazilian Ministerio Publico Federal, the Brazilian Departamento de Polícia Federal and the Office of the Attorney General of Switzerland provided significant cooperation.

2.5.4 From the US Department of Justice Website[26]

Thursday, April 15, 2021

Former CEO of Braskem Pleads Guilty to Bribery
Approximately $250 Million Diverted from Braskem Through a Secret Slush Fund Used to Pay Bribes to Government Officials and Political Parties in Brazil

BROOKLYN, NY—Earlier today, in federal court in Brooklyn, **Jose Carlos Grubisich, the former chief executive officer of Braskem S.A. (Braskem)**, a publicly traded Brazilian petrochemical company, pleaded guilty before United States District Judge Raymond J. Dearie to (1) conspiring to violate the anti-bribery provisions of the Foreign Corrupt Practices Act (FCPA) and (2) conspiring to violate the books and records provisions of the FCPA in failing to accurately certify Braskem's financial reports. Grubisich and his co-conspirators engaged in a massive bribery scheme involving Braskem and its parent company Odebrecht S.A. (Odebrecht), in which hundreds of millions of dollars were diverted from Braskem to a secret slush fund that was used, in part, to pay bribes to government officials, political parties and others in Brazil to obtain and retain business for Braskem. Under the plea agreement, Grubisich has agreed to pay approximately $2.2 million in forfeiture.

Mark J. Lesko, Acting United States Attorney for the Eastern District of New York, Nicholas L. McQuaid, Acting Assistant Attorney General of the Justice Department's Criminal Division, and William F. Sweeney, Jr., Assistant Director-in-Charge, Federal Bureau of Investigation, New York Field Office (FBI), announced the guilty plea.

"Grubisich abused his position of trust as CEO of Braskem to both facilitate and conceal the payment of millions of dollars in bribes so that Braskem could increase its profits and its senior executives — including Grubisich himself — could personally benefit," stated Acting United States Attorney Lesko. "This Office is committed to the prosecution of corrupt gatekeepers, including officers and directors of public companies, who, like Grubisich, use the United States' financial system to commit crimes."

"As CEO of a publicly traded company, Grubisich and other senior executives at Braskem engaged in a large-scale, sophisticated international bribery and fraud scheme and then lied to U.S. shareholders and authorities to conceal their criminal conduct," stated Acting Assistant Attorney General McQuaid. "Today's guilty plea demonstrates the Department's commitment to holding individuals accountable for corrupt and fraudulent conduct, including those at the highest corporate echelons."

As set forth in court filings and at today's proceedings, between approximately 2002 and 2014, Grubisich, a citizen of Brazil, who served as the CEO and a member of the Board of Directors of Braskem as well as in various capacities for Odebrecht—engaged in a scheme to bribe Brazilian government officials in

---

[26] https://www.justice.gov/usao-edny/pr/former-ceo-braskem-pleads-guilty-bribery

violation of the FCPA. As part of the scheme, Grubisich and his co-conspirators diverted approximately $250 million from Braskem into a secret slush fund which Grubisich and others had set up through fraudulent contracts and offshore shell companies that were secretly controlled by Braskem. At the time of the conspiracy, Braskem's American Depositary Receipts were publicly traded on the New York Stock Exchange.

Grubisich admitted that, while CEO of Braskem, he agreed to pay bribes to Brazilian government officials to ensure Braskem's retention of a contract for a significant petrochemical project from Petroleo Brasileiro S.A.–Petrobras, Brazil's state-owned and state-controlled oil company. Grubisich further admitted that while CEO of Braskem, he agreed to falsify Braskem's books and records by causing Braskem to falsely record the payments to offshore shell companies controlled by Braskem as payments for legitimate services. Grubisich signed false Sarbanes-Oxley certifications submitted to the United States Securities and Exchange Commission (SEC) that, among other things, attested that Braskem's annual reports fairly and accurately represented Braskem's financial condition, and that Grubisich, as Braskem's principal officer, had disclosed all fraudulent conduct by Braskem's management and other employees with control over Braskem's financial reporting.

In December 2016, Braskem and Odebrecht pleaded guilty in the Eastern District of New York to one-count criminal informations charging each with conspiracy to violate the anti-bribery provisions of the FCPA. Braskem settled with the SEC in related proceedings on the same day.

The government's case is being prosecuted by Assistant U.S. Attorneys Julia Nestor and Alixandra Smith of the Office's Business and Securities Fraud Section, and Assistant Chief Lorinda Laryea and Trial Attorney Leila Babaeva of the Criminal Division's Fraud Section. Assistant U.S. Attorney Laura Mantell of the Office's Civil Division is handling forfeiture matters. The FBI's International Corruption squad in New York is investigating the case.

The Criminal Division's Office of International Affairs provided substantial assistance, as did the SEC's Division of Enforcement, Ministério Público Federal and the Departamento de Polícia Federal in Brazil, the Office of the Attorney General in Switzerland, and the governments of Portugal, Andorra, United Kingdom, and Panama.

The Defendant

JOSE CARLOS GRUBISICH
Age: 64
Sao Paulo, Brazil

E.D.N.Y. Docket No. 19-CR-102 (RJD)

2.5.5 From IDB's Website[27]

September 4, 2019

Odebrecht Reaches Settlement Agreement with IDB Group Resulting in Sanctions
Sanctions include debarment and contributions of US$ 50 million to go to NGOs and charities serving vulnerable communities in IDB member countries

Following an extensive investigation by the Office of Institutional Integrity (OII, an independent office of the Inter-American Development Bank), with the cooperation of the Brazilian company Odebrecht S.A. (Odebrecht), OII announced today the debarment of CNO S.A. (CNO), a subsidiary of Odebrecht, for six years in connection with prohibited practices in two IDB-financed projects. The debarment makes CNO ineligible to participate in IDB Group-financed projects.

The OII investigation uncovered bribes paid in two IDB-financed projects: the Tocoma Hydroelectric Power Plant Program in Venezuela and the Highway Rehabilitation Program in the State of São Paulo in Brazil.

As part of the Settlement, Odebrecht does not contest the evidence obtained by OII demonstrating that in both projects CNO committed corrupt practices when it made payments to public officials in order to facilitate either the award, contract execution payments and/or contract amendments.

According to OII's evidence, the illicit payments amounted to upward of 5–6% of each contract amount, including amendments. Specific to the Highway Rehabilitation Program, between 2006 and 2008, CNO paid government officials a total amount equivalent to approximately US$ 380,000. In the case of the Tocoma Hydroelectric Power Plant Program, evidence obtained by OII indicates that between 2007 and 2015, illicit payments and transactions of up to US$ 118 million were made utilizing a complex network of agents and offshore financial payment schemes.

The sanctions are the result of a Negotiated Resolution Agreement (the Settlement) between the IDB, the Inter-American Investment Corporation (IDB Invest) and Odebrecht on behalf of its subsidiaries, CNO and Odebrecht Engenharia e Construção S.A. (OEC). The Settlement also includes a conditional non-debarment applied to OEC for ten years and CNO for four years directly following CNO's six-year period of debarment. When conditionally non-debarred, a company remains eligible to participate in IDB Group-financed projects but only if it fully meets the conditions of the Settlement. If any of the conditions are not met, the company will be debarred.

As part of the sanctions, Odebrecht commits to make a total contribution of US$ 50 million, starting in 2024, directly to NGOs and charities managing social projects

---

[27] www.iadb.org/en/news/odebrecht-reaches-settlement-agreement-idb-group-resulting-sanctions-0

with the purpose of improving the quality of life of vulnerable communities in the IDB's developing member countries.

In addition to the sanctions against CNO and OEC, 19 CNO subsidiaries will be subject to debarment and a further 41 OEC subsidiaries will be subject to conditional non-debarment. CNO branches in Africa are excluded from the sanction. Separately, the Odebrecht group commits to comply with certain conditions necessary to demonstrate its reforms.

The Settlement allows for a reduced period of debarment in light of Odebrecht's continued cooperation, including internal investigations that are intended to uncover systemic integrity risks to IDB Group-financed activities. Under the terms of the Settlement, Odebrecht commits to report on its compliance program through an independent monitor.

The Settlement was negotiated by OII in accordance with the IDB Group's Sanctions Procedures. Settlements of this nature are used by the IDB Group and other multilateral development banks as an effective means to resolve investigations related to prohibited practices in exchange for cooperation and disclosures of systemic integrity risks.

The debarment of CNO and listed subsidiaries qualifies for cross-debarment by other multilateral development banks (MDBs) under the Agreement for Mutual Enforcement of Debarment Decisions that was signed on April 9, 2010.

For additional information on the IDB's Office of Institutional Integrity and its sanctions system, please click here.

Chapter 3
Financial Services

3.1 Malaysia Development Berhad

3.1.1 Text from Wikipedia[1] (January 21, 2022)

Malaysia Development Berhad Scandal

The 1Malaysia Development Berhad scandal (1MDB scandal) was a large corruption, bribery and money laundering scandal which began in 2009 in Malaysia but became global in scope and was exposed in 2015. It was as described as "one of the world's greatest financial scandals" [1, 2] and declared by the United States Department of Justice as the "largest kleptocracy case to date" in 2016 [3].

In 2015, Malaysia's then-Prime Minister Najib Razak was accused of channelling over RM 2.67 billion (approximately US$700 million) into his personal bank accounts from 1Malaysia Development Berhad (1MDB), a government-run strategic development company masterminded by Low Taek Jho [4]. Dismissal of charges triggered widespread outrage among Malaysians [5], with many calling for Najib Razak's resignation. Among Najib's critics was politician Mahathir Mohamad [6], who later defeated Najib in the 2018 general election and returned to power.

Anwar Ibrahim, a political leader in opposition to Najib, openly questioned 1MDB's credentials as early as 2010. He had told Parliament that, according to records held by the Companies Commission, the company "has no business address and no appointed auditor [7]." According to its publicly filed accounts, 1MDB had nearly RM 42 billion (US$11.73 billion) in debt by 2015 [8]. Some of this debt resulted from a $3 billion state-guaranteed 2013 bond issue led by the American investment bank Goldman Sachs, which had been reported to have received fees of up to $300 million for the deal, although the bank disputes this figure [9]. Nevertheless, Goldman Sachs was charged in a Foreign Bribery Case and agreed to pay over $2.9 billion in a settlement with the U.S. Department of Justice (DOJ) [10]. The

---

[1] Link: https://en.wikipedia.org/wiki/1Malaysia_Development_Berhad_scandal

Malaysian Conference of Rulers called for prompt investigation of the scandal, saying that it was causing a crisis of confidence in Malaysia [11, 12].

After the 2018 election, the newly elected prime minister, Mahathir Mohamad, reopened investigations into the 1MDB scandal [13]. Malaysian Immigration Department barred Najib [14] and 11 others [15] from leaving the country, while the police seized more than 500 handbags and 12,000 pieces of jewellery estimated to be worth US$270 million from property linked to Najib [16]. Najib was charged with criminal breach of trust, money laundering and abuse of power, while Low Taek Jho (commonly referred to as Jho Low), was charged with money laundering. The U.S. Department of Justice pursued its own investigation into 1MDB, alleging that more than US$4.5 billion was diverted from 1MDB by Jho Low and other conspirators including officials from Malaysia, Saudi Arabia and the United Arab Emirates [17]. Najib was subsequently found guilty of seven charges connected to SRC International, a dummy corporation associated with 1MDB, and was sentenced to twelve years imprisonment [18].

In September 2020, the alleged amount stolen from 1MDB was estimated to be US$4.5 billion and a Malaysian government report listed 1MBD's outstanding debts to be at US$7.8 billion [19]. The government has assumed 1MDB's debts, which includes 30-year bonds due in 2039 [20].

As of 5 August 2021, in an ongoing effort to fight global kleptocracy, the U.S. Department of Justice recovered and returned a total of US$1.2 billion of 1MDB funds misappropriated within U.S. jurisdiction to the people of Malaysia [21], joining a list of several countries which have initiated recovery or that have already repatriated smaller recovered amounts [22].

Contents
1. Email and newspaper exposés
2. Malaysian investigations and actions

    2.1. Change of auditors and transparency
    2.2. Debts and rating downgrade
    2.3. Donation explanation from government
    2.4. Bank Negara actions
    2.5. Police reports
    2.6. Local lawsuits
    2.7. Government actions
    2.8. Ramifications and debt restructuring default
    2.9. Renewed investigations after 14th general election

3. Investigations by foreign law enforcement agencies

    3.1. Australia
    3.2. Hong Kong
    3.3. Indonesia
    3.4. Luxembourg
    3.5. Seychelles
    3.6. Singapore

3.7. Switzerland
3.8. United Arab Emirates
3.9. United Kingdom
3.10. United States

4. Recovery of 1MDB assets

1. Email and Newspaper Exposés

It was reported by news portal Sarawak Report and British newspaper The Sunday Times, using leaked email correspondences, that Penang-based financier Jho Low, who has ties with Najib Razak's step son, siphoned out US$700 million from a joint venture deal between 1MDB and PetroSaudi International through Good Star Ltd [23–27]. Although Low never received an official position in 1MDB, he is described as someone who was regularly consulted about 1MDB without having any decision-making authority [28]. An email revealed that Low had the loan approval from Najib for $1 billion without getting any approval from Bank Negara [29, 30]. Sarawak Report showed, using minutes of a meeting at 1MDB, that CEO Arul Kanda gave out false bank statements pertaining to its subsidiary's accounts at the Singapore branch of BSI Bank [31, 32]. Arul Kanda denied the allegation that he gave false bank statements to Bank Negara [33].

It was claimed through a report by The Wall Street Journal that 1MDB made overpriced purchases of power assets in Malaysia through Genting Group in 2012. Genting then allegedly donated this money to a foundation controlled by Najib, who used these funds for election campaign purposes during the 2013 general elections [34–36]. According to a news report quoting 1MDB, the company denied that it overpaid for its energy assets. 1MDB was quoted as saying that their energy acquisitions were made only when the company was convinced of its long-term value [37].

Further allegations were made by The Wall Street Journal (WSJ) that $700 million was transferred from 1MDB and deposited in AmBank and Affin Bank accounts under Najib's name [38, 39]. A task force to investigate these claims had frozen six bank accounts linked to Najib and 1MDB [40, 41]. The Malaysian Anti-Corruption Commission (MACC) subsequently, in August 2015, cleared 1MDB of this allegation. MACC issued a statement saying, among other things, "Results of the investigation have found that the RM2.6bil which was allegedly transferred into the account belonging to Najib Razak came from the contribution of donors, and not from 1MDB" [42].

According to highly placed sources, three of the bank accounts that had been frozen belong to Najib [43, 44]. The WSJ revealed the bank account details online to rebut denials by Najib and his supporters [45–47]. Singapore police had frozen two Singapore bank accounts in connection with their own investigation into the alleged financial mismanagement at 1MDB, after reports stated that $700 million worth of deposits was moved through Falcon Bank in Singapore into Najib's personal accounts in Malaysia [48, 49]. However, 1MDB denied having any knowledge of their accounts being frozen, and said they have not been contacted by any of the foreign investigating authorities [50].

The WSJ also reported that 1MDB transferred around $850 million via three transactions in 2014 to a British Virgin Islands-registered company with a name disguising that it was controlled by International Petroleum Investment Company (IPIC), a United Arab Emirates state investment vehicle, according to wire transfer documents [51–53].

The WSJ released a report stating that 1MDB failed to pay $1.4 billion to IPIC. The money was owed to IPIC after it had guaranteed a US$3.5 billion bond issued by 1MDB to fund its purchase of power plant assets in 2012 [54–56]. The WSJ released another report saying that a further $993 million was missing that 1MDB was supposed to pay IPIC [57–59]. 1MDB responded to the WSJ report, saying that the company continues to enjoy a strong business relationship with IPIC, as proven by the execution of a binding term sheet that saw IPIC assume obligation for a $3.5 billion bond, currently held by 1MDB, and followed a $1 billion cash payment made by IPIC to 1MDB in June [60]. Earlier in October 2015, IPIC reaffirmed their commitment to working with 1MDB and the Malaysian Ministry of Finance [61].

Another report by the WSJ pointed out that 1MDB, in connection with a United States political fundraiser DuSable Capital Management LLC, signed a joint venture agreement creating a fund, Yurus PE Fund, to develop solar power plants in Malaysia [62, 63]. Six months after the joint venture agreement was signed, 1MDB bought out DuSable's stake of 49% of Yurus for $69 million before any construction took place [64, 65]. According to bank transfer information, the WSJ revealed that Najib spent close to $15 million on clothes, jewellery, and a car in places such as the United States, Singapore, and Italy using a credit card that was paid from one of several private bank accounts owned by Najib, that 1MDB funds had been diverted to [66–69].

2. Malaysian Investigations and Actions
2.1. Change of Auditors and Transparency

The RM 425 million profit declared between 25 September 2009 and 31 March 2010 raised many criticisms and controversies about the lack of transparency in 1MDB's published accounts. Tony Pua, DAP Member of Parliament for Petaling Jaya Utara, questioned Najib, 1MDB's advisory board chairman, as to whether the figures were the result of an asset injection into 1MDB by the government such as the transfer of land rights to the company [70, 71].

During the October 2010 parliamentary session, 1MDB explained that its accounts had been fully audited and signed off by KPMG, and closed as of 31 March 2010. Deloitte was involved in the valuation and analysis of the portfolio, while Ernst & Young provided tax advice for 1MDB.

1MDB eventually rang alarm bells by asking for a six-month extension on the filing of its annual report with the Companies Commission of Malaysia (CCM) due by 30 September 2013. At the same time, the change of three auditors since its inception in 2009 was considered suspicious [72, 73]. Responding to earlier criticism, CCM said that 1MDB had responded and lodged the necessary information, including registering an address, as required by law [74].

The Sungai Besi airport land transfer took place in June 2011 as a precedent for the development known as Bandar Malaysia, a mixed integrated project of commercial, residential, and hi-tech green environment [75]. Prior to this, there had been questions in parliament by the opposition regarding the lack of progress on Bandar Malaysia even though 1MDB had already raised RM 3.5 billion in loans and Islamic bonds to fund the project and take ownership of the land [76, 77]. In April 2013, 1MDB finally awarded a RM 2.1 billion contract to Perbadanan Perwira Harta Malaysia (PPHM), a subsidiary of Lembaga Tabung Angkatan Tentera (LTAT) to develop eight sites for the relocation of Pangkalan Udara Kuala Lumpur, the military base on the Sungai Besi land that was to be developed [78]. The construction of Bandar Malaysia was set to commence following the completion of this relocation. As part of its debt rationalisation plan, on 31 December 2015, 1MDB inked an agreement with a consortium comprising Iskandar Waterfront Holdings and China Railway Engineering Corporation to sell 60% of its stake in Bandar Malaysia Sdn Bhd [79]. This deal however eventually fell through [80].

On 7 September 2015, a member of the board of advisors to 1MDB, Abdul Samad Alias, resigned stating that he did so after many of his requests for information on 1MDB affairs were ignored [81, 82]. 1MDB subsequently denied receiving repeated requests from Abdul Samad, stating that its president, Arul Kanda, had personally met Abdul Samad in January and March that year to "discuss the company's affairs" [83].

1MDB had not had a proper external accounts audit since 2013, partly as a result of Deloitte Malaysia, their auditors at the start of that period, issuing a statement in July 2016 saying that their audit reports of 1MDB financial statements, dated 28 March 2014 and 5 November 2014 covering financial years 2013 and 2014 respectively, should no longer be relied upon [84, 85]. By early March 2015, with public discontent growing at the perceived lack of financial transparency at 1MDB, the Prime Minister, who was also the Chairman of 1MDB's Board of Advisors, ordered the Auditor General of Malaysia to carry out an audit of 1MDB [86]. However, on completion of the audit, the final report was classified as an Official Secret and only made available to the Public Accounts Committee (PAC) tasked to investigate improprieties at 1MDB [87, 88]. Purported copies of the report however surfaced on the internet [89–91]. After Najib's ouster in the 2018 general election, the much-leaked audit report was declassified by the new government on 12 May 2018 [92].

In May 2018, after the formation of the new Cabinet following Pakatan Harapan's victory in the General Elections, Finance Minister Lim Guan Eng ordered the appointment of PricewaterhouseCoopers (PwC) to conduct a special position audit and review of 1MDB [93].

2.2 Debts and Rating Downgrade

It was reported that by early 2015, 1MDB has accumulated debts of nearly RM 42 billion [94]. Further alleged financial challenges caused 1MDB bonds to trade at a record low [95, 96]. Additionally, the Malaysian cabinet rejected a requested RM 3 billion cash injection by 1MDB, narrowing its options to pay off its debts on time [97–99].

2.3 Donation Explanation from Government

Photo: Former Malaysian Prime Minister Najib has been heavily linked to 1MDB's eventual insolvency [100].

On 3 August 2015, the MACC stated that the RM 2.6 billion that had been banked into Najib's personal account came from donors, not 1MDB, but did not elaborate on who the donors were or why the funds were transferred, nor why this explanation had taken so long to emerge since the allegations were first made on 2 July 2015 [101, 102]. UMNO Kuantan division chief Wan Adnan Wan Mamat later claimed that the RM 2.6 billion was from Saudi Arabia as thanks for fighting ISIS. He further claimed that the Muslim community in the Philippines as well as southern Thailand had also received similar donations, and that since the donations were made to Najib personally as opposed to UMNO, the funds were deposited into Najib's personal accounts [103].

Saudi Foreign Minister Adel al-Jubeir said he was aware of the donation, and said that it was a genuine donation with nothing expected in return [104, 105]. Attorney-general Mohamad Apandi Ali has said that the donation was from one of the sons of the late Saudi King Abdullah [106, 107], namely Turki bin Abdullah Al Saud [108]. In an interview with ABC News, WSJ finance editor Ken Brown stated that the money did not come from the Saudis and they had evidence that it came from companies related to 1MDB [109–111].

2.4 Bank Negara Actions

Using the premise that 1MDB had used inaccurate or incomplete disclosure of information, Bank Negara, in early 2016, revoked permissions previously granted to 1MDB for investments abroad totalling $1.83 billion [112, 113]. Bank Negara then called for the Attorney General to begin criminal prosecution of 1MDB after completing its own investigations into 1MDB fund transfers [114, 115]. 1MDB responded that they were unable to repatriate the $1.83 billion demanded by Bank Negara because the funds had already been utilized [116].

2.5 Police Reports

The scandal took a dramatic twist on 28 August 2015 when a member of Najib Razak's own UMNO party filed a civil suit against him alleging a breach of duties as trustee and that he defrauded party members by failing to disclose receipt of the donated funds, and account for their use [117]. This suit was filed in the Kuala Lumpur High Court and also named party executive secretary Abdul Rauf Yusof. Expressing fear that Najib Razak would wield influence to remove any member of UMNO "for the sole purpose of avoiding liability", the court was also being moved for an injunction to restrain UMNO, its Supreme Council, state liaison body, divisions and branches from removing the nominal plaintiff as a party member pending the determination of the suit. The plaintiff is also seeking a repayment amounting to $650 million, the amount allegedly deposited by Najib to a Singapore bank, an account of all monies that he had received in the form of donations, details of all monies in an AmPrivate Banking Account (No. 2112022009694), allegedly belonging to Najib, along with damages, costs, and other reliefs [118]. One of the UMNO representatives, Anina Saadudin, who filed the lawsuit, was immediately expelled from the party [119–121].

Another police report was filed by a Johor UMNO member, Abdul Rashed Jamaludin, against Najib Razak, over the funds that went into his bank account and other wrongdoings at 1MDB [122, 123].

Another UMNO member, Khairuddin Abu Hassan, and his lawyer Matthias Chang, has submitted evidence on the 1MDB scandal to the Swiss attorney general for investigation into whether any Swiss banks had done business with 1MDB [124, 125]. Khairuddin also lodged a police report in Hong Kong against Najib Razak and Jho Low, pertaining to four companies: Alliance Assets International, Cityfield Enterprises, Bartingale International and Wonder Quest Investment, which had purported dealings with 1MDB [126, 127]. Khairuddin and Matthias were barred from leaving Malaysia [128–130]. Khairuddin and Matthias were charged under the Security Offenses Act (SOSMA) under the pretext of sabotaging Malaysia's banking and financial sector [131–133].

2.6 Local Lawsuits

The opposition People's Justice Party (PKR) has filed a lawsuit against Najib Razak, Tengku Adnan Tengku Mansor, 1MDB and the Election Commission accusing them of violating election laws on campaign expenses, using funds from 1MDB [134, 135]. However, the Malaysian High Court threw out the suit, stating PKR had no legal standing to bring the suit against Najib and 1MDB [136, 137].

Former Prime Minister Mahathir has filed a lawsuit against Najib Razak for alleged interference in government investigations on 1MDB and the RM 2.6 billion political donation [138–140].

2.7 Government Actions

Following criticisms of the 1MDB issue, deputy Prime Minister Muhyiddin Yassin was removed from office and his position was given to then Home Minister Ahmad Zahid Hamidi [141, 142]. Also removed from office was Rural and Regional Development Minister Shafie Apdal who was also critical of the 1MDB issue [143, 144]. Both were eventually expelled from UMNO in June 2016.

The attorney general Abdul Gani Patail, who was heading a multi-agency task force investigating claims of misappropriations of funds allegedly involving Najib Razak and 1MDB, was dismissed and his position given to Mohamed Apandi Ali, a former Federal Court judge [145, 146]. Additionally, the Public Action Committee that was investigating the purported losses in 1MDB was indefinitely postponed due to four of its members being given positions in Najib Razak's cabinet, namely the PAC chairman Nur Jazlan Mohamed, Reezal Merican Naina Merican, Wilfred Madius Tangau and Mas Ermieyati Samsudin [147–149].

The news publications The Edge Malaysia and The Edge Financial Daily were suspended, for three months in July 2015 for allegedly publishing false reports about 1MDB issues, by the Malaysian Home Ministry [150–152]. Also in 2015, the website Sarawak Report was blocked by Malaysian Communications and Multimedia Commission, which regulates Internet services in Malaysia [153, 154]. The Malaysian police also issued an arrest warrant for Clare Rewcastle Brown, who was managing the Sarawak Report, alleging involvement in activities detrimental to parliamentary democracy and disseminating false reports about prime minister Najib [155, 156].

The police also arrested UMNO member Khairuddin Abu Hassan after he lodged police reports in London, Singapore, France and Hong Kong regarding alleged financial improprieties by 1MDB [157–159]. According to his lawyer, Khairuddin was going to the United States to meet with the Federal Bureau of Investigation (FBI) to urge them to probe 1MDB over money laundering [160, 161]. However, the FBI's New York City office confirmed to the WSJ that no agent had arranged to meet Khairuddin or had any previous contact with him [162].

Former Kedah Menteri Besar Mukhriz Mahathir resigned his office on 3 February 2016, saying he did so because he had been told by Najib Razak that he was in the wrong by criticising him and 1MDB publicly [163, 164]. Four months later, in June, Mukhriz was expelled from UMNO. His father, Mahathir Mohamad, who had been Malaysia's fourth prime minister and who had been a Najib supporter since Najib assumed office, withdrew his support and quit UMNO later that same month [165].

Opposition member of parliament Rafizi Ramli was arrested and charged under the Official Secrets Act by the police and the government for leaking information about the Auditor General's report on 1MDB [166–168].

The Home Ministry stated that they and Interpol had been unsuccessful in locating various individuals linked to 1MDB to help in facilitating their investigations, including business tycoon Jho Low, 1MDB's former senior executives Casey Tang Keng Chee and Jasmine Loo Ai Swan, SRC International managing director Nik Faisal Ariff Kamil, and Deutsche Bank country manager Yusof Annuar Yaacob [169–171].

Internet access was blocked by the Malaysian Communications and Multimedia Commission (MCMC), to websites including Medium.com, a social journalism platform over just a single article posted by Sarawak Report [172, 173]. Another website, Asia Sentinel, was blocked after carrying a Sarawak Report article related to MACC completing a probe that allegedly resulted in 37 charges being drawn up against Najib [174–176]. The Malaysian Insider, was also blocked and its journalists investigated for carrying a report alleging that the MACC had found enough evidence in its investigations into Najib to charge him for corruption [177–179]. Blocks were removed shortly after Najib's government was deposed [180].

2.8 Ramifications and Debt Restructuring Default

The Malaysian Public Accounts Committee (PAC) inquiry into 1MDB revealed that the management of the fund acted without the board's approval and misled auditors several times [181–183], calling for the police to investigate its former manager [184, 185]. The PAC also found that the board of directors in which Najib Razak was the chairman failed in giving proper oversight of the fund's finances [186, 187]. The 1MDB board of directors immediately submitted their resignations after the PAC findings were made public [188–190]. The PAC report stated that US$3.5 billion was paid to a company, Aabar Investments PJS, but IPIC released a statement that neither it or its subsidiary Aabar Investments PJS have any links to a British Virgin Islands-incorporated firm Aabar BVI or received any money from that BVI firm [191–193].

International Petroleum Investment Company made an announcement in a filing in the London Stock Exchange that 1MDB failed to make a US$1.1 billion payment as part of its debt restructuring agreement, and that the debt deal between the two companies has been terminated [194–196].

2.9 Renewed Investigations after 14th General Election

After the 14th Malaysian general election on 9 May 2018 which marked a historic defeat for the Barisan Nasional coalition led by Najib Razak, Pakatan Harapan formed a new government led by Prime Minister Mahathir Mohamad. The government set up a special task force headed by former Attorney General Tan Sri Abdul Gani Patail to renew investigations into the 1MDB scandal [197].

The government barred Najib Razak from leaving the country, and the police seized cash and valuable items amounting to between RM 900 million and RM 1.1 billion ($220 million and $269 million) from residential units linked to Najib and his wife Rosmah Mansor. As claimed by the police, this was the biggest seizure in Malaysian history, with the seized items comprising more than 12,000 pieces of jewelry, 423 valuable watches and 567 handbags made up of 37 luxury brands [198, 199]. Najib was subsequently arrested by the MACC [200]. In September 2018, he faced 25 charges relating to abuse of power and money laundering amounting to RM 2.3 billion ($556 million), on top of seven charges with criminal breach of trust and power abuse brought against him in the preceding two months [201]. As of April 2019, he stands with 42 charges.

The government has also issued arrest warrants against Jho Low and former director of SRC International Nik Faisal Ariff Kamil in a graft probe related to the state fund 1MDB [202].

On 28 June 2018, two days before the end of his employment contract, 1MDB sacked its president and Chief Executive Officer Arul Kanda on grounds of dereliction of duties [203].

Media reports from June 2018 also indicate that the MACC froze bank accounts associated with UMNO, purportedly in relation to investigations into the 1MDB matter [204].

In August 2018, Malaysian police filed criminal charges against Jho Low and his father Larry Low over money laundering of US$457 million, which was allegedly stolen from 1MDB and most of the cash used for purchasing the superyacht Equanimity [205, 206]. From 29 October through 28 November 2018, the Equanimity was up for auction by investigators (pending a US$1 million deposit) [207]. It was eventually sold to the Genting Group at $126 million [208].

In December 2018, the Attorney-General Chambers of Malaysia filed criminal charges against subsidiaries of Goldman Sachs, their former employees Tim Leissner and Roger Ng Chong Hwa, former 1MDB employee Jasmine Loo, and Jho Low in connection with 1MDB bond offerings arranged and underwritten by Goldman Sachs in 2012 and 2013. The prosecutors were seeking criminal fines in excess of $2.7 billion misappropriated from the bonds proceeds, $600 million in fees received by Goldman Sachs, as well as custodial sentences against the individuals accused [209–211].

On 28 July 2020, Najib was found guilty in all seven charges related to SRC and was sentenced to 12 years' jail and a fine of RM 210 million ($49.5 million) [18].

3. Investigations by Foreign Law Enforcement Agencies

3.1 Australia

The Australian fund management company Avestra Asset Management, which managed up to RM 2.32 billion in 1MDB funds, is being liquidated, and is under investigation by the Australian Securities and Investments Commission for reported breaches of the law and potential losses to its members [212–214]. The Australian High Court has ordered five investment schemes run by Avestra to close down after discovering undisclosed related-party transactions, with 13 potential breaches of corporate law and failure to invest according to the fund's individual mandates [215, 216].

3.2 Hong Kong

Hong Kong police have begun investigations regarding $250 million in Credit Suisse branch deposits in Hong Kong linked to Najib Razak and 1MDB [217, 218].

3.3 Indonesia

Indonesia seized the superyacht Equanimity on 28 February 2018 on the island of Bali at the request of the U.S. Department of Justice, as part of a corruption investigation linked to the 1MDB scandal [219]. The Indonesian government returned the yacht to Malaysia in August 2018, following the activation of the Mutual Legal Assistance Treaties between Indonesia, the United States and Malaysia [220, 221].

3.4 Luxembourg

State prosecutors in Luxembourg have also started money laundering investigations concerning 1MDB as it involved transfers of several hundred million dollars to an offshore company involving a bank account from Luxembourg [222–225]. The bank in question is a private bank of the Edmond de Rothschild Group that manages money on behalf of wealthy clients [226–228].

3.5 Seychelles

The Seychelles's Financial Intelligence Unit is helping an international investigation into the troubled state fund 1MDB, by providing detailed information relating to offshore entities registered in Seychelles that are related to the international investigation [229–231].

1MBD has not contested, and appears unlikely to contest, any lawsuit which has arisen from the investigations of foreign investigating authorities [232].

3.6 Singapore

In Singapore, the Monetary Authority of Singapore (MAS) and the Commercial Affairs Department have seized a number of bank accounts in Singapore for possible money-laundering offences related to investigations into alleged financial mismanagement at 1MDB [233–235]. One of the bank accounts frozen belonged to Yak Yew Chee, who was the relationship manager for 1MDB Global Investments Ltd, Aabar Investment PJS Limited and SRC International and Low Taek Jho [236–238]. Singaporean Yeo Jiawei, an ex-BSI banker, has been charged with money laundering and cheating offences as part of the Singapore probe into 1MDB, and Yeo's dealings with firms linked to 1MDB, Brazen Sky Ltd. and Bridge Partners Investment Management [239, 240]. A second individual, Kelvin Ang Wee

Keng, was charged with corruption in connection with the Singaporean investigation into 1MDB [241, 242].

According to a joint statement from the Attorney General's Chambers and the Monetary Authority of Singapore, assets totalling S$240 million have been seized during their investigations into 1MDB [243, 244]. Of the bank accounts and properties seized were S$120 million belonging to Jho Low and his family [245–247].

In March 2017, MAS issued a 10-year prohibition order against former Goldman Sachs banker Tim Leissner for making false statements on behalf of his bank without its knowledge [248]. The prohibition order, which prevents him from performing any regulated activity under the Securities and Futures Act and from managing any capital market services firm in Singapore, was extended in December 2018 from 10 years to lifetime after he admitted to charges related to an investigation into the 1MDB scandal [249, 250].

In September 2018, the Singapore State Courts granted the return of 1MDB monies with a total value of S$15.3 million to Malaysia while solicitors for the Malaysian government stated that efforts to recover other unlawfully misappropriated assets were ongoing [251, 252].

3.7 Switzerland

Swiss authorities under the direction of the Office of the Attorney General of Switzerland began to freeze bank accounts amounting to several million US dollars linked to 1MDB [253–255]. The Swiss attorney general's office said its investigation revealed indications that funds estimated to be US$4 billion may have been misappropriated and said it was looking into four cases of potential criminal conduct [256, 257]. The Swiss prosecutor has said that money had been deposited into Swiss bank accounts of former Malaysian public officials and current and former officials of United Arab Emirates [258–260]. Swiss Financial Market Supervisory Authority (Finma) has begun investigations into several Swiss banks as part of the money laundering probe involving 1MDB [261–263].

On 15 March 2018, the Swiss parliament rejected a motion to return seized monies from their investigations into 1MDB to the Malaysian people, as had been lobbied for by Swiss politicians and non-governmental bodies [264]. However, on 10 July 2018, Swiss Attorney General Michael Lauber indicated that Switzerland would not enrich itself by keeping illicit or stolen assets and be able to have the monies returned by legal obligations [265].

3.8 United Arab Emirates

The United Arab Emirates has issued travel bans and frozen bank accounts of former Abu Dhabi sovereign-wealth fund International Petroleum Investment Company's employees Khadem al-Qubaisi and Mohammed Badawy Al Husseiny who had close connections to 1MDB, and may have used the British Virgin Islands-based Aabar Investments PJS to funnel money from 1MDB into various accounts and companies around the world [266, 267].

3.9 United Kingdom

The UK's Serious Fraud Office has begun an investigations into money laundering involving 1MDB, after it was highlighted by the investigative journalist Clare

Rewcastle Brown and the Sarawak Report [268, 269]. The UK's investigation is focusing on the transfer of money from 1MDB funds in Malaysia to Switzerland as it involved Royal Bank of Scotland's branch in Zurich [270, 271].

3.10 United States

The Wall Street Journal reported in 2015 that the Federal Bureau of Investigation had begun investigations into money laundering involving 1MDB [272–274]. The international corruption unit of the US Department of Justice (DOJ) began a probe into property purchases in the United States involving Najib Razak's stepson Riza Aziz and the transfer of millions of dollars into Najib Razak's personal account [275, 276]. The probe was looking at properties purchased by shell companies belonging to Riza Aziz and close family friend Jho Low [277, 278]. Investment banks such as JPMorgan Chase & Co., Deutsche Bank AG and Wells Fargo were asked by the DOJ to retain and turn over records that might be related to improper transfers from 1MDB [279–281]. The FBI issued subpoenas to several past and present employees of film production company Red Granite Pictures, co-founded by Najib Razak's stepson Riza Aziz, also its chairman, in regards to allegations that US$155 million was diverted from 1MDB to help finance the 2013 film The Wolf of Wall Street [282–285].

Also under scrutiny by the FBI and DOJ was the role of global investment bank Goldman Sachs in alleged money laundering and corruption [286–288]. The FBI probed the connection between Najib and a regional top executive of Goldman Sachs, and the nature of the latter's involvement in multibillion-dollar deals with 1MDB [289]. Tim Leissner, the former chairman of Goldman Sachs' Southeast Asia branch and husband of Kimora Lee Leissner, was issued a subpoena by the DOJ as part of their investigations [290–292]. In the July 2016 DOJ civil lawsuit [293], a high-ranking government official having control over 1MDB, who was referred to more than 30 times as "Malaysian Official 1" ("MO1"), was alleged to have received around US$681 million (RM 2.8 billion) of stolen 1MDB money via Falcon Bank in Singapore on 21 and 25 March 2013, of which US$650 million (RM 2.0 billion) was sent back to Falcon Bank on 30 August 2013 [294]. In September 2016, Najib Razak was identified as "MO1" by Datuk Abdul Rahman Dahlan, then Minister in the Prime Minister's Department [295, 296]. The wife of "MO1", Rosmah Mansor, was also alleged to have received US$30 million worth of jewels financed from pilfered 1MDB funds [297].

In June 2017, the DOJ began actions to recover more than US$1 billion from people close to Najib and 1MDB [298–301], seizing assets including high-end properties in Beverly Hills, Los Angeles, Manhattan, New York City and London [302, 303], as well as fine artwork, a private jet, a luxury yacht and royalties from the film The Wolf of Wall Street and its production company Red Granite Pictures [304–306]. On 7 March 2018, in California courts, the producers of the film agreed to pay US$60 million to settle DOJ's claims that they financed the movie with money siphoned from 1MDB [307]. The claims were settled in August 2018, with the settlement stipulating that the payment should not be construed as "an admission of wrongdoing or liability on the part of Red Granite" [308].

On 1 November 2018, the DOJ announced that two former Goldman Sachs bankers, Tim Leissner and Roger Ng, as well as Malaysian fugitive financier Jho Low, were charged over funds misappropriated from 1MDB and paying bribes to various Malaysian and Abu Dhabi officials. Tim Leissner admitted in a plea that more than US$200 million in proceeds from 1MDB bonds flowed into accounts controlled by him and a relative [309–311]. He agreed to forfeit US$43.7 million (RM 185 million) and pleaded guilty to conspiring to launder money and violate the Foreign Corrupt Practices Act, while Roger Ng was arrested in Malaysia at the request of DOJ and extradited to the US for prosecution before returning and facing charges in Malaysia [312–316]. According to Roger Ng's lawyers, he was infected with Dengue fever and leptospirosis while in Malaysian jail and lost a significant amount of weight [317, 318].

On 30 November 2018, the DOJ announced that George Higginbotham, a former DOJ employee, pleaded guilty to conspiracy to deceive US banks about the source and purpose of foreign funds for a lobbying campaign against the US investigations into the 1MDB scandal. The DOJ filed a lawsuit to recover more than US$73 million (RM 305 million) in American bank accounts that Higginbotham helped open on behalf of Jho Low to finance the lobbying campaign [319–321]. Further in May 2019, the DOJ announced that it had charged Jho Low and former Fugees rapper Pras for conspiring to funnel US$21.6 million from overseas accounts into the 2012 presidential election [322].

On 1 November 2019, Barron's reported that Jho Low had forfeited over $100 million in luxury homes as part of a settlement with prosecutors in the United States. Overall, he agreed to give up some $700 million in assets to the U.S. Department of Justice to have charges dropped, without admitting guilt [323].

US President Donald Trump's fundraiser Elliott Broidy was charged by the Federal authorities in the violation of Foreign Agents Registration Act as per public court filing published on 8th October 2020. Broidy reportedly took $6 million from agents of Malaysia and China to lobby officials from the administration to end the investigation 1MDB scandal. Broidy was also charged for lobbying White House officials in alignment to UAE's interest [324, 325].

4. Recovery of 1MDB Assets

Malaysia has so far recovered US$322 million (RM1.3 billion) worth of 1MDB assets since its renewed investigations into the 1MDB scandal after the 14th General Election in May 2018 [326].

Steps have been taken to preserve the value of the assets caught up in the case, including the sale of the Park Lane Hotel in New York in November 2018, a step endorsed by the U.S. DOJ, in accordance with the rule of law and on the basis of no admission of wrongdoing or liability [327]. In August 2018, Malaysian authorities seized a yacht allegedly purchased by Low, selling it some eight months later to minimize the costs associated with maintaining it. A spokesperson for Low described the seizure as "illegal" [328, 329].

The recovered funds include the sum of US$126 million from the Equanimity judicially sold to the Genting Group, US$139 million to be returned by the United

States after sale of Jho Low's interest in Park Lane Hotel in Manhattan, and US$57 million from a forfeiture settlement of Red Granite Pictures, which has been repatriated to Malaysia after deducting the costs incurred for investigations, seizures and litigation [326].

Apart from the above, another sum of S$50 million (RM152 million) related to 1MDB has been ordered by the Singapore Courts to be repatriated [326].

Malaysia has been working with at least six countries to recover about US$4.5 billion worth of assets allegedly stolen from 1MDB [330], in which US$1.7 billion (RM7 billion) worth of assets have been sought by the DOJ to forfeit [326].

On 15 April 2020, it was reported that the DOJ had returned US$300 million in funds stolen during the 1MDB scandal to Malaysia [331].

On 24 July 2020, it was announced that the Malaysian government would receive US$2.5 billion in cash from Goldman Sachs, and a guarantee from the bank they would also return US$1.4 billion in assets linked to 1MDB bonds [332]. Put together this was substantially less than the US$7.5 billion that had been previously demanded by the Malaysian finance minister. At the same time, the Malaysian government agreed to drop all criminal charges against the bank and that it would cease legal proceedings against 17 current and former Goldman directors. Some commentators argued that Goldman had got away with a very good deal [333].

In January 2022, the Malaysian government received RM 333 million ($111 million) as a fine from the local affiliate of KPMG in settlement of the lawsuit filed against it [334].....

(*See website for Timeline*)

References

1. "1MDB: The playboys, PMs and partygoers around a global financial scandal. It is one of the world's greatest financial scandals". BBC. 9 August 2019. Retrieved 24 August 2021.
2. "Shorenstein Journalism Award Winner Tom Wright Recounts Story of Global Financial Scandal". The Freeman Spogli Institute For International Studies, Stanford University. 6 November 2020. Retrieved 24 August 2021.
3. "International Corruption - U.S. Seeks to Recover $1 Billion in Largest Kleptocracy Case to Date". Federal Bureau of Investigation. 20 June 2016. Retrieved 24 August 2021.
4. "Malaysian taskforce investigates allegations $700 m paid to Najib". The Guardian. 6 July 2015. Retrieved 24 March 2018.
5. "Dismissal of Corruption Charges Against Malaysian Prime Minister Prompts Scorn". Time. 27 January 2016. Retrieved 27 August 2021.
6. "Former Malaysia PM Mahathir calls for removal of PM Najib Razak". BBC news. 30 August 2015. Retrieved 27 August 2021.
7. "Gov't 'gambling' on untested 1MDB". Malaysiakini. 18 October 2010.
8. "1MDB faces fresh debt payment test". Free Malaysia Today. 27 February 2015. Archived from the original on 1 March 2015.
9. "Jho says it ain't so: Malaysian tycoon denies role in 1MDB 'heist of the century'". Euromoney Magazine. April 2015.

10. "Goldman Sachs Charged in Foreign Bribery Case and Agrees to Pay Over $2.9 Billion". United States Department of Justice. 22 October 2020. Retrieved 26 August 2021.
11. "Malaysia's royal rulers urge quick completion of 1MDB probe". The Straits Times. Retrieved 1 March 2016.
12. "Royal rulers deplore Malaysia's 'crisis of confidence'". Al Jazeera. Retrieved 1 March 2016.
13. "Mahathir Picks Lim as Finance Minister, Returns Zeti to Council". Bloomberg.com. 12 May 2018. Retrieved 18 May 2018.
14. "Former Malaysia PM Najib Razak banned from leaving country". BBC. Retrieved 24 November 2020.
15. "12 people on Malaysia's travel blacklist over 1MDB probe". The Straits Times. 18 May 2018. Retrieved 23 August 2021.
16. "Malaysia's former first lady Rosmah Mansor's seized handbags damaged and government should pay, lawyer tells court". South China Morning Post. Retrieved 24 November 2020.
17. "US DOJ says pursuing investigations related to Malaysia's 1MDB". The Star. Retrieved 22 May 2018.
18. Jump up to: a b c Singh, Sharanjit; Khairulrijal, Khairah N. Karim and Rahmat (28 July 2020). "Najib sentenced to 12 years' jail, RM210 million fine | New Straits Times". NST Online. Retrieved 28 July 2020.
19. "Malaysia's 1MDB state fund still $7.8 billion in debt - government report". Reuters. 6 November 2020. Retrieved 11 July 2021.
20. "How 'Insolvent' 1MDB's Debt Stacks Up and Who's Saddled With It". Bloomberg News. 6 November 2020. Retrieved 26 August 2021.
21. "Over $1.6 billion in misappropriated 1MDB funds repatriated to Malaysia so far". Straits Times. 6 August 2021. Retrieved 6 August 2021.
22. "Singapore to return $11 million in 1MDB-linked funds to Malaysia". Reuters. 10 September 2018. Retrieved 7 August 2021.
23. Report, Sarawak. "HEIST OF THE CENTURY – How Jho Low Used PetroSaudi As "A Front" To Siphon Billions Out Of 1MDB!". Sarawak Report. Retrieved 29 July 2020.
24. Boswell, Jon Ungoed-Thomas, Clare Rewcastle and Josh. "Harrow playboy linked to troubled Malaysian fund". The Times. ISSN 0140–0460. Retrieved 29 July 2020.
25. "Jho Low allegedly siphoned off US$700 million from 1MDB, says website". Archived from the original on 1 July 2015. Retrieved 7 July 2015.
26. Jump up to: a b "Jho Low accused of siphoning US$700 m from 1MDB". Retrieved 7 July 2015.
27. "'Stolen' 1MDB Funds: The DOJ lawsuit revisited". Malaysiakini. 31 March 2018.
28. "Why are Najib, Jho Low giving similar answers on 1MDB, asks DAP". The Edge Markets. 19 March 2015. Retrieved 26 May 2019.
29. "Jho Low email said Najib approved US$1bn loan". Free Malaysia Today. Archived from the original on 20 July 2015. Retrieved 7 July 2015.

30. "Jho Low claims Najib okayed 1MDB's US$500 million loan to PetroSaudi, says Sarawak Report". Archived from the original on 1 July 2015. Retrieved 7 July 2015.
31. "1MDB gave out false info on Singapore's BSI Bank assets, says Sarawak Report". Archived from the original on 4 March 2016. Retrieved 1 March 2016.
32. "'Minutes of board meeting proves 1MDB's Arul a liar'". Malaysiakini. Retrieved 1 March 2016.
33. "1MDB CEO says never gave false bank statements to Bank Negara". The Malay Mail. Retrieved 5 February 2016.
34. "WSJ: Najib used 1MDB's funds for GE13". Retrieved 8 July 2015.
35. "Bersih 2.0 says GE13 rigged, shocked over links to 1MDB". Archived from the original on 8 July 2015. Retrieved 8 July 2015.
36. "Roadshow unnecessary, just come clean on 1MDB's objectives, Kit Siang tells BN". Retrieved 8 July 2015.
37. "1MDB refutes WSJ article, says acquisitions based on long-term value". The Star Online. Retrieved 5 February 2016.
38. Tom Wright and Simon Clark (2 July 2015). "Investigators Believe Money Flowed to Malaysian Leader Najib's Accounts Amid 1MDB Probe". The Wall Street Journal. Retrieved 8 July 2015.
39. "Special team to probe graft allegations against Malaysia PM Najib Razak". The Economic Times. Retrieved 8 July 2015.
40. "Task force freezes bank accounts as pressure mounts on PM Najib". Channel NewsAsia. Retrieved 8 July 2015.
41. Niluksi Koswanage (7 July 2015). "Malaysia Task Force to Freeze Accounts in Najib Money Probe". Bloomberg L.P. Retrieved 8 July 2015.
42. "MACC: RM2.6bil in Najib's account from donors, not 1MDB's – Nation | The Star Online". The Star. Malaysia. Retrieved 5 February 2016.
43. "3 frozen accounts belong to Najib, sources say". Archived from the original on 8 July 2015. Retrieved 8 July 2015.
44. "Three frozen accounts belong to PM, says source". Retrieved 8 July 2015.
45. Sarawak Report. "SENSATIONAL FINDINGS! – Prime Minister Najib Razak's Personal Accounts Linked To 1MDB Money Trail MALAYSIA EXCLUSIVE!". Sarawak Report. Retrieved 8 July 2015.
46. "DocumentCloud Document Viewer". Retrieved 8 July 2015.
47. "Take legal action against WSJ, PM urged". The Star. Retrieved 8 July 2015.
48. "Singapore police freeze two bank accounts linked to 1MDB probe". Channel NewsAsia. Retrieved 27 September 2015.
49. "Singapore freezes bank accounts over Malaysia 1MDB graft scandal". DW. Retrieved 27 September 2015.
50. "1MDB chief denies Singapore accounts frozen, says asset sales will put company in black by early 2016". The Malay Mail. Retrieved 5 February 2016.
51. Bradley Hope (17 December 2015). "Malaysia's 1MDB Sent $850 Million to Entity Set Up to Appear Owned by Abu Dhabi Wealth Fund". The Wall Street Journal. Retrieved 1 March 2016.

3.1 Malaysia Development Berhad

52. "WSJ drops US$850 m bombshell on 1MDB". Malaysiakini. Retrieved 1 March 2016.
53. "$850 M 1MDB payment sent to Virgin Island firm". CNBC. 17 December 2015.
54. "WSJ: UAE fund claims US$1.4b payment from 1MDB missing". Retrieved 27 September 2015.
55. Bradley Hope and Tom Wright (9 September 2015). "Malaysia's 1MDB Fund Scandal Spreads to U.A.E." The Wall Street Journal. Retrieved 27 September 2015.
56. "Abu Dhabi alleges US$1.4 billion from 1MDB missing, says WSJ". Archived from the original on 27 September 2015. Retrieved 27 September 2015.
57. "WSJ: Another US$1b payment from 1MDB to IPIC missing". Malaysiakini. Retrieved 27 September 2015.
58. "1MDB mystery deepens as Abu Dhabi questions another missing US$993 m to IPIC". Retrieved 27 September 2015.
59. "Another $1.4b payment from 1MDB to Abu Dhabi fund is missing: Wall Street Journal". The Straits Times. Retrieved 27 September 2015.
60. "We enjoy strong business relationship with UAE firm, says 1MDB – The Malaysian Insider". themalaysianinsider.com. Archived from the original on 20 December 2015. Retrieved 15 February 2016.
61. "Abu Dhabi's Ipic to pay interest on 1MDB bonds as Malaysia clears officials | The National". The National. Abu Dhabi. Retrieved 15 February 2016.
62. Bradley Hope (12 November 2015). "1MDB's Latest Act: Two Obama Fundraisers, One Fugee and $69 Million". The Wall Street Journal. Retrieved 1 March 2016.
63. "Wong Chen queries Obama link in 1MDB-DuSable 'JV'". Free Malaysia Today. Archived from the original on 16 January 2016. Retrieved 1 March 2016.
64. "WSJ picks up on 1MDB-DuSable links to former Obama fundraisers". The Malaysian Insider. Archived from the original on 4 March 2016. Retrieved 1 March 2016.
65. "Najib urged to disclose dealings of 1MDB and Yurus PE Fund". Theedgemarkets.com. Retrieved 1 March 2016.
66. "Malaysian Prime Minister Spent Lavishly From Accounts He Says Weren't 'Personal'". Fortune. 31 March 2016.
67. Wright, Tom; Hope, Bradley (31 March 2016). "1MDB Probe Shows Malaysian Leader Najib Spent Millions on Luxury Goods". The Wall Street Journal.
68. "1MDB probe shows Najib Razak spent millions on luxury goods: Report". Today.
69. Lee Seok Hwai (31 March 2016). "Malaysia PM Najib spent millions on luxury goods, political payments: WSJ". The Straits Times.
70. "Pua says 1MDB profits suspect". The Malaysian Insider. 9 October 2010. Archived from the original on 12 October 2010. Retrieved 26 July 2015.
71. "1Malaysia Development Berhad Malaysia Factbook". malaysiafactbook.com. Archived from the original on 16 March 2014.

72. Has 1MDB filed its accounts?. The Edge Malaysia. 1 April 2014. Retrieved 26 July 2015.
73. "Auditors highlight several critical areas in 1MDB's books". The Star. 22 April 2014.
74. The business address is also available on the company's website, www.1mdb.com.my
75. "Agreements inked to develop Sungai Besi airport land into Bandar Malaysia". The Star. 15 June 2011.
76. "Amid lack of progress in Bandar Malaysia, Rafizi questions 1MDB's RM3.5b debt". Retrieved 27 September 2015.
77. "Why is 1MDB raising RM2.4bil in loans?". Malaysiakini. Retrieved 27 September 2015.
78. "1MDB awards RM2.1bil contract to Armed Forces Fund Board unit – Business News | The Star Online". The Star. Malaysia. Retrieved 4 February 2016.
79. "1MDB to sell 60% stake in Bandar Malaysia for RM7.41bil – Nation – The Star Online". Retrieved 1 March 2016.
80. "Malaysia's $1.8 bln mega project with China Railway falls through". Reuters. 15 July 2021. Retrieved 26 August 2021.
81. "1MDB accepts adviser's resignation – Nation – The Star Online". Retrieved 27 September 2015.
82. "1MDB insists former adviser was not ignored". Malaysiakini. Retrieved 27 September 2015.
83. "1MDB denies receiving 'repeated requests' for info from former advisor". The Malay Mail. Retrieved 4 February 2016.
84. "Deloitte Malaysia's statement on 1MDB accounts". The Sun Daily. 27 July 2016. Retrieved 23 March 2018.
85. "Lack of concern about 1MDB's unaudited accounts shows cover-up, says MP". The Malaysian Insight. 21 November 2017. Retrieved 23 March 2018.
86. Ng, Jason (4 March 2015). "Malaysian Leader Orders Auditor to Verify 1MDB Accounts". wsj.com. Wall Street Journal. Retrieved 5 March 2015.
87. "Malaysia Auditor General's 1MDB Report Classified". Asia Sentinel. 6 April 2016. Retrieved 24 March 2018.
88. "Azmin fails to unseal 1MDB audit report". The Malaysian Insight. 24 January 2018. Retrieved 24 March 2018.
89. "Now Is The Best Time To Declassify AG's Report on 1MDB – There Should Be Nothing To Hide!". Transparency International Malaysia. 6 April 2016. Archived from the original on 24 March 2018. Retrieved 24 March 2018.
90. "Sarawak Report publishes AG's 1MDB report classified under Official Secrets Act". The Straits Times Singapore. 14 July 2016. Retrieved 24 March 2018.
91. "Rafizi charged under secrecy law over leak on 1MDB federal audit". The Malay Mail Malaysia. 8 April 2016. Retrieved 24 March 2018.
92. "1MDB audit report now declassified, says Auditor-General". The Edge (Malaysia). 15 May 2018. Retrieved 26 August 2021.

93. "1MDB Unable To Repay Debts – Guan Eng". Malaysian Digest. 23 May 2018. Archived from the original on 24 May 2018. Retrieved 24 May 2018.
94. "Ringgit under pressure over 1MDB debt". Archived from the original on 8 July 2015. Retrieved 7 July 2015.
95. "1MDB faces fresh debt payment test". Free Malaysia Today. Archived from the original on 1 March 2015. Retrieved 7 July 2015.
96. "1MDB bonds drop to junk status as investors consider wind-down". Retrieved 7 July 2015.
97. "Cabinet rejects RM3 billion for 1MDB as debt repayment options narrow". Retrieved 7 July 2015.
98. "RPT-MALAYSIA PRESS-Cabinet rejects $834 mln proposed injection into 1MDB-The Malaysian Insider". Reuters. Retrieved 7 July 2015.
99. "Cabinet rejects RM3 billion aid for 1MDB". Free Malaysia Today. Archived from the original on 8 July 2015. Retrieved 7 July 2015.
100. "1MDB insolvent, unable to repay debts: 2 directors". The Straits Times. 24 May 2018. Retrieved 21 August 2021.
101. "MACC: RM2.6bil in Najib's account from donors, not 1MDB's | The Star". www.thestar.com.my.
102. "Malaysia's anti-graft unit says funds in PM's account a 'donation', not from state fund". 3 August 2015 – via uk.reuters.com.
103. "Najib's RM2.6 billion is from Saudi Arabia as thanks for fighting Isis, claims Umno leader". Archived from the original on 17 August 2015.
104. "Malaysia 1MDB: Saudi minister says Najib funds were donation". BBC News. 15 April 2016. Retrieved 1 May 2016.
105. "Saudi Arabia says money sent to Malaysian PM was a 'genuine donation'". The Guardian. Retrieved 14 April 2016.
106. "Late Saudi king's son is RM2.6b donor, says Apandi". Malaysiakini. Retrieved 1 March 2016.
107. SHANNON TEOH. "KL graft-busters challenge A-G's decision on Najib". The Straits Times. Retrieved 1 March 2016.
108. "Malaysia's prime minister will call an election soon". The Economist. 8 November 2017.
109. "RM2.6 billion in Najib's accounts not from Saudis, says WSJ editor". TODAYonline. Retrieved 1 March 2016.
110. "RM2.6 bil in Najib's accounts not from Saudis, says WSJ editor". Retrieved 1 March 2016.
111. "WSJ refutes AG's Saudi donation claim". Malaysiakini. Retrieved 1 March 2016.
112. "Bank Negara: 1MDB breached exchange controls, three permissions revoked". Archived from the original on 7 March 2016.
113. "1MDB acknowledges BNM's right to revoke earlier permissions". NST Online. Retrieved 1 March 2016.
114. "Bank Negara urges criminal prosecution of 1MDB". Archived from the original on 4 March 2016. Retrieved 1 March 2016.

115. "BNM recommends criminal prosecution against 1MDB". Retrieved 1 March 2016.
116. "1MDB unable to repatriate US$1.83b ordered by Bank Negara". Malaysiakini. 9 October 2015. Retrieved 1 March 2016.
117. "Umno member files lawsuit against Malaysia PM Najib". Channel NewsAsia. Retrieved 27 September 2015.
118. "'Umno' sues Najib to retrieve chunk of RM2.6b". Archived from the original on 26 January 2018. Retrieved 28 August 2015.
119. "Anina sacked from Umno". The Rakyat Post. Retrieved 27 September 2015.
120. "Umno expels Langkawi woman rep for suing Najib, party executive secretary confirms". Retrieved 27 September 2015.
121. "Anina: 'I will continue to fight'". Retrieved 27 September 2015.
122. "The Malaysian Insider". Archived from the original on 25 September 2015. Retrieved 27 September 2015.
123. "Now, Johor UMNO member lodges report against Najib over RM2.6 billion". TODAYonline. Retrieved 27 September 2015.
124. "Umno man submits 1MDB evidence to Swiss AG". Malaysiakini. 20 August 2015. Retrieved 27 September 2015.
125. "1MDB whistleblower submits evidence to Swiss prosecutor". Retrieved 27 September 2015.
126. "Khairuddin lodges reports against Najib, Jho Low in HK". Free Malaysia Today. Archived from the original on 20 September 2017. Retrieved 27 September 2015.
127. "'These are traitors to the people, God and the country': Former Malaysian official asks Hong Kong police to investigate 1MDB scandal". South China Morning Post. 3 September 2015. Retrieved 27 September 2015.
128. "Pair who lodged reports on 1MDB barred from leaving M'sia". Malaysiakini. 18 September 2015. Retrieved 27 September 2015.
129. "Former Umno leader, lawyer allegedly barred from leaving country". AsiaOne. Archived from the original on 20 September 2015. Retrieved 27 September 2015.
130. "Khairuddin, Matthias Chang allegedly barred from leaving country – Nation – The Star Online". Retrieved 27 September 2015.
131. SHANNON TEOH (12 October 2015). "Mahathir, Umno leaders slam prosecution of 1MDB critic and his lawyer". The Straits Times. Retrieved 1 March 2016.
132. "Khairuddin and Matthias vow to fight on – Nation – The Star Online". Retrieved 1 March 2016.
133. Marzukhi, Hafiz (12 October 2015). "Khairuddin, Matthias Chang charged with sabotaging Malaysian banking, financial services | Astro Awani". Astro Awani.
134. "After WSJ exposé, PKR hauls PM, 1MDB to court for alleged electoral offences". 12 August 2015.
135. "PKR sues Najib over breach of election law in S$914 m 'donation'". TODAYonline.

136. "High Court strikes out PKR civil suit against Najib | The Star". www.thestar.com.my.
137. "Court throws out PKR's election overspending lawsuit against Najib over RM2.6b". 21 January 2016.
138. "Dr M sues Najib over alleged interference in 1MDB, RM2.6b probes". 23 March 2016.
139. Holmes, Oliver (23 March 2016). "Former Malaysian premier Mahathir sues PM Najib over 'abuse of power'".
140. "Malaysia Political Spat Escalates as Former Premier Sues Najib". www.bloomberg.com. 26 March 2016.
141. "Malaysia PM sacks top officials over corruption probe ahead of Cameron visit". The Daily Telegraph. 28 July 2015. Retrieved 30 August 2015.
142. "Malaysian PM Najib Razak sacks deputy after 1MDB graft scandal remarks". The Sydney Morning Herald. 28 July 2015. Retrieved 30 August 2015.
143. "Najib's manoeuvre cripples 1MDB probes". Malaysiakini. 28 July 2015. Retrieved 30 August 2015.
144. "Axed from Cabinet, Shafie says only speaking for grassroots". The Malay Mail. Retrieved 30 August 2015.
145. "Gani Patail no longer Attorney-General, chief secretary says". The Malay Mail. Retrieved 30 August 2015.
146. "Apandi Ali becomes new Attorney-General, replaces Gani Patail". themalaysianinsider.com. Archived from the original on 31 August 2015. Retrieved 30 August 2015.
147. "Cabinet reshuffled, AG replaced, PAC probe into 1MDB postponed". astroawani.com. Retrieved 30 August 2015.
148. "PAC delay allows time to check on 1MDB document tampering, says minister". themalaysianinsider.com. Archived from the original on 11 September 2015. Retrieved 30 August 2015.
149. "1MDB probe to continue as scheduled: PAC Deputy Chairman". NST Online. Retrieved 30 August 2015.
150. "The Edge weekly, daily suspended for 3 months from July 27". themalaysianinsider.com. Archived from the original on 10 September 2015. Retrieved 30 August 2015.
151. Jason Ng (25 July 2015). "Malaysia Orders Suspension of Two Publications". The Wall Street Journal. Retrieved 30 August 2015.
152. "The Edge daily and weekly suspended three months over 1MDB reports". The Malay Mail. Retrieved 30 August 2015.
153. "MCMC confirms Sarawak Report blocked to maintain 'national stability'". themalaysianinsider.com. Archived from the original on 21 August 2015. Retrieved 30 August 2015.
154. "Sarawak Report whistleblowing website blocked by Malaysia after PM corruption allegations". The Independent. Retrieved 30 August 2015.
155. "Malaysia issues arrest warrant for Gordon Brown's sister-in-law over allegations about prime minister Najib Razak". The Daily Telegraph. 5 August 2015. Retrieved 30 August 2015.

156. "Interpol alert for Clare Rewcastle Brown in 190 countries". The Rakyat Post. Retrieved 30 August 2015.
157. "Cops arrest former Umno man after barring him from leaving country". Archived from the original on 28 September 2015. Retrieved 27 September 2015.
158. "Cops arrest former Umno man after barring him from leaving country". 18 September 2015. Retrieved 27 September 2015.
159. "After travel ban, former Penang Umno leader nabbed by cops". Retrieved 27 September 2015.
160. "NYT: Khairuddin was supposed to meet FBI on 1MDB". Malaysiakini. 19 September 2015. Retrieved 27 September 2015.
161. "Malaysia Blocks Critic of Prime Minister From Taking Case to U.S." The New York Times. 19 September 2015. Retrieved 1 March 2016.
162. "FBI begins probe into 1MDB, says WSJ". Archived from the original on 28 September 2015. Retrieved 27 September 2015.
163. "Najib ticked me off over 1MDB, RM2.6 billion, Mukhriz tells supporters". Archived from the original on 16 February 2016. Retrieved 1 March 2016.
164. "Free from constraints as MB, Mukhriz says will speak out more". Retrieved 1 March 2016.
165. hermes (1 March 2016). "Mahathir quits Umno, calling it 'Najib's party'". The Straits Times. Retrieved 10 April 2019.
166. "Malaysian opposition MP charged over 1MDB scandal-related leak". 8 April 2016.
167. "Malaysian opposition MP charged over 1MDB leak".
168. "Malaysian opposition MP arrested for allegedly disclosing A-G's 1MDB report". TODAYonline.
169. "Cops unable to locate key people linked to 1MDB issue – Nation – The Star Online". Retrieved 1 March 2016.
170. "Interpol unable to locate Jho Low, others in 1MDB case". Free Malaysia Today. Archived from the original on 19 September 2017. Retrieved 1 March 2016.
171. "Interpol help not sought". Retrieved 1 March 2016.
172. "Why has Malaysia blocked Medium?". Engadget. Retrieved 31 January 2016.
173. Legal, Medium (26 January 2016). "The Post Stays Up". Medium. Retrieved 31 January 2016.
174. "Despite being blocked, Asia Sentinel says will continue reporting on corruption". Archived from the original on 2 March 2016. Retrieved 1 March 2016.
175. "Putrajaya blocks access to Asia Sentinel, says portal". Free Malaysia Today. Retrieved 1 March 2016.
176. "Najib is Indictable, M'sia's Anti-graft Body Believes". Asia Sentinel. Retrieved 1 March 2016.
177. "Minister defends Malaysia's free speech, as blocked news portal probed". Channel NewsAsia. Retrieved 1 March 2016.
178. "Malaysia blocks access to news portal for violating media law". Reuters. Reuters Editorial. 25 February 2016. Retrieved 1 March 2016.

179. Rachel Middleton. "Malaysia blocks another news portal as 1MDB scandal deepens over oversight panel probing fund". International Business Times UK. Retrieved 1 March 2016.
180. "Malaysian government unblocks media sites, raising hopes of new freedoms". EFE. 29 May 2018. Retrieved 28 August 2021.
181. "1mdb boss blamed by watchdog triggering boards resignation". The Australian.
182. "Malaysia parliament report calls for probe into 1MDB". 7 April 2016 – via Reuters.
183. "PAC report: 1MDB got special treatment from Putrajaya". The Malay Mail. 7 April 2016.
184. Reuters (7 April 2016). "Malaysian parliament calls for inquiry into 1MDB's former boss".
185. "1MDB report: PAC zeroes in on former CEO Shahrol as among the culprits | The Star". www.thestar.com.my.
186. Lumpur, Associated Press in Kuala (7 April 2016). "Malaysia: directors of scandal-hit 1MDB state investment fund offer mass resignation".
187. "Malaysia Panel Calls for Investigation of Former Head of 1MDB Fund". The New York Times. 8 April 2016.
188. "1MDB Board Resigns After Parliamentary Report".
189. "Malaysia 1MDB board offers resignations after inquiry". 7 April 2016.
190. Press, Eileen Ng The Associated. "Board of troubled Malaysia fund offers to resign".
191. "IPIC denies links with BVI-incorporated firm linked to 1MDB". 11 April 2016. Archived from the original on 14 April 2016. Retrieved 13 April 2016.
192. Shaffer, Leslie (13 April 2016). "1MDB payment may have ended up in movies".
193. "Mystery deepens over US$3.5 billion Malaysia's 1MDB sent to BVI entity". Reuters. 11 April 2016. Archived from the original on 14 April 2016. Retrieved 13 April 2016 – via Channel NewsAsia.
194. Hope, Bradley; Parasie, Nicolas; Wright, Tom (18 April 2016). "Abu Dhabi Fund Calls 1MDB in Default After Missed Payment" – via Wall Street Journal.
195. "UAE fund says Malaysia's 1MDB in default on $1 billion deal". 18 April 2016 – via Reuters.
196. "Abu Dhabi fund says 1MDB in default on rescue deal". CNBC. 18 April 2016.
197. "Special task force formed to look into 1MDB – Nation | The Star Online". www.thestar.com.my. Retrieved 9 June 2018.
198. "Amount of cash seized from Najib-linked condo is RM114m". www.thesundaily.my. Retrieved 9 June 2018.
199. "Value of cash and goods seized from Najib-linked residences amounted to about RM1bil (updated) – Nation | The Star Online". www.thestar.com.my. Retrieved 27 June 2018.
200. "Malaysian ex-prime minister Najib arrested in stunning fall from grace". Reuters. 3 July 2018. Retrieved 29 May 2019.

201. "Former Malaysian PM Najib Razak claims trial to 25 charges of abuse of power, money laundering". Channel NewsAsia. Retrieved 20 September 2018.
202. "MACC issues arrest warrants for Jho Low and Nik Faisal, ex Goldman Sachs banker is next – Business News | The Star Online". www.thestar.com.my. Retrieved 9 June 2018.
203. "1MDB sacks Arul Kanda". The Edge Market. 29 June 2018. Retrieved 6 July 2018.
204. Pei, Goh Pei (29 June 2018). "MACC has frozen SUPP's account | New Straits Times". NST Online.
205. "Malaysia files criminal charges against Jho Low in absentia". The Edge Markets. 24 August 2018. Retrieved 17 September 2018.
206. "Report: Criminal charges filed against Jho Low and his father – Nation | The Star Online". www.thestar.com.my. Retrieved 17 September 2018.
207. "Superyacht going cheap – 1MDB investigators auction off seized boat". The Thaiger. 27 October 2018. Retrieved 1 November 2018.
208. hermesauto (3 April 2019). "Malaysia to sell 1MDB-linked superyacht to casino operator Genting for $170 million". The Straits Times. Retrieved 10 April 2019.
209. Panirchellvum, Vathani. "Malaysia files charges against Goldman over 1MDB scandal (Updated)". www.thesundaily.my. Retrieved 17 December 2018.
210. "AGC files criminal charges against subsidiaries of Goldman Sachs and employees – Nation | The Star Online". www.thestar.com.my. Retrieved 17 December 2018.
211. Hamdan, Nurbaiti. "Ex-Goldman Sachs banker charged with abetting bank – Nation | The Star Online". www.thestar.com.my. Retrieved 20 December 2018.
212. staff, CNBC com (3 November 2015). "Australia firm caught up in 1MDB scandal: Report".
213. "Nocookies". The Australian. Retrieved 1 March 2016.
214. Peel, Michael; O'Murchu, Cynthia; Harris, Bryan (30 October 2015). "Caribbean dealings stalk Malaysia's 1MDB" – via Financial Times.
215. "Nocookies". The Australian. Retrieved 1 March 2016.
216. "Australia shuts down investment schemes run by fund linked to 1MDB". Archived from the original on 4 March 2016. Retrieved 1 March 2016.
217. "Hong Kong police launch probe into US$250 million linked to Najib". Archived from the original on 28 September 2015. Retrieved 27 September 2015.
218. Peel, Bryan Harris and Michael (11 September 2015). "The growing 1MDB scandal has now spread to Hong Kong".
219. "Indonesia seizes luxury yacht linked to 1MDB investigation – ASEAN/East Asia | The Star Online". www.thestar.com.my. Retrieved 10 August 2018.
220. "Indonesia Returns Yacht in Malaysia's 1MDB Corruption Probe". Time. Archived from the original on 7 August 2018. Retrieved 10 August 2018.
221. "Equanimity was properly seized under the laws of Malaysia, says AG – Nation | The Star Online". www.thestar.com.my. Retrieved 10 August 2018.

3.1 Malaysia Development Berhad

222. "Luxembourg Prosecutors Look for Embezzlement at Malaysia's 1MDB". www.bloomberg.com. 31 March 2016.
223. "Luxembourg launches money-laundering probe into 1MDB". 31 March 2016.
224. "Luxembourg launches money laundering inquiry into Malaysian state fund". Channel NewsAsia. 31 March 2016. Archived from the original on 13 April 2016. Retrieved 31 March 2016.
225. "UPDATE 2-Singapore seizes assets, to take action against major banks in 1MDB probe". reuters. 21 July 2016.
226. Clark, Simon (1 April 2016). "Edmond de Rothschild Bank Cooperating With Luxembourg 1MDB Probe" – via Wall Street Journal.
227. "Donation or 1MDB funds? Luxembourg probe may uncover missing link". 2 April 2016.
228. "Report: Foreign authorities investigating 1MDB's 2012 bond issue". 2 April 2016.
229. "Exclusive: Seychelles says helping worldwide probe into Malaysia's 1MDB fund". 24 April 2016 – via Reuters.
230. "Seychelles says helping worldwide probe into 1MDB fund news". Newsunited.com. Retrieved 26 August 2017.
231. "Seychelles assisting in 1MDB probe". 24 April 2016.
232. "Arul: More important for 1MDB to settle debts than take legal action". The Star Malaysia. 20 March 2018. Retrieved 24 March 2018.
233. "Singapore seizes bank accounts in 1MDB probe". Malaysiakini. Retrieved 1 March 2016.
234. "S'pore cracks down on money laundering". Free Malaysia Today. Retrieved 1 March 2016.
235. Jasmine Ng (1 February 2016). "Singapore Seizes 'Large Number' of Bank Accounts Amid 1MDB Probe". Bloomberg L.P. Retrieved 1 March 2016.
236. "Banker's accounts frozen in Singapore's 1MDB probe". Archived from the original on 6 March 2016. Retrieved 1 March 2016.
237. YASMINE YAHYA. "Businessman Jho Low's private banker is first name to emerge from Singapore probe into 1MDB". The Straits Times. Retrieved 1 March 2016.
238. "Singapore court to hear first case related to Government's 1MDB probe". Channel NewsAsia. Retrieved 1 March 2016.
239. "Ex-BSI Singapore banker involved in 1MDB probe faces new charge".
240. reatanjourno. "Singapore Brings 7th Charge Against Ex-BSI Banker in 1MDB Probe".
241. hermesauto (9 May 2016). "Singaporean Kelvin Ang, charged in 1MDB probe, out on bail".
242. "Second 1MDB probe-linked accused Kelvin Ang offered bail at $100,000".
243. Watts, Jake Maxwell; Venkat, P. R. (21 July 2016). "Singapore Finds Lapses Related to 1MDB Funds at Banks" – via Wall Street Journal.
244. "Assets worth S$240 m seized as part of Singapore's 1MDB probe".

245. Lai, Adrian (21 July 2016). "Singapore authorities seize S$240 million in assets linked to 1MDB probe | New Straits Times | Malaysia General Business Sports and Lifestyle News". Nst.com.my. Retrieved 25 September 2017.
246. "As 1MDB Scandal Unravels, Singapore Seizes $177 Million in Assets". 21 July 2016.
247. "Singapore financial institutions were used for dubious 1MDB deals, monetary authority says, citing 'serious lapses'". South China Morning Post. 21 July 2016.
248. "MAS bars former Goldman Sachs banker from trading in Singapore over 1MDB-related breaches". Channel NewsAsia. Retrieved 20 December 2018.
249. "Singapore central bank bans former Goldman Sachs director Tim Leissner for life". Channel NewsAsia. Retrieved 20 December 2018.
250. hermesauto (19 December 2018). "Ex-Goldman Sachs banker Tim Leissner banned for life by MAS over role in 1MDB scandal". The Straits Times. Retrieved 20 December 2018.
251. "Guan Eng: RM46mil 1MDB-linked funds from Singapore is just 'tip of the iceberg' – Nation | The Star Online". www.thestar.com.my. Retrieved 11 September 2018.
252. "S'pore returns 1MDB funds – Nation | The Star Online". www.thestar.com.my. Retrieved 11 September 2018.
253. "Swiss freeze millions amid 1MDB fund probe". Free Malaysia Today. Archived from the original on 25 September 2015. Retrieved 27 September 2015.
254. John Revill (2 September 2015). "Swiss Authorities Freeze Millions of Dollars Linked to Malaysian Fund 1MDB". The Wall Street Journal. Retrieved 27 September 2015.
255. "Swiss freeze millions amid Malaysian 1MDB fund probe". Reuters. Retrieved 27 September 2015.
256. John Revill (30 January 2016). "Swiss Prosecutors Investigating 1MDB Say Malaysia Funds Were Diverted". The Wall Street Journal. Retrieved 1 March 2016.
257. Vasagar, Jeevan (30 January 2016). "1MDB: Swiss probe finds 'indications' of $4bn being misappropriated" – via Financial Times.
258. "Swiss: US$4bn believed embezzled from 1MDB". Free Malaysia Today. Retrieved 1 March 2016.
259. "Malaysia 1MDB scandal: Investigators say about $4bn may be missing from fund". BBC News. Retrieved 1 March 2016.
260. "Swiss Suspect $4 Billion Misappropriated in Malaysia 1MDB Case". NASDAQ.com. 29 January 2016. Retrieved 1 March 2016.
261. Letzing, John (7 April 2016). "Swiss Banks at Risk of Harboring Corruption Proceeds, Says Regulator" – via Wall Street Journal.
262. "Swiss financial regulator calls 1MDB and Petrobras cases 'clear corruption'". 7 April 2016.
263. hugodmiller, Jeffrey Voegeli JeffVogeli Hugo Miller. "Swiss Regulator Probes Panama Alongside 1MDB, Petrobras".

3.1 Malaysia Development Berhad

264. "Swiss parliament rejects call to return 1MDB profits to Malaysia". The Straits Times, Singapore. Retrieved 16 March 2018.
265. "Swiss AG: '1MDB-linked funds will be returned' – Nation | The Star Online". www.thestar.com.my. Retrieved 11 July 2018.
266. "UAE bans travel, freezes ex-IPIC execs' assets in 1MDB probe". 2 April 2016.
267. York, Bradley Hope in New; London, Simon Clark in; Lumpur, Yantoultra Ngui in Kuala (1 April 2016). "Authorities Investigating Malaysia's 1MDB Fund Focusing on Bond Proceeds" – via Wall Street Journal.
268. "UK investigators latest to join 1MDB probe". Malaysiakini. Retrieved 27 September 2015.
269. "British anti-fraud agency joins 1MDB corruption probe". Retrieved 27 September 2015.
270. Rachel Middleton. "UK weighs in on Malaysia's 1MDB state fund as it launches own investigation". International Business Times UK. Retrieved 1 March 2016.
271. "UK probing Royal Bank of Scotland on 1MDB". Free Malaysia Today. Retrieved 1 March 2016.
272. Bradley Hope (19 September 2015). "FBI Probes Malaysia Development Fund". The Wall Street Journal. Retrieved 27 September 2015.
273. "FBI investigates 1MDB". Retrieved 27 September 2015.
274. "FBI launches investigation into Malaysian state fund 1MDB: WSJ". AsiaOne. Retrieved 27 September 2015.
275. Oliver Holmes. "US investigators launch probes into scandal-hit Malaysian Najib Razak – World news – The Guardian". The Guardian. Retrieved 27 September 2015.
276. Christopher Matthews And Bradley Hope (22 September 2015). "Malaysia Leader Najib Razak's Assets Probed by U.S." The Wall Street Journal. Retrieved 27 September 2015.
277. "Malaysian PM Najib faces US corruption inquiry". The Straits Times. Retrieved 27 September 2015.
278. Story, Louise (22 September 2015). "Malaysia's Najib faces US property probe".
279. "1MDB: US asks Deutsche, JPMorgan to give details on dealings". 1 April 2016.
280. Chew, Keri Geiger GeigerWire Elffie. "U.S. Asks JPMorgan, Wells Fargo to Save Records Tied to 1MDB".
281. "Banks in firing line over Malaysia fund". The Australian. 1 April 2016.
282. Hope, Bradley; Fritz, John R. Emshwiller And Ben (1 April 2016). "The Secret Money Behind 'The Wolf of Wall Street'"– via Wall Street Journal.
283. "Malaysia's 1MDB refutes report that it financed 'Wolf of Wall Street': Statement".
284. "FBI probes 1MDB-Red Granite US$155 m financing claim – WSJ". The Edge Markets. 2 April 2016.

285. "'The Wolf Of Wall Street' Financed By Wolf Of Malaysia?". www.inquisitr.com.
286. Mia Lamar in Hong Kong, and Bradley Hope and Justin Baer in New York (14 October 2015). "U.S. Examines Goldman Sachs Role in 1MDB Transactions". The Wall Street Journal. Retrieved 1 March 2016.
287. "Goldman Sachs under FBI, DOJ scrutiny over 1MDB probe: WSJ". Reuters. Reuters Editorial. 14 October 2015. Retrieved 1 March 2016.
288. "Goldman Sachs under FBI, US Department of Justice scrutiny over 1MDB probe: Wall Street Journal". The Economic Times. Retrieved 1 March 2016.
289. Maierbrugger, Arno. "1MDB scandal: Next suspect Goldman Sachs banker l Investvine". Investvine. Retrieved 28 February 2016.
290. hermesauto (8 March 2016). "Ex-Goldman Sachs banker Tim Leissner issued subpoena amid US probe into Malaysia's 1MDB".
291. "U.S. subpoenas ex-Goldman banker in 1MDB probe: Bloomberg". Business Insider.
292. staff, CNBC com (8 March 2016). "Ex-Goldman banker subpoenaed in Malaysia 1MDB probe: WSJ".
293. "U.S. lawsuits link Malaysian leader to stolen money from 1MDB fund". Reuters. 20 July 2016. Retrieved 20 March 2018.
294. "Malaysian Prime Minister transferred US$650 million back to Singapore Bank". StatesTimesReview, Singapore. 15 August 2015. Retrieved 17 March 2018.
295. "PM Najib is 'Malaysian Official 1' but not involved in 1MDB probe: Minister". The Straits Times. Retrieved 13 September 2016.
296. Vaswani, Karishma (September 2016). "Who is 'Malaysian Official 1'? Case closed". BBC News. Retrieved 13 September 2016.
297. Ananthalakshmi, A. (16 June 2017). "Malaysia's first lady linked to $30 mln worth of jewelry bought with 1MDB funds". Reuters. Retrieved 16 March 2018.
298. "Civil action in rem to forfeit assets involved in and traceable to an international conspiracy to launder money misappropriated from 1Malaysia Development Berhad (1MDB)". United States Department of Justice. Retrieved 17 March 2018.
299. "US goes after $1.4 billion in assets linked to Malaysian fund 1MDB". Stuff. 21 July 2016.
300. "US moves to seize USD1b in assets of M'sian 1MDB fund". 21 July 2016.
301. Jenkins, Nash. "U.S. to Seize $1 Billion in Assets in Malaysia's 1MDB Case".
302. "Malaysia 1MDB Scandal: Luxury Properties in US Linked To Najib Razak's Stepson Riza Aziz, Close Associate Jho Low Likely To Be Seized". 21 July 2016.
303. gregfarrel, Greg Farrell; Harris, rew M.; damclaugh, yNewsNowInDC Keri Geiger GeigerWire David McLaughlin. "U.S. Maps 1MDB Fraud Trail From Kuala Lumpur to Hollywood".
304. Hope, Bradley; Wright, Tom (21 July 2016). "U.S. Links Malaysian Prime Minister to Millions Stolen From Development Fund". Wall Street Journal.

305. "US seeks to seize $1bn in Malaysia probe". BBC News. 21 July 2016 – via www.bbc.com.
306. "US seeks $1bln in 1MDB-tied Assets, 'Wolf of Wall Street' royalties". Al Arabiya English. 21 July 2016. Retrieved 25 September 2017.
307. "Wolf of Wall Street producers to pay $60 m to US government". The Guardian UK. 7 March 2018. Retrieved 16 March 2018.
308. "'The Wolf of Wall Street' producers to pay $60 million to U.S. in...". Reuters. 7 March 2018. Retrieved 6 June 2019.
309. "The 1MDB deals that continue to haunt Goldman Sachs: QuickTake". The Edge Markets. 5 November 2018. Archived from the original on 14 November 2018. Retrieved 14 November 2018.
310. "Goldman Sachs Tumbles on 1MDB Scandal and 'Fear of the Unknown'". www.bloomberg.com. Retrieved 14 November 2018.
311. "1MDB: How did Leissner and other execs bypass Goldman's compliance rules? – Nation | The Star Online". www.thestar.com.my. Retrieved 14 November 2018.
312. "Ex-Goldman bankers face 1MDB charges". BBC News. 1 November 2018. Retrieved 2 November 2018.
313. "Goldman Sachs and 1MDB: what we learned from US charges – Business News | The Star Online". www.thestar.com.my. Retrieved 2 November 2018.
314. "US prosecutors file charges against two Goldman Sachs bankers, Jho Low". www.thesundaily.my. Retrieved 2 November 2018.
315. "DoJ has until Dec to extradite Ng, says Amar Singh – Nation | The Star Online". www.thestar.com.my. Retrieved 22 November 2018.
316. Loheswar, R. "AG: Roger Ng extradited to US for 10 months over 1MDB criminal charges | Malay Mail". www.malaymail.com. Retrieved 16 May 2019.
317. "Ex-Goldman Banker in Plea Talks Ahead of 1MDB Trial in New York". Bloomberg.com. 6 May 2019. Retrieved 12 May 2019.
318. "Lawyer claims Ng down with leptospirosis and dengue – Nation | The Star Online". www.thestar.com.my. Retrieved 12 May 2019.
319. "Ex-Justice Official Helped 1MDB's Jho Low Funnel Dirty Money". www.bloomberg.com. Retrieved 2 December 2018.
320. "Ex-US Justice Dept employee pleads guilty to 1MDB fraud – Nation | The Star Online". www.thestar.com.my. Retrieved 2 December 2018.
321. "US Justice official pleads guilty in 1MDB lobbying case | New Straits Times". NST Online. 1 December 2018.
322. "US charges Jho Low, ex-Fugees rapper, over funding in 2012 election – Business News | The Star Online". www.thestar.com.my. Retrieved 18 May 2019.
323. "Fugitive Businessman Jho Low to Forfeit Over $100 Million in Luxury Homes". Barron's. 1 November 2019. Retrieved 13 November 2019.
324. Vogel, Kenneth P. (8 October 2020). "Elliott Broidy, a Top Trump Fund-Raiser, Charged in Foreign Influence Case". The New York Times. Retrieved 8 October 2020.

325. "Mueller probe witness secretly backed UAE agenda in Congress". AP News. Retrieved 26 March 2018.
326. Jump up to: a b c d Bedi, Rashvinjeet S. "RM1.3bil in 1MDB assets recouped – Nation | The Star Online". www.thestar.com.my. Retrieved 8 May 2019.
327. "1MDB: Emboldened Trusts Wrangle Over Jho Low Assets". finews.asia. 16 February 2017. Retrieved 9 July 2019.
328. Harris, Elizabeth A.; Stevenson, Alexandra (9 December 2018). "A Yacht, a Monet, a See-Through Piano: The U.S. Collects on a Fugitive's Shopping Spree". The New York Times. ISSN 0362-4331. Archived from the original on 6 July 2020. Retrieved 9 July 2019.
329. Latiff, Rozanna (24 August 2018). Cameron-Moore, Simon (ed.). "Court gives Malaysia nod to sell superyacht seized in 1MDB probe". Reuters. Archived from the original on 22 April 2020. Retrieved 9 July 2019.
330. "US begins return of US$200 million in 1MDB funds to Malaysia". CNA. Retrieved 8 May 2019.
331. Jump up to: a b "US returns US$300 m of 1MDB money to Malaysia". The Sun Daily. 15 April 2020. Archived from the original on 15 April 2020. Retrieved 15 April 2020.
332. "Goldman Sachs, Malaysia agree to US$3.9 billion settlement over 1MDB". CNA. Retrieved 28 July 2020.
333. "Commentary: Goldman has done it again with its 1MDB Malaysia deal". CNA. Retrieved 28 July 2020.
334. "KPMG pays Malaysian government $111 million settlement over 1MDB audit scandal". ABC News Australia. 13 January 2022. Retrieved 15 January 2022.

3.1.2 Text from US Department of Justice Website[2] *(January 21, 2022)*

Department of Justice, Office of Public Affairs
FOR IMMEDIATE RELEASE
Tuesday, April 14, 2020

U.S. Repatriates $300 Million to Malaysia in Proceeds of Funds Misappropriated from 1Malaysia Development Berhad
The Department of Justice announced today that it has repatriated to Malaysia approximately $300 million (RM 1.292 billion) in additional funds misappropriated from 1Malaysia Development Berhad (1MDB), Malaysia's investment development

---

[2] Link: https://www.justice.gov/opa/pr/us-repatriates-300-million-malaysia-proceeds-funds-misappropriated-1malaysia-development

fund, and laundered through financial institutions in several jurisdictions, including the United States, Switzerland, Singapore and Luxembourg.

Combined with other funds that the department previously returned to Malaysia in May 2019, the United States has returned or assisted Malaysia in recovering over $600 million (RM 2.6 billion) of funds misappropriated from 1MDB. The department's efforts to recover funds misappropriated from 1MDB are continuing.

In 2019, the U.S. District Court for the Central District of California entered judgments forfeiting more than $700 million in assets acquired by Low Taek Jho, aka Jho Low, and his family located in the United States, the United Kingdom and Switzerland. To date, the United States has recovered or assisted in the recovery of more than $1 billion in assets associated with the 1MDB international money laundering and bribery scheme. This represents the largest recovery to date under the department's Kleptocracy Asset Recovery Initiative and the largest civil forfeiture ever concluded by the Justice Department.

"We are pleased to make this latest repatriation of an additional $300 million in stolen 1MDB funds," said Assistant Attorney General Brian A. Benczkowski of the Justice Department's Criminal Division. "The payment reflects the United States' continuing commitment to the Malaysian people to hunt down, seize, forfeit, and return assets that were acquired in connection with this brazen scheme."

"The repatriation of these stolen funds to the citizens of Malaysia is the result of the tireless efforts of prosecutors and federal agents to prevent foreign kleptocrats and their associates from using the United States as a playground where they can enjoy the fruits of their pilfered wealth," said U.S. Attorney Nick Hanna of the Central District of California. "The amount of money stolen from the people of Malaysia is staggering, and we have been relentless in recovering assets that always should have been used for their benefit."

"The FBI's International Corruption Squads are dedicated to protecting the United States from criminals attempting to benefit from our economy using their illicit, ill-gotten funds," said Assistant Director Calvin Shivers of the FBI's Criminal Investigative Division. "The repatriation announced today is a direct result of an FBI international corruption investigation, conclusively demonstrating that criminals will not be allowed to prosper in the United States. This money is now being returned to its rightful place—the country and people of Malaysia."

"This extraordinary sum of money is going back to the people of Malaysia where it belongs and where it can finally be used for its original intended purpose—to better the lives of everyday Malaysians," said Chief Don Fort of IRS-Criminal Investigations (IRS-CI). "Mr. Low attempted to launder these assets through multiple international jurisdictions and a web of shell corporations, but his greed finally caught up with him. This case is a model for international cooperation in significant cross-border money laundering investigations."

According to the civil forfeiture complaints, from 2009 through 2015, more than $4.5 billion in funds belonging to 1MDB were allegedly misappropriated by high-level officials of 1MDB and their associates, including Low, through a criminal conspiracy involving international money laundering and bribery. 1MDB was created by the government of Malaysia to promote economic development in Malaysia through global partnerships and foreign direct investment, and its funds were intended to be used for improving the well-being of the Malaysian people. The assets subject to the 2019 judgments include high-end real estate in Beverly Hills, New York and London; a luxury boutique hotel in Beverly Hills; and tens of millions of dollars in business investments that Low allegedly made with funds traceable to misappropriated 1MDB monies.

The FBI's International Corruption Squads in New York City and Los Angeles and the IRS-CI are investigating the case. Deputy Chief Woo S. Lee and Trial Attorneys Barbara Levy, Joshua L. Sohn and Jonathan Baum of the Criminal Division's Money Laundering and Asset Recovery Section and Assistant U.-S. Attorneys John Kucera, Michael R. Sew Hoy and Steven R. Welk of the Central District of California are prosecuting the case. The Criminal Division's Office of International Affairs is providing substantial assistance.

The department also appreciates the significant assistance provided by the Attorney General's Chambers of Malaysia, the Royal Malaysian Police, the Malaysian Anti-Corruption Commission, the Attorney General's Chambers of Singapore, the Singapore Police Force-Commercial Affairs Division, the Office of the Attorney General and the Federal Office of Justice of Switzerland, the judicial investigating authority of the Grand Duchy of Luxembourg and the Criminal Investigation Department of the Grand-Ducal Police of Luxembourg.

The Kleptocracy Asset Recovery Initiative is led by a team of dedicated prosecutors in the Criminal Division's Money Laundering and Asset Recovery Section, in partnership with federal law enforcement agencies, and often with U.S. Attorney's Offices, to forfeit the proceeds of foreign official corruption and, where appropriate, to use those recovered assets to benefit the people harmed by these acts of corruption and abuse of office. In 2015, the FBI formed International Corruption Squads across the country to address national and international implications of foreign corruption. Individuals with information about possible proceeds of foreign corruption located in or laundered through the U.S. should contact federal law enforcement or send an email to kleptocracy@usdoj.gov (link sends e-mail) or https://tips.fbi.gov/

A civil forfeiture complaint is merely an allegation that money or property was involved in or represents the proceeds of a crime. These allegations are not proven until a court awards judgment in favor of the United States...

3.1.3 Text from US Department of Justice Website[3] (January 21, 2022)

Department of Justice, Office of Public Affairs
FOR IMMEDIATE RELEASE
Thursday, August 5, 2021

Over $1 Billion in Misappropriated 1MDB Funds Now Repatriated to Malaysia
The Justice Department announced today that it has repatriated an additional $452 million in misappropriated 1Malaysia Development Berhad (1MDB) funds to the people of Malaysia, bringing the total returned to over $1.2 billion.

According to court documents, the funds from 1MDB, formerly Malaysia's investment development fund, were laundered through major financial institutions worldwide, including in the United States, Switzerland, Singapore, and Luxembourg.

Beginning in 2016, a landmark effort encompassing 41 civil forfeiture actions filed in the U.S. District Court for the Central District of California and one in the U.S. District Court for the District of Columbia by the Money Laundering and Asset Recovery Section (MLARS) of the Justice Department's Criminal Division led to the seizure of over $1.7 billion in stolen assets. This is the largest recovery to date under the Department's Kleptocracy Asset Recovery Initiative. The funds include both funds finally forfeited and funds the Department assisted in recovering and returning. The Department continues to litigate actions against additional assets allegedly linked to this scheme.

As alleged in the civil forfeiture complaints, from 2009 through 2015, more than $4.5 billion in funds belonging to 1MDB were allegedly misappropriated by high-level officials of 1MDB and their associates, and Low Taek Jho (aka Jho Low), through a criminal scheme involving international money laundering and embezzlement. Some of the embezzlement proceeds were also allegedly used to pay bribes.

1MDB was created by the government of Malaysia to promote economic development in Malaysia through global partnerships and foreign direct investment. Its funds were intended to be used for improving the well-being of the Malaysian people. Instead, funds held by 1MDB and proceeds of bonds issued for and on behalf of 1MDB were taken and spent on a wide variety of extravagant items, including luxury homes and properties in Beverly Hills, New York, and London; a 300-foot superyacht; and fine art by Monet and Van Gogh. The funds also were sent into numerous business investments, including a boutique hotel in Beverly Hills, a movie production company that made "The Wolf of Wall Street" while the embezzlement scheme was ongoing, the redevelopment of the Park Lane Hotel in Manhattan, and shares in EMI, the largest private music-rights holder. As alleged, other funds were provided to various public officials and co-conspirators.

---
[3] Link: https://www.justice.gov/opa/pr/over-1-billion-misappropriated-1mdb-funds-now-repatriated-malaysia

The FBI's International Corruption Squads in New York and Los Angeles and IRS-Criminal Investigation are leading the investigation.

MLARS Trial Attorneys Barbara Levy, Josh Sohn and Jonathon Baum are litigating the case. Assistant U.S. Attorney Jonathon Galatzan and Chief of the Asset Forefeiture Section Steven R. Welk of the Central District of California worked as MLARS partners, along with former MLARS Deputy Chief Woo S. Lee, Trial Attorney Kyle Freeny, and former Assistant U.S. Attorneys John Kucera and Michael Sew Hoy.

The Criminal Division's Office of International Affairs is providing substantial assistance. MLARS' Program Operations Unit has also provided significant support.

Significant assistance was also provided to the department by the Attorney General's Chambers of Malaysia, the Royal Malaysian Police, the Malaysian Anti-Corruption Commission, the Attorney General's Chambers of Singapore, the Singapore Police Force–Commercial Affairs Division, the Office of the Attorney General and the Federal Office of Justice of Switzerland, the judicial investigating authority of the Grand Duchy of Luxembourg, and the Criminal Investigation Department of the Grand-Ducal Police of Luxembourg.

The Kleptocracy Asset Recovery Initiative is led by a team of dedicated MLARS prosecutors in partnership with federal law enforcement agencies, and often with U.S. Attorneys' Offices, to forfeit the proceeds of foreign official corruption and, where appropriate, to seize, forfeit and repatriate those recovered assets to benefit the people harmed by these acts of corruption and abuse of office. In 2015, the FBI formed International Corruption Squads across the country to address national and international implications of foreign corruption. Individuals with information about possible proceeds of foreign corruption located in or laundered through the United States should email kleptocracy@usdoj.gov or submit information at https://tips.fbi.gov/.

A civil forfeiture complaint is merely an allegation that money or property was involved in or represents the proceeds of crime. These allegations are not proven until a court awards judgment in favor of the United States, which has occurred in the cases that have led to these recoveries.

3.2 Goldman Sachs: 1MDB[4]

3.2.1 Text from US Department of Justice Website[5] (11 February 2022)

Department of Justice
Office of Public Affairs
FOR IMMEDIATE RELEASE
Thursday, October 22, 2020

Goldman Sachs Charged in Foreign Bribery Case and Agrees to Pay Over $2.9 Billion

The Goldman Sachs Group Inc. (Goldman Sachs or the Company), a global financial institution headquartered in New York, New York, and Goldman Sachs (Malaysia) Sdn. Bhd. (GS Malaysia), its Malaysian subsidiary, have admitted to conspiring to violate the Foreign Corrupt Practices Act (FCPA) in connection with a scheme to pay over $1 billion in bribes to Malaysian and Abu Dhabi officials to obtain lucrative business for Goldman Sachs, including its role in underwriting approximately $6.5 billion in three bond deals for 1Malaysia Development Bhd. (1MDB), for which the bank earned hundreds of millions in fees. Goldman Sachs will pay more than $2.9 billion as part of a coordinated resolution with criminal and civil authorities in the United States, the United Kingdom, Singapore, and elsewhere.

Goldman Sachs entered into a deferred prosecution agreement with the department in connection with a criminal information filed today in the Eastern District of New York charging the Company with conspiracy to violate the anti-bribery provisions of the FCPA. GS Malaysia pleaded guilty in the U.S. District Court for the Eastern District of New York to a one-count criminal information charging it with conspiracy to violate the anti-bribery provisions of the FCPA.

Previously, Tim Leissner, the former Southeast Asia Chairman and participating managing director of Goldman Sachs, pleaded guilty to conspiring to launder money

---

[4] See also an article in the FCPA Blog entitled: (A US) Jury convicts former Goldman Sachs banker on FCPA conspiracy charges, by Harry Cassin dated April 8, 2022. The article notes that "Roger Ng, a former managing director of Goldman Sachs, was convicted by a New York jury Friday on three counts including conspiring to violate the anti-bribery provisions of the FCPA, conspiring to circumvent internal accounting controls in violation of the FCPA, and conspiracy to commit money laundering. Ng, a Malaysian citizen, was charged in 2018 as part of the looting of Malaysian sovereign wealth fund 1Malaysia Development Berhad in an unsealed three-count indictment. He was arrested in November 2018 in Malaysia and extradited to the United States in May 2019 and that: "The DOJ reached a $700 million civil forfeiture agreement in 2019 for assets (Low Taek Jho) Low allegedly acquired with money stolen from 1MDB. Low hasn't appeared in U.S. court to answer the criminal charges. He is currently a fugitive and his whereabouts are unknown." Link: https://fcpablog.com/2022/04/08/jury-convicts-former-goldman-sachs-banker-on-fcpa-conspiracy-charges/

[5] https://www.justice.gov/opa/pr/goldman-sachs-charged-foreign-bribery-case-and-agrees-pay-over-29-billion

and to violate the FCPA. Ng Chong Hwa, also known as "Roger Ng," former managing director of Goldman and head of investment banking for GS Malaysia, has been charged with conspiring to launder money and to violate the FCPA. Ng was extradited from Malaysia to face these charges and is scheduled to stand trial in March 2021. The cases are assigned to U.S. District Judge Margo K. Brodie of the Eastern District of New York.

In addition to these criminal charges, the department has recovered, or assisted in the recovery of, in excess of $1 billion in assets for Malaysia associated with and traceable to the 1MDB money laundering and bribery scheme.

"Goldman Sachs today accepted responsibility for its role in a conspiracy to bribe high-ranking foreign officials to obtain lucrative underwriting and other business relating to 1MDB," said Acting Assistant Attorney General Brian C. Rabbitt of the Justice Department's Criminal Division. "Today's resolution, which requires Goldman Sachs to admit wrongdoing and pay nearly three billion dollars in penalties, fines, and disgorgement, holds the bank accountable for this criminal scheme and demonstrates the department's continuing commitment to combatting corruption and protecting the U.S. financial system."

"Over a period of five years, Goldman Sachs participated in a sweeping international corruption scheme, conspiring to avail itself of more than $1.6 billion in bribes to multiple high-level government officials across several countries so that the company could reap hundreds of millions of dollars in fees, all to the detriment of the people of Malaysia and the reputation of American financial institutions operating abroad," said Acting U.S. Attorney Seth D. DuCharme of the Eastern District of New York. "Today's resolution, which includes a criminal guilty plea by Goldman Sachs' subsidiary in Malaysia, demonstrates that the department will hold accountable any institution that violates U.S. law anywhere in the world by unfairly tilting the scales through corrupt practices."

"When government officials and business executives secretly work together behind the scenes for their own illegal benefit, and not that of their citizens and shareholders, their behavior lends credibility to the narrative that businesses don't succeed based on the quality of their products, but rather their willingness to play dirty," said Assistant Director in Charge William F. Sweeney Jr. of the FBI's New York Field Office. "Greed eventually exacts an immense cost on society, and unchecked corrupt behavior erodes trust in public institutions and government entities alike. This case represents the largest ever penalty paid to U.S. authorities in an FCPA case. Our investigation into the looting of funds from 1MDB remains ongoing. If anyone has information that could assist the case, call us at 1-800-CALLFBI."

"1MDB was established to drive strategic initiatives for the long-term economic development of Malaysia. Goldman Sachs admitted today that one billion dollars of the money earmarked to help the people of Malaysia was actually diverted and used to pay bribes to Malaysian and Abu Dhabi officials to obtain their business," said Special Agent in Charge Ryan L. Korner of IRS Criminal Investigation's (IRS-CI) Los Angeles Field Office. "Today's guilty pleas demonstrate that the law applies to everyone, including large investment banks like Goldman Sachs. IRS Criminal

Investigation will work tirelessly alongside our law enforcement partners to identify and bring to justice those who engage in fraud and deceit around the globe. When the American financial system is misused for corruption, the IRS will take notice and we will take action."

According to Goldman's admissions and court documents, between approximately 2009 and 2014, Goldman conspired with others to violate the FCPA by engaging in a scheme to pay more than $1.6 billion in bribes, directly and indirectly, to foreign officials in Malaysia and Abu Dhabi in order to obtain and retain business for Goldman from 1MDB, a Malaysian state-owned and state-controlled fund created to pursue investment and development projects for the economic benefit of Malaysia and its people. Specifically, the Company admitted to engaging in the bribery scheme through certain of its employees and agents, including Leissner, Ng, and a former executive who was a participating managing director and held leadership positions in Asia (Employee 1), in exchange for lucrative business and other advantages and opportunities. These included, among other things, securing Goldman's role as an advisor on energy acquisitions, as underwriter on three lucrative bond deals with a total value of $6.5 billion, and a potential role in a highly anticipated and even more lucrative initial public offering for 1MDB's energy assets. As Goldman admitted — and as alleged in the indictment pending in the Eastern District of New York against Ng and Low — in furtherance of the scheme, Leissner, Ng, Employee 1, and others conspired to pay bribes to numerous foreign officials, including high-ranking officials in the Malaysian government, 1MDB, Abu Dhabi's state-owned and state-controlled sovereign wealth fund, International Petroleum Investment Company (IPIC), and Abu Dhabi's state-owned and state-controlled joint stock company, Aabar Investments PJS (Aabar).

Goldman admitted today that, in order to effectuate the scheme, Leissner, Ng, Employee 1, and others conspired with Low Taek Jho, aka Jho Low, to promise and pay over $1.6 billion in bribes to Malaysian, 1MDB, IPIC, and Aabar officials. The co-conspirators allegedly paid these bribes using more than $2.7 billion in funds that Low, Leissner, and other members of the conspiracy diverted and misappropriated from the bond offerings underwritten by Goldman. Leissner, Ng and Low also retained a portion of the misappropriated funds for themselves and other co-conspirators. Goldman admitted that, through Leissner, Ng, Employee 1 and others, the bank used Low's connections to advance and further the bribery scheme, ultimately ensuring that 1MDB awarded Goldman a role on three bond transactions between 2012 and 2013, known internally at Goldman as "Project Magnolia," "Project Maximus," and "Project Catalyze."

Goldman also admitted that, although employees serving as part of Goldman's control functions knew that any transaction involving Low posed a significant risk, and although they were on notice that Low was involved in the transactions, they did not take reasonable steps to ensure that Low was not involved. Goldman further admitted that there were significant red flags raised during the due diligence process and afterward — including but not limited to Low's involvement — that either were ignored or only nominally addressed so that the transactions would be approved and Goldman could continue to do business with 1MDB. As a result of the scheme,

Goldman received approximately $606 million in fees and revenue, and increased its stature and presence in Southeast Asia.

Under the terms of the agreements, Goldman will pay a criminal penalty and disgorgement of over $2.9 billion. Goldman also has reached separate parallel resolutions with foreign authorities in the United Kingdom, Singapore, Malaysia, and elsewhere, along with domestic authorities in the United States. The department will credit over $1.6 billion in payments with respect to those resolutions.

The department reached this resolution with Goldman based on a number of factors, including the Company's failure to voluntarily disclose the conduct to the department; the nature and seriousness of the offense, which included the involvement of high-level employees within the Company's investment bank and others who ignored significant red flags; the involvement of various Goldman subsidiaries across the world; the amount of the bribes, which totaled over $1.6 billion; the number and high-level nature of the bribe recipients, which included at least 11 foreign officials, including high-ranking officials of the Malaysian government; and the significant amount of actual loss incurred by 1MDB as a result of the co-conspirators' conduct. Goldman received partial credit for its cooperation with the department's investigation, but did not receive full credit for cooperation because it significantly delayed producing relevant evidence, including recorded phone calls in which the Company's bankers, executives, and control function personnel discussed allegations of bribery and misconduct relating to the conduct in the statement of facts. Accordingly, the total criminal penalty reflects a 10 percent reduction off the bottom of the applicable U.S. sentencing guidelines fine range.

Low has also been indicted for conspiracy to commit money laundering and violate the FCPA, along with Ng, E.D.N.Y. Docket No. 18-CR-538 (MKB). Low remains a fugitive. The charges in the indictment as to Low and Ng are merely allegations, and those defendants are presumed innocent until proven guilty beyond a reasonable doubt in a court of law.

The investigation was conducted by the FBI's International Corruption Unit and IRS-CI. The prosecution is being handled by the Criminal Division's Fraud Section and the Money Laundering and Asset Recovery Section (MLARS), and the Business and Securities Fraud Section of the U.S. Attorney's Office for the Eastern District of New York. Trial Attorneys Katherine Nielsen, Nikhila Raj, Jennifer E. Ambuehl, Woo S. Lee, Mary Ann McCarthy, Leo Tsao, and David Last of the Criminal Division, and Assistant U.S. Attorneys Jacquelyn M. Kasulis, Alixandra Smith and Drew Rolle of the Eastern District of New York are prosecuting the case. Additional Criminal Division Trial Attorneys and Assistant U.S. Attorneys within U.S. Attorney's Offices for the Eastern District of New York and Central District of California have provided valuable assistance with various aspects of this investigation, including with civil and criminal forfeitures. The Justice Department's Office of International Affairs of the Criminal Division provided critical assistance in this case.

The department also appreciates the significant assistance provided by the U.-S. Securities and Exchange Commission; the Board of Governors of the Federal Reserve System, including the Federal Reserve Bank of New York; the New York

State Department of Financial Services, the United Kingdom Financial Conduct Authority; the United Kingdom Prudential Regulation Authority; the Attorney General's Chambers of Singapore; the Singapore Police Force-Commercial Affairs Division; the Monetary Authority of Singapore; the Office of the Attorney General and the Federal Office of Justice of Switzerland; the judicial investigating authority of the Grand Duchy of Luxembourg and the Criminal Investigation Department of the Grand-Ducal Police of Luxembourg; the Attorney General's Chambers of Malaysia; the Royal Malaysian Police; and the Malaysian Anti-Corruption Commission. The department also expresses its appreciation for the assistance provided by the Ministry of Justice of France; the Attorney General's Office of the Bailiwick of Guernsey and the Guernsey Economic Crime Division.

3.3 Bernard L Madoff

3.3.1 Text from Wikipedia[6] (January 21, 2022)

Madoff Investment Scandal

The Madoff investment scandal was a major case of stock and securities fraud discovered in late 2008 [1]. In December of that year, Bernie Madoff, the former NASDAQ chairman and founder of the Wall Street firm Bernard L. Madoff Investment Securities LLC, admitted that the wealth management arm of his business was an elaborate multi-billion-dollar Ponzi scheme.

Madoff founded Bernard L. Madoff Investment Securities LLC in 1960, and was its chairman until his arrest [2–4]. The firm employed Madoff's brother Peter as senior managing director and chief compliance officer, Peter's daughter Shana Madoff as rules and compliance officer and attorney, and Madoff's sons Mark and Andrew. Peter was sentenced to 10 years in prison, and Mark committed suicide exactly two years after his father's arrest.

Alerted by his sons, federal authorities arrested Madoff on December 11, 2008. On March 12, 2009, Madoff pleaded guilty to 11 federal crimes and admitted to operating the largest private Ponzi scheme in history [5, 6]. On June 29, 2009, he was sentenced to 150 years in prison with restitution of $170 billion. He died in prison in 2021 [7].

According to the original federal charges, Madoff said that his firm had "liabilities of approximately US$50 billion."[8, 9] Prosecutors estimated the size of the fraud to be $64.8 billion, based on the amounts in the accounts of Madoff's 4,800 clients as of November 30, 2008 [10, 11]. Ignoring opportunity costs and taxes paid on fictitious profits, about half of Madoff's direct investors lost no money [12]. Harry Markopolos, a whistleblower whose repeated warnings about Madoff were ignored,

---

[6]Link: https://en.wikipedia.org/wiki/Madoff_investment_scandal

estimated that at least $35 billion of the money Madoff claimed to have stolen never really existed, but was simply fictional profits he reported to his clients [13].

Investigators determined that others were involved in the scheme [14]. The U.S. Securities and Exchange Commission (SEC) was criticized for not investigating Madoff more thoroughly; questions about his firm had been raised as early as 1999. The legitimate trading arm of Madoff's business that was run by his two sons was one of the top market makers on Wall Street, and in 2008 was the sixth-largest [15].

Madoff's personal and business asset freeze created a chain reaction throughout the world's business and philanthropic community, forcing many organizations to at least temporarily close, including the Robert I. Lappin Charitable Foundation, the Picower Foundation, and the JEHT Foundation [16–18].

Contents
1. Background
2. Modus operandi
   - 2.1. Purported strategy
   - 2.2. Sales methods
   - 2.3. Access to Washington
3. Previous investigations
   - 3.1. Avellino and Bienes
   - 3.2. SEC
   - 3.3. FINRA
   - 3.4. Other warnings
4. Final weeks and collapse
5. Investigation into co-conspirators
   - 5.1. Alleged co-conspirators
6. Charges and sentencing
   - 6.1. Criminal complaint
   - 6.2. Plea proceeding
   - 6.3. Sentencing, prison life and death
7. Recovery of funds
8. Affected clients
   - 8.1. Largest stake-holders
     - 8.1.1. IRS penalties
9. Impact and aftermath
   - 9.1. Criminal charges against Aurelia Finance
   - 9.2. Grupo Santander
   - 9.3. Union Bancaire Privee
   - 9.4. Bank Medici

9.5. The Innocence Project
9.6. Westport National Bank
9.7. Thema International Fund
9.8. The Picower Foundation
9.9. Peter Madoff
9.10. Suicides

    9.1.1. René-Thierry Magon de la Villehuchet
    9.1.2. William Foxton
    9.1.3. Mark Madoff
    9.1.4. Charles Murphy

9.11. U.S. Securities and Exchange Commission
9.12. JPMorgan Chase
9.13. Payouts

10. See also
11. References

    11.1. Sources

12. External links

1. Background

Madoff started his firm in 1960 as a penny stock trader with $5000, earned from working as a lifeguard and sprinkler installer [19]. His fledgling business began to grow with the assistance of his father-in-law, accountant Saul Alpern, who referred a circle of friends and their families [20]. Initially, the firm made markets (quoted bid and ask prices) via the National Quotation Bureau's Pink Sheets. To compete with firms that were members of the New York Stock Exchange trading on the stock exchange's floor, his firm began using innovative computer information technology to disseminate quotes [21]. After a trial run, the technology that the firm helped develop became the NASDAQ [22]. At one point, Madoff Securities was the largest buying-and-selling "market maker" at the NASDAQ [21].

He was active in the National Association of Securities Dealers (NASD), a self-regulatory securities industry organization, serving as the chairman of the board of directors and on the board of governors [23].

In 1992, The Wall Street Journal described him [24]:

> ... one of the masters of the off-exchange "third market" and the bane of the New York Stock Exchange. He has built a highly profitable securities firm, Bernard L. Madoff Investment Securities, which siphons a huge volume of stock trades away from the Big Board. The $740 million average daily volume of trades executed electronically by the Madoff firm off the exchange equals 9% of the New York exchange's. Mr. Madoff's firm can execute trades so quickly and cheaply that it actually pays other brokerage firms a penny a share to execute their customers' orders, profiting from the spread between bid and asked prices that most stocks trade for.
> —Randall Smith, Wall Street Journal

Several family members worked for him. His younger brother, Peter, was senior managing director and chief compliance officer [21], and Peter's daughter, Shana Madoff, was the compliance attorney. Madoff's sons, Mark and Andrew, worked in the trading section [21], along with Charles Weiner, Madoff's nephew [25]. Andrew Madoff invested his own money in his father's fund, but Mark stopped in about 2001 [26].

Federal investigators believe the fraud in the investment management division and advisory division may have begun in the 1970s [27]. However, Madoff himself stated his fraudulent activities began in the 1990s [28]. Madoff's fraudulent activities are believed to have accelerated after the 2001 change from fractional share trades to decimals in the NYSE, which cut significantly into his legitimate profits as a market-maker [29].

In the 1980s, Madoff's market-maker division traded up to 5% of the total volume made on the New York Stock Exchange [21]. Madoff was "the first prominent practitioner" [30] of payment for order flow, paying brokers to execute their clients' orders through his brokerage, a practice some have called a "legal kickback" [31]. This practice gave Madoff the distinction of being the largest dealer in NYSE-listed stocks in the U.S., trading about 15% of transaction volume [32]. Academics have questioned the ethics of these payments [33, 34]. Madoff has argued that these payments did not alter the price that the customer received [35]. He viewed payments for order flow as a normal business practice: "If your girlfriend goes to buy stockings at a supermarket, the racks that display those stockings are usually paid for by the company that manufactured the stockings. Order flow is an issue that attracted a lot of attention but is grossly overrated [35]."

By 2000, Madoff Securities, one of the top traders of US securities, held approximately $300 million in assets [21]. The business occupied three floors of the Lipstick Building in Manhattan, with the investment management division on the 17th floor, referred to as the "hedge fund", employing a staff of less than 24 [36]. Madoff also ran a branch office in London that employed 28 people, separate from Madoff Securities. The company handled investments for his family of approximately £80 million [37]. Two remote cameras installed in the London office permitted Madoff to monitor events from New York [38].

After 41 years as a sole proprietorship, Madoff converted his firm into a limited liability company in 2001, with himself as the sole shareholder [39].

2. Modus Operandi

In 1992, Bernard Madoff explained his purported strategy to The Wall Street Journal. He said his returns were really nothing special, given that the Standard & Poors 500-stock index generated an average annual return of 16.3% between November 1982 and November 1992. "I would be surprised if anybody thought that matching the S&P over 10 years was anything outstanding." The majority of money managers actually trailed the S&P 500 during the 1980s. The Journal concluded Madoff's use of futures and options helped cushion the returns against the market's ups and downs. Madoff said he made up for the cost of the hedges, which could have caused him to trail the stock market's returns, with stock-picking and market timing [24].

2.1 Purported Strategy

Madoff's sales pitch was an investment strategy consisting of purchasing blue-chip stocks and taking options contracts on them, sometimes called a split-strike conversion or a collar [40]. "Typically, a position will consist of the ownership of 30–35 S&P 100 stocks, most correlated to that index, the sale of out-of-the-money 'calls' on the index and the purchase of out-of-the-money 'puts' on the index. The sale of the 'calls' is designed to increase the rate of return, while allowing upward movement of the stock portfolio to the strike price of the 'calls'. The 'puts', funded in large part by the sales of the 'calls', limit the portfolio's downside."

In his 1992 "Avellino and Bienes" interview with The Wall Street Journal, Madoff discussed his supposed methods: In the 1970s, he had placed invested funds in "convertible arbitrage positions in large-cap stocks, with promised investment returns of 18% to 20%" [40], and in 1982, he began using futures contracts on the stock index, and then placed put options on futures during the 1987 stock market crash [40]. A few analysts performing due diligence had been unable to replicate the Madoff fund's past returns using historic price data for U.S. stocks and options on the indexes [41, 42]. Barron's raised the possibility that Madoff's returns were most likely due to front running his firm's brokerage clients [43].

Mitchell Zuckoff, professor of journalism at Boston University and author of Ponzi's Scheme: The True Story of a Financial Legend, says that "the 5% payout rule", a federal law requiring private foundations to pay out 5% of their funds each year, allowed Madoff's Ponzi scheme to go undetected for a long period since he managed money mainly for charities. Zuckoff notes, "For every $1 billion in foundation investment, Madoff was effectively on the hook for about $50 million in withdrawals a year. If he was not making real investments, at that rate the principal would last 20 years. By targeting charities, Madoff could avoid the threat of sudden or unexpected withdrawals [44].

In his guilty plea, Madoff admitted that he hadn't actually traded since the early 1990s, and all of his returns since then had been fabricated [45]. However, David Sheehan, principal investigator for trustee Irving Picard, believes the wealth management arm of Madoff's business had been a fraud from the start [46].

Madoff's operation differed from a typical Ponzi scheme. While most Ponzi schemes are based on nonexistent businesses, Madoff's brokerage operation arm was very real. At the time of its shuttering, it handled large trades for institutional investors.

2.2 Sales Methods

Madoff was a "master marketer" who, throughout the 1970s and 1980s, built a reputation as a wealth manager for a highly exclusive clientele [47, 48]. Investors who gained access, typically on word-of-mouth referral, believed that they had entered the inner circle of a money-making genius [47], and some were wary of removing their money from his fund, in case they could not get back in [15]. In later years, even as Madoff's operation accepted money from various countries through feeder funds, he continued to package it as an exclusive opportunity [47]. People who met him in person were impressed with his apparent humility despite his reported financial success and personal wealth [47, 48].

The New York Post reported that Madoff "worked the so-called 'Jewish circuit' of well-heeled Jews he met at country clubs on Long Island and in Palm Beach" [49]. (The scandal so affected Palm Beach that, according to The Globe and Mail, residents "stopped talking about the local destruction the Madoff storm caused only when Hurricane Trump came along" in 2016 [50].) The New York Times reported that Madoff courted many prominent Jewish executives and organizations and, according to the Associated Press, they "trusted [Madoff] because he is Jewish" [45]. One of the most prominent promoters was J. Ezra Merkin, whose fund Ascot Partners steered $1.8 billion towards Madoff's firm [47]. A scheme that targets members of a particular religious or ethnic community is a type of affinity fraud, and a Newsweek article identified Madoff's scheme as "an affinity Ponzi" [51].

Madoff's annual returns were "unusually consistent" [52], around 10%, and were a key factor in perpetuating the fraud [53]. Ponzi schemes typically pay returns of 20% or higher, and collapse quickly. One Madoff fund, which described its "strategy" as focusing on shares in the Standard & Poor's 100-stock index, reported a 10.5% annual return during the previous 17 years. Even at the end of November 2008, amid a general market collapse, the same fund reported that it was up 5.6%, while the same year-to-date total return on the S&P 500-stock index had been negative 38% [16]. An unnamed investor remarked, "The returns were just amazing and we trusted this guy for decades — if you wanted to take money out, you always got your check in a few days. That's why we were all so stunned [54]" [clarification needed] [55].

The Swiss bank Union Bancaire Privée explained that because of Madoff's huge volume as a broker-dealer, the bank believed he had a perceived edge on the market because his trades were timed well, suggesting they believed he was front running [56].

2.3 Access to Washington

The Madoff family gained unusual access to Washington's lawmakers and regulators through the industry's top trade group. The Madoff family maintained long-standing, high-level ties to the Securities Industry and Financial Markets Association (SIFMA), the primary securities industry organization.

Bernard Madoff sat on the board of directors of the Securities Industry Association, which merged with the Bond Market Association in 2006 to form SIFMA. Madoff's brother Peter then served two terms as a member of SIFMA's board of directors [57, 58]. Peter's resignation as the scandal broke in December 2008 came amid growing criticism of the Madoff firm's links to Washington, and how those relationships may have contributed to the Madoff fraud [59]. Over the years 2000–08, the two Madoff brothers gave $56,000 to SIFMA [59], and tens of thousands of dollars more to sponsor SIFMA industry meetings [60].

In addition, Bernard Madoff's niece Shana Madoff [61] who was the compliance officer and attorney at Bernard L. Madoff Investment Securities from 1995 until 2008, was active on the Executive Committee of SIFMA's Compliance & Legal Division, but resigned her SIFMA position shortly after her uncle's arrest [62]. She

3.3 Bernard L Madoff

in 2007 married former assistant director of the SEC's Office of Compliance Inspections and Examinations Eric Swanson [63], whom she had met in April 2003 while he was investigating her uncle Bernie Madoff and his firm [64–66]. The two had periodic contact thereafter in connection with Swanson speaking at industry events organized by a SIFMA committee on which Shana Madoff sat. During 2003 Swanson sent Shana's father Peter Madoff two regulatory requests [64–71]. In March 2004, SEC lawyer Genevievette Walker-Lightfoot, who was reviewing Madoff's firm, raised questions to Swanson (Walker-Lightfoot's boss's supervisor) about unusual trading at a Bernie Madoff fund; Walker-Lightfoot was told to instead concentrate on an unrelated matter [72, 73]. Swanson and Walker-Lightfoot's boss asked for her research, but did not act upon it [73]. In February 2006, Swanson was emailed by Assistant Director John Nee that the SEC's New York Regional Office was investigating a complaint that Bernard Madoff might be running "the biggest Ponzi scheme ever." [67].

In April 2006, Swanson began to date Shana Madoff. Swanson reported the relationship to his supervisor who wrote in an email "I guess we won't be investigating Madoff anytime soon." [74] On 15 September 2006, Swanson left the SEC [64, 75]. On December 8, 2006, Swanson and Shana Madoff became engaged [64, 76]. In 2007 the two married [77–79]. A spokesman for Swanson said he "did not participate in any inquiry of Bernard Madoff Securities or its affiliates while involved in a relationship" with Shana Madoff [80].

3. Previous Investigations

Madoff Securities LLC was investigated at least eight times over a 16-year period by the U.S. Securities and Exchange Commission (SEC) and other regulatory authorities [81].

3.1 Avellino and Bienes

In 1992, the SEC investigated one of Madoff's feeder funds, Avellino & Bienes, the principals being Frank Avellino, Michael Bienes, and his wife Dianne Bienes. Bienes began his career working as an accountant for Madoff's father-in-law, Saul Alpern. Then, he became a partner in the accounting firm Alpern, Avellino and Bienes. In 1962, the firm began advising its clients about investing all of their money with a mystery man, a highly successful and controversial figure on Wall Street—but until this episode, not known as an ace money manager—Madoff [24]. When Alpern retired at the end of 1974, the firm became Avellino and Bienes and continued to invest solely with Madoff [40, 82].

Avellino & Bienes, represented by Ira Sorkin, Madoff's former attorney, were accused of selling unregistered securities. In a report to the SEC they mentioned the fund's "curiously steady" yearly returns to investors of 13.5% to 20%. However, the SEC did not look any more deeply into the matter, and never publicly referred to Madoff [24, 40]. Through Sorkin, who once oversaw the SEC's New York office, Avellino & Bienes agreed to return the money to investors, shut down their firm, undergo an audit, and pay a fine of $350,000. Avellino complained to the presiding federal judge, John E. Sprizzo, that Price Waterhouse fees were excessive, but the judge ordered him to pay the bill of $428,679 in full. Madoff said that he did not realize the feeder fund was operating illegally, and that his own investment returns tracked the previous 10 years of the S&P 500 [40]. The SEC investigation came right in the middle of Madoff's three terms as the chairman of the NASDAQ stock market board [82].

The size of the pools mushroomed by word-of-mouth, and investors grew to 3200 in nine accounts with Madoff. Regulators feared it all might be just a huge scam. "We went into this thinking it could be a major catastrophe. They took in nearly a half a billion dollars in investor money, totally outside the system that we can monitor and regulate. That's pretty frightening," said Richard Walker, who at the time was the SEC's New York regional administrator [24].

Avellino and Bienes deposited $454 million of investors' money with Madoff, and until 2007, Bienes continued to invest several million dollars of his own money with Madoff. In a 2009 interview after the scam had been exposed, he said, "Doubt Bernie Madoff? Doubt Bernie? No. You doubt God. You can doubt God, but you don't doubt Bernie. He had that aura about him." [82].

3.2 SEC

The SEC investigated Madoff in 1999 and 2000 about concerns that the firm was hiding its customers' orders from other traders, for which Madoff then took corrective measures [81]. In 2001, an SEC official met with Harry Markopolos at their Boston regional office and reviewed his allegations of Madoff's fraudulent practices [81]. The SEC said it conducted two other inquiries into Madoff in the last several years, but did not find any violations or major issues of concern [83].

In 2004, after published articles appeared accusing the firm of front running, the SEC's Washington office cleared Madoff [81]. The SEC detailed that inspectors had examined Madoff's brokerage operation in 2005 [81], checking for three kinds of violations: the strategy he used for customer accounts; the requirement of brokers to obtain the best possible price for customer orders; and operating as an unregistered investment adviser. Madoff was registered as a broker-dealer, but doing business as an asset manager [84]. "The staff found no evidence of fraud". In September 2005 Madoff agreed to register his business, but the SEC kept its findings confidential [81]. During the 2005 investigation, Meaghan Cheung, a branch head of the SEC's New York's Enforcement Division, was the person responsible for the oversight and blunder, according to Markopolos [13, 85], who testified on February 4, 2009, at a hearing held by a House Financial Services Subcommittee on Capital Markets [81–86].

In 2007, SEC enforcement completed an investigation they had begun on January 6, 2006, into a Ponzi scheme allegation. This investigation resulted in neither a finding of fraud, nor a referral to the SEC Commissioners for legal action [87, 88].

3.3 FINRA

In 2007, the Financial Industry Regulatory Authority (FINRA), the industry-run watchdog for brokerage firms, reported without explanation that parts of Madoff's firm had no customers. "At this point in time we are uncertain of the basis for FINRA's conclusion in this regard," SEC staff wrote shortly after Madoff was arrested [81].

As a result, the chairman of the SEC, Christopher Cox, stated that an investigation would delve into "all staff contact and relationships with the Madoff family and firm, and their impact, if any, on decisions by staff regarding the firm" [89]. A former SEC compliance officer, Eric Swanson, had married Madoff's niece Shana, the Madoff firm compliance attorney [89].

3.4 Other Warnings

Outside analysts raised concerns about Madoff's firm for years [16]. Mathematician Edward O. Thorp noted irregularities in 1991 [90].

Rob Picard of the Royal Bank of Canada (RBC), seeking low-volatility investments, was referred to Madoff in 1997 by employees of Tremont Group who were one of Madoff's key "feeder funds". When pressed for details of his investing strategy, Madoff "stuttered" and became evasive. Picard later stated: "right away I realized he either didn't understand it or he wasn't doing what he said he was doing. [29]" Suspecting fraud, RBC declined to invest with Madoff and also cut off professional contact with Tremont.

The next major concern about Madoff's operation was raised in May 2000, when Harry Markopolos, a financial analyst and portfolio manager at Boston options trader Rampart Investment Management, alerted the SEC about his suspicions. A year earlier, Rampart had learned that Access International Advisors, one of its trading partners, had significant investments with Madoff. Markopolos' bosses at Rampart asked him to design a product that could replicate Madoff's returns [13]. However, Markopolos concluded that Madoff's numbers didn't add up. After four hours of trying and failing to replicate Madoff's returns, Markopolos concluded Madoff was a fraud. He told the SEC that based on his analysis of Madoff's returns, it was mathematically impossible for Madoff to deliver them using the strategies he claimed to use. In his view, there were only two ways to explain the figures—either Madoff was front running his order flow, or his wealth management business was a massive Ponzi scheme. This submission, along with three others, passed with no substantive action from the SEC [91, 92]. At the time of Markopolos' initial submission, Madoff managed assets from between $3 billion and $6 billion, which would have made his wealth management business the largest hedge fund in the world even then. The culmination of Markopolos' analysis was his third submission, a detailed 17-page memo entitled The World's Largest Hedge Fund is a Fraud [93]. He had also approached The Wall Street Journal about the existence of the Ponzi scheme in 2005, but its editors decided not to pursue the story [94]. The memo specified 30 "red flags" based on a little over 14 years of Madoff trades. The biggest red flag was that Madoff reported only seven losing months during this time, and those losses were statistically insignificant. This result produced a return stream that rose steadily upward at a nearly-perfect 45-degree angle. Markopolos argued that the markets were far too volatile even under the best of conditions for this to be possible [13]. Later, Markopolos testified before Congress that this was like a baseball player batting 0.966 for the season, compared to 0.300 to 0.400 for elite players, "and no one suspecting a cheat" [95]. In part, the memo concluded: "Bernie Madoff is running the world's largest unregistered hedge fund. He's organized this business as a 'hedge fund of funds' privately labeling their own hedge funds which Bernie

Madoff secretly runs for them using a split-strike conversion strategy getting paid only trading commissions which are not disclosed. If this is not a regulatory dodge, I do not know what is." Markopolos declared that Madoff's "unsophisticated portfolio management" was either a Ponzi scheme or front running [95] (buying stock for his own account based on knowledge of his clients' orders), and concluded it was most likely a Ponzi Scheme [81]. Markopolos later testified to Congress that to deliver 12% annual returns to the investor, Madoff needed to earn an extraordinary 16% gross on a regular basis, so as to distribute a 4% fee to the feeder fund managers, who Madoff needed to secure new victims, which encouraged the feeder funds to be "willfully blind, and not get too intrusive [86]". Though Markopolos's findings were neglected by regulators he did persuade some professional investors. Joel Tillinghast, a mutual fund manager at Fidelity Investments, had been intrigued by anecdotes of Madoff's steady gains. But after a 2000 meeting with Markopolos he became convinced "nothing in Madoff's ostensible strategy made sense [96]."

In 2001, financial journalist Erin Arvedlund wrote an article for Barron's entitled "Don't Ask, Don't Tell" [43], questioning Madoff's secrecy and wondering how he obtained such consistent returns. She reported that "Madoff's investors rave about his performance—even though they don't understand how he does it. 'Even knowledgeable people can't really tell you what he's doing,' one very satisfied investor told Barron's [43]." The Barron's article and one in MarHedge by Michael Ocrant suggested Madoff was front-running to achieve his gains [81]. In 2001 Ocrant, editor-in-chief of MARHedge, wrote he interviewed traders who were incredulous that Madoff had 72 consecutive gaining months, an unlikely possibility [15]. Hedge funds investing with him were not permitted to name him as money manager in their marketing prospectus. When high-volume investors who were considering participation wanted to review Madoff's records for purposes of due diligence, he refused, convincing them of his desire to keep his proprietary strategies confidential [citation needed].

By purportedly selling its holdings for cash at the end of each period, Madoff avoided filing disclosures of its holdings with the SEC, an unusual tactic. Madoff rejected any call for an outside audit "for reasons of secrecy", claiming that was the exclusive responsibility of his brother, Peter, the company's chief compliance officer" [97].

Concerns were also raised that Madoff's auditor of record was Friehling & Horowitz, a two-person accounting firm based in suburban Rockland County that had only one active accountant, David G. Friehling, a close Madoff family friend. Friehling was also an investor in Madoff's fund, which was seen as a blatant conflict of interest.[98] In 2007, hedge fund consultant Aksia LLC advised its clients not to invest with Madoff, saying it was inconceivable that a tiny firm could adequately service such a massive operation [99, 100].

Typically, hedge funds hold their portfolio at a securities firm (a major bank or brokerage), which acts as the fund's prime broker. This arrangement allows outside investigators to verify the holdings. Madoff's firm was its own broker-dealer, and purported to process all of its trades [42].

Ironically, Madoff, a pioneer in electronic trading, refused to provide his clients online access to their accounts [16]. He sent out account statements by mail [101], unlike most hedge funds, which email statements [102].

Madoff also operated as a broker-dealer, running an asset management division. In 2003, Joe Aaron, a hedge-fund professional, believed the structure suspicious and warned a colleague to avoid investing in the fund, "Why would a good businessman work his magic for pennies on the dollar?" he concluded [103]. Also in 2003, Renaissance Technologies, "arguably the most successful hedge fund in the world", reduced its exposure to Madoff's fund first by 50 percent and eventually completely because of suspicions about the consistency of returns, the fact that Madoff charged very little compared to other hedge funds, and the impossibility of the strategy Madoff claimed to use because options volume had no relation to the amount of money Madoff was said to administer. The options volume implied that Madoff's fund had $750 million, while he was believed to be managing $15 billion. And only if Madoff was assumed to be responsible for all the options traded in the most liquid strike price [104].

Charles J. Gradante, co-founder of hedge-fund research firm Hennessee Group, observed that Madoff "only had five down months since 1996" [105], and commented on Madoff's investment performance: "You can't go 10 or 15 years with only three or four down months. It's just impossible" [106].

Clients such as Fairfield Greenwich Group and Union Bancaire Privée said that they had been given an "unusual degree of access" to evaluate and analyze Madoff's funds, and found nothing unusual with his investment portfolio [52].

The Central Bank of Ireland failed to spot Madoff's gigantic fraud when he started using Irish funds, and had to supply large amounts of information that should have been enough to enable the Irish regulator to uncover the fraud much earlier than late 2008 when he was finally arrested in New York City [107–109].

4. Final Weeks and Collapse

The scheme began to unravel in the fall of 2008, when the general market downturn accelerated. Madoff had previously come close to collapse in the second half of 2005 after Bayou Group, a group of hedge funds, was exposed as a Ponzi scheme that used a bogus accounting firm to misrepresent its performance. By November, investors had requested $105 million in redemptions, though Madoff's Chase account only had $13 million. Madoff only survived by moving money from his broker-dealer's account into his Ponzi scheme account. Eventually, he drew on $342 million from his broker-dealer's credit lines to keep the Ponzi scheme afloat through 2006 [110]. Markopolos wrote that he suspected Madoff was on the brink of insolvency as early as June 2005, when his team learned he was seeking loans from banks. By then, at least two major banks were no longer willing to lend money to their customers to invest it with Madoff [13].

In June 2008, Markopolos' team uncovered evidence that Madoff was accepting leveraged money. To Markopolos' mind, Madoff was running out of cash and needed to increase his promised returns to keep the scheme going [13]. As it turned out, redemption requests from skittish investors ramped up in the wake of the collapse of Bear Stearns in March 2008. The trickle became a flood when Lehman Brothers was forced into bankruptcy in September, coinciding with the near-collapse of American International Group [111].

As the market's decline accelerated, investors tried to withdraw $7 billion from the firm. Unknown to them, however, Madoff had simply deposited his clients' money into his business account at Chase Manhattan Bank, and paid customers out of that account when they requested withdrawals. To pay off those investors, Madoff needed new money from other investors. However, in November, the balance in the account dropped to dangerously low levels. Only $300 million in new money had come in, but customers had withdrawn $320 million. He had just barely enough in the account to meet his redemption payroll on November 19. Even with a rush of new investors who believed Madoff was one of the few funds that was still doing well, it still wasn't enough to keep up with the avalanche of withdrawals [112] [page needed].

In the weeks prior to his arrest, Madoff struggled to keep the scheme afloat. In November 2008, Madoff Securities International (MSIL) in London made two fund transfers to Bernard Madoff Investment Securities of approximately $164 million. MSIL had neither customers nor clients, and there is no evidence that it conducted any trades on behalf of third parties [113].

Madoff received $250 million around December 1, 2008, from Carl J. Shapiro, a 95-year-old Boston philanthropist and entrepreneur who was one of Madoff's oldest friends and biggest financial backers. On December 5, he accepted $ten million from Martin Rosenman, president of Rosenman Family LLC, who later sought to recover the never-invested $ten million, deposited in a Madoff account at JPMorgan, wired six days before Madoff's arrest. Judge Lifland ruled that Rosenman was "indistinguishable" from any other Madoff client, so there was no basis for giving him special treatment to recover funds [114]. The judge separately declined to dismiss a lawsuit brought by Hadleigh Holdings, which claimed it entrusted $one million to the Madoff firm three days before his arrest [114].

Madoff asked others for money in the final weeks before his arrest, including Wall Street financier Kenneth Langone, whose office was sent a 19-page pitch book, purportedly created by the staff at the Fairfield Greenwich Group. Madoff said he was raising money for a new investment vehicle, between $500 million and $1 billion for exclusive clients, was moving quickly on the venture, and wanted an answer by the following week. Langone declined [115]. In November, Fairfield announced the creation of a new feeder fund. However, it was far too little and far too late [13].

By the week after Thanksgiving 2008, Madoff knew he was at the end of his tether. The Chase account, which at one point in 2008 had well over $5 billion, was down to only $234 million. With banks having all but stopped lending to anyone, he knew he could not even begin to borrow enough money to meet the outstanding redemption requests. On December 4, he told Frank DiPascali, who oversaw the Ponzi scheme's operation, that he was finished. He directed DiPascali to use the remaining balance in the Chase account to cash out the accounts of relatives and favored investors. On December 9, he told his brother Peter that he was on the brink of collapse [112, 116] [page needed].

The following morning, December 10, he suggested to his sons, Mark and Andrew, that the firm pay out over $170 million in bonuses two months ahead of schedule, from $200 million in assets that the firm still had [15]. According to the complaint, Mark and Andrew, reportedly unaware of the firm's pending insolvency, confronted their father, asking him how the firm could pay bonuses to employees if it could not pay investors. At that point, Madoff asked his sons to follow him to his apartment, where he admitted that he was "finished", and that the asset management arm of the firm was in fact a Ponzi scheme—as he put it, "one big lie". Mark and Andrew then reported him to the authorities [16, 112] [page needed].

Madoff intended to take a week to wind up the firm's operations before his sons alerted authorities. Instead, Mark and Andrew immediately called lawyers. When the sons revealed their father's plan to use the remaining money to pay relatives and favored investors, their lawyers put them in touch with federal prosecutors and the SEC. Madoff was arrested the following morning [112, 117] [page needed].

5. Investigation into Co-Conspirators
Main article: Participants in the Madoff investment scandal

Investigators looked for others involved in the scheme, despite Madoff's assertion that he alone was responsible for the large-scale operation [14]. Harry Susman, an attorney representing several clients of the firm, stated that "someone had to create the appearance that there were returns", and further suggested that there must have been a team buying and selling stocks, forging books, and filing reports [14]. James Ratley, president of the Association of Certified Fraud Examiners said, "In order for him to have done this by himself, he would have had to have been at work night and day, no vacation and no time off. He would have had to nurture the Ponzi scheme daily. What happened when he was gone? Who handled it when somebody called in while he was on vacation and said, 'I need access to my money'?" [118].

"Simply from an administrative perspective, the act of putting together the various account statements, which did show trading activity, has to involve a number of people. You would need office and support personnel, people who actually knew what the market prices were for the securities that were being traded. You would need accountants so that the internal documents reconcile with the documents being sent to customers at least on a superficial basis," said Tom Dewey, a securities lawyer [118].

Arvenlund wrote there was widespread suspicion of confederates to the fraud within Madoff's inner circle, but the secretive nature of the scheme made investigation difficult [29].

5.1 Alleged Co-Conspirators

- Jeffry Picower and his wife, Barbara, of Palm Beach, Florida, and Manhattan, had two dozen accounts. He was a lawyer, accountant, and investor who led buyouts of health-care and technology companies. Picower's foundation stated its investment portfolio with Madoff was valued at nearly $1 billion at one time [119]. In June 2009, Irving Picard, the trustee liquidating Madoff's assets, filed a lawsuit against Picower in the U.S. Bankruptcy Court for the Southern District of New York (Manhattan), seeking the return of $7.2 billion in profits, alleging that Picower and his wife Barbara knew or should have known that their rates of return were "implausibly high", with some accounts showing annual returns ranging from 120% to more than 550% from 1996 through 1998, and 950% in 1999 [120, 121]. On October 25, 2009, Picower, 67, was found dead of a massive heart attack at the bottom of his Palm Beach swimming pool [122]. On December 17, 2010, it was announced that a settlement of $7.2 billion had been reached between Irving Picard and Barbara Picower, Picower's widow, the executor of the Picower estate to resolve the Madoff trustee suit, and repay losses in the Madoff fraud [123]. It was the largest single forfeiture in American judicial history [124]. "Barbara Picower has done the right thing," US Attorney Preet Bharara said [123].

- Stanley Chais, of the Brighton Company: On May 1, 2009, Picard filed a lawsuit against Stanley Chais. The complaint alleged he "knew or should have known" he was involved in a Ponzi scheme when his family investments with Madoff averaged a 40% return. It also claimed Chais was a primary beneficiary of the scheme for at least 30 years, allowing his family to withdraw more than $1 billion from their accounts since 1995. The SEC filed a similar civil suit mirroring these claims [125, 126]. On September 22, 2009, Chais was sued by California Attorney General Jerry Brown who was seeking $25 million in penalties as well as restitution for victims, saying the Beverly Hills investment manager was a 'middleman' in Madoff's Ponzi Scheme [127]. Chais died in September 2010. The widow, children, family, and estate of Chais settled with Picard in 2016 for $277 million [128, 129]. Picard's lawyers said the settlement covered all of Chais' estate, and substantially all of his widow's assets [128].
- Fairfield Greenwich Group, based in Greenwich, Connecticut, had a "Fairfield Sentry" fund—one of many feeder funds that gave investors portals to Madoff. On April 1, 2009, the Commonwealth of Massachusetts filed a civil action charging Fairfield Greenwich with fraud and breaching its fiduciary duty to clients by failing to provide promised due diligence on its investments. The complaint sought a fine and restitution to Massachusetts investors for losses and disgorgement of performance fees paid to Fairfield by those investors. It alleged that, in 2005, Madoff coached Fairfield staff about ways to answer questions from SEC attorneys who were looking into Markopolos' complaint about Madoff's operations [130, 131]. The fund settled with the Commonwealth in September 2009 for $8 million [132]. On May 18, 2009, the hedge fund was sued by trustee Irving Picard, seeking a return of $3.2 billion during the period from 2002 to Madoff's arrest in December 2008 [133]. However, the money may already be in the hands of Fairfield's own clients, who are likely off-limits to Picard, since they weren't direct investors with Madoff [134]. In May 2011 the liquidator for the funds settled with Picard for $1 billion [135].
- Peter Madoff, chief compliance officer, worked with his brother Bernie for more than 40 years, and ran the daily operations for 20 years. He helped create the computerized trading system. He agreed to pay more than $90 million that he

does not have to settle claims that he participated in the Ponzi scheme, but Irving Picard agreed to forbear from seeking to enforce the consent judgment as long as Peter Madoff "makes reasonable efforts to cooperate with the Trustee in the Trustee's efforts to recover funds for the BLMIS Estate, including providing truthful information to the Trustee upon request." [136] He was sentenced to 10 years in prison [137].

- Ruth Madoff, Bernard's wife, agreed as part of his sentencing to keep from the federal government only $2.5 million of her claim of more than $80 million in assets, and to give up all of her possessions. The $2.5 million was not however protected from civil legal actions against her pursued by a court-appointed trustee liquidating Madoff's assets, or from investor lawsuits [138]. On July 29, 2009, she was sued by trustee Irving Picard who sought to recover from her $45 million in Madoff funds that were being used to support her "life of splendor" on the gains from the fraud committed by her husband [139]. On November 25, 2008, she had withdrawn $5.5 million, and $10 million on December 10, 2008, from her brokerage account at Cohmad, a feeder fund that had an office in Madoff's headquarters and was part-owned by him [140, 141]. In November she also received $2 million from her husband's London office [142, 143]. She has been seen riding the N.Y.C. subway, and did not attend her husband's sentencing [144, 145]. In May 2019, 77-year-old Ruth Madoff agreed to pay $594,000 ($250,000 in cash, and $344,000 of trusts for two of her grandchildren), and to surrender her remaining assets when she dies, to settle claims by the Irving Picard [128]. She is required to provide reports to Picard about her expenditures often, as to any purchase over $100, to ensure she does not have any hidden bank accounts [146–148]. The case is Picard v. Madoff, 1:09-ap-1391, U.S. Bankruptcy Court, Southern District of New York (Manhattan) [149–151].
- Madoff's sons, Mark and Andrew Madoff, worked in the legitimate trading arm in the New York office, but also raised money marketing the Madoff funds [152]. Their assets were frozen on March 31, 2009 [153]. The two became estranged from their father and mother in the wake of the fraud, which some contended was a charade to protect their assets from litigation [145, 154]. On October 2, 2009, a civil lawsuit was filed against them by trustee Irving Picard for a judgment in the aggregate amount of at least $198,743,299. Peter Madoff and daughter Shana were also defendants [155, 156]. On December 11, 2010, the second anniversary of Madoff's arrest, Mark Madoff was found having committed suicide and hanging from a ceiling pipe in the living room of his SoHo loft apartment [157]. Andrew Madoff died September 3, 2014, from cancer. He was 48, and had reconciled with his mother prior to his death [158]. Told that his father wanted to speak with him and explain what he had done, Andrew told Matt Lauer of the Today Show he wasn't interested. In June 2017 Irving Picard settled with the sons' estates for more than $23 million, stripping the estates of Andrew and Mark Madoff of "all assets, cash, and other proceeds" of their father's fraud, leaving them with a respective $2 million and $1.75 million [159].
- Tremont Group Holdings started its first Madoff-only fund in 1997. That group managed several funds marketed under the Re Select Broad Market Fund [160].

In July 2011, Tremont Group Holdings settled with Irving Picard for more than $1 billion [161].
- The Maxam Fund invested through Tremont. Sandra L. Manzke, founder of Maxam Capital, had her assets temporarily frozen by the same Connecticut court [which?] [162]. In August 2013, Irving Picard reached a $98 million settlement with Maxam Absolute Return Fund [163].
- Cohmad Securities Corp., of which Madoff owned a 10–20% stake: The brokerage firm listed its address as Madoff's firm's address in New York City. Its chairman, Maurice J. "Sonny" Cohn, his daughter and COO Marcia Beth Cohn, and Robert M. Jaffe, a broker at the firm, were accused by the SEC of four counts of civil fraud, "knowingly or recklessly disregarding facts indicating that Madoff was operating a fraud," and they settled that suit with the SEC in 2010 [125, 164]. Another lawsuit filed by bankruptcy trustee Irving Picard sought funds for Madoff victims [165]. In November 2016, Picard announced that the estate of "Sonny" Cohn, his widow Marilyn Cohn, and their daughter had agreed to settle with Picard for $32.1 million [164].
- Madoff Securities International Ltd. in London; individual and entities related to it were sued by Irving Picard and Stephen J. Akers, a joint liquidator of Madoff's London operation, in the United Kingdom's High Court of Justice Commercial Court [166].
- J. Ezra Merkin, a prominent investment advisor and philanthropist, was sued for his role in running a "feeder fund" for Madoff [167]. On April 6, 2009, New York Attorney General Andrew Cuomo filed civil fraud charges [168] against Merkin alleging he "betrayed hundreds of investors" by moving $2.4 billion of clients' money to Madoff without their knowledge. The complaint stated he lied about putting the money with Madoff, failed to disclose conflicts of interest, and collected over $470 million in fees for his three hedge funds, Ascot Partners LP with Ascot Fund Ltd., Gabriel Capital Corp., and Ariel Fund Ltd. He promised he would actively manage the money, but instead, he misguided investors about his Madoff investments in quarterly reports, in investor presentations, and in conversations with investors. "Merkin held himself out to investors as an investing guru... In reality, Merkin was but a master marketer [169–172]."
- Carl J. Shapiro, women's clothing entrepreneur, self-made millionaire, and philanthropist, and one of Madoff's oldest friends and biggest financial backers, who helped him start his investment firm in 1960. He was never in the finance business. In 1971, Shapiro sold his business, Kay Windsor, Inc., for $20 million. Investing most of it with Madoff, that sum grew to hundreds of millions of dollars and possibly to more than $1 billion. Shapiro personally lost about $400 million, $250 million of which he gave to Madoff 10 days before Madoff's arrest. His foundation lost more than $100 million [119].
- The Hadon Organisation, a UK-based company involved in mergers and acquisitions: Between 2001 and 2008 The Hadon Organisation established very close ties with Madoff Securities International Ltd. in London [173].
- David G. Friehling, the sole practitioner at Friehling & Horowitz CPAs, waived indictment and pleaded not guilty to criminal charges on July 10, 2009. He agreed

to proceed without having the evidence in the criminal case against him reviewed by a grand jury at a hearing before U.S. District Judge Alvin Hellerstein in Manhattan. Friehling was charged on March 18, 2009, with securities fraud, aiding and abetting investment adviser fraud, and four counts of filing false audit reports with the SEC [174]. On November 3, 2009, Friehling pled guilty to the charges [175]. His involvement in the scheme made it the largest accounting fraud in history, dwarfing the $11 billion accounting fraud masterminded by Bernard Ebbers at WorldCom. In May 2015, U.S. District Judge Laura Taylor Swain sentenced Friehling to one year of home detention and one year of supervised release, with Friehling avoiding prison because he cooperated extensively with federal prosecutors and because he had been unaware of the extent of Madoff's crimes [176]. Swain suggested that Friehling be forced to pay part of the overall $130 million forfeiture arising from the fraud [176].

- Frank DiPascali, who referred to himself as "director of options trading" and as "chief financial officer" at Madoff Securities, pled guilty on August 11, 2009, to 10 counts [177]: conspiracy, securities fraud, investment advisor fraud, mail fraud, wire fraud, perjury, income tax evasion, international money laundering, falsifying books and records of a broker-dealer and investment advisor. He agreed to "connect the dots" and to "name names", with sentencing originally scheduled for May 2010 [178]. Prosecutors sought more than $170 billion in forfeiture, the same amount sought from Madoff, which represents funds deposited by investors and later disbursed to other investors. The same day, an SEC civil complaint [179] was filed against DiPascali [180]. On May 7, 2015, while still awaiting sentencing, DiPascali died of lung cancer [181].
- Daniel Bonventre, former operations director for Bernard Madoff Investment Securities [182–184]. He was convicted on 21 counts, and sentenced to 10 years in jail [185, 186].
- Joann Crupi (Westfield, NJ; sentenced to six years in prison) and Annette Bongiorno (Boca Raton, FL; sentenced to six years in prison), both back office employees, were arrested in November 2010 [187]. "Authorities previously said Bongiorno was a staff supervisor and was responsible for answering questions from Madoff's clients about their purported investments. They allege she oversaw the fabrication of documents", according to the Associated Press.
- Jerome O'Hara (sentenced to two and a half years in prison) and George Perez (sentenced to two and a half years in prison), long-time employees of Bernard L. Madoff Investment Securities LLC (BLMIS), were charged in an indictment in November 2010, and in a 33-count superseding indictment on October 1, 2012 [188–190].
- Enrica Cotellessa-Pitz, controller of Bernard L. Madoff Investment Securities LLC, but not a licensed certified public accountant: Her signature is on checks from BLMIS to Cohmad Securities Corp. representing commission payments. She was the liaison between the SEC and BLMIS regarding the firm's financial statements. The SEC has removed the statements from its website [191]. She pled guilty to her role [192].

6. Charges and Sentencing

The criminal case is U.S.A. v. Madoff, 1:08-mJ-02735.

The SEC case is Securities and Exchange Commission v. Madoff, 1:08-cv-10,791, both U.S. District Court, Southern District of New York [193]. The cases against Fairfield Greenwich Group et al. were consolidated as 09–118 in U.S. District Court for the Southern District of New York (Manhattan) [194].

While awaiting sentencing, Madoff met with the SEC's Inspector General, H. David Kotz, who was conducting an investigation into how regulators failed to detect the fraud despite numerous red flags [195]. Because of concerns of improper conduct by Inspector General Kotz in conducting the Madoff investigation, Inspector General David C. Williams of the U.S. Postal Service was brought in to conduct an independent outside review of Kotz's actions [196]. The Williams Report questioned Kotz's work on the Madoff investigation, because Kotz was a "very good friend" with Markopolos [197, 198]. Investigators were not able to determine when Kotz and Markopolos became friends. A violation of the ethics rules took place if their friendship was concurrent with Kotz's investigation of Madoff [197, 199].

Former SEC chairman Harvey Pitt estimated the actual net fraud to be between $10 and $17 billion, because it does not include the fictional returns credited to the Madoff's customer accounts [200].

6.1 Criminal Complaint

U.S. v. Madoff, 08-MAG-02735 [201, 202].

The original criminal complaint estimated that investors lost $50 billion through the Scheme [203], though The Wall Street Journal reports "that figure includes the alleged false profits that Mr. Madoff's firm reported to its customers for decades. It is unclear exactly how much investors deposited into the firm [204]." He was originally charged with a single count of securities fraud and faced up to 20 years in prison, and a fine of $five million if convicted.

Court papers indicate that Madoff's firm had about 4,800 investment client accounts as of November 30, 2008, and issued statements for that month reporting that client accounts held a total balance of about $65 billion, but actually "held only a small fraction" of that balance for clients [205].

Madoff was arrested by the Federal Bureau of Investigation (FBI) on December 11, 2008, on a criminal charge of securities fraud [202]. According to the criminal complaint, the previous day [206] he had told his sons that his business was "a giant Ponzi scheme" [207, 208]. They called a friend for advice, Martin Flumenbaum, a lawyer, who called federal prosecutors and the SEC on their behalf. FBI Agent Theodore Cacioppi made a house call. "We are here to find out if there is an innocent explanation," Cacioppi said quietly. The 70-year-old financier paused, then said: "There is no innocent explanation [85, 203]." He had "paid investors with money that was not there" [209]. Madoff was released on the same day of his arrest after posting $ten million bail [207]. Madoff and his wife surrendered their passports, and he was subject to travel restrictions, a 7 p.m. curfew at his co-op, and electronic monitoring as a condition of bail. Although Madoff only had two co-signers for his $ten million bail, his wife and his brother Peter, rather than the four required, a judge allowed him free on bail but ordered him confined to his apartment [210]. Madoff reportedly received death threats that were referred to the FBI, and the SEC referred to fears of "harm or flight" in its request for Madoff to be confined to his Upper East Side apartment [210, 211]. Cameras monitored his apartment's doors, its communication devices sent signals to the FBI, and his wife was required to pay for additional security [211].

Apart from 'Bernard L. Madoff' and 'Bernard L. Madoff Investment Securities LLC ("BMIS")', the order to freeze all activities [212] also forbade trading from the companies Madoff Securities International Ltd. ("Madoff International") and Madoff Ltd.

On January 5, 2009, prosecutors requested that the Court revoke his bail, after Madoff and his wife allegedly violated the court-ordered asset freeze by mailing jewelry worth up to $one million to relatives, including their sons and Madoff's brother. It was also noted that $173 million in signed checks had been found in Madoff's office desk after he had been arrested [213, 214]. His sons reported the mailings to prosecutors. Up to that point, Madoff was thought to be cooperating with prosecutors [214]. The following week, Judge Ellis refused the government's request to revoke Madoff's bail, but required as a condition of bail that Madoff make an inventory of personal items and that his mail be searched [215].

On March 10, 2009, the U.S. Attorney for the Southern District of New York filed an 11-count criminal information, or complaint [216], charging Madoff [217] with 11 federal crimes: securities fraud, investment adviser fraud, mail fraud, wire fraud, three counts of money laundering, false statements, perjury, making false filings with the SEC, and theft from an employee benefit plan [202, 218]. The complaint stated that Madoff had defrauded his clients of almost $65 billion—thus spelling out the largest Ponzi scheme in history, as well as the largest investor fraud committed by a single person.

Madoff pleaded guilty to three counts of money laundering. Prosecutors alleged that he used the London Office, Madoff Securities International Ltd.m to launder more than $250 million of client money by transferring client money from the investment-advisory business in New York to London, and then back to the U.S., to support the U.S. trading operation of Bernard L. Madoff Investment Securities LLC. Madoff gave the appearance that he was trading in Europe for his clients [219].

6.2 Plea Proceeding

On March 12, 2009, Madoff appeared in court in a plea proceeding, and pleaded guilty to all charges [28]. There was no plea agreement between the government and Madoff; he simply pleaded guilty and signed a waiver of indictment. The charges carried a maximum sentence of 150 years in prison, as well as mandatory restitution and fines up to twice the gross gain or loss derived from the offenses. If the government's estimate were correct, Madoff would have to pay $7.2 billion in restitution [202, 218]. A month earlier, Madoff settled the SEC's civil suit against him. He accepted a lifetime ban from the securities industry, and also agreed to pay an undisclosed fine [220].

In his pleading allocution, Madoff admitted to running a Ponzi scheme and expressed regret for his "criminal acts" [4]. He stated that he had begun his scheme some time in the early 1990s. He wished to satisfy his clients' expectations of high returns he had promised, even though it was during an economic recession. He admitted that he hadn't invested any of his clients' money since the inception of his scheme. Instead, he merely deposited the money into his business account at Chase Manhattan Bank. He admitted to false trading activities masked by foreign transfers and false SEC returns. When clients requested account withdrawals, he paid them from the Chase account, claiming the profits were the result of his own unique "split-strike conversion strategy". He said he had every intention of terminating the scheme, but it proved "difficult, and ultimately impossible" to extricate himself. He eventually reconciled himself to being exposed as a fraud [28].

Only two of at least 25 victims who had requested to be heard at the hearing spoke in open court against accepting Madoff's plea of guilt [202, 221].

Judge Denny Chin accepted his guilty plea and remanded him to incarceration at the Manhattan Metropolitan Correctional Center until sentencing. Chin said that Madoff was now a substantial flight risk given his age, wealth, and the possibility of spending the rest of his life in prison [222].

Madoff's attorney, Ira Sorkin, filed an appeal, to return him back to his "penthouse arrest", await sentencing, and to reinstate his bail conditions, declaring he would be more amenable to cooperate with the government's investigation [223], and prosecutors filed a notice in opposition [224, 225]. On March 20, 2009, the appellate court denied his request [226].

On June 26, 2009, Chin ordered Madoff to forfeit $170 million in assets. His wife Ruth was to relinquish her claim to $80 million worth of assets, leaving her with $2.5 million in cash [144]. The settlement did not prevent the SEC and Irving Picard from continuing to make claims against Ruth Madoff's funds in the future [145]. Madoff had earlier requested to shield $70 million in assets for Ruth, arguing that it was unconnected to the fraud scheme.

6.3 Sentencing, Prison Life and Death

Prosecutors recommended a prison sentence of 150 years, the maximum possible under federal sentencing guidelines. They informed Chin that Irving Picard, the trustee overseeing bankruptcy proceedings for the Madoff organization, had indicated that "Mr. Madoff has not provided meaningful cooperation or assistance [227, 228]." The Bureau of US Prisons had recommended 50 years, while defense lawyer Ira Sorkin had recommended 12 years, arguing that Madoff had confessed. The judge granted Madoff permission to wear his personal clothing at sentencing [145].

On June 29, Judge Chin sentenced Madoff to 150 years in prison, as recommended by the prosecution. Chin said he had not received any mitigating letters from friends or family testifying to Madoff's good deeds, saying that "the absence of such support is telling [229]." Commentators noted that this was in contrast to other high-profile white collar trials such as those of Andrew Fastow, Jeffrey Skilling, and Bernard Ebbers who were known for their philanthropy and/or cooperation to help victims; however, Madoff's victims included several charities and foundations, and the only person who pleaded for mercy was his defense lawyer Ira Sorkin [230].

Chin called the fraud "unprecedented" and "staggering", and stated that the sentence would deter others from committing similar frauds. He stated, "Here the message must be sent that Mr. Madoff's crimes were extraordinarily evil." Many victims, some of whom had lost their life savings, applauded the sentence [231]. Chin agreed with prosecutors' contention that the fraud began at some point in the 1980s. He also noted Madoff's crimes were "off the charts" since federal sentencing guidelines for fraud only go up to $400 million in losses; Madoff swindled his investors out of several times that [232]. Prosecutors estimated that, at the very least, Madoff was responsible for a loss of $13 billion, more than 32 times the federal cap [227]; the commonly quoted loss of $65 billion is more than 162 times the cap.

Chin said "I have a sense Mr. Madoff has not done all that he could do or told all that he knows," noting that Madoff failed to identify accomplices, making it more difficult for prosecutors to build cases against others. Chin dismissed Sorkin's plea for leniency, stating that Madoff made substantial loans to family members and moved $15 million from the firm to his wife's account shortly before confessing [233]. Picard also said that Madoff's failure to provide substantial assistance complicated efforts to locate assets. A former federal prosecutor suggested Madoff would have had the possibility of a sentence with parole if he fully cooperated with investigators, but Madoff's silence implied that there were other accomplices in the fraud, which led the judge to impose the maximum sentence [234, 235]. Chin also ordered Madoff to pay $17 billion in restitution [236–238].

Madoff apologized to his victims at the sentencing, saying, "I have left a legacy of shame, as some of my victims have pointed out, to my family and my grandchildren. This is something I will live in for the rest of my life. I'm sorry.... I know that doesn't help you [239]."

Madoff was incarcerated at Butner Federal Correctional Complex outside Raleigh, North Carolina. His inmate number was #61727–054 [240].

On July 28, 2009, he gave his first jailhouse interview to Joseph Cotchett and Nancy Fineman, attorneys from San Francisco, because they threatened to sue his wife, Ruth, on behalf of several investors who lost fortunes. During the 4 1/2 hour session, he "answered every one of [the attorneys'] questions", and expressed remorse, according to Cotchett [241].

Madoff died of natural causes in a federal prison hospital in 2021 [7].

7. Recovery of Funds

Madoff's combined assets were worth about $826 million at the time that they were frozen. Madoff provided a confidential list of his and his firm's assets to the SEC on December 31, 2008, which was subsequently disclosed on March 13, 2009, in a court filing. Madoff had no IRAs, no 401(k), no Keogh plan, no other pension plan, and no annuities. He owned less than a combined $200,000 in securities in Lehman Brothers, Morgan Stanley, Fidelity, Bear Stearns, and M&T. No offshore or Swiss bank accounts were listed [242, 243].

Wikinews has related news: Madoff prosecutors want assets from wife and children

On March 17, 2009, a prosecutor filed a document listing more assets, including $2.6 million in jewelry and about 35 sets of watches and cufflinks, more than $30 million in loans owed to the couple by their sons, and Ruth Madoff's interest in real estate funds sponsored by Sterling Equities, whose partners included Fred Wilpon. Ruth Madoff and Peter Madoff invested as "passive limited partners" in real estate funds sponsored by the company, as well as other venture investments. Assets also included the Madoffs' interest in Hoboken Radiology LLC in Hoboken, New Jersey; Delivery Concepts LLC, an online food ordering service in midtown Manhattan that operated as "delivery.com"; an interest in Madoff La Brea LLC; an interest in the restaurant, PJ Clarke's on the Hudson LLC; and Boca Raton, Florida-based Viager II LLC [244, 245].

On March 2, 2009, Judge Louis Stanton modified an existing freeze order to surrender assets Madoff owned: his securities firm, real estate, artwork, and entertainment tickets, and granted a request by prosecutors that the existing freeze remain in place for the Manhattan apartment, and vacation homes in Montauk, New York, and Palm Beach, Florida. He also agreed to surrender his interest in Primex Holdings LLC, a joint venture between Madoff Securities and several large brokerages, designed to replicate the auction process on the New York Stock Exchange [246]. Madoff's April 14, 2009, opening day New York Mets tickets were sold for $7500 on eBay [247].

On April 13, 2009, a Connecticut judge dissolved the temporary asset freeze from March 30, 2009, and issued an order for Fairfield Greenwich Group executive Walter Noel to post property pledges of $10 million against his Greenwich home and $2 million against Jeffrey Tucker's [248]. Noel agreed to the attachment on his house "with no findings, including no finding of liability or wrongdoing". Andres Piedrahita's assets continued to remain temporarily frozen because he was never served with the complaint. The principals were all involved in a lawsuit filed by the town of Fairfield, Connecticut, pension funds, which lost $42 million. The pension fund case was Retirement Program for Employees of the Town of Fairfield v. Madoff, FBT-CV-09-5,023,735-S, Superior Court of Connecticut (Bridgeport) [249–251]. Maxam Capital and other firms that allegedly fed Madoff's fund, which could allow Fairfield to recover up to $75 million, were also part of the dissolution and terms [252, 253].

Professor John Coffee, of Columbia University Law School, said that much of Madoff's money may be in offshore funds. The SEC believed keeping the assets secret would prevent them from being seized by foreign regulators and foreign creditors [254, 255].

The Montreal Gazette reported on January 12, 2010, that there were unrecovered Madoff assets in Canada [256].

In December 2010, the widow Barbara Picower and others reached an agreement with Irving Picard to return $7.2 billion from the estate of her deceased husband Jeffrey Picower to other investors in the fraud [257]. It was the largest single forfeiture in American judicial history [124].

In connection with the victim compensation process, on December 14 and 17, 2012, the Government filed motions requesting that the Court find restitution to be impracticable, thereby permitting the Government to distribute to victims the more than $2.35 billion forfeited to date as part of its investigation through the remission process, in accordance with Department of Justice regulations [258]. Richard C. Breeden was retained to serve as Special Master on behalf of the Department of Justice to administer the process of compensating the victims through the Madoff Victim Fund [259].

The Madoff Recovery Initiative reports $14.377 billion in recoveries and settlement agreements as of December 18, 2020 [260].

8. Affected Clients

Main article: List of investors in Bernard L. Madoff Investment Securities

On February 4, 2009, the U.S. Bankruptcy Court in Manhattan released a 162-page client list with at least 13,500 different accounts, but without listing the amounts invested [261, 262]. Individual investors who invested through Fairfield Greenwich Group, Ascot Partners, and Chais Investments were not included on the list [263].

Clients included banks, hedge funds, charities, universities, and wealthy individuals who had disclosed about $41 billion invested with Bernard L. Madoff Investment Securities LLC, according to a Bloomberg News tally, which may have included double counting of investors in feeder funds [264].

Although Madoff filed a report with the SEC in 2008 stating that his advisory business had only 11–25 clients and about $17.1 billion in assets [265], thousands of investors reported losses, and Madoff estimated the fund's assets at $50 billion.

Other notable clients included former Salomon Brothers economist Henry Kaufman, Steven Spielberg, Jeffrey Katzenberg, screenwriter Eric Roth, actors Kevin Bacon, Kyra Sedgwick, John Malkovich, Zsa Zsa Gabor, and Rue McClanahan [266], politician Frank Lautenberg [267], Mortimer Zuckerman [268], Baseball Hall of Fame pitcher Sandy Koufax, the Wilpon family (owners of the New York Mets), broadcaster Larry King and World Trade Center developer Larry Silverstein. The Elie Wiesel Foundation for Humanity lost $15.2 million, and Wiesel and his wife, Marion, lost their life savings [269].

8.1 Largest Stake-Holders

According to The Wall Street Journal [270] the investors with the largest potential losses, including feeder funds, were:

- Fairfield Greenwich Group, $7.5 billion.
- Tremont Capital Management, which was owned by MassMutual [271], $3.3 billion.
- Banco Santander, $2.87 billion.
- Bank Medici, $2.1 billion.
- Ascot Partners, $1.8 billion.
- Access International Advisors, $1.4 billion.
- Fortis, $1.35 billion.
- HSBC, $1 billion.

The potential losses of these eight investors total $21.32 billion.

The feeder fund Thema International Fund as of November 30, 2008, had a then-purported net asset value invested in the fund of $1.1 billion [64, 272].

Eleven investors had potential losses between $100 million and $1 billion:

- Natixis SA
- Carl J. Shapiro (a 104-year-old Boston philanthropist)
- Royal Bank of Scotland Group PLC
- BNP Paribas
- BBVA
- Man Group PLC
- Reichmuth & Co.
- Nomura Holdings
- Maxam Capital Management
- EIM SA
- Union Bancaire Privée

The fund Defender Limited has a $523 million claim in the BLMIS liquidation [273].

Twenty-three investors with potential losses of $500,000 to $100 million were also listed, with a total potential loss of $540 million. The grand total potential loss in The Wall Street Journal table was $26.9 billion.

Some investors amended their initial estimates of losses to include only their original investment, since the profits Madoff reported were most likely fraudulent. Yeshiva University, for instance, said its actual incurred loss was its invested $14.5 million, not the $110 million initially estimated, which included falsified profits reported to the university by Madoff.

8.1.1 IRS Penalties

It was estimated the potential tax penalties for foundations invested with Madoff were $1 billion.

Although foundations are exempt from federal income taxes, they are subject to an excise tax, for failing to vet Madoff's proposed investments properly, to heed red flags, or to diversify prudently. Penalties may range from 10% of the amount invested during a tax year, to 25% if they fail to try to recover the funds. The foundation's officers, directors, and trustees faced up to a 15% penalty, with up to $20,000 fines for individual managers, per investment [274].

9. Impact and Aftermath
9.1 Criminal Charges against Aurelia Finance

Criminal charges against five directors proceeded against Swiss wealth manager Aurelia Finance, which lost an alleged $800 million of client money. The directors' assets were frozen [275, 276]. In September 2015 they paid "substantial compensation" to settle the criminal complaints [277].

9.2 Grupo Santander

Clients primarily located in South America who invested with Madoff through the Spanish bank Grupo Santander, filed a class action against Santander in Miami. Santander proposed a settlement that would give the clients $2 billion worth of preferred stock in Santander based on each client's original investment. The shares pay a 2% dividend [278]. Seventy percent of the Madoff/Santander investors accepted the offer [279].

9.3 Union Bancaire Privee

On May 8, 2009, a lawsuit against UBP was filed on behalf of New York investor Andrea Barron in the U.S. District Court in Manhattan [280]. Despite being a victim of Bernard Madoff's fraud, the bank offered in March 2009 to compensate eligible investors 50 percent of the money they initially invested with Madoff [281]. In March 2010, the US District Court for the Southern District of New York threw out the class action against Union Bancaire Privée that had been brought under state law, holding that private securities class actions alleging misrepresentations or omissions must be brought under the federal securities laws [282].

On December 6, 2010, Union Bancaire Privée announced it had reached a settlement with Irving Picard, the trustee for Madoff Investment Securities. UBP agreed to pay as much as $500 million to resolve the trustee's claims. UBP was the first bank to settle the Madoff trustee's claim [283]. With the settlement, the trustee agreed to discharge his "clawback" claims against UBP, its affiliates, and clients [284].

9.4 Bank Medici

Bank Medici is an Austrian bank founded by Sonja Kohn, who met Madoff in 1985 while living in New York [285]. Ninety percent of the bank's income was generated from Madoff investments [286].

In 1992 Kohn introduced Madoff to Mario Benbassat, founder of Genevalor Benbassat & Cie, and his two sons in New York, as a possible source of new funds for Madoff [287–289]. Genevalor set up five European feeder funds, including $1.1bn Irish fund Thema International Fund set up by Thema Asset Management, a British Virgin Islands-based company 55 per cent owned by Genevalor, and invested almost $2 billion with Madoff [287–290]. Thema International paid fees of 1.25 per cent ($13.75 m a year) to Genevalor Benbasset & Cie [290]. The Wall Street Journal reported in December 2008 that the company was said to be a key player distributing Madoff investments in the Madoff investment scandal [291].

In December 2008, Medici reported that two of its funds—Herald USA Fund and Herald Luxemburg Fund—were exposed to Madoff losses. On January 2, 2009, FMA, the Austria banking regulator, took control of Bank Medici and appointed a supervisor to control the bank [292]. Bank Medici was sued by its customers both in the U.S. and in Austria [293]. The Vienna State Prosecutor launched a criminal investigation of Bank Medici and Kohn, who had invested an estimated $2.1 billion with Madoff [294]. On May 28, 2009, Bank Medici lost its Austrian banking license. Kohn and the bank were under investigation, but she was not accused of criminal wrongdoing [295, 296].

9.5 The Innocence Project

The Innocence Project was partly funded by the JEHT Foundation, a private charity backed by a wealthy couple, Ken and Jeanne Levy-Church, financed with Madoff's mythical money. Jeanne Levy-Church's losses forced her to shut down both her foundation and that of her parents, the Betty and Norman F. Levy

Foundation, which lost $244 million. JEH helped the less fortunate, especially ex-convicts [297, 298]. (See Participants in the Madoff investment scandal: Norman F. Levy).

9.6 Westport National Bank

In April 2010, Connecticut Attorney General Richard Blumenthal sued the Westport National Bank and Robert L. Silverman for "effectively aiding and abetting" Madoff's fraud. The suit sought recovery of $16.2 million, including the fees that the bank collected as custodian of customers' holding in Madoff investments. Silverman's 240 clients invested about $10 million with Madoff using the bank as the custodian. The bank denied any wrongdoing [299].

9.7 Thema International Fund

In September 2017 in a case before the Irish High Court, Thema International Fund agreed to pay $687 million to resolve a trustee lawsuit brought on behalf of the fraud victims resulting from Madoff's frauds [300].

9.8 The Picower Foundation

The Picower Foundation, created in 2002, was one of the nation's leading philanthropies that supported groups such as the Picower Institute for Learning and Memory at the Massachusetts Institute of Technology, Human Rights First, the New York Public Library and the Children's Health Fund. It was listed as the 71st-largest in the nation by the Council on Foundations. The foundation reportedly invested $1 billion with Madoff. Jeffry Picower was a friend of Bernard Madoff for 30 years. The Picower Foundation, along with other smaller charities that invested with Madoff, announced in December 2008 that they would be closing [301].

9.9 Peter Madoff

In June 2012, Madoff's brother Peter was "expected to appear in Federal District Court in Manhattan and admit to, among other things, falsifying records, making false statements to securities regulators and obstructing the work of the Internal Revenue Service [302]". In December 2012 he was sentenced to 10 years in prison for his involvement in the Ponzi scheme [303].

9.10 Suicides

9.10.1 René-Thierry Magon de la Villehuchet

On December 23, 2008, one of the founders of Access International Advisors LLC, René-Thierry Magon de la Villehuchet, was found dead in his company office on Madison Avenue in New York City. His left wrist was slit, and de la Villehuchet had taken sleeping pills, in what appeared to be a suicide [304–306].

He lived in New Rochelle, New York and came from a prominent French family. Although no suicide note was found at the scene, his brother Bertrand in France received a note shortly after his death in which René-Thierry expressed remorse and a feeling of responsibility for the loss of his investors' money [304]. The FBI and SEC did not believe de la Villehuchet was involved in the fraud [306]. Harry Markopolos said he had met with de La Villehuchet several years before, and had warned him that Madoff might be breaking the law [307]. In 2002, Access invested about 45% of its $1.2 billion under management with Madoff. By 2008, Access managed $3 billion and raised its proportion of funds invested with Madoff to about 75%. De la Villehuchet had also invested all of his wealth and 20% of that of his brother, Bertrand, with Madoff [308]. Bertrand said that René-Thierry did not know Madoff, but the connection was through René-Thierry's partner in AIA, French banker Patrick Littaye [309].

9.10.2 William Foxton

On February 10, 2009, highly decorated British soldier William Foxton, OBE [310], 65, shot himself in a park in Southampton, England, having lost all of his family's savings. He had invested in the Herald USA Fund and Herald Luxembourg Fund, feeder funds for Madoff from Bank Medici in Austria [311–313].

9.10.3 Mark Madoff

Madoff's elder son, Mark Madoff, was found dead on December 11, 2010, two years to the day after he turned his father in. He was found hanged with a dog leash inside his New York apartment in an apparent suicide, but authorities said he left no suicide note [314, 315].

Mark had unsuccessfully sought a Wall Street trading job after the scandal broke, and it was reported that he was distraught over the possibility of criminal charges, as federal prosecutors were making criminal tax-fraud probes. Among the many Madoff family members being sued by the court-appointed trustee Irving Picard were Mark's two young children [316].

In his lawsuit, Picard stated that Mark and other Madoff family members improperly earned tens of millions of dollars, through "fictitious and backdated transactions", and falsely documented loans to buy real estate that weren't repaid. Picard also argued that Mark was in a position to recognize the fraud of his father's firm, as Mark was a co-director of trading, was the designated head of the firm in his father's absence, and held several securities licenses—Series 7, 24 and 55 with the Financial Industry Regulatory Authority. However, he worked in a division of Madoff's company distinct from the one involved with Madoff's fraud, which has not been accused of any wrongdoing [317].

9.10.4 Charles Murphy

Charles Murphy, a hedge fund executive with Fairfield Greenwich Group that invested more than $7 billion with Madoff, including nearly $50 million of personal wealth, leapt from the 24th floor of the Sofitel New York Hotel on March 27, 2017 [318].

9.11 U.S. Securities and Exchange Commission

Following the exposure of the Madoff investment scandal, the SEC's inspector general conducted an internal investigation into the agency's failures to uncover the scheme despite a series of red flags and tips. In September 2009, the SEC released a 477-page report on how the SEC missed these red flags, and identified repeated opportunities for SEC examiners to find the fraud and revealed how ineffective their efforts were [319, 320]. In response to the recommendations in the report, eight SEC employees were disciplined; none were fired [321].

9.12 JP Morgan Chase

On January 7, 2014, Forbes magazine and other news outlets reported that the bank JPMorgan Chase, "where Madoff kept the bank account at the center of his fraud", would pay a settlement of $1.7 billion. This resolved any potential criminal case against the bank arising from the Madoff scandal. JPMorgan entered into a deferred prosecution agreement with federal prosecutors to resolve two felony charges of violating the Bank Secrecy Act. The bank admitted to failing to file a "Suspicious Activity Report" after red flags about Madoff were raised, which, prosecutors alleged, did not have adequate anti-money laundering compliance procedures in place [322–324].

9.13 Payouts

Bloomberg Business News reported in 2016 that investors of approximately $2.5 billion of funds had made no effort to claim their lost funds. Analysts suspected that these parties remained silent because their investments were from illegal activities such as drug dealing or tax evasion, or because they had civil liabilities in the United States and did not wish to subject themselves to the jurisdiction of the U.S. courts [325].

Irving Picard and his team have been overseeing the liquidation of Bernard Madoff's firm in bankruptcy court, and by mid-2019 had recovered over $13 billion—about 76 percent of approved claims—by suing those who profited from the scheme, whether they knew of the scheme or not [326, 327]. Kathy Bazoian Phelps, a lawyer at Diamond McCarthy, said "That kind of recovery is extraordinary and atypical," as clawbacks in such schemes range from 5 percent to 30 percent, and many victims don't get anything [326]. Picard has successfully pursued not only investors, but also spouses and estates of those who profited, such as the wife of Bernard Madoff (Ruth Madoff), the widow and estate of the deceased Stanley Chais, and the widow and estate of the deceased Jeffry Picower, with whom he reached a $7.2 billion settlement (the largest civil forfeiture payment in US history) [128, 328, 329]. "You don't take this job if you're thin-skinned," Picard said [330].

In May 2019 Ruth Madoff settled with Picard, agreeing to surrender $250,000 in cash and another $344,000 in trusts for her grandchildren [331].

10. See Also

- Financial crisis of 2007–2008.
- The Wizard of Lies.

11. References

1. "Press Release: SEC Charges Bernard L. Madoff for Multi-Billion Dollar Ponzi Scheme; 2008-293; Dec. 11, 2008". www.sec.gov. Retrieved April 16, 2021.
2. "The Madoff Case: A Timeline". The Wall Street Journal. March 6, 2009. Retrieved March 6, 2009.
3. David Glovin (February 11, 2009). "Madoff Prosecutors Get 30 More Days for Indictment". Bloomberg L.P. Retrieved February 11, 2009.
4. Jump up to: a b DeStefano, Anthony M. (March 7, 2009). "Madoff expected to plead guilty in Ponzi scheme". Newsday. Retrieved March 7, 2009.[dead link].
5. Bray, Chad (March 12, 2009). "Madoff Pleads Guilty to Massive Fraud". The Wall Street Journal. Dow Jones, Inc. Retrieved October 16, 2015.
6. "Biggest Fraud in History $50 billion Madoff Ponzi Scheme". December 13, 2008.

3.3 Bernard L Madoff

7. Jump up to: a b Balsamo, Michael (April 14, 2021). "Ponzi schemer Bernie Madoff dies in prison at 82". Seattle Times. Archived from the original on April 18, 2021. Retrieved April 14, 2021.
8. "SEC Charges Bernard L. Madoff for Multi-Billion Dollar Ponzi Scheme (2008–293)". SEC.gov. U.S. Securities and Exchange Commission. December 11, 2008. Retrieved December 11, 2008.
9. Randall, David (December 14, 2008). "Rich investors 'wiped out' by Wall Street fraud". The Independent. London. Archived from the original on December 14, 2008. Retrieved December 17, 2008.
10. "US Prosecutors updated the size of Madoff's scheme from $50 billion to $64 billion". Reuters. March 11, 2009. Retrieved April 26, 2009.
11. Hipwell, Deirdre (December 12, 2008). "Wall Street legend Bernard Madoff arrested over '$50 billion Ponzi scheme'". Times Online. London: Times Newspapers Ltd. Retrieved December 13, 2008.
12. Prosecutors say half of Bernie Madoff's investors lost nothing in Ponzi scheme, a September 23, 2009 article from the New York Daily News. Retrieved September 23, 2009.
13. Jump up to: a b c d e f g Markopolos, Harry (2010). No One Would Listen: A True Financial Thriller. John Wiley & Sons. ISBN 978–0–470-55,373-2.
14. Jump up to: a b c Caruso, David (December 18, 2008). "Madoff Investigators Look for Partners". AOL. Associated Press. Archived from the original on September 22, 2018. Retrieved December 23, 2008.
15. Jump up to: a b c d Lieberman, David; Pallavi Gogoi; Theresa Howard; Kevin McCoy; Matt Krantz (December 15, 2008). "Investors remain amazed over Madoff's sudden downfall". USA Today. Retrieved December 24, 2008.
16. Jump up to: a b c d e Appelbaum, Binyamin; David S. Hilzenrath; Amit R. Paley (December 13, 2008). "All Just One Big Lie". The Washington Post. Washington Post Company. p. D01. Retrieved December 12, 2008.
17. "Madoff Wall Street fraud threatens Jewish philanthropy". Retrieved December 13, 2008.
18. Henriques (December 13, 2008). "For Investors, Trust Lost, and Money Too". The New York Times. Retrieved December 13, 2008.
19. "The Madoff files: Bernie's billions". The Independent. London. January 29, 2009. Retrieved April 26, 2009.
20. Bloomberg (February 1, 2009). "Madoff's tactics date to 1960s, when father-in-law was recruiter | Business Features | Jerusalem Post". Jpost.com. Archived from the original on June 15, 2011. Retrieved April 26, 2009.
21. Jump up to: a b c d e f de la Merced, Michael J. (December 24, 2008). "Effort Under Way to Sell Madoff Unit". The New York Times. Retrieved December 24, 2008.
22. Weiner, Eric J. (2005). What Goes Up: The Uncensored History of Modern Wall Street as Told by the Bankers, Brokers, CEOs, and Scoundrels who Made it Happen. Little, Brown and Company. pp. 188–192. ISBN 0–316-92,966-2. Retrieved March 13, 2009.

23. "The Owner's Name is on the Door". Madoff.com. Archived from the original on December 14, 2008. Retrieved December 11, 2008.
24. Jump up to: a b c d e Smith, Randall (December 16, 1992). "Wall Street Mystery Features a Big Board Rival". The Wall Street Journal.
25. Feuer, Alan; Haughney, Christine (December 12, 2008). "Standing Accused: A Pillar of Finance and Charity". The New York Times. Retrieved October 27, 2011.
26. Probe Eyes Role of Aide to Madoff, Accountant. The Wall Street Journal, December 23, 2008.
27. Kolker, Carlyn; Tiffany Kary; Saijel Kishan (December 23, 2008). "Madoff Victims May Have to Return Profits, Principal". Bloomberg News. Retrieved December 24, 2008.
28. Jump up to: a b c "Plea Allocution of Bernard Madoff (U.S. v. Bernard Madoff)" (PDF). The Wall Street Journal. March 12, 2009. Retrieved March 12, 2009.
29. Jump up to: a b c Erin Arvenlund (2010). Too Good to Be True: The Rise and Fall of Bernie Madoff. Portfolio, ISBN 1591842999.
30. Wilhelm, William J.; Joseph D. Downing (2001). Information Markets: What Businesses Can Learn from Financial Innovation. Harvard Business Press. p. 153. ISBN 1–57,851–278-6. Retrieved March 13, 2009. Madoff.
31. Princeton University Undergraduate Task Force (January 2005). "THE REGULATION OF PUBLICLY TRADED SECURITIES" (PDF). U.S. Securities and Exchange Commission. p. 58. Retrieved December 17, 2008.
32. Harris, Larry (2003). Trading and Exchanges: Market Microstructure for Practitioners. Oxford University Press. p. 290. ISBN 0–19–514,470-8. Retrieved March 13, 2009.
33. Ferrell, Allen (2001). "A Proposal for Solving the "Payment for Order Flow" Problem" (PDF). 74 S.Cal.L.Rev. 1027. Harvard. Retrieved December 12, 2008.
34. Battalio, Robert H.; Tim Loughran (January 15, 2007). "Does Payment for Order Flow to Your Broker Help or Hurt You?" (PDF). Notre Dame University. Retrieved December 12, 2008.
35. Jump up to: a b McMillan, Alex (May 29, 2000). "Q&A: Madoff Talks Trading". CNN. Retrieved December 11, 2008.
36. Henriques, Diana B.; Alex Berenson (December 14, 2008). "The 17th Floor, Where Wealth Went to Vanish". The New York Times. Retrieved December 23, 2008.
37. Dovkants, Keith; Alex Berenson (December 16, 2008). "Revealed: Magic Madoff's family 'piggy bank' in the heart of Mayfair". Evening Standard. Archived from the original on December 20, 2008. Retrieved December 25, 2008.
38. Creswell, Julie (January 24, 2009). "The Talented Mr. Madoff". The New York Times. Retrieved January 25, 2009.
39. "Madoff Securities International Ltd. v Raven & Ors [2013] EWHC 3147 (Comm) (18 October 2013)". Bailii.org. Retrieved April 14, 2021.

40. Jump up to: a b c d e f Moyer, Liz (December 23, 2008). "Could SEC Have Stopped Madoff Scam In 1992?". Forbes. Archived from the original on February 1, 2009. Retrieved December 24, 2008.
41. Interview with Jim Voss Bloomberg.
42. Jump up to: a b Berenson, Alex; Henriques, Diana B. (December 13, 2008). "Look at Wall St. Wizard Finds Magic Had Skeptics". The New York Times. Retrieved December 15, 2008.
43. Jump up to: a b c Arvedlund, Erin E. (May 7, 2001). "Don't Ask, Don't Tell – Bernie Madoff is so secretive, he even asks investors to keep mum" (PDF). Barron's. Retrieved August 12, 2009.
44. Zuckoff, Mitchell (December 29, 2008). "Were charities part of Madoff's secret formula? – Dec. 29, 2008". Money.cnn.com. Retrieved April 26, 2009.
45. Jump up to: a b "Tough task ahead to find Madoff money, co-schemers". Associated Press. March 13, 2009. Retrieved March 13, 2009.
46. Safer, Morley (September 27, 2009). "The Madoff Scam: Meet The Liquidator". 60 Minutes. CBS News. pp. 1–4. Retrieved September 28, 2009.
47. Jump up to: a b c d e Henriques, Diana B. (December 20, 2008). "Madoff Scheme Kept Rippling Outward, Across Borders". The New York Times. Retrieved December 22, 2008.
48. Jump up to: a b Chernoff, Allan (December 26, 2008). "What drove Bernie Madoff". CNN. Retrieved December 26, 2008.
49. "Investor Furor Over '50B Scam'". New York Post. December 14, 2008. Archived from the original on December 17, 2008. Retrieved December 17, 2008.
50. Brown, Ian (December 31, 2016). "A look inside Palm Beach, where wealthy Canadians are one degree of separation from Donald Trump". The Globe and Mail.
51. Biggs, Barton (January 3, 2009). "The Affinity Ponzi Scheme". Newsweek. Retrieved March 9, 2009.
52. Jump up to: a b Schwartz, Nelson D. (December 24, 2008). "Madoff Dealings Tarnish a Private Swiss Bank". The New York Times. Retrieved December 23, 2008.
53. "Marketing Advisory: Madoff Knew His Target Market" Archived March 16, 2009, at the Wayback Machine Marketing Doctor Blog. December 18, 2008.
54. ALEX BERENSON; DIANA B. HENRIQUES (December 12, 2008). "Look at Wall St. Wizard Finds Magic Had Skeptics". The New York Times. Retrieved March 9, 2009.
55. "Prominent Trader Accused of Defrauding Clients", The New York Times December 12, 2008.
56. Sender, Henry (December 21, 2008). "Madoff had 'perceived edge' in the markets". Financial Times. Retrieved December 25, 2008.
57. Barlyn, Suzanne (December 23, 2008). "Madoff Case Raises Compliance Questions". The Wall Street Journal. Retrieved March 1, 2008.

58. Williamson, Elizabeth; Kara Scannell (December 18, 2008). "Family Filled Posts at Industry Groups". The Wall Street Journal. Retrieved March 1, 2009.
59. Jump up to: a b Lerer, Lisa (December 18, 2008). "Peter Madoff resigns". Politico. Retrieved March 1, 2009.
60. Williamson, Elizabeth (December 22, 2008). "Shana Madoff's Ties to Uncle Probed". The Wall Street Journal. Retrieved March 1, 2009.
61. Javers, Eamon; Lisa Lerer (December 16, 2008). "Madoff bought influence in Washington". Politico. Retrieved March 1, 2009.
62. Madoff, Shana. "San Francisco Topical Breakfast". Compliance and Legal Division of the Securities Industry and Financial Markets Association. Archived from the original on September 3, 2014. Retrieved March 1, 2009.
63. Zachary A. Goldfarb, Staffer at SEC Had Warned Of Madoff; Lawyer Raised Alarm, Then Was Pointed Elsewhere, The Washington Post, July 2, 2009.
64. Jump up to: a b c d e Jerome De Lavenere Lussan (2012). The Financial Times Guide to Investing in Funds: How to Select Investments, Assess Managers and Protect Your Wealth. FT Press. ISBN 9780273732853. Retrieved February 9, 2013.
65. Williamson, Elizabeth (December 22, 2008). "Shana Madoff's Ties to Uncle Probed". Wall Street Journal. Retrieved February 15, 2013.
66. Nigel Da Costa Lewis (2012). The Fundamental Rules of Risk Management. CRC Press. ISBN 9781439816189. Retrieved February 14, 2013.
67. Jump up to: a b U.S. SEC Office of Investigations (August 31, 2009). "Investigation of Failure of the SEC to uncover Bernard Madoff's Ponzi Scheme (Public Version); B. Swanson's Initial Contact with Shana Madoff for SEC Office of Investigations Investigation of the SEC to Uncover Madoff Ponzi Scheme". Retrieved February 15, 2013.
68. "E-Mails Reveal Internal Drama at SEC Over Maddoff Firm". Fox Business. March 4, 2006. Retrieved February 15, 2013.
69. Deborah Hart Strober; Gerald Strober; Gerald S. Strober (2009). Catastrophe: The Story of Bernard L. Madoff, the Man Who Swindled the World. Phoenix Books, Inc. ISBN 9781597776400. Retrieved February 14, 2013.
70. Alexander Davidson (2010). How the Global Financial Markets Really Work: The Definitive Guide to Understanding International Investment and Money Flows. Kogan Page Publisher. p. 118. ISBN 9780749458218. Retrieved February 14, 2013.
71. Charles Gasparino (December 15, 2008). "Madoff Victims Claim Conflict of Interest at SEC". CNBC. Archived from the original on December 16, 2013. Retrieved February 15, 2013.
72. Zachary A. Goldfarb (July 2, 2009). "SEC Investigator Raised Madoff Concerns Years Ago, Was Asked to Look Elsewhere". Washington Post. Retrieved February 15, 2013.
73. Jump up to: a b Pressler, Jessica (July 2, 2009). "SEC Lawyer Raised Questions About Madoff Back in 2004". New York Magazine. Retrieved February 15, 2013.

74. Al Lewis (September 12, 2009). "True love can never be regulated". The Denver Post. Retrieved February 19, 2013.
75. Sandler, Linda (December 22, 2008). "Facebook Removes Madoff Web Page After Jeers, Cheers". Bloomberg. Retrieved February 15, 2013.
76. "Unlikely Player Pulled Into Madoff Swirl", by Stephen Labaton, December 18, 2008, The New York Times
77. David Kotz, H. (2009). Investigation of Failure of the SEC to Uncover Bernard Madoff's Ponzi Scheme ... ISBN 9781437921861. Retrieved March 1, 2013.
78. Labaton, Stephen (December 16, 2008). "Unlikely Player Pulled Into Madoff Swirl". The New York Times.
79. David Kotz, H. (2009). Investigation of Failure of the SEC to Uncover Bernard Madoff's Ponzi Scheme ... ISBN 9781437921861. Retrieved March 1, 2013.
80. "SEC Official Married into Madoff Family – ABC News". Abcnews.go.com. December 16, 2008. Retrieved April 26, 2009.
81. Jump up to: a b c d e f g h i j Scannell, Kara (January 5, 2009). "Madoff Chasers Dug for Years, to No Avail". The Wall Street Journal. Retrieved January 5, 2009.
82. Jump up to: a b c Johnson, Harriet (March 8, 2009). "Sun Sentinel exclusive: Former Madoff associate Michael Bienes breaks his silence – South Florida Sun-Sentinel.com". Sun-sentinel.com. Retrieved April 5, 2016.
83. Healy (December 13, 2008). "Boston donors bilked out of millions". Boston Globe. Retrieved March 13, 2009.
84. Jump up to: a b House of Representatives Financial Services Committee (2009). "Madoff Fraud Investigations and Financial Markets Regulation". C-SPAN.[permanent dead link].
85. Jump up to: a b "The Madoff files: Bernie's billions". The Independent. London. January 29, 2009. Retrieved April 26, 2009.
86. Jump up to: a b "Markopolos Testimony" (PDF). The Wall Street Journal.
87. Madoff fraud case raises questions about SEC Associated Press. Archived December 19, 2008, at the Wayback Machin.
88. "Man who warned about Bernard Madoff to testify – BostonHerald.com". BostonHerald.com <!. Associated Press. February 3, 2009. Retrieved April 26, 2009.
89. Jump up to: a b Serchuk, David (December 20, 2008). "Love, Madoff And The SEC". Forbes. Retrieved December 24, 2008.[dead link].
90. Lenzner, Robert. "The Card Sharp Who Cottoned Onto Madoff's Fraud In 1991". Forbes.com. Retrieved April 14, 2021.
91. "The Man Who Figured Out Madoff's Scheme". CBS News. February 27, 2009.
92. Tangled Webs by James B. Stewart c. 2011 James B. Stewart 2011(Penguin Press, USA; 2011) p.387.
93. Markopolos, Harry (November 7, 2005). "The World's Largest Hedge Fund is a Fraud" (PDF). Wall Street Journal Online. Archived (PDF) from the original on June 22, 2010. Retrieved December 22, 2008.

94. E&P Staff (February 4, 2009). "Whistleblower Claims He Tipped 'WSJ' to Madoff Fraud, Paper Failed to Act".
95. Jump up to: a b Chew, Robert (February 4, 2009). "A Madoff Whistle-Blower Tells His Story". TIME. Archived from the original on February 7, 2009. Retrieved April 26, 2009.
96. Joel Tillinghast (2017). Big Money Thinks Small: Biases, Blind Spots and Smarter Investing. Columbia Business School Publishing, pp. 123–124.
97. "Madoff's Brother Said to Audit Firm's Investments". Bloomberg. February 4, 2009.
98. Tangled Webs by James B. Stewart c. 2011 James B. Stewart 2011(Penguin Press, USA; 2011) pp.366–367.
99. Fitzgerald, Jim (December 18, 2008). "Madoff's financial empire audited by tiny firm: one guy". Seattle Times. Associated Press. Retrieved December 18, 2008.
100. Voreacos, David (December 16, 2008). "New York Prosecutor Drops Madoff Auditor Probe; Defers to U.S". Bloomberg News. Retrieved December 24, 2008.
101. Kouwe, Zachery (December 15, 2008). Andrew Ross Sorkin (ed.). "A Look at Madoff Trading Records". Deal Book. The New York Times. Retrieved December 22, 2008.
102. "Wall Street Titan May Have Fooled Investors for Years". CNBC. Archived from the original on June 11, 2011. Retrieved December 13, 2008.
103. Zuckerman (December 13, 2008). "Fees, Even Returns and Auditor All Raised Flags". The Wall Street Journal.
104. Tangled Webs by James B. Stewart c. 2011 James B. Stewart 2011(Penguin Press, USA; 2011) pp.363–371.
105. David B. Caruso (December 13, 2008). "A trusted man, $50B, a "giant Ponzi scheme"". The Seattle Times. Associated Press. Retrieved March 9, 2009.
106. Hamilton (December 13, 2008). "Madoff's reliable returns aroused doubts". LA Times. Retrieved December 13, 2008.
107. I4U News. "Bernard Madoff". Archived from the original on September 12, 2013. Retrieved September 26, 2014.
108. "Today in the press – Taiwan Sun". Archived from the original on September 12, 2013. Retrieved September 26, 2014.
109. Pyramid Games: Bernie Madoff and his Willing Disciples by Michael Leidig, pages 287–311, Medusa Publishing, ISBN 9780957619142.
110. Henriques 2011, p. 166.
111. Henriques 2011, pp. 195–196.
112. Jump up to: a b c d Ross, Brian (2015). The Madoff Chronicles. Kingswell. ISBN 9781484781401.
113. McCool, Grant (February 27, 2009). "Receiver says Madoff moved $164 million from UK firm to U.S. | Reuters". Uk.reuters.com. Retrieved April 26, 2009.
114. Jump up to: a b Bray, Chad (February 25, 2009). "Investor's Suit Is Dismissed – WSJ.com". Online.wsj.com. Retrieved April 26, 2009.

115. "Madoff Sought, Got Cash in Days Before Arrest". SmartMoney. January 9, 2009. Retrieved January 29, 2009.
116. Henriques 2011, pp. 5–6.
117. Henriques 2011, pp. 12–13.
118. Jump up to: a b David Glovin, David Voreacos and David Scheer (February 24, 2009). "Madoff Must Have Had Help, Lawyers Say, Citing Trustee Report". Bloomberg.com. Retrieved April 28, 2011.
119. Jump up to: a b Efrati, Amir (May 18, 2009). "Madoff Victims Investigated". Wall Street Journal. Retrieved March 16, 2010.
120. Santosh Nadgir and Grant McCool (May 13, 2009). "Lawsuit claims Picower profits from Madoff $5 billion". Reuters. Retrieved July 2, 2009.
121. Diana B. Henriques and Zachery Kouwe (May 12, 2009). "Billions Withdrawn Before Madoff Arrest". New York Times. Retrieved July 2, 2009.
122. "Madoff pal Jeffry Picower laid to rest on Long Island | Jose Lambiet's". Page2live.com. Archived from the original on November 1, 2009. Retrieved March 16, 2010.
123. Jump up to: a b "Madoff Trustee Gets 'game Changing' 7.2 Billion Settlement", NECN.
124. Jump up to: a b ""ORDER PURSUANT TO SECTION 105(a) OF THE BANKRUPTCY CODE AND RULES 2002 AND 9019 OF THE FEDERAL RULES OF BANKRUPTCY PROCEDURE APPROVING AN AGREEMENT BY AND AMONG THE TRUSTEE AND THE PICOWER BLMIS ACCOUNT HOLDERS AND ISSUING A PERMANENT INJUNCTION""(PDF). Madofftrustee.com. Retrieved April 14, 2021.
125. Jump up to: a b Henriques, Diana B. (June 22, 2009). "Brokerage Firm and 4 Others Sued in Madoff Case". The New York Times. Retrieved June 22, 2009.
126. Standora, Leo (May 2, 2009). "Los Angeles investment manager Stanley Chais sued for funneling cash to Bernie Madoff fund". New York Daily News.
127. Pfeifer, Stuart (September 23, 2009). "Financial advisor Stanley Chais sued in Bernie Madoff scheme". Los Angeles Times. Retrieved March 16, 2010.
128. Jump up to: a b c d "Madoff trustee reaches $277 million accord with money manager's family," Reuters.
129. "ORDER PURSUANT TO SECTION 105(a) OF THE BANKRUPTCY CODE AND RULES 2002 AND 9019 OF THE FEDERAL RULES OF BANKRUPTCY PROCEDURE APPROVING AN AGREEMENT BY AND AMONG THE TRUSTEE AND THE ESTATE OF STANLEY CHAIS AND OTHER DEFENDANTS," November 18, 2016.
130. "Securities: Fairfield Greenwich". Sec.state.ma.us. April 1, 2009. Retrieved April 26, 2009.
131. Frank, Robert; Lauricella, Tom (April 2, 2009). "Madoff Feeder Is Charged in Fraud". Wall Street Journal. Retrieved April 26, 2009.
132. "Madoff feeder fund settles with Massachusetts". ABC News. Retrieved April 14, 2021.

133. Henriques, Diana B. (May 19, 2009). "Trustee Sues Hedge Funds Over Losses to Madoff". The New York Times. Retrieved May 12, 2010.
134. Jones, Ashby (May 19, 2009). "Picard's Latest: A Huge Lawsuit Against Fairfield Greenwich". Wall Street Journal. Retrieved March 16, 2010.
135. Stempel, Jonathan (May 9, 2011). "Madoff trustee in $1 billion pact with Fairfield funds". reuters.com. Retrieved August 24, 2019.
136. "Madoff's Brother Agrees To $90 Million Settlement In Trustee Lawsuit - Litigation Blog - Litigation - LexisNexis® Legal Newsroom". Lexisnexis.com. Retrieved April 14, 2021.
137. "10 years later, here's what became of Bernie Madoff's inner circle," CNBC.
138. "Ruth Madoff Asks to Keep Her Fur Coat as U.S. Marshals Seize Penthouse". FOX News. July 2, 2009. Retrieved March 16, 2010.
139. "Trustee Sues Ruth Madoff for More Than $44 Million," The Wall Street Journal.
140. Groendahl, Boris (February 12, 2009). "Medici's Kohn says did not get Madoff payments". Reuters. Retrieved April 26, 2009.
141. "Galvin seeks to shut down firm with Madoff ties". The Boston Globe. February 11, 2009. Archived from the original on February 14, 2009. Retrieved April 26, 2009.
142. "Madoff's Wife Got $two Million from UK Unit". CNBC. March 27, 2009. Retrieved April 26, 2009.
143. "Madoff Fraud Charges Could Be Filed in U.K. This Year (Update4)". Bloomberg. March 27, 2009. Retrieved April 26, 2009.
144. Jump up to: a b "Madoff to Forfeit $170 Billion In Assets Ahead of Sentencing". Washington Post. June 27, 2009. Retrieved March 16, 2010.
145. Jump up to: a b c d Efrati, Amir (June 28, 2009). "Madoff's Wife Cedes Asset Claim". Wall Street Journal. Retrieved March 16, 2010.
146. "Life After Madoff: Ruth Living on $2.5 Million in Connecticut," ABC News.
147. "Bernie Madoff's Ponzi Scheme - How the Scandal Affected His Family, Ruth, Mark & Andrew," Town and Country.
148. Gearty, Robert; Standora, Leo (August 4, 2009). "Bernie Madoff's wife, Ruth, agrees to account for monthly spending". New York Daily News. New York. Retrieved March 16, 2010.
149. E-mail This (July 29, 2009). "Trustee Sues Ruth Madoff for $44.8 Million". The New York Times. Retrieved March 16, 2010.
150. Fitzgerald, Patrick (July 30, 2009). "Trustee Sues Ruth Madoff for More Than $44 Million". Wall Street Journal. Retrieved March 16, 2010.
151. "Lawsuit Against Ruth Madoff (Irving Picard)". March 1, 2009. Retrieved March 16, 2010.
152. Mike Greenlar / The Post Standard (March 29, 2009). "How warning signs eluded Bernard Madoff's man in Syracuse". Syracuse.com. Retrieved April 26, 2009.
153. Efrati, Amir (April 1, 2009). "Judge Freezes Assets of Madoff's Family". Wall Street Journal. Retrieved April 26, 2009.

154. Margolick, David (July 2009). "The Madoff Chronicles, Part III: Did the Sons Know". Vanity Fair. Retrieved June 25, 2009.
155. Lucchetti, Aaron (October 3, 2009). "Madoff Trustee Sues Swindler's Family". Wall Street Journal. Retrieved March 16, 2010.
156. "Baker & Hostetler LLP" (PDF). ABC News. Retrieved October 7, 2012.
157. Larry Neumeister (December 12, 2010). "Madoff son's suicide followed battle with trustee". Associated Press. Retrieved December 13, 2010.
158. Henriques, Diana B. (September 3, 2014). "Andrew Madoff, Who Told of His Father's Swindle, Dies at 48". The New York Times. ISSN 0362-4331. Retrieved December 11, 2018.
159. "Madoff sons' estates in $23 million settlement over Ponzi scheme," Reuters.
160. "Tremont Group Funds Invested $3.3 Billion With Madoff (Update1)". Bloomberg. December 15, 2008. Retrieved April 26, 2009.
161. "Madoff trustee in $1 billion settlement with Tremont," Reuters.
162. Randall, David (March 31, 2009). "Judge Freezes Madoff Assets". Forbes. Archived from the original on January 23, 2013. Retrieved April 26, 2009.
163. Reuters Staff (August 27, 2013). "Madoff trustee reaches $98 mln settlement with Maxam fund". Reuters.com. Retrieved April 14, 2021.
164. Jump up to: a b Stempel, Jonathan (November 4, 2016). "Madoff victims to recoup $32.1 million in Cohmad settlement". Reuters.com. Retrieved April 14, 2021.
165. Jonathan Stempel (August 21, 2009). "Madoff friend wants SEC, trustee charges dismissed". Reuters. Retrieved March 16, 2010.
166. "Madoff's London Operations Targeted In Suit - Financial Fraud Law Blog - Financial Fraud Law - LexisNexis® Legal Newsroom". Lexisnexis.com. Retrieved April 14, 2021.
167. Bray, Chad (December 16, 2008). "3rd UPDATE: Merkin, Ascot Fund Sued Over Madoff Investments". CNN. Dow Jones Newswires. Retrieved December 23, 2008.[dead link].
168. "Merkin Complaint" (PDF). The Wall Street Journal.
169. Graybow, Martha (April 6, 2009). "Fund operator Merkin charged with civil fraud". Reuters.
170. "Merkin Exhibit One" (PDF). The Wall Street Journal.
171. "Merkin Exhibit Two" (PDF). The Wall Street Journal.
172. "Merkin Exhibit Three" (PDF). The Wall Street Journal.
173. "UniCredit wins dismissal in Madoff case". Financial Times. December 15, 2008. Retrieved February 26, 2009.
174. Bray, Chad (July 18, 2009). "Madoff Ex-Auditor Friehling Enters a Plea of Not Guilty". Wall Street Journal. Retrieved March 16, 2010.
175. Dienst, Jonathan (October 30, 2009). "Madoff Accountant Set to Make a Deal". NBC New York. Retrieved March 16, 2010.
176. Jump up to: a b Matthew Goldstein, Madoff Accountant Avoids Prison Term, New York Times (May 28, 2015).
177. "United States v. Frank DiPascali, Jr" (PDF). ABC News. Retrieved October 7, 2012.

178. "Frank DiPascali Pleads Guilty, Bernard Madoff's Accomplice". ABC News. August 11, 2009. Retrieved March 16, 2010.
179. "SEC CHARGES KEY MADOFF LIEUTENANT FOR OPERATING AND CONCEALING FRAUD THROUGH BOGUS TRADES AND DOCUMENTS" (PDF). The Wall Street Journal.
180. Bray, Chad (August 12, 2009). "'All Fake': Key Madoff Executive Admits Guilt". Wall Street Journal. Retrieved March 16, 2010.
181. Yang, Stephanie (May 11, 2015). "Former Madoff Aide Frank DiPascali Dies at Age 58 of Lung Cancer". Wall Street Journal.
182. "Former Madoff operations exec arrested". Los Angeles Times. February 25, 2010. Retrieved February 25, 2010.[dead link]
183. "Madoff's Director of Operations Arrested". Traders Magazine. February 25, 2010. Archived from the original on July 17, 2011. Retrieved February 25, 2010.
184. "Press Release: Manhattan U.S. Attorney Charges Daniel Bonventre, Former Director Of Operations For Bernard L. Madoff Investment Securities, Llc, With Conspiracy, Securities Fraud, And Tax Crimes" (PDF). US DOJ United States Attorney Southern District of New York. February 25, 2010. Archived from the original (PDF) on March 2, 2010. Retrieved March 4, 2010.
185. Cohn, Scott (March 24, 2014). "Five Madoff employees convicted for aiding scam". Cnbc.com. Retrieved April 14, 2021.
186. "Madoff accomplice Daniel Bonventre jailed for 10 years," BBC News.
187. "Ex-Madoff manager sentenced to six years prison for fraud," Reuters.
188. "FBI — Manhattan U.S. Attorney Files Additional Charges Against Former Employees of Bernard L. Madoff Investment Securities LLC". Fbi.gov. Retrieved October 7, 2012.
189. "Ex-Madoff manager, computer programmer get prison terms," Reuters.
190. "Madoff computer programmer George Perez sentenced to 2–1/2 years," Newsday.
191. "Bernie Madoff: Why Is Bernie's Controller, Enrica Cotellessa-Pitz, Getting A Pass In The Press?". talkingpointsmemo.com. May 11, 2009. Archived from the original on July 5, 2009. Retrieved March 16, 2010.
192. "No jail time for Bernard Madoff's former controller," Newsday.
193. "Madoff Trustee Picard May Take Five Years to Pay Back Investors – Bloomberg.com". Bloomberg.com <!. January 21, 2009. Retrieved April 26, 2009.
194. McCool, Grant (January 22, 2009). "Fairfield fund wins order in Madoff-related suit". Reuters.
195. E-mail This (June 23, 2009). "Madoff Lawyers Seek Leniency in Sentencing – DealBook Blog – NYTimes.com". Dealbook.blogs.nytimes.com. Retrieved March 16, 2010.
196. Schmidt, Robert; Gallu, Joshua (January 25, 2013). "SEC Said to Back Hire of U.S. Capitol Police Inspector General". Bloomberg L.P. Retrieved October 15, 2015.

197. Jump up to: a b Schmidt, Robert; Joshua Gallu (October 26, 2012). "Former SEC Watchdog Kotz Violated Ethics Rules, Review Finds". Bloomberg. Retrieved February 10, 2013.
198. "David Kotz, Ex-SEC Inspector General, May Have Had Conflicts Of Interest". Huffington Post. October 5, 2012. Retrieved February 10, 2013.
199. Sarah N. Lynch (November 15, 2012). "David Weber Lawsuit: Ex-SEC Investigator Accused Of Wanting To Carry A Gun At Work, Suing For $20 Million". Huffingtonpost.com. Retrieved February 10, 2013.
200. Hays, Tom; Larry Neumeister; Shlomo Shamir (March 6, 2009). "Extent of Madoff fraud now estimated at far below $50b". Haaretz. Associated Press. Retrieved March 7, 2009.
201. Glovin, Dan; Bradley Keoun (December 11, 2008). "Madoff Charged in $50 Billion Fraud at Investment Advisory Firm". Bloomberg News. Retrieved December 11, 2008.
202. Jump up to: a b c d e "The United States Department of Justice – United States Attorney's Office". Usdoj.gov. Archived from the original on August 22, 2007. Retrieved April 26, 2009.
203. Jump up to: a b Henriques, Diana; Zachery Kouwe (December 11, 2008). "Prominent Trader Accused of Defrauding Clients". The New York Times. Retrieved December 11, 2008.
204. Efrati, Amir; Aaron Lucchetti; Tom Lauricella (December 23, 2008). "Probe Eyes Audit Files, Role of Aide To Madoff". The Wall Street Journal. Dow Jones. Retrieved December 23, 2008.
205. "Madoff faces life in prison on 11 criminal charges". Reuters. March 11, 2009.
206. "Madoff Securities Employees Sue Madoff Sons, Allege Fraud". The Wall Street Journal. June 16, 2009. Archived from the original on June 20, 2009. Retrieved July 27, 2009.
207. Jump up to: a b Neumeister, Larry (December 11, 2008). "Ex-Nasdaq chair arrested on fraud charge". Associated Press. Yahoo-Finance document http://biz.yahoo.com/ap/081211/wall_street_arrest.html accessed December 11, 2008 has expired.
208. Efrati, Amir; Lauricella, Tom; Searcey, Dionne (December 11, 2008). "Top Broker Accused of Fraud; Madoff, Money Manager for the Wealthy, Said to Have Run '$50 Billion Ponzi Scheme'". The Wall Street Journal. Retrieved December 11, 2008.
209. Honan, Edith; Dan Wilchins (December 12, 2008). "Former Nasdaq chair arrested over alleged £33 billion fraud". International Herald Tribune. Retrieved December 12, 2008.
210. Jump up to: a b Rush, George; Thomas Zambito; Phyllis Furman; Greg B. Smith (December 18, 2008). "Bernard Madoff Housebound After Failing to Get Enough Co-signers for Bail Bond in $50B Ponzi Scheme". New York Daily News. Retrieved December 26, 2008.
211. Jump up to: a b Zambito, Thomas; Corky Siemaszko (December 20, 2008). "Feds confine Bernie Madoff to his $seven million penthouse until trial". New York Daily News. Retrieved December 26, 2008.

212. "SIPC page 7, VII. U.S. Securities and Exchange Commission" (PDF). Retrieved March 1, 2013.
213. Glovin, David (January 6, 2009). "Madoff Sons Reported Jewelry Violations to U.S., Lawyer Says". Bloomberg.com. Retrieved January 6, 2009.
214. Jump up to: a b Berenson, Alex (January 6, 2009). "Bid to Revoke Madoff's Bail Cites His Gifts". The New York Times. Retrieved January 6, 2009.
215. Henrique, Diana (January 12, 2009). "Judge Rules Madoff Can Remain Free on Bail". The New York Times. Retrieved January 12, 2009.
216. "(PDF)" (PDF). Usdoj.gov. Retrieved April 14, 2021.
217. "Criminal Information (U.S. v. Bernard Madoff". FindLaw. March 10, 2009. Retrieved March 10, 2009.
218. Jump up to: a b "U.S. Department of Justice: United States v. Bernard L. Madoff" (PDF). Usdoj.gov. Retrieved October 16, 2015.
219. Lauricella, Tom (March 12, 2009). "Madoff Used U.K. Office in Cash Ploy, Filing Says – WSJ.com". Online.wsj.com. Retrieved April 26, 2009.
220. Jones, Ashby (February 9, 2009). "Madoff Makes Peace with the SEC, Amount of Fine TBD". The Wall Street Journal. Retrieved March 29, 2009.
221. "Madoff Lawyer Ira Sorkin Invested $18,860 With Madoff (Update2)". Bloomberg.com. March 10, 2009. Retrieved April 26, 2009.
222. DOJ Madoff hearing.
223. "Madoff to appeal bail, net worth revealed | U.S". Reuters. March 13, 2009. Retrieved April 26, 2009.
224. "United States Court of Appeals for the Second Circuit: United States v. Bernard L. Madoff" (PDF). Usdoj.gov. Retrieved October 7, 2012.
225. Zambito, Thomas; Connor, Tracy (March 17, 2009). "Bernard Madoff's sons, Andrew and Mark, latest targets of feds' efforts to seize ill-gotten loot". New York: Nydailynews.com. Retrieved April 26, 2009.
226. "Bernard Madoff's Bid for Freedom Denied by U.S. Court (Update5)". Bloomberg.com. March 20, 2009. Archived from the original on March 12, 2010. Retrieved April 26, 2009.
227. Jump up to: a b "Prosecutors' sentencing recommendation" (PDF). Usdoj.gov. Retrieved April 14, 2021.
228. Henriques, Dana. Prosecutors propose 150-year sentence for Madoff. The New York Times, June 26, 2009.
229. Zambito, Thomas; Martinez, Jose; Siemaszko, Corky (June 29, 2009). "Bye, Bye Bernie: Ponzi king Madoff sentenced to 150 years". New York: Nydailynews.com. Retrieved March 16, 2010.
230. "Madoff Lacks What Skilling, Ebbers, Fastow Had: Ann Woolner". Bloomberg.com. July 1, 2009. Retrieved March 16, 2010.
231. Frank, Robert (June 30, 2009). "Bernard Madoff, Convicted Ponzi-Scheme Operator, Sentenced to 150 Years". wsj.com. Retrieved March 16, 2010.
232. Murakami Tse, Tomoeh (June 30, 2009). "Madoff Sentenced to 150 Years Calling Ponzi Scheme 'Evil,' Judge Orders Maximum Term". Washington Post. Retrieved September 24, 2009.
233. [1][dead link]

234. "Inquirer.com: Philadelphia local news, sports, jobs, cars, homes". Inquirer.com. Retrieved April 14, 2021.
235. "Madoff's Failure to Name Accomplices Cripples His Leniency Bid". Bloomberg.com. June 26, 2009. Retrieved March 16, 2010.
236. "Bernard Madoff gets 150 years behind bars for fraud scheme". CBC News. June 29, 2009. Archived from the original on July 2, 2009. Retrieved June 29, 2009.
237. Healy, Jack (June 29, 2009). "Madoff Sentenced to 150 Years for Ponzi Scheme". The New York Times. Retrieved June 29, 2009.
238. "Fraudster Madoff gets 150 years". BBC News. June 29, 2009. Retrieved June 29, 2009.
239. Zambito, Thomas; Martinez, Jose; Siemaszko, Corky (June 29, 2009). "Bye, Bye Bernie: Ponzi king Madoff sentenced to 150 years". New York: Nydailynews.com. Retrieved March 16, 2010.
240. Perez, Evan; Bray, Chad (July 13, 2009). "Madoff is Moved to a Prison in Butner N.C". The Wall Street Journal.
241. "Bernard Madoff surprised by long run of luck". Theaustralian.com/au. Archived from the original on September 12, 2012. Retrieved April 14, 2021.
242. "Madoff Finance" (PDF). Archived from the original (PDF) on March 17, 2009. Retrieved March 16, 2009.
243. Madoff assets worth more than $820 million – Newsday.com Archived March 16, 2009, at the Wayback Machine.
244. "Prosecutors Seek to Claim More Madoff Assets — DealBook Blog — NYTimes.com". Dealbook.blogs.nytimes.com. March 17, 2009. Retrieved April 26, 2009.
245. "Madoff Prosecutors Seek to Take Businesses, Loans (Update1)". Bloomberg.com. March 17, 2009. Retrieved April 26, 2009.
246. "Ruth Madoff Says Her $62 Million 'Unrelated' to Fraud (Update2) – Bloomberg.com". Bloomberg.com <!. March 2, 2009. Retrieved April 26, 2009.
247. Goldsmith, Samuel (April 12, 2009). "Now that's a decent return! Madoff's opening day Mets tickets sell for $7500 on eBay". New York: Nydailynews.com. Retrieved April 26, 2009.
248. "Minuteman News Center". Zwire.com. Archived from the original on July 6, 2009. Retrieved March 16, 2010.
249. "Madoff-Linked Asset Freeze Lifted in Connecticut Suit (Update1)". Bloomberg.com. April 13, 2009. Retrieved March 16, 2010.
250. "Judge freezes assets of Madoff sons, executives". Reuters. March 31, 2009. Retrieved March 16, 2010.
251. "Town of Fairfield suit against NEPC and KPMG". Scribd.com. Retrieved March 16, 2010.
252. "Town sues Madoff, hedge funds over losses". Newsday.com. March 31, 2009. Retrieved April 26, 2009.[dead link]
253. "Fairfield gets freeze on Madoff assets". Wtnh.com. Retrieved April 26, 2009.

254. "ABC News: Madoff Set to Disclose List of Holdings". Abcnews.go.com. December 17, 2008. Retrieved April 26, 2009.
255. Scheer, David (January 2, 2009). "Madoff's assets to be kept secret". Business. smh.com.au. Retrieved April 26, 2009.
256. Madoff trustee finds assets in Canada, Montreal Gazette, January 12, 2010.
257. "Picower estate returns $7.2 billion from Madoff scam". JTA. December 17, 2010. Archived from the original on September 26, 2012. Retrieved October 7, 2012.
258. "United States V. Bernard L. Madoff And Related Cases". Justice.gov. May 13, 2015. Retrieved April 14, 2021.
259. "Madoff Victim Fund | Reaching Victims". Madoffvictimfund.com. Retrieved April 14, 2021.
260. "The Madoff Recovery Initiative". Madoff (SIPA) Trustee. Retrieved December 28, 2020.
261. Fleury, Michelle (February 19, 2009). "Business | Madoff victims count their losses". BBC News. Retrieved April 26, 2009.
262. "WSJ: Madoff Client List" (PDF). The Wall Street Journal.
263. Chew, Robert (February 5, 2009). "The Bernie Madoff Client List Is Made Public". TIME. Archived from the original on February 7, 2009. Retrieved April 26, 2009.
264. "Madoff's Firm Owed $600 Million in Stock, SIPC Says (Update1)". Bloomberg.com <!. January 27, 2009. Retrieved April 26, 2009.
265. "Banks face huge losses from $50B 'scam'". CNN. December 15, 2008.
266. Darmon, Aynslee (April 7, 2021). "Leslie Jordan Let's It Slip That 'Golden Girls' Star Rue McClanahan 'Lost' Money In The Bernie Madoff Scandal". Etcanada.com. Retrieved April 14, 2021.
267. Conklin, Audrey (April 14, 2021). "Look back at Bernie Madoff's most high-profile victims". FOXBusiness.
268. Bennett, Chuck; Rosario, Frank (December 15, 2008). ""Zuckerman Sounds Off on Madoff", New York Daily News (December 14, 2008)". New York Post.
269. Strom, Stephanie (February 27, 2009). "Elie Wiesel Levels Scorn at Madoff". The New York Times. Retrieved May 12, 2010.
270. "Madoff's Victims". The Wall Street Journal. December 16, 2008. Retrieved December 17, 2008.
271. Healy, Beth (July 29, 2011). "Madoff clients get $1b in deal". The Boston Globe.
272. International Currency Review, Volume 34. 2008. Retrieved February 9, 2013.
273. Stempel, Jonathan (March 23, 2015). "Madoff feeder fund settles; victims' recovery tops $10.6 billion". Reuters. Retrieved August 1, 2019.
274. Browning, Lynnley (February 12, 2009). "For Investing With Madoff, Private Foundations Could Face Tax Fines". The New York Times. Retrieved May 12, 2010.
275. "Swiss judge allows charges in Madoff losses case | Reuters". Uk.reuters.com. February 9, 2009. Retrieved April 26, 2009.

276. "Aurelia managers sought safety in Madoff: report | Reuters". Uk.reuters.com. April 28, 2009. Retrieved March 16, 2010.
277. Reuters Staff (September 4, 2015). "UPDATE 1-Geneva wealth managers pay defrauded investors to settle Madoff case". Reuters.com. Retrieved April 14, 2021.
278. Granby, Rachael (February 22, 2009). "Clients Lose Again with Santander's Madoff Compensation – Barron's". Barron's. Retrieved March 13, 2009.
279. "70% of Santander Clients Take Madoff Settlement". The New York Times. Reuters. February 19, 2009. Retrieved March 13, 2009.
280. "Barron v. Igolnikov et al". Justia.com.
281. "UBP Makes Offer to Madoff Victims". The New York Times. March 13, 2009.
282. Kleinhaus, Emil; Meli, Graham; Wachtell, Herbert; DiPrima, Stephen (March 24, 2010). "Court Dismisses Madoff-Related Class Action as Preempted". Corpgov.law.harvard.edu. Retrieved April 14, 2021.
283. McCool, Grant (December 6, 2010). "HSBC fights Madoff claim; new settlement reached". Reuters.
284. "Madoff Trustee Announces Approximately $500 Million Recovery Agreement With Swiss Bank Union Bancaire Privee". PR Newswire. December 6, 2010.
285. Espinoza, Javier (February 1, 2009). "Austria Takes Control Of Madoff-Tainted Bank". Forbes. Retrieved February 24, 2010.
286. "Austria: Madoff-Exposed Bank Medici Reportedly on Brink of Collapse, Class Action May Be in Works". Securities Docket. January 21, 2009. Retrieved March 13, 2009.
287. Jump up to: a b Henriques 2011, p. 168.
288. Jump up to: a b Keena, Colm (December 10, 2010). "Dublin-registered Thema part of complaint filed to recoup $9bn received under Madoff". The Irish Times.
289. Allan Dodds Frank (February 20, 2011). "Sonja Kohn, Bernie Madoff's Bag Lady". Newsweek.
290. Jump up to: a b "Madoff looking for new money as scandal hit". Financial Times. December 22, 2008.
291. Forelle, Charles (December 17, 2008). "In Geneva, Spotlight Casts an Unwelcome Glare on Banks". The Wall Street Journal.
292. "Austria takes over bank hit by Madoff case". CNN. January 3, 2009. Retrieved March 13, 2009.
293. Groendahl, Boris (March 12, 2009). "Austria's Madoff-hit Bank Medici seeks buyers". Reuters. Retrieved March 13, 2009.
294. Blodget, Henry (March 1, 2009). "Madoff Feeder Bank Medici Probed Criminally In Vienna". Business Insider. Retrieved March 13, 2009.
295. Hansen, Flemming E. (May 28, 2009). "Madoff-Hit Bank Medici Loses License – WSJ.com". Online.wsj.com. Retrieved March 16, 2010.
296. Stempel, Jonathan (September 6, 2017). "Madoff trustee recoups $687 million in biggest settlement since 2011". Reuters.com. Retrieved April 14, 2021.

297. Wayne, Leslie; Rashbaum, William K. (March 12, 2009). "Investigation Into Madoff Fraud Turns to a Small Circle of Accountants". The New York Times. Retrieved May 12, 2010.
298. "Was Madoff 'Victim' and Best Friend an Accomplice? – Page 1". The Daily Beast. Retrieved April 26, 2009.
299. Bray, Chad (April 20, 2010). "Connecticut Sues Madoff-Tied Adviser, Bank". The Wall Street Journal. p. C7.
300. "Irish fund Thema International to pay $687 m to Madoff victims". The Irish Times. Retrieved April 14, 2021.
301. Fabrikant, Geraldine (December 20, 2008). "Foundation That Relied On Madoff Fund Closes". New York Times.
302. Lattman, Peter, "Peter Madoff Expected to Plead Guilty", The New York Times, June 27, 2012. Retrieved June 27, 2012.
303. "Madoff Brother To Serve 10 Years In Prison For Role In Ponzi Scheme". NY1. Archived from the original on January 30, 2013. Retrieved December 20, 2012.
304. Jump up to: a b "Madoff Investor's Suicide Leaves Questions" by Alex Berenson and Matthew Saltmarsh, The New York Times, January 2, 2009, p. B1 New York edition.
305. "Police: Madoff Investor Found Dead of Suicide" (text and audio). AP Newswire. 1010 WINS. Retrieved December 23, 2008.
306. Jump up to: a b Marino, Joe; Schapiro, Rich (December 25, 2008). "Bernie Madoff should rot with rats, victim's pal says". New York Daily News. Retrieved December 26, 2008.
307. Zuckerman, Gregory; Gauthier-Villars, David (February 3, 2009). "A Lonely Lament From a Whistle-Blower – WSJ.com". Online.wsj.com. Retrieved April 26, 2009.
308. "U.K.'s Prince Charles Targeted by Madoff Marketer, Witness Says". Bloomberg.com <!. February 6, 2009. Retrieved April 26, 2009.
309. "Madoff Investor's Suicide Leaves Questions" by Alex Berenson and Matthew Saltmarsh, The New York Times, 2009-01-02, p. B1 NY edition.
310. "Bernard Madoff fraud victim committed suicide to avoid bankruptcy shame". telegraph.co.uk. London. June 11, 2009. Retrieved June 28, 2009.
311. Thompson, Susan (February 12, 2009). "Bernard Madoff has 'blood on his hands' over William Foxton suicide". London: Business.timesonline.co.uk. Retrieved April 26, 2009.
312. Little (February 12, 2009). "Banking crisis killed my father". BBC. Retrieved February 13, 2009.
313. AFP (December 16, 2008). "Madoff: la banque autrichienne Medici impliquée avec 2,1 milliards de dollars". Romandie News (in French). Retrieved March 13, 2009.
314. [2]. The Guardian, December 11, 2010
315. Erik Larson. "Estates of Madoff's dead sons reach $23 million U.-S. settlement". Inquirer.com. Retrieved April 14, 2021.

316. Martha Graybow and Daniel Trotta. "Mark Madoff found hanged on anniversary of father Bernie's arrest". Vancouver Sun. Retrieved December 13, 2010.
317. Lucchetti, Aaron (December 14, 2010). "Madoff Won't Attend Son's Funeral". The Wall Street Journal.
318. "Investor burned by Madoff leaps to death from luxury hotel balcony". The New York Post. March 27, 2017.
319. Investigation of Failure of the SEC to Uncover Bernard Madoff's Ponzi Scheme. U.S. Securities and Exchange Commission, Office of Investigations, August 31, 2009.
320. Madoff Report Reveals Extent of Bungling. The Wall Street Journal, September 5, 2009.
321. Eight SEC employees disciplined over failures in Madoff fraud case; none are fired. Washington Post, November 11, 2011.
322. Vardi, Nathan (January 7, 2014). "J P Morgan Chase pays $1.7 billion and settles Madoff related criminal case". Forbes.
323. JP Morgan to pay $1.7bn to victims of the Madoff fraud BBC January 7, 2014.
324. Hiltzik, Michael (January 7, 2014). "The Madoff settlement is an enormous win for a guilty JPMorgan". Los Angeles Times. Retrieved January 8, 2014.
325. Erik Larson, "The Mystery Madoff Victims Who Left $2.5 Billion on the Table", Bloomberg Business News (March 4, 2016).
326. Jump up to: a b "Madoff's Victims Are Close to Getting Their $19 Billion Back," Bloomberg.
327. "Madoff customer payout tops $12 billion," Reuters.
328. "Record-Setting Madoff Settlement Announced with Picower Estate," The Am Law Daily.
329. "$7.2 Billion Picower Settlement: Payday for Madoff Victims," The Daily Beast.
330. "Meet Irving Picard, the lawyer with the toughest task in the world," Financial News.
331. Andrew Scurria (May 7, 2019). "Ruth Maddoff Reaches Trustee Deal". Wall Street Journal. p. B5.

Sources

Henriques, Diana (2011). The Wizard of Lies. Times Books. ISBN 9781250007438.

External Links

Wikimedia Commons has media related to Madoff investment scandal.

- Criminal complaint, transcripts of hearings and other documents from the United States Department of Justice
- 113 Victim Impact Statements: Letters urging Justice June 12, 2009
- Defense Attorney pre-sentencing request for leniency letter, June 22, 2009
- Madoff Client List February 4, 2009
- Bernard Madoff Victim Support and Advocacy Group
- SEC civil complaint

- SEC press release and update for investors
- Bernard L. Madoff Investment Securities
- Jewish charities hit by Madoff scandal BBC
- Madoff Scandal ongoing coverage from the Financial Times
- Serious Fraud Office broadens investigation to Madoff feeders The Guardian, March 27, 2009, British government's investigation into the London activities of certain feeder funds that channeled investments to Madoff
- Deposition of J. Ezra Merkin: Madoff Charities Investigation, State of New York (January 30, 2009)
- Merkin Civil Fraud Complaint State of New York (April 6, 2009)
- Merkin Exhibits, Civil Fraud Complaint
- continued Merkin Exhibits, Civil Fraud Complaint State of New York, (April 6, 2009)
- Complaint against J P Morgan Chase (April 23, 2009)
- Complaint against J. Ezra Merkin (May 7, 2009)
- Complaint against Harley International (Cayman) Limited (May 12, 2009)
- Commonwealth of Massachusetts Secretary of State Complaint (January 14, 2009)
- Picard v. Cohmad Securities Corp. 09-AP-1305 (June 22, 2009)
- SEC v. Cohmad Securities Corp., 09 Civ. 5680 (June 22, 2009)
- Picard v. Chais et al. 08-01789 (May 1, 2009)
- SEC v. Stanley Chais, 09 CIV 5681 (June 22, 2009)
- Picard v. Ruth Madoff, 1:09-ap-1391 (July 29, 2009)
- Example of a Madoff Investment Securities LLC monthly statement
- June 3, 2011: Letter to Gene L. Dodaro Comptroller General of the United States Government Accountability Office from Congress requesting probe
- June 3, 2011: Madoff Trustee, SEC Should be Probed -US Reps
- July 27, 2011: Madoff Trustee's Actions to Be Probed by GAO, Representative Garrett Says

3.4 Wells Fargo

3.4.1 Text from Wikipedia[7] (January 23, 2022)

Wells Fargo Account Fraud Scandal
The Wells Fargo account fraud scandal is a controversy brought about by the creation of millions of fraudulent savings and checking accounts on behalf of Wells Fargo clients without their consent. News of the fraud became widely known in late 2016 after various regulatory bodies, including the Consumer

---

[7] Link: https://en.wikipedia.org/wiki/Wells_Fargo_account_fraud_scandal

Financial Protection Bureau (CFPB), fined the company a combined US$185 million as a result of the illegal activity. The company faces additional civil and criminal suits reaching an estimated $2.7 billion by the end of 2018 [1]. The creation of these fake accounts continues to have legal and financial ramifications for Wells Fargo and former bank executives as of early 2021 [2].

Wells Fargo clients began to notice the fraud after being charged unanticipated fees and receiving unexpected credit or debit cards or lines of credit. Initial reports blamed individual Wells Fargo branch workers and managers for the problem, as well as sales incentives associated with selling multiple "solutions" or financial products. This blame was later shifted to a top-down pressure from higher-level management to open as many accounts as possible through cross-selling.

The bank took relatively few risks in the years leading up to the financial crisis of 2007–2008, which led to an image of stability on Wall Street and in the financial world. The bank's stable reputation was tarnished by the widespread fraud, the subsequent coverage, and the revelation of other fraudulent practices employed by the company. The controversy resulted in the resignation of CEO John Stumpf, an investigation into the bank led by U.S. Senator Elizabeth Warren, a number of settlements between Wells Fargo and various parties, and pledges from new management to reform the bank.

Contents

1. Background

    1.1. Cross-selling
    1.2. Early coverage
    1.3. Fraud
    1.4. Initial fines and broader coverage
    1.5. Initial response from Wells Fargo and management

2. Initial impact of the fraud, legal action, and press coverage

    2.1. On Wells Fargo management
    2.2. Wells Fargo costs
    2.3. On consumers
    2.4. On non-management Wells Fargo employees

3. Later government investigations and fines

    3.1. First hearing
    3.2. Other investigations

4. External reactions[8]

    4.1. Divestitures by major clients
    4.2. Lawsuit by Navajo Nation
    4.3. From the media

---

[8] Sections 4–6 are not produced below but are available on the website.

5. Legacy at Wells Fargo and long-term impact
   5.1. Leadership implications
   5.2. Financial and business implications
   5.3. Workplace culture
   5.4. Rebranding
6. Contemporaneous allegations
7. References

1. Background
1.1 Cross-Selling

Cross-selling, the practice underpinning the fraud, is the concept of attempting to sell multiple products to consumers. For instance, a customer with a checking account might be encouraged to take out a mortgage, or set up credit card or online banking account [3]. Success by retail banks was measured in part by the average number of products held by a customer, and Wells Fargo was long considered the most successful cross-seller [4]. Richard Kovacevich, the former CEO of Norwest Corporation and, later, Wells Fargo, allegedly invented the strategy while at Norwest [5, 6]. In a 1998 interview, Kovacevich likened mortgages, checking and savings accounts, and credit cards offered by the company to more typical consumer products, and revealed that he considered branch employees to be "salespeople", and consumers to be "customers" rather than "clients" [6]. Under Kovacevich, Norwest encouraged branch employees to sell at least eight products, in an initiative known as "Going for Gr-Eight".

1.2 Early Coverage

Wells Fargo's sales culture and cross-selling strategy, and their impact on customers, were documented by the Wall Street Journal as early as 2011 [4]. In 2013, a Los Angeles Times investigation revealed intense pressure on bank managers and individual bankers to produce sales against extremely aggressive and even mathematically impossible [6] quotas [7]. In the Los Angeles Times article, CFO Timothy Sloan was quoted stating he was unaware of any "...overbearing sales culture". Sloan would later replace John Stumpf as CEO.

Under pressure from their supervisors, employees would often open accounts without customer consent. In an article from the American Bankruptcy Institute Journal, Wells Fargo employees reportedly "opened as many as 1.5 million checking and savings accounts, and more than 500,000 credit cards, without customers' authorization [8]." The employees received bonuses for opening new credit cards and checking accounts and enrolling customers in products such as online banking. California Treasurer John Chiang [9] stated: "Wells Fargo's fleecing of its customers...demonstrates, at best, a reckless lack of institutional control and, at worst, a culture which actively promotes wanton greed."

Verschoor explains the findings of the Wells Fargo investigation shows employees also opened online banking services and ordered debit cards without customer consent. "Blame is being placed on the bank's marketing incentive plan, which set extremely high sales goals for employees to cross-sell additional banking products to existing customers whether or not the customers needed or wanted them [9]." Cross-selling products is not a new practice, but if employees feel pushed to sell more than is needed, and are incentivized to do so, there is no surprise that unethical practices began.

In 2010, New York Department of Financial Services (NY DFS) issued the Interagency Guidance on Sound Incentive Compensation Policies. These policies monitor incentive-based compensation structures, and requires that banks appropriately balance risk and rewards, be compatible with effective controls and risk management, and that they are supported by effective corporate governance [10].

1.3 Fraud

Employees were encouraged to order credit cards for pre-approved customers without their consent, and to use their own contact information when filling out requests to prevent customers from discovering the fraud. Employees also created fraudulent checking and savings accounts, a process that sometimes involved the movement of money out of legitimate accounts. The creation of these additional products was made possible in part through a process known as "pinning". By setting the client's PIN to "0000", bankers were able to control client accounts and were able to enroll them in programs such as online banking [11].

Measures taken by employees to satisfy quotas included the enrollment of the homeless in fee-accruing financial products [7]. Reports of unreachable goals and inappropriate conduct by employees to supervisors did not result in changes to expectations [7].

After the Los Angeles Times article, the bank made nominal efforts to reform the company's sales culture [12]. Despite alleged reforms, the bank was fined $185 million in early September 2016 due to the creation of some 1,534,280 unauthorized deposit accounts and 565,433 credit-card accounts between 2011 and 2016 [11]. Later estimates, released in May 2017, placed the number of fraudulent accounts at closer to a total of 3,500,000 [13].

In December 2016, it was revealed that employees of the bank also issued unwanted insurance policies [14]. These included life insurance policies by Prudential Financial and renters' insurance policies by Assurant [14]. Three whistleblowers, Prudential employees, brought the fraud to light. Prudential later fired these employees [15], and announced that it might seek damages from Wells Fargo [16].

1.4 Initial Fines and Broader Coverage

John Stumpf, former CEO of Wells Fargo

Despite the earlier coverage in the Los Angeles Times, the controversy achieved national attention only in September 2016, with the announcement by the Consumer Financial Protection Bureau that the bank would be fined $185 million for the illegal activity. The Consumer Financial Protection Bureau received $100 million, the Los Angeles City Attorney received $50 million, and the Office of the Comptroller of the Currency received the last $35 million [11]. The fines received substantial media coverage in the following days, and triggered attention from further interested parties [17, 18].

1.5 Initial Response from Wells Fargo and Management [edit]

After news of the fines broke, the bank placed ads in newspapers taking responsibility for the controversy [19]. However, the bank rejected the notion that its sales culture led to the actions of employees, stating "...[the fraud] was not part of an intentional strategy" [19]. Stumpf also expressed that he would be willing to accept some personal blame for the problems.

Company executives and spokespeople referred to the problem as an issue with sales practices, rather than the company's broader culture [20].

2. Initial Impact of the Fraud, Legal Action, and Press Coverage

2.1 On Wells Fargo Management

The bank fired approximately 5300 employees between 2011 and 2016 as a result of fraudulent sales [21], and discontinued sales quotas at its individual branches after the announcement of the fine in September 2016 [22]. John Shrewsberry, the bank's CFO, said the bank had invested $50 million to improve oversight in individual branches. Stumpf accepted responsibility for the problems, but in September 2016, when the story broke, indicated he had no plans to resign [22].

Stumpf was subject to a hearing before the Senate Banking Committee on September 21, 2016, in an effort led by Senator Elizabeth Warren [23]. Before the hearing, Stumpf agreed to forgo $41 million in stock options that had not yet vested after being urged to do so by the company's board [24]. Stumpf resigned on October 12, roughly a month after the fines by the CFPB were announced, to be replaced by COO Timothy Sloan [25]. Sloan indicated there had not been internal pressure for Stumpf's resignation, and that he had chosen to do so after "...deciding that the best thing for Wells Fargo to move forward was for him to retire..." [24]. In November 2016, the Office of the Comptroller of the Currency levied further penalties against the bank, removing provisions from the September settlement [26]. As a result of the OCC adding new restrictions, the bank received oversight similar to that used for troubled or insolvent financial institutions [26].

Stumpf received criticism for praising former head of retail banking, Carrie Tolstedt, upon her retirement earlier in 2016, given that the bank had been conducting an investigation into retail banking practices for several years at the time [27]. In April 2017, the bank utilized a clawback provision in Stumpf's contract to take back $28 million of his earnings [28]. Tolstedt was also forced to forfeit earnings, though she denied involvement [28]. Tolstedt was responsible for the pressure placed on middle management to dramatically increase the bank's "cross-sell ratio", a metric for how many accounts each customer had.

The bank experienced decreased profitability in the first quarter after the news of the scandal broke [29]. Payments to law firms and other external advisers resulted in increased expenses [29]. After earnings were reported in January 2017, the bank announced it would close over 400 of its approximately 6000 branches by the end of 2018 [30]. In May 2017, the bank announced that they would cut costs through investment in technology while decreasing reliance on its "sales organization" [31]. The bank also revised up its 2017 efficiency-ratio goal from 60 to 61 [31].

2.2 Wells Fargo Costs

The CFPB fined Wells Fargo $100 million on September 8, 2016 for the "widespread illegal practice of secretly opening unauthorized accounts." The order also required Wells Fargo to pay an estimated $2.5 million in refunds to customers and hire an independent consultant to review its procedures [32].

Wells Fargo Incurred Additional Costs due to Refunds and Lawsuits:

$6.1 million in customer refunds due to inappropriate fees and charges;[33]
$142 million in customer compensation due to a class-action settlement;[33]
$480 million settlement for a shareholder class-action lawsuit;[34] and
$575 million 50-state Attorneys General (AG) settlement for a combination of opening unauthorized accounts and charging for unnecessary auto insurance and mortgage fees [1].

The December 2018 AG settlement announcement indicated that Wells Fargo had already paid $2.3 billion in settlements and consent orders, so its $575 million settlement brought the total to nearly $3 billion [1].

2.3 On Consumers

Approximately 85,000 of the accounts opened incurred fees, totaling $two million [11]. Customers' credit scores were also likely hurt by the fake accounts [35]. The bank was able to prevent customers from pursuing legal action as the opening of an account mandated customers enter into private arbitration with the bank [21].

The bank agreed to settle for $142 million with consumers who had accounts opened in their names without permission in March 2017 [36, 37]. The money repaid fraudulent fees and paid damages to those affected [37].

2.4 On Non-Management Wells Fargo Employees

Wells Fargo employees described intense pressure, with expectations of sales as high as 20 products a day [38]. Others described frequent crying, levels of stress that led to vomiting, and severe panic attacks [12, 38]. At least one employee consumed hand sanitizer to cope with the pressure [12]. Some indicated that calls to the company's ethics hotline were met with either no reaction [38] or resulted in the termination of the employee making the call [39].

During the period of the fraud, some Wells Fargo branch-level bankers encountered difficulty gaining employment at other banks. Banks issue U5 documents to departing employees, a record of any misbehavior or unethical conduct [39]. Wells Fargo issued defamatory U5 documents to bankers who reported branch-level malfeasance, indicating that they had been complicit in the creation of unwanted accounts [39], a practice that received media attention as early as 2011 [40]. There is no regulatory process to appeal a defamatory U5, other than to file a lawsuit against the issuing corporation.

Wells Fargo created a special internal group to rehire employees who had left the bank but were not implicated in the scandal. In April 2017, Timothy Sloan stated that the bank would rehire some 1000 employees who had either been wrongfully terminated or who had quit in protest of fraud [41]. Sloan emphasized that those being rehired would not be those who had participated in the creation of fake accounts [41]. The announcement was made shortly after the news was released that the bank had clawed back income from both Carrie Tolstedt and John Stumpf.

3. Later Government Investigations and Fines
3.1 First Hearing

John Stumpf appeared before the Senate Banking Committee on September 20, 2016. Stumpf delivered prepared testimony and was then questioned. Senators, including Committee Chairman Richard Shelby, asked about whether the bank would clawback income from executives and how the bank would help consumers it harmed [42]. Stumpf gave prepared testimony, but deferred from answering some of the questions, citing lack of expertise concerning the legal ramifications of the fraud [42].

Elizabeth Warren referred to Stumpf's leadership as "gutless" and told him he should resign [42]. Patrick Toomey expressed doubt that the 5300 employees fired by Wells Fargo had acted independently and without orders from supervisors or management [42]. Stumpf was later replaced as CEO by Tim Sloan, and Warren has expressed apprehension about leadership so closely associated with the period during which the fraud occurred. In October 2018, Warren urged the Fed Chairman to restrict any additional growth by Wells Fargo until Sloan is replaced as CEO [43].

3.2 Other Investigations

Prosecutors including Preet Bharara in New York City, and others in San Francisco and North Carolina, opened their own investigations into the fraud [44]. The Securities and Exchange Commission opened its own investigation into the bank in November 2016 [45].

Maxine Waters, chair of the House Financial Services Committee, announced her intention to investigate the bank further in early 2019. She previously released a report about the bank's malpractice, and had called for the government to dismantle the bank [46, 47]. Former Wells Fargo Chairwoman Elizabeth "Betsy" Duke and James Quigley resigned on March 9, 2020 three days before House Committee on Financial Services hearings on the fraud scandal [48].

The Department of Justice and the Securities and Exchange Commission reached a settlement with the bank in February 2020 for a total fine of US$3 billion to address the bank's criminal and civil violations. However, this settlement does not cover any future litigation against any individual employee of the bank [49].

In November 2020, the SEC filed civil charges against two former senior executives, Stumpf and Tolstead, accusing them of misrepresentation to investors of key performance metrics [50]....

References

1. Jump up to: a b c "Attorney General Shapiro Announces $575 Million 50-State Settlement with Wells Fargo Bank for Opening Unauthorized Accounts and Charging Consumers for Unnecessary Auto Insurance, Mortgage Fees".
2. Eisen, Dave Michaels and Ben (13 November 2020). "Wells Fargo Ex-CEO Settles SEC Claims, Former Consumer-Unit Head Faces Fraud Case". The Wall Street Journal. The Wall Street Journal. Retrieved 3 December 2020.

3. Kolhatkar, Sheelah (21 September 2016). "Elizabeth Warren and the Wells Fargo Scandal". The New Yorker. Retrieved 6 May 2017.
4. Jump up to: a b Smith, Randall (28 February 2011). "Copying Wells Fargo, Banks Try Hard Sell". The Wall Street Journal. Retrieved 6 May 2017.
5. Davidson, Adam (12 September 2016). "How Regulation Failed with Wells Fargo". The New Yorker. Retrieved 6 May 2017.
6. Jump up to: a b c McLean, Bethany (31 May 2017). "How Wells Fargo's Cutthroat Corporate Culture Allegedly Drove Bankers to Fraud". Vanity Fair. Retrieved 12 June 2017.
7. Jump up to: a b c Reckard, E. Scott (21 December 2013). "Wells Fargo's pressure-cooker sales culture comes at a cost". The Los Angeles Times. Retrieved 6 May 2017.
8. Rules amendments effective in December; Wells Fargo under fire for sales practices. (2016). American Bankruptcy Institute Journal, 35(10), 8–9.
9. Jump up to: a b Verschoor, C. (2016). Lessons from the Wells Fargo scandal. Strategic Finance, 98(5), 19–20.
10. Biben, M. L., Kini, S. M., Luigs, D. A., Lyons, G. J., & Alspector, L. (2016). Banking regulators focus on sales practices. Banking & Financial Services Policy Report, 35(11), 15–17.
11. Jump up to: a b c d Levine, Matt (9 September 2016). "Wells Fargo Opened a Couple Million Fake Accounts". Bloomberg.com. Bloomberg. Retrieved 6 May 2017.
12. Jump up to: a b c Cowley, Stacy (20 October 2016). "Voices From Wells Fargo: 'I Thought I Was Having a Heart Attack'". The New York Times. Retrieved 10 May 2017.
13. Keller, Laura (12 May 2017). "Wells Fargo's Fake Accounts Grow to 3.5 Million in Suit". Bloomberg.com. Bloomberg. Retrieved 13 May 2017.
14. Jump up to: a b Cowley, Stacy (12 December 2016). "Prudential Suspends Sales of Its Life Policies by Wells Fargo". The New York Times. Retrieved 16 May 2017.
15. Voreacos, David (26 January 2017). "Prudential Says Trio in Whistle-Blower Case Fired for Misconduct". Bloomberg.com. Bloomberg. Retrieved 16 May 2017.
16. Chiglinsky, Katherine (22 February 2017). "Prudential May Press Wells Fargo as Account Fallout Spreads". Bloomberg.com. Bloomberg. Retrieved 16 May 2017.
17. Levine, Wells Fargo Opened a Couple Million Fake Accounts.
18. Corkery, Michael (8 September 2016). "Wells Fargo Fined $185 Million for Fraudulently Opening Accounts". The New York Times. Retrieved 16 May 2017.
19. Jump up to: a b Corkery, Michael (9 September 2016). "Wells Fargo Offers Regrets, but Doesn't Admit Misconduct". The New York Times. Retrieved 6 May 2017.

20. Agnes, Melissa (12 September 2016). "Wells Fargo Is Not Addressing The Right Questions Within Their Crisis Response". Fortune. Retrieved 16 May 2017.
21. Jump up to: a b Olen, Helaine (8 September 2016). "Wells Fargo Must Pay $185 Million After Opening Customer Accounts Without Asking. That's Not Enough". Slate. Retrieved 6 May 2017.
22. Jump up to: a b Puzzanghera, Jim (13 September 2016). "Wells Fargo is eliminating retail sales goals after settlement over aggressive tactics". The Wall Street Journal. Retrieved 6 May 2017.
23. Phillips, Matt (21 September 2016). "You should resign". Vice. Retrieved 13 May 2017.
24. Jump up to: a b Faux, Zeke (13 October 2016). "Wells Fargo CEO Stumpf Quits in Fallout From Fake Accounts". Bloomberg.com. Bloomberg. Retrieved 14 May 2017.
25. Gonzales, Richard (12 October 2016). "Wells Fargo CEO John Stumpf Resigns Amid Scandal". NPR. Retrieved 14 May 2017.
26. Jump up to: a b Koren, James Rufus (21 September 2016). "Wells Fargo hit with new sanctions following fake-accounts scandal". The New Yorker. Retrieved 6 May 2017.
27. Maxfield, John (13 September 2016). "Why Is Wells Fargo CEO John Stumpf Making These 3 Major Mistakes?". The Motley Fool. Retrieved 16 May 2017.
28. Jump up to: a b Keller, Laura (10 April 2017). "Wells Fargo Board Claws Back $28 Million More From Ex-CEO". Bloomberg. Retrieved 14 May 2017.
29. Jump up to: a b Gray, Alistair (9 January 2017). "Wells Fargo counts cost of sham accounts scandal". The Financial Times. Retrieved 13 February 2019.
30. Keller, Laura (13 January 2017). "Wells Fargo Plans to Close More Than 400 Branches Through 2018". Bloomberg. Retrieved 14 May 2017.
31. Jump up to: a b Keller, Laura (11 May 2017). "Wells Fargo Doubles Cost Slashing as Scandal Spurs Tech Push". Bloomberg. Retrieved 14 May 2017.
32. "Consumer Financial Protection Bureau Fines Wells Fargo $100 Million for Widespread Illegal Practice of Secretly Opening Unauthorized Accounts". Consumer Financial Protection Bureau.

3.5 NatWest

3.5.1 Text from the US Department of Justice[9]

FOR IMMEDIATE RELEASE
Tuesday, December 21, 2021

NatWest Markets Pleads Guilty to Fraud in U.S. Treasury Markets
Global Banking and Financial Services Firm to Pay $35 Million in Fine, Restitution, and Forfeiture

NatWest Markets Plc (NatWest), a London, U.K.-based global banking and financial services firm, pleaded guilty today to various fraud schemes in the markets for U.S. Treasury securities and futures contracts.

NatWest pleaded guilty to one count of wire fraud and one count of securities fraud in connection with a criminal information filed today in the District of Connecticut. U.S. District Judge Omar A. Williams accepted the pleas and sentenced NatWest to pay approximately $35 million in a criminal fine, restitution, and forfeiture. NatWest also will serve three years of probation and will agree to the imposition of an independent compliance monitor.

"As we have previously warned, there will be serious consequences for a company that breaches the terms of an agreement with the government. Today's guilty plea by NatWest and the associated penalty show exactly that," said Deputy Attorney General Lisa O. Monaco. "Company executives should realize that investment in compliance programs can avoid situations like this, and take action accordingly."

"NatWest is a repeat offender," said Acting U.S. Attorney Leonard C Boyle for the District of Connecticut. "In this instance, a criminal conviction was an appropriate penalty, given the conduct of NatWest's supervisors, its compliance deficiencies, and its decision not to take the steps required to fulfill its agreement with this office that resolved a prior securities fraud scheme."

"NatWest's schemes were egregious—spanning multiple years and countries—and the sentencing today reflects that," said Deputy Director Paul M. Abbate of the FBI. "Let this case be an example that the FBI will not tolerate companies that fraudulently interfere in U.S. markets for their own gain. The FBI and our law enforcement partners are dedicated to protecting the integrity of our financial institutions and the Americans who use them."

"For over six years, NatWest engaged in separate fraud schemes to manipulate the market and unlawfully enrich themselves," said Inspector in Charge Eric Shen of the U.S. Postal Inspection Service's Criminal Investigations Group. "Those who engage in this type of abuse of power should know they cannot escape detection and will be held accountable for their actions. The U.S. Postal Inspection Service is

---

[9] https://www.justice.gov/opa/pr/natwest-markets-pleads-guilty-fraud-us-treasury-markets

proud to work alongside our fellow law enforcement partners to protect the integrity of the financial marketplace and it's participants."

According to court documents and NatWest admissions, between January 2008 and May 2014, NatWest traders in London and Stamford, Connecticut, independently engaged in schemes to defraud in connection with the purchase and sale of U.S. Treasury futures contracts. Separately, in 2018, two other traders employed at NatWest's Singapore branch engaged in a fraud scheme in connection with the purchase and sale of U.S. Treasury securities in the secondary (cash) market.

In each scheme, NatWest traders engaged in "spoofing" by placing orders with the intent to cancel those orders before execution, attempting to profit by deceiving other market participants by injecting false and misleading information regarding the existence of genuine supply and demand in the market. The spoof orders were designed to artificially push up or down the prevailing market price so that the NatWest traders could trade more profitably as a result of these schemes. In some instances, one of the NatWest traders took advantage of the close correlation between U.S. Treasury securities and U.S. Treasury futures contracts and engaged in cross-market manipulation by placing spoof orders in the futures market in order to profit from trading in the cash market.

The 2018 securities fraud scheme constituted a material breach of the Oct. 25, 2017 Non-Prosecution Agreement between the U.S. Attorney's Office for the District of Connecticut and NatWest's U.S. broker-dealer subsidiary, NatWest Markets Securities Inc. (formerly RBS Securities Inc.), and occurred while NatWest (formerly The Royal Bank of Scotland Plc) was on probation following its May 20, 2015 guilty plea and Jan. 5, 2017 sentencing for conspiring to manipulate the foreign currency exchange market.

A number of relevant considerations contributed to the department's criminal resolution with NatWest, including the nature and seriousness of the offense, NatWest's substantial prior history of other criminal conduct and civil and regulatory actions against it, its breach of a prior agreement, and the state of NatWest's compliance program.

The FBI and U.S. Postal Inspection Service investigated this matter. . . .

3.6 Credit Suisse (Mozambique)

3.6.1 Text from US DoJ Website (February 5, 2022)[10]

FOR IMMEDIATE RELEASE
Tuesday, October 19, 2021

---

[10] Link: https://www.justice.gov/opa/pr/credit-suisse-resolves-fraudulent-mozambique-loan-case-547-million-coordinated-global

3.6 Credit Suisse (Mozambique)

Credit Suisse Resolves Fraudulent Mozambique Loan Case in $547 Million Coordinated Global Resolution

Credit Suisse Securities (Europe) Limited Pleads Guilty to Conspiracy to Commit Wire Fraud

Credit Suisse Group AG, a global financial institution headquartered in Switzerland, and Credit Suisse Securities (Europe) Limited (CSSEL), its subsidiary in the United Kingdom (together, Credit Suisse), have admitted to defrauding U.S. and international investors in the financing of an $850 million loan for a tuna fishing project in Mozambique, and have been assessed more than $547 million in penalties, fines, and disgorgement as part of coordinated resolutions with criminal and civil authorities in the United States and the United Kingdom. After taking account of crediting by the department of the other resolutions, Credit Suisse will pay approximately $475 million to authorities in the United States and the United Kingdom, as well as restitution to victims in an amount to be determined by the court.

"Credit Suisse Group AG, through its U.K. subsidiary CSSEL, defrauded U.S. and international investors in connection with a lending project in Mozambique," said Assistant Attorney General Kenneth A. Polite Jr. of the Justice Department's Criminal Division. "Among other things, Credit Suisse Group AG, CSSEL, and their co-conspirators deceived investors by hiding information about the risk that loan proceeds were used for illegal purposes in connection with the restructuring of the loan. Today's coordinated resolution with the U.S. Securities and Exchange Commission and the Financial Conduct Authority in the United Kingdom shows that the department will not tolerate fraud by international financial institutions and is committed to working in parallel to domestic and foreign authorities to use all tools at our disposal to hold corporate wrongdoers accountable."

According to court documents filed today in the U.S. District Court for the Eastern District of New York and statements made during the proceeding, Credit Suisse Group AG entered into a three-year deferred prosecution agreement with the department in connection with a criminal information charging Credit Suisse Group AG with conspiracy to commit wire fraud, and CSSEL pleaded guilty to a one-count criminal information charging it with conspiracy to commit wire fraud.

This resolution follows the prior entry of guilty pleas by three CSSEL bankers. In July 2019, Andrew Pearse, a former managing director of CSSEL, pleaded guilty to conspiracy to commit wire fraud. In September 2019, Surjan Singh, a former managing director of CSSEL, pleaded guilty to conspiracy to commit money laundering, and in May 2019, Detelina Subeva, a former vice president of CSSEL, also pleaded guilty to conspiracy to commit money laundering.

"Over the course of several years, Credit Suisse, through its subsidiary in the United Kingdom, engaged in a global criminal conspiracy to defraud investors, including investors in the United States, by failing to disclose material information to investors, including millions of dollars in kickbacks to its bankers and a high risk of corruption, in connection with an $850 million fraudulent loan to a Mozambique state-owned entity," said U.S. Attorney Breon Peace for the Eastern District of New York. "This coordinated global resolution demonstrates this Office's commitment to working across borders with our global law enforcement partners to root out abuse and fraud by financial institutions in order to protect investors here in the United States."

According to Credit Suisse's admissions and court documents, between 2013 and March 2017, Credit Suisse, through CSSEL, and co-conspirators used U.S. wires and the U.S. financial system to defraud investors in securities related to a Mozambican state-owned entity, Empresa Moçambicana de Atum S.A. (EMATUM), which Mozambique created to develop a state-owned tuna fishing project. Credit Suisse, through its employees and agents, conspired to and did defraud investors and potential investors in EMATUM by making numerous material misrepresentations and omissions relating to, among other things, (1) the use of loan proceeds; (2) kickback payments to CSSEL bankers and the risk of bribes to Mozambican officials; and (3) the existence and maturity dates of debt owed by Mozambique, including another loan that Credit Suisse arranged to a Mozambique state-owned entity (ProIndicus) and a different loan another bank arranged with Credit Suisse's knowledge. Credit Suisse represented to investors that the loan proceeds would only be used for the tuna fishing project. Instead, co-conspirators diverted loan proceeds obtained from investors. Specifically, a contractor that supplied boats and equipment for EMATUM and that received the loan proceeds from Credit Suisse paid kickbacks of approximately $50 million to CSSEL bankers and bribes totaling approximately $150 million to Mozambican government officials.

Credit Suisse also admitted that it identified significant red flags prior to and during the EMATUM financing. For example, Credit Suisse had learned of significant corruption and bribery concerns associated with the contractor. In addition, in or about 2015, Credit Suisse became aware that EMATUM had encountered problems servicing the loan, raising the risk of default. Credit Suisse agreed to arrange the restructuring and exchange of the original EMATUM security into a bond with a longer maturity date. During the restructuring, Credit Suisse employees raised concerns about corruption allegations made in the press and disparities in the use of loan proceeds. To address these concerns, Credit Suisse retained two independent industry experts to conduct a market valuation of the tuna fishing boats and other goods the contractor provided for the EMATUM project. Credit Suisse knew that the experts identified a shortfall of between $265 million and $394 million between the funds raised for the EMATUM loan and the fair market value of the boats and accompanying infrastructure and training the contractor sold to EMATUM. Credit Suisse did not disclose this material information to investors during the restructuring and the exchange. Aspects of Credit Suisse's fraudulent conduct were revealed beginning in April 2016, causing the price of the EMATUM securities to drop and resulting in losses to investors.

Under the terms of its agreements, Credit Suisse's penalty is approximately $247.5 million. After crediting by the department for payments to other authorities, Credit Suisse will pay approximately $175.5 million to the United States. Credit Suisse has also agreed to a methodology to calculate proximate fraud loss for victims of its criminal conduct; the amount of restitution payable to victims will be determined at a future proceeding. Credit Suisse also reached separate parallel resolutions with the U.S. Securities and Exchange Commission (SEC) and the United

Kingdom's Financial Conduct Authority (FCA). Switzerland's Financial Market Supervisory Authority (FINMA) also engaged in an enforcement action, which includes the appointment of an independent third-party to review the implementation and effectiveness of compliance measures for business conducted in financially weak and high-risk countries, subject to FINMA's administrative process.

The department reached this resolution with Credit Suisse based on several factors, including its failure to voluntarily disclose the conduct to the department and the nature and seriousness of the offense, which included the involvement of bankers within CSSEL. Credit Suisse received only partial credit for its cooperation with the department's investigation because it significantly delayed producing relevant evidence. Accordingly, the total penalty reflects a 15% reduction off the bottom of the applicable U.S. Sentencing Guidelines range. Credit Suisse has also agreed to continue to cooperate with the department, to enhance its compliance program and internal controls, and to provide enhanced reporting to the department on the Credit Suisse's remediation and compliance program. Among other things, the enhanced reporting provisions require Credit Suisse to meet with the department at least quarterly and to submit yearly reports regarding the status of its remediation efforts, the results of its testing of its compliance program, and its proposals to ensure that its compliance program is reasonably designed, implemented, and enforced so that it is effective in deterring and detecting violations of fraud, money laundering, the Foreign Corrupt Practices Act, and other applicable anti-corruption laws.

The FBI is investigating the case.

Trial Attorneys Margaret A. Moeser of the Criminal Division's Money Laundering and Asset Recovery Section (MLARS), David M. Fuhr and Katherine Nielsen of the Criminal Division's Fraud Section, and Assistant U.S. Attorney Hiral D. Mehta of the U.S. Attorney's Office for the Eastern District of New York are prosecuting the case. The Criminal Division's Office of International Affairs provided critical assistance in this case.

The department appreciates the significant assistance provided by the SEC and the FCA. The department also expresses its appreciation for the assistance provided by authorities in Switzerland and the United Kingdom in responding to Mutual Legal Assistance requests.

MLARS' Bank Integrity Unit investigates and prosecutes banks and other financial institutions, including their officers, managers, and employees, whose actions threaten the integrity of the individual institution or the wider financial system...

3.7 Deutsche Bank AG

Deutsche Bank have been involved in a number of issues including:

3,7.1 Text from Wikipedia[11] (February 5, 2022)

Fine for Business with Jeffrey Epstein, 2020
Deutsche Bank lent money and traded currencies for the well-known sex offender Jeffrey Epstein up to May 2019, long after Epstein's 2008 guilty plea in Florida to soliciting prostitution from underage girls, according to news reports [165–167]. Epstein and his businesses had dozens of accounts through the private-banking division [168, 169]. From 2013 to 2018, "Epstein, his related entities and his associates" had opened over forty accounts with Deutsche Bank [170].

According to The New York Times, Deutsche Bank managers overruled compliance officers who raised concerns about Epstein's reputation [166].

The bank found suspicious transactions in which Epstein moved money out of the United States, The Times reported [168].

On 7 July 2020, the New York Department of Financial Services (DFS) imposed a $150 million penalty on Deutsche Bank, in connection with Epstein. The bank had "ignored red flags on Epstein" [170, 171].

Criminal Cartel Charges in Australia, 2018
On 1 June 2018, the Australian Competition & Consumer Commission announced that criminal cartel charges were laid by the Commonwealth Director of Public Prosecutions against ANZ Bank, its group treasurer Rick Moscati, along with Deutsche Bank, Citigroup, and a number of individuals [172, 173]. The case was going to trial in December 2020 [174].

Involvement in Danske Bank Money-Laundering Scandal, 2018
On 19 November 2018, a whistleblower of the Danske Bank money laundering scandal stated that a large European bank was involved in helping Danske process $150 billion in suspect funds [175]. Although the whistleblower, Howard Wilkinson, did not name Deutsche Bank directly, another inside source claimed the institute in question was Deutsche Bank's U.S. unit [176]. In 2020 it became known that the U.S. arm of Deutsche Bank processed more than $150 billion of the $230 billion dirty money through New York, for which it was fined 150 million $. After a raid in 2019, Frankfurt-based prosecutors imposed a fine of $15.8 million in 2020 for DB's failure on more than 600 occasions to promptly report suspicious transactions [177].

---

[11] Link: https://en.wikipedia.org/wiki/Deutsche_Bank#Criminal_cartel_charges_in_Australia,_2018

3.7 Deutsche Bank AG

Improper Handling of ADRs, 2018

On 20 July 2018, Deutsche Bank agreed to pay nearly $75 million to settle charges of improper handling of "pre-released" American depositary receipt (ADRs) under investigation of the U.S. Securities and Exchange Commission (SEC). Deutsche Bank didn't admit or deny the investigation findings but agreed to pay disgorgement of more than $44.4 million in ill-gotten gains plus $6.6 million in prejudgment interest and a penalty of $22.2 million [178, 179].

Malaysian 1MDB Fund, 2019-Today

In July 2019 U.S. prosecutors investigated Deutsche Bank's role in a multibillion-dollar fraud scandal involving the 1Malaysia Development Berhad, or 1MDB [180, 181]. Deutsche Bank helped raise $1.2 billion for the 1MDB in 2014 [181]. As of May 2021 Malaysia sued Deutsche Bank to recover billions in alleged losses from a corruption scandal at the fund [182].

Commodities Trading, Bribery Fine, 2021

In January 2021, Deutsche Bank agreed to pay a U.S. fine of more than $130 million for a scheme to conceal bribes to foreign officials in countries such as Saudi Arabia and China, and the city of Abu Dhabi, between 2008 and 2017 and a commodities case where it spoofed precious metals futures [183–185].

References

165. David Enrich [@davidenrich] (10 July 2019). "Exclusive: @DeutscheBank had an extensive relationship with Jeffrey Epstein, lending him money and providing trading services — up until May 2019, when the bank cut him off. www.nytimes.com/2019/07/10/business/jeffrey-epstein-net-worth.html" (Tweet). Retrieved 11 July 2019 – via Twitter.
166. Jump up to: a b Stewart, James B.; Goldstein, Matthew; Kelly, Kate; Enrich, David (10 July 2019). "Jeffrey Epstein's 'Infinite Means' May Be a Mirage". The New York Times. ISSN 0362-4331. Retrieved 11 July 2019.
167. Metcalf, Tom; Robinson, Matt (10 July 2019). "Deutsche Bank ended its relationship with Jeffrey Epstein this year". The Boston Globe. Retrieved 11 July 2019.
168. Jump up to: a b Enrich, David; Becker, Jo (23 July 2019). "Jeffrey Epstein Moved Money Overseas in Transactions His Bank Flagged to U.S." The New York Times. ISSN 0362-4331. Retrieved 24 July 2019.
169. Hong, Jenny Strasburg and Nicole. "Jeffrey Epstein's Financial Trail Goes Through Deutsche Bank". WSJ. Retrieved 24 July 2019.
170. Jump up to: a b Goldstein, Matthew (7 July 2020). "Deutsche Bank Settles Over Ignored Red Flags on Jeffrey Epstein". The New York Times. ISSN 0362-4331. Retrieved 7 July 2020.
171. "Superintendent Lacewell Announces DFS Imposes $150 Million Penalty on Deutsche Bank in Connection with Bank's Relationship with Jeffrey Epstein and Correspondent Relationships with Danske Estonia And FBME Bank". Department of Financial Services (Press release). 7 July 2020. Retrieved 7 July 2020.

172. "Update: Criminal cartel charges to be laid against Deutsche Bank". Australian Competition & Consumer Commission. 1 June 2018. Retrieved 1 June 2018.
173. "Update: Criminal cartel charges to be laid against Citigroup". Australian Competition & Consumer Commission. 1 June 2018. Retrieved 4 August 2018.
174. "Criminal cartel case against ANZ, investment banks heading to trial". ABC News. 8 December 2020. Retrieved 13 October 2021.
175. Jensen, Teis; Gronholt-Pedersen, Jacob (19 November 2018). "Danske whistleblower says big European bank handled $150 billion in..." Reuters. Archived from the original on 17 December 2018. Retrieved 20 November 2018.
176. Arons, Steven; Barnert, Jan-Patrick; Comfort, Nicholas (20 November 2018). "Deutsche Bank Hits Record Low on New Worry Over Danske Role". bloomberg.com. Archived from the original on 29 November 2018. Retrieved 20 November 2018.
177. Simon Bowers (16 October 2020). "German prosecutors drop probe into Deutsche Bank ties to Estonian dirty money scandal - ICIJ". Retrieved 13 October 2021.
178. SEC.gov | Deutsche Bank to Pay Nearly $75 Million for Improper Handling of ADRs". sec.gov. Retrieved 8 March 2019.
179. "Deutsche to pay $75 million to settle ADRs abuses case, U.S. SEC says". Reuters. 20 July 2018. Retrieved 8 March 2019.
180. Strasburg, Aruna Viswanatha, Bradley Hope and Jenny. "U.S. Investigating Deutsche Bank's Dealings With Malaysian Fund 1MDB". Wall Street Journal. Retrieved 11 July 2019.
181. Jump up to: a b Flitter, Emily (10 July 2019). "Deutsche Bank Caught Up in Scandal Over Malaysian 1MDB Fund". The New York Times. ISSN 0362–4331. Retrieved 11 July 2019.
182. Reuters (10 May 2021). "Malaysia sues Deutsche Bank, JP Morgan, Coutts over 1MDB". Reuters. Retrieved 13 October 2021.
183. Wolf, Brett (13 January 2021). "Deutsche Bank reaches $130 million settlement over U.S. bribery, commodities". Reuters. Retrieved 24 February 2021.
184. "Deutsche Bank Agrees to Pay over $130 Million to Resolve Foreign Corrupt Practices Act and Fraud Case". www.justice.gov. 8 January 2021. Retrieved 24 February 2021.
185. Welle (www.dw.com), Deutsche Welle (8 January 2021). "Deutsche Bank handed $124 million in bribery fines by US court". DW.COM. Retrieved 24 February 2021.

3.8 BCCI

3.8.1 Text from Wikipedia[12] *(February 5, 2022)*

Bank of Credit and Commerce International

The Bank of Credit and Commerce International (BCCI) was an international bank founded in 1972 by Agha Hasan Abedi, a Pakistani financier [1]. The bank was registered in Luxembourg with head offices in Karachi and London. A decade after opening, BCCI had over 400 branches in 78 countries and assets in excess of US$20 billion, making it the seventh largest private bank in the world [2, 3].

BCCI came under the scrutiny of financial regulators and intelligence agencies in the 1980s, due to concerns that it was poorly regulated. Subsequent investigations revealed that it was involved in massive money laundering and other financial crimes, and had illegally gained the controlling interest in a major American bank. BCCI became the focus of a massive regulatory battle in 1991, and, on 5 July of that year, customs and bank regulators in seven countries raided and locked down records of its branch offices [4] during Operation C-Chase [5–7].

Investigators in the United States and the UK determined that BCCI had been "set up deliberately to avoid centralized regulatory review, and operated extensively in bank secrecy jurisdictions. Its affairs were extraordinarily complex. Its officers were sophisticated international bankers whose apparent objective was to keep their affairs secret, to commit fraud on a massive scale, and to avoid detection" [8].

The liquidators, Deloitte & Touche, filed a lawsuit against the bank's auditors, Price Waterhouse and Ernst & Young, which was settled for $175 million in 1998. By 2013, Deloitte & Touche claimed to have recovered about 75% of the creditors' lost money [9].

Contents
1. History
2. Lending practices
3. Money laundering
4. Investigations begin
5. The Sandstorm report
6. Forced closure
7. American inquiries and legal actions
8. British inquiry and litigation
9. Litigation elsewhere
10. Former directors
11. Legal cases involving BCCI
12. See also
13. References

---

[12] Link: https://en.wikipedia.org/wiki/Bank_of_Credit_and_Commerce_International

14. Bibliography
15. External links

1. History

BCCI's founder, Agha Hasan Abedi, established the bank in 1972. Abedi, a prolific banker, had previously set up the United Bank Limited in Pakistan in 1959 sponsored by Saigols. Preceding the nationalization of the United Bank in 1974, he sought to create a new supranational banking entity. BCCI was created with capital of which 25% was from the Bank of America and the remaining 75% from Sheikh Zayed bin Sultan Al Nahyan, the ruler of Abu Dhabi in the United Arab Emirates.

BCCI expanded rapidly in the 1970s, pursuing long-term asset growth over profits, seeking high-net-worth individuals and regular large deposits. The company itself divided into BCCI Holdings with the bank under that splitting into BCCI SA (Luxembourg) and BCCI Overseas (Grand Cayman). BCCI also acquired parallel banks through acquisitions: buying the Banque de Commerce et Placements (BCP) of Geneva in 1976, and creating KIFCO (Kuwait International Finance Company), Credit & Finance Corporation Ltd., and a series of Cayman-based companies held together as ICIC (International Credit and Investment Company Overseas, International Credit and Commerce [Overseas], etc.). Overall, BCCI expanded from 19 branches in five countries in 1973 to 27 branches in 1974 and 108 branches by 1976, with assets growing from $200 million to $1.6 billion [10]. This growth caused extensive underlying capital problems. The Guardian alleged that BCCI was using cash from deposits to fund operating expenses, rather than making investments. Investigative journalist and author Joseph J. Trento has argued that the bank's transformation was guided by the head of Saudi intelligence with a view to enabling it to finance covert American intelligence operations at a time, in the aftermath of Watergate, when the American intelligence agencies were defending themselves from investigations by domestic authorities [11].

BCCI entered the African markets in 1979, and Asia in the early 1980s. BCCI was among the first foreign banks awarded a license to operate in the Chinese Shenzhen Special Economic Zone which bore testament to Agha Hasan Abedi's public relations skills, a feat that had yet to be achieved by the likes of Citicorp and JP Morgan. Some of China's largest state banks were depositors in BCCI's Shenzhen branch [12, 13].

There was rigid compartmentalization; the 248 managers and general managers reported directly to Abedi and the CEO Swaleh Naqvi. It was structured in such a way that no single country had overall regulatory supervision over it so as not to hinder potential growth and expansion opportunities [14]. Its two holding companies were based in Luxembourg and the Cayman Islands—two jurisdictions where banking regulation was notoriously weak. It was also not regulated by a country that had a central bank. On several occasions, the Office of the Comptroller of the Currency, a bureau within the U.S. Department of the Treasury, told the Federal Reserve in no uncertain terms that BCCI must not be allowed to buy any American bank because it was poorly regulated.

3.8 BCCI

By 1980, BCCI was reported to have assets of over $4 billion with over 150 branches in 46 countries. Bank of America was "bewildered" by BCCI and reduced its holding in 1980, and the company came to be held by a number of groups, with International Credit and Investment Corp ('ICIC') owning 70% [15]. By 1989, ICIC's shareholding was reduced to 11% with Abu Dhabi groups holding almost 40%. However, large numbers of shares were held by BCCI nominees.

In 1982, 15 Middle Eastern investors bought Financial General Bankshares, a large bank holding company headquartered in Washington, D.C. All the investors were BCCI clients, but the Fed received assurances that BCCI would be in no way involved in the management of the company, which was renamed First American Bankshares. To alleviate regulators' concerns, Clark Clifford, an adviser to five presidents, was named First American's chairman. Clifford headed a board composed of himself and several other distinguished American citizens, including former United States Senator Stuart Symington. In truth, BCCI had been involved in the purchase of FGB/First American from the beginning. Abedi had been approached about buying it as early as 1977, but by this time BCCI's reputation in the United States was so poor that it could not hope to buy an American bank on its own (as mentioned above, the OCC was adamantly opposed to BCCI being allowed to buy its way into the American banking industry). Rather, it used the First American investors as nominees. Moreover, Clifford's law firm was retained as general counsel, and also handled most of BCCI's American legal work. BCCI was also heavily involved in First American personnel matters. The relationship between the two was so close that rumors spread BCCI was the real owner of First American.

BCCI had an unusual annual auditing system: Price Waterhouse were the accountants for BCCI Overseas, while Ernst & Young audited BCCI and BCCI Holdings (London and Luxembourg). Other companies such as KIFCO and ICIC were audited by neither. In October 1985, the Bank of England and the Monetary Institute of Luxembourg (Luxembourg's bank regulator) ordered BCCI to change to a single accountant, alarmed at reported BCCI losses on the commodities and financial markets. Price Waterhouse became the banks sole accountant in 1987.

In 1990, a Price Waterhouse audit of BCCI revealed an unaccountable loss of hundreds of millions of dollars. The bank approached Sheikh Zayed bin Sultan Al Nahyan, who made good the loss in exchange for an increased shareholding of 78%. Much of BCCI's documentation was then transferred to Abu Dhabi. The audit also revealed numerous irregularities. Most seriously, BCCI had made a staggering $1.48 billion worth of loans to its own shareholders, who used BCCI stock as collateral.

The audit also confirmed what many Americans who watched BCCI long suspected—that BCCI secretly (and illegally) owned First American. When the Fed cleared the group of Arab investors to buy First American, it did so on condition that they supplement their personal funds with money borrowed from banks with no connection to BCCI. Contrary to that agreement, several stockholders had borrowed heavily from BCCI. Even more seriously, they pledged their First American stock as collateral. When they failed to make interest payments, BCCI took control of the shares. It was later estimated that in this manner, BCCI had ended up with 60% or more of First American's stock.

Despite these problems, Price Waterhouse signed BCCI's 1989 annual report, largely due to Zayed's firm commitment to propping up the bank. Abedi was succeeded by Swaleh Naqvi as the bank's chief, who, in the aftermath following controversy over BCCI, was replaced by Zafar Iqbal Chaudhry in the late 1990s.

2. Lending Practices

BCCI contended that its growth was fueled by the increasingly large number of deposits by oil-rich states that owned stock in the bank as well as by sovereign developing nations. However, this claim failed to mollify the regulators. For example, the Bank of England ordered BCCI to cap its branch network in the United Kingdom at 45 branches [16].

There was particular concern over BCCI's loan portfolio, because of its roots in areas where modern banking was still an alien concept. For instance, a large number of its customers were devout Muslims who believed charging interest on loans—a major pillar of modern banking—was riba, or usury. In many third-world countries, a person's financial standing did not matter as much as his relationship with his banker. One particularly notable example is the Gokal family, a prominent family of shipping magnates. The three Gokal brothers, Abbas, Mustafa and Murtaza, were owners of the Gulf Group. They had a relationship with Abedi dating back to his days at United Bank. Abedi personally handled their loans, with little regard for details such as loan documents or creditworthiness. At one point, BCCI's loans to the Gokal companies were equivalent to US$1.2 billion, three times the bank's capital [17]. The case of Nazmu Virani the UK based property tycoon also borrow £500 million unsecured which was widely reported [18]. Longstanding banking practice dictates that a bank not lend more than 10% of its capital to a single customer [16].

3. Money Laundering

In addition to violations of lending laws, BCCI was also accused of opening accounts or laundering money for figures such as Saddam Hussein, Manuel Noriega, Hussain Muhammad Ershad, and Samuel Doe [16], and for criminal organizations such as the Medellin Cartel and Abu Nidal [19]. Police and intelligence experts nicknamed BCCI the "Bank of Crooks and Criminals International" for its penchant for catering to customers who dealt in arms, drugs, and hot money [20]. Both Syed A. Hussain (b. 1960 or 1961) and Amjad Awan, (b. 1946 or 1947) a Pakistani banker that headed the Panamanian branch of BCCI in the early 1980s, assisted Noriega with Noriega's accounts at BCCI [21, 22].

William von Raab, a former U.S. Commissioner of Customs, also told the Kerry Committee that the U.S. Central Intelligence Agency held "several" accounts at BCCI. According to a 1991 article in Time magazine, the National Security Council also had accounts at BCCI, which were used for a variety of covert operations, including transfers of money and weapons during the Iran–Contra affair [23].

4. Investigations Begin

BCCI's demise began in 1986, when a U.S. Customs undercover operation led by Special Agent Robert Mazur infiltrated the bank's private client division at Tampa,

Florida, and uncovered their active role soliciting deposits from drug traffickers and money launderers [24]. This two-year undercover operation concluded in 1988 with a fake wedding that was attended by BCCI officers and drug dealers from around the world, who had established a personal friendship and working relationship with undercover agent Mazur. At the same time he was dealing undercover with BCCI executives, Mazur used his undercover operation to establish a relationship with the hierarchy of the Medellin Cartel as one of their sources for laundering drug proceeds. Mazur's and others' roles in the sting operation were highlighted in the film The Infiltrator (2016).

In 1988, the bank was implicated for being the center of a major money laundering scheme. After a six-month trial, BCCI, under immense pressure from U.-S. authorities, pleaded guilty in 1990, but only on the grounds of respondeat superior. While federal regulators took no action, Florida regulators forced BCCI to pull out of the state [16].

In 1990, U.S. Senator Orrin Hatch presented an impassioned defense of the bank in a speech on the Senate floor. He and his aide, Michael Pillsbury, were involved in efforts to counter the negative publicity that surrounded the bank, and Hatch solicited the bank to approve a $ten million loan to a close friend, Monzer Hourani [25].

5. The Sandstorm Report

In March 1991, the Bank of England asked Price Waterhouse to carry out an inquiry. On 24 June 1991, using the code name "Sandstorm" for BCCI, Price Waterhouse submitted the Sandstorm report showing that BCCI had engaged in "widespread fraud and manipulation" that made it difficult, if not impossible, to reconstruct BCCI's financial history.

The Sandstorm report, parts of which were leaked to The Sunday Times, included details of how the Abu Nidal terrorist group had manipulated details and through using fake identities had opened accounts at BCCI's Sloane Street branch in London. Britain's internal security service, MI5, had signed up two sources inside the branch to hand over copies of all documents relating to Abu Nidal's accounts. One source was the Syrian-born branch manager, Ghassan Qassem, the second a young British employee.

The Abu Nidal link man for the BCCI accounts was a man based in Iraq named Samir Najmeddin or Najmedeen. Throughout the 1980s, BCCI had set up millions of dollars worth of letters of credit for Najmeddin, largely for arms deals with Iraq. Qassem later swore in an affidavit that Najmeddin was often accompanied by an American, whom Qassem subsequently identified as the financier Marc Rich. Rich was later indicted in the United States for tax evasion and racketeering in an apparently unrelated case and fled the country.

Qassem also told reporters that he had once escorted Abu Nidal, who was allegedly using the name Shakir Farhan, around town to buy a tie, without realizing who he was. This revelation led in 1991 to one of the London Evening Standard's best-known front-page headlines: "I Took Abu Nidal Shopping".

6. Forced Closure

BCCI was awaiting final approval for a restructuring plan in which it would have re-emerged as the "Oasis Bank". However, after the Sandstorm report, regulators concluded BCCI was so fraught with problems that it had to be seized. It had already been ordered to shut down its American operations in March for its illegal control of First American.

On 5 July 1991, regulators persuaded a court in Luxembourg to order BCCI liquidated on the grounds that it was hopelessly insolvent. According to the court order, BCCI had lost more than its entire capital and reserves the year before. At 1 pm London time that day (8 am in New York City), regulators marched into BCCI's offices and shut them down. Around a million depositors were immediately affected by this action.

On 7 July 1991, Hong Kong Office of the Commissioner of Banking (forerunner of the Hong Kong Monetary Authority) ordered BCCI to shut down its business in Hong Kong on the grounds that BCCI had problem loans and the Sheikh of Abu Dhabi, the major shareholder of BCCI, refused to provide funds to the Hong Kong BCCI. Hong Kong BCCI was liquidated on 17 July 1991.

A few weeks after the seizure, on 29 July, Manhattan District Attorney Robert Morgenthau announced that a Manhattan grand jury had indicted BCCI, Abedi and Naqvi on twelve counts of fraud, money laundering, and larceny. Morgenthau, who had been investigating BCCI for over two years, claimed jurisdiction because millions of dollars laundered by the bank flowed through Manhattan. Also, Morgenthau cited BCCI's secret ownership of First American, which operated a subsidiary in New York City. Morgenthau said that all of BCCI's deposits had been fraudulently collected because the bank misled depositors about its ownership structure and financial condition. He described BCCI as "the largest bank fraud in world financial history" [26].

On 15 November, BCCI, Abedi and Naqvi were indicted on federal charges that it had illegally bought control of another American bank, Independence Bank of Los Angeles, using Saudi businessman Ghaith Pharaon as the puppet owner.

Just a month later, BCCI's liquidators (Deloitte, PWC) pleaded guilty to all criminal charges pending against the bank in the United States (both those lodged by the federal government and by Morgenthau), clearing the way for BCCI's formal liquidation that fall. BCCI paid $ten million in fines and forfeited all $550 million of its American assets—at the time, the largest single criminal forfeiture ever obtained by federal prosecutors. The money was used to repay losses to First American and Independence and to make restitution to BCCI's depositors. None of this was enough to rescue both banks, however; Independence was seized later in 1992, while First American was forced into a sale to First Union in 1993.

Many of the major players in the scandal have never been brought to trial in American or UK courts. Abedi, for example, died in 1995. He was under indictment in the United States and UK for crimes related to BCCI, but Pakistani officials refused to give him up for extradition because they felt the charges were politically motivated. Even without this to consider, he had been in poor health since suffering a stroke in the 1980s. Pharaon remained a fugitive until his death in 2017 [27].

In 2002, Denis Robert and Ernest Backes, former number three of financial clearing house Clearstream, discovered that BCCI had continued to maintain its activities after its official closure, with microfiches of Clearstream's illegal unpublished accounts [28].

7. American Inquiries and Legal Actions

In 1991, Robert Mueller declared the government had been investigating BCCI since 1986 resulting in intense media coverage [29].

In 1992, United States Senators John Kerry and Hank Brown became the co-authors of a report on BCCI, which was delivered to the Committee on Foreign Relations. The BCCI scandal was one of a number of disasters that influenced thinking leading to the Public Interest Disclosure Act (PIDA) of 1998. The report found that Clifford and his legal/business partner Robert A. Altman had been closely involved with the bank from 1978, when they were introduced to BCCI by Bert Lance, the former director of the Office of Management and Budget, to 1991. Earlier, Pharaon was revealed to have been the puppet owner of National Bank of Georgia, a bank formerly owned by Lance before being sold back to First American (it had previously been an FGB subsidiary before Lance bought it). Clifford and Altman testified that they had never observed any suspicious activity, and had themselves been deceived about BCCI's control of First American. However, the federal government and Morgenthau contended that the two men knew, or should have known, that BCCI controlled First American. Pharaon also was revealed to be the puppet controlling owner of CenTrust Bank in Miami, Florida.

Morgenthau and the federal government brought indictments against Clifford and Altman, but did not pursue Clifford due to his age and deteriorating health (he died in 1998). Altman was indicted and tried in New York, though he was ultimately acquitted following a jury verdict of not guilty. Altman later accepted a de facto lifetime ban from any role in the banking industry to settle a civil suit by the Fed.

8. British Inquiry and Litigation

The British government set up an independent inquiry, chaired by Lord Justice Bingham, in 1992. Its House of Commons Paper, Inquiry into the Supervision of the Bank of Credit and Commerce International, was published in October of that year. Following the report, BCCI liquidators Deloitte Touche filed suit against the Bank of England for £850 m, claiming that the Bank was guilty of misfeasance in public office. The suit lasted 12 years. It ended in November 2005, when Deloitte withdrew its claims after England's High Court ruled that it was "no longer in the best interests of creditors" for the litigation to continue [30, 31]. Deloitte eventually paid the Bank of England £73 m for its legal costs. According to news reports at the time, it was the most expensive case in British legal history [31].

9. Litigation Elsewhere

Although major litigation has ended in the case, suits and legal actions relating to the bank were still being brought in 2013, over 20 years after the bank's failure [32].

10. Former Directors
- Khalid bin Mahfouz—non-executive director. Mahfouz and his brothers owned a 20% stake in BCCI between 1986 and 1990 [33].
- Alfred Hartman.
- Shaikh Mohammed Ishaq.

11. Legal Cases Involving BCCI
Bank of Credit and Commerce International SA v Aboody [1992] 4 All ER 955, pre-collapse case, later overturned, on the criteria for undue influence if someone is pressured into signing a mortgage agreement.

Mahmud and Malik v Bank of Credit and Commerce International SA [1998] AC 20, where employees sued the bank for breach of mutual trust and confidence by carrying on unlawful activities and thereby tarnishing the employees' reputations.

Bank of Credit and Commerce International (Overseas) Ltd. v Akindele [2000] EWCA Civ 502.

12. See Also
- Banks portal
- ABLV Bank
- Agha Hasan Abedi
- Kamal Adham
- Abbas Gokal
- The Infiltrator (2016 film)
- The International (2009 film)

13. References
1. Adams and Frantz, p. ix.
2. Kanas, Angelos (May 2005). "Pure Contagion Effects in International Banking: The Case of BCCI's Failure" (PDF). Journal of Applied Economics. 8 (1): 101–123. doi:https://doi.org/10.1080/15140326.2005.12040620.
3. "Biographical data on Agha Hasan Abedi". Salaam Knowledge.
4. Trento. Prelude to Terror. p. 370.
5. "The BCCI Affair - 8 BCCI and Law Enforcement - The Justice Department and the US Customs Service". irp.fas.org. Archived from the original on 13 September 2021.
6. Lohr, Steve (22 November 1991). "Agent Tells Of Failures On B.C.C.I." The New York Times. Archived from the original on 25 January 2017.
7. Castro, Janice (24 June 2001). "The Cash Cleaners". Time. Archived from the original on 10 June 2020.
8. Kerry, John. The BCCI Affair: A Report to the Committee on Foreign Relations. Lulu.com. p. 60. ISBN 978–1,105,096,853.
9. "BCCI bank fraud begets silver lining 13 years later". Deloitte.com. Archived from the original on 20 November 2007. Retrieved 28 February 2009.

10. Hemraj, Mohammed B. (October 2005). "The Regulatory Failure: The Saga of BCCI". Journal of Money Laundering Control. 8 (4): 346–353. doi:https://doi.org/10.1108/13685200510735329.
11. Trento. Prelude to Terror. pp. 99–105 & 370.
12. "BCCI Reportedly Moved Millions of Dollars Out of China". Associated Press. 9 August 1991. Retrieved 11 July 2019.
13. "CHINA'S WEAPONS MAFIA". The Washington Post. 27 October 1991. Retrieved 11 July 2019.
14. Passas, Nikos; Groskin, Richard B. (1 January 2001). Overseeing and Overlooking: The US Federal Authorities' Response to Money Laundering and Other Misconduct at BCCI. The Organized Criminal Activities of the Bank of Credit and Commerce International: Essays and Documentation. Springer Netherlands. pp. 141–175. doi:https://doi.org/10.1007/978-94-017-3413-4_5. ISBN 978–90–481-5731-0.
15. Kerry, John; Hank Brown (December 1992). "The Origin and Early Years of BCCI". The BCCI Affair: A Report to the Committee on Foreign Relations, United States Senate. 102d Congress 2d Session Senate Print 102–140. pp. Chapter 3. Archived from the original on 30 September 2007. Retrieved 28 September 2007.
16. Jump up to: a b c d Truell, Peter& Gurwin, Larry (1992). False Profits. The Inside Story of BCCI, The World's Most Corrupt Financial Empire. Boston & New York: Houghton, Mifflin Company. ISBN 978–0–395-62,339-8.
17. "12bn-bcci-fraudster-faces-17-years". The Independent. UK.
18. Merchant, Khozem (31 May 1994). "Asian millionaire Nazmu Virani convicted over BCCI". India Today.
19. "Follow The Money". Washington Monthly. 4 September 2004. Archived from the original on 11 September 2004. Retrieved 11 September 2004.
20. "world-class-fraud-bcci-pulled-it-off-special-report-end-twisted-trail-piggy-bank". The New York Times. 12 August 1991.
21. Rohter, Larry (10 December 1991). "Banker Tells How Noriega Used B.C.C.I. Account". The New York Times. Retrieved 7 April 2021.
22. "Three Convicted BCCI Bankers Win Sentence Reductions". Associated Press. 4 February 1992. Retrieved 7 April 2021.
23. "Iran-Contra: The Cover-Up Begins to Crack". Time. 22 July 1991. Archived from the original on 11 February 2010.
24. Hasan, Saad (12 April 2015). "Robert Mazur: The man behind the downfall of a Pakistani's greatest commercial achievement: Former US customs agent, Robert Mazur, reflects on the past; says it wasn't personal". The Express Tribune. Pakistan. Archived from the original on 14 April 2015. Retrieved 7 April 2021.
25. Baquet, Dean; Gerth (26 August 1992). "Lawmaker's Defense of B.C.C.I. Went Beyond Speech in Senate". The New York Times. Retrieved 16 January 2020.
26. Spalek, Basia (1 May 2001). "Regulation, White–Collar Crime and the Bank of Credit and Commerce International". The Howard Journal of Criminal Justice. 40 (2): 166–179. doi:https://doi.org/10.1111/1468-2311.00199. ISSN 1468-2311.

27. Spike, Justin (11 January 2017). "Saudi businessman Ghaith Pharaon confirmed dead in Beirut". The Budapest Beacon.
28. "L'affaire BCCI". arenes.fr. Archived from the original on 1 March 2007.
29. Mufson, Steven; McGee, Jim (28 July 1991). "BCCI SCANDAL: BEHIND THE 'BANK OF CROOKS AND CRIMINALS'". The Washington Post. Last week Assistant Attorney General Robert Mueller, the head of the department's criminal division, undertook an unusual media blitz to declare that the federal government had been investigating BCCI since 1986 when a federal money-laundering prosecution ensnared BCCI.
30. Gray, Joanna (2006). "Court castigates BCCI liquidators' claim against Bank of England". Journal of Financial Regulation and Compliance. 14 (4): 411–417. doi:https://doi.org/10.1108/13581980610711180
31. Jump up to: a b Tait, Nikki (8 June 2006). "Costs settlement brings to an end record-breaking BCCI litigation 12-Year Action". Financial Times. London (UK), United Kingdom. p. 4. ISSN 0307–1766.
32. Pujol, Veronique (8 November 2013). "Comment ressusciter la BCCI?". Paperjam Luxembourg. Paperjam.lu. Archived from the original on 11 November 2013. Retrieved 11 November 2013.
33. Kerry, John; Brown, Hank (December 1992). "BCCI in the United States, Part Two: Acquisition, Consolidation, and Consequences". The BCCI Affair, A Report to the Committee on Foreign Relations. United States Senate Committee on Foreign Relations. Retrieved 26 June 2006.

14. Bibliography
- Adams, James Ring & Frantz, Douglas (1991). A Full Service Bank. London.
- Brisard, Jean-Charles & Dasquié, Guillaume (2002). Ben Laden: La Vérité interdite. Gallimard. pp. 166–168. ISBN 978-2-07-042377-4.
- Ehrenfeld, Rachel (1992). Evil Money. Encounters along the Money Trail. Harper Business. ISBN 978-0-88730-560-3.
- Kerry, John & Brown, Hank (December 1992). The BCCI Affair, Report to the Committee on Foreign Relations States Senate; held at FAS] – (A Report to the Committee on Foreign Relations United States Senate by Senator John Kerry and Senator Hank Brown (Print ed.). 102d Congress 2d Session Senate. pp. 102–140.
- Robert, Denis & Backes, Ernest (2001). Révélations. Arènes Editions. ISBN 978-2-912485-28-1.

Chapter 4
Transport

4.1 Airbus

4.1.1 Text from the US DoJ Website[1] Friday, January 31, 2020

(The Deferred Prosecution Agreement is available at: https://www.justice.gov/criminal-fraud/fcpa/cases/airbus-se).

Airbus Agrees to Pay Over $3.9 Billion in Global Penalties to Resolve Foreign Bribery and ITAR Case

Airbus SE (Airbus or the Company), a global provider of civilian and military aircraft based in France, has agreed to pay combined penalties of more than $3.9 billion to resolve foreign bribery charges with authorities in the United States, France and the United Kingdom arising out of the Company's scheme to use third-party business partners to bribe government officials, as well as non-governmental airline executives, around the world and to resolve the Company's violation of the Arms Export Control Act (AECA) and its implementing regulations, the International Traffic in Arms Regulations (ITAR), in the United States. This is the largest global foreign bribery resolution to date.

Airbus entered into a deferred prosecution agreement with the department in connection with a criminal information filed on Jan. 28, 2020 in the District of Columbia charging the Company with conspiracy to violate the anti-bribery provision of the Foreign Corrupt Practices Act (FCPA) and conspiracy to violate the AECA and its implementing regulations, the ITAR. The FCPA charge arose out of Airbus's scheme to offer and pay bribes to foreign officials, including Chinese officials, in order to obtain and retain business, including contracts to sell aircraft.

---

[1] https://www.justice.gov/opa/pr/airbus-agrees-pay-over-39-billion-global-penalties-resolve-foreign-bribery-and-itar-case.

The AECA charge stems from Airbus's willful failure to disclose political contributions, commissions or fees to the U.S. government, as required under the ITAR, in connection with the sale or export of defense articles and defense services to the Armed Forces of a foreign country or international organization. The case is assigned to U.S. District Judge Thomas F. Hogan of the District of Columbia.

"Airbus engaged in a multi-year and massive scheme to corruptly enhance its business interests by paying bribes in China and other countries and concealing those bribes," said Assistant Attorney General Brian A. Benczkowski of the Justice Department's Criminal Division. "This coordinated resolution was possible thanks to the dedicated efforts of our foreign partners at the Serious Fraud Office in the United Kingdom and the PNF in France. The Department will continue to work aggressively with our partners across the globe to root out corruption, particularly corruption that harms American interests."

"International corruption involving sensitive U.S. defense technology presents a particularly dangerous combination. Today's announcement demonstrates the Department's continuing commitment to ensuring that those who violate our export control laws are held to account," said Principal Deputy Assistant Attorney General David P. Burns of the Justice Department's National Security Division (NSD). "The resolution, however, also reflects the significant benefits available under NSD's revised voluntary self-disclosure policy for companies that choose to self-report export violations, cooperate, and remediate as to those violations, even where there are aggravating circumstances. We hope other companies will make the same decision as Airbus to report potential criminal export violations timely and directly to NSD so that they too can avail themselves of the policy's benefits."

"Today, Airbus has admitted to a years-long campaign of corruption around the world, said U.S. Attorney Jessie K. Liu of the District of Columbia. "Through bribes, Airbus allowed rampant corruption to invade the U.S. system. Additionally, Airbus falsely reported information about their conduct to the U.S. government for more than five years in order to gain valuable licenses to export U.S. military technology. This case exemplifies the ability of our prosecutors and law enforcement to work with our foreign counterparts to ensure that corruption around the world is prevented and punished at the highest levels."

"Airbus SE, the second largest Aerospace company world-wide, engaged in a systematic and deliberate conspiracy, that knowingly and willfully violated U.-S. fraud and export laws," said Special Agent in Charge Peter C. Fitzhugh of U.S. Immigration and Customs Enforcement's Homeland Security Investigations (HSI) New York. "Airbus's fraud and bribery in commercial aircraft transactions strengthened corrupt airlines and bad actors worldwide, at the expense of straightforward enterprises. Additionally, the bribery of government officials, specifically those involved in the procurement of U.S. military technology, posed a national security threat to both the U.S. and its allies. The global threats facing the U.S. have never been greater than they are today, and HSI New York is committed to working with our federal and international partners to assure sensitive U.S. technologies are not unlawfully and fraudulently acquired. As this investigation reflects, national security continues to be a top priority not just for Department of Homeland Security, but for HSI New York."

The Company's payment to the United States will be $527 million for the FCPA and ITAR violations, and an additional 50 million Euros (approximately $55 million) as part of a civil forfeiture agreement for the ITAR-related conduct, and the department will credit a portion of the amount the Company pays to the Parquet National Financier (PNF) in France under the Company's agreement with the PNF. In addition, the Company has agreed to pay a $10 million penalty to the U.-S. Department of State's Directorate of Defense Trade Controls (DDTC), of which the department is crediting $5 million. In related proceedings, the Company settled with the PNF in France over bribes paid to government officials and non-governmental airline executives in China and multiple other countries and the Company has agreed to pay more than 2 billion Euros (more than approximately $2.29 billion) pursuant to the PNF agreement. As part of this coordinated global resolution, the Company also entered into a deferred prosecution agreement with the United Kingdom's Serious Fraud Office (SFO) over bribes paid in Malaysia, Sri Lanka, Taiwan, Indonesia and Ghana, and the Company has agreed to pay approximately 990 million Euros equivalent (approximately $1.09 billion) pursuant to the SFO agreement. The PNF and SFO had investigated the Company as part of a Joint Investigative Team.

According to admissions and court documents, beginning in at least 2008 and continuing until at least 2015, Airbus engaged in and facilitated a scheme to offer and pay bribes to decision makers and other influencers, including to foreign officials, in order to obtain improper business advantages and to win business from both privately owned enterprises and entities that were state-owned and state-controlled. In furtherance of the corrupt bribery scheme, Airbus employees and agents, among other things, sent emails while located in the United States and participated in and provided luxury travel to foreign officials within the United States.

The admissions and court documents establish that in order to conceal and to facilitate the bribery scheme, Airbus engaged certain business partners, in part, to assist in the bribery scheme. Between approximately 2013 and 2015, Airbus engaged a business partner in China and knowingly and willfully conspired to make payments to the business partner that were intended to be used as bribes to government officials in China in connection with the approval of certain agreements in China associated with the purchase and sale of Airbus aircraft to state-owned and state-controlled airlines in China. In order to conceal the payments and to conceal its engagement of the business partner in China, Airbus did not pay the business partner directly but instead made payments to a bank account in Hong Kong in the name of a company controlled by another business partner.

Pursuant to the AECA and ITAR, the DDTC regulates the export and import of U.S. defense articles and defense services, and prohibits their export overseas without the requisite licensing and approval of the DDTC. According to admissions and court documents, between December 2011 and December 2016, Airbus filed numerous applications for the export of defense articles and defense services to foreign armed forces. As part of its applications, Airbus was required under Part 130 of the ITAR to provide certain information related to political contributions, fees or commissions paid in connection with the sale of defense articles or defense services. The admissions and court documents reveal, however, that the Company engaged in a criminal conspiracy to knowingly and willfully violate the AECA and ITAR, by failing to provide DDTC with accurate information related to commissions paid by Airbus to third-party brokers who were hired to solicit, promote or otherwise secure the sale of defense articles and defense services to foreign armed forces.

As part of the deferred prosecution agreement with the department, Airbus has agreed to continue to cooperate with the department in any ongoing investigations and prosecutions relating to the conduct, including of individuals, and to enhance its compliance program.

For the FCPA-related conduct, the department reached this resolution with Airbus based on a number of factors, including the Company's cooperation and remediation. In addition, for the FCPA-related conduct, the U.S. resolution recognizes the strength of France's and the United Kingdom's interests over the Company's corruption-related conduct, as well as the compelling equities of France and the United Kingdom to vindicate their respective interests as those countries deem appropriate, and the department has taken into account these countries' determination of the appropriate resolution into all aspects of the U.S. resolution.

With respect to the AECA and ITAR-related conduct, the department reached this resolution with Airbus based on the voluntary and timely nature of its disclosure to the department as well as the Company's cooperation and remediation.

HSI's New York Field Office Counter Proliferation Investigations Group is investigating the case. Deputy Chief Christopher Cestaro, Assistant Chief Vanessa Sisti and Trial Attorney Elina A. Rubin Smith of the Criminal Division's Fraud Section, Deputy Chief Elizabeth L. D. Cannon and Trial Attorney David Lim of the National Security Division's Counterintelligence and Export Control Section, and Assistant U.S. Attorneys Michelle Zamarin, Gregg Maisel, David Kent and Karen Seifert of the District of Columbia are prosecuting the case. The Criminal Division's Office of International Affairs provided assistance.

The Department of Justice acknowledges and expresses its appreciation of the significant assistance provided by France's Parquet National Financier and the UK's Serious Fraud Office.

The Fraud Section is responsible for all investigations and prosecutions of the Foreign Corrupt Practices Act, and conducts other investigations into sophisticated economic crimes. The Counterintelligence and Export Control Section supervises the investigation and prosecution of cases involving the export of military and strategic commodities and technology, including cases under the AECA and ITAR.

4.2 VW

Wednesday, December 6, 2017
From US Department of Justice[2]

Volkswagen Senior Manager Sentenced to 84 Months in Prison for Role in Conspiracy to Cheat U.S. Emissions Tests

The former general manager of Volkswagen AG's (VW) U.S. Environment and Engineering Office was sentenced today to 84 months in prison for his role in VW's scheme to sell diesel "clean diesel" vehicles containing software designed to cheat U.S. emissions tests.

Acting Assistant Attorney General John P. Cronan of the Justice Department's Criminal Division, Deputy Assistant Attorney General Jean E. Williams of the Justice Department's Environment and Natural Resources Division, Acting U.-S. Attorney Daniel L. Lemisch of the Eastern District of Michigan, Special Agent in Charge David P. Gelios of FBI's Detroit Field Office and Acting Assistant Administrator Larry Starfield, for the Environmental Protection Agency (EPA)'s Office of Enforcement and Compliance Assurance made the announcement.

Oliver Schmidt, 48, a citizen and resident of Germany, was sentenced by U.-S. District Judge Sean F. Cox of the Eastern District of Michigan, who also ordered Schmidt to pay a criminal penalty of $400,000. Schmidt pleaded guilty on Aug. 4 to one count of conspiracy to defraud the United States, to commit wire fraud and to violate the Clean Air Act, and to one count of violating the Clean Air Act.

"Upon learning of Volkswagen's massive scheme to defraud and mislead U.-S. consumers and regulators, Oliver Schmidt chose to join the conspiracy and deceive U.S. regulators," said Acting Assistant Attorney General Cronan. "This case, along with the prior prosecution of the company and another Volkswagen engineer, further demonstrate the Criminal Division's unwavering commitment to hold both corporations and individuals accountable for their wrongdoing."

"Oliver Schmidt cheated the American people, and today's sentencing shows that such behavior will be prosecuted to the fullest extent of the law," said Deputy Assistant Attorney General Williams. "The Department of Justice and its partner agencies will continue to work together to ensure a level playing field for all competitors and a cleaner environment for all Americans."

"This sentence reflects how seriously we take environmental crime," said Acting U.S. Attorney Lemisch. "Protecting natural resources is a priority of this office. Corporations, and individuals acting on behalf of corporations, will be brought to justice for harming our environment."

"Americans expect corporations to follow laws and regulations designed to protect consumers and the environment," said FBI Special Agent in Charge Gelios. "The sentence of Mr. Schmidt demonstrates the Department of Justice's

---

[2] https://www.justice.gov/opa/pr/volkswagen-senior-manager-sentenced-84-months-prison-role-conspiracy-cheat-us-emissions-tests.

commitment to hold companies that defraud their customers both personally, as well as, corporately accountable for their crimes."

"As this case demonstrates, EPA is committed to ensuring a level playing field for companies that follow the rules and pursuing individuals whose actions create an unfair competitive advantage for their employer," said EPA Acting Assistant Administrator Starfield.

In connection with his guilty plea, Schmidt admitted that he agreed with VW employees to mislead and defraud the United States and domestic customers who purchased diesel vehicles, and to violate the Clean Air Act. Schmidt first learned during the summer of 2015 that certain VW diesel vehicle models contained a defeat device, or software that detected the difference between when the car was undergoing standard U.S. emissions testing and when it was being driven under normal conditions on the road. If the vehicle recognized that it was not being tested, many of its emissions control systems were significantly reduced, resulting in NOx emissions that were sometimes 30 times higher than U.S. standards. Schmidt admitted to participating in discussions with other VW employees in the summer of 2015 on how to coordinate responses to questions from U.S. regulators about VW's diesel vehicles without admitting to the defeat device contained in vehicles. On the instructions of management, Schmidt met with U.S. regulators twice in August 2015 and attempted to obtain approval for the sale of additional VW diesel vehicles without disclosing what he knew was the truth—that the real reason for the high emissions on the road was that VW had intentionally installed software designed to cheat emissions testing.

Schmidt further admitted that he knew during his participation in the conspiracy that the VW "clean diesel" vehicles were being marketed to the public as being environmentally friendly and promoting increased fuel economy while complying with U.S. environmental regulations. Schmidt knew that VW's diesel vehicles were not compliant with U.S. standards and regulations and that these representations made to domestic customers were false, he admitted.

As part of his guilty plea, Schmidt agreed that during his participation in the scheme, he and his co-conspirators caused losses to victims of more than $150 million and that he obstructed justice.

The FBI's Detroit Field Office and the EPA's Criminal Investigation Division are investigating the case, with assistance from U.S. Immigration and Customs Enforcement's Homeland Security Investigations. Securities and Financial Fraud Unit Chief Benjamin D. Singer and Trial Attorney David M. Fuhr of the Criminal Division's Fraud Section, Senior Trial Attorney Jennifer Blackwell of the Environment and Natural Resources Division's Environmental Crimes Section and White Collar Chief John K. Neal of the U.S. Attorney's Office for the Eastern District of Michigan are prosecuting the case.

Friday, April 21, 2017

4.2.1 Text from US Department of Justice[3]

Volkswagen AG Sentenced in Connection with Conspiracy to Cheat U.S. Emissions Tests

Volkswagen AG (VW) was sentenced in federal court in Detroit today after pleading guilty on March 10, 2017, to three felony counts of:

1. Conspiracy to defraud the United States, engage in wire fraud, and violate the Clean Air Act
2. Obstruction of justice; and
3. Importation of merchandise by means of false statements

During the sentencing hearing, the court accepted the parties' plea agreement, which requires VW to pay a $2.8 billion penalty stemming from the company's decade-long scheme to sell diesel vehicles containing software designed to cheat on U.S. emissions tests.

Acting Assistant Attorney General Kenneth A. Blanco of the Justice Department's Criminal Division, Acting U.S. Attorney Daniel L. Lemisch of the Eastern District of Michigan, Deputy Assistant Attorney General Jean E. Williams of the Justice Department's Environment and Natural Resources Division, Acting Assistant Administrator Larry Starfield of the EPA's Office of Enforcement and Compliance and Special Agent in Charge David Gelios of the FBI's Detroit Field Office made the announcement.

U.S. District Judge Sean F. Cox of the Eastern District of Michigan accepted the plea agreement, resulting in VW's conviction on three felony charges. VW was convicted, first, of participating in a conspiracy to defraud the United States and its U.S. customers and to violate the Clean Air Act by lying and misleading the EPA and U.S. customers about whether certain VW, Audi and Porsche branded diesel vehicles complied with U.S. emissions standards. Moreover, the company used cheating software to circumvent the U.S. testing process, and concealed material facts about its cheating from U.S. regulators. Second, VW was convicted of obstruction of justice for destroying documents related to the scheme. And third, VW was convicted of importing these cars into the United States by means of false statements about the vehicles' compliance with emissions limits.

As part of the plea agreement, VW will pay a $2.8 billion criminal penalty to the U.S. and fully cooperate in the government's ongoing investigation and prosecution of individuals responsible for these crimes. The parties also announced that the government had selected Larry D. Thompson as an independent corporate compliance monitor who will oversee the company during its three-year term of probation. Thompson is a former Deputy U.S. Attorney General. His team includes experts in automotive regulatory compliance, as well as the corporate monitors for Deutsche

---

[3] https://www.justice.gov/opa/pr/volkswagen-ag-sentenced-connection-conspiracy-cheat-us-emissions-tests.

Bank in the London Interbank Offered Rate (LIBOR) manipulation prosecution and Duke Energy in the coal ash environmental prosecution.

"The sentencing of Volkswagen marks a significant milestone in this historic case," said Acting U.S. Attorney Lemisch. "Volkswagen has been punished for its scheme to defeat U.S. environmental standards and cheat U.S. consumers. This prosecution sends a strong message to Volkswagen and others that we take our environmental laws seriously and that federal prosecution awaits those who defraud the EPA."

"The Criminal Division will continue to be vigilant in assuring that all companies—foreign and domestic—that choose to benefit from our valuable economy and consumers abide by our laws, said Acting Assistant Attorney General Blanco. "The sentencing of VW vindicates the rights of U.S. consumers who for over a decade were victims of the calculated corporate decisions of VW and its senior management to fraudulently employ a device intended to deceive U.S. consumers and to defeat our environmental laws."

"With today's sentence, VW is being held fully accountable for its deception and fraud perpetrated against American consumers and the environment, as well as the deliberate obstruction of the criminal investigation into its wrongdoing," said Deputy Assistant Attorney General Williams. "We also hope this sends a message around the world that those who violate American environmental laws will be vigorously investigated and prosecuted."

"Today's strong sentence recognizes the egregious nature of VW's violations, and VW's attempt to gain an unfair competitive advantage over automakers that follow the law," said Acting Assistant Administrator Starfield. "Vehicle emissions standards help protect clean air and ensure a level playing field for companies that play by the rules. When those standards are broken, violators can expect to be held accountable."

"Americans expect corporations doing business in the United States to conduct their business honestly," said Special Agent in Charge Gelios. "Today's sentencing sends a clear message that the FBI, along with its federal partners, will continue to hold corporations, like Volkswagen AG, accountable when they defraud consumers and violate federal laws."

Along with the January 2017 plea agreement, the United States also announced separate civil resolutions of environmental, customs and financial claims, in which VW agreed to pay an additional $1.5 billion to settle EPA's claim for civil penalties in connection with the importation and sale of these cars, as well as U.S. Customs and Border Protection (CBP) claims for customs fraud. In addition, that agreement requires injunctive relief to prevent future violations. The agreements also resolved alleged violations of the Financial Institutions Reform, Recovery and Enforcement Act (FIRREA).

The FBI and EPA investigated the case. This case is being prosecuted by members of the Department of Justice's Criminal Division, Fraud Section, including: Chief of the Securities and Financial Fraud Unit Benjamin D. Singer, as well as Trial Attorneys David Fuhr, Alison Anderson, Christopher Fenton and Gary Winters. Also prosecuting the case are members of the Department of Justice's

Environment and Natural Resources Division, Environmental Crimes Section, including: Senior Trial Attorney Jennifer Blackwell. Additionally, the case is being prosecuted by members of the U.S. Attorney's Office for the Eastern District of Michigan, including Criminal Division Chief Mark Chutkow, Economic Crimes Unit Chief John K. Neal and Assistant U.S. Attorney Timothy J. Wyse. The Justice Department's Office of International Affairs also assisted in the case. The Justice Department extends its thanks to the Office of the Public Prosecutor in Braunschweig, Germany.

Thursday, May 3, 2018

4.2.2 Text from US Department of Justice Website[4]

Former CEO of Volkswagen AG Charged with Conspiracy and Wire Fraud in Diesel Emissions Scandal

An indictment was unsealed earlier today charging Martin Winterkorn, 70, the former chairman of the management board of Volkswagen AG (VW), with conspiracy and wire fraud in connection with VW's long-running scheme to cheat U.S. diesel vehicle emissions requirements.

Attorney General Jeff Sessions, Acting Assistant Attorney General John P. Cronan of the Justice Department's Criminal Division, U.S. Attorney Matthew J. Schneider of the Eastern District of Michigan, Deputy Assistant Attorney General Jean E. Williams of the Justice Department's Environment and Natural Resources Division, EPA Administrator Scott Pruitt, and Special Agent in Charge Timothy R. Slater of FBI's Detroit Division, made the announcement.

The superseding indictment was issued by a federal grand jury sitting in the Eastern District of Michigan and charges Winterkorn with four counts of violating federal law. The first count charges that Winterkorn conspired with other senior VW executives and employees to defraud the United States, defraud VW's U.S. customers and violate the Clean Air Act by making false representations to regulators and the public about the ability of VW's supposedly "clean diesel" vehicles to comply with U.S. emissions requirements. The remaining three counts charge Winterkorn with wire fraud in connection with the scheme.

"If you try to deceive the United States, then you will pay a heavy price," said Attorney General Sessions. "The indictment unsealed today alleges that Volkswagen's scheme to cheat its legal requirements went all the way to the top of the company. These are serious allegations, and we will prosecute this case to the fullest extent of the law. I want to thank the Criminal Division's Fraud Section, the Department's Environment and Natural Resources Division and the U.S. Attorney's

---

[4] https://www.justice.gov/opa/pr/former-ceo-volkswagen-ag-charged-conspiracy-and-wire-fraud-diesel-emissions-scandal.

Office for the Eastern District of Michigan as well as our partners at the EPA, FBI and in Germany for their hard work on this important case."

"Volkswagen deceived American regulators and defrauded American consumers for years," said U.S. Attorney Schneider. "The fact that this criminal conduct was allegedly blessed at Volkswagen's highest levels is appalling. The U.S. Attorney's Office is committed to pursuing accountability for corporate crimes, and the Winterkorn prosecution is a reflection of that commitment."

"The indictment of former VW CEO Martin Winterkorn should send a clear message that EPA and its law enforcement partners will seek to hold corporate officers accountable for alleged criminal activities at their company," said EPA Administrator Pruitt.

"Today's indictment of Volkswagen AG's former CEO, Martin Winterkorn, sends a clear message that businesses both here in the United States and abroad are expected to conduct their business honestly," said FBI Special Agent in Charge Slater. "Accountability will be sought for any individuals or corporations that cheat American consumers or harm the environment by circumventing the standards set by our legal system."

The indictment of Winterkorn represents the most recent charges in an ongoing investigation by U.S. criminal authorities into unprecedented emissions cheating by VW. In March 2017, VW pleaded guilty to criminal charges that it deceived U.-S. regulatory agencies, including the Environmental Protection Agency (EPA) and the California Air Resources Board (CARB), by installing so-called defeat devices in diesel vehicles emissions control systems that were designed to cheat emissions tests. The defeat devices consisted of software designed to recognize whether a vehicle was undergoing standard U.S. emissions testing on a dynamometer or being driven on the road under normal driving conditions, in which case harmful nitrogen oxide (NOx) emissions increased significantly.

As part of its plea agreement with the Department, VW paid a criminal penalty of \$2.8 billion. VW also agreed to the imposition of an independent corporate compliance monitor for the duration of its probation, which is at least 3 years. Subsequently, Larry Thompson was appointed as VW's monitor.

Winterkorn, who served as VW's management board chairman and thus VW's highest ranking executive from January 2007 until September 2015, is the ninth individual against whom U.S. criminal authorities have announced charges in connection with this matter. Two former VW engineers, Oliver Schmidt, 48, and James Liang, 63, both German citizens, pleaded guilty to participating in the conspiracy alleged in the indictment and are currently serving sentences of 84 months and 40 months in prison, respectively, imposed by U.S. District Judge Sean F. Cox of the Eastern District of Michigan. Five additional defendants, including former VW executives and senior managers, were indicted in January 2017, but have not been apprehended. Similar to Winterkorn, each of them is believed to be a German citizen and to reside in Germany. Finally, one former manager of VW's subsidiary Audi AG, Giovanni Pamio, 61, an Italian citizen, has been charged by complaint and currently remains in Germany pending extradition.

The indictment of Winterkorn alleges that he was informed of VW's diesel emissions cheating in May 2014 and again in July 2015. The indictment further alleges that Winterkorn, after having been clearly informed of the emissions cheating, agreed with other senior VW executives to continue to perpetrate the fraud and deceive U.S. regulators.

As the indictment sets forth, in the spring of 2014 a study commissioned by the International Council on Clean Transportation (the ICCT study) tested road emissions of two VW diesel vehicles sold in the United States. The results of the study showed significantly elevated NOx levels of the two VW vehicles, with one emitting up to 35 times above the allowable legal limit. VW management quickly learned of the results of the study and discussed potential consequences flowing from the revelations. Specifically, the indictment alleges that Bernd Gottweis, a senior manager then responsible for product safety issues, met with employees of the engine development department to discuss the ICCT study. Upon learning of the facts revealed by the study and the risks facing the company, Gottweis remarked that he needed to speak with Winterkorn immediately. Shortly thereafter, on May 22, 2014, Gottweis wrote a one-page memorandum describing the results of the ICCT study and warning that VW could not give a well-grounded explanation for the dramatically increased NOx emissions and that it could be assumed that the authorities would investigate whether the vehicles contained test-recognition software. Gottweis's memorandum was then attached to a cover note authored by a then-senior VW executive, and addressed to Winterkorn.

As alleged in the indictment, following publication of the ICCT study in the spring of 2014 the company knowingly continued to deny the existence of emissions cheating in its vehicles until late summer 2015. Instead, VW sought to deceive U.S. regulators about the causes for the significant discrepancies between emissions tests and emissions values measured on the road.

By the summer of 2015, however, the indictment alleges that U.S. regulators threatened to withhold authorization for VW to sell Model Year 2016 diesel vehicles in the United States until VW answered their questions about the discrepancies uncovered by the ICCT study. The diesel situation in the United States became increasingly alarming to VW senior management, culminating in a meeting on July 27, 2015 at VW's headquarters in Wolfsburg, Germany, internally referred to as the "damage table meeting." During that meeting, which was chaired by Winterkorn and attended by several senior VW executives, engine development department employees, with the help of a PowerPoint presentation, described to the attendees, and Winterkorn specifically: (1) how VW was deceiving U.S. regulators, including precisely what information had been disclosed and what had not yet been disclosed; and (2) the potential consequences of VW being caught cheating.

The indictment alleges that upon being presented with those and other facts, Winterkorn did not order his subordinates to disclose the cheating but instead agreed to continue to deceive U.S. authorities. Part of that strategy, which Winterkorn allegedly approved at the July 27, 2015 meeting, and which informed VW's steps over the next several weeks, included sending Oliver Schmidt to meet with a senior CARB official on Aug. 5, 2015, in order to obtain the release of the Model Year

2016 vehicles without revealing the fundamental reason for the higher NOx measurements on the road: that software had been intentionally installed in VW vehicles so the vehicles could detect and evade emissions testing. Consistent with Winterkorn's alleged directive from the July 27 meeting, VW executives also approved a script for an Aug. 19, 2015 meeting with CARB that continued to conceal VW's cheating. At the meeting, however, in direct contravention of the instructions from his superiors, a VW employee, in answering a direct question from CARB, revealed that VW had been using software in its 2.0 L diesel vehicles to cheat U.S. emissions tests. On Sept. 3, 2015, VW officially admitted that it had installed defeat devices in various 2.0 L diesel vehicles sold in the United States.

An indictment is merely an allegation and all defendants are presumed innocent until proven guilty beyond a reasonable doubt in a court of law.

FBI and EPA Criminal Investigation Division are investigating the case. The prosecution is being handled by Deputy Chief Benjamin D. Singer and Trial Attorney David M. Fuhr from the Criminal Division's Fraud Section, White Collar Crime Unit Chief John K. Neal of the U.S. Attorney's Office for the Eastern District of Michigan and Senior Trial Attorney Jennifer L. Blackwell from the DOJ's Environment and Natural Resources Division. The Justice Department's Office of International Affairs also assisted in the case. The Justice Department also extends its thanks to the Office of the Public Prosecutor in Braunschweig, Germany.

Tuesday, December 18, 2018

4.2.3 Text from US Department of Justice Website[5]

IAV GmbH to Pay $35 Million Criminal Fine in Guilty Plea for Its Role in Volkswagen AG Emissions Fraud

IAV GmbH (IAV), a German company that engineers and designs automotive systems, has agreed to plead guilty to one criminal felony count and pay a $35 million criminal fine as a result of the company's role in a long-running scheme for Volkswagen AG (VW) to sell diesel vehicles in the United States by using a defeat device to cheat on U.S. vehicle emissions tests required by federal law.

Principal Deputy Assistant Attorney General John P. Cronan of the Justice Department's Criminal Division, U.S. Attorney Matthew J. Schneider of the Eastern District of Michigan, Deputy Assistant Attorney General Jean E. Williams of the Justice Department's Environment and Natural Resources Division, Assistant Administrator Susan Bodine of the EPA's Office of Enforcement and Compliance Assurance and Special Agent in Charge Timothy R. Slater of FBI's Detroit Division made the announcement.

---

[5] https://www.justice.gov/opa/pr/iav-gmbh-pay-35-million-criminal-fine-guilty-plea-its-role-volkswagen-ag-emissions-fraud.

IAV is charged with and has agreed to plead guilty to one count of conspiracy to defraud the United States and VW's U.S. customers and to violate the Clean Air Act by misleading the EPA and U.S. customers about whether certain VW- and Audi-branded diesel vehicles complied with U.S. vehicle emissions standards. IAV and its co-conspirators knew the vehicles did not meet U.S. emissions standards, worked collaboratively to design, test, and implement cheating software to cheat the U.-S. testing process, and IAV was aware that VW concealed material facts about its cheating from federal and state regulators and U.S. customers. Under the terms of the plea agreement, which must be accepted by the court, IAV will plead guilty to this crime, will serve probation for 2 years, will be under an independent corporate compliance monitor who will oversee the company for 2 years, and will fully cooperate in the Justice Department's ongoing investigation and prosecution of individuals responsible for these crimes. Pursuant to the U.S. Sentencing Guidelines, IAV's $35 million fine was set according to the company's inability to pay a higher fine amount without jeopardizing its continued viability. IAV is scheduled to appear for a change of plea hearing before the Honorable Sean F. Cox of the U.S. District Court for the Eastern District of Michigan on Jan. 18, 2019 at 9:30 a.m.

"Today's guilty plea shows that this scheme to evade automotive emissions tests and cheat the American public and the U.S. government extended well beyond Volkswagen," said Principal Deputy Assistant Attorney General Cronan. "Our investigation into emissions cheating is ongoing and we will follow the evidence wherever it leads."

"By helping VW cheat on U.S. emissions tests in violation of the Clean Air Act, IAV put its corporate success over public health and unfairly disadvantaged its competitors," said Deputy Assistant Attorney General Williams. "The Department of Justice will continue to work with its law enforcement partners to ensure that companies like IAV play fair and that all Americans can enjoy the protections of our nation's environmental laws."

"IAV participated in Volkswagen's deception of American regulators and fraud on American consumers," said U.S. Attorney Matthew Schneider. "As this guilty plea demonstrates, our office will continue to aggressively prosecute corporate criminals, even when they work at some of the world's largest, most prominent companies."

"IAV designed the software that allowed VW to cheat U.S. air emissions standards," said EPA Office of Enforcement and Compliance Assurance Assistant Administrator Susan Bodine. "EPA and its law enforcement partners will not tolerate actions like this that put profit above public health and environmental protection."

"Americans rightly expect corporations to operate honestly," said FBI Special Agent in Charge Slater. "This case sends a clear message that the FBI and its partners will hold corporations accountable when they defraud consumers and violate federal laws."

The guilty plea of IAV represents the most recent charges in an ongoing investigation by U.S. criminal authorities into unprecedented emissions cheating by VW. In March 2017, VW pleaded guilty to criminal charges that it deceived U.-S. regulatory agencies, including the EPA and the California Air Resources Board, by installing defeat devices in diesel vehicles emissions control systems that were designed to cheat emissions tests. As part of its plea agreement with the Department, VW paid a criminal fine of $2.8 billion and agreed to an independent corporate compliance monitor for 3 years. Eight individuals were previously indicted in connection with this matter, two of whom have pleaded guilty and been sentenced. The other six charged defendants are believed to reside in Germany.

According to the statement of facts that will be filed with the court in IAV's case, in 2006, VW engineers began to design a new diesel engine to meet stricter U.-S. emissions standards that would take effect by model year 2007. This new engine would be the cornerstone of a new project to sell diesel vehicles in the United States that would be marketed to buyers as "clean diesel." When the co-conspirators realized that they could not design a diesel engine that would both meet the stricter standards for nitrogen oxides (Nox) and attract sufficient customer demand in the U.S. market, they decided they would use a software function to cheat the U.-S. emissions tests.

VW delegated certain tasks associated with designing its new "Gen 1" diesel engine to IAV, including parts of software development, diesel development and exhaust after-treatment. In November 2006, a VW employee requested that an IAV employee assist in the design of defeat device software for use in the diesel engine. The IAV employee agreed to do so and prepared documentation for a software design change to recognize whether a vehicle was undergoing standard U.-S. emissions testing on a dynamometer or it was being driven on the road under normal driving conditions. If the software detected that the vehicle was not being tested, the vehicle's emissions control systems were reduced substantially, causing the vehicle to emit substantially higher NOx, sometimes 35 times higher than U.S. standards.

By at least 2008, an IAV manager knew the purpose of the defeat device software, instructed IAV employees to continue working on the project and directed IAV employees to route VW's requests regarding the defeat device software through him; the manager was involved in coordinating IAV's continued work on it.

Starting with the first model year (2009) of VW's new "clean diesel" Gen 1 engine, through model year 2014, IAV and its co-conspirators caused defeat device software to be installed on all of the approximately 335,000 Gen 1 vehicles that VW sold in the United States.

This case was investigated by the FBI and EPA-Criminal Investigation Division. The prosecution and corporate investigation are being handled by Trial Attorneys Philip Trout, Mark Cipolletti and Gary Winters of the Criminal Division's Fraud Section; Senior Trial Attorney Jennifer Blackwell of the Environment and Natural Resources Division's Environmental Crimes Section; and White Collar Crime Unit Chief John K. Neal of the Eastern District of Michigan. The Criminal Division's Office of International Affairs also assisted in the case. The Justice Department also extends its thanks to the Office of the Public Prosecutor in Braunschweig, Germany.

VW and EIB Agreement

4.2.4 Text from EIB's Website[6]

The European Investment Bank has today published a detailed summary of the investigation report by the European Anti-Fraud Office (OLAF) into alleged misuse of EIB loan by Volkswagen AG. This was done in accordance with the EIB Group Transparency Policy and considering the strong public interest in this highly exceptional case.

The summary includes all information relevant to the public interest and also includes extracts of the report, providing the public with an informative and meaningful account of the OLAF investigation. The investigation concerns practices which have been the centre of controversy and legal action ever since 2015, when environmental authorities in the US issued a notice of violation against Volkswagen AG for producing and selling diesel cars that featured sophisticated software to circumvent emissions standards for air pollutants. Notably, the report states: "The investigation established that VW never informed the EIB throughout the duration of the loan from 24 February 2009 to 24 February 2014 about the continuous use and implementation of this 'defeat device' on the EA 189 engine in the context of the Research and Development activities financed by the EIB loan." OLAF's report further indicates that this information should have been communicated to the EIB and, had the EIB been informed of this relevant information, the EIB would not have granted the loan or would have requested full repayment.

OLAF opened its investigation in November 2015. The OLAF investigation focused on one sub-project under the loan "VW Antrieb RDI", which was granted to Volkswagen AG by the EIB in February 2009. The aim of EIB loan "Antrieb RDI" was to provide financing for the development of power engines and power train components for passenger cars and commercial vehicles. The notion of 'defeat device' was used in the OLAF report to refer to VW's sophisticated" software which aimed at circumventing emissions standards for air pollutants, in particular nitrogen oxides (NOx) [...] The 'defeat device' deployed on the EA 189 engine detected if the car was operated under testing conditions and accordingly activated and deactivated certain functionalities in order to meet emission standards during tests while offering full performance of the vehicle under normal driving conditions."

The end of legal proceedings arising from the OLAF investigation and the implementation by the Bank of OLAF's recommendation gives the possibility to the Bank to publish the summary of the OLAF report.

EIB and Volkswagen AG finalised an agreement in December 2018, following the OLAF investigation. As part of the agreement Volkswagen AG voluntarily committed to contribute EUR 10 million to environmental and/or sustainability projects in Europe. In addition, according to this agreement, the European

---

[6] www.eib.org/en/press/all/2019-049-eib-publishes-a-summary-of-the-european-anti-fraud-office-report-into-alleged-misuse-of-eib-loan-by-volkswagen-ag.

Investment Bank concluded its investigation and Volkswagen AG in turn agreed voluntarily not to participate in any European Investment Bank project for an exclusion period of 18 months. Since October 2015, the consideration of loans by the European Investment Bank to Volkswagen AG had been under suspension.

Summary of the European Anti-Fraud Office (OLAF) report on the European Investment Bank (EIB) loan "Antrieb RDI" to Volkswagen AG.

Agreement reached between the European Investment Bank and Volkswagen AG in relation to EIB loan "Antrieb RDI".[7]

4.3 Rolls Royce

4.3.1 Text from UK SFO Website[8] (February 11, 2022)

1. **Rolls-Royce PLC**

17 January 2017

Following a 4 year investigation, the SFO and Rolls-Royce entered into a Deferred Prosecution Agreement (DPA) which was approved by Sir Brian Leveson, President of the Queen's Bench Division on 17 January 2017. The DPA enables Rolls-Royce to account to a UK court for criminal conduct spanning three decades in seven jurisdictions and involving three business sectors.

The DPA involved payments of £497,252,645 (comprising disgorgement of profits of £258,170,000 and a financial penalty of £239,082,645) plus interest. Rolls-Royce also reimbursed the SFO's costs in full (c£13 m).

Full information is available in the Statement of Facts, agreed by the SFO and Rolls-Royce. The Agreement itself and Sir Brian Leveson's judgment are published below.

- 17 January 2017

  – Deferred Prosecution Agreement—SFO v Rolls Royce PLC
  – Deferred Prosecution Agreement—Statement of Facts—SFO v Rolls Royce PLC
  – Judgment of Sir Brian Leveson, President of the Queen's Bench Division.

- 28 January 2022

  – Detail of compliance—Discontinuance of proceedings on expiry of deferred prosecution agreement

---

[7] See also FCPA Blog article: Compliance dialog: What happens when an "air of innocence" fills the halls? by Richard Bistrong, June 27, 2019.

[8] https://www.sfo.gov.uk/cases/rolls-royce-plc/.

Following a detailed review of the available evidence and an assessment of the public interest, there will be no prosecution of individuals associated with the company. For more information, please see the statement here.

Page published on September 11, 2014 | Page modified on January 28, 2022.

2. **SFO Completes £497.25 m Deferred Prosecution Agreement with Rolls-Royce PLC**

4.3.2 *Text from UK SFO Website[9] (February 11, 2022):*

17 January, 2017

The SFO has entered into a significant Deferred Prosecution Agreement (DPA) with Rolls-Royce PLC following its approval today by Sir Brian Leveson, President of the Queen's Bench division.

The agreement with the company follows the SFO's four-year investigation into bribery and corruption, an investigation which continues into the conduct of individuals.

The indictment, which has been suspended for the term of the DPA, covers 12 counts of conspiracy to corrupt, false accounting and failure to prevent bribery. The conduct spans three decades and involves Rolls-Royce's Civil Aerospace and Defence Aerospace businesses and its former Energy business and relates to the sale of aero engines, energy systems and related services. The conduct covered by the UK DPA took place across seven jurisdictions: Indonesia, Thailand, India, Russia, Nigeria, China and Malaysia.

A DPA is a statutory means by which a company can account to a court for conduct without suffering the full consequences of a criminal conviction, which might include international disbarment from competition for public contracts.

The Judge ruled today in a public hearing at the Royal Courts of Justice that the DPA's terms were fair, reasonable and proportionate and that the DPA was in the interests of justice. He also agreed that the total sum in the UK settlement (£497.25 m plus interest and the SFO's costs of £13 m) reflected the gravity of the conduct, the full cooperation of Rolls-Royce PLC in the investigation, and the programme of corporate reform and compliance put in place by new leadership at the top of the company. The resolution is the highest ever enforcement action against company in the UK for criminal conduct.

As part of a DPA, a company agrees to a number of terms. If the company does not honour the conditions, the prosecution may resume. Arrangements for monitoring compliance with the conditions are set out in the terms of the DPA. In this case the terms included paying a financial penalty and co-operating with future prosecutions of individuals.

---

[9] https://www.sfo.gov.uk/2017/01/17/sfo-completes-497-25m-deferred-prosecution-agreement-rolls-royce-plc/.

Rolls-Royce has also reached an Agreement with the US Department of Justice and a Leniency Agreement with Brazil's Ministério Público Federal today. In total, these agreements result in the payment of approximately £671 million (including US$170 m to the US and $25 m to Brazil) by Rolls-Royce at the current exchange rate.

In his judgment, Sir Brian Leveson said:

"[T]he investigation into the conduct of individuals continues and nothing in this agreement in any way affects the prospects of criminal prosecutions being initiated if the full code test for prosecution is met. . . . .

"[T]he question becomes whether it is necessary to inflict the undeniably adverse consequences on Rolls-Royce that would flow from prosecution because of the gravity of its offending even though it may now be considered a dramatically changed organisation.

"In any event, it will have to suffer the undeniably adverse publicity that will flow from the facts of its business practices which will be exposed by the DPA so that the way in which it has done business will be obvious. Any public procurement exercise will be conducted in the light of its history and it will doubtless only win contracts on the merits of its products. That, of course, is as it should be. Neither will the conduct of Rolls-Royce escape sanction: it could only ever be fined and the DPA has to be approached on the basis that it must be broadly comparable to the fine that a court would have imposed on conviction following a guilty plea."

Director of the SFO, David Green CB QC, said:

"Bribery harms the reputation of the UK as a safe place to do business. I welcome this DPA, a significant enforcement action by the SFO, using relatively new statutory powers in respect of an important British company. It allows Rolls-Royce to draw a line under conduct spanning seven countries, three decades and three sectors of its business.

"I am grateful to the excellent SFO team who led on this case and for the assistance and cooperation of our trusted international partners."

This is the largest ever single investigation carried out by the SFO, costing £13 m and involving some 70 SFO personnel. It is the third use of a DPA since the power became available to prosecutors in 2014.

The SFO conducted its investigation with trusted partners around the globe, resulting in a coordinated resolution with the US Department of Justice and Brazil's Ministério Público Federal. The SFO is grateful for the cooperation and support those partners provided.

Notes to Editors

1. The full DPA and Statement of Facts can be accessed here.
2. The SFO announced its investigation into Rolls-Royce PLC in December 2012.
3. For more background on the introduction and purpose DPAs, please see here.
4. The first DPA the SFO reached was with Standard Bank PLC. The second is with a company currently referred to as XYZ due to ongoing related legal proceedings.

3. **Guilty Pleas in the United States Arising from Investigations into Rolls-Royce's Former Energy Division**

4.3.3 Text from UK SFO Website[10] *(February 11, 2022)*

November, 2017

Three ex-employees of Rolls-Royce's former Energy division, James Finley, Keith Barnett and Louis Zuurhout, have pleaded guilty to bribery and corruption offences in the United States District Court for the Southern District of Ohio Eastern Division.

A further individual, Andreas Kohler, who worked for an international engineering consulting firm instructed by Rolls-Royce's former customer in Kazakhstan has entered a guilty plea. Another individual, Petros Contoguris, who worked as an intermediary for Rolls-Royce has been indicted.

This followed parallel investigations by the US authorities and the UK's SFO into corruption and failure to prevent bribery in relation to the sale of energy systems and related services.

The SFO provided significant assistance to the US authorities throughout the course of their investigation. The pleas and indictment arise from the US authorities' investigation into Rolls-Royce's former Energy division with James Finley, Keith Barnett and Louis Zuurhout's pleas also covering conduct arising from the SFO's investigation, including conduct which was addressed by the deferred prosecution agreement between the SFO and Rolls-Royce on 17 January 2017.

- James Finley was a Vice President and Global Head of Sales of Rolls-Royce's Energy Division.
- Keith Barnett was a Regional Director of Rolls-Royce's Energy Division.
- Louis Zuurhout was a Sales Manager of Rolls-Royce's Energy Division.
- Andreas Kohler was a Director of an international engineering consulting firm which worked for Rolls-Royce's former customer in Kazakhstan.
- Petros Contoguris acted as an intermediary of Rolls-Royce in Kazakhstan.

Please see the following link to the United States Department of Justice's press release.

The SFO's investigation in respect of the conduct of individuals in Rolls-Royce Civil, Defence, Marine, and former Energy Divisions continues. The SFO and DOJ continue to cooperate in their parallel investigations.

---

[10] https://www.sfo.gov.uk/2017/11/08/guilty-pleas-united-states-arising-investigations-rolls-royces-former-energy-division/.

4. **Rolls-Royce plc Agrees to Pay $170 Million Criminal Penalty to Resolve Foreign Corrupt Practices Act Case**

4.3.4 Text from US DoJ Website[11] (February 11, 2022)

FOR IMMEDIATE RELEASE
Tuesday, January 17, 2017
Company Agrees to $800 Million Global Resolution with authorities in the United States, the United Kingdom and Brazil.

Rolls-Royce plc, the United Kingdom-based manufacturer and distributor of power systems for the aerospace, defense, marine and energy sectors, has agreed to pay the U.S. nearly $170 million as part of an $800 million global resolution to investigations by the department, U.K. and Brazilian authorities into a long-running scheme to bribe government officials in exchange for government contracts.

U.S. Attorney Benjamin C. Glassman of the Southern District of Ohio, Chief Andrew Weissmann of the Fraud Section of the Justice Department's Criminal Division, Assistant Director Stephen Richardson of the FBI's Criminal Investigative Division, Assistant Director in Charge Paul M. Abbate of the FBI's Washington Field Office and Inspector in Charge Regina Faulkerson of the U.S. Postal Inspection Service's Criminal Investigations Group made the announcement.

"Bribery of government officials undermines the integrity of a free and fair market," said U.S. Attorney Glassman. "This multinational resolution imposes significant criminal penalties on Rolls-Royce for its multinational corruption."

"For more than a decade, Rolls-Royce repeatedly resorted to bribes to secure contracts and get a competitive edge in countries throughout the world," said Chief Weissmann. "The global nature of this crime requires a global response, and this case is yet another example of the strong relationship between the United States and U.K. Serious Fraud Office and Brazilian Ministério Público Federal, and the collective efforts to ensure that ethical companies can compete on an even playing field anywhere in the world."

"Rolls-Royce knowingly acted outside the law by conspiring to bribe foreign officials to gain an unfair advantage," said Assistant Director Richardson. "No company is above the law. This resolution will stand as a warning to big and small companies all across the world that the FBI will not tolerate the foreign corruption that threatens our fair and competitive markets."

"This successful parallel investigation is a tremendous example of the central importance of working cooperatively alongside our international partners to achieve a fair and meaningful resolution," said Assistant Director in Charge Abbate. "This outcome is a reflection of the immense reach and capabilities of the FBI's

---

[11] https://www.justice.gov/opa/pr/rolls-royce-plc-agrees-pay-170-million-criminal-penalty-resolve-foreign-corrupt-practices-act.

4.3 Rolls Royce

Washington Field Office international corruption squad and the global impact of the anti-corruption program."

According to admissions made in court papers unsealed today, Rolls-Royce admitted that between 2000 and 2013, the company conspired to violate the Foreign Corrupt Practices Act (FCPA) by paying more than $35 million in bribes through third parties to foreign officials in various countries in exchange for those officials' assistance in providing confidential information and awarding contracts to Rolls-Royce, RRESI and affiliated entities (collectively, Rolls-Royce):

In Thailand, Rolls-Royce admitted to using intermediaries to pay approximately $11 million in bribes to officials at Thai state-owned and state-controlled oil and gas companies that awarded approximately seven contracts to Rolls-Royce during the same time period.

In Brazil, Rolls-Royce used intermediaries to pay approximately $9.3 million in bribes to bribe foreign officials at a state-owned petroleum corporation that awarded multiple contracts to Rolls-Royce during the same time period.

In Kazakhstan, between approximately 2009 and 2012, Rolls-Royce paid commissions of approximately $5.4 million to multiple advisors, knowing that at least a portion of the commission payments would be used to bribe foreign officials with influence over a joint venture owned and controlled by the Kazakh and Chinese governments that was developing a gas pipeline between the countries. In 2012, the company also hired a local Kazakh distributor, knowing it was beneficially owned by a high-ranking Kazakh government official with decision-making authority over Rolls-Royce's ability to continue operating in the Kazakh market. During this time, the state-owned joint venture awarded multiple contracts to Rolls-Royce.

In Azerbaijan, between approximately 2000 and 2009, Rolls-Royce used intermediaries to pay approximately $7.8 million in bribes to foreign officials at the state-owned and state-controlled oil company, which awarded multiple contracts to Rolls-Royce during the same time period.

In Angola, between approximately 2008 and 2012, Rolls-Royce used an intermediary to pay approximately $2.4 million in bribes to officials at a state-owned and state-controlled oil company, which awarded three contracts to Rolls-Royce during this time period.

In Iraq, from approximately 2006 to 2009, Rolls-Royce supplied turbines to a state-owned and state-controlled oil company. Certain Iraqi foreign officials expressed concerns about the turbines and subsequently threatened to blacklist Rolls-Royce from doing future business in Iraq. In response, Rolls-Royce's intermediary paid bribes to Iraqi officials to persuade them to accept the turbines and not blacklist the company.

Rolls-Royce entered into a deferred prosecution agreement (DPA) in connection with a criminal information, filed on Dec. 20, 2016, in the Southern District of Ohio and unsealed today, charging the company with conspiring to violate the anti-bribery provisions of the FCPA. Pursuant to the DPA, Rolls-Royce agreed to pay a criminal penalty of $195,496,880, subject to a credit discussed below. The company has also agreed to continue to cooperate fully with the department's ongoing investigation, including its investigation of individuals.

In related proceedings, Rolls-Royce also settled with the United Kingdom's Serious Fraud Office (SFO) and the Brazilian Ministério Público Federal (MPF). As part of its resolution with the SFO, Rolls-Royce entered into a DPA and admitted to paying additional bribes or failing to prevent bribery payments in connection with Rolls-Royce's business operations in China, India, Indonesia, Malaysia, Nigeria, Russia and Thailand between in or around 1989 and in or around 2013, and Rolls-Royce agreed to pay a total fine of £497,252,645 ($604,808,392). As part of its leniency agreement with the MPF, Rolls-Royce also agreed to pay a penalty of approximately $25,579,170 for the company's role in a conspiracy to bribe foreign officials in Brazil between 2005 and 2008. Because the conduct underlying the MPF resolution overlaps with the conduct underlying part of the department's resolution, the department credited the $25,579,170 that Rolls-Royce agreed to pay in Brazil against the total fine in the United States. Therefore, the total amount to be paid to the United States is $169,917,710, and the total amount of penalties that Rolls-Royce has agreed to pay is more than $800 million.

A number of factors contributed to the department's criminal resolution with the company, including that Rolls-Royce did not disclose the criminal conduct to the department until after the media began reporting allegations of corruption and after the SFO had initiated an inquiry into the allegations and that the conduct was extensive and spanned 12 countries. However, the company did cooperate with the department's investigation. Rolls-Royce has also taken significant remedial measures, including terminating business relationships with multiple employees and third-party intermediaries who were implicated in the corrupt scheme; enhancing compliance procedures to review and approve intermediaries; and implementing new and enhanced internal controls to address and mitigate corruption and compliance risks. Thus, the criminal penalty reflects a 25-percent reduction from the bottom of the U.S. Sentencing Guidelines fine range. In addition, the department considered the parallel resolutions reached by the SFO and MPF in determining the resolution....

Chapter 5
Communications

5.1 Ericsson

5.1.1 Text from US Department of Justice Website[1] (January 21, 2022)

FOR IMMEDIATE RELEASE
Friday, December 6, 2019

Ericsson Agrees to Pay More Than $1 Billion to Resolve Foreign Corrupt Practices Act Case
Geoffrey S. Berman, the United States Attorney for the Southern District of New York ("SDNY"), Brian A. Benczkowski, the Assistant Attorney General for the Criminal Division of the Department of Justice ("DOJ"), and Don Fort, Chief of the Criminal Investigation Division, Internal Revenue Service ("IRS-CI"), announced today the filing of criminal charges against TELEFONAKTIEBOLAGET LM ERICSSON ("ERICSSON"), a multinational telecommunications company headquartered in Sweden, and its subsidiary ERICSSON EGYPT LTD. ("ERICSSON EGYPT") for conspiring to violate the Foreign Corrupt Practices Act ("FCPA") by bribing government officials, falsifying books and records, and failing to implement reasonable internal accounting controls. The resolutions cover criminal conduct in Djibouti, China, Vietnam, Indonesia, and Kuwait.

Mr. Berman also announced that in connection with the filed charges, ERICSSON EGYPT pled guilty today before United States District Judge Alison J. Nathan, and SDNY and DOJ entered into a deferred prosecution agreement ("DPA") with ERICSSON. Pursuant to the DPA, ERICSSON admitted to participating in the

---

[1] https://www.justice.gov/usao-sdny/pr/ericsson-agrees-pay-more-1-billion-resolve-foreign-corrupt-practices-act-case.

charged conspiracy. ERICSSON will pay a total criminal penalty of $520,650,432 to the United States, which includes a $9,520,000 criminal fine that ERICSSON agreed to pay on behalf of ERICSSON EGYPT. ERICSSON also agreed to implement rigorous internal controls, retain an independent compliance monitor for a term of 3 years, and cooperate fully with the Government in any ongoing investigations.

In related proceedings, ERICSSON reached a settlement with the U.S. Securities and Exchange Commission ("SEC"). Under the terms of its civil resolution with the SEC, ERICSSON agreed to pay $539,920,000 in disgorgement of profits and prejudgment interest, which, together with the criminal penalty paid to the United States, yields total criminal and regulatory penalties to be paid by ERICSSON of $1,060,570,432.

U.S. Attorney Geoffrey S. Berman said: "Today Swedish telecom giant Ericsson has admitted to a years-long campaign of corruption in five countries to solidify its grip on telecommunications business. Through slush funds, bribes, gifts, and graft, Ericsson conducted telecom business with the guiding principle that 'money talks.' Today's guilty plea and surrender of over a billion dollars in combined penalties should communicate clearly to all corporate actors that doing business this way will not be tolerated."

Assistant Attorney General Brian A. Benczkowski said: "Ericsson's corrupt conduct involved high-level executives and spanned 17 years and at least five countries, all in a misguided effort to increase profits. Such wrongdoing called for a strong response from law enforcement, and through a tenacious effort with our partners in the Southern District of New York, the SEC, and the IRS, today's action not only holds Ericsson accountable for these schemes, but should deter other companies from engaging in similar criminal conduct."

IRS Criminal Investigation Chief Don Fort said: "Implementing strong compliance systems and internal controls are basic principles that international companies must follow to steer clear of illegal activity. Ericsson's shortcomings in these areas made it easier for its executives and employees to pay bribes and falsify its books and records. We will continue to pursue cases such as these in order to preserve a global commerce system free of corruption."

According to the allegations contained in the criminal informations, which were filed today in Manhattan federal court, the statement of facts set forth in the DPA, and other publicly available information:

From approximately 2000 to 2016, ERICSSON and ERICSSON EGYPT, through various executives, employees, and affiliated entities, used third-party agents and consultants to bribe foreign government officials and/or manage off-the-books slush funds in countries where it pursued contracts to conduct telecommunications business. The agents were often engaged through sham contracts and paid pursuant to false invoices, with those payments accounted for improperly in ERICSSON's books and records.

In Djibouti, from approximately 2010 to 2014, ERICSSON, via subsidiaries, paid approximately $2.1 million in bribes to high-ranking government officials in order to obtain a contract valued at approximately €20.3 million. To conceal the bribe payments, an ERICSSON subsidiary entered into a sham contract with a consulting company and approved fake invoices to conceal the bribe payments, and ERICSSON employees completed a draft due diligence report that failed to disclose that the owner of the consulting company was married to a high-ranking official in Djibouti's government.

In China, from approximately 2000 to 2016, ERICSSON, via subsidiaries, paid various agents, consultants, and service providers tens of millions of dollars, a portion of which was used to fund an expense account that covered gifts, travel, and entertainment for foreign officials. ERICSSON used the expense account to win business with Chinese state-owned customers. In addition, from approximately 2013 to 2016, ERICSSON subsidiaries paid third-party service providers approximately $31.5 million pursuant to sham contracts for services that were never performed. The payments were intended to allow ERICSSON's subsidiaries to continue to use and pay third-party agents in China in contravention of ERICSSON's policies and procedures. ERICSSON knowingly mischaracterized the payments and improperly recorded them in its books and records.

In Vietnam, from approximately 2012 to 2015, ERICSSON, via subsidiaries, paid a consulting company approximately $4.8 million in order to create off-the-books slush funds. The slush funds were then used to make payments to third parties who would not be able to pass ERICSSON's due diligence processes. ERICSSON knowingly mischaracterized these payments, which were made pursuant to sham contracts for services that were never performed, and improperly recorded them in ERICSSON's books and records.

In Indonesia, from approximately 2012 to 2015, ERICSON, via a subsidiary, paid a consulting company approximately $45 million in order to create off-the-books slush funds. ERICSSON took active steps to conceal the payments, which were made pursuant to sham contracts for services that were never performed.

In Kuwait, from approximately 2011 to 2013, ERICSSON, via a subsidiary, paid a consulting company approximately $450,000 at the request of a sales agent who had given ERICSSON inside information about the bidding process for a lucrative contract with a state-owned telecommunications company. ERICSSON made the payment after one of its subsidiaries was awarded the contract, which was valued at approximately $182 million. The payment was made pursuant to a sham contract for services that were never performed.

ERICSSON EGYPT was charged with, and pled guilty to, one count of conspiring to violate the anti-bribery provisions of the FCPA. ERICSSON was charged in a two-count Information with one count of conspiracy to violate the anti-bribery provisions of the FCPA and one count of conspiracy to violate the internal-controls and books-and-records provisions of the FCPA.

Mr. Berman thanked the Fraud Section of the DOJ's Criminal Division for its collaboration, and praised the investigative efforts of IRS-CI and law enforcement authorities in Sweden. He also thanked the SEC's Division of Enforcement for its significant assistance and cooperation in the investigation. . . .

5.2 Telia

5.2.1 Text from Wikipedia[2] (22 January 2022)

Telecom Corruption Scandal
The Telecom corruption scandal is a 2012 corruption case involving the daughter of President Islam Karimov of Uzbekistan, Gulnara Karimova, accepting bribes from several foreign telecom companies in exchange for contracts to do business within Uzbekistan. Revelations showed that Karimova was paid bribes through a series of shell companies by a series of firms seeking to negotiate with her directly. In addition, it was discovered that more industries had paid bribes for access to Uzbekistan than simply telecom firms [1, 2].

Contents
1. Background
2. Revelations
3. Results
4. Reactions
5. References

1. Background

Gulnara Karimova
A Swiss criminal investigation begun in 2012 was directed at first against four Uzbek citizens who had connections to Karimova. Two of them were arrested that year and freed on bail [citation needed]. Also in 2012, a Swedish TV documentary stated that a Swedish telecom group, TeliaSonera, in exchange for licenses and frequencies in Uzbekistan, had paid $320 million to a Gibraltar-based shell company, Takilant, that was reportedly linked to Karimova. TeliaSonera denied the charges [1].

2. Revelations

In January 2013, Swedish investigators released new documents apparently showing that TeliaSonera had tried to negotiate directly with Karimova [2]. In the same year, US and Dutch authorities began investigating her [3].

In February 2014, the chief executive of TeliaSonera was forced resign after serious failures of due diligence were uncovered. In May, the Swedish media made documents public that suggested Karimova had aggressively dictated the terms of the TeliaSonera contract and threatened it with obstruction by several Uzbek government ministries if it did not agree to make illegal payments. Related money-laundering investigations in Switzerland and Sweden continued throughout the year, and hundreds of millions of dollars in accounts connected to the case being frozen by

---

[2] https://en.wikipedia.org/wiki/Telecom_corruption_scandal.

authorities [4]. By the end of the year, Swedish criminal proceedings were underway [1].

It was reported in March 2014 that Swiss authorities had begun a money-laundering investigation into Karimova and corruption in Uzbekistan, and prosecutors in Bern said that the evidence had led their investigation into Sweden and France and that they had "seized assets in excess of 800 million Swiss francs ($912 million)" [1, 5].

It was also revealed in 2014 that the US Justice Department and SEC were investigating Vimpelcom Ltd., based in Amsterdam; the Russian firm Mobile TeleSystems PJSC; and Sweden's TeliaSonera AB. These three firms had funneled hundreds of millions of dollars to firms controlled by Karimova. An August 2015 report stated that US prosecutors were asking authorities in Ireland, Belgium, Luxembourg, Sweden, and Switzerland to seize assets of about $1 billion in connection with their investigation into corruption by the three above-mentioned global telecoms and other firms liked to Karimova. US authorities believed Karimova was the principal of a "$1 billion fortune scattered across the continent" [6]. In November 2015, it was reported that Karimova was possibly on the run. Reports stated that she had been seen at a restaurant in Tashkent [3].

It was reported in January 2015 that although executives at the Norwegian telecom firm Telenor, which owns one-third of Vimpelcom, claimed that they had uncovered no signs of corruption, a newly released document indicated that Telenor had knowledge about millions in bribes [7].

3. Results

On March 20, 2015, the US Department of Justice (DOJ) "asked Sweden to freeze $30 million in funds held by a Stockholm-based bank", as part of its activities ending the corruption scheme [8] of Karimova and Talikant. At the time, Karimova was reportedly under house arrest in connection with a corruption investigation. Meanwhile, investigations were underway in Switzerland, Sweden, Norway, France and the Netherlands focusing on shell companies allegedly used by the three multinational telecoms "to pay bribes and gain access to the lucrative Uzbek mobile phone market" [8]. The DOJ probe uncovered the fact that all three firms had "paid bribes to Uzbek officials to obtain mobile telecommunications business in Uzbekistan and that funds involved in the scheme were laundered through shell companies and financial accounts around the world, including accounts held in Sweden, to conceal the true nature of these illegal payments" [8]. European investigators revealed that Takilant was run by Gayane Avakyan, a former Karimova aide [8].

According to Swiss newspaper Le Temps, "500 million francs of the seized funds involved TeliaSonera, a major telephone company and mobile network operator in Sweden and Finland, and the rest involved Karimova's personal assets" [1, 5].

A July 1, 2015, report stated that US authorities were seeking to seize $300 million in bank accounts in Ireland, Luxembourg and Belgium, alleging that the funds were the proceeds of corrupt payments in Uzbekistan by MTS and Vimpelcom, presumably to Karimova, between 2004 and 2011 [1, 9].

An August 2015 Radio Free Europe/Radio Liberty (RFE/RL) report stated that Uzbek authorities had arrested nine suspects in connection with their probe of Karimova's corruption activities. Among those taken into custody were two top executives at a Coca-Cola bottling plant in Uzbekistan, which Karimova formerly owned [10].

On September 17, 2015, it was reported that TeliaSonera was "deeply shaken" [11] by the corruption scandal in Uzbekistan, and that it would be pulling out of all of central Asia as a result of "heavy investor and public pressure." It was revealed that the US Department of Justice, along with Swedish prosecutors, had initiated investigations into corruption allegations at TeliaSonera [11].

In October 2015, Norway's government demanded the resignation of Telenor chairman Svein Aaser on account of the Uzbekistan corruption scandal [7].

4. Reactions

Reportedly, Karimova "ran afoul of her father" [12] who refused to comment on the accusations against her. Previously, in 2013, Karimova accused Uzbek security services on Twitter of harassing her and deceiving her father about her [5].

Her sister, Lola, rejected her, however. In return, Karimova accused Lola, Uzbekistan's UNESCO ambassador, who lives in a $40 million mansion in Geneva, of hiding secret stashes of dollars somewhere in the president's palace [12]. In early 2014, Gulnara claimed her sister had sent goons to physically harm her because she wished to go to Israel for medical care. Gulnara smuggled out a letter informing the media of her arrest, claiming the "reason for the Pinochet-style persecution is that I dared to speak up about things that millions are quiet about" [5]. Karimova was put under house arrest in February 2014. She stated that she and her 16-year-old daughter were prohibited from visiting the president. She claimed to have been the target of police violence and asserted that she had been refused medical and psychological treatment [12].

References

1. Keena, Colm (Jul 1, 2015). "US wants to seize allegedly corrupt funds in Irish banks". Irish Times.
2. Boehler, Patrick (Dec 5, 2012). "Where Corruption in King: 2012 Rankings". Newsfeed.
3. "Presidentdatteren mistenkes for å ha fått Vimpelcom-penger - nå kan hun være på frifot". Dagbladet.
4. "Uzbekistan". Freedom House.
5. "Uzbek first daughter, a prisoner in her home, probed for corruption". Times of Israel. Mar 27, 2014.
6. Patterson, Scott (Aug 13, 2015). "U.S. Seeks to Seize $1 Billion in Telecom Probe". Wall Street Journal.
7. Kates, Glenn (Jan 17, 2015). "'Whistle-Blower' Details Alleged Corruption By Western Telecoms In Uzbekistan". Radio Free Europe.

8. Eckel, Mike (Apr 1, 2015). "US Asks Sweden to Freeze $30 M Linked to Uzbek Corruption Case". Voice of America.
9. Lillis, Joanna (Jul 1, 2015). "Uzbekistan: US Seeks Recovery of Millions from Corruption 'Conspiracy'". Eurasia Net.
10. "Uzbekistan: More Karimova Associates Arrested in Corruption Probe". OCCRP. Aug 24, 2015.
11. "TeliaSonera set for Eurasia exodus in wake of corruption claims". Financial Times.
12. Follath, Erich (3 Apr 2015). "Tashkent's Shakespearean Drama: Scandal Shakes Uzbekistan's". Spiegel.

5.2.2 Text from US Department of Justice Website[3]

FOR IMMEDIATE RELEASE
Thursday, September 21, 2017
Telia Company AB and Its Uzbek Subsidiary Enter Into a Global Foreign Bribery Resolution of More Than $965 Million for Corrupt Payments in Uzbekistan.

Companies Agree to Coordinated Resolution between the Department of Justice, U.S. Securities and Exchange Commission (SEC) and the Kingdom of the Netherlands Representing the Second Major Resolution Involving Corruption by Telecom Companies in Uzbekistan.

Stockholm-based Telia Company AB, an international telecommunications company that was formerly an issuer of publicly traded securities in the U.S., and its Uzbek subsidiary, Coscom LLC, entered into a global foreign bribery resolution and agreed to pay a combined total penalty of more than $965 million to resolve charges arising out of a scheme to pay bribes in Uzbekistan.

Acting Assistant Attorney General Kenneth A. Blanco of the Justice Department's Criminal Division, Acting U.S. Attorney Joon H. Kim of the Southern District of New York, Chief Don Fort of Internal Revenue Service-Criminal Investigation (IRS-CI) and Special Agent in Charge Patrick J. Lechleitner of U.-S. Immigration and Customs Enforcement's Homeland Security Investigations (ICE-HSI) Washington, D.C., Field Office made the announcement.

"This resolution underscores the Department's continued and unwavering commitment to robust FCPA and white-collar criminal enforcement. It also demonstrates the Department's cooperative posture with its foreign counterparts to stamp out international corruption and to reach fair, appropriate and coordinated resolutions," said Acting Assistant Attorney General Blanco. "Foreign and domestic companies that pay bribes put honest companies at a disadvantage and distort the free and fair market and the rule of law. Today's resolution reflects the significant efforts of law enforcement, the Criminal Division and the U.S. Attorney's Office for the Southern

---

[3] https://www.justice.gov/opa/pr/telia-company-ab-and-its-uzbek-subsidiary-enter-global-foreign-bribery-resolution-more-965.

District of New York to bring such companies to justice, and to maintain a competitive and level playing field for companies to do business, create jobs and thrive."

"Today, we announce one of the largest criminal corporate bribery and corruption resolutions ever, with penalties totaling just under a billion dollars," said Acting U.S. Attorney Kim. "Swedish telecom company Telia and its Uzbek subsidiary Coscom have admitted to paying, over many years, more than $331 million in bribes to an Uzbek government official. Telia, whose securities traded publicly in New York, corruptly built a lucrative telecommunications business in Uzbekistan, using bribe payments wired around the world through accounts here in New York City. If your securities trade on our exchanges and you use our banks to move ill-gotten money, then you have to abide by our country's laws. Telia and Coscom refused to do so, and they have been held accountable in Manhattan federal court today."

"Today marks the second resolution of proceedings against corporate entities who have engaged in a global bribery scheme of government officials," said Chief Fort. "It also further demonstrates the dedication we have to identifying illegal financial transactions being used for bribery in the international community. It is important that the global economy remain on a fair playing field and IRS-CI will remain committed in our efforts to dismantle these kinds of corrupt financial schemes."

"Today's resolution marks a win against a foreign corruption scheme where millions of dollars in bribery funds were paid to Uzbekistan officials and laundered through the U.S. financial system." said Special Agent in Charge Lechleitner. "HSI, working hand in hand with our partners at IRS Criminal Investigation, leveled the playing field for publicly traded companies by exposing these corrupt practices and helped the U.S. government collect nearly $275 million in criminal penalties".

Telia entered into a deferred prosecution agreement in connection with a criminal information filed today in the Southern District of New York charging the company with conspiracy to violate the anti-bribery provisions of the Foreign Corrupt Practices Act (FCPA). The case is assigned to U.S. District Judge George B. Daniels. In addition, Coscom pleaded guilty and was sentenced by Judge Daniels on a one-count criminal information charging the company with conspiracy to violate the anti-bribery provisions of the FCPA. Pursuant to its agreement with the Department, Telia agreed to pay a total criminal penalty of $274,603,972 to the U.S., including a $500,000 criminal fine and $40 million in criminal forfeiture that Telia agreed to pay on behalf of Coscom. Telia also agreed to implement rigorous internal controls and cooperate fully with the Department's ongoing investigation, including its investigation of individuals.

The U.S. Securities and Exchange Commission (SEC) and the Public Prosecution Service of the Netherlands (Openbaar Ministrie, or OM) announced separate settlements with Telia in connection with related proceedings. Under the terms of its resolution with the SEC, Telia agreed to a total of $457,169,977 in disgorgement of profits and prejudgment interest, and the SEC agreed to credit any disgorged profits that Telia pays to the Swedish Prosecution Authority (SPA) or OM, up to half of the total. Telia agreed to pay the OM a criminal penalty of $274,000,000 for a total criminal penalty of $548,603,972, and a total resolution amount of more than $1 billion. The Department of Justice agreed to credit the criminal penalty paid to the OM as part of its agreement with the company. The SEC agreed to credit the $40 million in forfeiture paid to the Department as part of its agreement with the company. Thus, the combined total amount of criminal and regulatory penalties paid by Telia and Coscom to the U.S., Dutch, and Swedish authorities will be $965,773,949.

According to the companies' admissions, Telia and Coscom, through various managers and employees within Telia, Coscom and affiliated entities, paid approximately $331 million in bribes to an Uzbek government official, who was a close relative of a high-ranking government official and had influence over the Uzbek governmental body that regulated the telecom industry. The companies structured and concealed the bribes through various payments including to a shell company that certain Telia and Coscom management knew was beneficially owned by the foreign official. The bribes were paid on multiple occasions between approximately 2007 and 2010, so that Telia could enter the Uzbek market and Coscom could gain valuable telecom assets and continue operating in Uzbekistan. Certain Telia and Coscom management also contemplated structuring an additional bribe payment in late 2012, after Swedish media began reporting about Telia's corrupt payments in Uzbekistan, Swedish authorities began a criminal investigation and Telia opened an internal investigation.

A number of significant factors contributed to the Department's criminal resolution with the companies. Among these, the companies received significant credit for their extensive remedial measures and cooperation with the Department's investigation. Specifically, the criminal penalty reflects a 25 percent reduction off the bottom of the U.S. Sentencing Guidelines fine range. However, the companies did not receive more significant mitigation credit, either in the penalty or the form of resolution, because the companies did not voluntarily self-disclose their misconduct to the Department.

The resolution, reached in coordination with the SEC and authorities in the Netherlands, marks the second such resolution by a major international telecommunciations provider for bribery in Uzbekistan. On Feb. 18, 2016, Amsterdam-based VimpelCom Limited and its Uzbek subsidiary, Unitel LLC, also entered into resolutions with the Department of Justice and admitted to a conspiracy to make more than $114 million in bribery payments to the same Uzbek government official between 2006 and 2012. The investigation has thus far yielded a combined total of over $1.76 billion in global fines and disgorgement, including over $500 million in criminal penalties to the Department of Justice. In related actions, the Department has also filed civil complaints seeking the forfeiture of more than $850 million held in bank accounts in Switzerland, Belgium, Luxembourg and Ireland, which constitute bribe payments made by VimpelCom, Telia and a third telecommunications company, or funds involved in the laundering of those corrupt payments, to the Uzbek official.

Law enforcement colleagues within the OM and the SPA provided significant cooperation and assistance in this matter. Law enforcement colleagues in Austria, Belgium, Cyprus, France, Ireland, Latvia, Luxembourg, Norway, Switzerland, the

Isle of Man and the United Kingdom have also provided valuable assistance. The Criminal Division's Office of International Affairs provided significant assistance, as well. The SEC referred the matter to the Department and also provided extensive cooperation and assistance.

The IRS-CI and ICE-HSI are investigating the cases as part of the IRS Global Illicit Financial Team in Washington, D.C....[4]

5.3 WorldCom

5.3.1 Text from Wikipedia[5] (26 January 2022)

WorldCom Scandal

The WorldCom scandal was a major accounting scandal that came to light in the summer of 2002 at WorldCom, the USA's second-largest long-distance telephone company at the time. From 1999 to 2002, senior executives at WorldCom led by founder and CEO Bernard Ebbers orchestrated a scheme to inflate earnings in order to maintain WorldCom's stock price [1]. The fraud was uncovered in June 2002 when the company's internal audit unit, led by the vice president Cynthia Cooper, discovered over $3.8 billion of fraudulent balance sheet entries. Eventually, WorldCom was forced to admit that it had overstated its assets by over $11 billion. At the time, it was the largest accounting fraud in American history.

Background

In December 2000, WorldCom financial analyst Kim Emigh was told to allocate labour for capital projects in WorldCom's network systems division as an expense rather than book it as a capital project. By Emigh's estimate, the order would have affected at least $35 million in capital spending. Believing that he was being asked to commit tax fraud, Emigh pressed his concerns up the chain of command, notifying an assistant to WorldCom chief operating officer Ron Beaumont. Within 24 h, it was decided not to implement the directive. However, Emigh was reprimanded by his immediate superiors and subsequently laid off in March 2001 [2].

Emigh, who was from the MCI half of the 1997 WorldCom/MCI merger, later told Fort Worth Weekly in May 2002 that he had expressed concerns about MCI's spending habits for years. He believed that things had been reined in somewhat after WorldCom took over, but he was still unnerved by vendors billing WorldCom for exorbitant amounts [2]. The Fort Worth Weekly article was eventually read by Glyn

---

[4] Please note also that in March 2019, Russia's biggest mobile phone company (MTS) paid $850 million in penalties to the DOJ and SEC to resolve FCPA violations and entered into a 2-year deferred prosecution agreement. Recently, the company agreed to extend the DPA by a year as noted by the FCPA Blog article: https://fcpablog.com/2022/03/08/russia-telecom-mts-agrees-to-voluntary-one-year-dpa-extension/.

[5] https://en.wikipedia.org/wiki/WorldCom_scandal.

Smith, an internal audit manager at WorldCom headquarters in Clinton, Mississippi. After examining it, he suggested to his boss, Cynthia Cooper, that she should start that year's scheduled capital expenditure audit a few months early. Cooper agreed, and the audit began in late May [3]: 220–221.

Prepaid Capacity

During a meeting with the auditors, corporate finance director Sanjeev Sethi explained that differing amounts in two capital spending expenditures related to "prepaid capacity." No one in the room had ever heard that term before. When pressed for an explanation, Sethi said that he did not know what the term meant, even though his division approved capital spending requests. He referred the auditors to corporate controller David Myers [3]: 223–225. Suspicious, Cooper asked Mark Abide, head of property, about the term. Abide was not familiar with it either, even though he had made several entries about prepaid capacity in WorldCom's computerized accounting system [3]: 225.

Cooper and Smith asked senior associate Eugene Morse, one of the "techies" on the internal audit team, to peruse the accounting system for any references to prepaid capacity. Morse was eventually able to find one and trace it through the system. However, the amounts were bouncing between accounts in an unusual manner, resulting in a large round amount moving from WorldCom's income statement to its balance sheet. Cooper asked Morse to see if there was another prepaid capacity entry that moved around in similar fashion [3]: 225–227. Morse went to work, but pulled so much data that he frequently clogged up the accounting servers. Eventually, he and the rest of the team began working at night. Finally, on June 10, Morse found more entries about "prepaid capacity"; large amounts had been transferred from the income statement to the balance sheet from the third quarter of 2001 to the first quarter of 2002 [3]: 231–233.

Suspicions Mount

Soon afterward, chief financial officer Scott Sullivan, Cooper's immediate supervisor, called Cooper in for a meeting about audit projects, and asked the internal audit team to walk him through recently completed audits. When Smith's turn came, Cooper asked about the prepaid capacity entries. Sullivan claimed that it referred to costs related to SONET rings and lines that were either not being used at all or were seeing low usage. He claimed those costs were being capitalized because the costs associated with line leases were fixed even as revenue dropped. He planned to take a restructuring charge in the second quarter of 2002, after which WorldCom would allocate these costs between restructuring charges and expenses. He asked Cooper to postpone the capital-expenditure audit until the third quarter, heightening Cooper's suspicions [3]: 233–237.

That night, Cooper and Smith called Max Bobbitt, a WorldCom board member and the chairman of the Audit Committee, to discuss their concerns. Bobbitt was concerned enough to tell Cooper to discuss the matter with Farrell Malone of KPMG, WorldCom's external auditor [3]: 237–238. KPMG had inherited the WorldCom account when it bought Arthur Andersen's Jackson practice in the wake of Andersen's indictment for its role in the accounting scandal at Enron [3]:

229. By this time, the internal audit team had found 28 prepaid capacity entries dating back to the second quarter of 2001. By their calculations, if not for those entries, WorldCom's $130 million profit in the first quarter of 2002 would have become a $395 million loss. Despite this, Bobbitt thought it was premature to discuss the matter with the Audit Committee at that point. He did, however, discuss the matter with Sullivan, and assured Cooper that he would have support for those entries by the following Monday [3]: 240–241.

Fraud Revealed
Cooper decided not to wait to discuss the matter with Sullivan. She decided to ask the accountants who made those entries to provide support for them herself. Beforehand, she asked Kenny Avery, who had been Andersen's lead partner on the WorldCom account before KPMG took over, if he knew about prepaid capacity. Avery had never heard of the term, and knew of nothing in Generally Accepted Accounting Principles that allowed for capitalizing line costs. Andersen, it turned out, had never tested WorldCom's capital expenditures for it [3].

Cooper and Smith then questioned Betty Vinson, the accounting director who made the entries. To their surprise, Vinson admitted she had made the entries without knowing what they were for or seeing support for them. She had done so at the direction of Myers and general accounting director Buford Yates. When Cooper and Smith spoke with Yates, he admitted that he did not know what prepaid capacity was. Yates also claimed that accountants reporting to him booked entries at Myers' direction [3]: 243–245.

Finally, the internal auditors spoke with Myers. He admitted that there was no support for the entries. In fact, they had been booked "based on what we thought the margins should be," and there were no accounting standards that supported them. He admitted that the entries should have never been made, but it was difficult to stop once they started. Although he was uncomfortable with the entries, he never thought that he would have to explain them to regulators [3]: 246–247. The following day, Farrell met with Sullivan and Myers, and concluded that their rationale for the entries made sense "from a business perspective, but not an accounting perspective." In response, Sullivan, Myers, Yates and Abide scrambled to find amounts that were expensed when they should have been capitalized in hopes of offsetting the prepaid capacity entries. They believed that the only other alternative was an earnings restatement [3].

Bobbitt finally called an Audit Committee meeting for June 20. By this time, Cooper's team had discovered over $3 billion in questionable transfers from line cost expense accounts to assets from 2001 to 2002. At the meeting, Farrell stated that there was nothing in GAAP that would allow those entries. Sullivan claimed that WorldCom had invested in expanding the telecom network from 1999 onward, but the anticipated expansion in customer usage never occurred. He argued that the entries were justified on the basis of the matching principle, which allowed costs to be booked as expenses so they align with any future benefit accrued from an asset. He also contended that since capital assets were worth less than what the books said they should be, he reiterated his proposal for a restructuring charge, or an "impairment charge," as he called it, for the second quarter of 2002. He claimed that Myers could provide support for the entries. The committee gave him until the following Monday to get support [3]: 256–258.

Over the weekend, Cooper and her team discovered several more suspicious "prepaid capacity" entries. All told, the internal audit unit had discovered a total of 49 prepaid capacity entries detailing $3.8 billion in transfers spread out across all of 2001 and the first quarter of 2002. Several of them were keyed in on explicit directions from Sullivan and Myers under the line "SS entry." While some of the suspicious entries were made by directors and managers, others were made by lower-level accountants who didn't understand the seriousness of what they were doing [3]: 258–259. While meeting with another accounting director, Troy Normand, they learned about more potentially illicit accounting. According to Normand, management had drawn down the company's cost reserves in portions of 2000 and 2001 to artificially reduce expenses [3]: 261.

At the same time, the Audit Committee asked KPMG to conduct its own review. KPMG discovered that Sullivan had moved system costs across a number of property accounts, allowing them to be booked as capital expenditures. The expenses were spread out so they weren't initially obvious. When KPMG asked Andersen's former WorldCom engagement team about the entries, the Andersen accountants said they would have never approved of the entries had they known about them. Sullivan was asked to present a written explanation for his actions by Monday [4].

At an Audit Committee meeting that Monday, Sullivan presented a white paper explaining his reasoning. The Audit Committee and KPMG were not persuaded. They concluded that the amounts were transferred with the sole purpose of meeting Wall Street targets, and the only acceptable remedy was to restate corporate earnings for all of 2001 and the first quarter of 2002. Andersen withdrew its audit opinion for 2001, and the board demanded Sullivan and Myers' resignations [3]: 262–264.

SEC Begins Investigation

On June 25, after the amount of the illicit entries was confirmed, the board accepted Myers' resignation and fired Sullivan when he refused to resign. On the same day, WorldCom executives briefed the SEC, revealing that it would have to restate its earnings for the previous five quarters [3, 4]: 265. Later that day, WorldCom publicly admitted that it had overstated its cash flow by over $3.8 billion over the previous five quarters. The disclosure came at a particularly bad time for WorldCom. Even before the scandal broke, its credit had been reduced to junk status, and its stock had lost over 94 percent of its value. It had been facing a separate SEC investigation into its accounting that had started earlier in the year, and was laboring under $30 billion in debt. Amid rumors of bankruptcy, WorldCom said it would lay off 17,000 employees [5].

The federal government had already begun an informal inquiry earlier in June, when Vinson, Yates, and Normand secretly met with SEC and Justice Department officials [3]: 261. The SEC filed civil fraud charges against WorldCom on June 26, speculating that WorldCom had engaged in a concerted effort to manipulate its earnings in order to meet Wall Street targets and support its stock price. Additionally, it claimed that the scheme had been "directed and approved by senior management"–thus hinting that executives higher up on the org chart than Sullivan and Myers had known about the Scheme [6].

Trial
In 2005, Ebbers was found guilty by a jury for fraud, conspiracy, and filing false documents with regulators. He was subsequently sentenced to 25 years in prison [7]. However he was released in December 2019 due to declining health. Ebbers died February 2, 2020 [8].

Aftermath
The Sarbanes–Oxley Act is said to have passed due to scandals such as WorldCom and Enron.

WorldCom, by then renamed MCI, was acquired by Verizon Communications in January 2006 [9].

References

1. "Worldcom, Inc. 2002 Form 10-K Annual Report". U.S. Securities and Exchange Commission.
2. Jump up to: a b Gale Reaves (May 16, 2002). "Accounting for Anguish". Fort Worth Weekly.
3. Jump up to: a b c d e f g h i j k l m n o p q r s Cooper, Cynthia (April 15, 2009). Extraordinary Circumstances: The Journey of a Corporate Whistleblower. Hoboken, New Jersey: John Wiley & Sons. ISBN 978-0-470-12,429-1.
4. Jump up to: a b Kurt Eichenwald; Simon Romero (June 27, 2002). "The Latest Corporate Scandal Is Sudden, Vast and Simple". The New York Times.
5. Simon Romero; Alex Berenson (June 26, 2002). "WorldCom Says It Hid Expenses, Inflating Cash Flow $3.8 Billion". The New York Times.
6. Simon Romero (June 27, 2002). "WorldCom Facing Charges Of Fraud, Inquiries Expand". The New York Times.
7. "Ebbers found guilty in WorldCom trial". the Guardian. 2005-03-15. Retrieved 2020-10-19.
8. "Bernard Ebbers, Telecom CEO Sent To Prison In Accounting Scandal, Dies". NPR.org. Retrieved 2020-10-19.
9. "WorldCom". www.verizon.com. Retrieved 2020-10-19.

Chapter 6
Education

6.1 US College Corruption

6.1.1 Wikipedia[1] Summary of US College Corruption (August 10, 2022)

2019 College Admissions Bribery Scandal
"Operation Varsity Blues" redirects here. For the documentary film about the scandal, see Operation Varsity Blues: The College Admissions Scandal.

In 2019, a scandal arose over a criminal conspiracy to influence undergraduate admissions decisions at several top American universities. The investigation into the conspiracy was code named **Operation Varsity Blues** [1, 2]. The investigation and related charges were made public on March 12, 2019, by United States federal prosecutors. At least 53 [3] people have been charged as part of the conspiracy [4, 5], a number of whom pleaded guilty or agreed to plead guilty. Thirty-three parents of college applicants are accused of paying more than $25 million between 2011 and 2018 to **William Rick Singer**, organizer of the scheme, who used part of the money to fraudulently inflate entrance exam test scores and bribe college officials [6, 7].

Singer controlled the two firms involved in the scheme, Key Worldwide Foundation and The Edge College & Career Network (also known as "The Key"). He pleaded guilty and cooperated with the Federal Bureau of Investigation (FBI) in gathering incriminating evidence against co-conspirators [8, 9]. He said he unethically facilitated college admission for children in more than 750 families [10]. Singer faces up to 65 years in prison, and a fine of $1.25 million.

Prosecutors in the Office of the U.S. Attorney for the District of Massachusetts, led by United States Attorney Andrew Lelling, unsealed indictments and complaints for felony conspiracy to commit mail fraud and honest services mail fraud against 50 people, including Singer, who has been "portrayed [...] as a criminal mastermind"

---
[1] https://en.wikipedia.org/wiki/2019_college_admissions_bribery_scandal.

© The Author(s), under exclusive license to Springer Nature Switzerland AG 2022
D. Smith, *Fraud and Corruption*, Contributions to Finance and Accounting,
https://doi.org/10.1007/978-3-031-10063-5_6

[11], university staff he bribed, and parents who are alleged to have used bribery and fraud to secure admission for their children to 11 universities [12–15]. Among the accused parents are prominent business-people and well-known actors [16, 17]. Those charges have a maximum term of 20 years in prison, supervised release of 3 years, and a $250,000 fine. One month later, 16 of the parents were also indicted by prosecutors for alleged felony conspiracy to commit money laundering. This third charge has a maximum sentence of 20 years in prison, supervised release of 3 years, and a $500,000 fine.

The investigation's name, Operation Varsity Blues, comes from a 1999 film of the same name [1, 2]. The case is the largest of its kind to be prosecuted by the US Justice Department [18].

Contents
    1. Discovery and Charges
        1.1. Allegations
        1.2. Methods of Fraudulent Admission
    2. Involved Parties and Organizations
        2.1. Key Worldwide Foundation/The Edge College & Career Network
        2.2. Universities and Accused Personnel
        2.3. Parents
    3. Responses
        3.1. Extrajudicial Actions
        3.2. Lawsuits
        3.3. Commentary
    4. Documentaries and Adaptation
    5. See Also
    6. Notes
    7. References
    8. External Links

Discovery and Charges

The FBI alleged that beginning in 2011, 33 parents of high school students conspired with other people to use bribery and other forms of fraud to illegally arrange to have their children admitted to top colleges and universities [19]. The first reporter was Julie Taylor-Vaz, a Buckley School guidance counselor, who in 2017 learned that a Buckley student identified as "Eliza" Bass—a pseudonym given by Vanity Fair—had been accepted to Tulane University, Georgetown and Loyola Marymount as an "African-American tennis whiz, ranked in the Top 10 in California," according to the report. The problem was that "Eliza" was white and did not play tennis. Eliza's father, Adam J. Bass, a member of the Buckley School Board, initially denied that he had used an outside admissions consultant before finally admitting to Buckley that his family had hired Rick Singer, the Newport Beach man who became infamous in March for spearheading the admissions scandal [20]. Bass was a business partner of Singer's and therefore did not have to pay any fees. Authorities became aware of the scheme around April 2018 when Los Angeles businessman Morrie Tobin, who was under investigation in an unrelated case for alleged pump-and-dump conspiracy and securities fraud, offered information in exchange for leniency in the previously existing, unrelated case [21]. Tobin, who attended but did not graduate from Yale, told authorities that the Yale women's soccer head coach, Rudolph "Rudy" Meredith, had asked him for $450,000 in exchange for helping his youngest daughter gain admission to the school [22]. As part of his cooperation with the FBI, Tobin wore a recording device while talking to Meredith in a Boston hotel on April 12, 2018; Meredith subsequently agreed to cooperate with the authorities and led them to Singer [23, 24]. Meredith pled guilty as part of his cooperation with the prosecution [22, 23]. Tobin has not been charged in this case, but in February 2019 he pled guilty in the unrelated securities fraud case [23]. US sentencing guidelines, to which judges often refer when deciding sentences, call for between eight and 10 years behind bars [21]. According to *The Wall Street Journal*, *Vanity Fair*, and CBS, prosecutors are recommending 36 months of supervised release [22, 23, 25]. In addition, Tobin has agreed to forfeit $4 million as part of his plea deal [21]. Tobin was scheduled for sentencing at a hearing in June 2019, but this did not in fact take place [25, 26].

On March 12, 2019, federal prosecutors in Boston unsealed a criminal complaint charging 50 people with conspiracy to commit felony mail fraud and honest services mail fraud in violation of Title 18 United States Code, Section 1349 [15, 19]. Those charges have a maximum term of 20 years in prison, supervised release of 3 years, and a $250,000 fine [27]. The charges were announced by Andrew Lelling, United States Attorney for the District of Massachusetts [28, 29]. Assistant U.S. Attorneys Eric Rosen, Justin O'Connell, Leslie Wright, and Kristen Kearney of the securities and financial fraud unit are prosecuting the case [30, 31]. FBI special agent Laura Smith signed the 204-page affidavit in support of the charges [32].

On April 9, 16 of the original 33 charged parents (e.g., Lori Loughlin, her husband Mossimo Giannulli, Gamal Aziz, Douglas M. Hodge, Bill McGlashan, Diane and Todd Blake, I-Hsin "Joey" Chen, Michelle Janavs, Elizabeth and Manuel Henriquez, Elisabeth Kimmel, Marci Palatella, John Wilson, Homayoun Zadeh, and Robert Zangrillo), who had not pled guilty to the original charges, were additionally charged with conspiracy to commit money laundering by federal prosecutors in Boston in a superseding indictment [27, 33]. The indictment added those defendants to an existing case against David Sidoo, another of the 33 parents, that was already pending before Judge Nathaniel Gorton [34]. The indictment alleged that the parents engaged in a conspiracy to launder bribes paid to Singer "by funneling them through Singer's purported charity and his for-profit corporation" [27]. This third charge has a maximum sentence of 20 years in prison, supervised release of 3 years, and a $500,000 fine [27].

In June 2022, the final defendant in the investigation, Amin Khoury, was acquitted at trial of bribing a Georgetown University tennis coach to get his daughter into Georgetown. Mr. Khoury was accused of delivering $180,000 in a paper bag to the tennis coach through a middleman [35]. Mr. Khoury, who was represented by attorney Roy Black, was the only defendant in the Varsity Blues investigation to gain an acquittal [36].

Allegations
Federal prosecutors alleged a college-admission scheme that involved:

- bribing exam administrators to facilitate cheating on college and university entrance exams [19];
- bribing coaches and administrators of elite universities to nominate unqualified applicants as elite recruited athletes, thus facilitating the applicants' admission [19];
- using a charitable organization to conceal the source and nature of laundered bribery payments [19].

Court documents unsealed in March 2019 detail a scheme led by William Rick Singer, a 58-year-old resident of Newport Beach, California. Wealthy parents paid Singer to illegally arrange to have their children admitted to elite schools by bribing admissions testing officials, athletics staff, and coaches at universities. Payments were made to Key Worldwide Foundation, a nonprofit organization owned by Singer and previously granted 501(c)(3) status; that status allowed him to avoid federal income taxes on the payments, while parents could deduct their "donations" from their own personal taxes. Singer offered college counseling services as The Edge College & Career Network, a limited liability company registered in 2012, which he operated out of his home in Newport Beach [31, 37].

Methods of Fraudulent Admission
Singer primarily used two fraudulent techniques to help clients' children gain admission to elite universities: cheating on college entrance exams and fabrication of elite sports credentials [38].

Cheating on College Entrance Exams
Singer arranged to allow clients' children to cheat on the SAT or ACT college admission tests [17]. Singer worked with psychologists to complete the detailed paperwork required to falsely certify clients' children as having a learning disability; this in turn gave them access to accommodations, such as extra time, while taking the tests. Singer said he could obtain a falsified disability report from a psychologist for $4000 to $5000 [39], and that the report could be re-used to fraudulently obtain similar benefits at the schools.

Once the paperwork was complete, Singer told clients to invent false travel plans to arrange to have their children's test locations moved to a test center under his control, either in West Hollywood or Houston. Parents might also be advised to fabricate a family event that could provide a pretense for the student to take the SAT, ACT, or other test at a private location where Singer could have complete control over the testing process [38].

In some cases, the student was involved directly in the fraud. In others, the fraud was kept secret from the student and corrupt proctors altered tests on their behalf after the fact [40]. In some cases, other people posed as the students to take the tests. Mark Riddell, a Harvard alumnus and college admission exam preparation director at IMG Academy, was one of the stand-in test takers who took over two dozen exams; he pled guilty to one count of conspiracy to commit mail fraud and honest services mail fraud and one count of money laundering, and agreed to cooperate with investigators [41–43]. Prosecutors said he was paid $10,000 per test, and the government is seeking to recover almost $450,000 from him in forfeiture [44]. Riddell did not have advance access to the test papers, but was described as "just a really smart guy" [45]. He could be sentenced to up to 20 years in prison, but reportedly prosecutors said that because of his cooperation they will instead likely recommend 33 months' imprisonment at his November 1 (originally July 18) sentencing hearing [43, 46, 47].

According to recorded phone calls, the transcripts of which were included in court filings, Singer claimed that the practice of fraudulently obtaining accommodations such as extra testing time, intended for those with legitimate learning disabilities, was widespread outside of his particular scheme:

Yeah, everywhere around the country. What happened is, all the wealthy families that figured out that if I get my kid tested and they get extended time, they can do better on the test. So most of these kids don't even have issues, but they're getting time. The playing field is not fair [48].

For example, Jane Buckingham was arrested on March 12, 2019, for allegedly submitting false paperwork saying her son had a learning disability, and paying $50,000 to Key Worldwide Foundation for a proctor to take the ACT on her son's behalf, scoring a 35 out of 36. The goal was entrance to the University of Southern California (USC) [49]. Portions of recorded conversations between Buckingham and a cooperating witness were included in the FBI's affidavit [19, 42, 50].

Fabrication of Sports Credentials
Singer also bribed college athletics staff and coaches. At certain colleges, these personnel can submit a certain number of sports recruit names to the admissions office, which then views those applications more favorably. Singer used his Key Worldwide Foundation as a money-laundering operation to pay coaches a bribe for labeling applicants as athletic recruits. He also fabricated profiles highlighting each applicant's purported athletic prowess. In some cases, image editing software (e.g., Photoshop) was used to insert a photograph of a student's face onto a photograph of another person participating in the sport to document purported athletic activity [38].

In one such incident, Michael Center, the men's tennis coach at the University of Texas (UT), accepted about $100,000 to designate an applicant as a recruit for the Texas Longhorns tennis team [7]. A similar fraud occurred at Yale [22], where the then-head coach of the women's soccer team, Rudolph "Rudy" Meredith, allegedly accepted a $450,000 bribe to falsely identify an applicant as a recruit [51, 52]. USC's senior associate athletic director Donna Heinel and water polo coach Jovan Vavic allegedly received $1.3 million and $250,000, respectively, for similar frauds [53]. They were indicted alongside former USC women's soccer coaches Ali Khosroshahin and Laura Janke [54]. Coaches at two other Pac-12 programs, University of California, Los Angeles (UCLA) men's soccer coach Jorge Salcedo and Stanford sailing coach John Vandemoer, have been charged with accepting bribes [55]. Vandemoer admitted that he accepted $270,000 to classify two applicants as prospective sailors, and agreed to plead guilty to a charge of racketeering conspiracy

[56]. At Wake Forest, head volleyball coach William "Bill" Ferguson was placed on administrative leave following charges of racketeering [57]. Former Georgetown tennis coach Gordon "Gordie" Ernst is alleged to have facilitated as many as 12 students through fraudulent means while accepting bribes of up to $950,000 [58]. On March 20, 2019, the University of San Diego (USD) revealed that its former men's basketball head coach Lamont Smith allegedly accepted bribes [59]. Hours after that revelation, Smith resigned from his position as assistant coach at the University of Texas at El Paso [60]. Two San Diego families were accused of paying $875,000 as part of the scheme [61].

Bill McGlashan, a private equity investor, allegedly discussed using Adobe Photoshop to create a fake profile for his son as a football kicker to help him get into USC [62, 63]. Similarly, Marci Palatella, wife of former San Francisco 49ers player Lou Palatella, allegedly conspired with Singer to pass her son off as a long snapper recruit for USC [63, 64]. In one of the most notable cases, actress Lori Loughlin, famous for her role on the American sitcom *Full House* and the drama *When Calls the Heart*, and her husband, fashion designer Mossimo Giannulli of Mossimo fashion, allegedly paid $500,000 in bribes to arrange to have their two daughters accepted into USC as members of the rowing team, although neither girl had participated in the sport [39]. On March 13, 2019 [65, 66], media sources reported that, when news of the scandal broke, Loughlin's younger daughter was on Rick Caruso's yacht in the Bahamas with her friend, Gianna, Caruso's daughter [67, 68]. Caruso is the chairman of the USC Board of Trustees [69, 70].

Singer pleaded guilty on March 12, 2019, in the U.S. District Court in Boston to four felony counts of conspiracy to commit money laundering, conspiracy to defraud the United States, and obstruction of justice for alerting a number of subjects to the investigation after he began cooperating with the government [71]. He faces up to 65 years in prison and a fine of $1.25 million [72].

Involved Parties and Organizations

A total of 50 people have been charged in the investigations [73]. This number includes 33 parents of college applicants [50] and 11 named collegiate coaches or athletic administrators from eight universities [17, 73, 74]. Three additional universities are involved, but no staff members from those schools have been directly named or implicated, believed to be Stanford, Harvard, and Northwestern [12, 13, 75].

Key Worldwide Foundation/The Edge College & Career Network
- William Rick Singer, purported college counselor, and author of self-help books for college admission. Singer organized and sold fraudulent college admission services [16, 17]. Singer pled guilty and cooperated with the prosecution [53].
- Mark Riddell, a Harvard alumnus and former director of college entrance exams at IMG Academy [76]. Riddell was paid by Singer to fraudulently take admission tests, impersonating the clients' children; he also paid College Board (which develops and administers the SAT and related tests), Educational Testing Service, and ACT contractors to deliberately mis-administer the tests [44, 77, 78]. He was fired from IMG Academy and pled guilty [46, 76].

- Steven Masera, officer at Singer's companies [77, 78]. Pleaded guilty to conspiracy to commit racketeering.
- Mikaela Sanford, employee at Singer's companies [77, 78]. Pleaded guilty to conspiracy to commit racketeering.

Other Involved Conspirators
- Igor Dvorskiy, administrator of standardized tests (including those from ACT and the College Board), and director of an LA-area private school [77, 78]. Pleaded guilty to conspiracy to commit racketeering [79].
- Martin Fox, Houston tennis academy president [77, 78]. Pleaded guilty to conspiracy to commit racketeering [80]. Sentenced to 3 months in prison, 15 months' supervised release with 3 months' home confinement, $95,000 fine, forfeiture of $245,000 & 250 h of community service.
- Niki Williams, administrator of standardized tests for ACT and College Board, Houston-area assistant high school teacher [77, 78]. Pleaded guilty to mail and wire fraud.

Universities and Accused Personnel

The following universities, their associated athletic programs, and 11 university personnel were involved in the case [12, 14, 74]:

Please consult full list on the internet

Parents

Officials said Singer had many legitimate clients, who did not engage in any fraud [118]. Singer cited famous clients on his Facebook page while promoting his 2014 book *Getting In* [118, 119] and, as a result of this and other public endorsements by Singer [120], many former clients have made statements to distance themselves and their children from any perceived involvement in the scandal [118, 120].

The table below lists parents in connection with the nationwide college admissions prosecution as listed by CNN [12], CBS News [50], and *People* [77, 78]. Morrie Tobin is not included in the above total due to the fact that he is an unindicted cooperating witness supporting the prosecution's case [22, 23, 121, 122]. To date, 38 of the indicted parents have either pled guilty or have been convicted [123].

Please consult full list on the internet

Responses

In response to the scandal, the National Collegiate Athletic Association (NCAA), the chief governing body for college sports in the United States, announced plans to review the allegations "to determine the extent to which NCAA rules may have been violated" [55, 208].

U.S. Senator Ron Wyden (D-OR), of the Senate Finance Committee, plans to sponsor a bill making donations to schools taxable if the donor has children attending or applying to the college [209]. Separately, Senators Chris Coons (D-DE) and Johnny Isakson (R-GA) have agreed to reintroduce 2017 legislation that imposes a fine on colleges and universities that have the smallest proportion of low-income students [209].

One of the parents who was convicted, Robert Zangrillo, was pardoned by President Donald Trump on his final day in office [178, 210].

Extrajudicial Actions
Indicted coaches were fired or suspended, or had already left the university at the time of the charges [211]. Mark Riddell, who took tests on behalf of the students, was suspended from his position as director of college entrance exam preparation at IMG Academy and fired a week later [46, 76, 212].

On March 12, 2019, William Singer, the CEO of Edge College & Career Network who masterminded the scandal, pleaded guilty to four criminal charges involving racketeering conspiracy money laundering conspiracy, conspiracy to defraud the U.S. government and obstruction of justice [213]. The U.S. government has not yet imposed a sentence on Singer [214]. On March 26, 2019, Yale became the first university to rescind the admission of a student associated with the scandal [207]. On April 2, Stanford announced they also expelled a student connected to the fraud [215]. In June 2019, Grand Canyon University ended its relationship with Singer, who was enrolled as a student of the university's psychiatric school since November 2019 [216].

Actress Felicity Huffman formally pleaded guilty to honest services fraud, which involved hiring someone to test SAT scores while using the name of her daughter Sophia, on May 13, 2019, and on September 13 she was sentenced to 14 days in jail, 1 year of supervised release, fined $30,000 and ordered to undertake 250 h of community service [217–219]. On October 15, 2019, Huffman reported to the Federal Correctional Institution in Dublin, California, to begin her sentence [220]. She was meant to be released from prison on October 27, 2019, but was released 2 days early because October 27 fell on a weekend [221]. As of October 2020, when Huffman completed her full sentence, no charges have filed against Huffman's husband and Sophia's father, actor and director William H. Macy [222].

The Hallmark Channel cut its ties to Lori Loughlin, star of the program *Garage Sale Mystery* and *When Calls the Heart*, after she was named as a parent in the indictments [120]. According to *The Hill*, Netflix decided to drop Loughlin from *Fuller House* as well [223]. Her younger daughter Olivia Jade also lost her partnership with TRESemmé and the Sephora chain of beauty products [224]. It was reported by TMZ, Page Six, and others that Loughlin's daughters dropped out of USC due to fears of being "viciously bullied" [138]; however, a USC spokesperson confirmed in March that they both remained enrolled at the school [120, 225] and in October the school's registrar stated they were no longer enrolled [226]. According to the *San Jose Mercury News*, USC scheduled a hearing in March 2019 to determine if Olivia Jade should be designated a "disruptive individual", which would result in her lifetime ban from the university's campus and properties [227]. Loughlin was found guilty and began serving a 2-month prison sentence on October 30, 2020 [228, 229]. Giannulli, who was also found guilty, began serving a 5-month prison sentence on November 19, 2020 [230].

On September 8, 2021, the scandal's first criminal trial, which saw parents John Wilson and Gamal Aziz as defendants, officially began, with jury selection commencing in a Boston federal court [128]. This trial was centered around phony credentials which the two defendants paid to admit their children into the University of Southern California [128]. Both men were convicted by a jury on October 8, 2021, after 10 h of deliberation [231].

On March 10, 2022, the first criminal trial involving a former coach, former USC water polo coach Jovan Vavic, got underway in the same Boston federal court as well [106, 107]. Vavic was the only coach implicated in the case who opted to challenge the charges brought against them in court [106, 108]. On April 9, 2022, a federal jury in Boston convicted Vavic of fraud and bribery [110].

Lawsuits

Multiple lawsuits were immediately filed against universities and individuals. Three students from Tulane University, Rutgers University, and a California community college filed a complaint against Singer and the affected universities that they hope will be certified as a class-action suit [232]. A Stanford undergraduate claimed a loss for the time and money she spent applying to schools named in the scandal, as well as the possibility that the stain on Stanford's reputation will decrease the value of her degree. A parent filed a $500 billion civil suit in San Francisco against all the indicted individuals, claiming that her son was denied admission to some schools because of other parents buying access [233].

Commentary

After the scandal broke, multiple American news sources including *The Atlantic* [234], *Vox* [235], *Rolling Stone* [236], and *The New York Times* [237] characterized it as a symptom of a broken college admissions system [238, 239]. Alan Dershowitz, professor emeritus at Harvard Law School, said it was "the worst scandal involving elite universities in the history of the United States" [240]. Elizabeth Warren, United States Senator from Massachusetts (where all the criminal cases were filed), told news media that the scandal represented "just one more example of how the rich and powerful know how to take care of their own" [241].

Much of the news coverage attempted to explain why anyone would have been tempted by Singer's scheme. A common attribute among the defendants was that many were rich, but not ultra-rich. According to *The New York Times* [242], college admissions at certain elite American universities had become so selective that a family would have to make a minimum donation of $ten million to inspire an admission committee to take a second look at their child, and even for families of such means, there would be no guarantee of return on investment, while Singer was selling certainty [242]. In open court, he said: "I created a guarantee" [242]. The *Los Angeles Times* explained that there was probably also a social signaling element at work, in that admission to an elite university based purely upon an applicant's apparent merit publicly validates both the child's innate talent and the parents' own parenting skills in a way that an admission coinciding with a sizable donation does not [243].

In turn, others examined why certain universities had become so selective in the first place. *The Atlantic* pointed out that college seats are not scarce in the United States, except at a handful of universities which became selective on purpose: "[S] carcity has the added benefit of increasing an institution's prestige. The more students who apply, and the fewer students who get in, the more selective an institution becomes, and, subsequently, the more prestigious. And parents are clawing over one another to get a taste of the social capital that comes with that" [244]. Arizona State University (ASU) president Michael M. Crow described the "crisis of access to these social-status-granting institutions" as a full-blown "hysteria" [244]. It was alleged in court filings that one of the defendant parents had named ASU as a university they were specifically trying to avoid; the non-selective university has been the "butt of jokes" in American television shows for many years, as well as the 2015 film *Ted 2* [245]. The inevitable result, according to *Newsweek*, was that the most elite institutions had created a situation in which purely meritocratic admissions had become impossible because they were already turning away too many overqualified candidates—former Harvard president Drew Gilpin Faust had once said, "we could fill our class twice over with valedictorians" [246]. It was also recognized that any workable long-term solution would need to alleviate the underlying anxiety driving the crisis, either by restructuring the college admissions process or the American labor market [244, 246].

The HuffPost explained that such anxiety barely exists in Canada, whose 4-year universities do not show such extreme disparities in selectivity and prestige, and in turn, most Canadian employers do not rigidly discriminate between job candidates based upon where they graduated. In contrast, selective American universities have evolved into gatekeepers for the highest echelons of certain socially prestigious and financially lucrative industries like law and finance [247]. University of Oklahoma history professor Wilfred M. McClay told *Newsweek*: "I'm not going to pretend there isn't a difference between Harvard and Suffolk County Community College, but I think this situation where the Supreme Court is made up entirely of Harvard[a] or Yale Law School graduates is wrong. The thing driving the current scandal seems to be that ultimately parents were willing to do anything to game the system to get their kids these advantages, not because the education was better but because the legitimation of social position would be better" [246].

Writing for *The Washington Post*, psychologists Jonathan Wai, Matt Brown and Christopher Chabris cited research on the predictive powers of the SAT and the doubtful value of costly SAT preparation programs, and concluded, "If the SAT were nothing but a wealth test, then Lori Loughlin, Mossimo Giannulli and other super-rich parents would not have had to cheat to get their kids into the latter two schools. In reality, they had to fake intellectual ability—the one thing they could not buy" [248].

Documentaries and Adaptation
In 2019, Lifetime produced and broadcast a television film about this event called *The College Admissions Scandal*. The film stars Penelope Ann Miller as Caroline DeVere, Mia Kirshner as Bethany Slade, and Michael Shanks as Rick Singer [249].

On April 4, 2019, 3 weeks after Operation Varsity Blues' charges were made public, Granite Bay High School debuted *Ranked*, a new musical. The show, written from 2018 to 2019 by the school's drama teacher and musical director, focused on academic pressure in schools, specifically telling the story of a student whose parents were paying for his grades without his knowledge [250]. The timing of the musical's debut in relation to the scandal was serendipitous, and earned the high school national attention. Rick Singer worked in the Granite Bay community a decade prior as a college coach for local high school students [251].

In 2019, Lifetime released a movie based on the incident called *The College Admissions Scandal* [252, 253] and a documentary called *Beyond the Headlines: The College Admissions Scandal* with Gretchen Carlson [254].

A fictionalized account of the events was in the book *Admissions* by Julie Buxbaum on December 1, 2020. It tells the story from the point of view of the child of a fictional actress who was charged [255].

Netflix released a documentary on the subject, *Operation Varsity Blues: The College Admissions Scandal*, in 2021, mostly focusing on Singer played by Matthew Modine [256, 257].

In 2021, Casey Lyons and Caroline Miller wrote and self-produced *Bars of Ivy: The College Admissions Scandal Musical* about the scandal from the perspective of a student affected by it [258].

See Also
- National Association for College Admission Counselinghttps://en.wikipedia.org/wiki/National_Association_for_College_Admission_Counseling
- University of Bristol admissions controversyhttps://en.wikipedia.org/wiki/University_of_Bristol_admissions_controversy
- University of Illinois clout scandalhttps://en.wikipedia.org/wiki/University_of_Illinois_clout_scandal
- University of Texas at Austin admissions controversyhttps://en.wikipedia.org/wiki/University_of_Texas_at_Austin_admissions_controversy
- Legacy preferences

Notes
- The one exception to Professor McClay's statement (at the time it was made in 2019) was that Associate Justice Ruth Bader Ginsburg had attended Harvard for her first 2 years of law school but did not graduate from Harvard. After her husband found a job in New York City, Dean Erwin Griswold denied Ginsburg's request to earn credit at Columbia Law School towards her Harvard law degree. Ginsburg stayed with her husband, formally transferred to Columbia for her third year of law school, and earned her law degree from Columbia [259].

References
1. Kates, Graham (March 12, 2019). "Lori Loughlin and Felicity Huffman among dozens charged in college bribery scheme". CBS News. Archived from the original on March 12, 2019. Retrieved March 12, 2019.
2. Richer, Alanna; Binkley, Collin (March 12, 2019). "TV stars and coaches charged in college bribery scheme". AP News. Archived from the original on January 10, 2021. Retrieved March 12, 2019.

3. Levenson, Eric (December 9, 2019). "Mom to plead guilty to paying for son to cheat through Georgetown classes in college admissions scam". CNN. Archived from the original on December 17, 2019. Retrieved December 17, 2019.
4. Garrison, Joey (June 28, 2019). "Dad pleads guilty to paying $250,000 to get son into USC as fake volleyball recruit". USA Today. Archived from the original on June 29, 2019. Retrieved June 29, 2019.
5. Ormseth, Matthew; Rubin, Joel (August 19, 2019). "A $100,000 bribe got teen a UCLA soccer scholarship without even playing". Los Angeles Times. Archived from the original on August 19, 2019. Retrieved August 19, 2019.
6. Eustachewich, Lia (March 12, 2019). "Felicity Huffman, Lori Loughlin busted in college admissions cheating scandal". New York Post. Archived from the original on September 18, 2019. Retrieved March 12, 2019.
7. Trevino, Robert (March 12, 2019). "Michael Center, University of Texas men's tennis coach implicated in admissions scheme, placed on administrative leave". The Daily Texan. Archived from the original on July 20, 2019. Retrieved March 12, 2019.
8. Siemaszko, Corky; Kaplan, Ezra (March 12, 2019). "College admissions scheme mastermind William Rick Singer wore wire to expose scam". NBC News. Archived from the original on January 1, 2021. Retrieved March 13, 2019.
9. Raymond, Nate (March 13, 2019). "Ex-Stanford sailing coach pleads guilty to college admission bribe scheme". Reuters. Archived from the original on November 8, 2020. Retrieved March 13, 2019.
10. Winter, Tom (March 13, 2019). "College cheating ringleader says he helped more than 750 families with admissions scheme". NBC. Archived from the original on January 1, 2021. Retrieved March 13, 2019.
11. Golden, Daniel; Burke, Doris (October 8, 2019). "An Unseen Victim of the College Admissions Scandal: The High School Tennis Champion Aced Out by a Billionaire Family". ProPublica. Archived from the original on October 12, 2019. Retrieved October 12, 2019.
12. "Full indictment on the nationwide college admission scheme". CNN. March 12, 2019. Archived from the original on November 5, 2020. Retrieved April 8, 2019.
13. Woods, Amanda (March 16, 2019). "UC Berkeley joins list of schools ensnared in college admissions scandal". New York Post. Archived from the original on November 12, 2020. Retrieved March 16, 2019.
14. "Northwestern Student Linked To Nationwide College Cheating Scandal". CBS. March 13, 2019. Archived from the original on November 11, 2020. Retrieved April 8, 2019.
15. "Felicity Huffman Announces Guilty Plea in College Admissions Scandal: 'My Daughter Knew Nothing'". PEOPLE.com. Archived from the original on August 23, 2020. Retrieved May 14, 2019.
16. Medina, Jennifer; Benner, Katie; Taylor, Kate (March 12, 2019). "Actresses, Business Leaders and Other Wealthy Parents Charged in U.S. College Entry

Fraud". The New York Times. ISSN 0362-4331. Archived from the original on March 14, 2019. Retrieved March 12, 2019.
17. Korn, Melissa; Levitz, Jennifer; Ailworth, Erin (March 13, 2019). "Federal Prosecutors Charge Dozens in College Admissions Cheating Scheme". The Wall Street Journal. ISSN 0099-9660. Archived from the original on November 8, 2020. Retrieved March 12, 2019.
18. Garrison, Joey; Puente, Maria (March 12, 2019). "Felicity Huffman, Lori Loughlin among 50 indicted in largest-ever case alleging bribery to get kids into colleges". USA Today. Archived from the original on September 18, 2019. Retrieved March 12, 2019.
19. Smith, Laura, Special Agent FBI (March 12, 2019). "College admissions bribery scheme affidavit" (PDF). The Washington Post. Archived from the original on January 9, 2021. Retrieved March 12, 2019.
20. "Buckley School Whistleblower Stumbled Onto Rick Singer's Fake College Applications Long Before Admissions Scandal". July 31, 2019. Retrieved February 7, 2022.
21. Rubin, Joel; Ormseth, Matthew; Hussain, Suhauna; Winton, Richard (March 31, 2019). "The bizarre story of the L.A. dad who exposed the college admissions scandal". Los Angeles Times. Archived from the original on March 31, 2019. Retrieved March 31, 2019.
22. Levitz, Jennifer; Korn, Melissa (March 14, 2019). "The Yale Dad Who Set Off the College-Admissions Scandal". The Wall Street Journal. Archived from the original on March 15, 2019. Retrieved March 15, 2019.
23. "Only On 2: Tipster Who Touched Off Campus Bribery Admissions Scandal Lives In Larchmont". CBS Los Angeles. March 14, 2019. Archived from the original on October 24, 2020. Retrieved March 15, 2019.
24. Chen, David W.; Tracy, Marc (March 15, 2019). "At Yale, a Once Respected Soccer Coach Becomes an Enigma". The New York Times. p. A1. Archived from the original on March 16, 2019. Retrieved March 16, 2019.
25. Levin, Bess (March 14, 2019). "HOW A CROOKED FINANCE EXEC NARC'D ON THE COLLEGE-ADMISSIONS SCAM". Vanity Fair. Archived from the original on August 7, 2020. Retrieved April 11, 2019.
26. Pavlo, Walter. "Felicity Huffman And America's Failing Criminal Justice System". Forbes. Archived from the original on September 26, 2019. Retrieved October 11, 2019.
27. "Lori Loughlin indicted on money-laundering charge in college admissions scandal". Los Angeles Daily News. April 9, 2019. Archived from the original on January 29, 2022. Retrieved May 14, 2019.
28. Frank, Robert; Newburger, Emma (March 12, 2019). "A slew of CEOs charged in alleged college entrance cheating scam". CNBC. Archived from the original on March 12, 2019. Retrieved March 12, 2019.
29. Levenson, Eric; Morales, Mark (March 13, 2019). "Wealthy parents, actresses, coaches, among those charged in massive college cheating admission scandal, federal prosecutors say". CNN. Archived from the original on March 12, 2019. Retrieved March 13, 2019.

30. United States Attorney's Office, District of Massachusetts (March 12, 2019). "Arrests Made in Nationwide College Admissions Scam: Alleged Exam Cheating & Athletic Recruitment Scheme". Department of Justice. Archived from the original on March 12, 2019. Retrieved March 12, 2019.
31. Lelling, Andrew E. (March 5, 2019). "Criminal Information 1:19-CR-10078-RWZ, United States of America vs. William Rick Singer". U.S. Department of Justice. Archived from the original on March 12, 2019. Retrieved March 12, 2019.
32. Ferris, Jolene (March 15, 2019). "Utica College grad lead investigator on college scandal". News Channel 2 WKTV. Utica, NY: Heartland Media. Retrieved March 16, 2019.[permanent dead link].
33. "Loughlin, 15 others hit with more charges in college scam". WKMG. April 9, 2019. Archived from the original on June 20, 2019. Retrieved May 14, 2019.
34. Newsham, Jack (April 9, 2019). "College Scandal Defense Teams Accuse Feds of Judge-Shopping". The American Lawyer. Archived from the original on April 10, 2019. Retrieved May 14, 2019.
35. Hartocollis, Anemona (June 16, 2022). "A Businessman Is Acquitted in a Georgetown Admissions Trial". The New York Times. ISSN 0362-4331. Retrieved July 24, 2022.
36. Richer, Alanna Durkin (June 16, 2022). "Georgetown dad acquitted in final college bribery scam trial". ABC News. Retrieved July 24, 2022.
37. "Newport Beach and Laguna Beach connections abound in college admissions scandal". Los Angeles Times. March 12, 2019. Archived from the original on January 1, 2021. Retrieved March 16, 2019.
38. Quintana, Chris (March 12, 2019). Fake disabilities, photoshopped faces: How feds say celebrities, coaches and scammers got kids into elite colleges Archived March 15, 2019, at the Wayback Machine USA Today.
39. Taylor, Kate (March 13, 2019). "Fallout From College Admissions Scandal: Arrests, Damage Control and a Scramble for Answers". The New York Times. ISSN 0362-4331. Archived from the original on March 13, 2019. Retrieved March 13, 2019.
40. Breaux, Aimee (March 12, 2019). "The ACT says 'few bad actors' undermined fair testing in college admissions scandal". Iowa City Press-Citizen. Archived from the original on January 29, 2022. Retrieved March 13, 2019.
41. Baker, Matt (March 13, 2019). "IMG Academy suspends Mark Riddell after college admissions bribery scandal". Tampa Bay Times. Archived from the original on March 15, 2019. Retrieved March 13, 2019.
42. Barrett, Devlin; Zapotosky, Matt (March 12, 2019). "FBI accuses wealthy parents, including celebrities, in college-entrance bribery scheme". The Washington Post. Archived from the original on March 13, 2019. Retrieved March 13, 2019.
43. "Mark Riddell, test-taker ace in college admissions cheating case, pleads guilty in court". USA TODAY. Archived from the original on May 14, 2019. Retrieved May 14, 2019.

44. Li, David K. (March 13, 2019). "Harvard alum 'profoundly sorry' for taking tests for students in college cheating scheme". NBC News. Archived from the original on March 14, 2019. Retrieved March 13, 2019.
45. Baker, Vicky (March 15, 2019). "Celebrity parents and the bizarre 'cheating' scandal". BBC News. Archived from the original on March 22, 2019. Retrieved March 22, 2019. According to the FBI, he would fly in, take the test for students in a hotel room, or sneak them the correct answers in the exam room, or inflate their scores when they finished. Sometimes he would be given a sample of the teen's handwriting so he could copy it. Riddell did not know the questions in advance, according to Andrew Lelling, US attorney for the District of Massachusetts. He was "just a really smart guy".
46. "Mark Riddell, college admissions scandal test-taker, pleads guilty". NBC News. Archived from the original on May 13, 2019. Retrieved May 14, 2019.
47. Martin, Susan Taylor. "Sentencing reset for Mark Riddell, Tampa Bay man involved in the college admissions scandal". Tampa Bay Times. Archived from the original on July 20, 2019. Retrieved September 12, 2019.
48. Smith, Laura, Special Agent FBI. Affidavit in Support of Criminal Complaint Archived March 12, 2019, at the Wayback Machine, filed in the United States District Court for the District of Massachusetts. Retrieved March 12, 2019.
49. Reiss, Jaclyn (March 12, 2019). "College bribery plot: A list of names of those charged in the nationwide scheme". The Boston Globe. Archived from the original on March 21, 2019. Retrieved March 15, 2019.
50. Pascus, Brian (March 14, 2019). "Every charge and accusation facing the parents in the college admissions scandal". CBS News. Archived from the original on May 14, 2019. Retrieved March 22, 2019.
51. Stannard, Ed; Friedmann, Meghan (March 12, 2019). "Ex-Yale soccer coach, Greenwich businessman charged in college admissions scandal". New Haven Register. Archived from the original on March 13, 2019. Retrieved March 12, 2019.
52. Wong, Alia (March 12, 2019). "Why the College-Admissions Scandal Is So Absurd". The Atlantic. Archived from the original on March 12, 2019. Retrieved March 12, 2019.
53. Fry, Hannah; Winton, Richard; Ormseth, Matthew; Newberry, Laura (March 12, 2019). "College cheating scandal snares actresses, CEOs and coaches; alleged mastermind pleads guilty". Los Angeles Times. Archived from the original on January 3, 2021. Retrieved March 12, 2019.
54. Klick, Rea; Speier, Mia (March 12, 2019). "Athletic director, water polo coach fired in wake of FBI investigation of admission scam". Daily Trojan. Archived from the original on November 28, 2020. Retrieved March 13, 2019.
55. "3 Pac-12 Programs Dismiss Top Coaches Amid Admissions Bribery Scandal; NCAA Investigating". KTLA. Associated Press. March 12, 2019. Archived from the original on April 1, 2019. Retrieved March 13, 2019.
56. Dahlberg, Tim (March 13, 2019). "Column: A twist in the usual college sports scandal". The Oakland Press. Archived from the original on April 1, 2019. Retrieved March 14, 2019.

57. Craver, Richard (March 12, 2019). "Wake Forest coach accused of accepting six-figure bribe to help student get into the university". Winston-Salem Journal. Archived from the original on March 31, 2019. Retrieved March 13, 2019.
58. Brennan, George (March 13, 2019). "Martha's Vineyard tie to college admissions scandal". The Martha's Vineyard Times. Archived from the original on April 1, 2019. Retrieved March 13, 2019.
59. Ziegler, Mark; Davis, Kristina (March 21, 2019). "Lamont Smith identified as USD coach in bribery scheme; resigns as UTEP assistant". San Diego Union-Tribune. Archived from the original on January 1, 2021. Retrieved March 21, 2019.
60. "UTEP assistant basketball coach resigns, implicated in college admissions scandal". KTSM-TV. March 21, 2019. Archived from the original on March 22, 2019. Retrieved March 21, 2019.
61. Davis, Kristina; Robbins, Gary (March 12, 2019). "University of San Diego, local families caught up in college admissions scandal". San Diego Union-Tribune. Archived from the original on March 26, 2019. Retrieved March 13, 2019.
62. Sulek, Julia Prodis (March 12, 2019). "How Silicon Valley became epicenter of college-entry cheating scandal". The Mercury News. Archived from the original on March 31, 2019. Retrieved March 13, 2019.
63. Sallee, Barrett (March 12, 2019). "College admissions scandal indictment alleges use of fake USC football profiles for students". CBS Sports. Archived from the original on January 1, 2021. Retrieved March 13, 2019.
64. Swindell, Bill; Callahan, Mary (March 12, 2019). "What 2 locals charged in the college admissions scandal allegedly did". The Press Democrat. Archived from the original on August 12, 2019. Retrieved March 13, 2019.
65. Schmidt, Ingrid (March 13, 2019). "Lori Loughlin's Daughter Vacationed on Billionaire USC Official's Yacht". The Hollywood Reporter. Archived from the original on January 29, 2022. Retrieved March 14, 2019. Lori Loughlin and Mossimo Giannulli's 19-year-old daughter was on the yacht of billionaire Rick Caruso, the chairman of USC's Board of Trustees, during Tuesday's indictment that charged the couple in a nationwide college cheating scandal.
66. "Lori Loughlin Daughter Olivia Leaves Yacht Owned By Top USC Official". TMZ. March 13, 2019. Archived from the original on March 14, 2019. Retrieved March 14, 2019. As Lori Loughlin traveled from Vancouver to L. A. Tuesday night to surrender to federal authorities in the college bribery scandal – which got her daughter, Olivia Jade, into USC – Olivia spent the night on the yacht of the Chairman of USC's Board of Trustees
67. Blum, Steven (March 13, 2019). "Olivia Jade Found Out Her Mom Had Schemed Her Into USC While On Rick Caruso's Yacht". Los Angeles. Archived from the original on March 14, 2019. Retrieved March 14, 2019. Olivia Jade, social media influencer and daughter of actress Lori Loughlin, was apparently spending her spring break on a yacht owned by USC board of trustees member Rick Caruso when the news broke that her mother was part of an epic college bribery case.

68. Ross, Martha (March 13, 2019). "Will Lori Loughlin's Instagram-famous daughters get kicked out of USC, face other fallout because of parents?". The Mercury News. Archived from the original on March 27, 2019. Retrieved March 14, 2019. TMZ reported late Wednesday afternoon that Lori Loughlin's daughter Olivia Jade Giannulli had been traveling in the Bahamas on a yacht owned by Rick Caruso, the chairman of the USC Board of Trustees
69. "Board of Trustees | USC". University of Southern California. Archived from the original on January 6, 2022. Retrieved January 29, 2022.
70. Moore, Annette (February 9, 2011). "Rick J. Caruso Elected to USC Board". University of Southern California. Archived from the original on August 26, 2011. Retrieved September 3, 2011.
71. Anderson, Travis; Ellement, John R.; Fernandes, Deirdre; Finucane, Martin (March 12, 2019). "'A catalog of wealth and privilege': Feds allege college bribery scam". The Boston Globe. Archived from the original on March 12, 2019. Retrieved March 12, 2019.
72. Brokaw, Sommer; Uria, Daniel (March 12, 2019). "Parents, coaches, actors among 50 charged in college scandal". UPI. Archived from the original on March 13, 2019. Retrieved March 13, 2019.
73. 73 Winter, Tom; Williams, Pete; Ainsley, Julia; Schapiro, Rich (March 12, 2019). "TV actresses among 50 people charged in college exam cheating plot". NBC News. Archived from the original on January 3, 2021. Retrieved March 12, 2019.
74. Yan, Holly (March 13, 2019). "What we know so far in the college admissions cheating scandal". CNN. Archived from the original on December 23, 2020. Retrieved March 14, 2019.
75. Kim, Catherine (March 13, 2019). "Parents of NU student implicated in Key Worldwide cheating scandal". The Daily Northwestern. Archived from the original on November 7, 2020. Retrieved March 26, 2019.
76. Munoz, Carlos R. "IMG Academy fires director involved in college admissions scam". Sarasota Herald-Tribune. Archived from the original on January 1, 2021. Retrieved May 14, 2019.
77. Merrett, Robyn (March 13, 2019). "Everyone Who Has Been Charged in the College Admissions Cheating Scandal". People. Archived from the original on November 12, 2020. Retrieved March 22, 2019.
78. "Investigations of College Admissions and Testing Bribery Scheme". Justice.gov. March 11, 2019. Archived from the original on January 22, 2021. Retrieved April 8, 2019.
79. "Former SAT/ACT test administrator pleads guilty in college admissions scandal". NBC News. Archived from the original on November 14, 2019. Retrieved November 14, 2019.
80. "4 more parents to plead guilty in college admissions scandal". ABC News. Archived from the original on October 22, 2019. Retrieved October 22, 2019.
81. Beaujon, Andrew (March 12, 2019). 5 Facts About the DC Life of Gordon Ernst, the Tennis Coach Named in the Admissions-Scandal Indictment, he left

Georgetown University under a cloud Archived March 23, 2019, at the Wayback Machine, Washingtonian.
82. Lothspeich, Jennifer (March 12, 2019). "A closer look at those with San Diego ties indicted in college admissions scandal". CBS8. KFMB-TV. Archived from the original on March 31, 2019. Retrieved March 14, 2019.
83. "NEW: URI Puts Women's Tennis Coach Ernst on Administrative Leave Following Federal Charges". GoLocalProv. Archived from the original on April 21, 2021. Retrieved April 21, 2021.
84. Amaral, Brian. "Gordie Ernst's fall from grace in college-admissions scandal". providencejournal.com. Archived from the original on April 21, 2021. Retrieved April 21, 2021.
85. Reynolds, Mark (October 25, 2021). "RI tennis legend 'Gordie' Ernst pleads guilty in Varsity Blues college admissions scandal". Providence Journal. Archived from the original on November 5, 2021. Retrieved November 6, 2021.
86. Lumpkin, Lauren (September 15, 2021). "Former Georgetown tennis coach to plead guilty following college admissions scandal". Washington Post. Archived from the original on September 16, 2021. Retrieved September 21, 2021.
87. Hartocollis, Anemona (September 15, 2021). "Former Georgetown Tennis Coach Agrees to Plead Guilty in Admissions Scandal". New York Times. Archived from the original on September 20, 2021. Retrieved September 21, 2021.
88. Billy, Witz (September 27, 2021). "A Cog in the College Admissions Scandal Speaks Out". The New York Times. Archived from the original on May 6, 2022. Retrieved May 5, 2022.
89. Shao, Elena; Foreman, Holden (March 12, 2019). "Head sailing coach fired after agreeing to plead guilty to bribery charges in admissions scandal". The Stanford Daily. Archived from the original on March 27, 2019. Retrieved March 26, 2019.
90. Garrison, Joey (June 12, 2019). "Former Stanford sailing coach avoids prison in first sentence of college admissions scandal". USA Today. Archived from the original on June 12, 2019. Retrieved June 12, 2019.
91. Bolch, Ben (March 12, 2019). "UCLA men's soccer coach placed on leave after indictment in college admissions scam". Los Angeles Times. Archived from the original on June 21, 2019. Retrieved March 13, 2019.
92. Owens, Jason (March 22, 2019). "Report: UCLA soccer coach Jorge Salcedo resigns after allegedly taking $200 K in college admissions scandal". Yahoo Sports. Archived from the original on March 27, 2019. Retrieved March 24, 2019.
93. "Former UCLA soccer coach Jorge Salcedo agrees to guilty plea in college admissions case". www.dailynews.com. April 21, 2020. Archived from the original on May 22, 2020. Retrieved May 22, 2020.

94. "Former UCLA Soccer Coach Sentenced in College Admissions Case". www.justice.gov. March 19, 2021. Archived from the original on April 18, 2021. Retrieved April 21, 2021.
95. Helsel, Phil (March 19, 2021). "Former UCLA coach sentenced to 8 months in college admissions cheating case". NBC News. Archived from the original on April 12, 2021. Retrieved April 21, 2021.
96. "Ex-UCLA men's soccer coach Jorge Salcedo gets 8 months in prison for admissions scam". ESPN. Associated Press. March 19, 2021. Archived from the original on April 12, 2021. Retrieved April 21, 2021.
97. Ziegler, Mark (November 13, 2020). "Man who bribed USD basketball coach is sentenced in admissions scandal". San Diego Tribune. Archived from the original on April 21, 2021. Retrieved April 21, 2021.
98. "Investigations of College Admissions and Testing Bribery Scheme". United States Department of Justice. Retrieved April 14, 2022.
99. Kaufman, Joey (March 12, 2019). "USC fires associate AD Donna Heinel, legendary water polo coach Jovan Vavic in college admissions bribery scandal". Orange County Register. Archived from the original on September 18, 2019. Retrieved March 14, 2019.
100. Wolf, Scott (March 12, 2019). "USC Fires Jovan Vavic And Donna Heinel". InsideUSC with Scott Wolf. Archived from the original on April 12, 2021. Retrieved April 21, 2021.
101. "Former USC official pleads guilty in college bribery scheme". Midland Reporter Telegram. Associated Press. November 5, 2021. Archived from the original on November 6, 2021. Retrieved November 6, 2021.
102. Andersen, Travis. "Former coach and parent plead guilty in college admissions cheating scandal". The Boston Globe. Archived from the original on April 23, 2019. Retrieved April 23, 2019.
103. Garrison, Joey (June 3, 2019). "Ex-USC soccer coach reverses course, agrees to plead guilty in college admissions scandal". USA Today. Archived from the original on June 4, 2019. Retrieved June 10, 2019.
104. Greene, Nick (March 13, 2019). "America's Best College Water Polo Coach Also Allegedly Excelled at Taking Bribes From Rich Parents". Slate Magazine. Archived from the original on November 11, 2020. Retrieved April 8, 2019.
105. Leiterberg, Neal J. (April 16, 2019). "Ex-USC water polo coach Jovan Vavic, arrested in college bribing scandal, lists South Bay home". Los Angeles Times. Archived from the original on April 10, 2021. Retrieved April 21, 2021.
106. Marcelo, Philip (March 10, 2022). "Trial opens for ex-USC coach in college bribery scandal". Associated Press. Retrieved March 20, 2022.
107. Raymond, Nate (March 10, 2022). "Former USC water polo coach goes on trial in 'Varsity Blues' college scandal". Reuters. Retrieved March 20, 2022.
108. Korn, Melissa; Levitz, Jennifer (March 7, 2022). "Last Coach Charged in Varsity Blues College Admissions Case Heads to Trial". Wall Street Journal. Retrieved March 20, 2022.

109. Ormseth, Matthew (April 8, 2022). "Former USC water polo coach found guilty in final conviction of college admissions case". Los Angeles Times. Retrieved April 9, 2022.
110. "Former USC Water Polo Coach Convicted in College Admissions Scandal".
111. Sakelaris, Nicholas (March 13, 2019). "Investment chief, Texas coach step down over college cheating scandal". UPI. Archived from the original on November 8, 2020. Retrieved March 13, 2019.
112. Moyle, Nick (March 13, 2019). "UT fires tennis coach Michael Center in wake of college admissions scandal". Houston Chronicle. Archived from the original on March 14, 2019. Retrieved March 14, 2019.
113. "Actress Felicity Huffman, 13 others to plead guilty in U.S. college admissions scandal". WKZO. Midwest Communications, Inc. Archived from the original on September 10, 2019. Retrieved May 14, 2019.
114. Theresa Waldrop; Eric Levenson (February 24, 2020). "Former University of Texas tennis coach sentenced in admissions scam". CNN. Archived from the original on February 26, 2020. Retrieved February 27, 2020.
115. Murphy, Kate (August 23, 2019). "Wake Forest volleyball coach charged in national college admissions scandal resigns". Archived from the original on April 21, 2021. Retrieved April 21, 2021.
116. "Former Wake Forest University volleyball coach William Ferguson can pay $50 k fine, avoid prosecution in college admissions bribery scandal". ESPN. Associated Press. October 12, 2021. Archived from the original on November 8, 2021. Retrieved November 8, 2021.
117. "Frequently Asked Questions Related to Admissions Fraud Scheme – Office of the President". Yale University. March 15, 2019. Archived from the original on April 13, 2019. Retrieved April 8, 2019.
118. Gafni, Matthias (March 15, 2019). "Joe Montana says he used company charged with college admissions fraud". San Francisco Chronicle. Archived from the original on November 8, 2020. Retrieved March 16, 2019.
119. "Getting In by Rick Singer". Goodreads. Archived from the original on March 7, 2021. Retrieved March 16, 2019.
120. Mangan, Dan (March 15, 2019). "'Full House' actress Lori Loughlin's kids remain enrolled in USC amid college bribe scandal; Phil Mickelson, Joe Montana say they did nothing wrong". CNBC. Archived from the original on March 16, 2019. Retrieved March 15, 2019.
121. Levitz, Jennifer; Korn, Melissa. "Tipster who alerted feds to college-admissions scheme was dad seeking leniency in securities fraud case". MarketWatch. Archived from the original on June 20, 2019. Retrieved April 8, 2019.
122. "Alleged Tipster in College-Cheating Scandal Bribed a Coach, Source Says". The Wall Street Journal. Archived from the original on November 8, 2020. Retrieved March 26, 2019.
123. Woolfolk, John (December 16, 2021). "College admission scandal: Here's the tally after final parent pleads guilty". Mercury News. Archived from the original on December 16, 2021. Retrieved December 17, 2021.

124. "2 Nevada executives charged in college bribery scheme". Las Vegas Sun. Associated Press. March 12, 2019. Archived from the original on January 1, 2021. Retrieved March 14, 2019.
125. Executive Profile, Gamal Mohammed Abdelaziz, Member of Advisory Board, Kiwi Collection, Inc. Archived April 1, 2019, at the Wayback Machine, Bloomberg.
126. Prince, Todd (March 12, 2019). "Suspect in college bribery case opened Las Vegas, Macau casinos". Las Vegas Review-Journal. Archived from the original on April 21, 2021. Retrieved April 21, 2021.
127. Stutz, Howard (March 12, 2021). "Nevada gaming executive indicted in college admissions and bribery scandal". Nevada Independent. Archived from the original on April 21, 2021. Retrieved April 21, 2021.
128. 128 "The first Trial Is Kicking Off Over The 'Varsity Blues' College Admissions Scandal". NPR. Associated Press. September 8, 2021. Archived from the original on September 8, 2021. Retrieved September 8, 2021.
129. Levenson, Michael (February 9, 2022). "Ex-Casino Executive Gets 1 Year and 1 Day in Prison in College Admissions Scheme". New York Times. Retrieved February 10, 2022.
130. "California Businessman Sentenced in College Admissions Case". www.justice.gov. October 30, 2019. Archived from the original on December 29, 2019. Retrieved February 11, 2020.
131. "Marin County couple latest to plead guilty in college admissions scandal". July 13, 2020. Archived from the original on May 14, 2021. Retrieved May 14, 2021.
132. The Washington Post [dead link].
133. Raymond, Adam K. (March 12, 2019). "Here Are All the Parents Named in the College Admissions Scandal Indictment". The Daily Intelligencer. New York. Archived from the original on November 7, 2020. Retrieved April 8, 2019.
134. Cain, Áine (March 13, 2019). "Fashion designer Mossimo Giannulli – whose self-titled brand once ran at Target – is accused of shelling out $500,000 to get his daughters into USC". Business Insider. Archived from the original on June 8, 2020. Retrieved March 13, 2019.
135. CNN Lori Loughlin sentenced to 2 months in prison in college admissions scam. Her husband, Mossimo Giannulli, got 5 months Archived August 21, 2020, at the Wayback Machine, August 21, 2020.
136. Kesslen, Ben (March 12, 2019). "Lori Loughlin's daughter, Olivia Jade, comes under fire online over college-cheating scandal". NBC News. Archived from the original on January 1, 2021. Retrieved March 13, 2019.
137. Rao, Sonia; Yahr, Emily (March 12, 2019). "Before Lori Loughlin's alleged cheating scandal, daughter Olivia Jade made her life at USC a YouTube brand". The Washington Post. Archived from the original on March 13, 2019. Retrieved March 13, 2019.
138. Lapin, Tamar (March 14, 2019). "Lori Loughlin's daughter Drop Out of USC After Admissions Scandal" Archived March 18, 2019, at the Wayback Machine, New York Post-Page Six.

139. Ormseth, Matthew (February 7, 2020). "Ex-CEO of investment giant Pimco given longest sentence to date in college admissions scandal". Los Angeles Times. Archived from the original on February 11, 2020. Retrieved February 11, 2020.
140. 40th Annual Conference of IOSCO - London, June 18, 2015, Panel 3. Douglas M. Hodge, Chief Executive, PIMCO Archived January 1, 2021, at the Wayback Machine (PDF), International Organization of Securities Commissions (2015). Retrieved March 13, 2019.
141. McLaughlin, Kelly (March 13, 2019). [https://web.archive.org/web/201 90411011138/https://www.thisisinsider.com/college-cheating-scandal-pimco-former-ceo-douglas-hodge-2019-3 Archived April 11, 2019, at the Wayback Machine A former CEO's daughter was allegedly listed as co-captain of a Japanese national soccer team as part of a $25 million college admission scheme], Insider Inc., March 13, 2019.
142. Phillips, Morgan (October 4, 2019). "Fifth parent receives sentence in college admissions scandal and it's the stiffest one yet". Fox News. Archived from the original on October 7, 2019. Retrieved October 7, 2019.
143. Korn, Melissa (April 9, 2019). "Prosecutors Net 14 New Guilty Plea Agreements in College Cheating Probe". The Wall Street Journal. Archived from the original on November 25, 2020. Retrieved May 14, 2019.
144. Dremann, Sue (May 17, 2021). "Former Palo Altan sentenced in college admissions scam". Palo Alto Weekly. Archived from the original on July 24, 2021. Retrieved July 24, 2021.
145. "Ex-USC coach, couple avoid prison time in college scandal".
146. "USC coach who created fake athletic profiles for children of wealthy parents sentenced". June 29, 2022.
147. "Ex-USC coach, couple avoid prison time in college scandal".
148. "USC coach who created fake athletic profiles for children of wealthy parents sentenced". June 29, 2022.
149. Moran, Greg (March 19, 2019). "San Diego media executive appears in federal court on college admissions scandal charges". Los Angeles Times. Archived from the original on October 25, 2020. Retrieved March 19, 2019.
150. Gotfredson, David (August 16, 2021). "Former KFMB Stations owner Elisabeth Kimmel pleads guilty in college admissions scandal". KFMB-TV. Archived from the original on August 18, 2021. Retrieved August 16, 2021.
151. Lothspeich, Jennifer (March 14, 2019). "Who is Elisabeth Kimmel? Former owner of KFMB Stations in San Diego named in college admissions scandal". CBS 8. Archived from the original on April 12, 2021. Retrieved April 21, 2021.
152. Davis, Kristina (March 17, 2019). "A prominent La Jolla family is linked to the massive college admissions scandal. Who are the Kimmels?". The San Diego Union-Tribune. Archived from the original on May 12, 2021. Retrieved May 12, 2021.

153. Kristina Davis, San Diego Union-Tribune (August 12, 2021). "Former San Diego TV exec to plead guilty in college bribery scandal". Los Angeles Times. Archived from the original on August 18, 2021. Retrieved August 18, 2021.
154. "Ex-media CEO sentenced to prison in college admissions scam". Associated Press. December 9, 2021. Retrieved February 18, 2022.
155. "Parent in College Admissions Case Pleads Guilty". U.S. Department of Justice. August 16, 2021. Archived from the original on August 17, 2021. Retrieved August 18, 2021.
156. "College admissions scandal: California exec gets longest sentence yet". NBC News. Archived from the original on November 14, 2019. Retrieved November 14, 2019.
157. https://www.courier-journal.com/story/news/2019/04/16/kentucky-distillery-owner-charged-college-admissions-scandal-enters-plea/3484979002/%7Ctitle=Kentucky distillery owner will plead not guilty in college admissions scandal|first=Billy|last=Kobin|publisher=Courier Journal|date=April 16, 2019|accessdate=April 21, 2021}}
158. "Parent in College Admissions Case Agrees to Plead Guilty". United States Attorney's Office:District of Massachusetts. August 24, 2021. Archived from the original on September 8, 2021. Retrieved September 8, 2021.
159. Alanna Durkin Richer, Associated Press (August 25, 2021). "Kentucky distillery owner to plead guilty in nationwide college admissions scandal case". Courier Journal. Archived from the original on January 29, 2022. Retrieved September 8, 2021.
160. "Investigations of College Admissions and Testing Bribery Scheme". U.S. Department of Justice. March 11, 2019. Archived from the original on January 22, 2021. Retrieved November 15, 2021.
161. Yee, Gregory (December 16, 2021). "Bay Area liquor company CEO sentenced to six weeks in prison in college admissions case". Los Angeles Times. Retrieved February 18, 2022.
162. "Parent Charged and Agrees to Plead Guilty in College Admissions Case". www.justice.gov. May 26, 2020. Archived from the original on October 31, 2020. Retrieved November 19, 2020.
163. Li, David K. (May 26, 2021). "Pennsylvania man pleads guilty to paying bribe for daughter's admission to Georgetown". NBC News. Archived from the original on August 1, 2021. Retrieved August 1, 2021.
164. "Dad gets 4 months for $400,000 bribe to get son into Georgetown". NBC News. Archived from the original on October 5, 2019. Retrieved October 1, 2019.
165. CNN.com (September 26, 2019). "California business executive who paid $400,000 to get his child into Georgetown sentenced to 4 months in prison". Mercury News. Archived from the original on August 1, 2021. Retrieved August 1, 2021.
166. "Executive gets 4 months for bribing son's way into USC". KSTP. September 24, 2019. Archived from the original on September 24, 2019. Retrieved September 24, 2019.

167. Garrison, Joey (February 24, 2020). "UCLA mom pleads guilty in college admissions case after spending 5 months in Spanish prison". USA Today. Archived from the original on February 27, 2020. Retrieved March 11, 2020.
168. "Lynnfield father charged in college bribery case". ItemLive. March 14, 2019. Archived from the original on October 30, 2020. Retrieved April 8, 2019.
169. Borchers, Callum (March 14, 2019). "Mass. Businessman Charged In College Admissions Case Has A Resume On LinkedIn. So We Fact-Checked It". WBUR. Archived from the original on May 12, 2021. Retrieved May 12, 2021.
170. Ormseth, Matthew (January 14, 2020). "Financier charged in admissions scandal indicted again on new tax fraud allegation". Los Angeles Times. Archived from the original on May 12, 2021. Retrieved May 12, 2021.
171. Levenson, Michael (February 16, 2022). "Private Equity Investor Sentenced to 15 Months in College Bribery Case". New York Times. Retrieved February 18, 2022.
172. Genter, Ethan. "3 men with Cape ties charged in nationwide college cheating scandal". Cape Cod Times. Archived from the original on January 1, 2021. Retrieved April 8, 2019 – via SouthCoastToday.com.
173. "USC professor admits to tax charge in admissions scandal". Associated Press. July 9, 2021. Archived from the original on July 24, 2021. Retrieved July 24, 2021.
174. Helsel, Phil (November 11, 2021). "California parent sentenced to 6 weeks in college admissions scheme". NBC News. Retrieved February 18, 2022.
175. Andersen, Travis (April 4, 2019). "Dentist charged in college admissions scandal lost book deals because of case, lawyers say". Boston Globe. Archived from the original on May 12, 2021. Retrieved May 12, 2021.
176. Melin, Anders (March 12, 2019). "Bloomberg – Venture Capitalist Robert Zangrillo Charged in College Admission Scheme". Bloomberg LP. Archived from the original on June 20, 2019. Retrieved March 22, 2019.
177. Alanna Durkin Richer, The Associated Press (January 21, 2021). "Robert Zangrillo, parent charged in college admissions scandal, pardoned by President Trump". Masslive.com. Archived from the original on July 24, 2021. Retrieved July 24, 2021.
178. Hamilton, Matt (January 21, 2021). "Finger-pointing and outrage follow Trump's pardon for USC father in college admission scandal". Los Angeles Times. Archived from the original on January 22, 2021. Retrieved January 22, 2021.
179. Anderson, Nick. "California developer gets one month of prison in college admissions scandal". The Washington Post. Archived from the original on October 21, 2019. Retrieved October 22, 2019.
180. Meadows, Jonah (March 14, 2019). "College Cheating Scandal: Northwestern Student's Parents Charged". Evanston, IL Patch. Patch Media. Archived from the original on June 20, 2019. Retrieved March 26, 2019.
181. Gibson, Kate (March 13, 2019). "Venture capitalist charged in college admissions cheating scandal loses job". CBS News. Archived from the original on September 18, 2019. Retrieved March 13, 2019.

182. "Hercules Capital CEO Manuel Henriquez Resigns; Chief Investment Officer Scott Bluestein Named Interim CEO". NASDAQ.com. March 13, 2019. Archived from the original on August 1, 2019. Retrieved April 8, 2019.
183. "2 Chicago universities tied to college admissions scandal". WGNTV. March 14, 2019. Archived from the original on April 3, 2019. Retrieved April 8, 2019.
184. Waldrop, Theresa (February 25, 2020). "Hot Pockets heiress Michelle Janavs sentenced in college admissions scam". CNN. Archived from the original on February 27, 2020. Retrieved February 27, 2020.
185. Garrison, Joey (February 25, 2020). "Hot Pockets heiress Michelle Janavs gets 5 months in prison in admissions scandal". USA Today. Archived from the original on August 1, 2021. Retrieved August 1, 2021.
186. "Admissions scandal: Heir to Hot Pockets fortune sentenced to 5 month". Los Angeles Times. February 25, 2020. Archived from the original on August 1, 2021. Retrieved August 1, 2021.
187. Oreskes, Benjamin (March 21, 2019). "A wiretap brings privilege and helicopter parenting to the fore in the college admissions scandal". Los Angeles Times. Archived from the original on December 30, 2020. Retrieved April 8, 2019.
188. Shoot, Brittany (March 12, 2019). "TPG Growth Founder Bill McGlashan Placed on Immediate, Indefinite Leave Over College Admissions Cheating Scandal". Fortune. Archived from the original on November 7, 2020. Retrieved March 13, 2019.
189. "Former executive pleads guilty in college admissions scandal". ABC News. Archived from the original on February 21, 2021. Retrieved March 5, 2021.
190. "Ex-TPG Executive McGlashan Pleads Guilty in College Scandal". Bloomberg News. February 10, 2021. Archived from the original on April 21, 2021. Retrieved April 21, 2021.
191. Raymond, Nate (May 12, 2021). "Former TPG Capital exec sentenced to three months in prison for U.S. college scam". Reuters. Archived from the original on May 12, 2021. Retrieved May 12, 2021.
192. Casiano, Louis (October 8, 2019). "Husband, wife each get one month in jail in college admissions scandal". Fox News. Archived from the original on October 15, 2019. Retrieved October 16, 2019.
193. Ng, David; Faughnder, Ryan (March 13, 2019). "Marketing guru Jane Buckingham caught up in college admissions scandal". Los Angeles Times. Archived from the original on December 30, 2020. Retrieved March 14, 2019.
194. "Author and CEO Jane Buckingham gets 3 weeks in prison for college admissions scandal". NBC News. Archived from the original on November 22, 2019. Retrieved October 29, 2019.
195. Zafar, Maryam; Cronin, Amanda H. (March 13, 2019). "Gordon Caplan '88 Paid $75,000 to Rig His Daughter's ACT Score, the FBI Says. He and Nearly 50 Others Were Charged With Fraud". The Cornell Daily Sun. Archived from the original on November 26, 2020. Retrieved March 14, 2019.
196. Dillon, Nancy (October 3, 2019). "Millionaire Manhattan lawyer becomes fourth parent sentenced to prison in college admissions scandal". New York

Daily News. Archived from the original on October 3, 2019. Retrieved October 4, 2019.
197. "Final Parent Charged In College Admissions Scam Agrees To Plead Guilty". CBS Boston. December 9, 2021. Archived from the original on December 17, 2021. Retrieved December 17, 2021.
198. Ho, Catherine (March 14, 2019). "Medical board reviewing charges against Bay Area doctor indicted in college admissions scam". San Francisco Chronicle. Archived from the original on May 14, 2021. Retrieved May 14, 2021.
199. Raymond, Nate (December 2, 2021). "California couple to plead guilty in U.S. college admissions scandal". Reuters. Archived from the original on December 17, 2021. Retrieved December 17, 2021.
200. "List of local residents charged in college admissions scandal". Palo Alto Daily Post. March 14, 2019. Archived from the original on October 28, 2020. Retrieved April 8, 2019.
201. Taylor, Kate (September 13, 2019). "By Turns Tearful and Stoic, Felicity Huffman Gets 14-Day Prison Sentence". The New York Times. Archived from the original on September 13, 2019. Retrieved September 14, 2019.
202. "Admissions scandal: Mom who rigged son's ACT, lied about his race gets 3 weeks in prison". Los Angeles Times. October 16, 2019. Archived from the original on October 16, 2019. Retrieved October 16, 2019.
203. latimes.com/california/story/2020-07-15/admissions-scandal-newport-beach-mother-sentenced-to-in-prison
204. "Operation Varsity Blues: Bay Area parent avoids prison time in college admissions scandal". ABC7 San Francisco. October 11, 2019. Archived from the original on October 16, 2019. Retrieved October 16, 2019.
205. Brown, Scott; Griffin, Kevin; Fraser, Keith (March 13, 2019). "Vancouver's David Sidoo charged in U.S. college-entrance scandal". The Vancouver Sun. Archived from the original on January 1, 2021. Retrieved March 13, 2019.
206. latimes.com/california/story/2020-07-15/college-admissions-scandal-david-sidoo-sentenced
207. "Yale rescinds admission of a student whose family paid $1.2 million to get her in". CNN. March 26, 2019. Archived from the original on November 21, 2020. Retrieved March 26, 2019.
208. Wang, Amy B.; Bieler, Des (March 13, 2019). "College coaches took bribes to pass kids off as star athletes, FBI says. The NCAA is investigating". The Denver Post. Archived from the original on October 21, 2020. Retrieved March 14, 2019.
209. Hackman, Michelle (March 15, 2019). College-Admission Scandal Draws Scrutiny in Washington Archived November 10, 2020, at the Wayback Machine, The Wall Street Journal.
210. Stieb, Charlotte Klein, Matt (January 20, 2021). "Who Did Trump Pardon on His Last Night As President?". Intelligencer. Archived from the original on January 20, 2021. Retrieved January 20, 2021.

6.1 US College Corruption

211. Caron, Emily (March 12, 2019). "Every Coach Charged in the FBI's College Admission Recruiting, Bribery Scandal". Sports Illustrated. Archived from the original on November 28, 2020. Retrieved March 15, 2019.
212. Garrison, Joey (March 13, 2019). "The 'really smart guy' who aced SATs for rich students: 'I will always regret' the scandal". USA Today. Archived from the original on January 1, 2021. Retrieved March 16, 2019.
213. Taylor, Kate; Lyons, Patrick J. (March 12, 2020). "William Singer, the Man in the Middle of the College Bribery Scanda". The New York Times. Archived from the original on December 9, 2020. Retrieved December 28, 2020. <? ref. > Garrison, Joey (May 23, 2019). "College admissions scandal tracker: Who's pleaded guilty, who's gone to prison — and who's still fighting". USA Today. Archived from the original on January 1, 2021. Retrieved December 28, 2020.
214. "Investigations of College Admissions and Testing Bribery Scheme". www.justice.gov. March 11, 2019. Archived from the original on January 22, 2021. Retrieved March 12, 2019.
215. Sheyner, Gennady. "Stanford expels student in connection with college-fraud scheme". Palo Alto Weekly. Archived from the original on January 1, 2021. Retrieved May 14, 2019.
216. Oldman, Grace (June 22, 2019). "Rick Singer, mastermind behind college admissions scandal, was GCU student". Arizona Republic. Archived from the original on January 29, 2022. Retrieved December 28, 2020.
217. Winton, Richard (May 13, 2019). "Will Felicity Huffman get prison time for her role in college admissions scandal?". Los Angeles Times. Archived from the original on May 13, 2019. Retrieved May 13, 2019.
218. Miller, Hayley (May 13, 2019). "Felicity Huffman Pleads Guilty In College Admissions Scandal". HuffPost. Archived from the original on December 29, 2019. Retrieved December 28, 2019.
219. Romo, Vanessa (September 13, 2019). "Actress Felicity Huffman Sentenced To 14 Days In College Admissions Scandal". National Public Radio. Archived from the original on January 22, 2021. Retrieved December 28, 2020.
220. Levenson, Eric (October 15, 2019). "Felicity Huffman reports to prison to start two-week sentence for college admissions scam". CNN. Archived from the original on December 6, 2020. Retrieved December 28, 2020.
221. Fieldstadt, Elisha; Kaplan, Ezra (October 25, 2019). "Felicity Huffman released from prison on 11th day of 14-day sentence". NBC News. Archived from the original on December 29, 2020. Retrieved December 28, 2020.
222. Foussianes, Chloe (October 26, 2020). "How Felicity Huffman and William H. Macy Became Involved the College Admissions Scandal". Town and Country Magazine. Archived from the original on November 29, 2020. Retrieved December 28, 2020.
223. "Netflix's 'Fuller House' drops Lori Loughlin after college bribery scandal: report". The Hill. March 16, 2019. Archived from the original on March 27, 2019. Retrieved March 16, 2019.

224. Richwine, Lisa (March 14, 2019). "C elebrities lose work, students sue U.S. colleges in admissions scandal". Reuters. Archived from the original on June 20, 2019. Retrieved March 15, 2019.
225. Lieber, Chavie (March 15, 2019). "Olivia Jade, the influencer at the center of the college admissions scandal, explained". Vox. Archived from the original on March 21, 2019. Retrieved March 15, 2019.
226. Bailey, Alyssa (October 22, 2019). "USC Confirms Lori Loughlin's Daughters Olivia Jade And Isabella Are No Longer Enrolled". Elle. Archived from the original on October 26, 2019. Retrieved October 25, 2019.
227. "Olivia Jade and Isabella Giannulli may face lifetime ban from USC, report says". The Mercury News. March 24, 2019. Archived from the original on March 22, 2019. Retrieved March 23, 2019.
228. "Lori Loughlin begins 2-month prison sentence in college admissions scandal". NBC News. Archived from the original on October 30, 2020. Retrieved October 30, 2020.
229. "Lori Loughlin Begins Serving 2 Month Prison Sentence For College Admissions Scam". October 30, 2020. Archived from the original on November 1, 2020. Retrieved October 30, 2020.
230. "Lori Loughlin's husband, Mossimo Giannulli, reports to prison for admissions scandal sentence". NBC News. Archived from the original on November 20, 2020. Retrieved November 19, 2020.
231. "2 parents are convicted in the first trial of the 'Varsity Blues' admission scandal". NPR. Associated Press. October 8, 2021. Archived from the original on October 8, 2021. Retrieved October 9, 2021.
232. Li, David K. (March 14, 2019). "College cheating scandal: Lawsuits filed by students at elite schools". NBC News. Archived from the original on January 1, 2021. Retrieved March 15, 2019.
233. Seemayer, Zach (March 14, 2019). "Felicity Huffman, Lori Loughlin & Others Sued by Angry Parent for $500 Billion Over College Admissions Scandal". ET Online. Archived from the original on October 23, 2020. Retrieved March 15, 2019.
234. Wong, Alia (March 12, 2019). "Why the College-Admissions Scandal Is So Absurd". The Atlantic. Archived from the original on March 19, 2019. Retrieved March 17, 2019.
235. Nelson, Libby (March 12, 2019). "The real college admissions scandal is what's legal". Vox. Archived from the original on November 7, 2020. Retrieved March 16, 2019.
236. Dickson, E.J. (March 13, 2019). "The College Admissions Scandal Proves the System Is Broken". Rolling Stone. Archived from the original on March 27, 2019. Retrieved March 16, 2019.
237. Hartocollis, Anemona (March 15, 2019). "College Admissions: Vulnerable, Exploitable, and to Many Americans, Broken". The New York Times. Archived from the original on March 15, 2019. Retrieved March 16, 2019.

238. "College admissions scandal exposes a corrupt and broken system". The Star-Ledger. March 13, 2019. Archived from the original on March 27, 2019. Retrieved March 16, 2019.
239. Khadaroo, Stacy Teicher (March 15, 2019). "America to elite colleges: Shape up (but please let us in)". The Christian Science Monitor. Archived from the original on June 6, 2021. Retrieved March 17, 2019.
240. Fox News Insider (March 12, 2019). "Dershowitz: Alleged College Admissions Scam Is 'One of the Great Scandals of the 21st Century'". Outnumbered. Fox News. Archived from the original on March 22, 2019. Retrieved March 13, 2019.
241. Katersky, Aaron (March 12, 2019). "Ringleader pleads guilty in $25 million nationwide college admissions cheating scam". ABC News. Archived from the original on March 12, 2019. Retrieved March 12, 2019.
242. Goldstein, Dana; Healy, Jack (March 13, 2019). "Inside the Pricey, Totally Legal World of College Consultants". The New York Times. Archived from the original on December 19, 2020. Retrieved March 16, 2019.
243. Roy, Jessica (March 14, 2019). "A lingering question in the college admissions scandal: Why?". Los Angeles Times. Archived from the original on March 15, 2019. Retrieved March 16, 2019.
244. Harris, Adam (March 13, 2019). "One Way to Stop College-Admissions Insanity: Admit More Students". The Atlantic. Archived from the original on April 20, 2021. Retrieved March 25, 2019.
245. Leingang, Rachel (March 12, 2019). "Arizona State University gets dissed in college bribery scandal court documents". The Arizona Republic. Gannett. Archived from the original on January 29, 2022. Retrieved March 25, 2019.
246. Goodkind, Nicole (March 22, 2019). "An End to Affirmative Action? Why the College Admissions Scandal Could Fulfill Critics' Wish to Scrap Race-Based Program". Newsweek. Archived from the original on December 4, 2020. Retrieved March 25, 2019.
247. Kingkade, Tyler (April 26, 2019). "This Is Why Canadian Universities Don't Have College Admissions Scandals". HuffPost. Verizon Media. Archived from the original on November 24, 2020. Retrieved April 27, 2019.
248. Wai, Jonathan; Brown, Matt; Chabris, Christopher (2019). "No one likes the SAT. It's still the fairest thing about admissions". The Washington Post. Archived from the original on November 17, 2020. Retrieved February 15, 2021.
249. "Felicity Huffman & Lori Loughlin-Inspired 'College Admissions Scandal' Movie Gets First Trailer (Exclusive)". Archived from the original on November 24, 2020. Retrieved October 7, 2019.
250. "A Dystopian High School Musical Foresaw The College Admissions Scandal". NPR.org. Archived from the original on January 2, 2021. Retrieved January 1, 2020.
251. Cova, Spencer. "Local families affected by college scandal". Granite Bay Today. Archived from the original on October 31, 2020. Retrieved January 1, 2020.

252. "Watch the Trailer for Lifetime's 'College Admissions Scandal'". Entertainment Tonight. Archived from the original on November 24, 2020. Retrieved March 31, 2021.
253. Petski, Denise (August 12, 2019). "'The College Admissions Scandal': Penelope Ann Miller & Mia Kirshner To Headline Lifetime Movie". Deadline. Archived from the original on April 18, 2021. Retrieved March 31, 2021.
254. "Gretchen Carlson on her college admissions scandal doc for Lifetime: 'I understand the immense anger'". EW.com. Archived from the original on October 15, 2020. Retrieved March 31, 2021.
255. "Admissions". Amazon. 2021. Archived from the original on April 26, 2020. Retrieved February 6, 2021.
256. What to Know About Netflix's Operation Varsity Blues—and the College Admissions Scandal That Inspired It Archived March 21, 2021, at the Wayback Machine, Time.
257. Park, Kelly. "Netflix's 'Operation Varsity Blues' Misses the Mark". Arc Publishing. Archived from the original on April 11, 2021. Retrieved March 31, 2021.
258. https://www.caseyandcaroline.com/barsofivy
259. Sherron de Hart, Jane (2018). Ruth Bader Ginsburg: A Life (2020 1st Vintage Books ed.). New York: Vintage Books. pp. 73–77. ISBN 9781984897831. Archived from the original on January 29, 2022. Retrieved December 20, 2020.

6.2 Oxford University Press

6.2.1 Text from the Website of the UK SFO[2]

Oxford Publishing Ltd to Pay Almost £1.9 Million as Settlement After Admitting Unlawful Conduct in Its East African Operations: 3 July 2012
The Director of the Serious Fraud Office (SFO) has taken action in the High Court, which has resulted in an Order that Oxford Publishing Limited (OPL) pay £1,895,435 in recognition of sums it received which were generated through unlawful conduct related to subsidiaries incorporated in Tanzania and Kenya.

Background
OPL is a wholly owned subsidiary of Oxford University Press (OUP), which pursues its mission through five publishing divisions, including the International Division. (See note 1 for editors.) The International Division has ten overseas publishing entities with a head office in Oxford. Oxford University Press East Africa

---
[2] www.sfo.gov.uk/2012/07/03/oxford-publishing-ltd-pay-almost-1-9-million-settlement-admitting-unlawful-conduct-east-african-operations/.

(OUPEA) is based in Kenya but covers a geographical region which includes Kenya, Burundi, Malawi, Rwanda, Sudan and Uganda. Oxford University Press Tanzania (OUPT) is based in mainland Tanzania but also has responsibility for the semi-autonomous Zanzibar archipelago. Both OUPT and OUPEA are wholly owned subsidiaries of OPL and part of the International Division of OUP.

The business of all the International Division entities is focused on the school text book market but most entities also have well established local dictionary programmes and growing higher education lists. The business activities include participating in public tenders for contracts to supply governments with text books and other educational materials for the school curricula. These tenders may lead to contracts which are supported or funded by the World Bank Group which is the collective title for the International Bank for Reconstruction and Development and the International Development Association.

Self Referral

In 2011, OUP became aware of the possibility of irregular tendering practices involving its education business in East Africa. OUP acted immediately to investigate the matter, instructing independent lawyers and forensic accountants to undertake a detailed investigation.

As a result of the investigation, in November 2011 OUP voluntarily reported certain concerns in relation to contracts arising from a number of tenders which its Kenyan and Tanzanian subsidiaries, OUPEA and OUPT, entered into between the years 2007 and 2010. The SFO required OUP to follow a procedure based on the guidance contained within its published protocol document—"The Serious Fraud Office's Approach to Dealing with Overseas Corruption".

Because two of the tenders were funded by the World Bank, OUP also voluntarily reported on a potential breach of the World Bank's Procurement Guidelines to the World Bank.

The SFO remit was broader in its scope than the World Bank investigation in that it required investigation of all public tender contracts whether or not funded by the World Bank.

The costs of the investigation were met by OUP.

The investigation was thorough—involving numerous interviews and an extensive review of documents and electronic data—and completed to the satisfaction of the SFO. The substantial product of those investigations was presented to the SFO and, in a separate presentation, to the World Bank. The product of that work led the SFO and the World Bank to believe that OUPEA and OUPT had offered and made payments, directly and through agents, intended to induce the recipients to award competitive tenders and/or publishing contracts for schoolbooks to OUPEA and OUPT.

Chapter 7
Health

7.1 Fresenius

Friday, March 29, 2019

7.1.1 Text from US DoJ Website[1]

Fresenius Medical Care Agrees to Pay $231 Million to Resolve Foreign Corrupt Practices Act Charges
BOSTON—**Fresenius Medical Care AG & Co. KGaA** (Fresenius), a German-based provider of medical products and services, has agreed to pay approximately $231 million to resolve the Department of Justice (DOJ) and Securities and Exchange Commission's (SEC) investigation into violations of the Foreign Corrupt Practices Act (FCPA) in connection with Fresenius's participation in various corrupt schemes to obtain business in multiple countries.

"Bribery, in all forms, is corrosive and illegal," said United States Attorney Andrew E. Lelling of the District of Massachusetts. "As today's announcement makes clear, this Office will continue its long tradition of aggressively investigating companies and individuals who use bribes and kickbacks to gain an unfair and illicit business advantage, or who deliberately turn a blind eye to that conduct."

"Fresenius doled out millions of dollars in bribes across the globe to gain a competitive advantage in the medical services industry, profiting to the tune of over $140 million," said Assistant Attorney General Benczkowski. "Today's resolution, under which Fresenius has agreed to retain an independent compliance monitor for at least two years, reflects the Department's firm commitment to both

---

[1] https://www.justice.gov/usao-ma/pr/fresenius-medical-care-agrees-pay-231-million-resolve-foreign-corrupt-practices-act.

rooting out bribery and promoting the kind of effective corporate compliance programs that will prevent misconduct going forward."

"This case shows the continued commitment of the FBI and our partners to investigate bribery and corruption worldwide," said FBI Assistant Director Robert Johnson. "The FBI's dedicated International Corruption Squads across the United States will continue to combat foreign corruption that reaches our shores and send a strong message that, no matter how long it takes, we will not wane in our efforts to uphold the law."

"This case shows the FBI will hold accountable those who treat corruption as the cost of doing business," said Joseph R. Bonavolonta, Special Agent in Charge of the Federal Bureau of Investigation, Boston Field Division. "Fresenius's admissions are incredibly concerning because no company should break the law by paying-off international partners to obtain or retain business. We will continue to work with our law enforcement partners to root out corrupt schemes and ensure they do not become common practice at the expense of other hard-working businesses."

According to Fresenius's admissions, between 2007 and 2016, the company paid bribes to publicly-employed health and/or government officials to obtain or retain business in Angola and Saudi Arabia. In Angola and Saudi Arabia, as well as in Morocco, Spain, Turkey, and countries in West Africa, Fresenius knowingly failed to implement reasonable internal accounting controls over financial transactions, and failed to maintain books and records that accurately and fairly reflected the transactions.

In Angola, Fresenius offered or provided bribes to an Angolan military health officer and his family, as well as prominent Angolan government-employed nephrologists. Specifically, Fresenius offered these individuals shares in a joint venture, storage contracts, and consultancy agreements, all for the purpose of securing an improper advantage and assisting Fresenius with obtaining and retaining business in Angola.

In Saudi Arabia, Fresenius employed a check cashing scheme, entered into sham consulting and commission agreements for which no services were ever performed, entered into fake collection commission agreements, made payments to a government charity, gave gifts, and made payments for travel with no business or educational justification, the company admitted.

In Morocco, Fresenius paid bribes to a Moroccan state official for the purpose of obtaining contracts to develop kidney dialysis centers at Moroccan state-owned military hospitals.

In Spain, Fresenius entered into fake consulting agreements with publicly-employed doctors or professionals who could influence or provide information about public tenders, gave gifts or provided other benefits such as travel to medical conferences, and made donations to fund projects for the doctors.

In Turkey, Fresenius entered into joint ventures with publicly-employed doctors in exchange for those doctors directing business from their public employer to Fresenius Turkey clinics.

In West Africa, Fresenius paid bribes to publicly-employed health officials in various countries, including Benin, Burkina Faso, Cameroon, the Ivory Coast,

Niger, Gabon, Chad, and Senegal. Fresenius paid these bribes through a combination of direct payments, payments made through third parties, and payments through a third-party distributorship, all to obtain and retain business in those countries.

In total, Fresenius earned more than $140 million in profits from the corrupt schemes.

To resolve the case, Fresenius entered into a non-prosecution agreement (NPA) with DOJ and agreed to pay a total criminal penalty of $84,715,273. As part of the NPA, Fresenius also agreed to continue to cooperate with DOJ's investigation, enhance its compliance program, implement rigorous internal controls, and retain an independent corporate compliance monitor for at least two years.

DOJ reached this resolution based on a number of factors. Notably, although Fresenius voluntarily self-disclosed the misconduct in April 2012, the company did not timely respond to certain requests by the DOJ and, at times, did not provide fulsome responses to requests for information. In addition, misconduct occurred in 13 countries, yielded profits of more than $140 million, and continued in certain countries until 2016, and the company has not yet had the opportunity to test the effectiveness of its compliance enhancements. Therefore, the company did not qualify for a declination under the Corporate Enforcement Policy, and instead received a discount of 40 percent below the low end of the U.S. Sentencing Guidelines fine range, and an independent compliance monitor for a term of two years, followed by an additional year of self-reporting to the DOJ.

Fresenius settled a related FCPA matter with the SEC today and will pay $147 million in disgorgement and prejudgment interest to the SEC, which the DOJ credited in its resolution, bringing the total monetary amount to over $231 million.

Assistant U.S. Attorney Jordi de Llano of the District of Massachusetts and Trial Attorneys Paul A. Hayden and Sonali D. Patel of the Department's Criminal Division's Fraud Section are prosecuting this matter. The Department appreciates the significant cooperation and assistance provided by the U.S. Securities and Exchange Commission in this matter.

Wednesday, October 9, 2019

7.1.2 Text from US DoJ Website[2] (February 10, 2022)

Fresenius Agrees to Pay $5.2 Million to Resolve Allegations That It Overbilled Medicare for Hepatitis B Tests

BOSTON—The United States Attorney's Office announced today that **Fresenius Medical Care Holdings, Inc., d/b/a Fresenius Medical Care North America, Inc.**, the largest operator of kidney dialysis clinics in the United States, has agreed to pay $5.2 million to resolve allegations that the company tested dialysis patients for

---

[2] https://www.justice.gov/usao-ma/pr/fresenius-agrees-pay-52-million-resolve-allegations-it-overbilled-medicare-hepatitis-b.

Hepatitis B surface antigen more frequently than medically necessary and then billed Medicare for the unnecessary tests.

"Providers are expected to closely follow Medicare rules and bill properly—nothing more, nothing less," said United States Attorney Andrew E. Lelling. "When that obligation is violated, government health care programs—and American taxpayers—pay the price. This settlement is an example of how whistleblowers and government can work together to recoup and deter overbilling practices."

Patients suffering from end stage renal disease (ESRD) and chronic renal disease (CRD) require dialysis treatments 3-4 times a week because their kidneys no longer can perform some functions naturally. Because certain ESRD and CRD patients are at risk of contracting hepatitis B, a virus-borne disease that affects the liver, Medicare established a testing frequency schedule for dialysis clinics to follow for reimbursement. The schedule depended on each patient's immunity to hepatitis B infection, as determined through the result of a hepatitis B antibody test. The schedule provided for reimbursement of monthly hepatitis B surface antigen tests for patients who were not immune, but Fresenius also conducted, and billed Medicare for, frequent tests of patients it knew to be immune between Feb. 10, 2003 and Dec. 31, 2010. In many cases, Fresenius performed and billed Medicare for these tests for immune patients against their treating physicians' orders and without any accompanying documentation of medical necessity. These tests were not eligible for Medicare reimbursement under Medicare's testing frequency schedule, and the government alleged that Fresenius's bills for these tests were false.

A former employee of Fresenius, Christopher Drennen, brought these allegations through a whistleblower lawsuit. Under the qui tam provisions of the False Claims Act, private individuals, known as relators, can sue on behalf of the government for false claims and share in any recovery. In connection with today's announced settlement, Mr. Drennen will receive 27.5% of the recovery.

U.S. Attorney Lelling and Phillip M Coyne, Special Agent in Charge of the Office of the Inspector General for the U.S. Department of Health and Human Services made the announcement today. Assistant U.S. Attorneys Abraham George, Kriss Basil, Steven Sharobem, Jessica Weber, and Christine Wichers handled the case.

Tuesday, February 9, 2021

7.1.3 Text from US DoJ Website[3]

Indian Cancer Drug Manufacturer Agrees to Plead Guilty and Pay $50 Million for Concealing and Destroying Records in Advance of FDA Inspection

Indian drug manufacturer **Fresenius Kabi Oncology Limited** (FKOL) has agreed to plead guilty to concealing and destroying records prior to a 2013 U.S. Food and

---

[3] https://www.justice.gov/usao-nv/pr/indian-cancer-drug-manufacturer-agrees-plead-guilty-and-pay-50-million-concealing-and.

Drug Administration (FDA) plant inspection and pay $50 million in fines and forfeiture, the Department of Justice announced today.

In a criminal information filed in federal court in the District of Nevada and unsealed today, the United States charged FKOL with violating the Federal Food, Drug and Cosmetic Act by failing to provide certain records to FDA investigators. As part of a criminal resolution, FKOL agreed to plead guilty to the misdemeanor offense, pay a criminal fine of $30 million, and forfeit an additional $20 million. FKOL also agreed to implement a compliance and ethics program designed to prevent, detect, and correct violations of U.S. law relating to FKOL's manufacture of cancer drugs intended for terminally ill patients.

"By hiding and deleting manufacturing records, FKOL sought to obstruct the FDA's regulatory authority and prevent the FDA from doing its job of ensuring the purity and potency of drugs intended for U.S. consumers," said Acting Assistant Attorney General Brian Boynton of the Justice Department's Civil Division. "FKOL's conduct put vulnerable patients at risk. The Department of Justice will continue to work with FDA to prosecute drug manufacturers who obstruct these inspections."

"Pharmaceutical companies that obstruct FDA inspections jeopardize patient safety," said U.S. Attorney Nicholas A. Trutanich for the District of Nevada. "Maintaining the integrity of records and data is a critical part of drug manufacturing, and our office will continue prosecuting those that obstruct FDA inspections by destroying records or other means."

"FDA inspections of pharmaceutical manufacturing facilities help ensure the strength, quality and purity of our medicines. Any attempt to obstruct or interfere with these inspections threatens the public health," said Judy McMeekin, Pharm.D., Associate Commissioner for Regulatory Affairs of the FDA. "We will continue to aggressively investigate and present any such obstruction for prosecution."

According to court documents, FKOL owned and operated a manufacturing plant in Kalyani, West Bengal, India, that manufactured active pharmaceutical ingredients (APIs) used in various cancer drug products distributed to the United States. The government alleges that prior to a January 2013 FDA inspection of the Kalyani facility, FKOL plant management directed employees to remove certain records from the premises and delete other records from computers that would have revealed FKOL was manufacturing drug ingredients in contravention of FDA requirements. Kalyani plant employees removed computers, hardcopy documents, and other materials from the premises and deleted spreadsheets that contained evidence of the plant's violative practices.

This case is being prosecuted by Assistant Director Clint Narver and Trial Attorney Natalie Sanders of the Department of Justice's Consumer Protection Branch, with assistance from Assistant U.S. Attorney Nicholas D. Dickinson of the U.S. Attorney's Office for the District of Nevada. The FDA's Office of Criminal Investigations, Los Angeles Field Office, investigated the case. The Central Bureau of Investigation in India provided invaluable assistance to U.S. authorities in the investigation of this matter.

Also, the non-prosecution agreement is available at:
https://www.justice.gov/criminal-fraud/fcpa/cases/fresenius-medical-care-ag-co.

7.2 HealthSouth

7.2.1 From Wall Street to Prison: The HealthSouth Story[4]

May 31, 2011

The story of HealthSouth in the 1990s and early 2000s is about a corporate network of rehabilitation hospitals that skyrocketed up Wall Street and then plunged off a cliff. It's a story about sketchy ethics, tyrannical leadership, and crossing the line so often that boundaries disappeared.

HealthSouth's former CFO's, Aaron Beam and Weston Smith, candidly shared the ugly story of their rise and descent with students at Chicago Booth on May 9. The event was sponsored by Booth's Leadership Development office in the Full-Time MBA program.

Founded in 1984 by Beam and Richard Scrushy, the company's former chairman and CEO, HealthSouth went public two years later after Scrushy dazzled a group of Wall Street investors with a presentation on the company's potential. By 1990 it ballooned to a $1 billion dollar corporation of hospitals and health care centers offering diagnostic services and rehabilitation therapy. As CFO with a large chunk of shares in the company, Beam became a millionaire. He remembers people asking how a company on such a steep upward trajectory was handling the start up costs. "From the beginning, we were putting things on the balance sheet that probably should have stayed on the profit and loss statement."

By 1995 the company had health centers in all 50 states, plus 40,000 employees, 10 to 12 jets and a spot on the Fortune 500 list. Beam spent his millions on cars, condos and a collection of French neckties that equaled an entry-level salary.

All the while, Beam said he was allowing Scrushy to bully him and other HealthSouth executives into manipulating financial reports to reflect the numbers Scrushy promised investors. During a meeting in 1996, Beam told Scrushy they would have to finally report a bad quarter. Scrushy said no, and they devised a way to hide the earnings shortfall.

"I should have had the courage to stand up and say, 'No, we can't cross this line,'" Beam said. Scrushy promised to deny everything if Beam reported the fraud and accused Beam of not being a team player. "I couldn't sleep," Beam added. "I didn't understand what crossing that line would do to me emotionally and mentally. I hated my job, hated myself. I started drinking more than I should."

In 1997, Beam retired from HealthSouth, selling his company stock and walking away from a half-million dollar annual salary. He thought the deception was behind him—until March of 2003 when he heard on national television that a massive fraud had been uncovered at HealthSouth.

Prior to Beam's FBI visit, Weston Smith had joined Scrushy in 1987 and in 2001 became CFO, manipulating ledgers to scheme auditors and keeping sold assets on

---

[4] https://www.chicagobooth.edu/media-relations-and-communications/press-releases/From-Wall-Street-to-Prison-The-HealthSouth-Story.

the balance sheets, among other tricks. At its height in the late 90s, HealthSouth reported $4.5 billion in revenue— but those numbers were grossly inflated. "We had to come up with elaborate schemes to perpetuate the fraud," Smith said. "It was a time of absolute nauseating excess, though the company wasn't doing anything."

Scandals at Enron, Tyco, and WorldCom pushed Congress to pass the Sarbanes-Oxley Act of July 2002, which mandated transparent financial reporting to protect investors from fraud. Scrushy abruptly sold $75 million in HealthSouth stock just as the legislation became law. That law is what led Smith to blow the whistle on Scrushy and HealthSouth.

Federal prosecutors tapped Beam and Smith to be a witnesses in a six-month trial against Scrushy that ended in a not guilty verdict in 2005. Two years later Scrushy was convicted of unrelated political bribery charges and is now serving a seven-year sentence in a Texas prison.

Smith served 14 months in federal prison, followed by a four-month stay in a halfway house in Alabama. Beam served three months of jail time and has recently self-published a book about his experience, titled HealthSouth: The Wagon to Disaster. The two now lecture business students on corporate ethics. "How does a fraud start?" Smith told students. "With thoughts like, 'This is just temporary...We can't disappoint Wall Street...Everybody does it.' We saw that a lot of people were doing the same types of things we were doing. So, you start believing this is just business. "

Nurkholisoh Ibnu Aman was a risk management consultant and internal auditor in Indonesia when he followed news about the massive scandals at HealthSouth and other companies. "I was a distance away, and now I get to sit in the US, listening to the true story itself," said Aman, a first-year student in Booth's Full-Time MBA program. "This is very enlightening, exactly what I expect from a business school."— Kadesha Thomas

7.3 Guralp

7.3.1 Text from UK SFO Website[5] (February 11, 2022)

Three Individuals Acquitted as SFO Confirms DPA with Güralp Systems Ltd
20 December 2019

Cansun Güralp, Andrew Bell and Natalie Pearce were acquitted of conspiracy to make corrupt payments in relation to payments made to a South Korean public official between 2002 and 2015.

The conclusion of the trial removes reporting restrictions on the Deferred Prosecution Agreement reached by the SFO and Güralp Systems Ltd, which was agreed in October 2019. Güralp Systems Ltd accept the charges of conspiracy to make

---

[5] https://www.sfo.gov.uk/2019/12/20/three-individuals-acquitted-as-sfo-confirms-dpa-with-guralp-systems-ltd/.

corrupt payments and a failure to prevent bribery by employees in relation to the payments made between 2002 and 2015.

As a result of this DPA, Güralp Systems Ltd has agreed to pay a total of £2,069,861 for disgorgement of gross profits to the SFO for onward transmission to the Consolidated Fund. The DPA also requires Güralp Systems Ltd to cooperate fully and truthfully with the SFO and to review and maintain its existing internal controls, policies, and procedures regarding compliance with the Bribery Act 2010.

Director of the Serious Fraud Office, Lisa Osofsky, said:

> The Deferred Prosecution Agreement with Güralp Systems Ltd ensures that the company will pay the price for the wrongdoing that occurred under its roof. The DPA is a result of Güralp Systems Ltd's timely self-reporting and full cooperation, and holds the company to account whilst also promoting positive changes in corporate culture.

Güralp Systems Ltd appointed a new Executive Chairman in December 2014, who identified wrongdoing and ordered an internal investigation. Following this internal investigation, Güralp Systems Ltd self-reported to both the SFO and the US Department of Justice on 23 October 2015. The SFO commenced its own independent and comprehensive investigation on 3 December 2015.

Notes to Editors

1. The SFO investigation began on 3 December 2015.
2. Cansun Güralp, Andrew Bell and Natalie Pearce were each charged of conspiracy to make corrupt payments, contrary to section 1(1) of the Criminal Law Act 1977.
3. Cansun Güralp and Andrew Bell were charged by requisition with conspiracy to make corrupt payments on 26 July 2018. Natalie Pearce was charged with the same offences on 28 September 2018.
4. Andrew Bell was acquitted by the jury on 18 December 2019. Cansun Güralp and Natalie Pearce were acquitted on 20 December 2019, following a majority verdict.
5. Under the DPA, Güralp Systems Ltd is charged with conspiracy to make corrupt payments, contrary to section 1 of the Criminal Law Act 1971 and failure to prevent bribery by employees, contrary to section 7 of the Bribery Act 2010...

The Deferred Prosecution Agreement, Statement of Facts and full Judgment can be found here.

This press release was amended to reflect the earlier acquittal of Andrew Bell.

7.4 Theranos/Elisabeth Holmes

7.4.1 Text from Wikipedia[6] (February 11, 2022)

Theranos (/ˈθɛr.ən.oʊs/) was an American privately held corporation [1] that was touted as a breakthrough health technology company. The company claimed that it devised blood tests that required very small amounts of blood and could be performed rapidly, thanks to the small automated devices the company had developed. However, these claims were later proven to be false [2–4].

Founded in 2003 by 19-year-old Elizabeth Holmes [5], Theranos raised more than US$700 million from venture capitalists and private investors [6], resulting in a $10 billion valuation at its peak in 2013 and 2014 [7, 8].

A turning point came in 2015, when medical research professor John Ioannidis, and later Eleftherios Diamandis, along with investigative journalist John Carreyrou of *The Wall Street Journal*, questioned the validity of Theranos's technology. The company faced a string of legal and commercial challenges from medical authorities, investors, the U.S. Securities and Exchange Commission (SEC), Centers for Medicare and Medicaid Services (CMS), state attorneys general, former business partners, patients, and others [9]. By June 2016, it was estimated that Holmes's personal net worth had dropped from $4.5 billion to virtually nothing [10]. After several years of struggle, lawsuits, and sanctions from CMS, what remained of the company was dissolved on September 4, 2018 [11].

On March 14, 2018, Theranos, Holmes, and former company president Ramesh "Sunny" Balwani were charged with fraud by the SEC [12]. On June 15, 2018, the United States Attorney for the Northern District of California announced the indictment of Holmes on wire fraud and conspiracy charges. Balwani was also indicted on the same charges [13]. The trial was scheduled to commence in August 2020 [14], but it was delayed due to the COVID-19 pandemic and Holmes's pregnancy. Holmes's trial began on August 31, 2021 [15], while Balwani's trial has been postponed until January 11, 2022 [16]. Holmes was found guilty on four counts on January 3, 2022 [17].

Contents
   1 History
      1.1 Partnerships
      1.2 Exposure and Downfall
      1.3 Criminal Proceedings
      1.4 Shutdown
   2 Technology and Products
   3 Corporate Affairs
      3.1 Location
      3.2 Management
      3.3 Valuation

---

[6] https://en.wikipedia.org/wiki/Theranos.

4 Books and Documentaries
5 See Also
6 References
7 External Links

1. History

While at Stanford University, Elizabeth Holmes had an idea to develop a wearable patch that could adjust the dosage of drug delivery and notify doctors of variables in patients' blood [18]. She started developing lab-on-a-chip technology for blood tests, with the idea to start a company that would make blood tests cheaper, more convenient and accessible to consumers [19]. Holmes dropped out of Stanford in 2003 and used the education trust from her parents to found the company that would later be called Theranos, derived from a combination of the words "therapy" and "diagnosis" [20, 21]. The company's original name was "Real-Time Cures" [7, 22, 23], which Holmes changed after deciding that too many people were skeptical of the word "cure" [7].

1.1 Partnerships

In 2012, Safeway invested $350 million into retrofitting 800 locations with clinics that would offer in-store blood tests. However, after many missed deadlines and questionable results from a trial clinic at Safeway's corporate offices, the deal was called off in 2015.[24] In 2013, Theranos partnered with Walgreens to offer in-store blood tests at more than 40 locations.[25] Although Theranos blood tests were reportedly used on drug trial patients for GlaxoSmithKline and Pfizer, both companies stated that there were no active projects with Theranos in October 2015 [26, 27]. In November 2016, Walgreen Co. filed suit against Theranos in a federal court in Delaware, for breach of contract. In June 2017, Theranos reported to investors that the suit, which originally sought $140 million in damages, was settled for less than $30 million [28, 29].

In March 2015, the Cleveland Clinic announced a partnership with Theranos in order to test its technology and decrease the cost of lab tests [30, 31]. In July 2015, Theranos became the lab-work provider for Pennsylvania insurers AmeriHealth Caritas and Capital BlueCross [32, 33].

In July 2015, the Food and Drug Administration approved the use of the company's fingerstick blood testing device for the herpes simplex virus (HSV-1) outside a clinical laboratory setting [34, 35]. Theranos was named the 2015 Bioscience Company of the Year by the Arizona BioIndustry Association (AzBio) [36].

1.2 Exposure and Downfall

In February 2015, Stanford professor John Ioannidis wrote in the *Journal of the American Medical Association* that no peer-reviewed research from Theranos had been published in medical research literature [37, 38]. In May 2015, University of Toronto Professor Eleftherios Diamandis analyzed Theranos technology and concluded that "most of the company's claims are exaggerated" [39, 40]. Attempting to boost the company's credibility, Holmes invited then U.S. Vice President Joe Biden to tour their facility. Biden praised what he saw [41], but in order to conceal the lab's true operating conditions, Holmes and Balwani had created a fake lab for the Vice President's tour [42]. In October 2015, John Carreyrou of *The Wall Street Journal* reported that Theranos was using traditional blood testing machines instead of the company's Edison devices to run its tests, and that the company's Edison machines might provide inaccurate results [43, 44]. Tyler Shultz, a Theranos employee from 2013 to 2014 and the grandson of then-Theranos director, former U.S. Secretary of State George P. Shultz, was a key source for the WSJ story. Shultz had attempted to bring his concerns to company management, and when that had failed, he had spoken to Carreyrou and also, under an alias, reported the company to the New York State Department of Health [45].

Theranos claimed that the allegations were "factually and scientifically erroneous" [46, 47]. Walgreens suspended plans to expand blood-testing centers in their stores following the report [48, 49]. At that time, the Cleveland Clinic announced that it would work to verify Theranos technology [31]. Theranos fought back against the *Journal's* investigation, sending lawyers after sources in the story, including Shultz, in an effort to stop them from providing information to the press [3, 45]. Former employees of reputation management firm Status Labs said that Theranos had hired the firm to discreetly erase mentions of the *WSJ*'s reporting from its Wikipedia article, despite the activity being a violation of the website's terms of use [50].

Following the *WSJ* story, the history of FDA interactions with Theranos was scrutinized. The FDA had received a formal inquiry to look at Theranos blood test devices by the U.S. Department of Defense in 2012, before the devices were commercially available and did not require FDA approval [51]. FDA inspection reports from 2014 and 2015 stated that its containers for blood collection were "not validated under actual or simulated use conditions" and "were not reviewed and not approved by designated individual(s) prior to issuance" [52]. In 2015, an FDA inspection resulted in multiple observed violations of FDA Title 21 Regulations [53, 54]. It was eventually revealed that the FDA had classified Theranos's device, called a nanotainer, as a Class II medical device, meaning that Theranos would need to use special labels, meet certain performance standards and perform post-market surveillance of the device. Theranos asserted that the nanotainer was a Class I medical device and therefore was not subject to any regulatory requirements [55]. After the 2015 inspection, Theranos announced that it would voluntarily suspend its tests apart from the FDA-approved herpes simplex virus (HSV-1) test [56, 57].

The Arizona Department of Health Services reported issues with the company's Scottsdale lab meeting regulations in September 2015. The reports were revealed in the *Arizona Republic* in November 2015 [58].

In January 2016, the Centers for Medicare and Medicaid Services (CMS) sent a letter to Theranos based on an inspection of its Newark, California lab in 2015, reporting that the facility caused "immediate jeopardy to patient health and safety" due to a test to determine the correct dose of the blood-thinning drug warfarin [59, 60]. In 2016, Walgreens and Capital BlueCross announced a suspension of Theranos blood tests from the Newark lab [61].

In March 2016, CMS regulators announced plans to enact sanctions that included suspending Holmes and Balwani from owning or operating any certified clinical laboratory for two years and that they would revoke the facility's certification as a clinical laboratory [62, 63].

By April 2016, Theranos came under criminal investigation by federal prosecutors and the SEC for allegedly misleading investors and government officials about its technology [64]. The U.S. House of Representatives Committee on Energy and Commerce requested information on what Theranos was doing to correct its testing inaccuracies and adherence to federal guidelines in June 2016 [65, 66].

In May 2016, Theranos announced that it had voided two years of results from its Edison device [67]. The company announced that about one percent of test results had been voided or corrected from its proprietary machines in June 2016 [68].

In July 2016, Theranos announced that the CMS had revoked its CLIA certificate and issued sanctions prohibiting its owners and operators from owning or operating a clinical laboratory for two years, suspension of approval to receive Medicare and Medicaid payments, and a civil monetary penalty. The company discontinued testing at its Newark location while attempting to resolve the issues [69]. Theranos announced plans to appeal the decision by regulators to revoke its license to operate a lab in California and other sanctions [70].

In August 2016, the company withdrew its request for emergency clearance of a Zika virus blood test after a lack of essential safeguards during the testing process was found by federal inspectors [71, 72].

Theranos announced that it would close its laboratory operations and wellness centers and lay off about 40 percent of its work force to work on miniature medical testing machines in October 2016 [73–76].

In January 2017, Theranos announced that it had laid off 41 percent of its workforce, or approximately 155 people, and closed the last remaining blood-testing facility after the lab failed a second major U.S. regulatory inspection [77, 78]. Also that month, the company faced lawsuits from several different entities including Walgreens [79, 80] and Arizona Attorney General Mark Brnovich [81].

In April 2017, lawyers for Partner Investments LP and two other funds, with combined stakes totaling more than $96 million in Theranos preferred shares, charged that Theranos had threatened to seek bankruptcy protection if the investors did not agree to accept additional stock equity in lieu of litigation. Theranos officials said the funds had mischaracterized the exchange offer, which was discussed before the suit was filed [82]. The suit also alleged that Theranos had misled company directors about its practices concerning laboratory testing and that it had secretly bought lab equipment to run fake demonstrations [83]. On May 1, 2017, Theranos announced that it had reached an undisclosed settlement with Partner Fund Management LP (PFM). Theranos's General Counsel, David Taylor, stated: "Theranos is pleased to have resolved both lawsuits with PFM. Although we are confident that we would have prevailed at trial, resolution of these two cases allows our tender offer to go forward and enables us to return our focus where it belongs, which is on executing our business plans and delivering value for our shareholders" [84]. In April 2017, Theranos reached a settlement with CMS agreeing to stay out of the blood-testing business for at least two years in exchange for reduced penalties [85], and signed a consent decree with Arizona Attorney General Mark Brnovich over violations of the Arizona Consumer Fraud Act. Alleged violations included false advertisement and inaccurate blood testing. Theranos agreed to refund $4.65 million to the state's residents for Theranos blood testing services, providing a refund to every resident who had received a test, regardless of whether the test results were voided or corrected [86–89].

In August 2017, Theranos announced it had reached a settlement with Walgreens [90].

In December 2017, Fortress Investment Group, a wholly owned company of Softbank Group, loaned $100 million to Theranos for 4% of the company [91]. Theranos had reportedly been on the verge of bankruptcy, with the loan meant to keep the company solvent into 2018 [92–94]. The loan was secured by Theranos's patents [95]. On April 10, 2018, the company laid off the majority of workers in a renewed bid to avoid bankruptcy. The company's total headcount was down to fewer than 25 employees, after having 800 employees at its peak [96, 97]. Softbank's Fortress bought up Theranos patents and later, taking advantage of the new market conditions in the midst of the COVID-19 pandemic, set up a shell company called Labrador Diagnostics which sued one of the companies making COVID-19 tests, saying that its test violated those Theranos patents [98].

1.3 Criminal Proceedings

In March 2018 the US Securities and Exchange Commission charged Theranos, its CEO Elizabeth Holmes and former president Ramesh "Sunny" Balwani, claiming they had engaged in an "elaborate, years-long fraud" wherein they "deceived investors into believing that its key product—a portable blood analyzer—could conduct comprehensive blood tests from finger drops of blood" [99, 100]. Holmes reached a settlement with the SEC which required her to pay $500,000, forfeit 19 million shares of company stock, and be barred from having a leadership position in any public company for ten years [101]. Balwani did not settle with the SEC [102].

On June 15, 2018, Holmes and Balwani were indicted on multiple counts of wire fraud and conspiracy to commit wire fraud. According to the indictment, investors, doctors and patients were defrauded. It is alleged the defendants were aware of the unreliability and inaccuracy of their products, but concealed that information. If convicted, they each face a maximum fine of $250,000 and 20 years in prison. The case, *United States v. Elizabeth A. Holmes, et al.*, has been assigned to Lucy H. Koh, United States District Judge of the United States District Court for the Northern District of California [103, 104]. The jury selection for the trial was to begin on July 28, 2020, and the trial was to have commenced in August 2020; however, the COVID-19 pandemic led to a proposed October date [105], before the trial for Holmes was rescheduled to begin on August 31, 2021, with Balwani's trial pushed back further to 2022.

In February 2021, federal prosecutors accused Holmes and other executives of destroying evidence in Theranos's final days in business. The specific evidence in question is the history of internal testing, including accuracy and failure rates of Theranos's blood-testing systems [106].

On January 3, 2022, Holmes was found guilty of three counts of wire fraud and one count of conspiracy to commit wire fraud [17].

1.4 Shutdown

On September 4, 2018, Theranos announced in an email to investors that it would cease operations and release its assets and remaining cash to creditors after all efforts to find a buyer came to nothing. Most of the company's remaining employees had been laid off on the previous Friday, August 31. However, Theranos general counsel and new CEO David Taylor and a few support staffers remained on payroll for a few more days [11]. *The Wall Street Journal* reported that any equity investments in the company were made worthless by the shutdown.

2. Technology and Products

Theranos claimed to have developed devices to automate and miniaturize blood tests using microscopic blood volumes. Theranos dubbed its blood collection vessel the "nanotainer" and its analysis machine the "Edison" [107–109]. Holmes reportedly named the device "Edison" after inventor Thomas Edison, stating, "We tried everything else and it failed, so let's call it the Edison." This was likely because of a well-known Edison quote: "I've not failed. I've just found 10,000 ways that won't work" [110].

The blood sample was to be collected via a finger prick and then transferred to the nanotainer through Theranos's sample collection device. At just 12.9 millimetres (0.51 in) in height, the nanotainer held a couple of drops of blood [111].

One of the patents for the Edison described a point of care system that could communicate with the Internet to receive instructions for which blood tests to run on the samples, before communicating these results back through the Internet. The results would then be compared to medical data available on the Internet, with the Edison running supplementary blood tests that were more targeted based on the results of the comparison. The patent was unclear on how much blood the Edison would actually require to conduct these blood tests. In one section, the patent claimed the sample needed to consist of about 10 drops of blood, but in another section, the patent claimed the Edison would need less than one drop of blood [112]. The technology was criticized for not being peer reviewed [113, 114]. Theranos claimed to have data verifying the accuracy and reliability of its tests that would be published [115]. In February 2016, Theranos announced that it would permit the Cleveland Clinic to complete a validation study of its technology [116]. In March 2016, a study authored by 13 scientists appeared in the *Journal of Clinical Investigation*, where it was stated that the company's blood test results were flagged "outside their normal range 1.6x more often than other testing services", that 68 percent of lab measurements evaluated "showed significant interservice variability", and that "lipid panel test results between Theranos and other clinical services" were "nonequivalent" [117].

In August 2016, the company introduced a new robotic capillary blood testing unit named "miniLab" at the 2016 annual meeting of the American Association for Clinical Chemistry, but did not present any data supporting the claimed abilities of the device [118–120]. The miniLab was allegedly capable of carrying out a range of tests from a small amount of blood. After failing to address concerns that Theranos exaggerated the capabilities of the miniLab, Walgreens withdrew from their partnership. It was later revealed that Theranos had voided two years of test results showing inaccuracies with the Edison technology [121].

3. Corporate Affairs

3.1 Location

Theranos was headquartered in Palo Alto, California. It previously had laboratories in Newark, California and Scottsdale, Arizona [122].

3.2 Management

Elizabeth Holmes, the chief executive officer and founder of Theranos in 2013

From its incorporation in 2003 until 2018, Holmes was the company's chief executive officer. She recruited Channing Robertson, a chemical-engineering professor at Stanford, to be a technical advisor and the company's first board member during its early years. Holmes's then-boyfriend Ramesh Balwani, a software engineer whom Holmes had met during high school, joined the company as its president and chief operating officer in 2009 [123]. In July 2011, Holmes was introduced to former U.S. Secretary of State George Shultz, who joined the Theranos board of directors that month [124]. Over the next three years, Shultz helped to introduce almost all the outside directors on the "all-star board", which included William Perry (former U.S. Secretary of Defense), Henry Kissinger (former U.S. Secretary of State), Sam Nunn (former U.S. Senator), Bill Frist (former U.S. Senator, senate majority leader and heart-transplant surgeon), Gary Roughead (Admiral, USN, retired), Jim Mattis (General, USMC), Richard Kovacevich (former Wells Fargo Chairman and CEO) and Riley P. Bechtel (chairman of the board and former CEO at Bechtel Group) [124–126]. The board was criticized for consisting "mainly of directors with diplomatic or military backgrounds" [19].

In April 2016, Theranos announced its medical advisory board which included past presidents or board members of the American Association for Clinical Chemistry [127]. Members were invited to review the company's proprietary technologies and advise on the integration into clinical practice [127]. The board included members with relevant biomedical expertise such as past president of the American Association for Clinical Chemistry Susan A. Evans; William Foege, former director of the U.S. Centers for Disease Control and Prevention (CDC); David Helfet, director of the Orthopedic Trauma Service at the Hospital for Special Surgery; and professors Ann M. Gronowski, Larry J. Kricka, Jack Ladenson, Andy O. Miller and Steven Spitalnik [128, 129].

Balwani left his position as president and COO in May 2016. At that time, the company announced its new board members, Fabrizio Bonanni (former executive vice president of Amgen), Richard Kovacevich and William Foege, who would help to publicly introduce its technologies [130–132].

In May 2016 members of the Theranos board of directors were [133]:

- Elizabeth Holmes, founder and CEO
- Riley Bechtel, former Bechtel Group CEO
- David Boies, a founder and the chairman of Boies Schiller Flexner
- William Foege, former director of the CDC

- Richard Kovacevich, former CEO and chairman of Wells Fargo
- Jim Mattis, later U.S. Secretary of Defense
- Fabrizio Bonanni, former executive vice president of Amgen

In December 2016, it was announced the Theranos management team would be restructured with the departure of Riley Bechtel. In January 2017, incoming U.-S. Secretary of Defense nominee James Mattis resigned from the Theranos board. In January 2017 the Theranos board of directors included [134]:

- Elizabeth Holmes
- William Foege
- Fabrizio Bonanni
- Daniel Warmenhoven, former NetApp CEO, replacing Riley Bechtel

It was also announced in November 2016 that the celebrity-studded "board of counsulors" would be scrapped in January 2017 [135].

3.3 Valuation

Theranos raised millions of dollars in its first years. In 2004, Theranos was based in a rented basement near the Stanford campus [136]. By December 2004, the company had raised more than $6 million from investors at a valuation of $30 million [137]. The company had about $45 million total fundraising after Series B and Series C funding in 2006 [138]. Theranos raised an additional $45 million in 2010 at a valuation of $1 billion [137, 139]. The company moved to the former headquarters of Facebook in June 2012 [140, 141]. The company had significant news coverage starting in September 2013 after profiles in the *San Francisco Business Times* and *The Wall Street Journal* [19]. By 2014, Theranos had raised more than $400 million with an estimated value of $9 billion [142]. In 2016, *Forbes* revised the estimated net worth of the company to $800 million taking into account the $724 million of capital raised [10].

In May 2017, participating shareholders provided a release of any potential claims against Theranos in exchange for shares of the company's new preferred stock. Holders of more than 99 percent of the shares elected to participate. Holmes contributed shares to the company and gave up equity to offset potential dilution to non-participating shareholders [143].

In May 2018 John Carreyrou reported that American business and government leaders lost more than $600 million by privately investing in Theranos [144]. Major investments had been made by the Walton family ($150 million), Rupert Murdoch ($121 million), Betsy DeVos ($100 million), and the Cox family (of Cox Media Group) ($100 million) [69]. The final liquidation of the company in September 2018 rendered these investments worthless [11].

4. Books and Documentaries

John Carreyrou, a *Wall Street Journal* journalist whose work exposed Theranos, published a book-length treatment in May 2018 titled *Bad Blood: Secrets and Lies in a Silicon Valley Startup* [145]. A film version was reportedly scheduled for release in 2020, starring Jennifer Lawrence as Elizabeth Holmes, written by Vanessa Taylor and directed by Adam McKay [146, 147].

In January 2019, ABC News' *Nightline* released a podcast and documentary about the Holmes/Theranos story called *The Dropout* [148].

Also, in January 2019, a documentary film entitled *The Inventor: Out for Blood in Silicon Valley* about Holmes and Theranos was released. Directed by Alex Gibney, it made its debut at the Sundance Film Festival and was released to the general public in March 2019 on HBO platforms [149, 150].

5. See also

- Ian Gibbons, Theranos's chief scientist who died by suicide in 2013
- Nikola Corporation

References

1. *"Amended Statement by Foreign Corporation"* (PDF). California Secretary State Business Search. April 21, 2004. *Archived* from the original on February 8, 2021. Retrieved June 19, 2019. C2651481
2. Bilton, Nick (September 6, 2016). *"Exclusive: How Elizabeth Holmes's House of Cards Came Tumbling Down"*. Vanity Fair. *Archived* from the original on September 3, 2017. Retrieved June 19, 2019.
3. Jump up to:[a] [b] Carreyrou, John (2018). *Bad Blood: Secrets and Lies in a Silicon Valley Startup*. Knopf Doubleday Publishing Group. ISBN 9781524731663.
4. Levine, Matt (March 14, 2018). *"The Blood Unicorn Theranos Was Just a Fairy Tale"*. Bloomberg View. Retrieved June 19, 2019.
5. Rago, Joseph (September 8, 2013). *"Elizabeth Holmes: The Breakthrough of Instant Diagnosis"*. The Wall Street Journal. *Archived* from the original on February 8, 2021. Retrieved June 19, 2019.
6. Salzman, Avi. *"Theranos: From Unicorn Hype to 'Massive Fraud'"*. Barron's. *Archived* from the original on February 8, 2021. Retrieved June 19, 2019.
7. Jump up to:[a] [b] [c] Parloff, Roger (June 12, 2014). *"This CEO is out for blood"*. Fortune. *Archived* from the original on October 7, 2019. Retrieved June 19, 2019.
8. Johnson, Carolyn Y. (October 15, 2015). *"The wildly hyped $9 billion blood test company that no one really understands"*. The Washington Post. ISSN 0190-8286. *Archived* from the original on February 8, 2021. Retrieved June 19, 2019.
9. Ableson, Reed; Pollack, Andrew (April 18, 2016). *"Theranos Under Federal Criminal Investigation, Adding to Its Woes"*. The New York Times. *Archived* from the original on February 8, 2021. Retrieved June 19, 2019.
10. Jump up to:[a] [b] Herper, Matthew (June 1, 2016). *"From $4.5 Billion To Nothing: Forbes Revises Estimated Net Worth of Theranos Founder Elizabeth Holmes"*. Forbes. *Archived* from the original on December 16, 2019. Retrieved June 1, 2016.
11. Jump up to:[a] [b] [c] Carreyrou, John. *"Blood-Testing Firm Theranos to Dissolve"*. The Wall Street Journal. *Archived* from the original on April 14, 2020. Retrieved September 5, 2018.
12. della Cava, Marco (March 14, 2018). *"She was 'the next Steve Jobs.' Now, Theranos founder Elizabeth Holmes is charged with fraud"*. USA Today. *Archived* from the original on March 15, 2018. Retrieved March 14, 2018.
13. O'Brien, Sarah Ashley. *"Elizabeth Holmes indicted on wire fraud charges, steps down from Theranos"*. CNN. *Archived* from the original on February 8, 2021. Retrieved June 19, 2019.
14. *"Theranos founder Elizabeth Holmes to stand trial in 2020"*. TechCrunch. *Archived* from the original on February 8, 2021. Retrieved June 30, 2019.

15. Khorram, Yasmin. "Elizabeth Holmes trial pushed to August following surprise pregnancy announcement". cnbc.com. CNBC. Retrieved June 4, 2021.
16. Beale, Stephen (February 22, 2021). *"Theranos CEO Elizabeth Holmes Trial Delayed Again, This Time Due to COVID-19 Restrictions, as Lawyers Battle Over Destroyed Clinical Laboratory Test Evidence"*. Dark Daily. Retrieved March 9, 2021.
17. Jump up to:[a][b] Griffith, Erin; Woo, Erin (January 4, 2022). *"Elizabeth Holmes Found Guilty of Four Charges of Fraud"*. The New York Times. Retrieved January 4, 2022.
18. Weisul, Kimberly (September 16, 2015). *"How Playing the Long Game Made Elizabeth Holmes a Billionaire"*. Inc. Archived from the original on December 14, 2019. Retrieved June 19, 2019.
19. Jump up to:[a][b][c] Leuty, Ron (August 30, 2013). *"Theranos: The biggest biotech you've never heard of"*. San Francisco Business Times. Archived from the original on February 8, 2021. Retrieved June 19, 2019.
20. Roper, Caitlin (February 18, 2014). *"This Woman Invented a Way to Run 30 Lab Tests on Only One Drop of Blood"*. Wired. Archived from the original on February 8, 2021. Retrieved June 19, 2019.
21. Bolt, Beth (November 13, 2014). *"Bringing Painless Blood Testing to the Pharmacy"*. Pharmacy Times. Archived from the original on February 8, 2021. Retrieved September 27, 2016.
22. Hu, Charlotte; Ramsey, Lydia (May 25, 2018). *"The rise and fall of Theranos, the blood-testing startup that went from a rising star in Silicon Valley to facing fraud charges over a wild 15-year span"*. Business Insider. Archived from the original on February 8, 2021. Retrieved June 19, 2019.
23. Stockton, Nick (May 4, 2016). *"Everything You Need to Know About the Theranos Saga So Far"*. Wired. Archived from the original on June 8, 2016. Retrieved June 19, 2019.
24. *"Safeway severs ties with Theranos as $350M deal collapses"*. www.fiercebiotech.com. Archived from the original on February 8, 2021. Retrieved March 9, 2019.
25. Moon, Mariella (November 18, 2014). *"Walgreens to offer affordable and needle-free blood tests in more stores (updated)"*. Business Insider. Archived from the original on February 8, 2021. Retrieved September 4, 2016.
26. *"Young blood"*. The Economist. June 27, 2015. Archived from the original on February 8, 2021. Retrieved September 4, 2016.
27. Duhaime-Ross, Arielle (October 26, 2015). *"Theranos didn't work with the huge drug company it supposedly made money from, drug company says"*. The Verge. Archived from the original on February 8, 2021. Retrieved October 29, 2015.
28. Weaver, Christopher, John Carreyrou and Michael Siconolfi, "Walgreen Sues Theranos, Seeks $140 Million in Damages" Archived February 8, 2021, at the Wayback Machine, The Wall Street Journal, November 8, 2016.
29. Thomas, Lauren (June 21, 2017). *"Theranos, Walgreens reportedly reach a deal to settle suit for under $30 million"*. CNBC. Archived from the original on February 8, 2021. Retrieved June 21, 2017.
30. "Theranos, Cleveland Clinic CEO's on innovation partnership". *Fox Business*. March 9, 2015. Archived from the original on February 8, 2021. Retrieved September 4, 2016.
31. Jump up to:[a][b] DiChristopher, Tom (October 30, 2015). *"We'll test Theranos tech: Cleveland Clinic CEO"*. CNBC. Archived from the original on February 8, 2021. Retrieved October 23, 2016.
32. George, John (July 16, 2016). *"Philadelphia health insurer to make lab testing easier for Medicaid members"*. Philadelphia Business Journal. Archived from the original on February 8, 2021. Retrieved September 4, 2016.
33. Chen, Caroline; Tracer, Zachary (July 8, 2015). *"Fingerprick Lab Test Startup Theranos Strikes Insurance Deal"*. Bloomberg. Retrieved September 4, 2016.
34. Parloff, Roger (July 2, 2015). *"Disruptive diagnostics firm Theranos gets boost from FDA"*. Fortune. Archived from the original on February 8, 2021. Retrieved July 16, 2015.

References

35. Quinn, Michelle (July 16, 2015). *"Theranos gets another FDA approval for its blood test"*. Silicon Beat. *Archived* from the original on February 8, 2021. Retrieved September 27, 2016.
36. *"This technology firm was named Arizona's Bioscience Company of the Year"*. www.bizjournals.com. *Archived* from the original on February 8, 2021. Retrieved March 9, 2020.
37. Ioannidis, J. P. A. (2015). "Stealth Research: Is Biomedical Innovation Happening Outside the Peer-Reviewed Literature?". JAMA: The Journal of the American Medical Association. 313 (7): 663–664. *doi*: https://doi.org/10.1001/jama.2014.17662. PMID 25688775.
38. Khan, Roomy (February 17, 2017). *"Theranos' $9 Billion Evaporated: Stanford Expert Whose Questions Ignited The Unicorn's Trouble"*. Forbes. *Archived* from the original on February 8, 2021. Retrieved February 17, 2017.
39. Diamandis, E. P. (2015). "Theranos phenomenon: promises and fallacies". Clinical Chemistry and Laboratory Medicine. 53 (7): 989–993. *doi*: https://doi.org/10.1515/cclm-2015-0356. PMID 26030792. S2CID 13822780.
40. Friedman, Lauren F.; Loria, Kevin. *"A scientist just raised 4 serious questions about the blood test that made Elizabeth Holmes a billionaire"*. Business Insider. *Archived* from the original on February 8, 2021. Retrieved June 26, 2015.
41. della Cava, Marco (July 24, 2015). *"Biden visits Theranos lab as part of healthcare innovation summit"*. USA Today. Archived from *the original* on September 8, 2021. Retrieved January 6, 2022.
42. Carreyrou, John (May 18, 2018). *"Theranos Inc.'s Partners in Blood"*. Wall Street Journal. *ISSN 0099-9660*. Retrieved December 25, 2021.
43. Bilton, Nick. *"Exclusive: How Elizabeth Holmes's House of Cards Came Tumbling Down"*. The Hive. *Archived* from the original on April 10, 2017. Retrieved April 22, 2017.
44. Carreyrou, John. *"Hot Startup Theranos Has Struggled With Its Blood-Test Technology"*. The Wall Street Journal. *ISSN 0099-9660*. *Archived* from the original on August 23, 2020. Retrieved October 29, 2015.
45. Jump up to:[a] [b] Carreyrou, John (November 17, 2016). *"Theranos Whistleblower Shook the Company—And His Family"*. The Wall Street Journal. *Archived* from the original on March 4, 2017. Retrieved November 17, 2016.
46. *"Report Claims Theranos Struggling With Blood Test Tech"*. Fortune. *Archived* from the original on February 8, 2021. Retrieved October 16, 2015.
47. Chmielewski, Dawn (October 22, 2015). *"Theranos Attacks Wall Street Journal (Again) in a Rebuttal You'll Need a Medical Degree to Understand"*. Re/code. *Archived* from the original on February 8, 2021. Retrieved December 26, 2015.
48. *"Walgreens halts expansion of Theranos centers"*. Fortune. October 24, 2015. *Archived* from the original on February 8, 2021. Retrieved October 25, 2015.
49. Rosenbloom, Micah (November 21, 2015). *"In Defense Of Theranos"*. TechCrunch. *Archived* from the original on February 8, 2021. Retrieved October 23, 2016.
50. Levy, Rachael (December 13, 2019). *"How the 1% Scrubs Its Image Online"*. The Wall Street Journal. *Archived* from the original on December 15, 2019. Retrieved December 15, 2019.
51. Johnson, Carolyn Y. (December 2, 2015). *"E-mails reveal concerns about Theranos's FDA compliance date back years"*. Washington Post. *Archived* from the original on February 8, 2021. Retrieved December 26, 2015.
52. *"The FDA's notes from its visit to Theranos' labs don't look good"*. Business Insider. October 27, 2015. *Archived* from the original on February 8, 2021. Retrieved October 27, 2015.
53. *"FDA-483"* (PDF). FDA. September 16, 2015. *Archived* from the original on February 8, 2021. Retrieved October 20, 2018.
54. *"FDA-483"* (PDF). FDA. September 16, 2015. *Archived* from the original on February 8, 2021. Retrieved October 20, 2018.
55. *"Two FDA Inspection Reports Show Theranos' Blood-Collection 'Nanotainer' Was an Uncleared Class II Medical Device | Dark Daily"*. *Archived* from the original on February 8, 2021. Retrieved October 4, 2020.

56. Derla, Katherine (October 22, 2015). *"Blood-Testing Start-Up Theranos Is In 'Pause Period', Says CEO Elizabeth Holmes"*. Tech Times. Archived from the original on February 8, 2021. Retrieved October 23, 2016.
57. Lopatto, Elizabeth (October 27, 2015). *"FDA inspector slams Theranos for poor quality management"*. The Verge. Archived from the original on February 8, 2021. Retrieved March 10, 2020.
58. *"Arizona inspectors find Theranos lab issues"*. Arizona Republic. November 27, 2015. Retrieved March 20, 2019.
59. *"US government says Theranos lab poses 'immediate jeopardy to patient safety'"*. The Verge. January 27, 2016. Archived from the original on February 8, 2021. Retrieved January 27, 2016.
60. Weaver, John Carreyrou and Christopher (April 13, 2016). *"Regulators Propose Banning Theranos Founder Elizabeth Holmes for at Least Two Years"*. The Wall Street Journal. ISSN 0099-9660. Archived from the original on February 8, 2021. Retrieved March 13, 2020.
61. Ramsey, Lydia (January 29, 2016). *"Another partner just asked Theranos to stop running blood tests"*. Business Insider. Archived from the original on February 8, 2021. Retrieved October 23, 2016.
62. *"Theranos Under Fire as U.S. Threatens Crippling Sanctions"*. The New York Times. Archived from the original on February 8, 2021. Retrieved April 19, 2016.
63. Ramsey, Lydia (April 13, 2016). *"US regulators want to bar Elizabeth Holmes from Theranos for 2 years"*. Business Insider. Archived from the original on February 8, 2021. Retrieved October 23, 2016.
64. *"Don't Blame Silicon Valley for Theranos"*. The New York Times. April 27, 2016. Archived from the original on February 8, 2021. Retrieved June 1, 2016.
65. Lagasse, Jeff (July 1, 2016). *"Theranos founder Elizabeth Holmes asked by Congressional committee to detail company's compliance efforts"*. Healthcare Finance News. Archived from the original on February 8, 2021. Retrieved July 2, 2016.
66. Tracer, Zachary. *"Theranos Queried on Blood Test Failures by House Democrats"*. Retrieved July 5, 2016.
67. Carreyrou, John (May 19, 2016). *"Theranos Voids Two Years of Edison Blood-Test Results"*. The Wall Street Journal. ISSN 0099-9660. Archived from the original on February 8, 2021. Retrieved May 21, 2016.
68. Chen, Caroline; Spalding, Rebecca (June 3, 2016). *"Theranos Says Only 1% of Results Affected; Some Doubt Tests"*. Bloomberg. Retrieved June 29, 2016.
69. Jump up to:[a] [b] Carreyrou, John; Siconolfi, Michael; Weaver, Christopher (July 8, 2016). *"Theranos Dealt Sharp Blow as Elizabeth Holmes Is Banned From Operating Labs"*. The Wall Street Journal. ISSN 0099-9660. Archived from the original on March 9, 2017. Retrieved June 19, 2019.
70. *"Theranos to Appeal Regulatory Sanctions"* Archived February 8, 2021, at the Wayback Machine The Wall Street Journal, Retrieved August 26, 2016.
71. *"Troubled Theranos hits another wall as Zika test withdrawn"*. The Washington Post. Retrieved August 31, 2016.
72. Carreyrou, John; Weaver, Christopher (August 30, 2016). *"Theranos Halts New Zika Test After FDA Inspection"*. The Wall Street Journal. Archived from the original on February 8, 2021. Retrieved October 6, 2016.
73. *"Theranos to Close Labs and Lay Off 340 Workers"*. The New York Times. Archived from the original on December 9, 2016. Retrieved June 19, 2019.
74. *"An Open Letter From Elizabeth Holmes"*. Theranos. October 5, 2016. Archived from *the original* on September 13, 2018. Retrieved October 6, 2016.
75. Post, Washington. *"Theranos will close labs and Walgreens testing sites, laying off hundreds"*. Chicago Tribune. Archived from the original on February 8, 2021. Retrieved October 6, 2016.

References

76. Mole, Beth (October 5, 2016). *"Theranos throws in the towel on clinical labs, officially pivots to devices"*. Ars Technica. Archived from the original on February 8, 2021. Retrieved October 6, 2016.
77. Weaver, Christopher; Carreyrou, John (January 17, 2017). *"Second Theranos Lab Failed U.S. Inspection"*. The Wall Street Journal. Archived from the original on April 21, 2017. Retrieved May 26, 2019.
78. Russell, Jon (January 18, 2017). *"Theranos closes its last remaining blood-testing lab after it reportedly failed an inspection"*. TechCrunch. Archived from the original on February 8, 2021. Retrieved January 18, 2017.
79. O'Brien, Sara Ashley (January 6, 2017). *"Theranos fires 41% of staffers"*. CNN. Archived from the original on February 8, 2021. Retrieved January 10, 2017.
80. Chen, Caroline. *"Theranos to fire 41 percent of workforce in second round of cuts"*. Chicago Tribune. Archived from the original on February 8, 2021. Retrieved January 10, 2017.
81. *"Arizona AG plans to sue Theranos over blood-testing devices"*. Reuters. January 12, 2017. Archived from the original on February 8, 2021. Retrieved January 12, 2017.
82. *"Theranos Investors Say They Were Pressured to Abandon Lawsuit"*. Bloomberg. April 19, 2017. Retrieved April 20, 2017.
83. Weaver, Christopher (April 22, 2017). *"Theranos Secretly Bought Outside Lab Gear, Ran Fake Tests: Court Filings"*. The Wall Street Journal. ISSN 0099-9660. Archived from the original on April 21, 2017. Retrieved April 22, 2017.
84. *"Theranos Reaches Settlement with Partner Fund Management"*. Theranos. May 1, 2017. Archived from the original (Press release) on August 13, 2018. Retrieved May 2, 2017.
85. Weaver, Christopher. *"Theranos agrees to 2-year ban on clinical blood work"*. MarketWatch. Archived from the original on February 8, 2021. Retrieved April 28, 2017.
86. *"Theranos, Arizona Attorney General Reach Agreement on Full Restitution to State Consumers"*. Theranos. April 18, 2017. Archived from the original (Press release) on June 17, 2018.
87. Mole, Beth (April 18, 2017). *"With $4.65M deal, Arizonans will get their money back from Theranos"*. Ars Technica. Archived from the original on February 8, 2021. Retrieved April 18, 2017.
88. Sy Mukherjee, Theranos Just Reached a Deal With Investors to Avoid Lawsuits Archived February 8, 2021, at the Wayback Machine Fortune, May 16, 2017
89. Howard Fischer, Theranos will refund $4.6M to Arizonans who took its blood tests Archived February 8, 2021, at the Wayback Machine White Mountain Independent April 21, 2017
90. *"Theranos Reaches Settlement with Walgreens"*. Theranos. August 1, 2017. Archived from the original (Press release) on September 13, 2018.
91. Why Softbank invested in Theranos (CB Insights) https://www.cbinsights.com/research/why-softbank-invested-in-theranos/
92. Carreyrou, John (December 24, 2017). *"Blood-Testing Firm Theranos Gets $100 Million Lifeline From Fortress"*. The Wall Street Journal. Archived from the original on February 8, 2021. Retrieved June 19, 2019.
93. Morris, David Z. (December 23, 2017). *"Theranos Secures $100 Million in New Funding from Fortress Capital"*. Fortune. Archived from the original on February 8, 2021. Retrieved January 15, 2018.
94. Sheetz, Michael (December 26, 2017). *"Theranos dodges bankruptcy after $100 million loan: Report"*. CNBC. Archived from the original on February 8, 2021. Retrieved January 15, 2018.
95. Joel Rosentblatt, "Theranos Investors Turn Scavengers on Wounded Unicorn's Remains", *Bloomberg Technology*, 28 March, 2018
96. Jump up to:[a] [b] Mukherjee, Sy (April 10, 2018). *"Report: Theranos Just Laid Off the Vast Majority of Its Employees"*. Fortune. Archived from the original on February 8, 2021. Retrieved June 19, 2019.
97. *"Theranos Lays Off Most Of Its Workforce"*. PYMNTS. April 11, 2018. Retrieved April 12, 2018.

98. A SoftBank-owned company used Theranos patents to sue over COVID-19 tests (The Verge) https://www.theverge.com/2020/3/18/21185006/softbank-theranos-coronavirus-covid-lawsuit-patent-testing
99. Johnson, Carolyn Y. (March 14, 2018). *"Theranos chief executive Elizabeth Holmes charged with massive fraud"*. The Washington Post. Archived from the original on February 8, 2021. Retrieved March 15, 2018.
100. *"Securities and Exchange Commission, vs. Elizabeth Holmes and Theranos, Inc., Complaint"* (PDF). sec.gov. SEC. Archived (PDF) from the original on February 8, 2021. Retrieved March 14, 2018.
101. Robinson, Matt (March 14, 2018). *"Theranos and CEO Elizabeth Holmes Accused of Fraud by SEC"*. Bloomberg News. Archived from the original on March 14, 2018. Retrieved March 14, 2018.
102. Balakrishnan, Anita (March 14, 2018). *"Theranos CEO Holmes and former president Balwani charged with massive fraud"*. CNBC. Archived from the original on February 8, 2021. Retrieved March 14, 2018.
103. *"Theranos Founder and Former Chief Operating Officer Charged In Alleged Wire Fraud Schemes"* (Press release). justice.gov. United States Department of Justice. June 15, 2018. Archived from the original on February 8, 2021. Retrieved June 16, 2018. Elizabeth Holmes and Ramesh "Sunny" Balwani Are Alleged To Have Perpetrated Multi-million Dollar Schemes To Defraud Investors, Doctors, and Patients.
104. O'Brien, Sara Ashley (June 15, 2018). *"Elizabeth Holmes indicted on wire fraud charges, steps down from Theranos"*. CNNMoney. Archived from the original on February 8, 2021. Retrieved March 25, 2019.
105. *"Theranos founder Elizabeth Holmes' trial likely won't take place until next year"*. MassDevice. July 22, 2020. Archived from the original on February 8, 2021. Retrieved August 2, 2020.
106. Khorram, Yasmin (February 23, 2021). *"Elizabeth Holmes denies destroying evidence in Theranos case"*. CNBC. Retrieved February 24, 2021.
107. Rago, Joseph (September 8, 2013). *"Elizabeth Holmes: The Breakthrough of Instant Diagnosis"*. The Wall Street Journal. Archived from the original on February 8, 2021. Retrieved July 25, 2016.
108. Nguyen, Tuan C. *"How To Run 30 Health Tests On a Single Drop of Blood"*. Smithsonian Magazine. Smithsonian. Retrieved October 31, 2015.
109. Loria, Kevin (October 16, 2015). *"Here's what we know about how Theranos' 'revolutionary' technology works"*. Tech Insider. Archived from the original on February 8, 2021. Retrieved July 25, 2016.
110. Stieg, Cory. *"What Exactly Was The Theranos Edison Machine Supposed To Do?"*. www.refinery29.com. Archived from the original on February 8, 2021. Retrieved October 4, 2020.
111. Stieg, Cory. *"What Exactly Was The Theranos Edison Machine Supposed To Do?"*. www.refinery29.com. Archived from the original on February 8, 2021. Retrieved October 4, 2020.
112. Look, Vincent (May 1, 2019). *"Theranos Patent for Point of Care System"*. The Patent Geek. Archived from the original on February 8, 2021. Retrieved October 4, 2020.
113. Stewart, James B. (October 29, 2015). *"The Narrative Frays for Theranos and Elizabeth Holmes"*. The New York Times. Archived from the original on August 23, 2020. Retrieved October 31, 2015.
114. Lapowsky, Issie (October 15, 2015). *"Theranos' Scandal Exposes the Problem With Tech's Hype Cycle"*. Wired. Archived from the original on December 1, 2015. Retrieved November 15, 2015.
115. *"Theranos Chief Yields to Calls for Proof of Blood Test's Reliability"*. The New York Times. October 27, 2015. Archived from the original on July 22, 2016. Retrieved December 26, 2015.
116. *"Theranos Has Still Not Begun a Promised Validation Study"*. Fortune. Retrieved February 2, 2016.

117. Kidd, Brian; et al. (March 28, 2016). *"Evaluation of direct-to-consumer low-volume lab tests in healthy adults"*. Journal of Clinical Investigation. 126 (5): 1734–1744. *doi*: https://doi.org/10.1172/JCI86318. PMC 4855945.
118. Abelson, Reed (June 1, 2016). *"Elizabeth Holmes, Founder of Theranos, Falls From Highest Perch Off Forbes List"*. The New York Times. Archived from the original on February 8, 2021. Retrieved July 25, 2016.
119. Langreth, Robert; Chen, Caroline (August 1, 2016). *"Expecting Data From Theranos, Lab Experts Get New Product"*. Bloomberg. Retrieved August 1, 2016.
120. Herper, Matthew (August 1, 2016). *"Theranos Presents Data On New Blood Test Machine, Remains Mum On Previous Technology"*. Forbes. Archived from the original on February 8, 2021. Retrieved August 1, 2016.
121. Tracy, Abigail (August 2016). *"Elizabeth Holmes's First Public Presentation of Theranos Data Falls Short"*. Vanity Fair. Archived from the original on February 8, 2021. Retrieved October 4, 2020.
122. Abelson, Reed; Creswell, Julie (December 19, 2015). *"Theranos Founder Faces a Test of Technology, and Reputation"*. The New York Times. Archived from the original on January 20, 2017. Retrieved July 2, 2016.
123. Auletta, Ken (December 15, 2014). *"Blood, Simpler"*. The New Yorker. Archived from the original on October 28, 2019. Retrieved May 31, 2016.
124. Jump up to:[a] [b] Parloff, Roger (June 12, 2014). *"A singular board at Theranos"*. Fortune. Archived from the original on November 9, 2016. Retrieved May 11, 2016.
125. Leuty, Ron (August 2, 2013). *"Theranos adds Kovacevich to all-star board"*. San Francisco Business Times. Archived from the original on April 14, 2017. Retrieved March 9, 2014.
126. Leuty, Ron (July 29, 2013). *"Quiet Theranos adds former Wells chief Kovacevich, 'Mad Dog' Mattis to power-packed board"*. San Francisco Business Times. Archived from the original on February 8, 2021. Retrieved March 9, 2014.
127. Jump up to:[a] [b] Parloff, Roger (April 7, 2016). *"Theranos Adds Startlingly Well-Qualified Medical Board"*. Fortune. Retrieved April 14, 2016.
128. Ramsey, Lydia (April 7, 2016). *"Theranos just made a crucial move that could help its reputation"*. Business Insider. Archived from the original on February 8, 2021. Retrieved September 9, 2016.
129. Weisul, Kimberly (April 7, 2016). *"Heavy Hitters Join Theranos Advisory Board"*. Inc. Archived from the original on February 8, 2021. Retrieved September 9, 2016.
130. Masunaga, Samantha. *"Theranos shuffles leadership; president retires"*. Los Angeles Times. Archived from the original on February 8, 2021. Retrieved September 9, 2016.
131. Carreyrou, John. *"Theranos Executive Sunny Balwani to Depart Amid Regulatory Probes"*. The Wall Street Journal. Archived from the original on February 8, 2021. Retrieved May 12, 2016.
132. della Cava, Marco. *"Theranos COO departs as embattled startup adds to board"*. USA Today. Archived from the original on February 8, 2021. Retrieved May 12, 2016. Theranos also is adding former Amgen executive Fabrizio Bonanni to its board.
133. Abelson, Reed (May 11, 2016). *"Embattled Blood Lab Theranos Makes a Bid to Regain Confidence"*. The New York Times. Archived from the original on February 8, 2021. Retrieved May 17, 2016.
134. Ramsey, Lydia. *"Theranos Dissolves High-Profile Board of Counselors"*. Inc. Archived from the original on February 8, 2021. Retrieved December 3, 2016.
135. Weaver, Christopher; Minaya, Ezequiel. *"Theranos Investor Riley Bechtel Steps Down From Board"*. The Wall Street Journal. Archived from the original on February 8, 2021. Retrieved May 26, 2019.
136. Crow, David (April 8, 2016). *"Blood Simple"*. Financial Times. Archived from the original on February 8, 2021. Retrieved September 27, 2016.

137. Jump up to:ᵃ ᵇ Carreyrou, John (December 27, 2015). *"At Theranos, Many Strategies and Snags"*. The Wall Street Journal. *Archived* from the original on February 8, 2021. Retrieved December 28, 2015.
138. Leuty, Ron (June 29, 2015). *"Theranos: Testing times lie ahead for secretive blood-testing firm"*. American City Business Journals. *Archived* from the original on February 8, 2021. Retrieved September 27, 2016.
139. Klein, Julie (July 8, 2010). *"Theranos raises $45M to help patients track drug reactions"*. VentureBeat. *Archived* from the original on February 8, 2021. Retrieved September 16, 2013.
140. Segall, Eli (June 29, 2012). *"Theranos growing close to home in Palo Alto"*. Silicon Valley Business Journal. *Archived* from the original on February 8, 2021. Retrieved September 27, 2016.
141. Grossman, Lev (May 5, 2016). *"The Fall Of Theranos And The Future Of Science In Silicon Valley"*. Time. 187 (18): 25–6. *Archived* from the original on February 8, 2021. Retrieved September 27, 2016.
142. Loria, Kevin (September 29, 2014). *"This Woman's Revolutionary Idea Made Her A Billionaire—And Could Change Medicine"*. Business Insider. *Archived* from the original on February 8, 2021. Retrieved September 27, 2016.
143. *"Theranos Finalizes Shareholder Recapitalization"*. Businesswire. May 16, 2017. *Archived* from the original on August 25, 2017. Retrieved May 19, 2017.
144. Carreyrou, John (May 3, 2018). *"Theranos Cost Business and Government Leaders More Than $600 Million"*. The Wall Street Journal. *Archived* from the original on February 8, 2021. Retrieved May 5, 2018.
145. *"How One Company Scammed Silicon Valley. And How It Got Caught"*. The New York Times. May 21, 2018. ISSN 0362-4331. *Archived* from the original on August 23, 2020. Retrieved May 22, 2018.
146. McNary, Dave (June 23, 2016). *"Legendary Wins Bidding War for Jennifer Lawrence Movie 'Bad Blood'"*. Variety. *Archived* from the original on June 25, 2016. Retrieved July 23, 2018.
147. *"Bad Blood (2020)"*. www.filmaffinity.com. *Archived* from the original on February 8, 2021. Retrieved September 1, 2019.
148. *"The Dropout"*. ABC News (Press release). *Archived* from the original on February 8, 2021. Retrieved January 22, 2019.
149. Debruge, Peter (November 28, 2018). *"Sundance Film Festival Unveils 2019 Features Lineup"*. Variety. *Archived* from the original on November 29, 2018. Retrieved March 5, 2019.
150. O'Brien, Sara Ashley (March 12, 2019). *"HBO Theranos documentary goes inside the secretive, failed company"*. CNN Business. *Archived* from the original on February 8, 2021. Retrieved December 15, 2019.

Chapter 8
Energy

8.1 Petrofac Ltd

8.1.1 Text from the UK SFO Website[1] (January 14, 2022)

The SFO is investigating the activities of Petrofac Ltd, its subsidiaries, and their officers, employees and agents for suspected bribery, corruption and money laundering.

On Friday 24 September 2021, following requisition by the Serious Fraud Office (SFO), Petrofac Limited attended Westminster Magistrates' Court where the company was charged with seven separate offences of failing to prevent bribery between 2011 and 2017.

Having been heard at Westminster Magistrates' Court, the case was sent to the Crown Court, in line with the legal procedure for SFO cases into serious and complex financial crime.

Following a plea agreement with the SFO, Petrofac Limited pleaded guilty to each offence on Friday, 1 October. On Monday, 4 October, Petrofac Limited was ordered to pay confiscation of GBP 22,836,985, a fine of over GBP 47,197,640, and the SFO's costs of GBP 7 million.

Petrofac Limited admitted that it failed to prevent former senior executives of the Petrofac Group from paying GBP 32 million (USD 44 million) in bribes, to help the Petrofac Group win over GBP 2.6 billion (USD 3.5 billion) of contracts in the oil and gas industry in Iraq, Saudi Arabia and the United Arab Emirates.

The Court heard how, over a period of six years, senior executives within the Petrofac Group engaged in elaborate schemes to corrupt the awarding of contracts, using agents to systematically bribe officials to win lucrative contracts by unfair and dishonest means.

---

[1] https://www.sfo.gov.uk/cases/petrofac/.

A key feature of the case was the complex and deliberately opaque methods used by these senior executives to pay agents across borders, disguising payments through sub-contractors, creating fake contracts for fictitious services and, in some cases, passing bribes through more than one agent and one country, to disguise their actions.

Also on Monday, 4 October 2021, David Lufkin, a British national and previously Global Head of Sales for Petrofac International Limited, was sentenced to a two-year custodial sentence, which was suspended for 18 months.

David Lufkin pleaded guilty to 11 counts of bribery on 6 February 2019 and 3 further counts of bribery on 14 January 2021. The charges relate to payments or offers of over USD $181 million in bribes to win contracts worth a total of over USD $7.8 billion in the United Arab Emirates, Saudi Arabia, and Iraq.

In addition to pleading guilty, David Lufkin co-operated with SFO investigators and assisted with the investigation.

Petrofac Limited's conviction and sentencing brings to a conclusion the investigation into suspected bribery and corruption as far as the corporate entity (and its subsidiaries) is concerned. The investigation into the conduct of individual suspects continues.

8.1.2 Text from the SFO Website (14 Jan 2022)[2]

SFO Secures Confiscation Against Former Petrofac Executive
December 15, 2021

The Serious Fraud Office has secured a confiscation order worth over £140,000 against Petrofac's former Head of Sales, David Lufkin.

In October 2021, David Lufkin was handed a two-year suspended sentence, for making corrupt payments and offers to influence the awarding of oil and gas contracts for Petrofac in Iraq, Saudi Arabia and the United Arab Emirates.

Following a hearing today at Southwark Crown Court, the Serious Fraud Office (SFO) secured a confiscation order worth over £140,000 against former senior Petrofac executive, David Lufkin.

In October 2021, Mr Lufkin, Petrofac's former Head of Sales, was handed a two-year custodial sentence, suspended for 18 months. Mr Lufkin had previously pleaded guilty to 14 counts of bribery and admitted making corrupt payments between 2011 and 2018 to influence the awarding of contracts to the Petrofac Group. In addition to pleading guilty, Mr Lufkin co-operated with SFO investigators and assisted the wider investigation.

---

[2] https://www.sfo.gov.uk/2021/12/15/serious-fraud-office-secures-confiscation-against-former-petrofac-executive/.

This case has also seen the SFO secure convictions against Petrofac Ltd, with the company ordered to pay £77m in fines (including a confiscation order worth over £22m) after pleading guilty to seven counts of failing to prevent bribery between 2011 and 2017.

Serious Fraud Office Secures Third Set of Petrofac Bribery Convictions

8.1.3 Text from the UK SFO Website[3] (August 11, 2022)

4 October, 2021

The Serious Fraud Office (SFO) has secured the conviction of Petrofac Limited for seven separate counts of failure to prevent bribery between 2011 and 2017.

Petrofac Limited pleaded guilty to failing to prevent former senior executives of the Petrofac group of subsidiaries (the Petrofac Group) from using agents to systematically bribe officials, to win oil contracts in Iraq, Saudi Arabia and the United Arab Emirates.

Petrofac Limited admitted that senior executives of the Petrofac Group paid GBP 32 million (USD 44 million) in bribes to corrupt the awarding of contracts worth approximately GBP 2.6 billion (USD 3.5 billion).

Today, Petrofac Limited was ordered to pay confiscation of GBP 22,836,985, they were fined over GBP 47,197,640 and the SFO's costs of GBP 7 million.

David Lufkin, Petrofac Group's former Head of Sales, was also sentenced today. He received a two-year custodial sentence, which was suspended for 18 months, for committing 14 counts of bribery.

Petrofac Limited has been ordered to pay GBP 77 million after the SFO secured further convictions in its investigation into bribery and corruption at the Jersey-registered energy services company.

On Friday, Petrofac Limited pleaded guilty to seven separate counts of failing to prevent bribery between 2011 and 2017.

Petrofac Limited admitted that it failed to prevent former senior executives of the Petrofac Group from paying GBP 32 million (USD 44 million) in bribes, to help the Petrofac Group win over GBP 2.6 billion (USD 3.5 billion) of contracts in the oil and gas industry in Iraq, Saudi Arabia and the United Arab Emirates.

The Court heard how, over a period of six years, senior executives within the Petrofac Group engaged in elaborate schemes to corrupt the awarding of contracts, using agents to systematically bribe officials to win lucrative contracts by unfair and dishonest means.

A key feature of the case was the complex and deliberately opaque methods used by these senior executives to pay agents across borders, disguising payments through sub-contractors, creating fake contracts for fictitious services and, in some

---

[3] https://www.sfo.gov.uk/2021/10/04/serious-fraud-office-secures-third-set-of-petrofac-bribery-convictions/.

cases, passing bribes through more than one agent and one country, to disguise their actions.

Lisa Osofsky, Director, Serious Fraud Office, said: "By pleading guilty, Petrofac Limited has accepted that senior executives within the Petrofac Group acted deliberately and without conscience in the pursuit of greed. The company's failure to prevent this conduct distorted competitive market conditions and tainted the oil and gas industry.

"Today's result should serve as a warning; the SFO will use all the powers at its disposal to root out and prosecute companies and individuals, whose criminal activity detrimentally affects the reputation and integrity of the United Kingdom.

"The SFO welcomes Petrofac Limited taking responsibility for its conduct."

This is the third set of convictions secured by the SFO in its four-year investigation into cross-border corruption at the Petrofac Group. David Lufkin, former Head of Sales at Petrofac pleaded guilty to 11 counts of bribery in 2019 and 3 counts of bribery in 2021.

Lufkin was today sentenced to a two-year custodial sentence, which was suspended for 18 months. In addition to pleading guilty, David Lufkin co-operated with SFO investigators and assisted with the investigation.

Petrofac Limited's conviction and sentencing brings to a conclusion the investigation into suspected bribery and corruption as far as the corporate entity (and its subsidiaries) is concerned. The investigation into the conduct of individual suspects continues.

8.2 Enron

8.2.1 Text from Wikipedia[4] (August 11, 2022)

The **Enron scandal** was an accounting scandal involving Enron Corporation, an American energy company based in Houston, Texas. Upon being publicized in October 2001, the company declared bankruptcy and its accounting firm, Arthur Andersen—then one of the five largest audit and accountancy partnerships in the world—was effectively dissolved. In addition to being the largest bankruptcy reorganization in U.S. history at that time, Enron was cited as the biggest audit failure [1]:61.

Enron was formed in 1985 by Kenneth Lay after merging Houston Natural Gas and InterNorth. Several years later, when Jeffrey Skilling was hired, Lay developed a staff of executives that—by the use of accounting loopholes, special purpose entities, and poor financial reporting—were able to hide billions of dollars in debt from failed deals and projects. Chief Financial Officer Andrew Fastow and

---

[4] https://en.wikipedia.org/wiki/Enron_scandal.

other executives misled Enron's board of directors and audit committee on high-risk accounting practices and pressured Arthur Andersen to ignore the issues.

Enron shareholders filed a $40 billion lawsuit after the company's stock price, which achieved a high of US$90.75 per share in mid-2000, plummeted to less than $1 by the end of November 2001 [2]. The U.S. Securities and Exchange Commission (SEC) began an investigation, and rival Houston competitor Dynegy offered to purchase the company at a very low price. The deal failed, and on December 2, 2001, Enron filed for bankruptcy under Chap. 11 of the United States Bankruptcy Code. Enron's $63.4 billion in assets made it the largest corporate bankruptcy in U.S. history until the WorldCom scandal the following year [3].

Many executives at Enron were indicted for a variety of charges and some were later sentenced to prison, including Lay and Skilling. Arthur Andersen was found guilty of illegally destroying documents relevant to the SEC investigation, which voided its license to audit public companies and effectively closed the firm. By the time the ruling was overturned at the U.S. Supreme Court, Arthur Andersen had lost the majority of its customers and had ceased operating. Enron employees and shareholders received limited returns in lawsuits, despite losing billions in pensions and stock prices.

As a consequence of the scandal, new regulations and legislation were enacted to expand the accuracy of financial reporting for public companies [4]. One piece of legislation, the Sarbanes–Oxley Act, increased penalties for destroying, altering, or fabricating records in federal investigations or for attempting to defraud shareholders [5]. The act also increased the accountability of auditing firms to remain unbiased and independent of their clients [4].

Contents
1. Rise of Enron
   2. Causes of Downfall
      2.1. Revenue Recognition
      2.2. Mark-to-Market Accounting
      2.3. Special Purpose Entities
         2.3.1. JEDI and Chewco
         2.3.2. Whitewing
         2.3.3. LJM and Raptors
      2.4. Corporate Governance
         2.4.1. Executive Compensation
         2.4.2. Risk Management
         2.4.3. Financial Audit
         2.4.4. Audit Committee
         2.4.5. Ethical and Political Analyses
      2.5. Other Accounting Issues
      2.6. Speculative Business Ventures
   3. Timeline of Downfall
      3.1. Investors' Confidence Declines
      3.2. Restructuring Losses and SEC Investigation

      3.3. Credit Rating Downgrade
      3.4. Proposed Buyout by Dynegy
      3.5. Bankruptcy
   4. Trials
      4.1. Enron
      4.2. Arthur Andersen
      4.3. NatWest Three
   5. Aftermath
      5.1. Employees and Shareholders
      5.2. Sarbanes-Oxley Act
      5.3. Criticism of the Bush Administration
   6. See Also
   7. References
      7.1. Bibliography
   8. Further Reading
   9. External links

Rise of Enron Kenneth Lay in a July 2004 mugshot

In 1985, Kenneth Lay merged the natural gas pipeline companies of Houston Natural Gas and InterNorth to form Enron [6]:3. In the early 1990s, he helped to initiate the selling of electricity at market prices and, soon after, Congress approved legislation deregulating the sale of natural gas. The resulting markets made it possible for traders such as Enron to sell energy at higher prices, thereby significantly increasing its revenue [7]. After producers and local governments decried the resultant price volatility and asked for increased regulation, strong lobbying on the part of Enron and others prevented such regulation [7, 8].

As Enron became the largest seller of natural gas in North America by 1992, its trading of gas contracts earned $122 million (before interest and taxes), the second largest contributor to the company's net income. The November 1999 creation of the EnronOnline trading website allowed the company to better manage its contracts trading business [6]:7.

In an attempt to achieve further growth, Enron pursued a diversification strategy. The company owned and operated a variety of assets including gas pipelines, electricity plants, paper plants, water plants, and broadband services across the globe. Enron also gained additional revenue by trading contracts for the same array of products and services with which it was involved [6]:5. This included setting up power generation plants in developing countries and emerging markets including the Philippines (Subic Bay), Indonesia and India (Dabhol) [9].

Enron's stock increased from the start of the 1990s until year-end 1998 by 311%, only modestly higher than the average rate of growth in the Standard & Poor 500 index [6]:1. However, the stock increased by 56% in 1999 and a further 87% in 2000, compared to a 20% increase and a 10% decrease for the index during the same years. By December 31, 2000, Enron's stock was priced at $83.13 and its market capitalization exceeded $60 billion, 70 times earnings and six times book value, an indication of the stock market's high expectations about its future prospects. In addition, Enron was rated the most innovative large company in America in *Fortune*'s Most Admired Companies survey [6]:1.

Causes of Downfall The subject of this accounting scandal had published a manual of ethics earlier.

Enron's complex financial statements were confusing to shareholders and analysts [1]:6 [10]. In addition, its complex business model and unethical practices required that the company use accounting limitations to misrepresent earnings and modify the balance sheet to indicate favorable performance [6]:9. Further, some speculative business ventures proved disastrous.

The combination of these issues later resulted in the bankruptcy of Enron, and the majority of them were perpetuated by the indirect knowledge or direct actions of Lay, Skilling, Andrew Fastow, and other executives such as Rebecca Mark. Lay served as the chairman of Enron in its last few years, and approved of the actions of Skilling and Fastow, although he did not always inquire about the details. Skilling constantly focused on meeting Wall Street expectations, advocated the use of mark-to-market accounting (accounting based on market value, which was then inflated) and pressured Enron executives to find new ways to hide its debt. Fastow and other executives "created off-balance-sheet vehicles, complex financing structures, and deals so bewildering that few people could understand them" [11]:132–133.

Revenue Recognition *Further information: Revenue recognition*

Enron and other energy suppliers earned profits by providing services such as wholesale trading and risk management in addition to building and maintaining electric power plants, natural gas pipelines, storage, and processing facilities [12]. When accepting the risk of buying and selling products, merchants are allowed to report the selling price as revenues and the products' costs as cost of goods sold. In contrast, an "agent" provides a service to the customer, but does not take the same risks as merchants for buying and selling. Service providers, when classified as agents, may report trading and brokerage fees as revenue, although not for the full value of the transaction [13]:101–103.

Although trading companies such as Goldman Sachs and Merrill Lynch used the conventional "agent model" for reporting revenue (where only the trading or brokerage fee would be reported as revenue), Enron instead elected to report the entire value of each of its trades as revenue. This "merchant model" was considered much more aggressive in the accounting interpretation than the agent model [13]:102. Enron's method of reporting inflated trading revenue was later adopted by other companies in the energy trading industry in an attempt to stay competitive with the company's large increase in revenue. Other energy companies such as Duke Energy, Reliant Energy, and Dynegy joined Enron in the largest 50 of the revenue-based *Fortune* 500 owing mainly to their adoption of the same trading revenue accounting as Enron [13]:105.

Between 1996 and 2000, Enron's revenues increased by more than 750%, rising from $13.3 billion in 1996 to $100.7 billion in 2000. This expansion of 65% per year was extraordinary in any industry, including the energy industry, which typically considered growth of 2–3% per year to be respectable. For just the first nine months of 2001, Enron reported $138.7 billion in revenues, placing the company at the sixth position on the *Fortune* Global 500 [13]:97–100.

Enron also used creative accounting tricks and purposefully misclassified loan transactions as sales close to quarterly reporting deadlines, similar to the Lehman Brothers Repo 105 scheme in the 2008 financial crisis, or the currency swap concealment of Greek debt by Goldman Sachs. In Enron's case, Merrill Lynch bought Nigerian barges with an alleged buyback guarantee by Enron shortly before the earnings deadline. According to the government, Enron misreported a bridge loan as a true sale, then bought back the barges a few months later. Merrill Lynch executives were tried and in November 2004 convicted for aiding Enron in fraudulent accounting activities [14]. These charges were thrown out on appeal in 2006, after the Merrill Lynch executives had spent nearly a year in prison, with the 5th U.S. Circuit Court of Appeals in New Orleans calling the conspiracy and wire fraud charges "flawed". Expert observers said that the reversal was highly unusual for the 5th Circuit, commenting that the conviction must have had serious issues in order to be overturned [15]. The Justice Department decided not to retry the case after the reversal of the verdict [16, 17].

Mark-to-Market Accounting *Further information: Mark-to-market accounting*

In Enron's natural gas business, the accounting had been fairly straightforward: in each time period, the company listed actual costs of supplying the gas and actual revenues received from selling it. However, when Skilling joined Enron, he demanded that the trading business adopt mark-to-market accounting, claiming that it would represent "true economic value" [11]:39–42. Enron became the first nonfinancial company to use the method to account for its complex long-term contracts [18]. Mark-to-market accounting requires that once a long-term contract has been signed, income is estimated as the present value of net future cash flow. Often, the viability of these contracts and their related costs were difficult to estimate [6]:10. Owing to the large discrepancies between reported profits and cash, investors were typically given false or misleading reports. Under this method, income from projects could be recorded, although the firm might never have received the money, with this income increasing financial earnings on the books. However, because in future years the profits could not be included, new and additional income had to be included from more projects to develop additional growth to appease investors [11]: 39–42. As one Enron competitor stated, "If you accelerate your income, then you have to keep doing more and more deals to show the same or rising income" [18]. Despite potential pitfalls, the U.S. Securities and Exchange Commission (SEC) approved the accounting method for Enron in its trading of natural gas futures contracts on January 30, 1992 [11]:39–42. However, Enron later expanded its use to other areas in the company to help it meet Wall Street projections [11]:127.

For one contract, in July 2000, Enron and Blockbuster Video signed a 20-year agreement to introduce on-demand entertainment to various U.S. cities by year's end. After several pilot projects, Enron claimed estimated profits of more than $110 million from the deal, even though analysts questioned the technical viability and market demand of the service [6]:10. When the network failed to work, Blockbuster withdrew from the contract. Enron continued to claim future profits, even though the deal resulted in a loss [19].

Special Purpose Entities *Further information: Special purpose entity*

Enron used special purpose entities—limited partnerships or companies created to fulfill a temporary or specific purpose to fund or manage risks associated with specific assets. The company elected to disclose minimal details on its use of "special purpose entities" [6]:11. These shell companies were created by a sponsor, but funded by independent equity investors and debt financing. For financial reporting purposes, a series of rules dictate whether a special purpose entity is a separate entity from the sponsor. In total, by 2001, Enron had used hundreds of special purpose entities to hide its debt [6]:10. The company used a number of special purpose entities, such as partnerships in its Thomas and Condor tax shelters, financial asset securitization investment trusts (FASITs) in the Apache deal, real estate mortgage investment conduits (REMICs) in the Steele deal, and REMICs and real estate investment trusts (REITs) in the Cochise deal [20].

The special purpose entities were Tobashi schemes used for more than just circumventing accounting conventions. As a result of one violation, Enron's balance sheet understated its liabilities and overstated its equity, and its earnings were overstated [6]:11. Enron disclosed to its shareholders that it had hedged downside risk in its own illiquid investments using special purpose entities. However, investors were oblivious to the fact that the special purpose entities were actually using the company's own stock and financial guarantees to finance these hedges. This prevented Enron from being protected from the downside risk [6]:11.

JEDI and Chewco *Main article: Chewco*

In 1993, Enron established a joint venture in energy investments with CalPERS, the California state pension fund, called the Joint Energy Development Investments (JEDI) [11]:67. In 1997, Skilling, serving as Enron's chief operating officer (COO), asked CalPERS to join Enron in a separate investment. CalPERS was interested in the idea, but only if it could be terminated as a partner in JEDI [1]:30. However, Enron did not want to show any debt from assuming CalPERS' stake in JEDI on its balance sheet. Chief Financial Officer (CFO) Fastow developed the special purpose entity Chewco Investments, a limited partnership (L.P.) which raised debt guaranteed by Enron and was used to acquire CalPERS's joint venture stake for $383 million [6]:11. Because of Fastow's organization of Chewco, JEDI's losses were kept off of Enron's balance sheet.

In autumn 2001, CalPERS and Enron's arrangement was discovered, which required the discontinuation of Enron's prior accounting method for Chewco and JEDI. This disqualification revealed that Enron's reported earnings from 1997 to mid-2001 would need to be reduced by $405 million and that the company's indebtedness would increase by $628 million [1]:31.

Whitewing Whitewing was the name of a special purpose entity used as a financing method by Enron [21]. In December 1997, with funding of $579 million provided by Enron and $500 million by an outside investor, Whitewing Associates L.P. was formed. Two years later, the entity's arrangement was changed so that it would no longer be consolidated with Enron and be counted on the company's balance sheet. Whitewing was used to purchase Enron assets, including stakes in power plants, pipelines, stocks, and other investments [22]. Between 1999 and 2001, Whitewing bought assets from Enron worth $2 billion, using Enron stock as collateral. Although the transactions were approved by the Enron board, the asset transfers were not true sales and should have been treated instead as loans [23].

LJM and Raptors *Main article: LJM (Lea Jeffrey Matthew)*

In 1999, Fastow formulated two limited partnerships: LJM Cayman. L.P. (LJM1) and LJM2 Co-Investment L.P. (LJM2), for the purpose of buying Enron's poorly performing stocks and stakes to improve its financial statements. LJM 1 and 2 were created solely to serve as the outside equity investor needed for the special purpose entities that were being used by Enron [1]:31. Fastow had to go before the board of directors to receive an exemption from Enron's code of ethics (as he had the title of CFO) in order to manage the companies [11]:193,197. The two partnerships were funded with around $390 million provided by Wachovia, J.P. Morgan Chase, Credit Suisse First Boston, Citigroup, and other investors. Merrill Lynch, which marketed the equity, also contributed $22 million to fund the entities [1]:31.

Enron transferred to "Raptor I-IV", four LJM-related special purpose entities named after the velociraptors in *Jurassic Park*, more than "$1.2 billion in assets, including millions of shares of Enron common stock and long term rights to purchase millions more shares, plus $150 million of Enron notes payable" as disclosed in the company's financial statement footnotes [1, 24]:33 [25]. The special purpose entities had been used to pay for all of this using the entities' debt instruments. The footnotes also declared that the instruments' face amount totaled $1.5 billion, and the entities notional amount of $2.1 billion had been used to enter into derivative contracts with Enron [1]:33.

Enron capitalized the Raptors, and, in a manner similar to the accounting employed when a company issues stock at a public offering, then booked the notes payable issued as assets on its balance sheet while increasing the shareholders' equity for the same amount [1]:38. This treatment later became an issue for Enron and its auditor Arthur Andersen, as removing it from the balance sheet resulted in a $1.2 billion decrease in net shareholders' equity [26].

Eventually the derivative contracts worth $2.1 billion lost significant value. Swaps were established at the time the stock price achieved its maximum. During the ensuing year, the value of the portfolio under the swaps fell by $1.1 billion as the stock prices decreased (the loss of value meant that the special purpose entities technically now owed Enron $1.1 billion by the contracts). Enron, using its mark-to-market accounting method, claimed a $500 million gain on the swap contracts in its 2000 annual report. The gain was responsible for offsetting its stock portfolio losses and was attributed to nearly a third of Enron's earnings for 2000 (before it was properly restated in 2001) [1]:39.

Corporate Governance *Further information: Corporate governance*
On paper, Enron had a model board of directors comprising predominantly outsiders with significant ownership stakes and a talented audit committee. In its 2000 review of best corporate boards, *Chief Executive* included Enron among its five best boards [27]:21. Even with its complex corporate governance and network of intermediaries, Enron was still able to "attract large sums of capital to fund a questionable business model, conceal its true performance through a series of accounting and financing maneuvers, and hype its stock to unsustainable levels" [6]:4.

Executive Compensation Although Enron's compensation and performance management system was designed to retain and reward its most valuable employees, the system contributed to a dysfunctional corporate culture that became obsessed with short-term earnings to maximize bonuses. Employees constantly tried to start deals, often disregarding the quality of cash flow or profits, in order to get a better rating for their performance review. Additionally, accounting results were recorded as soon as possible to keep up with the company's stock price. This practice helped ensure dealmakers and executives received large cash bonuses and stock options [13]:112.

Enron was constantly emphasizing its stock price. Management was compensated extensively using stock options, similar to other U.S. companies. This policy of stock option awards caused management to create expectations of rapid growth in efforts to give the appearance of reported earnings to meet Wall Street's expectations [28]. Stock tickers were installed in lobbies, elevators, and on company computers [11]:187. At budget meetings, Skilling would develop target earnings by asking, "What earnings do you need to keep our stock price up?" and that number would be used, even if it was not feasible [11]:127. On December 31, 2000, Enron had 96 million shares outstanding as stock option plans (approximately 13% of common shares outstanding). Enron's proxy statement stated that, within three years, these awards were expected to be exercised [6]:13. Using Enron's January 2001 stock price of $83.13 and the directors' beneficial ownership reported in the 2001 proxy, the value of director stock ownership was $659 million for Lay, and $174 million for Skilling [27]:21.

Skilling believed that if Enron employees were constantly worried about cost, it would hinder original thinking [11]:119. As a result, extravagant spending was rampant throughout the company, especially among the executives. Employees had large expense accounts and many executives were paid sometimes twice as much as competitors [11]:401. In 1998, the top 200 highest-paid employees received $193 million from salaries, bonuses, and stock. Two years later, the figure jumped to $1.4 billion [11]:241.

Risk Management *Further information: Risk management*
Before its demise, Enron was lauded for its sophisticated financial risk management tools [29]. Risk management was crucial to Enron not only because of its regulatory environment, but also because of its business plan. Enron established long-term fixed commitments which needed to be hedged to prepare for the invariable fluctuation of future energy prices [30]:1171. Enron's downfall was attributed to

its reckless use of derivatives and special purpose entities. By hedging its risks with special purpose entities which it owned, Enron retained the risks associated with the transactions. This arrangement had Enron implementing hedges with itself [27]:17.

Enron's aggressive accounting practices were not hidden from the board of directors, as later learned by a Senate subcommittee. The board was informed of the rationale for using the Whitewing, LJM, and Raptor transactions, and after approving them, received status updates on the entities' operations. Although not all of Enron's widespread improper accounting practices were revealed to the board, the practices were dependent on board decisions [30]:1170. Even though Enron extensively relied on derivatives for its business, the company's finance committee and board did not have enough experience with derivatives to understand what they were being told. The Senate subcommittee argued that had there been a detailed understanding of how the derivatives were organized, the board would have prevented their use [30]:1175.

Financial Audit *Further information: Financial audit*

Enron's accounting firm, Arthur Andersen, was accused of applying reckless standards in its audits because of a conflict of interest over the significant consulting fees generated by Enron. During 2000, Andersen earned $25 million in audit fees and $27 million in consulting fees (this amount accounted for roughly 27% of the audit fees of public clients for Andersen's Houston office). The auditor's methods were questioned as either being completed solely to receive its annual fees or for its lack of expertise in properly reviewing Enron's revenue recognition, special entities, derivatives, and other accounting practices [6]:15.

Enron hired numerous Certified Public Accountants (CPAs) as well as accountants who had worked on developing accounting rules with the Financial Accounting Standards Board (FASB). The accountants searched for new ways to save the company money, including capitalizing on loopholes found in Generally Accepted Accounting Principles (GAAP), the accounting industry's standards. One Enron accountant revealed "We tried to aggressively use the literature [GAAP] to our advantage. All the rules create all these opportunities. We got to where we did because we exploited that weakness." [11]:142

Andersen's auditors were pressured by Enron's management to defer recognizing the charges from the special purpose entities as its credit risks became known. Since the entities would never return a profit, accounting guidelines required that Enron should take a write-off, where the value of the entity was removed from the balance sheet at a loss. To pressure Andersen into meeting earnings expectations, Enron would occasionally allow accounting companies Ernst & Young or PricewaterhouseCoopers to complete accounting tasks to create the illusion of hiring a new company to replace Andersen [11]:148. Although Andersen was equipped with internal controls to protect against conflicted incentives of local partners, it failed to prevent conflict of interest. In one case, Andersen's Houston office, which performed the Enron audit, was able to overrule any critical reviews of Enron's accounting decisions by Andersen's Chicago partner. In addition, after news of SEC investigations of Enron were made public, Andersen would later shred several tons of relevant documents and delete nearly 30,000 e-mails and computer files, leading to accusations of a cover-up [6]:15[11, 31]:383.

Revelations concerning Andersen's overall performance led to the break-up of the firm, and to the following assessment by the Powers Committee (appointed by Enron's board to look into the firm's accounting in October 2001): "The evidence available to us suggests that Andersen did not fulfill its professional responsibilities in connection with its audits of Enron's financial statements, or its obligation to bring to the attention of Enron's Board (or the Audit and Compliance Committee) concerns about Enron's internal contracts over the related-party transactions" [32].

Audit Committee Corporate audit committees usually meet just a few times during the year, and their members typically have only modest experience with accounting and finance. Enron's audit committee had more expertise than many others. It included: [33]

- Robert K. Jaedicke, an accounting professor at Stanford University and former dean of Stanford Business School
- John Mendelsohn, President of the University of Texas M.D. Anderson Cancer Center
- Paulo Pereira, former president and CEO of the State Bank of Rio de Janeiro in Brazil
- John Wakeham, former United Kingdom Secretary of State for Energy and Parliamentary Secretary to the Treasury
- Ronnie Chan, Chairman of Hong Kong Hang Lung Group
- Wendy Gramm, former Chair of U.S. Commodity Futures Trading Commission

Enron's audit committee was later criticized for its brief meetings that would cover large amounts of material. In one meeting on February 12, 2001, the committee met for an hour and a half. Enron's audit committee did not have the technical knowledge to question the auditors properly on accounting issues related to the company's special purpose entities. The committee was also unable to question the company's management due to pressures on the committee [6]:14. The United States Senate Permanent Subcommittee on Investigations of the Committee on Governmental Affairs' report accused the board members of allowing conflicts of interest to impede their duties as monitoring the company's accounting practices. When Enron's scandal became public, the audit committee's conflicts of interest were regarded with suspicion [34].

Ethical and Political Analyses Commentators attributed the mismanagement behind Enron's fall to a variety of ethical and political-economic causes. Ethical explanations centered on executive greed and hubris, a lack of corporate social responsibility, situation ethics, and get-it-done business pragmatism [35–39]. Political-economic explanations cited post-1970s deregulation, and inadequate staff and funding for regulatory oversight [40, 41]. A more libertarian analysis maintained that Enron's collapse resulted from the company's reliance on political lobbying, rent-seeking, and the gaming of regulations [42].

Other Accounting Issues Enron made a habit of booking costs of cancelled projects as assets, with the rationale that no official letter had stated that the project was cancelled. This method was known as "the snowball", and although it was initially dictated that such practices be used only for projects worth less than $90 million, it was later increased to $200 million [11]:77.

In 1998, when analysts were given a tour of the Enron Energy Services office, they were impressed with how the employees were working so vigorously. In reality, Skilling had moved other employees to the office from other departments (instructing them to pretend to work hard) to create the appearance that the division was larger than it was [11]:179–180. This ruse was used several times to fool analysts about the progress of different areas of Enron to help improve the stock price.

Speculative Business Ventures Enron division Azurix, slated for an IPO, initially planned to bid between $321 million and $353 million for the rights to operate water system services for areas around Buenos Aires. This was at the high end of what Enron's Risk Assessment and Control Group advised. But as pressure to outbid all others and win the deal grew more intense with the approaching IPO, the Azurix executives decided to up their bid. They eventually bid $438.6, which turned out to be about twice as much as the next highest sealed bid. But when Enron executives arrived at the Argentine facilities, they found them in a shambles with all of the customer records destroyed [43].

Timeline of downfall

At the beginning of 2001, the Enron Corporation, the world's dominant energy trader, appeared unstoppable. The company's decade-long effort to persuade lawmakers to deregulate electricity markets had succeeded from California to New York. Its ties to the Bush administration assured that its views would be heard in Washington. Its sales, profits and stock were soaring.

—A. Berenson and R. A. Oppel, Jr. *The New York Times*, October 28, 2001 [44].

On September 20, 2000, a reporter at *The Wall Street Journal* bureau in Dallas wrote a story about how mark-to-market accounting had become prevalent in the energy industry. He noted that outsiders had no real way of knowing the assumptions on which companies that used mark-to-market based their earnings. While the story only appeared in the *Texas Journal,* the Texas regional edition of the *Journal,* short-seller Jim Chanos happened to read it and decided to check Enron's 10-K report for himself. Chanos did not think it made sense that Enron's broadband unit appeared to far outpace a then-troubled broadband industry. He also noticed that Enron was spending much of its invested capital, and was alarmed by the large amounts of stock being sold by insiders. In November 2000, he decided to short Enron's stock [11]: 334–338.

In February 2001, Chief Accounting Officer Rick Causey told budget managers: "From an accounting standpoint, this will be our easiest year ever. We've got 2001 in the bag" [11]:299. On March 5, Bethany McLean's *Fortune* article "Is Enron Overpriced?" questioned how Enron could maintain its high stock value, which was trading at 55 times its earnings, arguing that analysts and investors did not know exactly how the company made money [45]. McLean was first drawn to the company's financial situation after Chanos suggested she view the company's 10-K for herself [11]:338. In a post-mortem interview with *The Washington Post*, she recalled finding "strange transactions", "erratic cash flow", and "huge debt". The debt was the biggest red flag to McLean; she wondered how a supposedly profitable company could be "adding debt at such a rapid rate" [46]. Later, in her book, *The Smartest Guys in the Room*, McLean recalled speaking off the record with a number of people in the investment community who were growing skeptical about Enron [11]:338.

McLean telephoned Skilling to discuss her findings prior to publishing the article, but he called her "unethical" for not properly researching his company [47]. Fastow claimed that Enron could not reveal earnings details as the company had more than 1,200 trading books for assorted commodities and did "... not want anyone to know what's on those books. We don't want to tell anyone where we're making money" [45].

In a conference call on April 17, 2001, then-Chief Executive Officer (CEO) Skilling verbally attacked Wall Street analyst Richard Grubman, [48] who questioned Enron's unusual accounting practices during a recorded conference call. When Grubman complained that Enron was the only company that could not release a balance sheet along with its earnings statements, Skilling stammered, "Well uh ... Thank you very much, we appreciate it ... Asshole." [49] This became an inside joke among many Enron employees, mocking Grubman for his perceived meddling rather than Skilling's offensiveness, with slogans such as, "Ask Why, Asshole", a variation on Enron's official slogan "Ask why" [50]. However, Skilling's comment was met with dismay and astonishment by press and public, as he had previously disdained criticism of Enron coolly or humorously.

By the late 1990s Enron's stock was trading for $80–90 per share, and few seemed to concern themselves with the opacity of the company's financial disclosures. In mid-July 2001, Enron reported revenues of $50.1 billion, almost triple year-to-date, and beating analysts' estimates by 3 cents a share [51]. Despite this, Enron's profit margin had stayed at a modest average of about 2.1%, and its share price had decreased by more than 30% since the same quarter of 2000 [51].

As time passed, a number of serious concerns confronted the company. Enron had recently faced several serious operational challenges, namely logistical difficulties in operating a new broadband communications trading unit, and the losses from constructing the Dabhol Power project, a large gas powered power plant in India that had been mired in controversy since the beginning in relation to its high pricing and bribery at the highest level [9]. These were subsequently confirmed in the 2002 Senate investigation [52]. There was also increasing criticism of the company for the role that its subsidiary Enron Energy Services had in the California electricity crisis of 2000–2001.

There are no accounting issues, no trading issues, no reserve issues, no previously unknown problem issues. I think I can honestly say that the company is probably in the strongest and best shape that it has probably ever been in.

—Kenneth Lay answering an analyst's question on August 14, 2001 [11]:347.

On August 14, Skilling announced he was resigning his position as CEO after only six months citing personal reasons [53]. Observers noted that in the months before his exit, Skilling had sold at minimum 450,000 shares of Enron at a value of around $33 million (though he still owned over a million shares at the date of his departure) [53]. Nevertheless, Lay, who was serving as chairman at Enron, assured surprised market watchers that there would be "no change in the performance or outlook of the company going forward" from Skilling's departure [53]. Lay announced he himself would re-assume the position of chief executive officer.

On August 15, Sherron Watkins, vice president for corporate development, sent an anonymous letter to Lay warning him about the company's accounting practices. One statement in the letter said: "I am incredibly nervous that we will implode in a wave of accounting scandals" [54]. Watkins contacted a friend who worked for Arthur Andersen and he drafted a memorandum to give to the audit partners about the points she raised. On August 22, Watkins met individually with Lay and gave him a six-page letter further explaining Enron's accounting issues. Lay questioned her as to whether she had told anyone outside of the company and then vowed to have the company's law firm, Vinson & Elkins, review the issues, despite Watkins arguing that using the law firm would present a conflict of interest [11]:357 [55]. Lay consulted with other executives, and although they wanted to dismiss Watkins (as Texas law did not protect company whistleblowers), they decided against it to prevent a lawsuit [11]:358. On October 15, Vinson & Elkins announced that Enron had done nothing wrong in its accounting practices as Andersen had approved each issue [56].

Investors' Confidence Declines Something is rotten with the state of Enron.
—*The New York Times*, September 9, 2001 [57].

By the end of August 2001, his company's stock value still falling, Lay named Greg Whalley, president and COO of Enron Wholesale Services, to succeed Skilling as president and COO of the entire company. He also named Mark Frevert as vice chairman, and appointed Whalley and Frevert to positions in the chairman's office. Some observers suggested that Enron's investors were in significant need of reassurance, not only because the company's business was difficult to understand (even "indecipherable") [57] but also because it was difficult to properly describe the company in financial statements [58]. One analyst stated "it's really hard for analysts to determine where [Enron] are making money in a given quarter and where they are losing money" [58]. Lay accepted that Enron's business was very complex, but asserted that analysts would "never get all the information they want" to satisfy their curiosity. He also explained that the complexity of the business was due largely to tax strategies and position-hedging [58]. Lay's efforts seemed to meet with limited success; by September 9, one prominent hedge fund manager noted that " [Enron] stock is trading under a cloud" [57]. The sudden departure of Skilling combined with the opacity of Enron's accounting books made proper assessment difficult for Wall Street. In addition, the company admitted to repeatedly using "related-party transactions", which some feared could be too-easily used to transfer losses that might otherwise appear on Enron's own balance sheet. A particularly troubling aspect of this technique was that several of the "related-party" entities had been or were being controlled by CFO Fastow [57].

After the September 11 attacks media attention shifted away from the company and its troubles; a little less than a month later Enron announced its intention to begin the process of selling its lower-margin assets in favor of its core businesses of gas and electricity trading. This policy included selling Portland General Electric to another Oregon utility, Northwest Natural Gas, for about $1.9 billion in cash and stock, and possibly selling its 65% stake in the Dabhol project in India [59].

Restructuring Losses and SEC Investigation On October 16, 2001, Enron announced that restatements to its financial statements for years 1997 to 2000 were necessary to correct accounting violations. The restatements for the period reduced earnings by $613 million (or 23% of reported profits during the period), increased liabilities at the end of 2000 by $628 million (6% of reported liabilities and 5.5% of reported equity), and reduced equity at the end of 2000 by $1.2 billion (10% of reported equity) [6]:11. Additionally, in January Jeff Skilling had asserted that the broadband unit alone was worth $35 billion, a claim also mistrusted [60]. An analyst at Standard & Poor's said, "I don't think anyone knows what the broadband operation is worth" [60].

Enron's management team claimed the losses were mostly due to investment losses, along with charges such as about $180 million in money spent restructuring the company's troubled broadband trading unit. In a statement, Lay said, "After a thorough review of our businesses, we have decided to take these charges to clear away issues that have clouded the performance and earnings potential of our core energy businesses" [60]. Some analysts were unnerved. David Fleischer at Goldman Sachs, an analyst termed previously 'one of the company's strongest supporters' asserted that the Enron management "... lost credibility and have to reprove themselves. They need to convince investors these earnings are real, that the company is for real and that growth will be realized" [60, 61].

Fastow disclosed to Enron's board of directors on October 22 that he earned $30 million from compensation arrangements when managing the LJM limited partnerships. That day, the share price of Enron decreased to $20.65, down $5.40 in one day, after the announcement by the SEC that it was investigating several suspicious deals struck by Enron, characterizing them as "some of the most opaque transactions with insiders ever seen" [62]. Attempting to explain the billion-dollar charge and calm investors, Enron's disclosures spoke of "share settled costless collar arrangements", "derivative instruments which eliminated the contingent nature of existing restricted forward contracts," and strategies that served "to hedge certain merchant investments and other assets." Such puzzling phraseology left many analysts feeling ignorant about just how Enron managed its business [62]. Regarding the SEC investigation, chairman and CEO Lay said, "We will cooperate fully with the SEC and look forward to the opportunity to put any concern about these transactions to rest" [62].

Two days later, on October 25, Fastow was removed as CFO, despite Lay's assurances as early as the previous day that he and the board had confidence in him. In announcing Fastow's ouster, Lay said, "In my continued discussions with the financial community, it became clear to me that restoring investor confidence would require us to replace Andy as CFO" [63]. The move came after several banks refused to issue loans to Enron as long as Fastow remained CFO [43]. However, with Skilling and Fastow now both departed, some analysts feared that revealing the company's practices would be made all the more difficult [63]. Enron's stock was now trading at $16.41, having lost half its value in a little more than a week [63].

Jeff McMahon, head of industrial markets, succeeded Fastow as CFO. His first task was to deal with a cash crisis. A day earlier, Enron discovered that it was unable to roll its commercial paper, effectively losing access to several billion dollars in financing. The company had actually experienced difficulty selling its commercial paper for a week, but was now unable to sell even overnight paper [43]. On October 27 the company began buying back all its commercial paper, valued at around $3.3 billion, in an effort to calm investor fears about Enron's supply of cash. Enron financed the re-purchase by depleting its lines of credit at several banks. While the company's debt rating was still considered investment-grade, its bonds were trading at levels slightly less, making future sales problematic [64]. It soon emerged that Fastow had been so focused on creating off-balance sheet vehicles that he had all but ignored some of the most rudimentary aspects of corporate finance. McMahon and a "financial SWAT team" put together to find a way out of the cash crisis discovered that Fastow never developed procedures for tracking cash or debt maturities. For all intents and purposes, Enron was illiquid [43].

As the month came to a close, serious concerns were being raised by some observers regarding Enron's possible manipulation of accepted accounting rules; however, analysis was claimed to be impossible based on the incomplete information provided by Enron [65]. Industry analysts feared that Enron was the new Long-Term Capital Management, the hedge fund whose bankruptcy in 1998 threatened systemic failure of the international financial markets. Enron's tremendous presence worried some about the consequences of the company's possible bankruptcy [44]. Enron executives accepted questions in written form only [44].

Credit Rating Downgrade The main short-term danger to Enron's survival at the end of October 2001 seemed to be its credit rating. It was reported at the time that Moody's and Fitch, two of the three biggest credit-rating agencies, had slated Enron for review for possible downgrade [44]. Such a downgrade would force Enron to issue millions of shares of stock to cover loans it had guaranteed, which would decrease the value of existing stock further. Additionally, all manner of companies began reviewing their existing contracts with Enron, especially in the long term, in the event that Enron's rating were lowered below investment grade, a possible hindrance for future transactions [44].

Analysts and observers continued their complaints regarding the difficulty or impossibility of properly assessing a company whose financial statements were so cryptic. Some feared that no one at Enron apart from Skilling and Fastow could completely explain years of mysterious transactions. "You're getting way over my head", said Lay during late August 2001 in response to detailed questions about Enron's business, a reaction that worried analysts [44].

On October 29, responding to growing concerns that Enron might have insufficient cash on hand, news spread that Enron was seeking a further $1–2 billion in financing from banks [66]. The next day, as feared, Moody's lowered Enron's credit rating from Baa1 to Baa2, two levels above junk status. Standard & Poor's affirmed Enron's rating of BBB+, the equivalent of Moody's Baa1. Moody's also warned that it would downgrade Enron's commercial paper rating, the consequence of which would likely prevent the company from finding the further financing it sought to keep solvent [67].

November began with the disclosure that the SEC was now pursuing a formal investigation, prompted by questions related to Enron's dealings with "related parties". Enron's board also announced that it would commission a special committee to investigate the transactions, directed by William C. Powers, the dean of the University of Texas law school [68]. The next day, an editorial in *The New York Times* demanded an "aggressive" investigation into the matter [69]. Enron was able to secure an additional $1 billion in financing from cross-town rival Dynegy on November 2, but the news was not universally admired in that the debt was secured by assets from the company's valuable Northern Natural Gas and Transwestern Pipeline [70].

Proposed Buyout by Dynegy Sources claimed that Enron was planning to explain its business practices more fully within the coming days, as a confidence-building gesture [71]. Enron's stock was now trading at around $7, and by this time it was obvious that Enron could not stay independent. However, investors worried that the company would not be able to find a buyer.

After Enron had received a wide spectrum of rejections, Enron management apparently found a buyer when the board of Dynegy, another energy trader based in Houston, voted late at night on November 7 to acquire Enron at a very low price of about $8 billion in stock [72]. Chevron Texaco, which at the time owned about a quarter of Dynegy, agreed to provide Enron with $2.5 billion in cash, specifically $1 billion at first and the rest when the deal was completed. Dynegy would also be required to assume nearly $13 billion of debt, plus any other debt hitherto occluded by the Enron management's secretive business practices [72], possibly as much as $10 billion in "hidden" debt [73]. Dynegy and Enron confirmed their deal on November 8, 2001.

With Enron in a state of near collapse, the deal was largely on Dynegy's terms. Dynegy would be the surviving company, and Dynegy CEO Charles Watson and his management team would head the merged company. Enron shareholders would get a 40 percent stake in the enlarged Dynegy, and Enron would get three seats on the merged company's board. Lay would not have any management role, though it was presumed he would get one of Enron's seats on the board. Of Enron's senior executives, only Whalley would join the merged company's C-suite, as an executive vice president. Dynegy agreed to invest $1.5 billion into Enron to keep it alive until the deal closed [11, 43]:395.

As a measure of how dire Enron's financial picture had become, the company initially balked at paying its bills for November until the credit agencies gave the merger their blessing and allowed Enron to keep its credit at investment grade. By this time, the Dynegy deal was virtually the only thing keeping the company alive, and Enron officials wanted to keep as much cash in the company's coffers in the event of bankruptcy [43]. Had the credit agencies balked at the deal and reduced Enron to junk status, its ability to trade would be severely limited if there was a reduction or elimination of its credit lines with competitors [43, 74]. Ultimately, after Enron and Dynegy retooled the deal to make it harder for Dynegy to trigger the "material adverse change" clause and pull out, Moody's and S&P agreed to drop Enron to one notch above junk status, allowing Enron to pay its bills one day late with interest [43].

Commentators remarked on the different corporate cultures between Dynegy and Enron, and on Watson's "straight-talking" personality [8]. Some wondered if Enron's troubles had not simply been the result of innocent accounting errors [75]. By November, Enron was asserting that the billion-plus "one-time charges" disclosed in October should in reality have been $200 million, with the rest of the amount simply corrections of dormant accounting mistakes [76]. Many feared other "mistakes" and restatements might yet be revealed [74].

Another major correction of Enron's earnings was announced on November 9, with a reduction of $591 million of the stated revenue of years 1997–2000. The charges were said to come largely from two special purpose partnerships (JEDI and Chewco). The corrections resulted in the virtual elimination of profit for fiscal year 1997, with significant reductions for the other years. Despite this disclosure, Dynegy declared it still intended to purchase Enron [76]. Both companies were said to be anxious to receive an official assessment of the proposed sale from Moody's and S&P presumably to understand the effect the completion of any buyout transaction would have on Dynegy and Enron's credit rating. In addition, concerns were raised regarding antitrust regulatory restrictions resulting in possible divestiture, along with what to some observers were the radically different corporate cultures of Enron and Dynegy [73].

Both companies promoted the deal aggressively, and some observers were hopeful; Watson was praised for attempting to create the largest company on the energy market [74]. At the time, Watson said: "We feel [Enron] is a very solid company with plenty of capacity to withstand whatever happens the next few months" [74]. One analyst called the deal "a whopper ... a very good deal financially, certainly should be a good deal strategically, and provides some immediate balance-sheet backstop for Enron" [77].

Credit issues were becoming more critical, however. Around the time the buyout was made public, Moody's and S&P publicly announced that they had reduced Enron to just above junk status [74]. In a conference call, S&P affirmed that, were Enron not to be bought, S&P would reduce its rating to low BB or high B, ratings noted as being within junk status [78]. Additionally, many traders had limited their involvement with Enron, or stopped doing business altogether, fearing more bad news. Watson again attempted to re-assure, attesting at a presentation to investors that there was "nothing wrong with Enron's business" [77]. He also acknowledged that remunerative steps (in the form of more stock options) would have to be taken to redress the animosity of many Enron employees towards management after it was revealed that Lay and other officials had sold hundreds of millions of dollars' worth of stock during the months prior to the crisis [77]. The situation was not helped by the disclosure that Lay, his "reputation in tatters" [79], stood to receive a payment of $60 million as a change-of-control fee subsequent to the Dynegy acquisition, while many Enron employees had seen their retirement accounts, which were based largely on Enron stock, ravaged as the price decreased 90% in a year. An official at a company owned by Enron stated "We had some married couples who both worked who lost as much as $800,000 or $900,000. It pretty much wiped out every employee's savings plan" [80].

Watson assured investors that the true nature of Enron's business had been made apparent to him: "We have comfort there is not another shoe to drop. If there is no shoe, this is a phenomenally good transaction" [78]. Watson further asserted that Enron's energy trading part alone was worth the price Dynegy was paying for the whole company [81].

By mid-November, Enron announced it was planning to sell about $8 billion worth of underperforming assets, along with a general plan to reduce its scale for the sake of financial stability [82]. On November 19 Enron disclosed to the public further evidence of its critical state of affairs. Most pressingly that the company had debt repayment obligations in the range of $9 billion by the end of 2002. Such debts were "vastly in excess" of its available cash [83]. Also, the success of measures to preserve its solvency were not guaranteed, specifically as regarded asset sales and debt refinancing. In a statement, Enron revealed "An adverse outcome with respect to any of these matters would likely have a material adverse impact on Enron's ability to continue as a going concern" [83].

Two days later, on November 21, Wall Street expressed serious doubts that Dynegy would proceed with its deal at all, or would seek to radically renegotiate. Furthermore, Enron revealed in a 10-Q filing that almost all the money it had recently borrowed for purposes including buying its commercial paper, or about $5 billion, had been exhausted in just 50 days. Analysts were unnerved at the revelation, especially since Dynegy was reported to have also been unaware of Enron's rate of cash use [84]. In order to end the proposed buyout, Dynegy would need to legally demonstrate a "material change" in the circumstances of the transaction; as late as November 22, sources close to Dynegy were skeptical that the latest revelations constituted sufficient grounds [85]. Indeed, while Lay assumed that one of his underlings had shared the 10-Q with Dynegy officials, no one at Dynegy saw it until it was released to the public. It subsequently emerged that Enron's traders had grabbed much of the money from Dynegy's cash infusion and used it to guarantee payment to their trading partners when it came time to settle up [43].

The SEC announced it had filed civil fraud complaints against Andersen [86]. A few days later, sources claimed Enron and Dynegy were renegotiating the terms of their arrangement [87]. Dynegy now demanded Enron agree to be bought for $4 billion rather than the previous $8 billion. Observers were reporting difficulties in ascertaining which of Enron's operations, if any, were profitable. Reports described an en masse shift of business to Enron's competitors for the sake of risk exposure reduction [87].

Bankruptcy Enron's stock price (former NYSE ticker symbol: ENE) from August 23, 2000 ($90) to January 11, 2002 ($0.12). As a result of the decrease of the stock price, shareholders incurred paper losses of nearly $11 billion [3].

On November 28, 2001, Enron's two worst possible outcomes came true. Credit rating agencies all reduced Enron's credit rating to junk status, and Dynegy's board tore up the merger agreement on Watson's advice. Watson later said, "At the end, you couldn't give it [Enron] to me" [11]:403. Although they had seemingly ironed out a number of outstanding issues at a meeting in New York over the previous weekend, ultimately Dynegy's concerns about Enron's liquidity and dwindling business proved insurmountable [43]. The company had very little cash with which to operate, let alone satisfy enormous debts. Its stock price fell to $0.61 at the end of the day's trading. One editorial observer wrote that "Enron is now shorthand for the perfect financial storm" [88].

Systemic consequences were felt, as Enron's creditors and other energy trading companies suffered the loss of several percentage points. Some analysts felt Enron's failure indicated the risks of the post-September 11 economy, and encouraged traders to lock in profits where they could [89]. The question now became how to determine the total exposure of the markets and other traders to Enron's failure. Early calculations estimated $18.7 billion. One adviser stated, "We don't really know who is out there exposed to Enron's credit. I'm telling my clients to prepare for the worst" [90].

Within 24 h, speculation abounded that Enron would have no choice but to file for bankruptcy. Enron was estimated to have about $23 billion in liabilities from both debt outstanding and guaranteed loans. Citigroup and JP Morgan Chase in particular appeared to have significant amounts to lose with Enron's bankruptcy. Additionally, many of Enron's major assets were pledged to lenders in order to secure loans, causing doubt about what, if anything, unsecured creditors and eventually stockholders might receive in bankruptcy proceedings [91]. As it turned out, new corporate treasurer Ray Bowen had known as early as the day Dynegy pulled out of the deal that Enron was headed for bankruptcy. He spent most of the next two days scrambling to find a bank who would take Enron's remaining cash after pulling all of its money out of Citibank. He was ultimately forced to make do with a small Houston bank [43].

By the close of business on November 30, 2001, it was obvious Enron was at the end of its tether. That day, Enron Europe, the holding company for Enron's operations in continental Europe, filed for bankruptcy [92]. The rest of Enron followed suit the following night, December 1, when the board voted unanimously to file for Chap. 11 protection [43]. It became the largest bankruptcy in U.S. history, surpassing the 1970 bankruptcy of the Penn Central (WorldCom's bankruptcy the next year surpassed Enron's bankruptcy so the title was short held), and resulted in 4,000 lost jobs [3, 93]. The day that Enron filed for bankruptcy, thousands of employees were told to pack their belongings and given 30 min to vacate the building [94]. Nearly 62% of 15,000 employees' savings plans relied on Enron stock that was purchased at $83 in early 2001 and was now practically worthless [95].

In its accounting work for Enron, Andersen had been sloppy and weak. But that's how Enron had always wanted it. In truth, even as they angrily pointed fingers, the two deserved each other.

—Bethany McLean and Peter Elkind in *The Smartest Guys in the Room* [11]:393.

On January 17, 2002, Enron dismissed Arthur Andersen as its auditor, citing its accounting advice and the destruction of documents. Andersen countered that it had already ended its relationship with the company when Enron became bankrupt [96].

Trials

Enron *Main article: Trial of Kenneth Lay and Jeffrey Skilling*

Fastow and his wife, Lea, both pleaded guilty to charges against them. Fastow was initially charged with 98 counts of fraud, money laundering, insider trading, and conspiracy, among other crimes [97]. Fastow pleaded guilty to two charges of conspiracy and was sentenced to ten years with no parole in a plea bargain to testify against Lay, Skilling, and Causey [98]. Lea was indicted on six felony counts, but prosecutors later dismissed them in favor of a single misdemeanor tax charge. Lea was sentenced to one year for helping her husband hide income from the government [99].

Lay and Skilling went on trial for their part in the Enron scandal in January 2006. The 53-count, 65-page indictment covers a broad range of financial crimes, including bank fraud, making false statements to banks and auditors, securities fraud, wire fraud, money laundering, conspiracy, and insider trading. United States District Judge Sim Lake had previously denied motions by the defendants to have separate trials and to relocate the case out of Houston, where the defendants argued the negative publicity concerning Enron's demise would make it impossible to get a fair trial. On May 25, 2006, the jury in the Lay and Skilling trial returned its verdicts. Skilling was convicted of 19 of 28 counts of securities fraud and wire fraud and acquitted on the remaining nine, including charges of insider trading. He was sentenced to 24 years and 4 months in prison [100]. In 2013 the United States Department of Justice reached a deal with Skilling, which resulted in ten years being cut from his sentence [101].

Lay pleaded not guilty to the eleven criminal charges, and claimed that he was misled by those around him. He attributed the main cause for the company's demise to Fastow [102]. Lay was convicted of all six counts of securities and wire fraud for which he had been tried, and he was subject to a maximum total sentence of 45 years in prison [103]. However, before sentencing was scheduled, Lay died on July 5, 2006. At the time of his death, the SEC had been seeking more than $90 million from Lay in addition to civil fines. The case of Lay's wife, Linda, is a difficult one. She sold roughly 500,000 shares of Enron 10–30 min before the information that Enron was collapsing went public on November 28, 2001 [104]. Linda was never charged with any of the events related to Enron [105].

Although Michael Kopper worked at Enron for more than seven years, Lay did not know of Kopper even after the company's bankruptcy. Kopper was able to keep his name anonymous in the entire affair [11]:153. Kopper was the first Enron executive to plead guilty [106]. Chief Accounting Officer Rick Causey was indicted with six felony charges for disguising Enron's financial condition during his tenure [107]. After pleading not guilty, he later switched to guilty and was sentenced to seven years in prison [108].

All told, sixteen people pleaded guilty for crimes committed at the company, and five others, including four former Merrill Lynch employees (three of whose convictions were subsequently overturned on appeal) [109–111], were found guilty. Eight former Enron executives testified—the main witness being Fastow—against Lay and Skilling, his former bosses [93]. Another was Kenneth Rice, the former chief of Enron Corp.'s high-speed Internet unit, who cooperated and whose testimony helped convict Skilling and Lay. In June 2007, he received a 27-month sentence [112].

Michael W. Krautz, a former Enron accountant, was among the accused who was acquitted [113] of charges related to the scandal. Represented by Barry Pollack [114], Krautz was acquitted of federal criminal fraud charges after a month-long jury trial.

Arthur Andersen *Main article: Arthur Andersen LLP v. United States*

Arthur Andersen was charged with and found guilty of obstruction of justice for shredding the thousands of documents and deleting e-mails and company files that tied the firm to its audit of Enron [115]. Although only a small number of Arthur Andersen's employees were involved with the scandal, the firm was effectively put out of business; the SEC is not allowed to accept audits from convicted felons. The company surrendered its CPA license on August 31, 2002, and 85,000 employees lost their jobs [116, 117]. The conviction was later overturned by the U.S. Supreme Court due to the jury not being properly instructed on the charge against Andersen [118]. The Supreme Court ruling theoretically left Andersen free to resume operations. However, the damage to the Andersen name has been so great that it has not returned as a viable business even on a limited scale.

NatWest Three *Main article: NatWest Three*

Giles Darby, David Bermingham, and Gary Mulgrew worked for Greenwich NatWest. The three British men had worked with Fastow on a special purpose entity he had started called Swap Sub. When Fastow was being investigated by the SEC, the three men met with the British Financial Services Authority (FSA) in November 2001 to discuss their interactions with Fastow [119]. In June 2002, the U.S. issued warrants for their arrest on seven counts of wire fraud, and they were then extradited. On July 12, a potential Enron witness scheduled to be extradited to the U.S., Neil Coulbeck, was found dead in a park in north-east London [120]. Coulbeck's death was eventually ruled to have been a suicide. The U.S. case alleged that Coulbeck and others conspired with Fastow [121]. In a plea bargain in November 2007, the trio plead guilty to one count of wire fraud while the other six counts were dismissed [122]. Darby, Bermingham, and Mulgrew were each sentenced to 37 months in prison [123]. In August 2010, Bermingham and Mulgrew retracted their confessions [124].

Aftermath

Employees and Shareholders Enron's headquarters in Downtown Houston was leased from a consortium of banks who had bought the property for $285 million in the 1990s. It was sold for $55.5 million, just before Enron moved out in 2004 [125].

While some employees, like John D. Arnold, received large bonuses in the final days of the company [126], Enron's shareholders lost $74 billion in the four years before the company's bankruptcy ($40 to $45 billion was attributed to fraud) [127]. As Enron had nearly $67 billion that it owed creditors, employees and shareholders received limited, if any, assistance aside from severance from Enron [128]. To pay its creditors, Enron held auctions to sell assets including art, photographs, logo signs, and its pipelines [129–131].

A class action lawsuit on behalf of about 20,000 Enron employees who alleged mismanagement of their 401(k) plans resulted in a July 2005 settlement of $356 million against Enron and 401(k) manager Northern Trust [132]. A year later the settlement was reduced to $37.5 million in an agreement by Federal judge Melinda Harmon, with Northern Trust neither admitting or denying wrongdoing [133].

In May 2004, more than 20,000 of Enron's former employees won a suit of $85 million for compensation of $2 billion that was lost from their pensions. From the settlement, the employees each received about $3,100 [134]. The next year, investors received another settlement from several banks of $4.2 billion [127]. In September 2008, a $7.2-billion settlement from a $40-billion lawsuit, was reached on behalf of the shareholders. The settlement was distributed among the main plaintiff, University of California (UC), and 1.5 million individuals and groups. UC's law firm Coughlin Stoia Geller Rudman and Robbins, received $688 million in fees, the highest in a U.S. securities fraud case [135]. At the distribution, UC announced in a press release "We are extremely pleased to be returning these funds to the members of the class. Getting here has required a long, challenging effort, but the results for Enron investors are unprecedented" [136].

Sarbanes-Oxley Act In the Titanic, the captain went down with the ship. And Enron looks to me like the captain first gave himself and his friends a bonus, then lowered himself and the top folks down the lifeboat and then hollered up and said, 'By the way, everything is going to be just fine.'
—U.S. Senator Byron Dorgan [137].
Main article: Sarbanes-Oxley Act

Between December 2001 and April 2002, the Senate Committee on Banking, Housing, and Urban Affairs and the House Committee on Financial Services held multiple hearings about the Enron scandal and related accounting and investor protection issues. These hearings and the corporate scandals that followed Enron led to the passage of the Sarbanes-Oxley Act on July 30, 2002 [138]. The Act is nearly "a mirror image of Enron: the company's perceived corporate governance failings are matched virtually point for point in the principal provisions of the Act" [139].

The main provisions of the Sarbanes-Oxley Act included the establishment of the Public Company Accounting Oversight Board to develop standards for the preparation of audit reports; the restriction of public accounting companies from providing any non-auditing services when auditing; provisions for the independence of audit committee members, executives being required to sign off on financial reports, and relinquishment of certain executives' bonuses in case of financial restatements; and expanded financial disclosure of companies' relationships with unconsolidated entities [138].

On February 13, 2002, due to the instances of corporate malfeasances and accounting violations, the SEC recommended changes of the stock exchanges' regulations. In June 2002, the New York Stock Exchange announced a new governance proposal, which was approved by the SEC in November 2003. The main provisions of the final NYSE proposal include [138]:

- All companies must have a majority of independent directors.
- Independent directors must comply with an elaborate definition of independent directors.
- The compensation committee, nominating committee, and audit committee shall consist of independent directors.
- All audit committee members should be financially literate. In addition, at least one member of the audit committee is required to have accounting or related financial management expertise.
- In addition to its regular sessions, the board should hold additional sessions without management.

Criticism of the Bush Administration Kenneth Lay was a longtime supporter of U.S. president George W. Bush and a donor to his various political campaigns, including his successful bid for the presidency in 2000. As such, critics of Bush and his administration attempted to link them to the scandal. A January 2002 article in *The Economist* claimed that Lay had been a close personal friend of Bush's family and had backed him financially since his unsuccessful campaign for Congress in 1978. Allegedly, Lay was even rumored at one point to be in the running to serve as Secretary of Energy for Bush [140].

In an article that same month, *Time* magazine accused the Bush administration of making desperate attempts to distance themselves from the scandal. According to author Frank Pellegrini, various Bush appointments held connections to Enron, including deputy White House Chief of Staff Karl Rove as a stockholder, Secretary of the Army Thomas E. White Jr. as a former executive, and SEC chairman Harvey Pitt, a former employee of Arthur Andersen. Former Montana governor Marc Racicot, whom Bush considered for appointment for Secretary of the Interior, briefly served as a lobbyist for the company after leaving office. After opening a criminal investigation into the scandal, Attorney General John Ashcroft recused himself and his chief of staff from the case when Democratic Congressman Henry Waxman accused Ashcroft of receiving $25,000 from Enron for his failed reelection campaign to the Senate in 2000. As Pellegrini wrote, "The Democrats will have the company-he-keeps, guilt-by-association thing on their side, and with all the ... general whiff of rich man's cover-up about the whole affair, they'll have a class warfare card to play this spring" [141].

See also

- *Texas portal*
- *The Crooked E: The Unshredded Truth About Enron*—television film about the rise and fall of Enron, based on *Anatomy of Greed*, a 2002 book by an ex-employee
- *Enron: The Smartest Guys in the Room*—2005 documentary based on the eponymous 2003 book about the scandal
- *Law & Order: Criminal Intent* episode "Tuxedo Hill"—2002 television episode inspired by the Enron Scandal
- *ENRON*—2009 play by British playwright Lucy Prebble about the scandal
- *Arthur Andersen LLP v. United States*—conviction in United States District Court subsequently overturned by United States Supreme Court

The Enron Corpus—a database of more than 600,000 emails between Enron executives, made public and used extensively in social networking research

References

1. Bratton, William W. (May 2002). "Does Corporate Law Protect the Interests of Shareholders and Other Stakeholders?: Enron and the Dark Side of Shareholder Value". Tulane Law Review. New Orleans: Tulane University Law School (1275). SSRN 301475.
2. "Enron shareholders look to SEC for support in court" (WEB). The New York Times. May 2007. Retrieved October 8, 2020.
3. Benston, George J. (November 6, 2003). "The Quality of Corporate Financial Statements and Their Auditors Before and After Enron" (PDF). Policy Analysis. Washington D.C.: Cato Institute (497): 12. Archived from the original (PDF) on June 15, 2010. Retrieved October 17, 2010.
4. Ayala, Astrid; Giancarlo Ibárgüen, Snr (March 2006). "A Market Proposal for Auditing the Financial Statements of Public Companies" (PDF). Journal of Management of Value. Universidad Francisco Marroquín: 1. Archived from the original (PDF) on July 21, 2011. Retrieved October 17, 2010.
5. Cohen, Daniel A.; Dey Aiyesha; Thomas Z. Lys (February 2005). "Trends in Earnings Management and Informativeness of Earnings Announcements in the Pre- and Post-Sarbanes Oxley Periods". Evanston, Illinois: Kellogg School of Management: 5. SSRN 658782.
6. Healy, Paul M.; Palepu, Krishna G. (Spring 2003). "The Fall of Enron". Journal of Economic Perspectives. 17 (2): 3–26. doi:https://doi.org/10.1257/089533003765888403.
7. Gerth, Jeff; Richard A. Oppel, Jr. (November 10, 2001). "Regulators struggle with a marketplace created by Enron". The New York Times. Archived from the original on March 22, 2012. Retrieved October 17, 2010.
8. Banerjee, Neela (November 9, 2001). "Surest steps, not the swiftest, are propelling Dynegy past Enron". The New York Times. Archived from the original on March 22, 2012. Retrieved October 17, 2010.
9. Bhushan, Ranjit (April 30, 2001). "The real story of Dabhol". Outlook India. Retrieved November 26, 2018.

10. Mack, Toni (October 14, 2002). "The Other Enron Story". Forbes. Archived from the original on January 18, 2012. Retrieved October 17, 2010.
11. McLean, Bethany; Elkind, Peter (2003). Enron: The Smartest Guys in the Room. ISBN 978-1-59184-008-4.
12. Foss, Michelle Michot (September 2003). "Enron and the Energy Market Revolution" (PDF). University of Houston Law Center: 1. Archived from the original (PDF) on July 19, 2011. Retrieved October 17, 2010.
13. Dharan, Bala G.; Bufkins, William R. (July 2008). "Red Flags in Enron's Reporting of Revenues and Key Financial Measures" (PDF). SSRN Electronic Journal. Social Science Research Network. doi:10.2139/ssrn.1172222. S2CID 166473994. Archived from the original (PDF) on June 4, 2011. Retrieved October 17, 2010.
14. "SEC Charges Merrill Lynch, Four Merrill Lynch Executives with Aiding and Abetting Enron Accounting Fraud". www.sec.gov. Retrieved September 28, 2019.
15. Roper, John C. (August 2, 2006). "4 ex-Merrill Lynch execs' convictions overturned". www.chron.com. Retrieved January 31, 2021.
16. CNN Money (February 16, 2007). "Feds won't fight overturned convictions". CNN. Retrieved January 31, 2021.
17. "Judge dismisses charges against ex-Merrill exec in Enron case at prosecutors' request". www.foxnews.com. March 27, 2015. Retrieved January 31, 2021.
18. Mack, Toni (May 24, 1993). "Hidden Risks". Forbes. ProQuest 194962870.
19. Hays, Kristen (April 17, 2005). "Next Enron trial focuses on broadband unit". USA Today. Archived from the original on August 26, 2009. Retrieved October 17, 2010.
20. Niskanen, William A. (2007). After Enron: Lessons for Public Policy. Rowman & Littlefield. pp. 306–307. ISBN 978-0-7425-4434-5.
21. McCullough, Robert (January 2002). "Understanding Whitewing" (PDF). Portland, Oregon: McCullough Research: 1. Archived from the original (PDF) on June 11, 2011. Retrieved October 17, 2010.
22. Cornford, Andrew (June 2004). "Internationally Agreed Principles For Corporate Governance And The Enron Case" (PDF). G-24 Discussion Paper Series No. 30. New York: United Nations Conference on Trade and Development: 18. Archived from the original (PDF) on March 4, 2011. Retrieved October 17, 2010.
23. Lambert, Jeremiah D. (September 2006). Energy Companies and Market Reform: How Deregulation Went Wrong. Tulsa: PennWell Corporation. p. 35. ISBN 978-1-59370-060-7.
24. Levine, Greg (March 7, 2006). "Fastow Tells Of Loss-Hiding Enron 'Raptors'". Forbes. Archived from the original on May 9, 2010. Retrieved October 17, 2010.
25. Hiltzik, Michael A. (January 31, 2002). "Enron's Web of Complex Hedges, Bets; Finances: Massive trading of derivatives may have clouded the firm's books, experts say" (Fee required). Los Angeles Times. Retrieved October 16, 2010.
26. Flood, Mary (February 14, 2006). "Spotlight falls on Enron's crash point". Houston Chronicle. Archived from the original on September 8, 2008. Retrieved October 17, 2010.
27. Gillan, Stuart; John D. Martin (November 2002). "Financial Engineering, Corporate Governance, and the Collapse of Enron". Alfred Lerner College of Business and Economics, The University of Delaware: 17–21. SSRN 354040.
28. Enron: The Smartest Guys in the Room (DVD). Magnolia Pictures. January 17, 2006. Event occurs at 32:58.
29. Kim, W. Chan; Renée Mauborgne (October 11, 1999). "New dynamics of strategy in the knowledge economy". Financial Times. Archived from the original on July 20, 2011. Retrieved October 17, 2010.
30. Rosen, Robert (2003). "Risk Management and Corporate Governance: The Case of Enron". Connecticut Law Review. 35 (1157): 1171–1175. SSRN 468168.
31. Enron: The Smartest Guys in the Room (DVD). Magnolia Pictures. January 17, 2006. Event occurs at 1:32:33.

32. Cornford, Andrew (June 2004). "Internationally Agreed Principles For Corporate Governance And The Enron Case" (PDF). G-24 Discussion Paper Series No. 30. New York: United Nations Conference on Trade and Development: 30. Archived from the original (PDF) on March 4, 2011. Retrieved October 17, 2010.
33. Lublin, Joann S. (February 1, 2002). "Enron Audit Panel Is Scrutinized For Its Cozy Ties With the Firm". The Wall Street Journal. Archived from the original on December 14, 2012. Retrieved August 9, 2009.
34. Deakin, Simon; Suzanne J. Konzelmann (September 2003). "Learning from Enron" (PDF). ESRC Centre for Business Research. University of Cambridge (Working Paper No 274): 9. Archived from the original (PDF) on December 24, 2010. Retrieved October 17, 2010.
35. Kristen Hayes, "Executives' greed big factor in Enron crash, probe shows" The Seattle Times, August 23, 2002.
36. Bethany McLean, "Why Enron Went Bust: Start with Arrogance," Fortune, December 24, 2001.
37. Duane Windsor, "Business Ethics at 'The Crooked E'" in Enron: Corporate Fiascos and Legal Implications, ed. Nanacy Rapoport and Bala Dharan, 659—87. New York: Foundation Press, 2004.
38. Alan Charles Raul, "In Era of Broken Rules, Society Breaks," Los Angeles Times, October 11, 2002
39. "Enron: Whatever happened to risk management?" Personnel Today, March 19, 2002.
40. David Leonhardt, "How Will Washington Read the Signs?" The New York Times, February 10, 2002.
41. Staff of the Committee on Governmental Affairs, United States Senate, "Financial Oversight of Enron: The SEC and the Private-Sector Watchdogs," October 7, 2002.
42. Robert L. Bradley Jr., "Enron: The Perils of Interventionism", Library of Economics and Liberty
43. Eichenwald, Kurt (2005). Conspiracy of Fools. Broadway Books. ISBN 0767911792.
44. Berenson, Alex; Richard A. Oppel, Jr. (October 28, 2001). "Once-Mighty Enron Strains Under Scrutiny". The New York Times. Archived from the original on December 13, 2009. Retrieved October 17, 2010.
45. McLean, Bethany (March 5, 2001). "Is Enron Overpriced?". Fortune. CNNMoney.com. Archived from the original on October 12, 2010. Retrieved October 17, 2010.
46. Kurtz, Howard (January 18, 2002). "The Enron Story That Waited To Be Told". The Washington Post. Archived from the original on June 9, 2012. Retrieved October 17, 2010.
47. Barringer, Felciity (January 28, 2002). "10 Months Ago, Questions on Enron Came and Went With Little Notice". The New York Times. Archived from the original on March 22, 2012. Retrieved October 17, 2010.
48. Pasha, Shaheen (April 10, 2006). "Skilling comes out swinging". CNNMoney.com. Archived from the original on October 24, 2010. Retrieved October 17, 2010.
49. Tolson, Mike; Katherine Feser (June 20, 2004). "Jeff Skilling's spectacular career". Houston Chronicle. Archived from the original on September 18, 2010. Retrieved October 17, 2010.
50. Niles, Sam (July 10, 2009). "In Pictures: 10 All-Time Great CEO Outbursts: Jeffrey Skilling". Forbes. Archived from the original on October 27, 2010. Retrieved October 17, 2010.
51. Norris, Floyd (July 13, 2001). "Enron Net Rose 40% in Quarter". The New York Times. Archived from the original on March 22, 2012. Retrieved October 17, 2010.
52. US Government Senate Minority Staff Committee on Government Reform. "FACT SHEET— Background on Enron's Dabhol Power Project (22 February 2002)" (PDF). U.S. House of Representatives. Archived from the original (PDF) on October 25, 2016. Retrieved October 25, 2016.
53. Oppel, Richard A., Jr.; Alex Berenson (August 15, 2001). "Enron's Chief Executive Quits After Only 6 Months in Job". The New York Times. Archived from the original on March 22, 2012. Retrieved October 17, 2010.

54. Foley, Stephen (March 16, 2006). "Enron whistleblower tells court of Lay lies". The Independent. Retrieved October 17, 2010.
55. Zellner, Wendy; Stephanie Forest Anderson; Laura Cohn (January 28, 2002). "A Hero—and a Smoking-Gun Letter". BusinessWeek. Archived from the original on April 16, 2011. Retrieved October 17, 2010.
56. Duffy, Michael (January 19, 2002). "By the Sign of the Crooked E". Time. Archived from the original on October 22, 2010. Retrieved October 17, 2010.
57. Berenson, Alex (September 9, 2001). "A self-inflicted wound aggravates angst over Enron". The New York Times. Archived from the original on March 22, 2012. Retrieved October 17, 2010.
58. Oppel, Richard A., Jr. (August 29, 2001). "Two are promoted as Enron seeks executive stability". The New York Times. Archived from the original on September 16, 2009. Retrieved October 17, 2010.
59. Sorkin, Andrew Ross (October 6, 2001). "Enron Reaches a Deal to Sell Oregon Utility for $1.9 Billion". The New York Times. Archived from the original on March 22, 2012. Retrieved October 17, 2010.
60. Gilpin, Kenneth N. (October 17, 2001). "Enron Reports $1 Billion In Charges And a Loss". The New York Times. Archived from the original on March 22, 2012. Retrieved October 17, 2010.
61. Norris, Floyd (October 24, 2001). "Enron Tries To Dismiss Finance Doubts". The New York Times. Archived from the original on September 14, 2009. Retrieved October 17, 2010.
62. Norris, Floyd (October 23, 2001). "Where Did The Value Go At Enron?". The New York Times. Archived from the original on September 16, 2009. Retrieved October 17, 2010.
63. Norris, Floyd (October 25, 2001). "Enron Ousts Finance Chief As S.E.C. Looks at Dealings". The New York Times. Archived from the original on September 16, 2009. Retrieved October 17, 2010.
64. Norris, Floyd (October 27, 2001). "Enron Taps All Its Credit Lines To Buy Back $3.3 Billion of Debt". The New York Times. Archived from the original on March 22, 2012. Retrieved October 17, 2010.
65. Norris, Floyd (October 28, 2001). "Plumbing Mystery Of Deals By Enron". The New York Times. Archived from the original on March 22, 2012. Retrieved October 17, 2010.
66. Oppel, Richard A., Jr. (October 29, 2001). "Enron Seeks Additional Financing". The New York Times. Archived from the original on March 22, 2012. Retrieved October 17, 2010.
67. "Enron Credit Rating Is Cut, And Its Share Price Suffers". The New York Times. October 30, 2001. Archived from the original on September 16, 2009. Retrieved October 17, 2010.
68. Berenson, Alex (November 1, 2001). "S.E.C. Opens Investigation Into Enron". The New York Times. Archived from the original on February 11, 2011. Retrieved October 17, 2010.
69. "The Rise and Fall of Enron" (PDF). The New York Times. November 1, 2001. Archived from the original on March 4, 2011. Retrieved October 17, 2010.
70. Oppel, Richard A., Jr. (November 2, 2001). "Enron's Shares Fall and Debt Rating Is Cut". The New York Times. Archived from the original on March 22, 2012. Retrieved October 17, 2010.
71. Oppel, Richard A., Jr.; Andrew Ross Sorkin (November 7, 2001). "Enron Looks for Investors, But Finds Them Skittish". The New York Times. Archived from the original on March 22, 2012. Retrieved October 17, 2010.
72. Oppel, Richard A., Jr.; Andrew Ross Sorkin (November 8, 2001). "Dynegy Is Said to Be Near to Acquiring Enron for $8 Billion". The New York Times. Archived from the original on March 22, 2012. Retrieved October 17, 2010.
73. Berenson, Alex; Andrew Ross Sorkin (November 10, 2001). "Rival to Buy Enron, Top Energy Trader, After Financial Fall". The New York Times. Archived from the original on March 22, 2012. Retrieved October 17, 2010.
74. Berenson, Alex; Richard A. Oppel, Jr. (November 12, 2001). "Dynegy's Rushed Gamble on Enron Carries Some Big Risks". The New York Times. Archived from the original on October 15, 2014. Retrieved October 17, 2010.

75. Norris, Floyd (November 9, 2001). "Does Enron Trust Its New Numbers? It Doesn't Act Like It". The New York Times. Archived from the original on March 22, 2012. Retrieved October 17, 2010.
76. Oppel, Richard A., Jr.; Andrew Ross Sorkin (November 9, 2001). "Enron Admits to Overstating Profits by About $600 Million". The New York Times. Archived from the original on March 22, 2012. Retrieved October 17, 2010.
77. Berenson, Alex (November 13, 2001). "Suitor for Enron Receives Approval From Wall St". The New York Times. Archived from the original on March 22, 2012. Retrieved October 17, 2010.
78. Norris, Floyd (November 13, 2001). "Gas Pipeline Is Prominent as Dynegy Seeks Enron". The New York Times. Archived from the original on November 9, 2012. Retrieved October 17, 2010.
79. Oppel, Richard A., Jr.; Floyd Norris (November 14, 2001). "Enron Chief Will Give Up Severance". The New York Times. Archived from the original on August 10, 2014. Retrieved October 17, 2010.
80. Oppel, Richard A., Jr. (November 22, 2001). "Employees' Retirement Plan Is a Victim as Enron Tumbles". The New York Times. Archived from the original on March 22, 2012. Retrieved October 17, 2010.
81. Norris, Floyd (November 16, 2001). "Did Ken Lay Understand What Was Happening at Enron?". The New York Times. Archived from the original on March 22, 2012. Retrieved October 17, 2010.
82. Oppel, Richard A., Jr. (November 15, 2001). "Enron Will Sell Some Assets In Hope of Raising Billions". The New York Times. Retrieved October 17, 2010.
83. Oppel, Richard A., Jr.; Floyd Norris (November 20, 2001). "In New Filing, Enron Reports Debt Squeeze". The New York Times. Archived from the original on March 22, 2012. Retrieved October 17, 2010.
84. Oppel, Richard A., Jr. (November 21, 2001). "Enron's Growing Financial Crisis Raises Doubts About Merger Deal". The New York Times. Archived from the original on March 22, 2012. Retrieved October 17, 2010.
85. Sorkin, Andrew Ross; Riva D. Atlas (November 22, 2001). "Circling the Wagons Around Enron; Risks Too Great To Let Trader Just Die". The New York Times. Archived from the original on March 22, 2012. Retrieved October 17, 2010.
86. Norris, Floyd (November 23, 2001). "From Sunbeam to Enron, Andersen's Reputation Suffers". The New York Times. Archived from the original on November 13, 2013. Retrieved October 17, 2010.
87. Oppel, Richard A., Jr. (November 28, 2001). "Trying to Restore Confidence in Enron to Salvage a Merger". The New York Times. Archived from the original on November 11, 2010. Retrieved October 17, 2010.
88. "An Implosion on Wall Street". The New York Times. November 29, 2001. Archived from the original on March 22, 2012. Retrieved October 17, 2010.
89. "Investors Pull Back as Enron Drags Down Key Indexes". The New York Times. Reuters. November 29, 2001. Archived from the original on March 2, 2016. Retrieved October 17, 2010.
90. Henriques, Diana B. (November 29, 2001). "Market That Deals in Risks Faces a Novel One". The New York Times. Archived from the original on January 4, 2013. Retrieved October 17, 2010.
91. Glater, Jonathan D. (November 29, 2001). "A Bankruptcy Filing Might Be the Best Remaining Choice". The New York Times. Archived from the original on March 22, 2012. Retrieved October 17, 2010.
92. Jennifer L. Rich; Saritha Rai (November 30, 2001). "Questions Surround Assets Abroad". The New York Times.

93. Pasha, Shaheen; Jessica Seid (May 25, 2006). "Lay and Skilling's Day of Reckoning". CNNMoney.com. Archived from the original on October 13, 2010. Retrieved October 17, 2010.
94. Enron: The Smartest Guys in the Room (DVD). Magnolia Pictures. January 17, 2006. Event occurs at 1:38:02.
95. Ayala, Astrid; Giancarlo Ibárgüen, Snr (March 2006). "A Market Proposal for Auditing the Financial Statements of Public Companies" (PDF). Journal of Management of Value. Universidad Francisco Marroquín: 51. Archived from the original (PDF) on July 21, 2011. Retrieved October 17, 2010.
96. DeVogue, Ariane; Peter Dizikes; Linda Douglass (January 18, 2002). "Enron Fires Arthur Andersen". ABC News. Archived from the original on January 31, 2011. Retrieved October 17, 2010.
97. "Key Witnesses in the Enron Trial". The Wall Street Journal. Associated Press. January 27, 2006. Archived from the original (Fee required) on May 24, 2012. Retrieved October 17, 2010.
98. Said, Carolyn (July 9, 2004). "Ex-Enron chief Ken Lay Enters Not Guilty Plea". San Francisco Chronicle. Archived from the original on January 28, 2012. Retrieved October 17, 2010.
99. Hays, Kristen (May 6, 2004). "Fastow's Wife Pleads Guilty in Enron Case". USA Today. Archived from the original on August 25, 2010. Retrieved October 17, 2010.
100. Johnson, Carrie (October 24, 2006). "Skilling Gets 24 Years for Fraud at Enron". The Washington Post. Archived from the original on November 8, 2012. Retrieved October 17, 2010.
101. "Ex-Enron Chief's Sentence is Cut by 10 Years to 14". The New York Times. Retrieved June 21, 2013.
102. Leung, Rebecca (March 14, 2005). "Enron's Ken Lay: I Was Fooled". 60 Minutes. CBS News. Archived from the original on November 14, 2010. Retrieved October 17, 2010.
103. Hays, Kristen (May 26, 2006). "Lay, Skilling Convicted in Enron Collapse". The Washington Post. Archived from the original on November 8, 2012. Retrieved October 17, 2010.
104. Eichenwald, Kurt (November 17, 2004). "Enron Inquiry Turns to Sales By Lay's Wife". The New York Times. Archived from the original on March 3, 2012. Retrieved October 17, 2010.
105. Johnson, Carrie (June 10, 2006). "A Woman Of Conviction". The Washington Post. Archived from the original on November 8, 2012. Retrieved October 17, 2010.
106. "Ex-Enron executive pleads guilty". guardian.co.uk. London. August 21, 2002. Archived from the original on March 6, 2016. Retrieved October 17, 2010.
107. Ackman, Dan (January 23, 2004). "Causey May Put GAAP On Trial". Forbes. Archived from the original on August 8, 2009. Retrieved October 17, 2010.
108. McCoy, Kevin (December 28, 2005). "Former Enron executive pleads guilty". USA Today. Archived from the original on October 25, 2012. Retrieved October 17, 2010.
109. "4 ex-Merrill Lynch execs' convictions overturned". www.chron.com. August 2, 2006. Retrieved January 31, 2021.
110. "Feds won't fight overturned convictions". www.cnn.com. Retrieved January 31, 2021.
111. "Judge dismisses charges against ex-Merrill exec in Enron case at prosecutors' request". www.foxnews.com. March 27, 2015. Retrieved January 31, 2021.
112. Porretto, John (June 18, 2007). "Ex-Enron broadband head sentenced". USA Today. Archived from the original on October 25, 2012. Retrieved October 17, 2010.
113. Murphy, Kate (June 2006). "One Guilty and One Acquitted in Enron Broadband Trial". The New York Times.
114. Ellison, Cara. "Michael Krautz: Sexy Accountant". The Enron Blog. Archived from the original on July 9, 2012.
115. Thomas, Cathy Booth (June 18, 2002). "Called to Account". Time. Archived from the original on October 13, 2010. Retrieved October 17, 2010.
116. Rosenwald, Michael S. (November 10, 2007). "Extreme (Executive) Makeover". The Washington Post. Archived from the original on November 7, 2012. Retrieved October 17, 2010.

117. Alexander, Delroy; Greg Burns; Robert Manor; Flynn McRoberts; and E.A. Torriero (November 1, 2002). "The Fall of Andersen". Hartford Courant. Archived from the original on April 24, 2011. Retrieved October 17, 2010.
118. "Supreme Court Overturns Arthur Andersen Conviction". Fox News. Associated Press. May 31, 2005. Archived from the original on February 9, 2011. Retrieved October 17, 2010.
119. Hays, Kristen (November 27, 2007). "Source: British bankers to plead guilty in Enron case". Houston Chronicle. Archived from the original on May 22, 2011. Retrieved October 17, 2010.
120. "Enron Witness Found Dead in Park". BBC News. July 12, 2006. Archived from the original on January 6, 2010. Retrieved October 17, 2010.
121. "Q&A: The NatWest Three". BBC News. November 29, 2007. Archived from the original on January 6, 2012. Retrieved October 17, 2010.
122. Clark, Andrew (November 28, 2007). "NatWest Three Plead Guilty to Wire Fraud". guardian.co.uk. London. Archived from the original on November 6, 2011. Retrieved October 17, 2010.
123. Murphy, Kate (February 22, 2008). "'NatWest 3' sentenced to 37 months each". The New York Times. Archived from the original on June 13, 2022. Retrieved October 17, 2010.
124. Tyler, Richard (August 15, 2010). "NatWest banker claims he was 'tortured' into pleading guilty over theft of $7.3m from RBS". The Daily Telegraph. Archived from the original on August 18, 2010. Retrieved October 17, 2010.
125. "Bankrupt Enron's HQ sold for $55m". BBC News. December 3, 2003. Archived from the original on April 30, 2009. Retrieved October 17, 2010.
126. Barboza, David (July 9, 2002). "CORPORATE CONDUCT: THE TRADER; Enron Trader Had a Year To Boast of, Even If . . ". The New York Times. ISSN 0362-4331. Retrieved June 25, 2019.
127. Axtman, Kris (June 20, 2005). "How Enron awards do, or don't, trickle down". The Christian Science Monitor. Archived from the original on March 5, 2012. Retrieved October 17, 2010.
128. "Enron's Plan Would Repay A Fraction of Dollars Owed". The New York Times. July 12, 2003. Archived from the original on March 22, 2012. Retrieved October 17, 2010.
129. Vogel, Carol (April 16, 2003). "Enron's Art to Be Auctioned Off". The New York Times. Archived from the original on March 22, 2012. Retrieved October 17, 2010.
130. "Enron's 'Tilted-E' Sign Goes for $44,000 at Auction". USA Today. Associated Press. September 25, 2002. Archived from the original on July 20, 2011. Retrieved October 17, 2010.
131. "Enron Gets Go Ahead to Sell Pipes". BBC News. September 10, 2004. Archived from the original on January 6, 2012. Retrieved October 17, 2010.
132. Shulz, Ellen (May 14, 2004). "Enron Settles With Employees Who Lost Retirement Money". The Wall Street Journal. New York City. Retrieved January 11, 2020.
133. Tom Fowler (July 26, 2006) Judge approves $37.5 million Enron 401(k) settlement, The Houston Chronicle, accessed January 11, 2020
134. Doran, James (May 14, 2004). "Enron Staff win $85m". The Times. London. Archived from the original on June 12, 2011. Retrieved October 17, 2010.
135. DeBare, Ilana (September 10, 2008). "Billions to be shared by Enron shareholders". San Francisco Chronicle. Archived from the original on January 11, 2012. Retrieved October 17, 2010.
136. Davis, Trey (December 18, 2008). "UC begins distributing Enron settlement money". University of California. Archived from the original on June 13, 2011. Retrieved October 17, 2010.
137. Enron: The Smartest Guys in the Room (DVD). Magnolia Pictures. January 17, 2006. Event occurs at 6:06.

138. Chhaochharia, Vidhi; Yaniv Grinstein (March 2007). "Corporate Governance and Firm Value: the Impact of the 2002 Governance Rules" (PDF). Johnson School Research Paper Series No. 23-06. Johnson School of Management: 7–9. Archived from the original (PDF) on July 16, 2011. Retrieved October 17, 2010.
139. Deakin, Simon; Suzanne J. Konzelmann (September 2003). "Learning from Enron" (PDF). ESRC Centre for Business Research. University of Cambridge (Working Paper No 274): 1. Archived from the original (PDF) on December 24, 2010. Retrieved October 17, 2010.
140. "Bush and Enron's collapse". The Economist. January 11, 2002. Retrieved June 20, 2018. The problem for Mr Bush is that the ties between the company and his administration were especially intricate and close. Mr Lay has been a supporter of Mr Bush ever since the president's unsuccessful campaign for Congress in 1978, and has been known as a close personal friend of Mr Bush and his family. At one stage, Mr Lay was mooted as a possible energy secretary under Mr Bush.
141. Pellegrini, Frank (January 10, 2002). "Bush's Enron Problem". Time. Time Inc. Retrieved June 20, 2018.

Chapter 9
Retail

9.1 Walmart Inc.[1]

9.1.1 Text from US Department of Justice Website

Office of Public Affairs
FOR IMMEDIATE RELEASE
Thursday, June 20, 2019

Walmart Inc. and Brazil-Based Subsidiary Agree to Pay $137 Million to Resolve Foreign Corrupt Practices Act Case
Walmart Inc. (Walmart), a U.S.-based multinational retailer and its wholly owned Brazilian subsidiary, WMT Brasilia S.a.r.l. (WMT Brasilia), have agreed to pay a combined criminal penalty of $137 million to resolve the government's investigation into violations of the Foreign Corrupt Practices Act (FCPA). WMT Brasilia pleaded guilty today in connection with the resolution.

Assistant Attorney General Brian A. Benczkowski of the Justice Department's Criminal Division, U.S. Attorney G. Zachary Terwilliger of the Eastern District of Virginia, Assistant Director Robert Johnson of the FBI's Criminal Investigative Division and Special Agent in Charge Kelly Jackson of IRS Criminal Investigation's (IRS-CI) Washington, D.C. office made the announcement.

"Walmart profited from rapid international expansion, but in doing so chose not to take necessary steps to avoid corruption," said Assistant Attorney General Benczkowski. "In numerous instances, senior Walmart employees knew of failures of its anti-corruption-related internal controls involving foreign subsidiaries, and yet Walmart failed for years to implement sufficient controls comporting with U.-S. criminal laws. As today's resolution shows, even the largest of U.S. companies

---

[1] Link: https://www.justice.gov/opa/pr/walmart-inc-and-brazil-based-subsidiary-agree-pay-137-million-resolve-foreign-corrupt

© The Author(s), under exclusive license to Springer Nature Switzerland AG 2022
D. Smith, *Fraud and Corruption*, Contributions to Finance and Accounting,
https://doi.org/10.1007/978-3-031-10063-5_9

operating abroad are bound by U.S. laws, and the Department of Justice will continue to aggressively investigate and prosecute foreign corruption."

"Walmart violated the Foreign Corrupt Practices Act because it failed to implement the internal controls necessary to ferret out corrupt conduct," said U.S. Attorney Terwilliger. "For more than a decade, Walmart experienced exponential international growth but failed to create safeguards to protect against corruption risks in various countries. This resolution is the result of several years of steadfast work by the prosecutors and our law enforcement partners at the FBI and IRS-CI."

"The FBI will hold corporations responsible when they turn a blind eye to corruption," said FBI Assistant Director Johnson. "If there is evidence of violations of FCPA, we will investigate. No corporation, no matter how large, is above the law."

"Walmart's guilty plea is another step in IRS-CI's ongoing effort to pursue corporations that engage in corruption that prevents fair competition around the world," said IRS-CI Special Agent in Charge Jackson. "Through our efforts, we delved through layers of transactions and uncovered the bribery of foreign officials. Today's announcement is a statement that no company, even one as large as Walmart, is above the law."

According to Walmart's admissions, from 2000 until 2011, certain Walmart personnel responsible for implementing and maintaining the company's internal accounting controls related to anti-corruption were aware of certain failures involving these controls, including relating to potentially improper payments to government officials in certain Walmart foreign subsidiaries, but nevertheless failed to implement sufficient controls that, among other things, would have ensured: (a) that sufficient anti-corruption-related due diligence was conducted on all third-party intermediaries (TPIs) who interacted with foreign officials; (b) that sufficient anti-corruption-related internal accounting controls concerning payments to TPIs existed; (c) that proof was required that TPIs had performed services before Walmart paid them; (d) that TPIs had written contracts that included anti-corruption clauses; (e) that donations ostensibly made to foreign government agencies were not converted to personal use by foreign officials; and (f) that policies covering gifts, travel and entertainment sufficiently addressed giving things of value to foreign officials and were implemented. Even though senior Walmart personnel responsible for implementing and maintaining the company's internal accounting controls related to anti-corruption knew of these issues, Walmart did not begin to change its internal accounting controls related to anti-corruption to comply with U.-S. criminal laws until 2011.

The internal controls failures allowed Walmart foreign subsidiaries in Mexico, India, Brazil and China to hire TPIs without establishing sufficient controls to prevent those TPIs from making improper payments to government officials in order to obtain store permits and licenses. In a number of instances, insufficiencies in Walmart's anti-corruption-related internal accounting controls in these foreign subsidiaries were reported to senior Walmart employees and executives. The internal control failures allowed the foreign subsidiaries in Mexico, India, Brazil and China to open stores faster than they would have with sufficient internal accounting controls related to anti-corruption. Consequently, Walmart earned additional profits through these subsidiaries by opening some of its stores faster.

In Mexico, a former attorney for Walmart's local subsidiary reported to Walmart in 2005 that he had overseen a scheme for several years prior in which TPIs made improper payments to government officials to obtain permits and licenses for the subsidiary and that several executives at the subsidiary knew of and approved of the scheme. Most of the TPI invoices included a code specifying why the subsidiary had made the improper payment, including: (1) avoiding a requirement; (2) influence, control or knowledge of privileged information known by the government official; and (3) payments to eliminate fines.

In India, because of Walmart's failure to implement sufficient internal accounting controls related to anti-corruption, from 2009 until 2011, Walmart's operations there were able to retain TPIs that made improper payments to government officials in order to obtain store operating permits and licenses. These improper payments were then falsely recorded in Walmart's joint venture's books and records with vague descriptions like "misc fees," "miscellaneous," "professional fees," "incidental" and "government fee."

In Brazil, as a result of Walmart's failure to implement sufficient internal accounting controls related to anti-corruption at its subsidiary, Walmart Brazil, despite repeated findings in internal audit reports that such controls were lacking, Walmart Brazil continued to retain and renew contracts with TPIs without conducting the required due diligence. Improper payments were in fact paid by some of these TPIs, including a construction company that made improper payments to government officials in connection with the construction of two Walmart Brazil stores in 2009 without the knowledge of Walmart Brazil. Walmart Brazil indirectly hired a TPI whose ability to obtain licenses and permits quickly earned her the nickname "sorceress" or "genie" within Walmart Brazil. Walmart Brazil employees, including a Walmart Brazil executive, knew they could not hire the intermediary directly because of several red flags. In 2009, the TPI made improper payments to government inspectors in connection with the construction of a Walmart Brazil store without the knowledge of Walmart Brazil. WMT Brasilia was a wholly-owned subsidiary of Walmart and was a majority-owner of Walmart Brazil, Walmart's wholly-owned subsidiary in Brazil, and the majority-owner of retail stores operating as Walmart Brazil.

In China, Walmart's local subsidiary's internal audit team flagged numerous weaknesses in internal accounting controls related to anti-corruption at the subsidiary between 2003 and 2011, sometimes repeatedly, but many of these weaknesses were not addressed. In fact, from 2007 until early 2010, Walmart and the subsidiary failed to address nearly all of the anti-corruption-related internal controls audit findings.

Walmart entered into a three-year non-prosecution agreement and agreed to retain an independent corporate compliance monitor for two years. The $137 million penalty reflects a 20 percent reduction off the bottom of the applicable U.-S. Sentencing Guidelines fine range for the portion of the penalty applicable to conduct in Mexico and 25 percent for the portion applicable to the conduct in Brazil,

China and India. Walmart fully cooperated with the investigation in Brazil, China and India. Walmart cooperated with the investigation in Mexico, but did not timely provide documents and information to the government and did not de-conflict with the government's request to interview one witness before Walmart interviewed that witness. Walmart did not voluntarily disclose the conduct in Mexico and only disclosed the conduct in Brazil, China and India after the government had already begun investigating the Mexico conduct. The $137 million penalty includes forfeiture of $3.6 million and a fine of $724,898 from WMT Brasilia.

In a related resolution with the U.S. Securities and Exchange Commission (SEC), Walmart agreed to disgorge $144 million in profits.

The FBI's International Corruption Squad in Washington, D.C. and IRS-CI are investigating the case....

9.2 Tesco

9.2.1 Text from UK SFO Website[2] (February 10, 2022)

Deferred Prosecution Agreement between the SFO and Tesco published
23 January, 2019

The SFO can now share in full the terms of a Deferred Prosecution Agreement (DPA) reached with Tesco Stores Ltd after reporting restrictions were lifted today.

Between February and September 2014, instead of working to safeguard the financial interests of the company and its shareholders, a culture existed at Tesco that encouraged illegal practices to meet accounting targets, including improperly recognised income in the UK accounts, by 'pulling forward' income from subsequent reporting periods.

Lisa Osofsky, Director of the Serious Fraud Office said:

"Tesco Stores Limited dishonestly created a false account of its financial position by overstating its profits.

"The DPA clearly outlines the extent of this criminal conduct for which the company has accepted full responsibility."

Under the DPA, Tesco agreed to pay a £129m fine and £3m investigation costs.

The company will also undertake and implement an ongoing compliance programme during the three year term of the DPA.

After discovering issues in their financial statements, Tesco referred itself to enforcement authorities after revealing that revenues had been incorrectly recorded as profit and made an announcement to the market.

---

[2] https://www.sfo.gov.uk/2019/01/23/deferred-prosecution-agreement-between-the-sfo-and-tesco-published/

Notes to editors:

1. The SFO began investigating this case in October 2014. See press releases here.
2. Tesco Stores Limited's Deferred Prosecution Agreement with the SFO was approved by the President of the Queen's Bench Division, the Right Honourable Sir Brian Leveson at Southwark Crown Court on 10 April 2017. See press release here.
3. The DPA with Tesco Stores Limited was the fourth ever agreed in the UK.
4. Tesco Plc has agreed to a separate £85m statutory compensation scheme for shareholders and bondholders with the Financial Conduct Authority (FCA) under the Market Abuse Regulations.
5. The SFO charged three former senior managers over alleged financial misreporting. Sir John Royce ruled that Christopher Bush and John Scouler had no case to answer on Monday 26 November 2018. Full details here.
6. A third defendant, Carl Rogberg, was severed from the trial. The SFO offered no evidence at a hearing on 23 January 2019 and Mr Rogberg was acquitted of all charges.
7. Counsel for the Prosecution
    1. Sasha Wass QC
    2. Esther Schutzer-Weissman

9.2.2 Text from UK SFO Website[3] (February 10, 2022)

SFO confirms end of Deferred Prosecution Agreement with Tesco Stores Ltd
10 April 2020

The Serious Fraud Office has confirmed to the courts that Tesco Stores Ltd has fulfilled the terms of its Deferred Prosecution Agreement (DPA) with the SFO, bringing an end to the SFO's case.

Under the three year term of the DPA, Tesco Stores Ltd agreed to pay a £129m fine and £3m investigation costs, as well as implementing an ongoing compliance programme.

The SFO is satisfied that Tesco has fully complied with the terms of the DPA.

Notes to editors:

1. The SFO served a Notice of Discontinuance on the Court on 7 April 2020. This can be found here.

---

[3] https://www.sfo.gov.uk/2020/04/10/sfo-confirms-end-of-deferred-prosecution-agreement-with-tesco-stores-ltd/

2. The SFO confirmed it had reached a Deferred Prosecution Agreement in principle with Tesco Stores Limited on 28 March 2017, before entering into the DPA on 10 April 2017.
3. The terms of the DPA ran for three years, from 10 April 2017 to 10 April 2020.
4. The full DPA, Statement of Facts, and Judgment from Sir Brian Leveson, can be found here.
5. This is the third DPA to have concluded with its terms fulfilled, after Standard Bank PLC and Sarclad Ltd. The remaining four of the SFO's seven DPAs—Rolls-Royce PLC, Serco Geografix Ltd, Güralp Systems Ltd, and Airbus SE—are currently open.

9.2.3 UK SFO Website[4] (February 10, 2022)

Tesco PLC

The SFO entered into a Deferred Prosecution Agreement (DPA) with Tesco Stores Limited on 10 April 2017.

Through the DPA Tesco Stores Limited accepted responsibility for false accounting practices. Between February and September 2014, instead of working to safeguard the financial interests of the company and its shareholders, a culture existed at Tesco that encouraged illegal practices to meet accounting targets, including improperly recognised income in the UK accounts, by 'pulling forward' income from subsequent reporting periods.

Carl Rogberg, John Scouler and Christopher Bush, former Tesco employees who held senior management roles in the Tesco UK business, were charged over allegations of fraud and false accounting on 9 September 2016.

John Scouler and Christopher Bush were acquitted of all charges after Sir John Royce ruled that they had no case to answer at trial. This decision was upheld in the Court of Appeal on 5 December 2018. A third defendant, Carl Rogberg, was severed from the trial. The SFO offered no evidence at a hearing on 23 January 2019 and Mr Rogberg was acquitted of all charges.

Terms of DPA

Under the DPA, Tesco agreed to pay a £129m fine and £3m investigation costs. The company also undertook and implemented an ongoing compliance programme during the three year term of the DPA.

On 7 April 2020, the SFO served a Notice of Discontinuance on the Court, confirming that Tessco Stores Ltd had fully complied with the terms of the DPA. The three-year term of the DPA came to end on 10 April 2020.

The Notice of Discontinuance is published below.

Notice of DPA Discontinuance—SFO v Tesco Stores Ltd

---

[4] https://www.sfo.gov.uk/cases/tesco-plc/

Full information on the DPA is available in the Statement of Facts, agreed by the SFO and Tesco Stores Ltd. The Agreement itself and Sir Brian Leveson's judgment are published below.

Deferred Prosecution Agreement—SFO v Tesco Stores Ltd
Deferred Prosecution Agreement—Statement of Facts—SFO v Tesco Stores Ltd
Judgment of Sir Brian Leveson, President of the Queen's Bench Division

9.2.4 Extract from UK SFO Website[5] (February 10, 2022)

Serious Fraud Office-v-Tesco Stores Limited: Statement of Facts Prepared Pursuant to Paragraph 6(1) of Schedule 17 to the Crime and Courts Act 2013
(Paras 54–62)

Evidence of False Accounting

54. In April 2013 Tesco had announced its first fall in profits in nearly twenty years as a result of a combination of adverse general economic conditions and competition from other retailers. It was against this background that Tesco's annual budget and financial targets were set by the CEO in consultation with the Group Executive Committee and approved by the Tesco Board. Once finalised in March 2014, the budgets were communicated to TSL's commercial and financial teams, where they were widely regarded as unachievable.

55. Tesco expected its employees to meet financial targets that were set. This gave rise to a culture in which TSL's employees were under great pressure to deliver in line with the budget. In the period between 1 February 2014 and 18 September 2014 and whilst under pressure to meet these targets TSL's employees misstated commercial income to the extent that by 23 August 2014 TSL had wrongly recognised £257m of commercial income, a figure made up of both legacy from earlier financial years and pulling forward of income from future accounting periods.

56. Every month in H1 2014/15, and in purported compliance with Tesco's procedures for financial reporting, Carl Rogberg had submitted to Group Finance financial reports for TSL which he certified (or authorised to be certified) as true and fair but which contained overstated commercial income figures for the UK Food Division. Group Finance used these figures to prepare reports on TSL's performance, including for a meeting of the Tesco Board held at 6pm on 28 August 2014 at which the only agenda item was Group performance. In advance of that meeting, Tesco Board members were provided with an analysis of expected performance for the half year and the full year, which indicated a reduction in expected trading profit. Nothing in that analysis alerted readers to the fact or risk of the overstatement.

57. The minutes of the meeting record that the Tesco Board was told that there was a reasonable degree of confidence that the figures on which the analysis had

---

[5]Link: https://webarchive.nationalarchives.gov.uk/ukgwa/20210301134047/https://www.sfo.gov.uk/download/deferred-prosecution-agreement-statement-of-facts-sfo-v-tesco-stores-ltd/

been based would not change materially as a result of the half year audit process. The Tesco Board then made a number of decisions including deciding immediately to inform the market of its revised profit forecast.

58. Carl Rogberg, Chris Bush and John Scouler were each told at various times in reports, meetings and emails that employees in TSL were pulling forward income. TSL employees did not like doing this: a number resigned as a consequence, and Carl Rogberg and John Scouler were aware of the toll this was taking. On 26 August 2014, Employee A informed them by email that staff were resigning, that H1 had left them "highly bruised", and that H2 had to be a different story or "they would lose credibility with colleagues". [B35]

59. All the Commercial teams within TSL were under pressure to meet targets or deliver more to cover shortfalls in other areas. The result was that the accounting and finance functions were also placed under pressure to help to deliver on the budgets including through illegitimate methods that ended up undermining their independence and true function to record and report accurately on the performance of the business.

60. At various points during H1 Carl Rogberg, Chris Bush and John Scouler were informed that the UK business was under-performing and could not meet its targets, that the challenge included filling the hole from previous years' pull forward and that pull forward was necessary to meet targets. This is illustrated as follows by reference to contemporaneous documents:

a. By the time the budget was set in March 2014 the UK business Commercial Food division entered the financial year with what was believed to be -£31 million of commercial income, a figure which the business would have to make up over the course of the year, whatever budget was fixed for it.

b. In April 2014 Chris Bush, Carl Rogberg and John Scouler received a presentation on a paper entitled Commercial Period 1 2014/15 Review which showed that at the end of P1 commercial income from the UK business Commercial Food division was £62.6m less than the budget anticipated.

a. On 26 May 2014 Carl Rogberg received a paper entitled H1 Phasing profit proposal identifying an anticipated miss to the H1 2014/15 budget for the trading profit of the UK business of £104m.

b. In early June 2014 Chris Bush, John Scouler and Carl Rogberg received and were taken through a report entitled Commercial Period 3 2014/15 Review to June 2014 which detailed a £69.8m profit shortfall to budget in the UK business Commercial Food division and included the £38.2m legacy of pull forwards from the previous year. A request to amend the budget was refused.

c. On 17 June 2014 Carl Rogberg, Chris Bush and John Scouler received and discussed a report with others entitled Review of Food Commercial Margin prepared by the UK Commercial department. It revealed the miss to the H1 2014/15 commercial gross margin ('CGM') target for the UK business Commercial Food Division was £72.1m. It suggested ways of closing the profit gap including an unpalatable option of "further pull forwards YOY". A request to amend the budget was refused.

9.2 Tesco

d. On 19 June 2014 Carl Rogberg emailed Chris Bush attaching a copy of a document entitled CGM review.pdf which he had annotated and which showed a miss of £72m to the CGM target for the UK Business Commercial Food division in H1 2014/15. Carl Rogberg informed ChrisBush that the prior year impact of £35m at the previous year end was now thought to be £57.7m.

e. On 19 June 2014 John Scouler emailed Chris Bush about H1. He informed Chris Bush that reducing the miss (presumably for the UK business Commercial Food division) from £71m to £35-40m involved a "number of very difficult actions we have put in place outside of price to get us to this figure. I have shared this with Carl". Chris Bush responded by email on the 21 June 2014 that the gap had to be closed to zero and suggested John Scouler meet with the "finance team . . . . to go through options yet again". John Scouler responded by email copying in Carl Rogberg that they would "go back again".

f. On 27 June 2014 John Scouler received a paper entitled H1 UK Commercial Margin, recording that the trading profit miss at H1 2014/15 in the UK business Commercial Food division could be £175m of which £102m was attributable to legacy and pull forward, £68m relating to the current half. It also detailed current stretch plans to include £46m of "pull forward income relating to future activity". He emailed the paper to Carl Rogberg and Chris Bush on 30 June.

g. On 2 July 2014 John Scouler emailed Chris Bush advising him that he would talk him through the assumptions in their £46m pull forward plan.

h. On 4 July 2014 the UK Leadership Team met. Chris Bush, Carl Rogberg and John Scouler attended along with others. A document entitled Risks and Ops to full year number from UKLT session 4th July 2014-Welham Green, generated as a result of the meeting, made no mention of legacy or a significant miss to the budget.

i. On 6 August 2014, Carl Rogberg and John Scouler were informed in an email from Employee A, who was requesting guidance, that a miss to the H1 target would be between £45m and £60m rather than £35m and there was a big risk at H2. A number of reasons for the miss were identified which included in the Packaged Category "13/14 Pull Forward". Employee A asked "if we are not going to hit (35), should we do what we are asking categories to do to hit the number".

j. On 8 August 2014 John Scouler emailed Chris Bush to inform him that what was being done to meet the H1 2014/15 target (for the UK business Commercial Food division) would mean there would be a miss to the margin in H2 of circa £100m. On 9 August Chris Bush emailed John Scouler that he would meet the UK commercial directors individually on his return from annual leave.

k. In mid-August 2014 a business plan review identified that by P5 2014/15 Tesco's UK Core profits were £408m lower than the year before. The business plan was circulated to recipients including Chris Bush, Carl Rogberg and John Scouler on 14 August and was presented at a meeting of the UK Leadership team on 15 August 2014 which was attended by Carl Rogberg (but not Chris Bush or John Scouler).

l. On 14 August 2014 Carl Rogberg received a document entitled UK Core—H2PP (6+6) 1415 H2 Risks and Ops outlook—unapproved draft, illustrating a profit forecast of £692m for the UK core business for H1 and various underlying risks for H2 which included a £90m Commercial accruals legacy.

m. On 15 August 2014 Carl Rogberg received a document entitled UK Core—H2PP (6+6) 1415 H2 Risks and Ops outlook—unapproved draft, detailing a £100m "Commercial: potential margin risk" to the UK Core business trading profit budget for H2 2014/15.

n. On 18 August 2014 Chris Bush, Carl Rogberg and John Scouler were emailed a paper reviewing P5 recording a miss to the CGM budget of £133.5 m to the budget, for the UK business Commercial Food division.

o. On 18 August 2014 Carl Rogberg was informed by Employee A by email that pull forward of at least £40m was used in the previous accounting year and the same number plus probably a further £10–15m was being used in H1 2014/15. Carl Rogberg was told that this contributed to the inability to meet the margin and that budget relief of £200m was required for the full year 2014/15.

p. On 19 August 2014 Carl Rogberg emailed John Scouler noting that there was a risk level of £100m + £100m of which an accrual risk of £100m was driven by legacy. He said Chris Bush understood the accrual risk of £100m driven by legacy and that Employee A had asked him to help get Chris Bush to understand the £100m 'rate' risk.

q. On 20 August 2014 John Scouler was advised in an email by Employee A that to get to the UK business Commercial Food trading budget for H1 2014/15 £50m had been pulled forward on top of the £45m "borrowed at full year 13/14". Employee A wrote that £100m in structural relief was required to get the "pull forward corrected (legacy)". He continued "whatthat will do is take the burden off the categories and help us have constructive conversations with suppliers. Also GSCOP risk is getting bigger, our legal team is asking for more discipline, our teams are walking away from it".

r. On 21 August 2014 a presentation was shown to and discussed with Chris Bush entitled Review of Food Commercial Margin—2014/15. It identified a gap of £444m on the UK Food H2 Margin Outlook to be filled in order to meet the full year budget. It also illustrated that £233m of the gap figure was legacy challenge.

s. On 1 September 2014 Employee A emailed John Scouler concerning the possibility of revising targets for H2 2014/15. In the email, Employee A said under the heading "How do we achieve it?"; "We don't test the integrity of our teams, we test their delivery. So, as a team we do discuss before passing accruals, especially where we are uncomfortable ..... We keep legacy conversation alive with Chris [Bush] and Dave [Lewis], and resolve it over next 6–9 months".

t. On 2 September 2014 John Scouler emailed his UK commercial directors about the H2 targets which they had to meet, save for the miss that had occurred at H1, referring to the need to "spend next two weeks getting to the bottom of the legacy and accrual position". The email was forwarded to Chris Bush by John Scouler and Carl Rogberg by Employee A.

u. On 15 September 2014 Employee A sent a draft position paper to John Scouler setting out legacy issues. The paper detailed that the UK Commercial Food margin in H1 2014/15 was overstated by c. £246m, the majority due to income being pulled forward from future periods. The paper explained that pulling forward income was a material audit risk and contrary to relevant accounting standards. It was also creating extra work for employees by collecting documentation to minimise audit risk. John Scouler agreed that much of what was said in the paper was fair and clear but asked for more balance to reflect "progress we have made in many areas".

v. On 16 September 2014, following a meeting between John Scouler, Employee A and a more junior finance colleague, a slightly amended legacy paper was submitted by the junior finance colleague to John Scouler. It contained details of a £246m legacy figure caused by the pulling forward of income, creating a material audit risk. The paper was presented to Chris Bush by John Scouler that day. A copy of the paper was emailed to Carl Rogberg.

61. Carl Rogberg knowingly signed off on false numbers in Tesco's accounting systems for every period in H1 2014/15. On 18 August 2014, Chris Bush was provided by the Tesco Investor Relations team with a Tesco Data Pack for the H1 2014/15 interim results which was based on data available for P5. The data pack contained a profit forecast for the UK for H1 2014/15 of £697m. Investor Relations requested that any concerns about the data pack should be raised by Chris Bush's team as this would be used to shape the interim results investor narrative at a meeting on 20 August 2014. There is no record that Chris Bush raised any concerns.

62. Throughout H1 and into H2 2014/15, Chris Bush, Carl Rogberg and John Scouler were provided with many opportunities to alert others including Group Finance, the TSL Board and the Tesco Board to the fact that the TSL numbers were false. They failed to take any of these opportunities and instead concealed the true position.

Chapter 10
Military

10.1 Fat Leonard/US Navy

Fat Leonard scandal
   From Wikipedia, the free encyclopedia
   The Fat Leonard scandal is a corruption scandal and ongoing investigation within the United States Navy involving ship support contractor Glenn Defense Marine Asia (GDMA), a Thai subsidiary of the Glenn Marine Group [1, 2]. The Washington Post called the scandal "perhaps the worst national-security breach of its kind to hit the Navy since the end of the Cold War [2]." The company's chief executive, president, and chairman, Malaysian national Leonard Glenn Francis ("Fat Leonard") [2] bribed a large number of uniformed officers of the United States Seventh Fleet with at least a half million dollars in cash, plus travel expenses, luxury items, and prostitutes, in return for classified material about the movements of U.S. ships and submarines, confidential contracting information, and information about active law enforcement investigations into Glenn Defense Marine Asia [2, 3]. Francis then "exploited the intelligence for illicit profit, brazenly ordering his moles to redirect aircraft carriers to ports he controlled in Southeast Asia so he could more easily bilk the Navy for fuel, tugboats, barges, food, water and sewage removal [2]." The Navy, through GDMA, even employed divers to search harbors for explosives [3]. He also

---

Please note that one possible reason in Russia's decision to invade Ukraine could be that Ukraine has taken a number of measures to prevent corruption, as discussed by the **FCPA Blog**: Reassessing Ukraine's 'failed' anti-corruption reforms by Richard L. Cassin (March 7, 2022) https://fcpablog.com/2022/03/07/reassessing-ukraines-failed-anti-corruption-reforms/ and the **Global Anti-Corruption Blog**: Hooray for Corruption (in the Russian Military) by Matthew Stephenson on March 8, 2022 https://globalanticorruptionblog.com/2022/03/08/hooray-for-corruption-in-the-russian-military/ ; and Why Has Ukrainian Military Corruption Been a Non-Story in the Current Conflict? by Matthew Stephenson on March 10, 2022 https://globalanticorruptionblog.com/2022/03/10/why-has-ukrainian-military-corruption-been-a-non-story-in-the-current-conflict/#more-19906

directed them to author "Bravo Zulu" memos, which is an informal term for a letter of commendation from the Navy given to civilians who have performed outstanding services for the Navy, in order to bolster GDMA's credibility for jobs "well done" [4].

The first activities of the conspiracy were confirmed to have existed in 2006 when Francis recruited numerous Navy personnel to engage in corruption, including directing contracts toward his firm, disfavoring competitors, and inhibiting legitimate fiscal and operational oversight. The initial co-conspirators labelled themselves "the cool kids" and "the wolf pack [5]."

U.S. federal prosecutors filed criminal charges against 33 people in connection with the Fat Leonard scandal. Of those, 22 pleaded guilty: Francis himself [6], four of his top aides, and 17 Navy officials (specifically, at least ten commissioned officers, two petty officers, one former Naval Criminal Investigative Service (NCIS) special agent, and two civilian Navy contracting officials) [7]. Nine others are awaiting trial in U.S. district court in San Diego. Separately, five Navy officers were charged with crimes under the Uniform Code of Military Justice (UCMJ) and have been subject to court-martial proceedings. An additional civilian pleaded guilty to a scandal-related crime in Singapore court [8, 9].

Suffering health problems, Francis was hospitalized and released in March 2018. Rather than returning to the custody of the U.S. Marshals Service, he was granted a medical furlough and allowed to stay in San Diego at a private residence owned by one of his physicians, under 24-hour surveillance for which his family paid [10, 11]. At a deposition taken in 2018 in the David A. Morales case, Francis said he is being treated for kidney cancer [11].

In 1989, when he was 21, Francis had been sentenced to three years in jail in Malaysia for firearms possession [12].

Contents
1. Initiation and conduct of investigation

    1.1 Discounting whistleblower warnings
    1.2 Tepid responses
    1.3 Eventual actions

2. Scope of inquiry and prosecutions
3. Corruption prevention
4. Similar corruption
5. Individuals involved
6. References
7. External links

1 Initiation and Conduct of Investigation
1.1 Discounting Whistleblower Warnings

In 2006, Dave Schaus, a Naval officer, became suspicious of GDMA contracts, but Francis was alerted by an informant, Paul Simpkins, to the scrutiny. Simpkins, a decorated veteran of the U.S. Air Force employed as a civilian contracting officer by the Navy in Singapore, managed to quash any inquiry and had Schaus' position eliminated [3]. "What else could I have done to expose this racket?," Schaus asked. Exposed as a whistleblower, he said officers, "made my life hell" after discovering he had attempted to initiate an investigation of GDMA [13].

In 2007, the Navy's Inspector General forwarded a document claiming GDMA was grossly overcharging the Navy for providing port security but NCIS may have failed to follow up the warning. According to a senior Navy officer, "Everybody knew that [Glenn Defense] had been under investigation." "Everybody also knew that nothing ever happened with those investigations." After that, the Manila NCIS office got an anonymous letter and documents, alleging GDMA had overcharged for fees, armed guards and other services during a Subic Bay, Philippines port visit by the Fred Stockham container support ship. "I hope you share the same concern when reading these documents and take swift action to stamp out this fraud, waste and abuse," the letter said.

Manila's NCIS agents forwarded the paperwork to the Navy's Singapore contracting office, but it had been infiltrated by GDMA's moles, and they claimed the allegations were false, closing the case. Mike Lang, a contracting officer who worked there from 2006 to 2008, said, "They'd always side with Glenn Defense and paint us as troublemakers. They'd say, 'Why are you harassing our contractors? You're making my job hard'."

Two officials from that office, Simpkins and his subordinate, Sharon Gursharan Kaur who was also a civilian Navy contracting officer, as well as a former GDMA employee, were sentenced to six years and 33 months, respectively, the latter doing her time in Singapore [13]. NCIS reportedly opened and closed as many as 27 investigations without taking action against GDMA. NCIS has yet to provide an explanation for this lack of action in a significant fraud investigation.

1.2 Tepid Responses

Documents obtained by the Washington Post via Freedom of Information Act Requests (FOIAs) revealed that after al-Qaeda committed the October 2000 suicide attack on the USS Cole and the September 11, 2001 attacks on the World Trade Center and the Pentagon, the Navy's Economic Crimes unit was reduced from a staff of 140 to only nine persons, most having been reassigned to focus on terrorism [3, 13]. At least 27 separate investigations had been opened, but later closed without action, thanks to the intervention of senior Navy personnel who were in league with Francis [13].

The lack of enthusiasm for oversight might have been motivated in part by GDMA's demonstrable ability to deliver the sometimes complex level of services the Navy sought. In 2016, Commander Mike Misiewicz, an officer who was later convicted, told Defense News, "He was a crook, but he was our crook [14]." John Hogan, the NCIS executive assistant director for criminal operations, admitted, "In hindsight, maybe we could have dug a little deeper than we did [13]."

Ray Mabus, who was appointed Navy Secretary by President Barack Obama in 2009, admitted his branch was vulnerable to contracting fraud and should have performed better oversight: "I'm not going to defend at all opening and closing 27 cases. Something should have raised a red flag along there somewhere...There were people inside the Navy who were trying to shut this down, who were coming up with reasons not to pursue it [13]." In 2010, a civilian Navy attorney drafted restrictive ethics guidelines for the 7th Fleet. Two admirals friendly to Francis were said to be responsible for seeing that it was delayed and diluted over the next 2 1/2 years, before being implemented [13].

1.3 Eventual Actions

In 2010, Navy officials became suspicious that some of the bills submitted by GDMA from Thailand were padded [15]. The escalating costs prompted the Navy to build a logistics team to keep contracts somewhat in check, but it was frustrated because Francis had a spy, Jose Luis Sanchez, feeding its information back to him [13]. (Sanchez has pleaded guilty to conspiracy and awaits sentencing.) Despite the increasing awareness that the Navy was being subjected to massive fraud, GDMA was able to contract to deliver $200 million in services in 2011 alone [13].

After a three-year investigation and having planted false information that their inquiries had been closed, putting Francis off his guard, federal agents lured him to the United States. In September 2013, he was arrested at a San Diego hotel in a sting operation [3]. He pleaded guilty in January 2015 and is awaiting sentencing [2, 16]. Leonard admitted to using his U.S. Navy contacts, including ship captains, to obtain classified information and to defraud the Navy of tens of millions of dollars by steering ships to specific ports in the Pacific and falsifying service charges [16]. In his plea, Francis identified seven Navy officials who accepted bribes [17]. He faces a maximum prison sentence of 25 years and agreed to forfeit $35 million in personal assets, an amount he admits to overcharging the Navy [18, 19].

2 Scope of Inquiry and Prosecutions

Since 2013, 31 people have been criminally charged in connection with the Fat Leonard bribery and corruption scandal. According to investigators, by November 2017, more than 440 people—including 60 admirals—have come under scrutiny under the inquiry [8, 20]. The Navy held a military trial for a still-serving commander, David A. Morales, the first not left to civilian prosecution. He was charged with bribery, conspiracy to commit bribery, false official statements, failure to obey lawful orders, and conduct unbecoming an officer. He was acquitted of the first three charges in a bench trial, only found guilty of failure to obey lawful orders and conduct unbecoming [21]. As of September 2018, 30 people have pleaded guilty; 12 others have been charged (including eight Navy officers who were indicted in March 2017); four admirals were disciplined by the military; two others, four-star admiral Robert Willard and three-star Joe Donnelly, were known to be under investigation [3]; and more than 150 other unidentified people have been scrutinized [8, 22–24].

A March 2017 indictment made reference to "AG", a former officer in the Royal Australian Navy (RAN), who had been employed for several years as a liaison officer aboard USS Blue Ridge. On May 3, 2018, the Australian Broadcasting Corporation identified "AG" as Lieutenant Commander Alex Gillett, reporting that he had resigned from the Navy after being questioned by the Australian Federal Police [25]. A second unidentified Australian of similar rank was also reported to be under investigation [12, 26]. A memo of understanding between the U.S. Navy and the RAN allows for the possible extradition of Australian personnel to the United States for the purposes of prosecution [25].

Among the nineteen people who have pleaded guilty to federal crimes, one was Francis himself, two others were his top deputies; and sixteen others were Navy personnel [13, 22]. The highest-ranking was Rear Admiral Robert Gilbeau, who was convicted in June 2016 after pleading guilty to making false statements to investigators about his contacts with Francis [27], becoming the first Navy admiral in modern American history to be convicted of a felony while on active duty [20]. On May 17, 2017, U.S. District Judge Janis Lynn Sammartino sentenced Gilbeau to 18 months in prison, although he was allowed to continue collecting his nearly $10,000 monthly pension [28]. He was being held in FCI Englewood, a low security federal prison in Littleton, Colorado, and was released on November 1, 2018 [29, 30].

National University of Singapore, corporate governance expert Mak Yuen Teen, noted that procurement in the defense industry is particularly vulnerable to bribery and corruption. "It is usually not that transparent," with infrequent bidding for large contracts. Blowing the whistle on superior officers might also be discouraged, he indicated. "Those at the top probably thought they could get away with it as their underlings were unlikely to squeal on them."

According to its spokesman Captain Amy Derrick, the U.S. Navy canceled all contracts with GDMA as the result of a 2013 audit [12].

In the case of former Naval Intelligence chief, Vice Admiral Ted N. Branch, both the Navy and the Department of Justice declined to prosecute after a three-year investigation [31].

3 Corruption Prevention

The scope of the GDMA investigation inadvertently hindered the Navy's ability to fill senior leadership roles, unintentionally delayed hundreds of officers' careers and depleted the Navy's admiralty. Hundreds of those who had not been compromised needed investigation and clearance. That stalled promotions for years according to Ray Mabus, the then-Secretary of the Navy (SECNAV). "If Leonard Francis mentioned somebody's name, or it seemed to us that if somebody had served in a senior position in the Pacific during this time, which covered a lot of folks, they were caught up in this until their name could be pulled out." "It took in a huge percentage of flag officers, and it really hamstrung the Navy in terms of promotions, in terms of positions," with his opinion widely shared. The Department of Justice, however, had forwarded to the USN almost 450 names that they declined to prosecute. The Navy elected to take only a handful to courts-martial, issuing at least twelve letters of censure from Mabus and his successor, Richard V. Spencer, with some forty other administrative actions. In early 2018, there were roughly 170 names still pending before the Consolidated Disposition Authority (CDA). "It's really been pretty devastating to the upper ranks of the Navy," said Mabus. "There were bad people here. You gotta catch them. You got to make sure they're punished. But there were a lot of people that didn't do anything that got caught up in this [14]."

A retired Admiral said. "At least with Tailhook, people knew that if they went to Tailhook they were being looked at. Right now, as far as anyone knows, if you ever went west of Hawaii, you're being looked at." Another senior U.S. Pacific Command staffer informed a room of Australians, regarding the ongoing case, "China could never have dreamt up a way to do this much damage to the U.S. Navy's Pacific leadership [14]."

GDMA's influence paralleled the Pacific Fleet's intentions to locate vessels into ports unfamiliar with its standards for services, that had been complicated by the al Qaida attack on the USS Cole in Yemen that killed 17 sailors. GDMA was able to provide services to meet more difficult standards than competitors could, 7th Fleet officers claimed. Francis had made himself indispensable [14].

In February 2018, Admiral Bill Moran, the Vice Chief of Naval Operations, announced the implementation of increased oversight and other measures and policies to deter a repeat of the widespread corruption in the "Fat Leonard" case. Glenn Fine, the principal deputy in the Office of the Inspector General (OIG) of the Department of Defense, said the Defense Criminal Investigative Service, the criminal investigative arm of the DOD's OIG, said GDMA, Francis' contract firm, created a scheme to defraud the Navy of tens of millions of dollars via overbilling for supplying goods and services. The Navy created a Consolidated Disposition Authority (CDA) which was tasked with determining whether hundreds of Navy officers should be charged under the UCMJ, or alternatively, to be subjected to administrative actions. Fine said the CDA has already adjudicated 300-plus cases [32]. The Navy, which had been posting the names of personnel who had been fired in the case on its website, announced in May 2018, that it will discontinue the practice. California Representative Jackie Speier, the ranking member of the House Armed Services Subcommittee on Military Personnel, objected to the change in policy, characterizing it as a reduction in transparency and a barrier to the public's "right to know [33]."

The private sector used feedback surveys to assess personnel performance, a method the Army adopted in 2001. The Army's initiative helped identify serious ethics problems amongst leaders. Besides "command climate" surveys, "360" evaluations identified causes for discipline or oversight among its upper ranks. The Navy has not extended such feedback to gather information from lower-ranking personnel, however [34].

Between Fat Leonard's arrest and the end of 2016, the Navy suspended 566 vendors, permanently debarring 548 more from contracts, according to the government's Interagency Suspension and Debarment Committee. Those included Glenn Defense Marine Asia and 55 of its Pacific Rim affiliates. Public corruption watchdogs say that the internal revisions to the way the Navy deals with contractors are important, but the more difficult problem to remedy is a culture of corruption that poisoned the highest ranks of the U.S. Navy. "Very few service members get promoted because they blew the whistle on their boss," "If you don't get promoted, you get forced out of the service. If that happens before you are eligible for a retirement, you lose out on the lifetime pension. For most people, it is much safer to simply put your head down and keep going until 20 years," according to Dan

Grazier, a Straus Military Reform Project fellow at Washington, D.C.'s Project on Government Oversight (POGO) [34].

Two of those who were involved in the investigation and prosecution became finalists for the 2019 Service to America medals. They were Mark Pletcher, an assistant U.S. attorney for the southern district of California who worked on the case for six years and Jim McWhirter of the Office of Inspector General (OIG) at the Defense Criminal Investigative Service (DCIS) [35].

4 Similar Corruption

Similar details of a ship husbandry corruption case similar to "Fat Leonard" but centered in Korea were aired in July 2019. The Department of Justice has charged Sung-Yol "David" Kim, head of DK Marine Service, with counts of conspiracy and bribery, according to pleadings filed with the Eastern District of Michigan. The case also alleged cover-ups and coordination to obscure the overcharges [36].

5 Individuals Involved

Except for the cases of Gursharan Kaur Sharon Rachael (who was tried in Singapore) [37], Alex Gillett (who was tried in the Supreme Court of the Australian Capital Territory) [38], and those of five persons charged in military courts (Captain John F. Steinberger, Commander David A. Morales, Commander Jason W. Starmer, Lt. Peter Vapor, and Chief Warrant Officer Brian T. Ware), all court proceedings as of March 15, 2021, have been in U.S. federal court [8]. As of January 27, 2022, 28 have pleaded guilty. Retired Rear Admiral Bruce Loveless, Captains David Newland, James Dolan, Donald Hornbeck and David Lausman [39], Commander Mario Herrera and Lieutenant Commander Stephen Shedd had entered not guilty pleas that remained outstanding; Shedd later entered a guilty plea [40]. The trial of those seven had been scheduled to begin on November 1, 2021, but was put off until February, 2022 [39].

(See table & names on website)

References

1. Craig Whitlock, 'Fat Leonard' scandal swells; three more Navy figures charges, *The Washington Post* (May 27, 2016).
2. Jump up to:[a b c d e f] Craig Whitlock, The man who seduced the 7th Fleet, *The Washington Post* (May 27, 2016).
3. Jump up to:[a b c d e f] Fat Leonard's Crimes on the High Seas, *Rolling Stone*, Jesse Hyde, March 11, 2018. Retrieved March 21, 2018.
4. Bravo Zulu, *U.S. Navy*. Retrieved July 22, 2018.
5. Jump up to:[a b c d e f g h i j k] Timeline: Fat Leonard Case, *U.S. Naval Institute News*, Cid Standifer, March 16, 2017. Retrieved July 22, 2018.
6. Jump up to:[a b c d] Dickstein, Corey (June 20, 2018). *"Officers Censured for Bringing 'Embarrassment' in Fat Leonard Scandal"*. Stars and Stripes.
7. Trump nominee sunk by 'Fat Leonard' corruption scandal, *Stars and Stripes*, Craig Whitlock, November 26, 2018. Retrieved February 11, 2019.

8. Jump up to:$^{a\ b\ c\ d\ e\ f\ g\ h\ i\ j\ k\ l\ m\ n\ o\ p\ q\ r\ s\ t\ u\ v\ w\ x\ y\ z\ aa\ ab\ ac\ ad\ ae\ af\ ag\ ah\ ai\ aj\ ak\ al\ am\ an\ ao\ ap\ aq\ ar\ as\ at\ au\ av\ aw\ ax\ ay\ az\ ba\ bb\ bc\ bd\ be\ bf\ bg}$ Craig Whitlock & Kevin Uhrmacher, Prostitutes, vacations and cash: The Navy officials 'Fat Leonard' took down, *The Washington Post* (last updated March 26, 2018).
9. Jump up to:$^{a\ b\ c}$ Former Pearl Harbor Navy Spokesman Sentenced In Corruption Scandal, *Honolulu Civil Beat*, February 8, 2019. Retrieved February 9, 2019.
10. 'Fat Leonard' is ailing and the prosecutors are keeping his whereabouts a secret, *The Washington Post*, Craig Whitlock, May 22, 2018. Retrieved May 26, 2018.
11. Jump up to:$^{a\ b}$ "Five Years After Arrest, Navy Bribery Mastermind Testifies at Deposition", Greg Moran, September 17, 2018. Retrieved October 21, 2018.
12. Jump up to:$^{a\ b\ c}$ Living large and loose, *The Straits Times*, Tan Tam Mei, April 20, 2017. Retrieved June 30, 2017.
13. Jump up to:$^{a\ b\ c\ d\ e\ f\ g\ h\ i\ j\ k\ l}$ Craig Whitlock, Navy repeatedly dismissed evidence that 'Fat Leonard' was cheating the 7th Fleet, *The Washington Post* (December 27, 2016).
14. Jump up to:$^{a\ b\ c\ d}$ Paying the Price: The Hidden Cost of the 'Fat Leonard' Investigation, *U.S. Naval Institute*, Sam LaGrone, January 24, 2019. Retrieved May 12, 2019.
15. Perry, Tony (January 15, 2015). "Navy captain admits providing classified info in massive bribery scheme". Stars and Stripes. Retrieved October 24, 2015.
16. Jump up to:$^{a\ b\ c}$ Whitlock, Craig (January 15, 2015). "Defense contractor pleads guilty in massive bribery case". The Washington Post. Retrieved November 24, 2015.
17. Watson, Julie (January 15, 2015). "Navy bribery probe far from over despite key figure's plea". Stars and Stripes. Associated Press. Retrieved November 24, 2015.
18. Jump up to:$^{a\ b}$ Admiral's illicit history with 'Fat Leonard' goes back 20 years, prosecutors say, *The Washington Post*, Craig Whitlock, April 19, 2017. Retrieved June 11, 2017.
19. Gault, Matthew. "How a Malaysian Playboy Controlled the Most Powerful Naval Force on the Planet". Medium. Retrieved April 14, 2015.
20. Jump up to:$^{a\ b\ c}$ Craig Whitlock, Navy officers convicted of corruption in 'Fat Leonard' scandal haven't lost their pensions, *The Washington Post* (March 18, 2017).
21. Jump up to:$^{a\ b}$ Navy files first charges under military law in 'Fat Leonard' scandal, *The Washington Post*, Craig Whitlock, June 19, 2017. Retrieved June 24, 2017.
22. Jump up to:$^{a\ b\ c\ d\ e\ f\ g\ h\ i\ j\ k\ l\ m}$ Navy's widening bribery and sex scandal has many Hawaii connections 18-month sentence for ex-Navy commander in 'Fat Leonard' bribery scandal, *Honolulu Civil Beat*, Kirstin Downey, June 7, 2017. Retrieved June 11, 2017.
23. Jump up to:$^{a\ b\ c\ d}$ Navy commander latest to plead guilty in 'Fat Leonard' bribery scandal, *U-T San Diego*, Kristina Davis, August 15, 2017. Retrieved September 4, 2017.
24. 'Fat Leonard' probe expands to ensnare more than 60 admirals, *The Washington Post*, Craig Whitlock, November 5, 2017. Retrieved November 15, 2017.
25. Jump up to:$^{a\ b\ c\ d\ e}$ Fat Leonard: Australian Navy Officer revealed as suspect in massive US Navy bribery and fraud conspiracy *ABC Australia*, May 3, 2018. Retrieved May 3, 2018.
26. Senior Australian sailors investigated over US Navy 'Fat Leonard' sex and bribery scandal, *ABC Australia*, Andrew Greene, March 16, 2017. Retrieved July 15, 2017.
27. Craig Whitlock, Admiral, seven others charged with corruption in new 'Fat Leonard' indictment, *The Washington Post* (March 14, 2017).
28. Craig Whitlock; Tony Perry (May 17, 2017). "Former admiral sentenced to 18 months in 'Fat Leonard' case". The Washington Post. Retrieved May 18, 2017.
29. FCI Englewood, *Federal Bureau of Prisons*. Retrieved July 22, 2018.
30. Robert Gilbeau Register Number: 56978-298, *Federal Bureau of Prisons*. Retrieved February 11, 2019.
31. Former Naval Intelligence Chief cleared in Fat Leonard case, *USNI News*, Sam LaGrone, September 22, 2017. Retrieved September 29, 2017.
32. Navy admiral: New measures in place to thwart another 'Fat Leonard' corruption scandal, *Stars and Stripes*, Claudia Grisales, February 7, 2018. Retrieved February 9, 2018.

33. Navy no longer will announce when a commander is fired for misconduct, *USA Today*, Tom Vanden Brook, May 2, 2018. Retrieved May 22, 2018.
34. Jump up to:[a] [b] Has Navy culture truly changed after Fat Leonard corruption crisis, *U-T San Diego*, Carl Prine, July 29, 2017. Retrieved May 12, 2019.
35. Navy bribery case steams on, *Federal News Network*, Tom Temin. July 12, 2019. Retrieved October 2, 2019.
36. Korean Fat Leonard? Feds probe new US Navy corruption case in Asia, *Defense News*, David B. Larter, July 30, 2019. Retrieved October 24, 2019.
37. Jump up to:[a] [b] Singapore woman in 'Fat Leonard' US Navy bribery scandal for leaking confidential info in exchange for cash, *South China Morning Post*, July 7, 2018. Retrieved July 10, 2018.
38. Jump up to:[a] [b] *Back, Alexandra (2019-02-14). "Fat Leonard scandal: Australian Navy lieutenant commander avoids jail". Canberra Times. Canberra. Retrieved 2021-11-26.*
39. Jump up to:[a] [b] [c] [d] [e] Retired Marine Corps colonel pleads guilty for role in 'Fat Leonard' scandal, *Navy Times*, Geoff Ziezulewicz, September 7, 2021.
40. Jump up to:[a] [b] "US Navy officer 'bribed by cash and prostitutes'". BBC News. 27 January 2022. Retrieved 27 January 2022.
41. Jump up to:[a] [b] Checkpoint Highest-ranking Navy officer yet sentenced in sex-for-secrets scandal, *The Washington Post*, Craig Whitlock March 25, 2016. Retrieved June 10, 2017.
42. Jump up to:[a] [b] Navy Admiral Plus Eight Officers Indicted in "Fat Leonard" Bribery and Sex Scandal, *Coronado Times*, March 16, 2017. Retrieved June 10, 2017.
43. Greg Moran, Another Navy officer charged in 'Fat Leonard' bribery scandal, *U-T San Diego* (February 16, 2017).
44. Jump up to:[a] [b] Navy May Move 'Fat Leonard' Court-Martial To San Diego, *KPBS-FM*, Steve Walsh, February 27, 2018. Retrieved March 20, 2018. He was found guilty of two lesser counts and was sentenced to 165 days in the brig, $40,000 in fines and assessments, but not discharged.
45. Jump up to:[a] [b] [c] "Navy's 'Fat Leonard' case implodes", *Navy Times*, Mark D. Faram, September 1, 2018. Retrieved September 6, 2018.
46. Top Stories 2019: Law, Policy and the Navy, *USNI*, Sam LaGrone, January 2, 2020, Retrieved February 26, 2020.
47. Court docket, Southern District of California. Retrieved June 10, 2017.
48. Another prison term handed down in Fat Leonard affair, *MarineLog*, March 20, 2017. Retrieved June 12, 2017.
49. Alex Wisidagama Register Number: 45416-298, *Federal Bureau of Prisons*. Retrieved February 11, 2019.
50. Jump up to:[a] [b] Another former executive for 'Fat Leonard' extradited to San Diego in Navy scandal, *San Diego Union-Tribune*, Kristina David, March 9, 2021. Retrieved March 14, 2021.
51. Jump up to:[a] [b] Former Australian Navy officer Alexander Gillett avoids jail over Fat Leonard bribery case, *ABC Net Australia*, Elizabeth Byrne, February 14, 2019. Retrieved April 6, 2019.
52. Jump up to:[a] [b] Craig Whitlock, Navy admiral pleads guilty in 'Fat Leonard' corruption scandal, *The Washington Post* (June 9, 2016).
53. [1][permanent dead link], *Federal Bureau of Prisons*. Retrieved February 11, 2019.
54. Robert Gilbeau Register Number: 56978-298, *Federal Bureau of Prisons*. Retrieved July 23, 2018.
55. *Davis, Kristina (May 17, 2017). "Former Navy admiral gets prison in 'Fat Leonard' bribery scam". U-T San Diego. Retrieved May 18, 2017.*
56. Craig Whitlock, Retired Navy captain becomes latest officer to admit taking bribes and prostitutes from 'Fat Leonard', *The Washington Post* (November 15, 2016).
57. Michael George Brooks Register Number: 90044-083, *Federal Bureau of Prisons*. Retrieved June 30, 2019.
58. Retired US Navy captain sentenced in 'Fat Leonard' case, CNN, Zachary Cohen, June 16, 2017. Retrieved June 18, 2017.

59. Tony Perry, Navy captain admits providing classified information as part of bribery scheme, *Los Angeles Times* (January 15, 2015).
60. Daniel Dusek Register Number: 43017-298, *Federal Bureau of Prisons*. Retrieved February 11, 2019.
61. 18-month sentence for ex-Navy commander in 'Fat Leonard' bribery scandal, *Navy Times*, Jennifer Sinco Kelleher, September 12, 2017. Retrieved September 16, 2017.
62. David Kapaun, *Federal Bureau of Prisons*. Retrieved April 6, 2019.
63. 'Fat Leonard' bribery scandal claims Navy officer who escaped Cambodia's killing fields as a child, *The Washington Post*, Craig Whitlock, April 29, 2016. Retrieved June 12, 2017.
64. Michael Misiewicz Register Number: 39883-013, *Federal Bureau of Prisons*. Retrieved February 11, 2019.
65. Greg Moran, Navy commander sentenced to 6 years in prison in 'Fat Leonard' bribery scandal, *Los Angeles Times* (April 29, 2016).
66. Slavin, Erik (January 6, 2015). "Former Yokosuka commander pleads guilty in Navy bribery scheme". Stars and Stripes. Retrieved October 24, 2015.
67. U.S. Navy Officer Sentenced to 40 Months in Prison for Selling Classified Ship Schedules as Part of Navy Bribery Probe, *Department of Justice*, January 29, 2016. Retrieved December 12, 2018.
68. Navy officer gets prison Fat Leonard bribery case, *Times of San Diego*, Hoa Quach, January 12, 2017. Retrieved June 22, 2017.
69. Craig Whitlock, Another Navy officer gets prison time for taking bribes and prostitutes from 'Fat Leonard', *The Washington Post* (January 12, 2017).
70. Gentry Debord Register Number: 56307-298, *Federal Bureau of Prisons*. Retrieved April 6, 2019.
71. One-time top Navy supply officer gets 30 months in prison for role in 'Fat Leonard' fraud scandal, *U-T San Diego* (January 12, 2017).
72. Ex-Navy officer gets prison in 'Fat Leonard' bribery case, *KSWB*, September 19, 2018.
73. Troy Amundson Register Number: 67630-298, *Federal Bureau of Prisons*. Retrieved October 18, 2021.
74. Brad Lendon (February 1, 2018) US Navy commander pleads guilty to bribery charge in 'Fat Leonard' scandal CNN. Retrieved February 1, 2018
75. Navy repeatedly dismissed evidence that 'Fat Leonard' was cheating the 7th Fleet, *The Washington Post*, Craig Whitlock, December 27, 2016. Retrieved June 18, 2017.
76. Jump up to:[a][b] Craig Whitlock, Former Navy official gets six years in prison for taking $350,000 in bribes from 'Fat Leonard', *The Washington Post* (December 2, 2016).
77. Morgantown FCI, *Federal Bureau of Prisons*. Retrieved July 22, 2018.
78. Paul Simpkins Register Number: 85297-083, *Federal Bureau of Prisons*. Retrieved July 22, 2018.
79. Jump up to:[a][b][c][d][e] 9 Navy officers, including an admiral, indicted in 'Fat Leonard' bribery scandal, *U-T San Diego*, March 14, 2017. Retrieved June 12, 2017.
80. Jump up to:[a][b][c][d][e][f][g][h][i][j] Meet Stephen Shedd, Prostitute-Loving Navy Exec in Fat Leonard Scandal, *Westword*, April 17, 2017. Retrieved July 4, 2017.
81. Bruce Loveless Register Number: 60755-298, *Federal Bureau of Prisons*. Retrieved June 30, 2019.
82. Stanfield, Frank. "No trial date set for Villager indicted in Navy scandal". DAILY COMMERCIAL. Gannett. Retrieved 14 August 2021.
83. Stephen Shedd Register Number: 44061-013, *Federal Bureau of Prisons*. Retrieved June 30, 2019.
84. Fighting Back: This Former Navy Officer Isn't Rolling Over In The Fat Leonard Bribery Case, *Honolulu Civil Beat*, Kirstin Downey, August 2, 2017. Retrieved August 2, 2017.
85. Jump up to:[a][b] Three U.S. Navy officers newly charged in "Fat Leonard" case, *Defense News*, Christopher P. Cavas, May 27, 2016. Retrieved January 17, 2019.

86. Navy commander sentenced for role in "Fat Leonard" bribery scandal, *CBS News*, December 1, 2017. Retrieved December 10, 2017.
87. First military case in Fat Leonard bribery scandal begins, *Navy Times*, Ben Finley (AP), June 26, 2017. Retrieved June 29, 2017.
88. Jump up to:[a] [b] [c] Navy commander latest to be charged in 'Fat Leonard' scandal, *Navy Times*, Mark D. Faram, September 1, 2017. Retrieved September 4, 2017.
89. Former Navy fighter pilot to be tried by military in "Fat Leonard" bribery scandal, *The Virginian-Pilot*, Courtney Mabeus, September 13, 2017. September 16, 2017.
90. Jump up to:[a] [b] [c] Two Navy officers plead guilty in "Fat Leonard" scandal in Norfolk courtrooms, *Virginian-Pilot*, Courtney Mabeus, March 7, 2018. Retrieved March 14, 2018.
91. Craig Whitlock, Another Navy officer pleads guilty to taking bribes from 'Fat Leonard', *The Washington Post* (August 18, 2017).
92. Navy Captain To Face Charges In Ongoing 'Fat Leonard' Scandal, *The Virginian-Pilot*, Courtney Mabeus, December 5, 2017. Retrieved December 10, 2017.
93. First military trial in Navy's 'Fat Leonard' scandal results in guilty plea in Norfolk, *The Virginian-Pilot*, Brock Vergakis, January 12, 2018. Retrieved January 12, 2018.
94. Trial set for navy supply officer accused of patronizing prostitutes, *Navy Times*, Mark D. Faram, January 31, 2018. Retrieved February 13, 2018.
95. Jump up to:[a] [b] 2 Former Executives Plead Guilty in Multi-Million Dollar Navy Bribery Scheme with 'Fat Leonard', *NBC San Diego*, Jaspreet Kaur, May 10, 2017. Retrieved June 24, 2017.
96. Jump up to:[a] [b] [c] [d] Two more Navy officers censured for Fat Leonard-related infractions, *Navy Times*, Geoff Ziezulewicz, May 16, 2019. Retrieved May 20, 2019.
97. Jump up to:[a] [b] [c] [d] Navy hired retired officer despite 'Fat Leonard' misconduct investigation, *Navy Times*, Geoff Ziezulewicz, June 22, 2018. Retrieved December 15, 2018.
98. Navy Office of Information, Rear Adm. Adrian Jansen Receives NJP at Admiral's Mast, *NNS*, Story Number: NNS170210-16 Release Date: October 2, 2017
99. U.S. Navy accepted gifts from Leonard, *Stars and Stripes*, Andrew Dyer, August 5, 2019. Retrieved September 4, 2019.
100. Jump up to:[a] [b] Trump nominee sunk by 'Fat Leonard' corruption scandal, *The Washington Post*, Craig Whitlock, November 20, 2018. Retrieved November 29, 2018.
101. Jump up to:[a] [b] [c] [d] [e] [f] [g] [h] Slavin, Erik (February 10, 2015). "3 rear admirals forced out amid massive Navy bribery investigation". *Stars and Stripes*.
102. Tritten, Travis J. (March 10, 2015). "McCaskill wants 'Fat Leonard' discipline to go 'to the very top'". *Stars and Stripes*.
103. Navy upbraids retired admiral caught up in 'Fat Leonard' scandal, *U-T San Diego*, Carl Prine, November 29, 2017. Retrieved December 10, 2017.
104. Whitlock, Craig (April 1, 2018). "How 'Fat Leonard' affected Pentagon's pick to lead Joint Chiefs". *The Washington Post*. Retrieved April 2, 2018.
105. Jump up to:[a] [b] [c] [d] [e] New indictments, same perks of hotels, booze, and sex in 'Fat Leonard' Navy bribery scandal, *Union Tribune*, John Wilkins, August 17, 2018. Retrieved August 19, 2018.
106. Jump up to:[a] [b] Retired CPO Gets Prison in Continuing Federal Probe into 'Fat Leonard' Navy Corruption Scandal, *USNI*, Gidget Fuentes, November 3, 2020. Retrieved November 27, 2020.
107. Jump up to:[a] [b] [c] 'Fat Leonard' scandal grows with indictment of three more retired Navy officials, *The Washington Post*, Craig Whitlock, August 17, 2018. Retrieved August 18, 2018.
108. Jump up to:[a] [b] Two retired Navy officials plead guilty in 'Fat Leonard' bribery prosecution, *The San Diego Union-Tribune*, Kristina Davis, June 9, 2020. Retrieved June 11, 2020.
109. Former Navy official pleads guilty in 'Fat Leonard' probe just weeks after indictment, *Union Tribune*, Kristina Davis, September 5, 2018. Retrieved September 6, 2018.

110. Former Master Chief Petty Officer Sentenced in Sweeping U.S. Navy Corruption and Fraud Probe, *United States Attorney for the Southern District of California*, Department of Justice, November 13, 2018.
111. Ricarte David Register Number: 78499-298, *Federal Bureau of Prisons*. Retrieved February 26, 2020.
112. Former Navy captain pleads guilty to ghostwriting 'Fat Leonard' emails, CNN, Euan McKirdy, November 14, 2018. Retrieved November 23, 2018.
113. Retired Navy Captain once assigned to Norfolk sentenced in 'Fat Leonard' corruption case, *WTKR*, Julia Varnier, February 12, 2019. Retrieved April 5, 2019.
114. Jeffrey Breslau Register Number: 79498-298, *Federal Bureau of Prisons*. Retrieved February 11, 2018.

Part II
Fraud and Corruption Materials

Chapter 11
International Treaties/Documents

11.1 United Nations Convention Against Corruption (UN CAC)

UNODC Summary[1] (Tuesday 25 January 2022): The United Nations Convention against Corruption is the only legally binding universal anti-corruption instrument. The Convention's far-reaching approach and the mandatory character of many of its provisions make it a unique tool for developing a comprehensive response to a global problem. The Convention covers five main areas: preventive measures, criminalization and law enforcement, international cooperation, asset recovery, and technical assistance and information exchange. The Convention covers many different forms of corruption, such as bribery, trading in influence, abuse of functions, and various acts of corruption in the private sector. A highlight of the Convention is the inclusion of a specific chapter on asset recovery, aimed at returning assets to their rightful owners, including countries from which they had been taken illicitly. The vast majority of United Nations Member States are parties to the Convention.

The United Nations Convention against Corruption is the only legally binding universal anti-corruption instrument. The Convention's far-reaching approach and the mandatory character of many of its provisions make it a unique tool for developing a comprehensive response to a global problem. The vast majority of United Nations Member States are parties to the Convention.[2]

---

[1] https://www.unodc.org/unodc/en/treaties/CAC/
[2] https://www.unodc.org/unodc/en/corruption/uncac.html

United Nations Convention against Corruption[3]
Preamble

The States Parties to this Convention,

Concerned about the seriousness of problems and threats posed by corruption to the stability and security of societies, undermining the institutions and values of democracy, ethical values and justice and jeopardizing sustainable development and the rule of law,

Concerned also about the links between corruption and other forms of crime, in particular organized crime and economic crime, including money-laundering,

Concerned further about cases of corruption that involve vast quantities of assets, which may constitute a substantial proportion of the resources of States, and that threaten the political stability and sustainable development of those States,

Convinced that corruption is no longer a local matter but a transnational phenomenon that affects all societies and economies, making international cooperation to prevent and control it essential,

Convinced also that a comprehensive and multidisciplinary approach is required to prevent and combat corruption effectively,

Convinced further that the availability of technical assistance can play an important role in enhancing the ability of States, including by strengthening capacity and by institution-building, to prevent and combat corruption effectively,

Convinced that the illicit acquisition of personal wealth can be particularly damaging to democratic institutions, national economies and the rule of law,

Determined to prevent, detect and deter in a more effective manner international transfers of illicitly acquired assets and to strengthen international cooperation in asset recovery,

Acknowledging the fundamental principles of due process of law in criminal proceedings and in civil or administrative proceedings to adjudicate property rights,

Bearing in mind that the prevention and eradication of corruption is a responsibility of all States and that they must cooperate with one another, with the support and involvement of individuals and groups outside the public sector, such as civil society, non-governmental organizations and community-based organizations, if their efforts in this area are to be effective,

Bearing also in mind the principles of proper management of public affairs and public property, fairness, responsibility and equality before the law and the need to safeguard integrity and to foster a culture of rejection of corruption,

Commending the work of the Commission on Crime Prevention and Criminal Justice and the United Nations Office on Drugs and Crime in preventing and combating corruption,

Recalling the work carried out by other international and regional organi-zations in this field, including the activities of the African Union, the Council of Europe, the Customs Cooperation Council (also known as the World Customs Organization), the

---

[3] https://www.unodc.org/documents/treaties/UNCAC/Publications/Convention/08-50026_E.pdf

European Union, the League of Arab States, the Organisation for Economic Cooperation and Development and the Organization of American States,

Taking note with appreciation of multilateral instruments to prevent and combat corruption, including, inter alia, the Inter-American Convention against Corruption, adopted by the Organization of American States on 29 March 1996[4], the Convention on the Fight against Corruption involving Officials of the European Communities or Officials of Member States of the European Union, adopted by the Council of the European Union on 26 May 1997[5], the Convention on Combating Bribery of Foreign Public Officials in International Business Transactions, adopted by the Organisation for Economic Cooperation and Development on 21 November 1997[6], the Criminal Law Convention on Corruption, adopted by the Committee of Ministers of the Council of Europe on 27 January 1999[7], the Civil Law Convention on Corruption, adopted by the Committee of Ministers of the Council of Europe on 4 November 1999[8], and the African Union Convention on Preventing and Combating Corruption, adopted by the Heads of State and Government of the African Union on 12 July 2003,

Welcoming the entry into force on 29 September 2003 of the United Nations Convention against Transnational Organized Crime,

Have agreed as follows:

Chapter I General Provisions
Article 1. Statement of Purpose

The purposes of this Convention are:

(a) To promote and strengthen measures to prevent and combat corruption more efficiently and effectively;
(b) To promote, facilitate and support international cooperation and technical assistance in the prevention of and fight against corruption, including in asset recovery;
(c) To promote integrity, accountability and proper management of public affairs and public property.

Article 2. Use of Terms

For the purposes of this Convention:

(a) "Public official" shall mean: (i) any person holding a legislative, executive, administrative or judicial office of a State Party, whether appointed or elected, whether permanent or temporary, whether paid or unpaid, irrespective of that person's seniority; (ii) any other person who performs a public function,

---

[4] See E/1996/99.
[5] Official Journal of the European Communities, C 195, 25 June 1997.
[6] See Corruption and Integrity Improvement Initiatives in Developing Countries (United Nations publication, Sales No. E.98.III.B.18).
[7] https://rm.coe.int/168007f3f5
[8] https://rm.coe.int/168007f3f6

including for a public agency or public enterprise, or provides a public service, as defined in the domestic law of the State Party and as applied in the pertinent area of law of that State Party; (iii) any other person defined as a "public official" in the domestic law of a State Party. However, for the purpose of some specific measures contained in chapter II of this Convention, "public official" may mean any person who performs a public function or provides a public service as defined in the domestic law of the State Party and as applied in the pertinent area of law of that State Party;

(b) "Foreign public official" shall mean any person holding a legislative, executive, administrative or judicial office of a foreign country, whether appointed or elected; and any person exercising a public function for a foreign country, including for a public agency or public enterprise;

(c) "Official of a public international organization" shall mean an international civil servant or any person who is authorized by such an organization to act on behalf of that organization;

(d) "Property" shall mean assets of every kind, whether corporeal or incorporeal, movable or immovable, tangible or intangible, and legal documents or instruments evidencing title to or interest in such assets;

(e) "Proceeds of crime" shall mean any property derived from or obtained, directly or indirectly, through the commission of an offence;

(f) "Freezing" or "seizure" shall mean temporarily prohibiting the transfer, conversion, disposition or movement of property or temporarily assuming custody or control of property on the basis of an order issued by a court or other competent authority;

(g) "Confiscation", which includes forfeiture where applicable, shall mean the permanent deprivation of property by order of a court or other competent authority;

(h) "Predicate offence" shall mean any offence as a result of which proceeds have been generated that may become the subject of an offence as defined in article 23 of this Convention;

(i) "Controlled delivery" shall mean the technique of allowing illicit or suspect consignments to pass out of, through or into the territory of one or more States, with the knowledge and under the supervision of their competent authorities, with a view to the investigation of an offence and the identification of persons involved in the commission of the offence.

Council of Europe, European Treaty Series, No. 173.
Ibid., No. 174.
General Assembly resolution 55/25, annex I.

Article 3. Scope of Application

1. This Convention shall apply, in accordance with its terms, to the prevention, investigation and prosecution of corruption and to the freezing, seizure, confiscation and return of the proceeds of offences established in accordance with this Convention.

2. For the purposes of implementing this Convention, it shall not be necessary, except as otherwise stated herein, for the offences set forth in it to result in damage or harm to state property.

Article 4. Protection of Sovereignty

1. States Parties shall carry out their obligations under this Convention in a manner consistent with the principles of sovereign equality and territorial integrity of States and that of non-intervention in the domestic affairs of other States.
2. Nothing in this Convention shall entitle a State Party to undertake in the territory of another State the exercise of jurisdiction and performance of functions that are reserved exclusively for the authorities of that other State by its domestic law.

Chapter II Preventive Measures
Article 5. Preventive Anti-corruption Policies and Practices

1. Each State Party shall, in accordance with the fundamental principles of its legal system, develop and implement or maintain effective, coordinated anti-corruption policies that promote the participation of society and reflect the principles of the rule of law, proper management of public affairs and public property, integrity, transparency and accountability.
2. Each State Party shall endeavour to establish and promote effective practices aimed at the prevention of corruption.
3. Each State Party shall endeavour to periodically evaluate relevant legal instruments and administrative measures with a view to determining their adequacy to prevent and fight corruption.
4. States Parties shall, as appropriate and in accordance with the fundamental principles of their legal system, collaborate with each other and with relevant international and regional organizations in promoting and developing the measures referred to in this article. That collaboration may include participation in international programmes and projects aimed at the prevention of corruption.

Article 6. Preventive Anti-corruption Body or Bodies

1. Each State Party shall, in accordance with the fundamental principles of its legal system, ensure the existence of a body or bodies, as appropriate, that prevent corruption by such means as:

    (a) Implementing the policies referred to in article 5 of this Convention and, where appropriate, overseeing and coordinating the implementation of those policies;
    (b) Increasing and disseminating knowledge about the prevention of corruption.

2. Each State Party shall grant the body or bodies referred to in paragraph 1 of this article the necessary independence, in accordance with the fundamental principles of its legal system, to enable the body or bodies to carry out its or their functions effectively and free from any undue influence. The necessary material resources and specialized staff, as well as the training that such staff may require to carry out their functions, should be provided.

3. Each State Party shall inform the Secretary-General of the United Nations of the name and address of the authority or authorities that may assist other States Parties in developing and implementing specific measures for the prevention of corruption.

Article 7. Public Sector

1. Each State Party shall, where appropriate and in accordance with the fundamental principles of its legal system, endeavour to adopt, maintain and strengthen systems for the recruitment, hiring, retention, promotion and retirement of civil servants and, where appropriate, other non-elected public officials:

   (a) That are based on principles of efficiency, transparency and objective criteria such as merit, equity and aptitude;
   (b) That include adequate procedures for the selection and training of individuals for public positions considered especially vulnerable to corruption and the rotation, where appropriate, of such individuals to other positions;
   (c) That promote adequate remuneration and equitable pay scales, taking into account the level of economic development of the State Party;
   (d) That promote education and training programmes to enable them to meet the requirements for the correct, honourable and proper performance of public functions and that provide them with specialized and appropriate training to enhance their awareness of the risks of corruption inherent in the performance of their functions. Such programmes may make reference to codes or standards of conduct in applicable areas.

2. Each State Party shall also consider adopting appropriate legislative and administrative measures, consistent with the objectives of this Convention and in accordance with the fundamental principles of its domestic law, to prescribe criteria concerning candidature for and election to public office.
3. Each State Party shall also consider taking appropriate legislative and administrative measures, consistent with the objectives of this Convention and in accordance with the fundamental principles of its domestic law, to enhance transparency in the funding of candidatures for elected public office and, where applicable, the funding of political parties.
4. Each State Party shall, in accordance with the fundamental principles of its domestic law, endeavour to adopt, maintain and strengthen systems that promote transparency and prevent conflicts of interest.

Article 8. Codes of Conduct for Public Officials

1. In order to fight corruption, each State Party shall promote, inter alia, integrity, honesty and responsibility among its public officials, in accordance with the fundamental principles of its legal system.
2. In particular, each State Party shall endeavour to apply, within its own institutional and legal systems, codes or standards of conduct for the correct, honourable and proper performance of public functions.

3. For the purposes of implementing the provisions of this article, each State Party shall, where appropriate and in accordance with the fundamental principles of its legal system, take note of the relevant initiatives of regional, interregional and multilateral organizations, such as the International Code of Conduct for Public Officials contained in the annex to General Assembly resolution 51/59 of 12 December 1996.
4. Each State Party shall also consider, in accordance with the fundamental principles of its domestic law, establishing measures and systems to facilitate the reporting by public officials of acts of corruption to appropriate authorities, when such acts come to their notice in the performance of their functions.
5. Each State Party shall endeavour, where appropriate and in accordance with the fundamental principles of its domestic law, to establish measures and systems requiring public officials to make declarations to appropriate authorities regarding, inter alia, their outside activities, employment, investments, assets and substantial gifts or benefits from which a conflict of interest may result with respect to their functions as public officials.
6. Each State Party shall consider taking, in accordance with the fundamental principles of its domestic law, disciplinary or other measures against public officials who violate the codes or standards established in accordance with this article.

Article 9. Public Procurement and Management of Public Finances

1. Each State Party shall, in accordance with the fundamental principles of its legal system, take the necessary steps to establish appropriate systems of procurement, based on transparency, competition and objective criteria in decision-making, that are effective, inter alia, in preventing corruption. Such systems, which may take into account appropriate threshold values in their application, shall address, inter alia:

   (a) The public distribution of information relating to procurement procedures and contracts, including information on invitations to tender and relevant or pertinent information on the award of contracts, allowing potential tenderers sufficient time to prepare and submit their tenders;
   (b) The establishment, in advance, of conditions for participation, including selection and award criteria and tendering rules, and their publication;
   (c) The use of objective and predetermined criteria for public procurement decisions, in order to facilitate the subsequent verification of the correct application of the rules or procedures;
   (d) An effective system of domestic review, including an effective system of appeal, to ensure legal recourse and remedies in the event that the rules or procedures established pursuant to this paragraph are not followed;
   (e) Where appropriate, measures to regulate matters regarding personnel responsible for procurement, such as declaration of interest in particular public procurements, screening procedures and training requirements.

2. Each State Party shall, in accordance with the fundamental principles of its legal system, take appropriate measures to promote transparency and accountability in the management of public finances. Such measures shall encompass, inter alia:

(a) Procedures for the adoption of the national budget;
(b) Timely reporting on revenue and expenditure;
(c) A system of accounting and auditing standards and related oversight;
(d) Effective and efficient systems of risk management and internal control; and
(e) Where appropriate, corrective action in the case of failure to comply with the requirements established in this paragraph.

3. Each State Party shall take such civil and administrative measures as may be necessary, in accordance with the fundamental principles of its domestic law, to preserve the integrity of accounting books, records, financial statements or other documents related to public expenditure and revenue and to prevent the falsification of such documents.

Article 10. Public Reporting

Taking into account the need to combat corruption, each State Party shall, in accordance with the fundamental principles of its domestic law, take such measures as may be necessary to enhance transparency in its public administration, including with regard to its organization, functioning and decision-making processes, where appropriate. Such measures may include, inter alia:

(a) Adopting procedures or regulations allowing members of the general public to obtain, where appropriate, information on the organization, functioning and decision-making processes of its public administration and, with due regard for the protection of privacy and personal data, on decisions and legal acts that concern members of the public;
(b) Simplifying administrative procedures, where appropriate, in order to facilitate public access to the competent decision-making authorities; and
(c) Publishing information, which may include periodic reports on the risks of corruption in its public administration.

Article 11. Measures Relating to the Judiciary and Prosecution Services

1. Bearing in mind the independence of the judiciary and its crucial role in combating corruption, each State Party shall, in accordance with the fundamental principles of its legal system and without prejudice to judicial independence, take measures to strengthen integrity and to prevent opportunities for corruption among members of the judiciary. Such measures may include rules with respect to the conduct of members of the judiciary.
2. Measures to the same effect as those taken pursuant to paragraph 1 of this article may be introduced and applied within the prosecution service in those States Parties where it does not form part of the judiciary but enjoys independence similar to that of the judicial service.

Article 12. Private Sector

1. Each State Party shall take measures, in accordance with the fundamental principles of its domestic law, to prevent corruption involving the private sector, enhance accounting and auditing standards in the private sector and, where appropriate, provide effective, proportionate and dissuasive civil, administrative or criminal penalties for failure to comply with such measures.
2. Measures to achieve these ends may include, inter alia:

   (a) Promoting cooperation between law enforcement agencies and relevant private entities;
   (b) Promoting the development of standards and procedures designed to safeguard the integrity of relevant private entities, including codes of conduct for the correct, honourable and proper performance of the activities of business and all relevant professions and the prevention of conflicts of interest, and for the promotion of the use of good commercial practices among businesses and in the contractual relations of businesses with the State;
   (c) Promoting transparency among private entities, including, where appropriate, measures regarding the identity of legal and natural persons involved in the establishment and management of corporate entities;
   (d) Preventing the misuse of procedures regulating private entities, including procedures regarding subsidies and licences granted by public authorities for commercial activities;
   (e) Preventing conflicts of interest by imposing restrictions, as appropriate and for a reasonable period of time, on the professional activities of former public officials or on the employment of public officials by the private sector after their resignation or retirement, where such activities or employment relate directly to the functions held or supervised by those public officials during their tenure;
   (f) Ensuring that private enterprises, taking into account their structure and size, have sufficient internal auditing controls to assist in preventing and detecting acts of corruption and that the accounts and required financial statements of such private enterprises are subject to appropriate auditing and certification procedures.

3. In order to prevent corruption, each State Party shall take such measures as may be necessary, in accordance with its domestic laws and regulations regarding the maintenance of books and records, financial statement disclosures and accounting and auditing standards, to prohibit the following acts carried out for the purpose of committing any of the offences established in accordance with this Convention:

   (a) The establishment of off-the-books accounts;
   (b) The making of off-the-books or inadequately identified transactions;
   (c) The recording of non-existent expenditure;
   (d) The entry of liabilities with incorrect identification of their objects;
   (e) The use of false documents; and

(f) The intentional destruction of bookkeeping documents earlier than foreseen by the law.

4. Each State Party shall disallow the tax deductibility of expenses that constitute bribes, the latter being one of the constituent elements of the offences established in accordance with articles 15 and 16 of this Convention and, where appropriate, other expenses incurred in furtherance of corrupt conduct.

Article 13. Participation of Society

1. Each State Party shall take appropriate measures, within its means and in accordance with fundamental principles of its domestic law, to promote the active participation of individuals and groups outside the public sector, such as civil society, non-governmental organizations and community-based organizations, in the prevention of and the fight against corruption and to raise public awareness regarding the existence, causes and gravity of and the threat posed by corruption. This participation should be strengthened by such measures as:

   (a) Enhancing the transparency of and promoting the contribution of the public to decision-making processes;
   (b) Ensuring that the public has effective access to information;
   (c) Undertaking public information activities that contribute to non-tolerance of corruption, as well as public education programmes, including school and university curricula;
   (d) Respecting, promoting and protecting the freedom to seek, receive, publish and disseminate information concerning corruption. That freedom may be subject to certain restrictions, but these shall only be such as are provided for by law and are necessary:

   (i) For respect of the rights or reputations of others;
   (ii) For the protection of national security or ordre public or of public health or morals.

2. Each State Party shall take appropriate measures to ensure that the relevant anti-corruption bodies referred to in this Convention are known to the public and shall provide access to such bodies, where appropriate, for the reporting, including anonymously, of any incidents that may be considered to constitute an offence established in accordance with this Convention.

Article 14. Measures to Prevent Money-Laundering

1. Each State Party shall:

   (a) Institute a comprehensive domestic regulatory and supervisory regime for banks and non-bank financial institutions, including natural or legal persons that provide formal or informal services for the transmission of money or value and, where appropriate, other bodies particularly susceptible to money-laundering, within its competence, in order to deter and detect all forms of money-laundering, which regime shall emphasize requirements for customer

and, where appropriate, beneficial owner identification, record-keeping and the reporting of suspicious transactions;
(b) Without prejudice to article 46 of this Convention, ensure that administrative, regulatory, law enforcement and other authorities dedicated to combating money-laundering (including, where appropriate under domestic law, judicial authorities) have the ability to cooperate and exchange information at the national and international levels within the conditions prescribed by its domestic law and, to that end, shall consider the establishment of a financial intelligence unit to serve as a national centre for the collection, analysis and dissemination of information regarding potential money-laundering.

2. States Parties shall consider implementing feasible measures to detect and monitor the movement of cash and appropriate negotiable instruments across their borders, subject to safeguards to ensure proper use of information and without impeding in any way the movement of legitimate capital. Such measures may include a requirement that individuals and businesses report the cross-border transfer of substantial quantities of cash and appropriate negotiable instruments.
3. States Parties shall consider implementing appropriate and feasible measures to require financial institutions, including money remitters:

   (a) To include on forms for the electronic transfer of funds and related messages accurate and meaningful information on the originator;
   (b) To maintain such information throughout the payment chain; and
   (c) To apply enhanced scrutiny to transfers of funds that do not contain complete information on the originator.

4. In establishing a domestic regulatory and supervisory regime under the terms of this article, and without prejudice to any other article of this Convention, States Parties are called upon to use as a guideline the relevant initiatives of regional, interregional and multilateral organizations against money-laundering.
5. States Parties shall endeavour to develop and promote global, regional, subregional and bilateral cooperation among judicial, law enforcement and financial regulatory authorities in order to combat money-laundering.

Chapter III Criminalization and Law Enforcement
Article 15. Bribery of National Public Officials

Each State Party shall adopt such legislative and other measures as may be necessary to establish as criminal offences, when committed intentionally:

(a) The promise, offering or giving, to a public official, directly or indirectly, of an undue advantage, for the official himself or herself or another person or entity, in order that the official act or refrain from acting in the exercise of his or her official duties;
(b) The solicitation or acceptance by a public official, directly or indirectly, of an undue advantage, for the official himself or herself or another person or entity, in order that the official act or refrain from acting in the exercise of his or her official duties.

Article 16. Bribery of Foreign Public Officials and Officials of Public International Organizations

1. Each State Party shall adopt such legislative and other measures as may be necessary to establish as a criminal offence, when committed intentionally, the promise, offering or giving to a foreign public official or an official of a public international organization, directly or indirectly, of an undue advantage, for the official himself or herself or another person or entity, in order that the official act or refrain from acting in the exercise of his or her official duties, in order to obtain or retain business or other undue advantage in relation to the conduct of international business.
2. Each State Party shall consider adopting such legislative and other measures as may be necessary to establish as a criminal offence, when committed intentionally, the solicitation or acceptance by a foreign public official or an official of a public international organization, directly or indirectly, of an undue advantage, for the official himself or herself or another person or entity, in order that the official act or refrain from acting in the exercise of his or her official duties.

Article 17. Embezzlement, Misappropriation or Other Diversion of Property by a Public Official

Each State Party shall adopt such legislative and other measures as may be necessary to establish as criminal offences, when committed intentionally, the embezzlement, misappropriation or other diversion by a public official for his or her benefit or for the benefit of another person or entity, of any property, public or private funds or securities or any other thing of value entrusted to the public official by virtue of his or her position.

Article 18. Trading in Influence

Each State Party shall consider adopting such legislative and other measures as may be necessary to establish as criminal offences, when committed intentionally:

(a) The promise, offering or giving to a public official or any other person, directly or indirectly, of an undue advantage in order that the public official or the person abuse his or her real or supposed influence with a view to obtaining from an administration or public authority of the State Party an undue advantage for the original instigator of the act or for any other person;
(b) The solicitation or acceptance by a public official or any other person, directly or indirectly, of an undue advantage for himself or herself or for another person in order that the public official or the person abuse his or her real or supposed influence with a view to obtaining from an administration or public authority of the State Party an undue advantage.

Article 19. Abuse of Functions

Each State Party shall consider adopting such legislative and other measures as may be necessary to establish as a criminal offence, when committed intentionally, the abuse of functions or position, that is, the performance of or failure to perform an act, in violation of laws, by a public official in the discharge of his or her functions, for the purpose of obtaining an undue advantage for himself or herself or for another person or entity.

Article 20. Illicit Enrichment

Subject to its constitution and the fundamental principles of its legal system, each State Party shall consider adopting such legislative and other measures as may be necessary to establish as a criminal offence, when committed intentionally, illicit enrichment, that is, a significant increase in the assets of a public official that he or she cannot reasonably explain in relation to his or her lawful income.

Article 21. Bribery in the Private Sector

Each State Party shall consider adopting such legislative and other measures as may be necessary to establish as criminal offences, when committed intentionally in the course of economic, financial or commercial activities:

(a) The promise, offering or giving, directly or indirectly, of an undue advantage to any person who directs or works, in any capacity, for a private sector entity, for the person himself or herself or for another person, in order that he or she, in breach of his or her duties, act or refrain from acting;

(b) The solicitation or acceptance, directly or indirectly, of an undue advantage by any person who directs or works, in any capacity, for a private sector entity, for the person himself or herself or for another person, in order that he or she, in breach of his or her duties, act or refrain from acting.

Article 22. Embezzlement of Property in the Private Sector

Each State Party shall consider adopting such legislative and other measures as may be necessary to establish as a criminal offence, when committed intentionally in the course of economic, financial or commercial activities, embezzlement by a person who directs or works, in any capacity, in a private sector entity of any property, private funds or securities or any other thing of value entrusted to him or her by virtue of his or her position.

Article 23. Laundering of Proceeds of Crime

1. Each State Party shall adopt, in accordance with fundamental principles of its domestic law, such legislative and other measures as may be necessary to establish as criminal offences, when committed intentionally:

    (a) The conversion or transfer of property, knowing that such property is the proceeds of crime, for the purpose of concealing or disguising the illicit origin of the property or of helping any person who is involved in the commission of the predicate offence to evade the legal consequences of his or her action;

    (i) The concealment or disguise of the true nature, source, location, disposition, movement or ownership of or rights with respect to property, knowing that such property is the proceeds of crime;

    (b) Subject to the basic concepts of its legal system:

    (ii) The acquisition, possession or use of property, knowing, at the time of receipt, that such property is the proceeds of crime;

(iii) Participation in, association with or conspiracy to commit, attempts to commit and aiding, abetting, facilitating and counselling the commission of any of the offences established in accordance with this article.

2. For purposes of implementing or applying paragraph 1 of this article:

   (a) Each State Party shall seek to apply paragraph 1 of this article to the widest range of predicate offences;
   (b) Each State Party shall include as predicate offences at a minimum a comprehensive range of criminal offences established in accordance with this Convention;
   (c) For the purposes of subparagraph (b) above, predicate offences shall include offences committed both within and outside the jurisdiction of the State Party in question. However, offences committed outside the jurisdiction of a State Party shall constitute predicate offences only when the relevant conduct is a criminal offence under the domestic law of the State where it is committed and would be a criminal offence under the domestic law of the State Party implementing or applying this article had it been committed there;
   (d) Each State Party shall furnish copies of its laws that give effect to this article and of any subsequent changes to such laws or a description thereof to the Secretary-General of the United Nations;
   (e) If required by fundamental principles of the domestic law of a State Party, it may be provided that the offences set forth in paragraph 1 of this article do not apply to the persons who committed the predicate offence.

Article 24. Concealment

Without prejudice to the provisions of article 23 of this Convention, each State Party shall consider adopting such legislative and other measures as may be necessary to establish as a criminal offence, when committed intentionally after the commission of any of the offences established in accordance with this Convention without having participated in such offences, the concealment or continued retention of property when the person involved knows that such property is the result of any of the offences established in accordance with this Convention.

Article 25. Obstruction of Justice

Each State Party shall adopt such legislative and other measures as may be necessary to establish as criminal offences, when committed intentionally:

(a) The use of physical force, threats or intimidation or the promise, offering or giving of an undue advantage to induce false testimony or to interfere in the giving of testimony or the production of evidence in a proceeding in relation to the commission of offences established in accordance with this Convention;
(b) The use of physical force, threats or intimidation to interfere with the exercise of official duties by a justice or law enforcement official in relation to the commission of offences established in accordance with this Convention. Nothing in this subparagraph shall prejudice the right of States Parties to have legislation that protects other categories of public official.

Article 26. Liability of Legal Persons

1. Each State Party shall adopt such measures as may be necessary, consistent with its legal principles, to establish the liability of legal persons for participation in the offences established in accordance with this Convention.
2. Subject to the legal principles of the State Party, the liability of legal persons may be criminal, civil or administrative.
3. Such liability shall be without prejudice to the criminal liability of the natural persons who have committed the offences.
4. Each State Party shall, in particular, ensure that legal persons held liable in accordance with this article are subject to effective, proportionate and dissuasive criminal or non-criminal sanctions, including monetary sanctions.

Article 27. Participation and Attempt

1. Each State Party shall adopt such legislative and other measures as may be necessary to establish as a criminal offence, in accordance with its domestic law, participation in any capacity such as an accomplice, assistant or instigator in an offence established in accordance with this Convention.
2. Each State Party may adopt such legislative and other measures as may be necessary to establish as a criminal offence, in accordance with its domestic law, any attempt to commit an offence established in accordance with this Convention.
3. Each State Party may adopt such legislative and other measures as may be necessary to establish as a criminal offence, in accordance with its domestic law, the preparation for an offence established in accordance with this Convention.

Article 28. Knowledge, Intent and Purpose as Elements of an Offence

Knowledge, intent or purpose required as an element of an offence established in accordance with this Convention may be inferred from objective factual circumstances.

Article 29. Statute of Limitations

Each State Party shall, where appropriate, establish under its domestic law a long statute of limitations period in which to commence proceedings for any offence established in accordance with this Convention and establish a longer statute of limitations period or provide for the suspension of the statute of limitations where the alleged offender has evaded the administration of justice.

Article 30. Prosecution, Adjudication and Sanctions

1. Each State Party shall make the commission of an offence established in accordance with this Convention liable to sanctions that take into account the gravity of that offence.
2. Each State Party shall take such measures as may be necessary to establish or maintain, in accordance with its legal system and constitutional principles, an appropriate balance between any immunities or jurisdictional privileges accorded to its public officials for the performance of their functions and the

possibility, when necessary, of effectively investigating, prosecuting and adjudicating offences established in accordance with this Convention.
3. Each State Party shall endeavour to ensure that any discretionary legal powers under its domestic law relating to the prosecution of persons for offences established in accordance with this Convention are exercised to maximize the effectiveness of law enforcement measures in respect of those offences and with due regard to the need to deter the commission of such offences.
4. In the case of offences established in accordance with this Convention, each State Party shall take appropriate measures, in accordance with its domestic law and with due regard to the rights of the defence, to seek to ensure that conditions imposed in connection with decisions on release pending trial or appeal take into consideration the need to ensure the presence of the defendant at subsequent criminal proceedings.
5. Each State Party shall take into account the gravity of the offences concerned when considering the eventuality of early release or parole of persons convicted of such offences.
6. Each State Party, to the extent consistent with the fundamental principles of its legal system, shall consider establishing procedures through which a public official accused of an offence established in accordance with this Convention may, where appropriate, be removed, suspended or reassigned by the appropriate authority, bearing in mind respect for the principle of the presumption of innocence.
7. Where warranted by the gravity of the offence, each State Party, to the extent consistent with the fundamental principles of its legal system, shall consider establishing procedures for the disqualification, by court order or any other appropriate means, for a period of time determined by its domestic law, of persons convicted of offences established in accordance with this Convention from:

(a) Holding public office; and
(b) Holding office in an enterprise owned in whole or in part by the State.

8. Paragraph 1 of this article shall be without prejudice to the exercise of disciplinary powers by the competent authorities against civil servants.
9. Nothing contained in this Convention shall affect the principle that the description of the offences established in accordance with this Convention and of the applicable legal defences or other legal principles controlling the lawfulness of conduct is reserved to the domestic law of a State Party and that such offences shall be prosecuted and punished in accordance with that law.
10. States Parties shall endeavour to promote the reintegration into society of persons convicted of offences established in accordance with this Convention.

Article 31. Freezing, Seizure and Confiscation

1. Each State Party shall take, to the greatest extent possible within its domestic legal system, such measures as may be necessary to enable confiscation of:
   (a) Proceeds of crime derived from offences established in accordance with this Convention or property the value of which corresponds to that of such proceeds;
   (b) Property, equipment or other instrumentalities used in or destined for use in offences established in accordance with this Convention.
2. Each State Party shall take such measures as may be necessary to enable the identification, tracing, freezing or seizure of any item referred to in paragraph 1 of this article for the purpose of eventual confiscation.
3. Each State Party shall adopt, in accordance with its domestic law, such legislative and other measures as may be necessary to regulate the administration by the competent authorities of frozen, seized or confiscated property covered in paragraphs 1 and 2 of this article.
4. If such proceeds of crime have been transformed or converted, in part or in full, into other property, such property shall be liable to the measures referred to in this article instead of the proceeds.
5. If such proceeds of crime have been intermingled with property acquired from legitimate sources, such property shall, without prejudice to any powers relating to freezing or seizure, be liable to confiscation up to the assessed value of the intermingled proceeds.
6. Income or other benefits derived from such proceeds of crime, from property into which such proceeds of crime have been transformed or converted or from property with which such proceeds of crime have been intermingled shall also be liable to the measures referred to in this article, in the same manner and to the same extent as proceeds of crime.
7. For the purpose of this article and article 55 of this Convention, each State Party shall empower its courts or other competent authorities to order that bank, financial or commercial records be made available or seized. A State Party shall not decline to act under the provisions of this paragraph on the ground of bank secrecy.
8. States Parties may consider the possibility of requiring that an offender demonstrate the lawful origin of such alleged proceeds of crime or other property liable to confiscation, to the extent that such a requirement is consistent with the fundamental principles of their domestic law and with the nature of judicial and other proceedings.
9. The provisions of this article shall not be so construed as to prejudice the rights of bona fide third parties.
10. Nothing contained in this article shall affect the principle that the measures to which it refers shall be defined and implemented in accordance with and subject to the provisions of the domestic law of a State Party.

Article 32. Protection of Witnesses, Experts and Victims

1. Each State Party shall take appropriate measures in accordance with its domestic legal system and within its means to provide effective protection from potential retaliation or intimidation for witnesses and experts who give testimony concerning offences established in accordance with this Convention and, as appropriate, for their relatives and other persons close to them.
2. The measures envisaged in paragraph 1 of this article may include, inter alia, without prejudice to the rights of the defendant, including the right to due process:

   (a) Establishing procedures for the physical protection of such persons, such as, to the extent necessary and feasible, relocating them and permitting, where appropriate, non-disclosure or limitations on the disclosure of information concerning the identity and whereabouts of such persons;

   (b) Providing evidentiary rules to permit witnesses and experts to give testimony in a manner that ensures the safety of such persons, such as permitting testimony to be given through the use of communications technology such as video or other adequate means.

3. States Parties shall consider entering into agreements or arrangements with other States for the relocation of persons referred to in paragraph 1 of this article.
4. The provisions of this article shall also apply to victims insofar as they are witnesses.
5. Each State Party shall, subject to its domestic law, enable the views and concerns of victims to be presented and considered at appropriate stages of criminal proceedings against offenders in a manner not prejudicial to the rights of the defence.

Article 33. Protection of Reporting Persons

Each State Party shall consider incorporating into its domestic legal system appropriate measures to provide protection against any unjustified treatment for any person who reports in good faith and on reasonable grounds to the competent authorities any facts concerning offences established in accordance with this Convention.

Article 34. Consequences of Acts of Corruption

With due regard to the rights of third parties acquired in good faith, each State Party shall take measures, in accordance with the fundamental principles of its domestic law, to address consequences of corruption. In this context, States Parties may consider corruption a relevant factor in legal proceedings to annul or rescind a contract, withdraw a concession or other similar instrument or take any other remedial action.

Article 35. Compensation for Damage

Each State Party shall take such measures as may be necessary, in accordance with principles of its domestic law, to ensure that entities or persons who have suffered damage as a result of an act of corruption have the right to initiate legal proceedings against those responsible for that damage in order to obtain compensation.

Article 36. Specialized Authorities

Each State Party shall, in accordance with the fundamental principles of its legal system, ensure the existence of a body or bodies or persons specialized in combating corruption through law enforcement. Such body or bodies or persons shall be granted the necessary independence, in accordance with the fundamental principles of the legal system of the State Party, to be able to carry out their functions effectively and without any undue influence. Such persons or staff of such body or bodies should have the appropriate training and resources to carry out their tasks.

Article 37. Cooperation with Law Enforcement Authorities

1. Each State Party shall take appropriate measures to encourage persons who participate or who have participated in the commission of an offence established in accordance with this Convention to supply information useful to competent authorities for investigative and evidentiary purposes and to provide factual, specific help to competent authorities that may contribute to depriving offenders of the proceeds of crime and to recovering such proceeds.
2. Each State Party shall consider providing for the possibility, in appropriate cases, of mitigating punishment of an accused person who provides substantial cooperation in the investigation or prosecution of an offence established in accordance with this Convention.
3. Each State Party shall consider providing for the possibility, in accordance with fundamental principles of its domestic law, of granting immunity from prosecution to a person who provides substantial cooperation in the investigation or prosecution of an offence established in accordance with this Convention.
4. Protection of such persons shall be, mutatis mutandis, as provided for in article 32 of this Convention.
5. Where a person referred to in paragraph 1 of this article located in one State Party can provide substantial cooperation to the competent authorities of another State Party, the States Parties concerned may consider entering into agreements or arrangements, in accordance with their domestic law, concerning the potential provision by the other State Party of the treatment set forth in paragraphs 2 and 3 of this article.

Article 38. Cooperation Between National Authorities

Each State Party shall take such measures as may be necessary to encourage, in accordance with its domestic law, cooperation between, on the one hand, its public authorities, as well as its public officials, and, on the other hand, its authorities responsible for investigating and prosecuting criminal offences. Such cooperation may include:

(a) Informing the latter authorities, on their own initiative, where there are reasonable grounds to believe that any of the offences established in accordance with articles 15, 21 and 23 of this Convention has been committed; or
(b) Providing, upon request, to the latter authorities all necessary information.

Article 39. Cooperation Between National Authorities and the Private Sector

1. Each State Party shall take such measures as may be necessary to encourage, in accordance with its domestic law, cooperation between national investigating and prosecuting authorities and entities of the private sector, in particular financial institutions, relating to matters involving the commission of offences established in accordance with this Convention.
2. Each State Party shall consider encouraging its nationals and other persons with a habitual residence in its territory to report to the national investigating and prosecuting authorities the commission of an offence established in accordance with this Convention.

Article 40. Bank Secrecy

Each State Party shall ensure that, in the case of domestic criminal investigations of offences established in accordance with this Convention, there are appropriate mechanisms available within its domestic legal system to overcome obstacles that may arise out of the application of bank secrecy laws.

Article 41. Criminal Record

Each State Party may adopt such legislative or other measures as may be necessary to take into consideration, under such terms as and for the purpose that it deems appropriate, any previous conviction in another State of an alleged offender for the purpose of using such information in criminal proceedings relating to an offence established in accordance with this Convention.

Article 42. Jurisdiction

1. Each State Party shall adopt such measures as may be necessary to establish its jurisdiction over the offences established in accordance with this Convention when:

    (a) The offence is committed in the territory of that State Party; or
    (b) The offence is committed on board a vessel that is flying the flag of that State Party or an aircraft that is registered under the laws of that State Party at the time that the offence is committed.

2. Subject to article 4 of this Convention, a State Party may also establish its jurisdiction over any such offence when:

    (a) The offence is committed against a national of that State Party; or
    (b) The offence is committed by a national of that State Party or a stateless person who has his or her habitual residence in its territory; or
    (c) The offence is one of those established in accordance with article 23, paragraph 1 (b) (ii), of this Convention and is committed outside its territory with a view to the commission of an offence established in accordance with article 23, paragraph 1 (a) (i) or (ii) or (b) (i), of this Convention within its territory; or
    (d) The offence is committed against the State Party.

3. For the purposes of article 44 of this Convention, each State Party shall take such measures as may be necessary to establish its jurisdiction over the offences established in accordance with this Convention when the alleged offender is present in its territory and it does not extradite such person solely on the ground that he or she is one of its nationals.
4. Each State Party may also take such measures as may be necessary to establish its jurisdiction over the offences established in accordance with this Convention when the alleged offender is present in its territory and it does not extradite him or her.
5. If a State Party exercising its jurisdiction under paragraph 1 or 2 of this article has been notified, or has otherwise learned, that any other States Parties are conducting an investigation, prosecution or judicial proceeding in respect of the same conduct, the competent authorities of those States Parties shall, as appropriate, consult one another with a view to coordinating their actions.
6. Without prejudice to norms of general international law, this Convention shall not exclude the exercise of any criminal jurisdiction established by a State Party in accordance with its domestic law.

Chapter IV International Cooperation
Article 43. International Cooperation

1. States Parties shall cooperate in criminal matters in accordance with articles 44 to 50 of this Convention. Where appropriate and consistent with their domestic legal system, States Parties shall consider assisting each other in investigations of and proceedings in civil and administrative matters relating to corruption.
2. In matters of international cooperation, whenever dual criminality is considered a requirement, it shall be deemed fulfilled irrespective of whether the laws of the requested State Party place the offence within the same category of offence or denominate the offence by the same terminology as the requesting State Party, if the conduct underlying the offence for which assistance is sought is a criminal offence under the laws of both States Parties.

Article 44. Extradition

1. This article shall apply to the offences established in accordance with this Convention where the person who is the subject of the request for extradition is present in the territory of the requested State Party, provided that the offence for which extradition is sought is punishable under the domestic law of both the requesting State Party and the requested State Party.
2. Notwithstanding the provisions of paragraph 1 of this article, a State Party whose law so permits may grant the extradition of a person for any of the offences covered by this Convention that are not punishable under its own domestic law.
3. If the request for extradition includes several separate offences, at least one of which is extraditable under this article and some of which are not extraditable by reason of their period of imprisonment but are related to offences established in

accordance with this Convention, the requested State Party may apply this article also in respect of those offences.

4. Each of the offences to which this article applies shall be deemed to be included as an extraditable offence in any extradition treaty existing between States Parties. States Parties undertake to include such offences as extraditable offences in every extradition treaty to be concluded between them. A State Party whose law so permits, in case it uses this Convention as the basis for extradition, shall not consider any of the offences established in accordance with this Convention to be a political offence.

5. If a State Party that makes extradition conditional on the existence of a treaty receives a request for extradition from another State Party with which it has no extradition treaty, it may consider this Convention the legal basis for extradition in respect of any offence to which this article applies.

6. A State Party that makes extradition conditional on the existence of a treaty shall:

    (a) At the time of deposit of its instrument of ratification, acceptance or approval of or accession to this Convention, inform the Secretary-General of the United Nations whether it will take this Convention as the legal basis for cooperation on extradition with other States Parties to this Convention; and

    (b) If it does not take this Convention as the legal basis for cooperation on extradition, seek, where appropriate, to conclude treaties on extradition with other States Parties to this Convention in order to implement this article.

7. States Parties that do not make extradition conditional on the existence of a treaty shall recognize offences to which this article applies as extraditable offences between themselves.

8. Extradition shall be subject to the conditions provided for by the domestic law of the requested State Party or by applicable extradition treaties, including, inter alia, conditions in relation to the minimum penalty requirement for extradition and the grounds upon which the requested State Party may refuse extradition.

9. States Parties shall, subject to their domestic law, endeavour to expedite extradition procedures and to simplify evidentiary requirements relating thereto in respect of any offence to which this article applies.

10. Subject to the provisions of its domestic law and its extradition treaties, the requested State Party may, upon being satisfied that the circumstances so warrant and are urgent and at the request of the requesting State Party, take a person whose extradition is sought and who is present in its territory into custody or take other appropriate measures to ensure his or her presence at extradition proceedings.

11. A State Party in whose territory an alleged offender is found, if it does not extradite such person in respect of an offence to which this article applies solely on the ground that he or she is one of its nationals, shall, at the request of the State Party seeking extradition, be obliged to submit the case without undue delay to its competent authorities for the purpose of prosecution. Those

authorities shall take their decision and conduct their proceedings in the same manner as in the case of any other offence of a grave nature under the domestic law of that State Party. The States Parties concerned shall cooperate with each other, in particular on procedural and evidentiary aspects, to ensure the efficiency of such prosecution.
12. Whenever a State Party is permitted under its domestic law to extradite or otherwise surrender one of its nationals only upon the condition that the person will be returned to that State Party to serve the sentence imposed as a result of the trial or proceedings for which the extradition or surrender of the person was sought and that State Party and the State Party seeking the extradition of the person agree with this option and other terms that they may deem appropriate, such conditional extradition or surrender shall be sufficient to discharge the obligation set forth in paragraph 11 of this article.
13. If extradition, sought for purposes of enforcing a sentence, is refused because the person sought is a national of the requested State Party, the requested State Party shall, if its domestic law so permits and in conformity with the requirements of such law, upon application of the requesting State Party, consider the enforcement of the sentence imposed under the domestic law of the requesting State Party or the remainder thereof.
14. Any person regarding whom proceedings are being carried out in connection with any of the offences to which this article applies shall be guaranteed fair treatment at all stages of the proceedings, including enjoyment of all the rights and guarantees provided by the domestic law of the State Party in the territory of which that person is present.
15. Nothing in this Convention shall be interpreted as imposing an obligation to extradite if the requested State Party has substantial grounds for believing that the request has been made for the purpose of prosecuting or punishing a person on account of that person's sex, race, religion, nationality, ethnic origin or political opinions or that compliance with the request would cause prejudice to that person's position for any one of these reasons.
16. States Parties may not refuse a request for extradition on the sole ground that the offence is also considered to involve fiscal matters.
17. Before refusing extradition, the requested State Party shall, where appropriate, consult with the requesting State Party to provide it with ample opportunity to present its opinions and to provide information relevant to its allegation.
18. States Parties shall seek to conclude bilateral and multilateral agreements or arrangements to carry out or to enhance the effectiveness of extradition.

Article 45. Transfer of Sentenced Persons

States Parties may consider entering into bilateral or multilateral agreements or arrangements on the transfer to their territory of persons sentenced to imprisonment or other forms of deprivation of liberty for offences established in accordance with this Convention in order that they may complete their sentences there.

Article 46. Mutual Legal Assistance

1. States Parties shall afford one another the widest measure of mutual legal assistance in investigations, prosecutions and judicial proceedings in relation to the offences covered by this Convention.
2. Mutual legal assistance shall be afforded to the fullest extent possible under relevant laws, treaties, agreements and arrangements of the requested State Party with respect to investigations, prosecutions and judicial proceedings in relation to the offences for which a legal person may be held liable in accordance with article 26 of this Convention in the requesting State Party.
3. Mutual legal assistance to be afforded in accordance with this article may be requested for any of the following purposes:

    (a) Taking evidence or statements from persons;
    (b) Effecting service of judicial documents;
    (c) Executing searches and seizures, and freezing;
    (d) Examining objects and sites;
    (e) Providing information, evidentiary items and expert evaluations;
    (f) Providing originals or certified copies of relevant documents and records, including government, bank, financial, corporate or business records;
    (g) Identifying or tracing proceeds of crime, property, instrumentalities or other things for evidentiary purposes;
    (h) Facilitating the voluntary appearance of persons in the requesting State Party;
    (i) Any other type of assistance that is not contrary to the domestic law of the requested State Party;
    (j) Identifying, freezing and tracing proceeds of crime in accordance with the provisions of chapter V of this Convention;
    (k) The recovery of assets, in accordance with the provisions of chapter V of this Convention.

4. Without prejudice to domestic law, the competent authorities of a State Party may, without prior request, transmit information relating to criminal matters to a competent authority in another State Party where they believe that such information could assist the authority in undertaking or successfully concluding inquiries and criminal proceedings or could result in a request formulated by the latter State Party pursuant to this Convention.
5. The transmission of information pursuant to paragraph 4 of this article shall be without prejudice to inquiries and criminal proceedings in the State of the competent authorities providing the information. The competent authorities receiving the information shall comply with a request that said information remain confidential, even temporarily, or with restrictions on its use. However, this shall not prevent the receiving State Party from disclosing in its proceedings information that is exculpatory to an accused person. In such a case, the receiving State Party shall notify the transmitting State Party prior to the disclosure and, if so requested, consult with the transmitting State Party. If, in

an exceptional case, advance notice is not possible, the receiving State Party shall inform the transmitting State Party of the disclosure without delay.
6. The provisions of this article shall not affect the obligations under any other treaty, bilateral or multilateral, that governs or will govern, in whole or in part, mutual legal assistance.
7. Paragraphs 9 to 29 of this article shall apply to requests made pursuant to this article if the States Parties in question are not bound by a treaty of mutual legal assistance. If those States Parties are bound by such a treaty, the corresponding provisions of that treaty shall apply unless the States Parties agree to apply paragraphs 9 to 29 of this article in lieu thereof. States Parties are strongly encouraged to apply those paragraphs if they facilitate cooperation.
8. States Parties shall not decline to render mutual legal assistance pursuant to this article on the ground of bank secrecy.

   (a) A requested State Party, in responding to a request for assistance pursuant to this article in the absence of dual criminality, shall take into account the purposes of this Convention, as set forth in article 1;
   (b) States Parties may decline to render assistance pursuant to this article on the ground of absence of dual criminality. However, a requested State Party shall, where consistent with the basic concepts of its legal system, render assistance that does not involve coercive action. Such assistance may be refused when requests involve matters of a de minimis nature or matters for which the cooperation or assistance sought is available under other provisions of this Convention;
   (c) Each State Party may consider adopting such measures as may be necessary to enable it to provide a wider scope of assistance pursuant to this article in the absence of dual criminality.

9. A person who is being detained or is serving a sentence in the territory of one State Party whose presence in another State Party is requested for purposes of identification, testimony or otherwise providing assistance in obtaining evidence for investigations, prosecutions or judicial proceedings in relation to offences covered by this Convention may be transferred if the following conditions are met:

   (a) The person freely gives his or her informed consent;
   (b) The competent authorities of both States Parties agree, subject to such conditions as those States Parties may deem appropriate.

10. For the purposes of paragraph 10 of this article:

    (a) The State Party to which the person is transferred shall have the authority and obligation to keep the person transferred in custody, unless otherwise requested or authorized by the State Party from which the person was transferred;
    (b) The State Party to which the person is transferred shall without delay implement its obligation to return the person to the custody of the State

Party from which the person was transferred as agreed beforehand, or as otherwise agreed, by the competent authorities of both States Parties;

(c) The State Party to which the person is transferred shall not require the State Party from which the person was transferred to initiate extradition proceedings for the return of the person;

(d) The person transferred shall receive credit for service of the sentence being served in the State from which he or she was transferred for time spent in the custody of the State Party to which he or she was transferred.

11. Unless the State Party from which a person is to be transferred in accordance with paragraphs 10 and 11 of this article so agrees, that person, whatever his or her nationality, shall not be prosecuted, detained, punished or subjected to any other restriction of his or her personal liberty in the territory of the State to which that person is transferred in respect of acts, omissions or convictions prior to his or her departure from the territory of the State from which he or she was transferred.

12. Each State Party shall designate a central authority that shall have the responsibility and power to receive requests for mutual legal assistance and either to execute them or to transmit them to the competent authorities for execution. Where a State Party has a special region or territory with a separate system of mutual legal assistance, it may designate a distinct central authority that shall have the same function for that region or territory. Central authorities shall ensure the speedy and proper execution or transmission of the requests received. Where the central authority transmits the request to a competent authority for execution, it shall encourage the speedy and proper execution of the request by the competent authority. The Secretary-General of the United Nations shall be notified of the central authority designated for this purpose at the time each State Party deposits its instrument of ratification, acceptance or approval of or accession to this Convention. Requests for mutual legal assistance and any communication related thereto shall be transmitted to the central authorities designated by the States Parties. This requirement shall be without prejudice to the right of a State Party to require that such requests and communications be addressed to it through diplomatic channels and, in urgent circumstances, where the States Parties agree, through the International Criminal Police Organization, if possible.

13. Requests shall be made in writing or, where possible, by any means capable of producing a written record, in a language acceptable to the requested State Party, under conditions allowing that State Party to establish authenticity. The Secretary-General of the United Nations shall be notified of the language or languages acceptable to each State Party at the time it deposits its instrument of ratification, acceptance or approval of or accession to this Convention. In urgent circumstances and where agreed by the States Parties, requests may be made orally but shall be confirmed in writing forthwith.

14. A request for mutual legal assistance shall contain:

(a) The identity of the authority making the request;
(b) The subject matter and nature of the investigation, prosecution or judicial proceeding to which the request relates and the name and functions of the authority conducting the investigation, prosecution or judicial proceeding;
(c) A summary of the relevant facts, except in relation to requests for the purpose of service of judicial documents;
(d) A description of the assistance sought and details of any particular procedure that the requesting State Party wishes to be followed;

A request for mutual legal assistance shall contain:

(a) The identity of the authority making the request;
(b) The subject matter and nature of the investigation, prosecution or judicial proceeding to which the request relates and the name and functions of the authority conducting the investigation, prosecution or judicial proceeding;
(c) A summary of the relevant facts, except in relation to requests for the purpose of service of judicial documents;
(d) A description of the assistance sought and details of any particular procedure that the requesting State Party wishes to be followed;
- A request for mutual legal assistance shall contain:
- The identity of the authority making the request;
- The subject matter and nature of the investigation, prosecution or judicial proceeding to which the request relates and the name and functions of the authority conducting the investigation, prosecution or judicial proceeding;

(e) Where possible, the identity, location and nationality of any person concerned; and
(f) The purpose for which the evidence, information or action is sought.

15. The requested State Party may request additional information when it appears necessary for the execution of the request in accordance with its domestic law or when it can facilitate such execution.
16. A request shall be executed in accordance with the domestic law of the requested State Party and, to the extent not contrary to the domestic law of the requested State Party and where possible, in accordance with the procedures specified in the request.
17. Wherever possible and consistent with fundamental principles of domestic law, when an individual is in the territory of a State Party and has to be heard as a witness or expert by the judicial authorities of another State Party, the first State Party may, at the request of the other, permit the hearing to take place by video conference if it is not possible or desirable for the individual in question to appear in person in the territory of the requesting State Party. States Parties may agree that the hearing shall be conducted by a judicial authority of the requesting State Party and attended by a judicial authority of the requested State Party.
18. The requesting State Party shall not transmit or use information or evidence furnished by the requested State Party for investigations, prosecutions or judicial

proceedings other than those stated in the request without the prior consent of the requested State Party. Nothing in this paragraph shall prevent the requesting State Party from disclosing in its proceedings information or evidence that is exculpatory to an accused person. In the latter case, the requesting State Party shall notify the requested State Party prior to the disclosure and, if so requested, consult with the requested State Party. If, in an exceptional case, advance notice is not possible, the requesting State Party shall inform the requested State Party of the disclosure without delay.

19. The requesting State Party may require that the requested State Party keep confidential the fact and substance of the request, except to the extent necessary to execute the request. If the requested State Party cannot comply with the requirement of confidentiality, it shall promptly inform the requesting State Party.

20. Mutual legal assistance may be refused:

    (a) If the request is not made in conformity with the provisions of this article;
    (b) If the requested State Party considers that execution of the request is likely to prejudice its sovereignty, security, ordre public or other essential interests;
    (c) If the authorities of the requested State Party would be prohibited by its domestic law from carrying out the action requested with regard to any similar offence, had it been subject to investigation, prosecution or judicial proceedings under their own jurisdiction;
    (d) If it would be contrary to the legal system of the requested State Party relating to mutual legal assistance for the request to be granted.

21. States Parties may not refuse a request for mutual legal assistance on the sole ground that the offence is also considered to involve fiscal matters.

22. Reasons shall be given for any refusal of mutual legal assistance.

23. The requested State Party shall execute the request for mutual legal assistance as soon as possible and shall take as full account as possible of any deadlines suggested by the requesting State Party and for which reasons are given, preferably in the request. The requesting State Party may make reasonable requests for information on the status and progress of measures taken by the requested State Party to satisfy its request. The requested State Party shall respond to reasonable requests by the requesting State Party on the status, and progress in its handling, of the request. The requesting State Party shall promptly inform the requested State Party when the assistance sought is no longer required.

24. Mutual legal assistance may be postponed by the requested State Party on the ground that it interferes with an ongoing investigation, prosecution or judicial proceeding.

25. Before refusing a request pursuant to paragraph 21 of this article or postponing its execution pursuant to paragraph 25 of this article, the requested State Party shall consult with the requesting State Party to consider whether assistance may be granted subject to such terms and conditions as it deems necessary. If the

requesting State Party accepts assistance subject to those conditions, it shall comply with the conditions.

26. Without prejudice to the application of paragraph 12 of this article, a witness, expert or other person who, at the request of the requesting State Party, consents to give evidence in a proceeding or to assist in an investigation, prosecution or judicial proceeding in the territory of the requesting State Party shall not be prosecuted, detained, punished or subjected to any other restriction of his or her personal liberty in that territory in respect of acts, omissions or convictions prior to his or her departure from the territory of the requested State Party. Such safe conduct shall cease when the witness, expert or other person having had, for a period of fifteen consecutive days or for any period agreed upon by the States Parties from the date on which he or she has been officially informed that his or her presence is no longer required by the judicial authorities, an opportunity of leaving, has nevertheless remained voluntarily in the territory of the requesting State Party or, having left it, has returned of his or her own free will.

27. The ordinary costs of executing a request shall be borne by the requested State Party, unless otherwise agreed by the States Parties concerned. If expenses of a substantial or extraordinary nature are or will be required to fulfil the request, the States Parties shall consult to determine the terms and conditions under which the request will be executed, as well as the manner in which the costs shall be borne.

28. The requested State Party:

    (a) Shall provide to the requesting State Party copies of government records, documents or information in its possession that under its domestic law are available to the general public;

    (b) May, at its discretion, provide to the requesting State Party in whole, in part or subject to such conditions as it deems appropriate, copies of any government records, documents or information in its possession that under its domestic law are not available to the general public.

29. States Parties shall consider, as may be necessary, the possibility of concluding bilateral or multilateral agreements or arrangements that would serve the purposes of, give practical effect to or enhance the provisions of this article.

Article 47. Transfer of Criminal Proceedings

States Parties shall consider the possibility of transferring to one another proceedings for the prosecution of an offence established in accordance with this Convention in cases where such transfer is considered to be in the interests of the proper administration of justice, in particular in cases where several jurisdictions are involved, with a view to concentrating the prosecution.

Article 48. Law Enforcement Cooperation

1. States Parties shall cooperate closely with one another, consistent with their respective domestic legal and administrative systems, to enhance the effectiveness of law enforcement action to combat the offences covered by this Convention. States Parties shall, in particular, take effective measures:

    (a) To enhance and, where necessary, to establish channels of communication between their competent authorities, agencies and services in order to facilitate the secure and rapid exchange of information concerning all aspects of the offences covered by this Convention, including, if the States Parties concerned deem it appropriate, links with other criminal activities;

    (b) To cooperate with other States Parties in conducting inquiries with respect to offences covered by this Convention concerning:

    (i) The identity, whereabouts and activities of persons suspected of involvement in such offences or the location of other persons concerned;
    (ii) The movement of proceeds of crime or property derived from the commission of such offences;
    (iii) The movement of property, equipment or other instrumentalities used or intended for use in the commission of such offences;

    (c) To provide, where appropriate, necessary items or quantities of substances for analytical or investigative purposes;

    (d) To exchange, where appropriate, information with other States Parties concerning specific means and methods used to commit offences covered by this Convention, including the use of false identities, forged, altered or false documents and other means of concealing activities;

    (e) To facilitate effective coordination between their competent authorities, agencies and services and to promote the exchange of personnel and other experts, including, subject to bilateral agreements or arrangements between the States Parties concerned, the posting of liaison officers;

    (f) To exchange information and coordinate administrative and other measures taken as appropriate for the purpose of early identification of the offences covered by this Convention.

2. With a view to giving effect to this Convention, States Parties shall consider entering into bilateral or multilateral agreements or arrangements on direct cooperation between their law enforcement agencies and, where such agreements or arrangements already exist, amending them. In the absence of such agreements or arrangements between the States Parties concerned, the States Parties may consider this Convention to be the basis for mutual law enforcement cooperation in respect of the offences covered by this Convention. Whenever appropriate, States Parties shall make full use of agreements or arrangements, including international or regional organizations, to enhance the cooperation between their law enforcement agencies.

3. States Parties shall endeavour to cooperate within their means to respond to offences covered by this Convention committed through the use of modern technology.

Article 49. Joint Investigations

States Parties shall consider concluding bilateral or multilateral agreements or arrangements whereby, in relation to matters that are the subject of investigations, prosecutions or judicial proceedings in one or more States, the competent authorities concerned may establish joint investigative bodies. In the absence of such agreements or arrangements, joint investigations may be undertaken by agreement on a case-by-case basis. The States Parties involved shall ensure that the sovereignty of the State Party in whose territory such investigation is to take place is fully respected.

Article 50. Special Investigative Techniques

1. In order to combat corruption effectively, each State Party shall, to the extent permitted by the basic principles of its domestic legal system and in accordance with the conditions prescribed by its domestic law, take such measures as may be necessary, within its means, to allow for the appropriate use by its competent authorities of controlled delivery and, where it deems appropriate, other special investigative techniques, such as electronic or other forms of surveillance and undercover operations, within its territory, and to allow for the admissibility in court of evidence derived therefrom.
2. For the purpose of investigating the offences covered by this Convention, States Parties are encouraged to conclude, when necessary, appropriate bilateral or multilateral agreements or arrangements for using such special investigative techniques in the context of cooperation at the international level. Such agreements or arrangements shall be concluded and implemented in full compliance with the principle of sovereign equality of States and shall be carried out strictly in accordance with the terms of those agreements or arrangements.
3. In the absence of an agreement or arrangement as set forth in paragraph 2 of this article, decisions to use such special investigative techniques at the international level shall be made on a case-by-case basis and may, when necessary, take into consideration financial arrangements and understandings with respect to the exercise of jurisdiction by the States Parties concerned.
4. Decisions to use controlled delivery at the international level may, with the consent of the States Parties concerned, include methods such as intercepting and allowing the goods or funds to continue intact or be removed or replaced in whole or in part.

Chapter V Asset Recovery
Article 51. General Provision

The return of assets pursuant to this chapter is a fundamental principle of this Convention, and States Parties shall afford one another the widest measure of cooperation and assistance in this regard.

Article 52. Prevention and Detection of Transfers of Proceeds of Crime

1. Without prejudice to article 14 of this Convention, each State Party shall take such measures as may be necessary, in accordance with its domestic law, to require financial institutions within its jurisdiction to verify the identity of customers, to take reasonable steps to determine the identity of beneficial owners of funds deposited into high-value accounts and to conduct enhanced scrutiny of accounts sought or maintained by or on behalf of individuals who are, or have been, entrusted with prominent public functions and their family members and close associates. Such enhanced scrutiny shall be reasonably designed to detect suspicious transactions for the purpose of reporting to competent authorities and should not be so construed as to discourage or prohibit financial institutions from doing business with any legitimate customer.
2. In order to facilitate implementation of the measures provided for in paragraph 1 of this article, each State Party, in accordance with its domestic law and inspired by relevant initiatives of regional, interregional and multilateral organizations against money-laundering, shall:
   (a) Issue advisories regarding the types of natural or legal person to whose accounts financial institutions within its jurisdiction will be expected to apply enhanced scrutiny, the types of accounts and transactions to which to pay particular attention and appropriate account-opening, maintenance and record-keeping measures to take concerning such accounts; and
   (b) Where appropriate, notify financial institutions within its jurisdiction, at the request of another State Party or on its own initiative, of the identity of particular natural or legal persons to whose accounts such institutions will be expected to apply enhanced scrutiny, in addition to those whom the financial institutions may otherwise identify.
3. In the context of paragraph 2 (a) of this article, each State Party shall implement measures to ensure that its financial institutions maintain adequate records, over an appropriate period of time, of accounts and transactions involving the persons mentioned in paragraph 1 of this article, which should, as a minimum, contain information relating to the identity of the customer as well as, as far as possible, of the beneficial owner.
4. With the aim of preventing and detecting transfers of proceeds of offences established in accordance with this Convention, each State Party shall implement appropriate and effective measures to prevent, with the help of its regulatory and oversight bodies, the establishment of banks that have no physical presence and that are not affiliated with a regulated financial group. Moreover, States Parties may consider requiring their financial institutions to refuse to enter into or continue a correspondent banking relationship with such institutions and to guard against establishing relations with foreign financial institutions that permit their accounts to be used by banks that have no physical presence and that are not affiliated with a regulated financial group.

5. Each State Party shall consider establishing, in accordance with its domestic law, effective financial disclosure systems for appropriate public officials and shall provide for appropriate sanctions for non-compliance. Each State Party shall also consider taking such measures as may be necessary to permit its competent authorities to share that information with the competent authorities in other States Parties when necessary to investigate, claim and recover proceeds of offences established in accordance with this Convention.
6. Each State Party shall consider taking such measures as may be necessary, in accordance with its domestic law, to require appropriate public officials having an interest in or signature or other authority over a financial account in a foreign country to report that relationship to appropriate authorities and to maintain appropriate records related to such accounts. Such measures shall also provide for appropriate sanctions for non-compliance.

Article 53. Measures for Direct Recovery of Property
Each State Party shall, in accordance with its domestic law:

(a) Take such measures as may be necessary to permit another State Party to initiate civil action in its courts to establish title to or ownership of property acquired through the commission of an offence established in accordance with this Convention;
(b) Take such measures as may be necessary to permit its courts to order those who have committed offences established in accordance with this Convention to pay compensation or damages to another State Party that has been harmed by such offences; and
(c) Take such measures as may be necessary to permit its courts or competent authorities, when having to decide on confiscation, to recognize another State Party's claim as a legitimate owner of property acquired through the commission of an offence established in accordance with this Convention.

Article 53. Measures for Direct Recovery of Property
Each State Party shall, in accordance with its domestic law:

(a) Take such measures as may be necessary to permit another State Party to initiate civil action in its courts to establish title to or ownership of property acquired through the commission of an offence established in accordance with this Convention;
(b) Take such measures as may be necessary to permit its courts to order those who have committed offences established in accordance with this Convention to pay compensation or damages to another State Party that has been harmed by such offences; and
(c) Take such measures as may be necessary to permit its courts or competent authorities, when having to decide on confiscation, to recognize another State Party's claim as a legitimate owner of property acquired through the commission of an offence established in accordance with this Convention.

Article 54. Mechanisms for Recovery of Property Through International Cooperation in Confiscation

1. Each State Party, in order to provide mutual legal assistance pursuant to article 55 of this Convention with respect to property acquired through or involved in the commission of an offence established in accordance with this Convention, shall, in accordance with its domestic law:

    (a) Take such measures as may be necessary to permit its competent authorities to give effect to an order of confiscation issued by a court of another State Party;

    (b) Take such measures as may be necessary to permit its competent authorities, where they have jurisdiction, to order the confiscation of such property of foreign origin by adjudication of an offence of money-laundering or such other offence as may be within its jurisdiction or by other procedures authorized under its domestic law; and

    (c) Consider taking such measures as may be necessary to allow confiscation of such property without a criminal conviction in cases in which the offender cannot be prosecuted by reason of death, flight or absence or in other appropriate cases.

2. Each State Party, in order to provide mutual legal assistance upon a request made pursuant to paragraph 2 of article 55 of this Convention, shall, in accordance with its domestic law:

    (a) Take such measures as may be necessary to permit its competent authorities to freeze or seize property upon a freezing or seizure order issued by a court or competent authority of a requesting State Party that provides a reasonable basis for the requested State Party to believe that there are sufficient grounds for taking such actions and that the property would eventually be subject to an order of confiscation for purposes of paragraph 1 (a) of this article;

    (b) Take such measures as may be necessary to permit its competent authorities to freeze or seize property upon a request that provides a reasonable basis for the requested State Party to believe that there are sufficient grounds for taking such actions and that the property would eventually be subject to an order of confiscation for purposes of paragraph 1 (a) of this article; and

    (c) Consider taking additional measures to permit its competent authorities to preserve property for confiscation, such as on the basis of a foreign arrest or criminal charge related to the acquisition of such property.

Article 55. International Cooperation for Purposes of Confiscation

1. A State Party that has received a request from another State Party having jurisdiction over an offence established in accordance with this Convention for confiscation of proceeds of crime, property, equipment or other instrumentalities referred to in article 31, paragraph 1, of this Convention situated in its territory shall, to the greatest extent possible within its domestic legal system:

   (a) Submit the request to its competent authorities for the purpose of obtaining an order of confiscation and, if such an order is granted, give effect to it; or

   (b) Submit to its competent authorities, with a view to giving effect to it to the extent requested, an order of confiscation issued by a court in the territory of the requesting State Party in accordance with articles 31, paragraph 1, and 54, paragraph 1 (a), of this Convention insofar as it relates to proceeds of crime, property, equipment or other instrumentalities referred to in article 31, paragraph 1, situated in the territory of the requested State Party.

2. Following a request made by another State Party having jurisdiction over an offence established in accordance with this Convention, the requested State Party shall take measures to identify, trace and freeze or seize proceeds of crime, property, equipment or other instrumentalities referred to in article 31, paragraph 1, of this Convention for the purpose of eventual confiscation to be ordered either by the requesting State Party or, pursuant to a request under paragraph 1 of this article, by the requested State Party.

3. The provisions of article 46 of this Convention are applicable, mutatis mutandis, to this article. In addition to the information specified in article 46, paragraph 15, requests made pursuant to this article shall contain:

   (a) In the case of a request pertaining to paragraph 1 (a) of this article, a description of the property to be confiscated, including, to the extent possible, the location and, where relevant, the estimated value of the property and a statement of the facts relied upon by the requesting State Party sufficient to enable the requested State Party to seek the order under its domestic law;

   (b) In the case of a request pertaining to paragraph 1 (b) of this article, a legally admissible copy of an order of confiscation upon which the request is based issued by the requesting State Party, a statement of the facts and information as to the extent to which execution of the order is requested, a statement specifying the measures taken by the requesting State Party to provide adequate notification to bona fide third parties and to ensure due process and a statement that the confiscation order is final;

   (c) In the case of a request pertaining to paragraph 2 of this article, a statement of the facts relied upon by the requesting State Party and a description of the actions requested and, where available, a legally admissible copy of an order on which the request is based.

4. The decisions or actions provided for in paragraphs 1 and 2 of this article shall be taken by the requested State Party in accordance with and subject to the

provisions of its domestic law and its procedural rules or any bilateral or multilateral agreement or arrangement to which it may be bound in relation to the requesting State Party.

5. Each State Party shall furnish copies of its laws and regulations that give effect to this article and of any subsequent changes to such laws and regulations or a description thereof to the Secretary-General of the United Nations.
6. If a State Party elects to make the taking of the measures referred to in paragraphs 1 and 2 of this article conditional on the existence of a relevant treaty, that State Party shall consider this Convention the necessary and sufficient treaty basis.
7. Cooperation under this article may also be refused or provisional measures lifted if the requested State Party does not receive sufficient and timely evidence or if the property is of a de minimis value.
8. Before lifting any provisional measure taken pursuant to this article, the requested State Party shall, wherever possible, give the requesting State Party an opportunity to present its reasons in favour of continuing the measure.
9. The provisions of this article shall not be construed as prejudicing the rights of bona fide third parties.

Article 56. Special Cooperation

Without prejudice to its domestic law, each State Party shall endeavour to take measures to permit it to forward, without prejudice to its own investigations, prosecutions or judicial proceedings, information on proceeds of offences established in accordance with this Convention to another State Party without prior request, when it considers that the disclosure of such information might assist the receiving State Party in initiating or carrying out investigations, prosecutions or judicial proceedings or might lead to a request by that State Party under this chapter of the Convention.

Article 57. Return and Disposal of Assets

1. Property confiscated by a State Party pursuant to article 31 or 55 of this Convention shall be disposed of, including by return to its prior legitimate owners, pursuant to paragraph 3 of this article, by that State Party in accordance with the provisions of this Convention and its domestic law.
2. Each State Party shall adopt such legislative and other measures, in accordance with the fundamental principles of its domestic law, as may be necessary to enable its competent authorities to return confiscated property, when acting on the request made by another State Party, in accordance with this Convention, taking into account the rights of bona fide third parties.
3. In accordance with articles 46 and 55 of this Convention and paragraphs 1 and 2 of this article, the requested State Party shall:
    (a) In the case of embezzlement of public funds or of laundering of embezzled public funds as referred to in articles 17 and 23 of this Convention, when confiscation was executed in accordance with article 55 and on the basis of a final judgement in the requesting State Party, a requirement that can be

waived by the requested State Party, return the confiscated property to the requesting State Party;

(b) In the case of proceeds of any other offence covered by this Convention, when the confiscation was executed in accordance with article 55 of this Convention and on the basis of a final judgement in the requesting State Party, a requirement that can be waived by the requested State Party, return the confiscated property to the requesting State Party, when the requesting State Party reasonably establishes its prior ownership of such confiscated property to the requested State Party or when the requested State Party recognizes damage to the requesting State Party as a basis for returning the confiscated property;

(c) In all other cases, give priority consideration to returning confiscated property to the requesting State Party, returning such property to its prior legitimate owners or compensating the victims of the crime.

4. Where appropriate, unless States Parties decide otherwise, the requested State Party may deduct reasonable expenses incurred in investigations, prosecutions or judicial proceedings leading to the return or disposition of confiscated property pursuant to this article.

5. Where appropriate, States Parties may also give special consideration to concluding agreements or mutually acceptable arrangements, on a case-by-case basis, for the final disposal of confiscated property.

Article 58. Financial Intelligence Unit

States Parties shall cooperate with one another for the purpose of preventing and combating the transfer of proceeds of offences established in accordance with this Convention and of promoting ways and means of recovering such proceeds and, to that end, shall consider establishing a financial intelligence unit to be responsible for receiving, analysing and disseminating to the competent authorities reports of suspicious financial transactions.

Article 59. Bilateral and Multilateral Agreements and Arrangements

States Parties shall consider concluding bilateral or multilateral agreements or arrangements to enhance the effectiveness of international cooperation undertaken pursuant to this chapter of the Convention.

Chapter VI Technical Assistance and Information Exchange
Article 60. Training and Technical Assistance

1. Each State Party shall, to the extent necessary, initiate, develop or improve specific training programmes for its personnel responsible for preventing and combating corruption. Such training programmes could deal, inter alia, with the following areas:

    (a) Effective measures to prevent, detect, investigate, punish and control corruption, including the use of evidence-gathering and investigative methods;
    (b) Building capacity in the development and planning of strategic anti-corruption policy;

(c) Training competent authorities in the preparation of requests for mutual legal assistance that meet the requirements of this Convention;
(d) Evaluation and strengthening of institutions, public service management and the management of public finances, including public procurement, and the private sector;
(e) Preventing and combating the transfer of proceeds of offences established in accordance with this Convention and recovering such proceeds;
(f) Detecting and freezing of the transfer of proceeds of offences established in accordance with this Convention;
(g) Surveillance of the movement of proceeds of offences established in accordance with this Convention and of the methods used to transfer, conceal or disguise such proceeds;
(h) Appropriate and efficient legal and administrative mechanisms and methods for facilitating the return of proceeds of offences established in accordance with this Convention;
(i) Methods used in protecting victims and witnesses who cooperate with judicial authorities; and
(j) Training in national and international regulations and in languages.

2. States Parties shall, according to their capacity, consider affording one another the widest measure of technical assistance, especially for the benefit of developing countries, in their respective plans and programmes to combat corruption, including material support and training in the areas referred to in paragraph 1 of this article, and training and assistance and the mutual exchange of relevant experience and specialized knowledge, which will facilitate international cooperation between States Parties in the areas of extradition and mutual legal assistance.
3. States Parties shall strengthen, to the extent necessary, efforts to maximize operational and training activities in international and regional organizations and in the framework of relevant bilateral and multilateral agreements or arrangements.
4. States Parties shall consider assisting one another, upon request, in conducting evaluations, studies and research relating to the types, causes, effects and costs of corruption in their respective countries, with a view to developing, with the participation of competent authorities and society, strategies and action plans to combat corruption.
5. In order to facilitate the recovery of proceeds of offences established in accordance with this Convention, States Parties may cooperate in providing each other with the names of experts who could assist in achieving that objective.
6. States Parties shall consider using subregional, regional and international conferences and seminars to promote cooperation and technical assistance and to stimulate discussion on problems of mutual concern, including the special problems and needs of developing countries and countries with economies in transition.
7. States Parties shall consider establishing voluntary mechanisms with a view to contributing financially to the efforts of developing countries and countries with

economies in transition to apply this Convention through technical assistance programmes and projects.
8. Each State Party shall consider making voluntary contributions to the United Nations Office on Drugs and Crime for the purpose of fostering, through the Office, programmes and projects in developing countries with a view to implementing this Convention.

Article 61. Collection, Exchange and Analysis of Information on Corruption

1. Each State Party shall consider analysing, in consultation with experts, trends in corruption in its territory, as well as the circumstances in which corruption offences are committed.
2. States Parties shall consider developing and sharing with each other and through international and regional organizations statistics, analytical expertise concerning corruption and information with a view to developing, insofar as possible, common definitions, standards and methodologies, as well as information on best practices to prevent and combat corruption.
3. Each State Party shall consider monitoring its policies and actual measures to combat corruption and making assessments of their effectiveness and efficiency.

Article 62. Other Measures: Implementation of the Convention Through Economic Development and Technical Assistance

1. States Parties shall take measures conducive to the optimal implementation of this Convention to the extent possible, through international cooperation, taking into account the negative effects of corruption on society in general, in particular on sustainable development.
2. States Parties shall make concrete efforts to the extent possible and in coordination with each other, as well as with international and regional organizations:

    (a) To enhance their cooperation at various levels with developing countries, with a view to strengthening the capacity of the latter to prevent and combat corruption;
    (b) To enhance financial and material assistance to support the efforts of developing countries to prevent and fight corruption effectively and to help them implement this Convention successfully;
    (c) To provide technical assistance to developing countries and countries with economies in transition to assist them in meeting their needs for the implementation of this Convention. To that end, States Parties shall endeavour to make adequate and regular voluntary contributions to an account specifically designated for that purpose in a United Nations funding mechanism. States Parties may also give special consideration, in accordance with their domestic law and the provisions of this Convention, to contributing to that account a percentage of the money or of the corresponding value of proceeds of crime or property confiscated in accordance with the provisions of this Convention;
    (d) To encourage and persuade other States and financial institutions as appropriate to join them in efforts in accordance with this article, in particular by

providing more training programmes and modern equipment to developing countries in order to assist them in achieving the objectives of this Convention.

3. To the extent possible, these measures shall be without prejudice to existing foreign assistance commitments or to other financial cooperation arrangements at the bilateral, regional or international level.
4. States Parties may conclude bilateral or multilateral agreements or arrangements on material and logistical assistance, taking into consideration the financial arrangements necessary for the means of international cooperation provided for by this Convention to be effective and for the prevention, detection and control of corruption.

Chapter VII Mechanisms for Implementation
Article 63. Conference of the States Parties to the Convention

1. A Conference of the States Parties to the Convention is hereby established to improve the capacity of and cooperation between States Parties to achieve the objectives set forth in this Convention and to promote and review its implementation.
2. The Secretary-General of the United Nations shall convene the Conference of the States Parties not later than one year following the entry into force of this Convention. Thereafter, regular meetings of the Conference of the States Parties shall be held in accordance with the rules of procedure adopted by the Conference.
3. The Conference of the States Parties shall adopt rules of procedure and rules governing the functioning of the activities set forth in this article, including rules concerning the admission and participation of observers, and the payment of expenses incurred in carrying out those activities.
4. The Conference of the States Parties shall agree upon activities, procedures and methods of work to achieve the objectives set forth in paragraph 1 of this article, including:

   (a) Facilitating activities by States Parties under articles 60 and 62 and chapters II to V of this Convention, including by encouraging the mobilization of voluntary contributions;
   (b) Facilitating the exchange of information among States Parties on patterns and trends in corruption and on successful practices for preventing and combating it and for the return of proceeds of crime, through, inter alia, the publication of relevant information as mentioned in this article;
   (c) Cooperating with relevant international and regional organizations and mechanisms and non-governmental organizations;
   (d) Making appropriate use of relevant information produced by other international and regional mechanisms for combating and preventing corruption in order to avoid unnecessary duplication of work;
   (e) Reviewing periodically the implementation of this Convention by its States Parties;

(f) Making recommendations to improve this Convention and its implementation;
(g) Taking note of the technical assistance requirements of States Parties with regard to the implementation of this Convention and recommending any action it may deem necessary in that respect.

5. For the purpose of paragraph 4 of this article, the Conference of the States Parties shall acquire the necessary knowledge of the measures taken by States Parties in implementing this Convention and the difficulties encountered by them in doing so through information provided by them and through such supplemental review mechanisms as may be established by the Conference of the States Parties.
6. Each State Party shall provide the Conference of the States Parties with information on its programmes, plans and practices, as well as on legislative and administrative measures to implement this Convention, as required by the Conference of the States Parties. The Conference of the States Parties shall examine the most effective way of receiving and acting upon information, including, inter alia, information received from States Parties and from competent international organizations. Inputs received from relevant non-governmental organizations duly accredited in accordance with procedures to be decided upon by the Conference of the States Parties may also be considered.
7. Pursuant to paragraphs 4 to 6 of this article, the Conference of the States Parties shall establish, if it deems it necessary, any appropriate mechanism or body to assist in the effective implementation of the Convention.

Article 64. Secretariat

1. The Secretary-General of the United Nations shall provide the necessary secretariat services to the Conference of the States Parties to the Convention.
2. The secretariat shall:

   (a) Assist the Conference of the States Parties in carrying out the activities set forth in article 63 of this Convention and make arrangements and provide the necessary services for the sessions of the Conference of the States Parties;
   (b) Upon request, assist States Parties in providing information to the Conference of the States Parties as envisaged in article 63, paragraphs 5 and 6, of this Convention; and
   (c) Ensure the necessary coordination with the secretariats of relevant international and regional organizations.

Chapter VIII Final Provisions
Article 65. Implementation of the Convention

1. Each State Party shall take the necessary measures, including legislative and administrative measures, in accordance with fundamental principles of its domestic law, to ensure the implementation of its obligations under this Convention.
2. Each State Party may adopt more strict or severe measures than those provided for by this Convention for preventing and combating corruption.

Article 66. Settlement of Disputes

1. States Parties shall endeavour to settle disputes concerning the interpretation or application of this Convention through negotiation.
2. Any dispute between two or more States Parties concerning the interpretation or application of this Convention that cannot be settled through negotiation within a reasonable time shall, at the request of one of those States Parties, be submitted to arbitration. If, six months after the date of the request for arbitration, those States Parties are unable to agree on the organization of the arbitration, any one of those States Parties may refer the dispute to the International Court of Justice by request in accordance with the Statute of the Court.
3. Each State Party may, at the time of signature, ratification, acceptance or approval of or accession to this Convention, declare that it does not consider itself bound by paragraph 2 of this article. The other States Parties shall not be bound by paragraph 2 of this article with respect to any State Party that has made such a reservation.
4. Any State Party that has made a reservation in accordance with paragraph 3 of this article may at any time withdraw that reservation by notification to the Secretary-General of the United Nations.

Article 67. Signature, Ratification, Acceptance, Approval and Accession

1. This Convention shall be open to all States for signature from 9 to 11 December 2003 in Merida, Mexico, and thereafter at United Nations Headquarters in New York until 9 December 2005.
2. This Convention shall also be open for signature by regional economic integration organizations provided that at least one member State of such organization has signed this Convention in accordance with paragraph 1 of this article.
3. This Convention is subject to ratification, acceptance or approval. Instruments of ratification, acceptance or approval shall be deposited with the Secretary-General of the United Nations. A regional economic integration organization may deposit its instrument of ratification, acceptance or approval if at least one of its member States has done likewise. In that instrument of ratification, acceptance or approval, such organization shall declare the extent of its competence with respect to the matters governed by this Convention. Such organization shall also inform the depositary of any relevant modification in the extent of its competence.
4. This Convention is open for accession by any State or any regional economic integration organization of which at least one member State is a Party to this Convention. Instruments of accession shall be deposited with the Secretary-General of the United Nations. At the time of its accession, a regional economic integration organization shall declare the extent of its competence with respect to matters governed by this Convention. Such organization shall also inform the depositary of any relevant modification in the extent of its competence.

Article 68. Entry into Force

1. This Convention shall enter into force on the ninetieth day after the date of deposit of the thirtieth instrument of ratification, acceptance, approval or accession. For the purpose of this paragraph, any instrument deposited by a regional economic integration organization shall not be counted as additional to those deposited by member States of such organization.
2. For each State or regional economic integration organization ratifying, accepting, approving or acceding to this Convention after the deposit of the thirtieth instrument of such action, this Convention shall enter into force on the thirtieth day after the date of deposit by such State or organization of the relevant instrument or on the date this Convention enters into force pursuant to paragraph 1 of this article, whichever is later.

Article 69. Amendment

1. After the expiry of five years from the entry into force of this Convention, a State Party may propose an amendment and transmit it to the Secretary-General of the United Nations, who shall thereupon communicate the proposed amendment to the States Parties and to the Conference of the States Parties to the Convention for the purpose of considering and deciding on the proposal. The Conference of the States Parties shall make every effort to achieve consensus on each amendment. If all efforts at consensus have been exhausted and no agreement has been reached, the amendment shall, as a last resort, require for its adoption a two-thirds majority vote of the States Parties present and voting at the meeting of the Conference of the States Parties.
2. Regional economic integration organizations, in matters within their competence, shall exercise their right to vote under this article with a number of votes equal to the number of their member States that are Parties to this Convention. Such organizations shall not exercise their right to vote if their member States exercise theirs and vice versa.
3. An amendment adopted in accordance with paragraph 1 of this article is subject to ratification, acceptance or approval by States Parties.
4. An amendment adopted in accordance with paragraph 1 of this article shall enter into force in respect of a State Party ninety days after the date of the deposit with the Secretary-General of the United Nations of an instrument of ratification, acceptance or approval of such amendment.
5. When an amendment enters into force, it shall be binding on those States Parties which have expressed their consent to be bound by it. Other States Parties shall still be bound by the provisions of this Convention and any earlier amendments that they have ratified, accepted or approved.

Article 70. Denunciation

1. A State Party may denounce this Convention by written notification to the Secretary-General of the United Nations. Such denunciation shall become effective one year after the date of receipt of the notification by the Secretary-General.
2. A regional economic integration organization shall cease to be a Party Convention when all of its member States have denounced it.

Article 71. Depositary and Languages

1. The Secretary-General of the United Nations is designated depositary of this Convention.
2. The original of this Convention, of which the Arabic, Chinese, English, French, Russian and Spanish texts are equally authentic, shall be deposited with the Secretary-General of the United Nations.

IN WITNESS WHEREOF, the undersigned plenipotentiaries, being duly authorized thereto by their respective Governments, have signed this Convention.

- **Organisation for Economic Co-operation and Development (OECD)** (16 February 2022)

(1) OECD Convention on Combating Bribery of Foreign Public Officials in International Business Transactions[9]

Adopted by the Negotiating Conference on 21 November 1997

Preamble

The Parties,

Considering that bribery is a widespread phenomenon in international business transactions, including trade and investment, which raises serious moral and political concerns, undermines good governance and economic development, and distorts international competitive conditions;

Considering that all countries share a responsibility to combat bribery in international business transactions;

Having regard to the Revised Recommendation on Combating Bribery in International Business Transactions, adopted by the Council of the Organisation for Economic Co-operation and Development (OECD) on 23 May 1997, C(97)123/FINAL, which, inter alia, called for effective measures to deter, prevent and combat the bribery of foreign public officials in connection with international business transactions, in particular the prompt criminalisation of such bribery in an effective and co-ordinated manner and in conformity with the agreed common elements set out in that Recommendation and with the jurisdictional and other basic legal principles of each country;

Welcoming other recent developments which further advance international understanding and co-operation in combating bribery of public officials, including

---

[9] https://www.oecd.org/corruption/oecdantibriberyconvention.htm

actions of the United Nations, the World Bank, the International Monetary Fund, the World Trade Organisation, the Organisation of American States, the Council of Europe and the European Union;

Welcoming the efforts of companies, business organisations and trade unions as well as other non-governmental organisations to combat bribery;

Recognising the role of governments in the prevention of solicitation of bribes from individuals and enterprises in international business transactions;

Recognising that achieving progress in this field requires not only efforts on a national level but also multilateral co-operation, monitoring and follow-up;

Recognising that achieving equivalence among the measures to be taken by the Parties is an essential object and purpose of the Convention, which requires that the Convention be ratified without derogations affecting this equivalence;

Have agreed as follows:

Article 1 The Offence of Bribery of Foreign Public Officials

1. Each Party shall take such measures as may be necessary to establish that it is a criminal offence under its law for any person intentionally to offer, promise or give any undue pecuniary or other advantage, whether directly or through intermediaries, to a foreign public official, for that official or for a third party, in order that the official act or refrain from acting in relation to the performance of official duties, in order to obtain or retain business or other improper advantage in the conduct of international business.
2. Each Party shall take any measures necessary to establish that complicity in, including incitement, aiding and abetting, or authorisation of an act of bribery of a foreign public official shall be a criminal offence. Attempt and conspiracy to bribe a foreign public official shall be criminal offences to the same extent as attempt and conspiracy to bribe a public official of that Party.
3. The offences set out in paragraphs 1 and 2 above are hereinafter referred to as "bribery of a foreign public official".
4. For the purpose of this Convention:
    (a) "foreign public official" means any person holding a legislative, administrative or judicial office of a foreign country, whether appointed or elected; any person exercising a public function for a foreign country, including for a public agency or public enterprise; and any official or agent of a public international organisation;
    (b) "foreign country" includes all levels and subdivisions of government, from national to local;
    (c) "act or refrain from acting in relation to the performance of official duties" includes any use of the public official's position, whether or not within the official's authorised competence.

Article 2 Responsibility of Legal Persons

Each Party shall take such measures as may be necessary, in accordance with its legal principles, to establish the liability of legal persons for the bribery of a foreign public official.

Article 3 Sanctions

1. The bribery of a foreign public official shall be punishable by effective, proportionate and dissuasive criminal penalties. The range of penalties shall be comparable to that applicable to the bribery of the Party's own public officials and shall, in the case of natural persons, include deprivation of liberty sufficient to enable effective mutual legal assistance and extradition.
2. In the event that, under the legal system of a Party, criminal responsibility is not applicable to legal persons, that Party shall ensure that legal persons shall be subject to effective, proportionate and dissuasive non-criminal sanctions, including monetary sanctions, for bribery of foreign public officials.
3. Each Party shall take such measures as may be necessary to provide that the bribe and the proceeds of the bribery of a foreign public official, or property the value of which corresponds to that of such proceeds, are subject to seizure and confiscation or that monetary sanctions of comparable effect are applicable.
4. Each Party shall consider the imposition of additional civil or administrative sanctions upon a person subject to sanctions for the bribery of a foreign public official.

Article 4 Jurisdiction

1. Each Party shall take such measures as may be necessary to establish its jurisdiction over the bribery of a foreign public official when the offence is committed in whole or in part in its territory.
2. Each Party which has jurisdiction to prosecute its nationals for offences committed abroad shall take such measures as may be necessary to establish its jurisdiction to do so in respect of the bribery of a foreign public official, according to the same principles.
3. When more than one Party has jurisdiction over an alleged offence described in this Convention, the Parties involved shall, at the request of one of them, consult with a view to determining the most appropriate jurisdiction for prosecution.
4. Each Party shall review whether its current basis for jurisdiction is effective in the fight against the bribery of foreign public officials and, if it is not, shall take remedial steps.

Article 5 Enforcement

Investigation and prosecution of the bribery of a foreign public official shall be subject to the applicable rules and principles of each Party. They shall not be influenced by considerations of national economic interest, the potential effect upon relations with another State or the identity of the natural or legal persons involved.

Article 6 Statute of Limitations

Any statute of limitations applicable to the offence of bribery of a foreign public official shall allow an adequate period of time for the investigation and prosecution of this offence.

Article 7 Money Laundering

Each Party which has made bribery of its own public official a predicate offence for the purpose of the application of its money laundering legislation shall do so on the same terms for the bribery of a foreign public official, without regard to the place where the bribery occurred.

Article 8 Accounting

1. In order to combat bribery of foreign public officials effectively, each Party shall take such measures as may be necessary, within the framework of its laws and regulations regarding the maintenance of books and records, financial statement disclosures, and accounting and auditing standards, to prohibit the establishment of off-the-books accounts, the making of off-the-books or inadequately identified transactions, the recording of non-existent expenditures, the entry of liabilities with incorrect identification of their object, as well as the use of false documents, by companies subject to those laws and regulations, for the purpose of bribing foreign public officials or of hiding such bribery.
2. Each Party shall provide effective, proportionate and dissuasive civil, administrative or criminal penalties for such omissions and falsifications in respect of the books, records, accounts and financial statements of such companies.

Article 9 Mutual Legal Assistance

1. Each Party shall, to the fullest extent possible under its laws and relevant treaties and arrangements, provide prompt and effective legal assistance to another Party for the purpose of criminal investigations and proceedings brought by a Party concerning offences within the scope of this Convention and for non-criminal proceedings within the scope of this Convention brought by a Party against a legal person. The requested Party shall inform the requesting Party, without delay, of any additional information or documents needed to support the request for assistance and, where requested, of the status and outcome of the request for assistance.
2. Where a Party makes mutual legal assistance conditional upon the existence of dual criminality, dual criminality shall be deemed to exist if the offence for which the assistance is sought is within the scope of this Convention.
3. A Party shall not decline to render mutual legal assistance for criminal matters within the scope of this Convention on the ground of bank secrecy.

Article 10 Extradition

1. Bribery of a foreign public official shall be deemed to be included as an extraditable offence under the laws of the Parties and the extradition treaties between them.

2. If a Party which makes extradition conditional on the existence of an extradition treaty receives a request for extradition from another Party with which it has no extradition treaty, it may consider this Convention to be the legal basis for extradition in respect of the offence of bribery of a foreign public official.
3. Each Party shall take any measures necessary to assure either that it can extradite its nationals or that it can prosecute its nationals for the offence of bribery of a foreign public official. A Party which declines a request to extradite a person for bribery of a foreign public official solely on the ground that the person is its national shall submit the case to its competent authorities for the purpose of prosecution.
4. Extradition for bribery of a foreign public official is subject to the conditions set out in the domestic law and applicable treaties and arrangements of each Party. Where a Party makes extradition conditional upon the existence of dual criminality, that condition shall be deemed to be fulfilled if the offence for which extradition is sought is within the scope of Article 1 of this Convention.

Article 11 Responsible Authorities

For the purposes of Article 4, paragraph 3, on consultation, Article 9, on mutual legal assistance and Article 10, on extradition, each Party shall notify to the Secretary-General of the OECD an authority or authorities responsible for making and receiving requests, which shall serve as channel of communication for these matters for that Party, without prejudice to other arrangements between Parties.

Article 12 Monitoring and Follow-up

The Parties shall co-operate in carrying out a programme of systematic follow-up to monitor and promote the full implementation of this Convention. Unless otherwise decided by consensus of the Parties, this shall be done in the framework of the OECD Working Group on Bribery in International Business Transactions and according to its terms of reference, or within the framework and terms of reference of any successor to its functions, and Parties shall bear the costs of the programme in accordance with the rules applicable to that body.

Article 13 Signature and Accession

1. Until its entry into force, this Convention shall be open for signature by OECD Members and by Non-Members which have been invited to become full participants in its Working Group on Bribery in International Business Transactions.
2. Subsequent to its entry into force, this Convention shall be open to accession by any non-signatory which is a member of the OECD or has become a full participant in the Working Group on Bribery in International Business Transactions or any successor to its functions. For each such non-signatory, the Convention shall enter into force on the sixtieth day following the date of deposit of its instrument of accession.

Article 14 Ratification and Depositary

1. This Convention is subject to acceptance, approval or ratification by the Signatories, in accordance with their respective laws.
2. Instruments of acceptance, approval, ratification or accession shall be deposited with the Secretary-General of the OECD, who shall serve as Depositary of this Convention.

Article 15 Entry into Force

1. This Convention shall enter into force on the sixtieth day following the date upon which five of the ten countries which have the ten largest export shares set out in DAFFE/IME/BR(97)18/FINAL (annexed), and which represent by themselves at least sixty per cent of the combined total exports of those ten countries, have deposited their instruments of acceptance, approval, or ratification. For each signatory depositing its instrument after such entry into force, the Convention shall enter into force on the sixtieth day after deposit of its instrument.
2. If, after 31 December 1998, the Convention has not entered into force under paragraph 1 above, any signatory which has deposited its instrument of acceptance, approval or ratification may declare in writing to the Depositary its readiness to accept entry into force of this Convention under this paragraph 2. The Convention shall enter into force for such a signatory on the sixtieth day following the date upon which such declarations have been deposited by at least two signatories. For each signatory depositing its declaration after such entry into force, the Convention shall enter into force on the sixtieth day following the date of deposit.

Article 16 Amendment

Any Party may propose the amendment of this Convention. A proposed amendment shall be submitted to the Depositary which shall communicate it to the other Parties at least sixty days before convening a meeting of the Parties to consider the proposed amendment. An amendment adopted by consensus of the Parties, or by such other means as the Parties may determine by consensus, shall enter into force sixty days after the deposit of an instrument of ratification, acceptance or approval by all of the Parties, or in such other circumstances as may be specified by the Parties at the time of adoption of the amendment.

Article 17 Withdrawal

A Party may withdraw from this Convention by submitting written notification to the Depositary. Such withdrawal shall be effective one year after the date of the receipt of the notification. After withdrawal, co-operation shall continue between the Parties and the Party which has withdrawn on all requests for assistance or extradition made before the effective date of withdrawal which remain pending.

See also[10]: Commentaries on the Convention on Combating Bribery of Foreign Public Officials in International Business Transactions, adopted by the Negotiating Conference on 21 November 1997

(2) 2021 OECD Anti-Bribery Recommendation[11] (January 26, 2022)

High Level Statement by the Parties to the Anti-Bribery Convention About the Recommendation

26/11/2021—The OECD Anti-Bribery Convention establishes legally binding standards to criminalise bribery of foreign public officials in international business transactions, and provides for a host of related measures to make this effective. It is the first and only international anti-corruption instrument focused on the "supply side" of the bribery transaction. The 2021 Recommendation for Further Combating Bribery of Foreign Public Officials in International Business Transactions complements the Anti-Bribery Convention with a view to further strengthening and supporting its implementation.

The OECD Working Group on Bribery—which brings together the 44 countries Party to the Anti-Bribery Convention—is responsible for monitoring the implementation and enforcement of the Anti-Bribery Convention and Recommendation. In 2018, the Working Group decided to conduct an extensive review of the 2009 Anti-Bribery Recommendation to ensure it continues to reflect the range of good practices, trends and challenges that have emerged in the foreign bribery field over the past ten years. After a rigorous process, including two rounds of extensive consultations with external partners, a stocktaking of ten years of implementation of the 2009 Anti-Bribery Recommendation, multiple written procedures and eight dedicated meetings of the Working Group, the 2021 Anti-Bribery Recommendation was adopted by the OECD Council on 26 November 2021.

With this Recommendation, the Parties to the Anti-Bribery Convention agree to new measures to reinforce their efforts to prevent, detect and investigate foreign bribery. In addition to enhancing the provisions already included in the 2009 Anti-Bribery Recommendation, the 2021 Recommendation includes sections on key topics that have emerged or significantly evolved in the anti-corruption area, including, inter alia, on strengthening enforcement of foreign bribery laws, addressing the demand side of foreign bribery, enhancing international co-operation, introducing principles on the use of non-trial resolutions in foreign bribery cases, incentivising anti-corruption compliance by companies, and providing comprehensive and effective protection for reporting persons. It is one of five OECD Recommendations which make up the strong OECD anti-corruption framework, covering areas such as tax, official development assistance, export credits and state-owned enterprises.

Key Elements of the Recommendation

- Promote a holistic approach to fighting foreign bribery through new measures to enhance awareness-raising and training of, as well as detection by, key

---

[10] https://www.oecd.org/daf/anti-bribery/ConvCombatBribery_ENG.pdf

[11] https://www.oecd.org/corruption/2021-oecd-anti-bribery-recommendation.htm

government agencies, including foreign representations, financial intelligence units, tax authorities and official development assistance agencies.
- Strengthen enforcement of foreign bribery laws, including through proactive detection and investigation of foreign bribery, more effective international co-operation among law enforcement authorities and co-operation in multi-jurisdictional cases.
- Address the demand side of foreign bribery cases by calling on countries to address the solicitation and acceptance of bribes and better support companies facing bribe solicitation risks.
- Introduce provisions on the key principles and features of non-trial resolutions.
- Include extensive provisions to ensure comprehensive and effective protection of whistleblowers in the public and private sectors.
- Encourage countries to incentivise enterprises to develop internal controls, ethics and compliance programmes or measures to prevent and detect foreign bribery.
- **World Economic Forum PACI**[12] **(26 January 2022)**

Global Future Council on Transparency and Anti-Corruption
Council Mission and Objectives

It is estimated that corruption costs the world economy 5% of GDP a year, equivalent to $3.6 trillion. There is an urgent imperative to collaborate towards greater integrity and ethical leadership. The Global Future Council on Transparency and Anti-Corruption has developed a forward-looking framework for business integrity, which supports and aligns with broader work to globally reset and embed a revised purpose of business based on a stakeholder economy. Building on this Agenda for Business Integrity, the council will continue to support global stakeholders to improve their integrity through an innovative playbook on the rise of the integrity officer and a deep dive into the role of investors on integrity. These deliverables aim to mobilize public and private sector leaders in delivering robust and responsible business conduct.

Forum Council Manager: Lisa Ventura, Practice Lead, Partnering Against Corruption Initiative (PACI), World Economic Forum
WEF: The agenda for business integrity[13]

The World Economic Forum's Global Future Council on Transparency and Anti-Corruption has developed a forward-looking framework for business integrity, which supports and aligns with broader work to globally reset and embed a revised purpose of business based on a stakeholder economy. 1 Our purpose is to provide a clearly defined and practical agenda for businesses to pursue integrity in a way that is aligned with the United Nations (UN) Sustainable Development Goals (SDGs), the Organisation for Economic Co-operation and Development (OECD) Guidelines for

---

[12] https://www.weforum.org/communities/gfc-on-transparency-and-anti-corruption

[13] https://www3.weforum.org/docs/WEF_GFC_on_Transparency_and_AC_pillar1_beyond_compliance_2020.pdf

Multinational Enterprises and the UN Guiding Principles on Business and Human Rights.

The framework is based on four pillars:

1. A conceptual foundation that requires a commitment to ethics and integrity beyond compliance
2. Strengthening corporate culture and incentives to drive continuous improvement and leadership
3. Leveraging innovative technologies to improve data collection, analysis, decision-making, reporting and overall accountability
4. Supporting collective action to increase scale and impact

- **EU Directive on Whistleblower Protection**[14] **(16 February 2022)**

26.11.2019, Official Journal of the European Union
Directive (EU) 2019/1937 of the European Parliament and of the Council of 23 October 2019 on the protection of persons who report breaches of Union law

The European Parliament and the Council of the European Union,

Having regard to the Treaty on the Functioning of the European Union, and in particular Article 16, Article 43(2), Article 50, Article 53(1), Articles 91, 100, and 114, Article 168(4), Article 169, Article 192(1) and Article 325(4) thereof and to the Treaty establishing the European Atomic Energy Community, and in particular Article 31 thereof,

Having regard to the proposal from the European Commission,

After transmission of the draft legislative act to the national parliaments,

Having regard to the opinion of the Court of Auditors,

Having regard to the opinion of the European Economic and Social Committee,

After consulting the Committee of the Regions,

Having regard to the opinion of 30 November 2018 of the Group of Experts referred to in Article 31 of the Treaty establishing the European Atomic Energy Community,

Acting in accordance with the ordinary legislative procedure,

Whereas:

1. Persons who work for a public or private organisation or are in contact with such an organisation in the context of their work-related activities are often the first to know about threats or harm to the public interest which arise in that context. By reporting breaches of Union law that are harmful to the public interest, such persons act as 'whistleblowers' and thereby play a key role in exposing and preventing such breaches and in safeguarding the welfare of society. However, potential whistleblowers are often discouraged from reporting their concerns or suspicions for fear of retaliation. In this context, the importance of providing balanced and effective whistleblower protection is increasingly acknowledged at both Union and international level.

---

[14] https://eur-lex.europa.eu/legal-content/EN/TXT/PDF/?uri=CELEX:32019L1937

2. At Union level, reports and public disclosures by whistleblowers are one upstream component of enforcement of Union law and policies. They feed national and Union enforcement systems with information, leading to effective detection, investigation and prosecution of breaches of Union law, thus enhancing transparency and accountability.
3. In certain policy areas, breaches of Union law, regardless of whether they are categorised under national law as administrative, criminal or other types of breaches, may cause serious harm to the public interest, in that they create significant risks for the welfare of society. Where weaknesses of enforcement have been identified in those areas, and whistleblowers are usually in a privileged position to disclose breaches, it is necessary to enhance enforcement by introducing effective, confidential and secure reporting channels and by ensuring that whistleblowers are protected effectively against retaliation . . .

Have Adopted This Directive:

Chapter I Scope, Definitions and Conditions for Protection
Article 1 Purpose

The purpose of this Directive is to enhance the enforcement of Union law and policies in specific areas by laying down common minimum standards providing for a high level of protection of persons reporting breaches of Union law.

Article 2 Material Scope

1. This Directive lays down common minimum standards for the protection of persons reporting the following breaches of Union law:

    (a) breaches falling within the scope of the Union acts set out in the Annex that concern the following areas:

       (i) public procurement;
       (ii) financial services, products and markets, and prevention of money laundering and terrorist financing;
       (iii) product safety and compliance;
       (iv) transport safety;
       (v) protection of the environment;
       (vi) radiation protection and nuclear safety;
       (vii) food and feed safety, animal health and welfare;
       (viii) public health;
       (ix) consumer protection;
       (x) protection of privacy and personal data, and security of network and information systems;

    (b) breaches affecting the financial interests of the Union as referred to in Article 325 TFEU and as further specified in relevant Union measures;
    (c) breaches relating to the internal market, as referred to in Article 26(2) TFEU, including breaches of Union competition and State aid rules, as well as breaches relating to the internal market in relation to acts which breach the rules of corporate tax or to arrangements the purpose of which is to obtain a

tax advantage that defeats the object or purpose of the applicable corporate tax law.

2. This Directive is without prejudice to the power of Member States to extend protection under national law as regards areas or acts not covered by paragraph 1.

Article 3 Relationship with Other Union Acts and National Provisions

1. Where specific rules on the reporting of breaches are provided for in the sector-specific Union acts listed in Part II of the Annex, those rules shall apply. The provisions of this Directive shall be applicable to the extent that a matter is not mandatorily regulated in those sector-specific Union acts.
2. This Directive shall not affect the responsibility of Member States to ensure national security or their power to protect their essential security interests. In particular, it shall not apply to reports of breaches of the procurement rules involving defence or security aspects unless they are covered by the relevant acts of the Union.
3. This Directive shall not affect the application of Union or national law relating to any of the following:

    (a) the protection of classified information;
    (b) the protection of legal and medical professional privilege;
    (c) the secrecy of judicial deliberations;
    (d) rules on criminal procedure.

4. This Directive shall not affect national rules on the exercise by workers of their rights to consult their representatives or trade unions, and on protection against any unjustified detrimental measure prompted by such consultations as well as on the autonomy of the social partners and their right to enter into collective agreements. This is without prejudice to the level of protection granted by this Directive.

Article 4 Personal Scope

1. This Directive shall apply to reporting persons working in the private or public sector who acquired information on breaches in a work-related context including, at least, the following:

    (a) persons having the status of worker, within the meaning of Article 45(1) TFEU, including civil servants;
    (b) persons having self-employed status, within the meaning of Article 49 TFEU;
    (c) shareholders and persons belonging to the administrative, management or supervisory body of an undertaking, including non-executive members, as well as volunteers and paid or unpaid trainees;
    (d) any persons working under the supervision and direction of contractors, subcontractors and suppliers.

11.1 United Nations Convention Against Corruption (UN CAC) 363

2. This Directive shall also apply to reporting persons where they report or publicly disclose information on breaches acquired in a work-based relationship which has since ended.
3. This Directive shall also apply to reporting persons whose work-based relationship is yet to begin in cases where information on breaches has been acquired during the recruitment process or other pre-contractual negotiations.
4. The measures for the protection of reporting persons set out in Chapter VI shall also apply, where relevant, to:

   (a) facilitators;
   (b) third persons who are connected with the reporting persons and who could suffer retaliation in a work-related context, such as colleagues or relatives of the reporting persons; and
   (c) legal entities that the reporting persons own, work for or are otherwise connected with in a work-related context.

Article 5 Definitions
For the purposes of this Directive, the following definitions apply:

1. 'breaches' means acts or omissions that:

   (a) are unlawful and relate to the Union acts and areas falling within the material scope referred to in Article 2; or
   (b) defeat the object or the purpose of the rules in the Union acts and areas falling within the material scope referred to in Article 2;

2. 'information on breaches' means information, including reasonable suspicions, about actual or potential breaches, which occurred or are very likely to occur in the organisation in which the reporting person works or has worked or in another organisation with which the reporting person is or was in contact through his or her work, and about attempts to conceal such breaches;
3. 'report' or 'to report' means, the oral or written communication of information on breaches;
4. 'internal reporting' means the oral or written communication of information on breaches within a legal entity in the private or public sector;
5. 'external reporting' means the oral or written communication of information on breaches to the competent authorities;
6. 'public disclosure' or 'to publicly disclose' means the making of information on breaches available in the public domain;
7. 'reporting person' means a natural person who reports or publicly discloses information on breaches acquired in the context of his or her work-related activities;
8. 'facilitator' means a natural person who assists a reporting person in the reporting process in a work-related context, and whose assistance should be confidential;
9. 'work-related context' means current or past work activities in the public or private sector through which, irrespective of the nature of those activities,

persons acquire information on breaches and within which those persons could suffer retaliation if they reported such information;

10. 'person concerned' means a natural or legal person who is referred to in the report or public disclosure as a person to whom the breach is attributed or with whom that person is associated;
11. 'retaliation' means any direct or indirect act or omission which occurs in a work-related context, is prompted by internal or external reporting or by public disclosure, and which causes or may cause unjustified detriment to the reporting person;
12. 'follow-up' means any action taken by the recipient of a report or any competent authority, to assess the accuracy of the allegations made in the report and, where relevant, to address the breach reported, including through actions such as an internal enquiry, an investigation, prosecution, an action for recovery of funds, or the closure of the procedure;
13. 'feedback' means the provision to the reporting person of information on the action envisaged or taken as follow up and on the grounds for such follow-up;
14. 'competent authority' means any national authority designated to receive reports in accordance with Chapter III and give feedback to the reporting person, and/or designated to carry out the duties provided for in this Directive, in particular as regards follow-up.

Article 6 Conditions for Protection of Reporting Persons

1. Reporting persons shall qualify for protection under this Directive provided that:
   (a) they had reasonable grounds to believe that the information on breaches reported was true at the time of reporting and that such information fell within the scope of this Directive; and
   (b) they reported either internally in accordance with Article 7 or externally in accordance with Article 10, or made a public disclosure in accordance with Article 15.
2. Without prejudice to existing obligations to provide for anonymous reporting by virtue of Union law, this Directive does not affect the power of Member States to decide whether legal entities in the private or public sector and competent authorities are required to accept and follow up on anonymous reports of breaches.
3. Persons who reported or publicly disclosed information on breaches anonymously, but who are subsequently identified and suffer retaliation, shall nonetheless qualify for the protection provided for under Chapter VI, provided that they meet the conditions laid down in paragraph 1.
4. Persons reporting to relevant institutions, bodies, offices or agencies of the Union breaches falling within the scope of this Directive shall qualify for protection as laid down in this Directive under the same conditions as persons who report externally.

Chapter II Internal Reporting and Follow-up
Article 7 Reporting Through Internal Reporting Channels

1. As a general principle and without prejudice to Articles 10 and 15, information on breaches may be reported through the internal reporting channels and procedures provided for in this Chapter.
2. Member States shall encourage reporting through internal reporting channels before reporting through external reporting channels, where the breach can be addressed effectively internally and where the reporting person considers that there is no risk of retaliation.
3. Appropriate information relating to the use of internal reporting channels referred to in paragraph 2 shall be provided in the context of the information given by legal entities in the private and public sector pursuant to point (g) of Article 9(1), and by competent authorities pursuant to point (a) of Article 12(4) and Article 13.

Article 8 Obligation to Establish Internal Reporting Channels

1. Member States shall ensure that legal entities in the private and public sector establish channels and procedures for internal reporting and for follow-up, following consultation and in agreement with the social partners where provided for by national law.
2. The channels and procedures referred to in paragraph 1 of this Article shall enable the entity's workers to report information on breaches. They may enable other persons, referred to in points (b), (c) and (d) of Article 4(1) and Article 4(2), who are in contact with the entity in the context of their work-related activities to also report information on breaches.
3. Paragraph 1 shall apply to legal entities in the private sector with 50 or more workers.
4. The threshold laid down in paragraph 3 shall not apply to the entities falling within the scope of Union acts referred to in Parts I.B and II of the Annex.
5. Reporting channels may be operated internally by a person or department designated for that purpose or provided externally by a third party. The safeguards and requirements referred to in Article 9(1) shall also apply to entrusted third parties operating the reporting channel for a legal entity in the private sector.
6. Legal entities in the private sector with 50 to 249 workers may share resources as regards the receipt of reports and any investigation to be carried out. This shall be without prejudice to the obligations imposed upon such entities by this Directive to maintain confidentiality, to give feedback, and to address the reported breach.
7. Following an appropriate risk assessment taking into account the nature of the activities of the entities and the ensuing level of risk for, in particular, the environment and public health, Member States may require legal entities in the private sector with fewer than 50 workers to establish internal reporting channels and procedures in accordance with Chapter II.
8. Member States shall notify the Commission of any decision they take to require legal entities in the private sector to establish internal reporting channels pursuant to paragraph 7. That notification shall include the reasons for the decision and the

criteria used in the risk assessment referred to in paragraph 7. The Commission shall communicate that decision to the other Member States.
9. Paragraph 1 shall apply to all legal entities in the public sector, including any entity owned or controlled by such entities.

Member States may exempt from the obligation referred to in paragraph 1 municipalities with fewer than 10 000 inhabitants or fewer than 50 workers, or other entities referred to in the first subparagraph of this paragraph with fewer than 50 workers.

Member States may provide that internal reporting channels can be shared between municipalities or operated by joint municipal authorities in accordance with national law, provided that the shared internal reporting channels are distinct from and autonomous in relation to the relevant external reporting channels.

Article 9 Procedures for Internal Reporting and Follow-up

1. The procedures for internal reporting and for follow-up as referred to in Article 8 shall include the following:

    (a) channels for receiving the reports which are designed, established and operated in a secure manner that ensures that the confidentiality of the identity of the reporting person and any third party mentioned in the report is protected, and prevents access thereto by non-authorised staff members;

    (b) acknowledgment of receipt of the report to the reporting person within seven days of that receipt;

    (c) the designation of an impartial person or department competent for following-up on the reports which may be the same person or department as the one that receives the reports and which will maintain communication with the reporting person and, where necessary, ask for further information from and provide feedback to that reporting person;

    (d) diligent follow-up by the designated person or department referred to in point (c);

    (e) diligent follow-up, where provided for in national law, as regards anonymous reporting;

    (f) a reasonable timeframe to provide feedback, not exceeding three months from the acknowledgment of receipt or, if no acknowledgement was sent to the reporting person, three months from the expiry of the seven-day period after the report was made;

    (g) provision of clear and easily accessible information regarding the procedures for reporting externally to competent authorities pursuant to Article 10 and, where relevant, to institutions, bodies, offices or agencies of the Union.

2. The channels provided for in point (a) of paragraph 1 shall enable reporting in writing or orally, or both. Oral reporting shall be possible by telephone or through other voice messaging systems, and, upon request by the reporting person, by means of a physical meeting within a reasonable timeframe.

Chapter III External Reporting and Follow-up
Article 10 Reporting Through External Reporting Channels

Without prejudice to point (b) of Article 15(1), reporting persons shall report information on breaches using the channels and procedures referred to in Articles 11 and 12, after having first reported through internal reporting channels, or by directly reporting through external reporting channels.

Article 11 Obligation to Establish External Reporting Channels and to Follow Up on Reports

1. Member States shall designate the authorities competent to receive, give feedback and follow up on reports, and shall provide them with adequate resources.
2. Member States shall ensure that the competent authorities:

    (a) establish independent and autonomous external reporting channels, for receiving and handling information on breaches;
    (b) promptly, and in any event within seven days of receipt of the report, acknowledge that receipt unless the reporting person explicitly requested otherwise or the competent authority reasonably believes that acknowledging receipt of the report would jeopardise the protection of the reporting person's identity;
    (c) diligently follow up on the reports;
    (d) provide feedback to the reporting person within a reasonable timeframe not exceeding three months, or six months in duly justified cases;
    (e) communicate to the reporting person the final outcome of investigations triggered by the report, in accordance with procedures provided for under national law;
    (f) transmit in due time the information contained in the report to competent institutions, bodies, offices or agencies of the Union, as appropriate, for further investigation, where provided for under Union or national law.

3. Member States may provide that competent authorities, after having duly assessed the matter, can decide that a reported breach is clearly minor and does not require further follow-up pursuant to this Directive, other than closure of the procedure. This shall not affect other obligations or other applicable procedures to address the reported breach, or the protection granted by this Directive in relation to internal or external reporting. In such a case, the competent authorities shall notify the reporting person of their decision and the reasons therefor.
4. Member States may provide that competent authorities can decide to close procedures regarding repetitive reports which do not contain any meaningful new information on breaches compared to a past report in respect of which the relevant procedures were concluded, unless new legal or factual circumstances justify a different follow-up. In such a case, the competent authorities shall notify the reporting person of their decision and the reasons therefor.
5. Member States may provide that, in the event of high inflows of reports, competent authorities may deal with reports of serious breaches or breaches of essential

provisions falling within the scope of this Directive as a matter of priority, without prejudice to the timeframe as set out in point (d) of paragraph 2.
6. Member States shall ensure that any authority which has received a report but does not have the competence to address the breach reported transmits it to the competent authority, within a reasonable time, in a secure manner, and that the reporting person is informed, without delay, of such a transmission.

Article 12 Design of External Reporting Channels

1. External reporting channels shall be considered independent and autonomous, if they meet all of the following criteria:

    (a) they are designed, established and operated in a manner that ensures the completeness, integrity and confidentiality of the information and prevents access thereto by non-authorised staff members of the competent authority;
    (b) they enable the durable storage of information in accordance with Article 18 to allow further investigations to be carried out.

2. The external reporting channels shall enable reporting in writing and orally. Oral reporting shall be possible by telephone or through other voice messaging systems and, upon request by the reporting person, by means of a physical meeting within a reasonable timeframe.
3. Competent authorities shall ensure that, where a report is received through channels other than the reporting channels referred to in paragraphs 1 and 2 or by staff members other than those responsible for handling reports, the staff members who receive it are prohibited from disclosing any information that might identify the reporting person or the person concerned, and that they promptly forward the report without modification to the staff members responsible for handling reports.
4. Member States shall ensure that competent authorities designate staff members responsible for handling reports, and in particular for:

    (a) providing any interested person with information on the procedures for reporting;
    (b) receiving and following up on reports;
    (c) maintaining contact with the reporting person for the purpose of providing feedback and requesting further information where necessary.

5. The staff members referred to in paragraph 4 shall receive specific training for the purposes of handling reports.

Article 13 Information Regarding the Receipt of Reports and Their Follow-up

Member States shall ensure that competent authorities publish on their websites in a separate, easily identifiable and accessible section at least the following information:

(a) the conditions for qualifying for protection under this Directive;
(b) the contact details for the external reporting channels as provided for under Article 12, in particular the electronic and postal addresses, and the phone numbers for such channels, indicating whether the phone conversations are recorded;
(c) the procedures applicable to the reporting of breaches, including the manner in which the competent authority may request the reporting person to clarify the information reported or to provide additional information, the timeframe for providing feedback and the type and content of such feedback;
(d) the confidentiality regime applicable to reports, and in particular the information in relation to the processing of personal data in accordance with Article 17 of this Directive, Articles 5 and 13 of Regulation (EU) 2016/679, Article 13 of Directive (EU) 2016/680 and Article 15 of Regulation (EU) 2018/1725, as applicable;
(e) the nature of the follow-up to be given to reports;
(f) the remedies and procedures for protection against retaliation and the availability of confidential advice for persons contemplating reporting;
(g) a statement clearly explaining the conditions under which persons reporting to the competent authority are protected from incurring liability for a breach of confidentiality pursuant to Article 21(2); and
(h) contact details of the information centre or of the single independent administrative authority as provided for in Article 20(3) where applicable.

Article 14 Review of the Procedures by Competent Authorities

Member States shall ensure that competent authorities review their procedures for receiving reports, and their follow-up, regularly, and at least once every three years. In reviewing such procedures, competent authorities shall take account of their experience as well as that of other competent authorities and adapt their procedures accordingly.

Chapter IV Public Disclosures
Article 15 Public Disclosures

1. A person who makes a public disclosure shall qualify for protection under this Directive if any of the following conditions is fulfilled:

   (a) the person first reported internally and externally, or directly externally in accordance with Chapters II and III, but no appropriate action was taken in response to the report within the timeframe referred to in point (f) of Article 9(1) or point (d) of Article 11(2); or
   (b) the person has reasonable grounds to believe that:

      (i) the breach may constitute an imminent or manifest danger to the public interest, such as where there is an emergency situation or a risk of irreversible damage; or
      (ii) in the case of external reporting, there is a risk of retaliation or there is a low prospect of the breach being effectively addressed, due to the particular circumstances of the case, such as those where evidence may

be concealed or destroyed or where an authority may be in collusion with the perpetrator of the breach or involved in the breach.
2. This Article shall not apply to cases where a person directly discloses information to the press pursuant to specific national provisions establishing a system of protection relating to freedom of expression and information.

Chapter V Provisions Applicable to Internal and External Reporting
Article 16 Duty of Confidentiality

1. Member States shall ensure that the identity of the reporting person is not disclosed to anyone beyond the authorised staff members competent to receive or follow up on reports, without the explicit consent of that person. This shall also apply to any other information from which the identity of the reporting person may be directly or indirectly deduced.
2. By way of derogation from paragraph 1, the identity of the reporting person and any other information referred to in paragraph 1 may be disclosed only where this is a necessary and proportionate obligation imposed by Union or national law in the context of investigations by national authorities or judicial proceedings, including with a view to safeguarding the rights of defence of the person concerned.
3. Disclosures made pursuant to the derogation provided for in paragraph 2 shall be subject to appropriate safeguards under the applicable Union and national rules. In particular, reporting persons shall be informed before their identity is disclosed, unless such information would jeopardise the related investigations or judicial proceedings. When informing the reporting persons, the competent authority shall send them an explanation in writing of the reasons for the disclosure of the confidential data concerned.
4. Member States shall ensure that competent authorities that receive information on breaches that includes trade secrets do not use or disclose those trade secrets for purposes going beyond what is necessary for proper follow-up.

Article 17 Processing of Personal Data

Any processing of personal data carried out pursuant to this Directive, including the exchange or transmission of personal data by the competent authorities, shall be carried out in accordance with Regulation (EU) 2016/679 and Directive (EU) 2016/680. Any exchange or transmission of information by Union institutions, bodies, offices or agencies shall be undertaken in accordance with Regulation (EU) 2018/1725. Personal data which are manifestly not relevant for the handling of a specific report shall not be collected or, if accidentally collected, shall be deleted without undue delay.

Article 18 Record Keeping of the Reports

1. Member States shall ensure that legal entities in the private and public sector and competent authorities keep records of every report received, in compliance with the confidentiality requirements provided for in Article 16. Reports shall be stored for no longer than it is necessary and proportionate in order to comply with the

requirements imposed by this Directive, or other requirements imposed by Union or national law.

2. Where a recorded telephone line or another recorded voice messaging system is used for reporting, subject to the consent of the reporting person, legal entities in the private and public sector and competent authorities shall have the right to document the oral reporting in one of the following ways:

   (a) by making a recording of the conversation in a durable and retrievable form; or
   (b) through a complete and accurate transcript of the conversation prepared by the staff members responsible for handling the report.

   Legal entities in the private and public sector and competent authorities shall offer the reporting person the opportunity to check, rectify and agree the transcript of the call by signing it.

3. Where an unrecorded telephone line or another unrecorded voice messaging system is used for reporting, legal entities in the private and public sector and competent authorities shall have the right to document the oral reporting in the form of accurate minutes of the conversation written by the staff member responsible for handling the report. Legal entities in the private and public sector and competent authorities shall offer the reporting person the opportunity to check, rectify and agree the minutes of the conversation by signing them.

4. Where a person requests a meeting with the staff members of legal entities in the private and public sector or of competent authorities for reporting purposes pursuant to Articles 9(2) and 12(2), legal entities in the private and public sector and competent authorities shall ensure, subject to the consent of the reporting person, that complete and accurate records of the meeting are kept in a durable and retrievable form.

   Legal entities in the private and public sector and competent authorities shall have the right to document the meeting in one of the following ways:

   (a) by making a recording of the conversation in a durable and retrievable form; or
   (b) through accurate minutes of the meeting prepared by the staff members responsible for handling the report.

   Legal entities in the private and public sector and competent authorities shall offer the reporting person the opportunity to check, rectify and agree the minutes of the meeting by signing them.

Chapter VI Protection Measures
Article 19 Prohibition of Retaliation

Member States shall take the necessary measures to prohibit any form of retaliation against persons referred to in Article 4, including threats of retaliation and attempts of retaliation including in particular in the form of:

(a) suspension, lay-off, dismissal or equivalent measures;
(b) demotion or withholding of promotion;

(c) transfer of duties, change of location of place of work, reduction in wages, change in working hours;
(d) withholding of training;
(e) a negative performance assessment or employment reference;
(f) imposition or administering of any disciplinary measure, reprimand or other penalty, including a financial penalty;
(g) coercion, intimidation, harassment or ostracism;
(h) discrimination, disadvantageous or unfair treatment;
(i) failure to convert a temporary employment contract into a permanent one, where the worker had legitimate expectations that he or she would be offered permanent employment;
(j) failure to renew, or early termination of, a temporary employment contract;
(k) harm, including to the person's reputation, particularly in social media, or financial loss, including loss of business and loss of income;
(l) blacklisting on the basis of a sector or industry-wide informal or formal agreement, which may entail that the person will not, in the future, find employment in the sector or industry;
(m) early termination or cancellation of a contract for goods or services;
(n) cancellation of a licence or permit;
(o) psychiatric or medical referrals.

Article 20 Measures of Support

1. Member States shall ensure that persons referred to in Article 4 have access, as appropriate, to support measures, in particular the following:

    (a) comprehensive and independent information and advice, which is easily accessible to the public and free of charge, on procedures and remedies available, on protection against retaliation, and on the rights of the person concerned;

    (b) effective assistance from competent authorities before any relevant authority involved in their protection against retaliation, including, where provided for under national law, certification of the fact that they qualify for protection under this Directive; and

    (c) legal aid in criminal and in cross-border civil proceedings in accordance with Directive (EU) 2016/1919 and Directive 2008/52/EC of the European Parliament and of the Council (48), and, in accordance with national law, legal aid in further proceedings and legal counselling or other legal assistance.
    (48) Directive 2008/52/EC of the European Parliament and of the Council of 21 May 2008 on certain aspects of mediation in civil and commercial matters (OJ L 136, 24.5.2008, p. 3).

2. Member States may provide for financial assistance and support measures, including psychological support, for reporting persons in the framework of legal proceedings.

3. The support measures referred to in this Article may be provided, as appropriate, by an information centre or a single and clearly identified independent administrative authority.

Article 21 Measures for Protection Against Retaliation

1. Member States shall take the necessary measures to ensure that persons referred to in Article 4 are protected against retaliation. Such measures shall include, in particular, those set out in paragraphs 2 to 8 of this Article.
2. Without prejudice to Article 3(2) and (3), where persons report information on breaches or make a public disclosure in accordance with this Directive they shall not be considered to have breached any restriction on disclosure of information and shall not incur liability of any kind in respect of such a report or public disclosure provided that they had reasonable grounds to believe that the reporting or public disclosure of such information was necessary for revealing a breach pursuant to this Directive.
3. Reporting persons shall not incur liability in respect of the acquisition of or access to the information which is reported or publicly disclosed, provided that such acquisition or access did not constitute a self-standing criminal offence. In the event of the acquisition or access constituting a self-standing criminal offence, criminal liability shall continue to be governed by applicable national law.
4. Any other possible liability of reporting persons arising from acts or omissions which are unrelated to the reporting or public disclosure or which are not necessary for revealing a breach pursuant to this Directive shall continue to be governed by applicable Union or national law.
5. In proceedings before a court or other authority relating to a detriment suffered by the reporting person, and subject to that person establishing that he or she reported or made a public disclosure and suffered a detriment, it shall be presumed that the detriment was made in retaliation for the report or the public disclosure. In such cases, it shall be for the person who has taken the detrimental measure to prove that that measure was based on duly justified grounds.
6. Persons referred to in Article 4 shall have access to remedial measures against retaliation as appropriate, including interim relief pending the resolution of legal proceedings, in accordance with national law.
7. In legal proceedings, including for defamation, breach of copyright, breach of secrecy, breach of data protection rules, disclosure of trade secrets, or for compensation claims based on private, public, or on collective labour law, persons referred to in Article 4 shall not incur liability of any kind as a result of reports or public disclosures under this Directive. Those persons shall have the right to rely on that reporting or public disclosure to seek dismissal of the case, provided that they had reasonable grounds to believe that the reporting or public disclosure was necessary for revealing a breach, pursuant to this Directive. Where a person reports or publicly discloses information on breaches falling within the scope of this Directive, and that information includes trade secrets, and where that person meets the conditions of this Directive, such reporting or public disclosure shall be

considered lawful under the conditions of Article 3(2) of the Directive (EU) 2016/943.

8. Member States shall take the necessary measures to ensure that remedies and full compensation are provided for damage suffered by persons referred to in Article 4 in accordance with national law.

Article 22 Measures for the Protection of Persons Concerned

1. Member States shall ensure, in accordance with the Charter, that persons concerned fully enjoy the right to an effective remedy and to a fair trial, as well as the presumption of innocence and the rights of defence, including the right to be heard and the right to access their file.
2. Competent authorities shall ensure, in accordance with national law, that the identity of persons concerned is protected for as long as investigations triggered by the report or the public disclosure are ongoing.
3. The rules set out in Articles 12, 17 and 18 as regards the protection of the identity of reporting persons shall also apply to the protection of the identity of persons concerned.

Article 23 Penalties

1. Member States shall provide for effective, proportionate and dissuasive penalties applicable to natural or legal persons that:
   (a) hinder or attempt to hinder reporting;
   (b) retaliate against persons referred to in Article 4;
   (c) bring vexatious proceedings against persons referred to in Article 4;
   (d) breach the duty of maintaining the confidentiality of the identity of reporting persons, as referred to in Article 16.
2. Member States shall provide for effective, proportionate and dissuasive penalties applicable in respect of reporting persons where it is established that they knowingly reported or publicly disclosed false information. Member States shall also provide for measures for compensating damage resulting from such reporting or public disclosures in accordance with national law.

Article 24 No Waiver of Rights and Remedies

Member States shall ensure that the rights and remedies provided for under this Directive cannot be waived or limited by any agreement, policy, form or condition of employment, including a pre-dispute arbitration agreement.

Chapter VII Final Provisions
Article 25 More Favourable Treatment and Non-regression Clause

1. Member States may introduce or retain provisions more favourable to the rights of reporting persons than those set out in this Directive, without prejudice to Article 22 and Article 23(2).

2. The implementation of this Directive shall under no circumstances constitute grounds for a reduction in the level of protection already afforded by Member States in the areas covered by this Directive.

Article 26 Transposition and Transitional Period

1. Member States shall bring into force the laws, regulations and administrative provisions necessary to comply with this Directive by 17 December 2021.
2. By way of derogation from paragraph 1, as regards legal entities in the private sector with 50 to 249 workers, Member States shall by 17 December 2023 bring into force the laws, regulations and administrative provisions necessary to comply with the obligation to establish internal reporting channels under Article 8(3).
3. When Member States adopt the provisions referred to in paragraphs 1 and 2, those provisions shall contain a reference to this Directive or be accompanied by such a reference on the occasion of their official publication. Member States shall determine how such reference is to be made. They shall forthwith communicate to the Commission the text of those provisions.

Article 27 Reporting, Evaluation and Review

1. Member States shall provide the Commission with all relevant information regarding the implementation and application of this Directive. On the basis of the information provided, the. Commission shall, by 17 December 2023, submit a report to the European Parliament and the Council on the implementation and application of this Directive.
2. Without prejudice to reporting obligations laid down in other Union legal acts, Member States shall, on an annual basis, submit the following statistics on the reports referred to in Chapter III to the Commission, preferably in an aggregated form, if they are available at a central level in the Member State concerned:
   (a) the number of reports received by the competent authorities;
   (b) the number of investigations and proceedings initiated as a result of such reports and their outcome; and
   (c) if ascertained, the estimated financial damage, and the amounts recovered following investigations and proceedings, related to the breaches reported.
3. The Commission shall, by 17 December 2025, taking into account its report submitted pursuant to paragraph 1 and the Member States' statistics submitted pursuant to paragraph 2, submit a report to the European Parliament and to the Council assessing the impact of national law transposing this Directive. The report shall evaluate the way in which this Directive has functioned and consider the need for additional measures, including, where appropriate, amendments with a view to extending the scope of this Directive to further Union acts or areas, in particular the improvement of the working environment to protect workers' health and safety and working conditions. In addition to the evaluation referred to in the first subparagraph, the report shall evaluate how Member States made use of existing cooperation mechanisms as part of their obligations to follow up

on reports regarding breaches falling within the scope of this Directive and more generally how they cooperate in cases of breaches with a cross-border dimension.
4. The Commission shall make the reports referred to in paragraphs 1 and 3 public and easily accessible.

Article 28 Entry into Force
This Directive shall enter into force on the twentieth day following that of its publication in the Official Journal of the European Union.

Article 29 Addressees
This Directive is addressed to the Member States.

- **ISO 37001 ANTI-BRIBERY MANAGEMENT SYSTEMS**

Summary from ISO website[15] (22 January 2022)

Transparency and trust are the building blocks of any organization's credibility. Nothing undermines effective institutions and equitable business more than bribery, which is why there's ISO 37001.

It's the International Standard that allows organizations of all types to prevent, detect and address bribery by adopting an anti-bribery policy, appointing a person to oversee anti-bribery compliance, training, risk assessments and due diligence on projects and business associates, implementing financial and commercial controls, and instituting reporting and investigation procedures.

Providing a globally recognized way to address a destructive criminal activity that turns over a trillion dollars of dirty money each year, ISO 37001 addresses one of the world's most destructive and challenging issues head-on, and demonstrates a committed approach to stamping out corruption.

Who Is ISO 37001 for?
ISO 37001 can be used by any organization, large or small, whether it be in the public, private or voluntary sector, and in any country. It is a flexible tool, which can be adapted according to the size and nature of the organization and the bribery risk it faces.

Where Can I Find Out More About ISO 37001?
ISO 37001 can be purchased from your national ISO member or through the ISO Store. You can also learn more about the standard in this PowerPoint presentation, which can be used whole, or in part, to demonstrate the advantages of ISO 37001 to your organization.

ISO 37001:2016 ANTI-BRIBERY MANAGEMENT SYSTEMS: A PRACTICAL GUIDE Published jointly by ISO and UNIDO, this handbook helps users put in place an effective anti-bribery management system

---

[15] https://www.iso.org/iso-37001-anti-bribery-management.html

- **Transparency International Integrity Pacts**[16]

Each year, governments spend huge sums of money on public procurement—funding roads, bridges, schools, housing, water and power supply, other community improvements... But with these vast expenditures, opportunities for corruption are rife.

Integrity Pacts were developed as a tool for preventing corruption in public contracting.

An Integrity Pact is both a signed document and approach to public contracting which commits a contracting authority and bidders to comply with best practice and maximum transparency. A third actor, usually a civil society organisation (often one of our chapters), monitors the process and commitments made. Monitors commit to maximum transparency and all monitoring reports and results are made available to the public on an ongoing basis.

Integrity Pacts have been around since the 1990s, and have been applied in more than 15 countries and 300 separate situations. They help save taxpayer money, ensure that infrastructure projects and other public works are delivered efficiently, and close off avenues for illicit gain. An update to the Integrity Pact concept in 2016 has seen it draw on major advances in the areas of technology and civic participation.

The Integrity Pact is co-created by TI national chapters, or other civil society partners, and government officials responsible for a particular procurement process. Its clauses are drawn from both international open contracting principles as well as the local legal and social context. In this way the tool is constantly evolving based on lessons learned and best practice around the world as well as up-to-date analysis regarding the country and sector's corruption risk profile. In this way, the Integrity Pact avoids being a one-size fits all approach but rather a living tool that adapts to local opportunities and challenges.

Examples from Around the World

Since 2002, our chapter in **Mexico** has implemented pacts in over 100 contracts worth US$ 30 billion. It has also emphasised the use of independent monitors, dubbed 'social witnesses', and since 2004 the country's Public Administration Authority has made social witnesses mandatory for public contracts above a certain threshold.

In 2013, Transparency International's partner in **Honduras** exposed massive corruption in the purchase, sales and distribution of medicines to state hospitals that was endangering the lives of untold numbers of Hondurans. As a result, an Integrity Pact was signed with the Ministry of Health and with major pharmaceutical companies to monitor the purchase and supply of medicines in the country. This IP came into force in 2017. As part of the IP, individual Ministry of Health employees and external actors that provide services to the Ministry, such as the College of Chemists and Pharmacists of Honduras and Banco de Occidente, have signed an ethics

---

[16] https://www.transparency.org/en/tool-integrity-pacts

statement. The IP has already lead to increased access to information, and increased compliance with open data principles.

In 2016, Transparency International together with 11 national chapters in the **European Union** and five other local civil society partners embarked on a process to apply the updated clean contracting approach. Involving just short of EUR 1 billion of funding, this pilot incorporates projects across the spectrum from flood protection to road building to tram construction. Learn more about the project here.

What Are the Benefits?
While Integrity Pacts help ensure clean operations on the part of contractors and public officials during the execution of a project, they also yield other benefits. Integrity Pacts provide enhanced access to information, increasing the level of transparency in public contracts. This, in turn, leads to greater confidence and trust in public decision-making, less litigation over procurement processes and more bidders competing for contracts.

Integrity pacts can also encourage institutional changes, such as increased commitment to making data available in a truly open format, simplified administrative procedures and improved regulatory action.

Resources
The following resources provide extensive information on the concept, design and implementation of Integrity Pacts.

Engaging Civil Society for Better Procurement Outcomes
The Integrity Pact (IP) is a powerful tool developed by Transparency International to help governments, businesses and civil society fight corruption in public contracting. Here are some of the concrete ways in which the IP tool has been used to engage civil society and improve public procurement across the world.

The Case for Integrity Pacts
The Business Case for Integrity Pacts
It's all too common for companies to encounter corruption during public procurement processes. In the EU alone, corrupt bidding processes have increased annual contract costs by US$5 billion. The effects can be disastrous, including exposing companies to serious risks. The Integrity Pact (IP) is a powerful tool developed by Transparency International to help governments, businesses and civil society fight corruption in public contracting. This publication looks specifically at how the IP tool can benefit businesses.

How Citizen Monitoring Benefits Businesses
Implementation Guide
The Integrity Pact (IP) is a powerful tool developed by Transparency International to help governments, businesses and civil society fight corruption in public contracting. With this implementation manual, we aim to help leaders and champions within their own governments across the world who are determined to overcome corruption in public contracting. This manual is a hands-on, practical guide to familiarise government officials in charge of public procurement

processes with the Integrity Pact and to provide them with tools and ideas for its application.

Integrity Pacts in Public Procurement: An Implementation Guide
A How-to Guide from Practitioners

The purpose of this publication is to contribute to the already existing literature on Integrity Pacts, but from a civil society perspective. Representatives from 10 Transparency International chapters were brought together to review the challenges that are faced in the different stages of Integrity Pacts, and to document the ways they have found to overcome them. These span from the moment IP implementation is being considered, until the time when the final results are evaluated. This guide does not intend to convince anyone of the usefulness of Integrity Pacts: rather, it is designed for those who are considering implementing, or have already decided to implement, an Integrity Pact. It is for those who are new to Integrity Pacts—who have questions about where, when and how to start implementing them.

Integrity Pacts: A How-to Guide from Practitioners
Integrity Pacts in the Water Sector

This collaboration between the Water Integrity Network (WIN) and Transparency International seeks to help determined leaders and champions to overcome corruption in public contracting within their own governments. Government officials and other interested parties can use the manual to familiarise themselves with the Integrity Pact and apply it to their situation. The manual emphasises the water sector but can serve as a more general set of guidelines in other sectors.

Integrity Pacts in the Water Sector: An Implementation Guide for Government Officials
Lessons from Indonesia, Malaysia and Pakistan

This handbook is designed to provide a basic introduction to the challenge of overcoming corruption in the field of public procurement. It provides readers with examples of counter-corruption efforts including the use of Integrity Pacts. The publication was issued as a result of a project carried out with our chapters from Indonesia, Malaysia and Pakistan.

Handbook for Curbing Corruption in Public Procurement (2006)

Chapter 12
Integrity Materials of International Organisations

12.1 Multilateral Development Bank (MDB) Documents

12.1.1 International Financial Institutions (IFI) Task Force on Anti-Corruption: Uniform Framework Agreement[1]

This is the framework (signed in September 2006) for preventing and combating fraud and corruption in the activities and operations of the IFIs which includes the agreed definitions of fraud, corruption, collusion and coersion.

12.1.2 MDB Cross Debarment Agreement[2]

Cross debarment makes multilateral development bank funding more effective by preventing corrupt entities from participating in projects financed by the signatory Banks. The heads of five multilateral development banks signed the Agreement for Mutual Enforcement of Debarment Decisions on April 9, 2010 in Luxembourg, thus closing a problematic loophole of how to prevent corrupt entities from participating in MDB-financed development programs. The agreement stipulates that entities debarred by one MDB will also be debarred on the same terms by the other signatories for which the Agreement has entered into force.

Current signatories are the Asian Development Bank, African Development Bank Group, European Bank for Reconstruction and Development, Inter-American Development Bank Group, and the World Bank Group (not EIB for legal reasons).

---

[1] https://www.eib.org/en/about/documents/ifi-anti-corruption-task-force-uniform-framework.htm
[2] http://crossdebarment.org/oai001p.nsf/Content.xsp?documentId=EF42202683A26B52482 5789A00839502&action=openDocument&SessionID=CWO0W588ZO

The Agreement is currently in force for the Asian Development Bank, the European Bank for Reconstruction and Development, Inter-American Development Bank Group, and the World Bank Group.

12.1.3 MDB Harmonised Guidelines

These guidelines agreed between each of the participating MDBs provide harmonized approaches that each participating institution may incorporate into their respective processes for consideration of sanctions.

(a) **General Principles and Guidelines for Sanctions**[3]

Adopted in furtherance of the IFI Uniform Framework, these are a set of General Principles to ensure consistent treatment of individuals and firms in the determination of sanctions.

(b) **MDB Harmonized Principles on Treatment of Corporate Groups**[4]

Adopted in September 2012, the guidelines agreed between each of the participating MDBs provide harmonized approaches that each participating institution may incorporate into their respective processes for consideration of sanctions.

(c) **MDB General Principles for Settlements**[5]

Adopted in July 2021, the General Principles for Settlements outline the basic features considered by the respective MDBs regarding settlements of investigations of Prohibited Practices.

12.2 European Investment Bank (EIB)

12.2.1 Anti-Fraud Policy[6]

This sets forth the policy of the EIB Group in preventing and deterring corruption, fraud, collusion, coercion, obstruction, theft at EIB Group premises, misuse of EIB Group resources or assets, money laundering and terrorist financing (jointly

---

[3] http://lnadbg4.adb.org/oai001p.nsf/0/CE3A1AB934F345F048257ACC002D8448/$FILE/Harmonized%20Sanctioning%20Guidelines.pdf

[4] http://lnadbg4.adb.org/oai001p.nsf/0/A7912C61C52A85AD48257ACC002DB7EE/$FILE/MDB%20Harmonized%20Principles%20on%20Treatment%20of%20Corporate%20Groups.pdf

[5] http://lnadbg4.adb.org/oai001p.nsf/0/299CA009578916A84825870F007B1604/$FILE/General%20Principles%20for%20MDB%20Settlements.pdf

[6] https://www.eib.org/en/publications/anti-fraud-policy.htm

"Prohibited Conduct") in its activities. It was approved by the EIF and the EIB Boards of Directors on 21 and 22 July 2021 respectively and becomes effective upon its publication on 5 August 2021.

12.2.2 Exclusion Policy[7]

The EIB's Exclusion Policy sets out the policy and procedures for the exclusion of entities and individuals found to have engaged in Prohibited Conduct from EIB-financed projects and other EIB-related activities for a certain period of time. It enforces the prohibitions contained in the EIB's Anti-Fraud Policy and, in doing so, contributes to safeguarding the financial interests, the integrity and reputation of the Bank and the activities it finances.

Proceedings instigated under this Exclusion Policy follow a three-stage review process to determine whether the evidence presented convincingly supports the conclusion that an entity or individual engaged in Prohibited Conduct.

12.2.3 List of Settlements and Excluded Entities[8]

The EIB Exclusion Policy includes a provision which allows the EIB to enter into negotiated settlements with individuals or entities that have engaged in Prohibited Conduct. The list contains historical settlements, agreed by the EIB and the respective parties.

12.2.4 Whistleblower Policy[9]

The EIB Group Whistleblowing Policy applies to all members of staff of the EIB Group and any other person working for the EIB Group, including consultants and other service providers to the extent that their contractual agreements with the EIB Group so provide.

By setting out clear reporting lines, ensuring maximum protection for any whistleblower acting in good faith, for any person who supports the Whistleblower and for any person associated with a Whistleblower (i.e. a relative, partner or spouse working in the EIB Group), granting information rights to the Whistleblower, and

---

[7] https://www.eib.org/en/publications/exclusion-policy.htm

[8] https://www.eib.org/en/about/accountability/anti-fraud/exclusion/index.htm?f=search&media=search

[9] https://www.eib.org/en/publications/eib-group-whistleblowing-policy

condemning any retaliatory action or reprisals, the EIB Group Whistleblowing Policy allows any relevant persons to fulfil their duty to report serious misconduct.

12.2.5 Covenant of Integrity (Annex 5 of the EIB Guide to Procurement)[10]

The purpose of the Guide to Procurement is to inform the Promoters of a project whose contracts are financed in whole or in part by the European Investment Bank—or are financed under loans guaranteed by the Bank—of the arrangements to be made for procuring works, goods and services required for the project.

This Guide applies specifically to those components of a project identified for the Bank's financing. However, in order to ensure the overall feasibility of the project, the Bank requires that procurement of the other project components does not compromise the project's technical, economic and financial viability.

---

[10] https://www.eib.org/en/publications/guide-to-procurement.htm

Chapter 13
National Legislation

13.1 UK Bribery Act 2010[1]

Latest version (as at 9 January 2022): https://www.legislation.gov.uk

An Act to make provision about offences relating to bribery; and for connected purposes. [8th April 2010]

Be it enacted by the Queen's most Excellent Majesty, by and with the advice and consent of the Lords Spiritual and Temporal, and Commons, in this present Parliament assembled, and by the authority of the same, as follows:—

Section 1. Offences of bribing another person

1. A person ("P") is guilty of an offence if either of the following cases applies.
2. Case 1 is where—

    (a) P offers, promises or gives a financial or other advantage to another person, and

    (b) P intends the advantage—

---

[1] An FCPA Blog article recently noted that there were: "Three Big Lessons from Amec Foster Wheeler's UK DPA" (with the SFO) by Lloydette Bai-Marrow dated April 7, 2022. The article noted that: "On February 7, 2022 the Serious Fraud Office released the Statement of Facts following its July 2021 Deferred Prosecution Agreement (DPA) with Amec Foster Wheeler Energy. It was ... the SFO's 10th DPA since the DPA regime was introduced in February 2014. The conduct set out in the Statement of Facts is egregious and endemic. In approving the DPA, the judge was scathing in his assessment of the conduct of senior leaders at Amec. He noted that, but for the fact that the company had been acquired by an innocent party, the John Wood Group, he would not have granted the DPA. The Statement of Facts offers some valuable insights and lessons for corporations who may find themselves entangled in a law enforcement investigation of a similar nature." The lessons noted by Lloydette are: 1. Have a clear strategy for dealing with material that is covered by legal professional privilege (LPP); 2. Policies and procedures don't effect change; people do and 3. Avoid "paper" internal investigations and reviews. Link: https://fcpablog.com/2022/04/07/three-big-lessons-from-amec-foster-wheelers-uk-dpa/

© The Author(s), under exclusive license to Springer Nature Switzerland AG 2022
D. Smith, *Fraud and Corruption*, Contributions to Finance and Accounting,
https://doi.org/10.1007/978-3-031-10063-5_13

(i) to induce a person to perform improperly a relevant function or activity, or
   (ii) to reward a person for the improper performance of such a function or activity.
3. Case 2 is where—
   (a) P offers, promises or gives a financial or other advantage to another person, and
   (b) P knows or believes that the acceptance of the advantage would itself constitute the improper performance of a relevant function or activity.
4. In case 1 it does not matter whether the person to whom the advantage is offered, promised or given is the same person as the person who is to perform, or has performed, the function or activity concerned.
5. In cases 1 and 2 it does not matter whether the advantage is offered, promised or given by P directly or through a third party.

Section 2. Offences relating to being bribed

1. A person ("R") is guilty of an offence if any of the following cases applies.
2. Case 3 is where R requests, agrees to receive or accepts a financial or other advantage intending that, in consequence, a relevant function or activity should be performed improperly (whether by R or another person).
3. Case 4 is where—
   (a) R requests, agrees to receive or accepts a financial or other advantage, and
   (b) the request, agreement or acceptance itself constitutes the improper performance by R of a relevant function or activity.
4. Case 5 is where R requests, agrees to receive or accepts a financial or other advantage as a reward for the improper performance (whether by R or another person) of a relevant function or activity.
5. Case 6 is where, in anticipation of or in consequence of R requesting, agreeing to receive or accepting a financial or other advantage, a relevant function or activity is performed improperly—
   (a) by R, or
   (b) by another person at R's request or with R's assent or acquiescence.
6. In cases 3 to 6 it does not matter—
   (a) whether R requests, agrees to receive or accepts (or is to request, agree to receive or accept) the advantage directly or through a third party,
   (b) whether the advantage is (or is to be) for the benefit of R or another person.
7. In cases 4 to 6 it does not matter whether R knows or believes that the performance of the function or activity is improper.

8. In case 6, where a person other than R is performing the function or activity, it also does not matter whether that person knows or believes that the performance of the function or activity is improper.

Section 3. Function or activity to which bribe relates

1. For the purposes of this Act a function or activity is a relevant function or activity if—

    (a) it falls within subsection (2), and
    (b) meets one or more of conditions A to C.

2. The following functions and activities fall within this subsection—

    (a) any function of a public nature,
    (b) any activity connected with a business,
    (c) any activity performed in the course of a person's employment,
    (d) any activity performed by or on behalf of a body of persons (whether corporate or unincorporate).

3. Condition A is that a person performing the function or activity is expected to perform it in good faith.
4. Condition B is that a person performing the function or activity is expected to perform it impartially.
5. Condition C is that a person performing the function or activity is in a position of trust by virtue of performing it.
6. A function or activity is a relevant function or activity even if it—

    (a) has no connection with the United Kingdom, and
    (b) is performed in a country or territory outside the United Kingdom.

7. In this section "business" includes trade or profession.

Section 4. Improper performance to which bribe relates

1. For the purposes of this Act a relevant function or activity—

    (a) is performed improperly if it is performed in breach of a relevant expectation, and
    (b) is to be treated as being performed improperly if there is a failure to perform the function or activity and that failure is itself a breach of a relevant expectation.

2. In subsection (1) "relevant expectation"—

    (a) in relation to a function or activity which meets condition A or B, means the expectation mentioned in the condition concerned, and
    (b) in relation to a function or activity which meets condition C, means any expectation as to the manner in which, or the reasons for which, the function or activity will be performed that arises from the position of trust mentioned in that condition.

3. Anything that a person does (or omits to do) arising from or in connection with that person's past performance of a relevant function or activity is to be treated for the purposes of this Act as being done (or omitted) by that person in the performance of that function or activity.

Section 5. Expectation test

1. For the purposes of sections 3 and 4, the test of what is expected is a test of what a reasonable person in the United Kingdom would expect in relation to the performance of the type of function or activity concerned.
2. In deciding what such a person would expect in relation to the performance of a function or activity where the performance is not subject to the law of any part of the United Kingdom, any local custom or practice is to be disregarded unless it is permitted or required by the written law applicable to the country or territory concerned.
3. In subsection (2) "written law" means law contained in—

    (a) any written constitution, or provision made by or under legislation, applicable to the country or territory concerned, or
    (b) any judicial decision which is so applicable and is evidenced in published written sources.

Bribery of Foreign Public Officials
Section 6. Bribery of foreign public officials

1. A person ("P") who bribes a foreign public official ("F") is guilty of an offence if P's intention is to influence F in F's capacity as a foreign public official.
2. P must also intend to obtain or retain—

    (a) business, or
    (b) an advantage in the conduct of business.

3. P bribes F if, and only if—

    (a) directly or through a third party, P offers, promises or gives any financial or other advantage—

        (i) to F, or
        (ii) to another person at F's request or with F's assent or acquiescence, and

    (b) F is neither permitted nor required by the written law applicable to F to be influenced in F's capacity as a foreign public official by the offer, promise or gift.

4. References in this section to influencing F in F's capacity as a foreign public official mean influencing F in the performance of F's functions as such an official, which includes—

(a) any omission to exercise those functions, and
(b) any use of F's position as such an official, even if not within F's authority.

5. "Foreign public official" means an individual who—

   (a) holds a legislative, administrative or judicial position of any kind, whether appointed or elected, of a country or territory outside the United Kingdom (or any subdivision of such a country or territory),
   (b) exercises a public function—
       (i) for or on behalf of a country or territory outside the United Kingdom (or any subdivision of such a country or territory), or
       (ii) for any public agency or public enterprise of that country or territory (or subdivision), or
   (c) is an official or agent of a public international organisation.

6. "Public international organisation" means an organisation whose members are any of the following—

   (a) countries or territories,
   (b) governments of countries or territories,
   (c) other public international organisations,
   (d) a mixture of any of the above.

7. For the purposes of subsection (3)(b), the written law applicable to F is—

   (a) where the performance of the functions of F which P intends to influence would be subject to the law of any part of the United Kingdom, the law of that part of the United Kingdom,
   (b) where paragraph (a) does not apply and F is an official or agent of a public international organisation, the applicable written rules of that organisation,
   (c) where paragraphs (a) and (b) do not apply, the law of the country or territory in relation to which F is a foreign public official so far as that law is contained in—
       (i) any written constitution, or provision made by or under legislation, applicable to the country or territory concerned, or
       (ii) any judicial decision which is so applicable and is evidenced in published written sources.

8. For the purposes of this section, a trade or profession is a business.

Failure of Commercial Organisations to Prevent Bribery
Section 7. Failure of commercial organisations to prevent bribery

1. A relevant commercial organisation ("C") is guilty of an offence under this section if a person ("A") associated with C bribes another person intending—

   (a) to obtain or retain business for C, or
   (b) to obtain or retain an advantage in the conduct of business for C.

2. But it is a defence for C to prove that C had in place adequate procedures designed to prevent persons associated with C from undertaking such conduct.
3. For the purposes of this section, A bribes another person if, and only if, A—
    (a) is, or would be, guilty of an offence under section 1 or 6 (whether or not A has been prosecuted for such an offence), or
    (b) would be guilty of such an offence if section 12(2)(c) and (4) were omitted.
4. See section 8 for the meaning of a person associated with C and see section 9 for a duty on the Secretary of State to publish guidance.
5. In this section—

"partnership" means—
   (a) a partnership within the Partnership Act 1890, or
   (b) a limited partnership registered under the Limited Partnerships Act 1907,
   (c) or a firm or entity of a similar character formed under the law of a country or territory outside the United Kingdom,

"relevant commercial organisation" means—
   (a) a body which is incorporated under the law of any part of the United Kingdom and which carries on a business (whether there or elsewhere),
   (b) any other body corporate (wherever incorporated) which carries on a business, or part of a business, in any part of the United Kingdom,
   (c) a partnership which is formed under the law of any part of the United Kingdom and which carries on a business (whether there or elsewhere), or
   (d) any other partnership (wherever formed) which carries on a business, or part of a business, in any part of the United Kingdom, and, for the purposes of this section, a trade or profession is a business.

Section 8. Meaning of associated person

1. For the purposes of section 7, a person ("A") is associated with C if (disregarding any bribe under consideration) A is a person who performs services for or on behalf of C.
2. The capacity in which A performs services for or on behalf of C does not matter.
3. Accordingly A may (for example) be C's employee, agent or subsidiary.
4. Whether or not A is a person who performs services for or on behalf of C is to be determined by reference to all the relevant circumstances and not merely by reference to the nature of the relationship between A and C.
5. But if A is an employee of C, it is to be presumed unless the contrary is shown that A is a person who performs services for or on behalf of C.

Section 9. Guidance about commercial organisations preventing bribery

1. The Secretary of State must publish guidance about procedures that relevant commercial organisations can put in place to prevent persons associated with them from bribing as mentioned in section 7(1).
2. The Secretary of State may, from time to time, publish revisions to guidance under this section or revised guidance.
3. The Secretary of State must consult the Scottish Ministers [F1 and the Department of Justice in Northern Ireland] before publishing anything under this section.
4. Publication under this section is to be in such manner as the Secretary of State considers appropriate.
5. Expressions used in this section have the same meaning as in section 7.

Textual Amendments
F1. Words in s. 9(3) inserted (18.10.2012) by The Northern Ireland Act 1998 (Devolution of Policing and Justice Functions) Order 2012 (S.I. 2012/2595), arts. 1(2), 19(2) (with arts. 24–28)

Prosecution and Penalties
Section 10. Consent to prosecution

1. No proceedings for an offence under this Act may be instituted in England and Wales except by or with the consent of—

    (a) the Director of Public Prosecutions,[F1 or]
    (b) the Director of the Serious Fraud Office F2...F2(c). . . . .

2. No proceedings for an offence under this Act may be instituted in Northern Ireland except by or with the consent of—

    (a) the Director of Public Prosecutions for Northern Ireland, or
    (b) the Director of the Serious Fraud Office.

3. No proceedings for an offence under this Act may be instituted in England and Wales or Northern Ireland by a person—

    (a) who is acting—

        (i) under the direction or instruction of the Director of Public Prosecutions [F3 or the Director of the Serious Fraud Office], or
        (ii) on behalf of such a Director, or

    (b) to whom such a function has been assigned by such a Director, except with the consent of the Director concerned to the institution of the proceedings.

4. The Director of Public Prosecutions [F4 and the Director of the Serious Fraud Office] must exercise personally any function under subsection (1), (2) or (3) of giving consent.
5. The only exception is if—

(a) the Director concerned is unavailable, and
(b) there is another person who is designated in writing by the Director acting personally as the person who is authorised to exercise any such function when the Director is unavailable.

6. In that case, the other person may exercise the function but must do so personally.
7. Subsections (4) to (6) apply instead of any other provisions which would otherwise have enabled any function of the Director of Public Prosecutions [F5 or the Director of the Serious Fraud Office] under subsection (1), (2) or (3) of giving consent to be exercised by a person other than the Director concerned.
8. No proceedings for an offence under this Act may be instituted in Northern Ireland by virtue of section 36 of the Justice (Northern Ireland) Act 2002 (delegation of the functions of the Director of Public Prosecutions for Northern Ireland to persons other than the Deputy Director) except with the consent of the Director of Public Prosecutions for Northern Ireland to the institution of the proceedings.
9. The Director of Public Prosecutions for Northern Ireland must exercise personally any function under subsection (2) or (8) of giving consent unless the function is exercised personally by the Deputy Director of Public Prosecutions for Northern Ireland by virtue of section 30(4) or (7) of the Act of 2002 (powers of Deputy Director to exercise functions of Director).
10. Subsection (9) applies instead of section 36 of the Act of 2002 in relation to the functions of the Director of Public Prosecutions for Northern Ireland and the Deputy Director of Public Prosecutions for Northern Ireland under, or (as the case may be) by virtue of, subsections (2) and (8) above of giving consent.

Textual Amendments

F1 Word in s. 10(1)(a) inserted (27.3.2014) by The Public Bodies (Merger of the Director of Public Prosecutions and the Director of Revenue and Customs Prosecutions) Order 2014 (S.I. 2014/834), art. 1(1), Sch. 2 para. 74(2)(a)

F2. S. 10(1)(c) and preceding word omitted (27.3.2014) by virtue of The Public Bodies (Merger of the Director of Public Prosecutions and the Director of Revenue and Customs Prosecutions) Order 2014 (S.I. 2014/834), art. 1(1), Sch. 2 para. 74(2)(b)

F3. Words in s. 10(3)(a)(i) substituted (27.3.2014) by The Public Bodies (Merger of the Director of Public Prosecutions and the Director of Revenue and Customs Prosecutions) Order 2014 (S.I. 2014/834), art. 1(1), Sch. 2 para. 74(3)

F4. Words in s. 10(4) substituted (27.3.2014) by The Public Bodies (Merger of the Director of Public Prosecutions and the Director of Revenue and Customs Prosecutions) Order 2014 (S.I. 2014/834), art. 1(1), Sch. 2 para. 74(4)

F5. Words in s. 10(7) substituted (27.3.2014) by The Public Bodies (Merger of the Director of Public Prosecutions and the Director of Revenue and Customs Prosecutions) Order 2014 (S.I. 2014/834), art. 1(1), Sch. 2 para. 74(5)

Section 11. Penalties

1. An individual guilty of an offence under section 1, 2 or 6 is liable—

    (a) on summary conviction, to imprisonment for a term not exceeding 12 months, or to a fine not exceeding the statutory maximum, or to both,
    (b) on conviction on indictment, to imprisonment for a term not exceeding 10 years, or to a fine, or to both.

2. Any other person guilty of an offence under section 1, 2 or 6 is liable—

    (a) on summary conviction, to a fine not exceeding the statutory maximum,
    (b) on conviction on indictment, to a fine.

3. A person guilty of an offence under section 7 is liable on conviction on indictment to a fine.
4. The reference in subsection (1)(a) to 12 months is to be read—

    (a) in its application to England and Wales in relation to an offence committed before the commencement of [F1 paragraph 24(2) of Schedule 22 to the Sentencing Act 2020], and
    (b) in its application to Northern Ireland,

    as a reference to 6 months.

Textual Amendments
F1 Words in s. 11(4)(a) substituted (1.12.2020) by Sentencing Act 2020 (c. 17), s. 416(1), Sch. 24 para. 443(1) (with Sch. 24 para. 447, Sch. 27); S.I. 2020/1236, reg. 2

Other Provisions About Offences
Section 12. Offences under this Act: territorial application

1. An offence is committed under section 1, 2 or 6 in England and Wales, Scotland or Northern Ireland if any act or omission which forms part of the offence takes place in that part of the United Kingdom.
2. Subsection (3) applies if—

    (a) no act or omission which forms part of an offence under section 1, 2 or 6 takes place in the United Kingdom,
    (b) a person's acts or omissions done or made outside the United Kingdom would form part of such an offence if done or made in the United Kingdom, and
    (c) that person has a close connection with the United Kingdom.

3. In such a case—

    (a) the acts or omissions form part of the offence referred to in subsection (2)(a), and
    (b) proceedings for the offence may be taken at any place in the United Kingdom.

4. For the purposes of subsection (2)(c) a person has a close connection with the United Kingdom if, and only if, the person was one of the following at the time the acts or omissions concerned were done or made—

   (a) a British citizen,
   (b) a British overseas territories citizen,
   (c) a British National (Overseas),
   (d) a British Overseas citizen,
   (e) a person who under the British Nationality Act 1981 was a British subject,
   (f) a British protected person within the meaning of that Act,
   (g) an individual ordinarily resident in the United Kingdom,
   (h) a body incorporated under the law of any part of the United Kingdom,
   (i) a Scottish partnership.

5. An offence is committed under section 7 irrespective of whether the acts or omissions which form part of the offence take place in the United Kingdom or elsewhere.
6. Where no act or omission which forms part of an offence under section 7 takes place in the United Kingdom, proceedings for the offence may be taken at any place in the United Kingdom.
7. Subsection (8) applies if, by virtue of this section, proceedings for an offence are to be taken in Scotland against a person.
8. Such proceedings may be taken—

   (a) in any sheriff court district in which the person is apprehended or in custody, or
   (b) in such sheriff court district as the Lord Advocate may determine.

9. In subsection (8) "sheriff court district" is to be read in accordance with section 307(1) of the Criminal Procedure (Scotland) Act 1995.

Section 13. Defence for certain bribery offences etc.

1. It is a defence for a person charged with a relevant bribery offence to prove that the person's conduct was necessary for—

   (a) the proper exercise of any function of an intelligence service, or
   (b) the proper exercise of any function of the armed forces when engaged on active service.

2. The head of each intelligence service must ensure that the service has in place arrangements designed to ensure that any conduct of a member of the service which would otherwise be a relevant bribery offence is necessary for a purpose falling within subsection (1)(a).
3. The Defence Council must ensure that the armed forces have in place arrangements designed to ensure that any conduct of—

(a) a member of the armed forces who is engaged on active service, or
(b) a civilian subject to service discipline when working in support of any person falling within paragraph (a),

which would otherwise be a relevant bribery offence is necessary for a purpose falling within subsection (1)(b).

4. The arrangements which are in place by virtue of subsection (2) or (3) must be arrangements which the Secretary of State considers to be satisfactory.
5. For the purposes of this section, the circumstances in which a person's conduct is necessary for a purpose falling within subsection (1)(a) or (b) are to be treated as including any circumstances in which the person's conduct—

   (a) would otherwise be an offence under section 2, and
   (b) involves conduct by another person which, but for subsection (1)(a) or (b), would be an offence under section 1.

6. In this section—"active service" means service in—

   (a) an action or operation against an enemy,
   (b) an operation outside the British Islands for the protection of life or property, or
   (c) the military occupation of a foreign country or territory,

   "armed forces" means Her Majesty's forces (within the meaning of the Armed Forces Act 2006),
   "civilian subject to service discipline" and "enemy" have the same meaning as in the Act of 2006,
   "GCHQ" has the meaning given by section 3(3) of the Intelligence Services Act 1994,
   "head" means—

(a) in relation to the Security Service, the Director General of the Security Service,
(b) in relation to the Secret Intelligence Service, the Chief of the Secret Intelligence Service, and
(c) in relation to GCHQ, the Director of GCHQ,

   "intelligence service" means the Security Service, the Secret Intelligence Service or GCHQ,
   "relevant bribery offence" means—

(a) an offence under section 1 which would not also be an offence under section 6,
(b) an offence under section 2,
(c) an offence committed by aiding, abetting, counselling or procuring the commission of an offence falling within paragraph (a) or (b),
(d) an offence of attempting or conspiring to commit, or of inciting the commission of, an offence falling within paragraph (a) or (b), or
(e) an offence under Part 2 of the Serious Crime Act 2007 (encouraging or assisting crime) in relation to an offence falling within paragraph (a) or (b).

Section 14. Offences under sections 1, 2 and 6 by bodies corporate etc.

1. This section applies if an offence under section 1, 2 or 6 is committed by a body corporate or a Scottish partnership.
2. If the offence is proved to have been committed with the consent or connivance of—
   (a) a senior officer of the body corporate or Scottish partnership, or
   (b) a person purporting to act in such a capacity,
   the senior officer or person (as well as the body corporate or partnership) is guilty of the offence and liable to be proceeded against and punished accordingly.
3. But subsection (2) does not apply, in the case of an offence which is committed under section 1, 2 or 6 by virtue of section 12(2) to (4), to a senior officer or person purporting to act in such a capacity unless the senior officer or person has a close connection with the United Kingdom (within the meaning given by section 12(4)).
4. In this section—

"director", in relation to a body corporate whose affairs are managed by its members, means a member of the body corporate,
"senior officer" means—

(a) in relation to a body corporate, a director, manager, secretary or other similar officer of the body corporate, and
(b) in relation to a Scottish partnership, a partner in the partnership.

Section 15. Offences under section 7 by partnerships

1. Proceedings for an offence under section 7 alleged to have been committed by a partnership must be brought in the name of the partnership (and not in that of any of the partners).
2. For the purposes of such proceedings—
   (a) rules of court relating to the service of documents have effect as if the partnership were a body corporate, and
   (b) the following provisions apply as they apply in relation to a body corporate—
      (i) section 33 of the Criminal Justice Act 1925 and Schedule 3 to the Magistrates' Courts Act 1980,
      (ii) section 18 of the Criminal Justice Act (Northern Ireland) 1945 (c. 15 (N.I.)) and Schedule 4 to the Magistrates' Courts (Northern Ireland) Order 1981 (S.I. 1981/1675 (N.I.26)),
      (iii) section 70 of the Criminal Procedure (Scotland) Act 1995.
3. A fine imposed on the partnership on its conviction for an offence under section 7 is to be paid out of the partnership assets.
4. In this section "partnership" has the same meaning as in section 7.

Section 16. Application to Crown

This Act applies to individuals in the public service of the Crown as it applies to other individuals.

Section 17. Consequential provision

1. The following common law offences are abolished—
   (a) the offences under the law of England and Wales and Northern Ireland of bribery and embracery,
   (b) the offences under the law of Scotland of bribery and accepting a bribe.
2. Schedule 1 (which contains consequential amendments) has effect.
3. Schedule 2 (which contains repeals and revocations) has effect.
4. The relevant national authority may by order make such supplementary, incidental or consequential provision as the relevant national authority considers appropriate for the purposes of this Act or in consequence of this Act.
5. The power to make an order under this section—
   (a) is exercisable by statutory instrument[F1(subject to subsection (9A))],
   (b) includes power to make transitional, transitory or saving provision,
   (c) may, in particular, be exercised by amending, repealing, revoking or otherwise modifying any provision made by or under an enactment (including any Act passed in the same Session as this Act).
6. Subject to subsection (7), a statutory instrument containing an order of the Secretary of State under this section may not be made unless a draft of the instrument has been laid before, and approved by a resolution of, each House of Parliament.
7. A statutory instrument containing an order of the Secretary of State under this section which does not amend or repeal a provision of a public general Act or of devolved legislation is subject to annulment in pursuance of a resolution of either House of Parliament.
8. Subject to subsection (9), a statutory instrument containing an order of the Scottish Ministers under this section may not be made unless a draft of the instrument has been laid before, and approved by a resolution of, the Scottish Parliament.
9. A statutory instrument containing an order of the Scottish Ministers under this section which does not amend or repeal a provision of an Act of the Scottish Parliament or of a public general Act is subject to annulment in pursuance of a resolution of the Scottish Parliament.

[F2(9A) The power of the Department of Justice in Northern Ireland to make an order under this section is exercisable by statutory rule for the purposes of the Statutory Rules (Northern Ireland) Order 1979 (and not by statutory instrument).

(9B) Subject to subsection (9C), an order of the Department of Justice in Northern Ireland made under this section is subject to affirmative resolution (within the meaning of section 41(4) of the Interpretation Act (Northern Ireland) 1954).

(9C) An order of the Department of Justice in Northern Ireland made under this section which does not amend or repeal a provision of an Act of the Northern Ireland Assembly or of a public general Act is subject to negative resolution (within the meaning of section 41(6) of the Interpretation Act (Northern Ireland) 1954).]

10. In this section—

"devolved legislation" means an Act of the Scottish Parliament, a Measure of the National Assembly for Wales or an Act of the Northern Ireland Assembly,

"enactment" includes an Act of the Scottish Parliament and Northern Ireland legislation,

"relevant national authority" means—

(a) in the case of provision which would be within the legislative competence of the Scottish Parliament if it were contained in an Act of that Parliament, the Scottish Ministers, F3...

(aa) [F4 in the case of provision which could be made by an Act of the Northern Ireland Assembly without the consent of the Secretary of State (see sections 6 to 8 of the Northern Ireland Act 1998), the Department of Justice in Northern Ireland, and]

(b) in any other case, the Secretary of State.

Textual Amendments
F1. *Words in s. 17(5)(a) inserted (18.10.2012) by The Northern Ireland Act 1998 (Devolution of Policing and Justice Functions) Order 2012 (S.I. 2012/2595), arts. 1(2), 19(3)(a) (with arts. 24–28)*
F2. *S. 17(9A)–(9C) inserted (18.10.2012) by The Northern Ireland Act 1998 (Devolution of Policing and Justice Functions) Order 2012 (S.I. 2012/2595), arts. 1(2), 19(3)(b) (with arts. 24–28)*
F3. *Word in s. 17(10) omitted (18.10.2012) by virtue of The Northern Ireland Act 1998 (Devolution of Policing and Justice Functions) Order 2012 (S.I. 2012/2595), arts. 1(2), 19(3)(c) (with arts. 24–28)*
F4. *Words in s. 17(10) inserted (18.10.2012) by The Northern Ireland Act 1998 (Devolution of Policing and Justice Functions) Order 2012 (S.I. 2012/2595), arts. 1(2), 19(3)(c) (with arts. 24–28)*

Commencement Information
I1. *S. 17 wholly in force at 1.7.2011; s. 17(4)–(10) in force at Royal Assent, see s. 19(2) ; s. 17 in force otherwise at 1.7.2011 by S.I. 2011/1418 , art. 2*

Section 18. Extent

1. Subject as follows, this Act extends to England and Wales, Scotland and Northern Ireland.
2. Subject to subsections (3) to (5), any amendment, repeal or revocation made by Schedule 1 or 2 has the same extent as the provision amended, repealed or revoked.
3. The amendment of, and repeals in, the Armed Forces Act 2006 do not extend to the Channel Islands.

4. The amendments of the International Criminal Court Act 2001 extend to England and Wales and Northern Ireland only.
5. Subsection (2) does not apply to the repeal in the Civil Aviation Act 1982.

Section 19. Commencement and transitional provision etc.

1. Subject to subsection (2), this Act comes into force on such day as the Secretary of State may by order made by statutory instrument appoint.
2. Sections 16, 17(4) to (10) and 18, this section (other than subsections (5) to (7)) and section 20 come into force on the day on which this Act is passed.
3. An order under subsection (1) may—
   (a) appoint different days for different purposes,
   (b) make such transitional, transitory or saving provision as the Secretary of State considers appropriate in connection with the coming into force of any provision of this Act.
4. The Secretary of State must consult the Scottish Ministers before making an order under this section in connection with any provision of this Act which would be within the legislative competence of the Scottish Parliament if it were contained in an Act of that Parliament.
5. This Act does not affect any liability, investigation, legal proceeding or penalty for or in respect of—
   (a) a common law offence mentioned in subsection (1) of section 17 which is committed wholly or partly before the coming into force of that subsection in relation to such an offence, or
   (b) an offence under the Public Bodies Corrupt Practices Act 1889 or the Prevention of Corruption Act 1906 committed wholly or partly before the coming into force of the repeal of the Act by Schedule 2 to this Act.
6. For the purposes of subsection (5) an offence is partly committed before a particular time if any act or omission which forms part of the offence takes place before that time.
7. Subsections (5) and (6) are without prejudice to section 16 of the Interpretation Act 1978 (general savings on repeal).

Subordinate Legislation Made
P1 S. 19(1) power fully exercised: 1.7.2011 appointed by {S.I. 2011/1418}, art. 2
Commencement Information
I1. S. 19 wholly in force at 1.7.2011; s. 19(1)–(4) in force at Royal Assent, see s. 19(2); s. 19 in force otherwise at 1.7.2011 by S.I. 2011/1418, art. 2

Section 20. Short title

This Act may be cited as the Bribery Act 2010.

13.2 US Foreign and Corrupt Practices Act (FCPA)

US Department of Justice Summary[2]
An Overview

The Foreign Corrupt Practices Act of 1977, as amended, 15 U.S.C. §§ 78dd-1, et seq. ("FCPA"), was enacted for the purpose of making it unlawful for certain classes of persons and entities to make payments to foreign government officials to assist in obtaining or retaining business. Specifically, the anti-bribery provisions of the FCPA prohibit the willful use of the mails or any means of instrumentality of interstate commerce corruptly in furtherance of any offer, payment, promise to pay, or authorization of the payment of money or anything of value to any person, while knowing that all or a portion of such money or thing of value will be offered, given or promised, directly or indirectly, to a foreign official to influence the foreign official in his or her official capacity, induce the foreign official to do or omit to do an act in violation of his or her lawful duty, or to secure any improper advantage in order to assist in obtaining or retaining business for or with, or directing business to, any person.

Since 1977, the anti-bribery provisions of the FCPA have applied to all U.-S. persons and certain foreign issuers of securities. With the enactment of certain amendments in 1998, the anti-bribery provisions of the FCPA now also apply to foreign firms and persons who cause, directly or through agents, an act in furtherance of such a corrupt payment to take place within the territory of the United States.

The FCPA also requires companies whose securities are listed in the United States to meet its accounting provisions. See 15 U.S.C. § 78m. These accounting provisions, which were designed to operate in tandem with the anti-bribery provisions of the FCPA, require corporations covered by the provisions to (a) make and keep books and records that accurately and fairly reflect the transactions of the corporation and (b) devise and maintain an adequate system of internal accounting controls..."

US Department of Justice Website[3]
Anti-Bribery and Books & Records Provisions of the Foreign Corrupt Practices Act

Current through Pub. L. 105–366 (November 10, 1998)
UNITED STATES CODE
TITLE 15. COMMERCE AND TRADE
CHAPTER 2B--SECURITIES EXCHANGES

---

[2] Link: https://www.justice.gov/criminal-fraud/foreign-corrupt-practices-act
[3] https://www.justice.gov/sites/default/files/criminal-fraud/legacy/2012/11/14/fcpa-english.pdf

§ 78m. Periodical and Other Reports
(a) Reports by issuer of security; contents

Every issuer of a security registered pursuant to section 78l of this title shall file with the Commission, in accordance with such rules and regulations as the Commission may prescribe as necessary or appropriate for the proper protection of investors and to insure fair dealing in the security--

1. such information and documents (and such copies thereof) as the Commission shall require to keep reasonably current the information and documents required to be included in or filed with an application or registration statement filed pursuant to section 78l of this title, except that the Commission may not require the filing of any material contract wholly executed before July 1, 1962.
2. such annual reports (and such copies thereof), certified if required by the rules and regulations of the Commission by independent public accountants, and such quarterly reports (and such copies thereof), as the Commission may prescribe.

Every issuer of a security registered on a national securities exchange shall also file a duplicate original of such information, documents, and reports with the exchange.

(b) Form of report; books, records, and internal accounting; directives

* * *

(2) Every issuer which has a class of securities registered pursuant to section 78l of this title and every issuer which is required to file reports pursuant to section 78o (d) of this title shall--

(A) make and keep books, records, and accounts, which, in reasonable detail, accurately and fairly reflect the transactions and dispositions of the assets of the issuer; and

(B) devise and maintain a system of internal accounting controls sufficient to provide reasonable assurances that--

(i) transactions are executed in accordance with management's general or specific authorization;

(ii) transactions are recorded as necessary (I) to permit preparation of financial statements in conformity with generally accepted accounting principles or any other criteria applicable to such statements, and (II) to maintain accountability for assets;

(iii) access to assets is permitted only in accordance with management's general or specific authorization; and

(iv) the recorded accountability for assets is compared with the existing assets at reasonable intervals and appropriate action is taken with respect to any differences.

(3) (A) With respect to matters concerning the national security of the United States, no duty or liability under paragraph (2) of this subsection shall be imposed upon any person acting in cooperation with the head of any Federal department or agency responsible for such matters if such act in cooperation with such head of a department or agency was done upon the specific, written directive of the head of such department or agency pursuant to Presidential authority to issue such directives.

Each directive issued under this paragraph shall set forth the specific facts and circumstances with respect to which the provisions of this paragraph are to be invoked. Each such directive shall, unless renewed in writing, expire one year after the date of issuance.

(B) Each head of a Federal department or agency of the United States who issues such a directive pursuant to this paragraph shall maintain a complete file of all such directives and shall, on October 1 of each year, transmit a summary of matters covered by such directives in force at any time during the previous year to the Permanent Select Committee on Intelligence of the House of Representatives and the Select Committee on Intelligence of the Senate.

(4) No criminal liability shall be imposed for failing to comply with the requirements of paragraph (2) of this subsection except as provided in paragraph (5) of this subsection.

(5) No person shall knowingly circumvent or knowingly fail to implement a system of internal accounting controls or knowingly falsify any book, record, or account described in paragraph (2).

(6) Where an issuer which has a class of securities registered pursuant to section 78l of this title or an issuer which is required to file reports pursuant to section 78o(d) of this title holds 50 per centum or less of the voting power with respect to a domestic or foreign firm, the provisions of paragraph (2) require only that the issuer proceed in good faith to use its influence, to the extent reasonable under the issuer's circumstances, to cause such domestic or foreign firm to devise and maintain a system of internal accounting controls consistent with paragraph (2). Such circumstances include the relative degree of the issuer's ownership of the domestic or foreign firm and the laws and practices governing the business operations of the country in which such firm is located. An issuer which demonstrates good faith efforts to use such influence shall be conclusively presumed to have complied with the requirements of paragraph (2).

(7) For the purpose of paragraph (2) of this subsection, the terms "reasonable assurances" and "reasonable detail" mean such level of detail and degree of assurance as would satisfy prudent officials in the conduct of their own affairs.

* * *

§ 78dd-1 [Section 30A of the Securities & Exchange Act of 1934]
Prohibited foreign trade practices by issuers

(a) **Prohibition**

It shall be unlawful for any issuer which has a class of securities registered pursuant to section 78l of this title or which is required to file reports under section 78o(d) of this title, or for any officer, director, employee, or agent of such issuer or any stockholder thereof acting on behalf of such issuer, to make use of the mails or any means or instrumentality of interstate commerce corruptly in furtherance of an offer, payment, promise to pay, or authorization of the payment of any money, or offer, gift, promise to give, or authorization of the giving of anything of value to--

13.2 US Foreign and Corrupt Practices Act (FCPA)

(1) any foreign official for purposes of--

(A) (i) influencing any act or decision of such foreign official in his official capacity, (ii) inducing such foreign official to do or omit to do any act in violation of the lawful duty of such official, or (iii) securing any improper advantage; or

(B) inducing such foreign official to use his influence with a foreign government or instrumentality thereof to affect or influence any act or decision of such government or instrumentality, in order to assist such issuer in obtaining or retaining business for or with, or directing business to, any person;

(2) any foreign political party or official thereof or any candidate for foreign political office for purposes of--

(A) (i) influencing any act or decision of such party, official, or candidate in its or his official capacity, (ii) inducing such party, official, or candidate to do or omit to do an act in violation of the lawful duty of such party, official, or candidate, or (iii) securing any improper advantage; or

(B) inducing such party, official, or candidate to use its or his influence with a foreign government or instrumentality thereof to affect or influence any act or decision of such government or instrumentality in order to assist such issuer in obtaining or retaining business for or with, or directing business to, any person; or

(3) any person, while knowing that all or a portion of such money or thing of value will be offered, given, or promised, directly or indirectly, to any foreign official, to any foreign political party or official thereof, or to any candidate for foreign political office, for purposes of--

(A) (i) influencing any act or decision of such foreign official, political party, party official, or candidate in his or its official capacity, (ii) inducing such foreign official, political party, party official, or candidate to do or omit to do any act in violation of the lawful duty of such foreign official, political party, party official, or candidate, or (iii) securing any improper advantage; or

(B) inducing such foreign official, political party, party official, or candidate to use his or its influence with a foreign government or instrumentality thereof to affect or influence any act or decision of such government or instrumentality, in order to assist such issuer in obtaining or retaining business for or with, or directing business to, any person.

(b) **Exception for routine governmental action**

Subsections (a) and (g) of this section shall not apply to any facilitating or expediting payment to a foreign official, political party, or party official the purpose of which is to expedite or to secure the performance of a routine governmental action by a foreign official, political party, or party official.

(c) **Affirmative defenses**

It shall be an affirmative defense to actions under subsection (a) or (g) of this section that--

(1) the payment, gift, offer, or promise of anything of value that was made, was lawful under the written laws and regulations of the foreign official's, political party's, party official's, or candidate's country; or

(2) the payment, gift, offer, or promise of anything of value that was made, was a reasonable and bona fide expenditure, such as travel and lodging expenses, incurred by or on behalf of a foreign official, party, party official, or candidate and was directly related to--

(A) the promotion, demonstration, or explanation of products or services; or

(B) the execution or performance of a contract with a foreign government or agency thereof.

(d) **Guidelines by Attorney General**

Not later than one year after August 23, 1988, the Attorney General, after consultation with the Commission, the Secretary of Commerce, the United States Trade Representative, the Secretary of State, and the Secretary of the Treasury, and after obtaining the views of all interested persons through public notice and comment procedures, shall determine to what extent compliance with this section would be enhanced and the business community would be assisted by further clarification of the preceding provisions of this section and may, based on such determination and to the extent necessary and appropriate, issue--

(1) guidelines describing specific types of conduct, associated with common types of export sales arrangements and business contracts, which for purposes of the Department of Justice's present enforcement policy, the Attorney General determines would be in conformance with the preceding provisions of this section; and

(2) general precautionary procedures which issuers may use on a voluntary basis to conform their conduct to the Department of Justice's present enforcement policy regarding the preceding provisions of this section.

The Attorney General shall issue the guidelines and procedures referred to in the preceding sentence in accordance with the provisions of subchapter II of chapter 5 of Title 5 and those guidelines and procedures shall be subject to the provisions of chapter 7 of that title.

(e) **Opinions of Attorney General**

(1) The Attorney General, after consultation with appropriate departments and agencies of the United States and after obtaining the views of all interested persons through public notice and comment procedures, shall establish a procedure to provide responses to specific inquiries by issuers concerning conformance of their conduct with the Department of Justice's present enforcement policy regarding the preceding provisions of this section. The Attorney General shall, within 30 days after receiving such a request, issue an opinion in response to that request. The opinion shall state whether or not certain specified prospective conduct would, for purposes of the Department of Justice's present enforcement policy, violate the preceding provisions of this section. Additional requests for opinions may be filed with the Attorney General regarding other specified prospective conduct that is beyond the scope of conduct specified in previous requests. In any action brought under the applicable provisions of this section, there shall be a rebuttable presumption that conduct, which is specified in a request by an issuer and for which the Attorney

General has issued an opinion that such conduct is in conformity with the Department of Justice's present enforcement policy, is in compliance with the preceding provisions of this section. Such a presumption may be rebutted by a preponderance of the evidence. In considering the presumption for purposes of this paragraph, a court shall weight all relevant factors, including but not limited to whether the information submitted to the Attorney General was accurate and complete and whether it was within the scope of the conduct specified in any request received by the Attorney General. The Attorney General shall establish the procedure required by this paragraph in accordance with the provisions of subchapter II of chapter 5 of Title 5 and that procedure shall be subject to the provisions of chapter 7 of that title.

(2) Any document or other material which is provided to, received by, or prepared in the Department of Justice or any other department or agency of the United States in connection with a request by an issuer under the procedure established under paragraph (1), shall be exempt from disclosure under section 552 of Title 5 and shall not, except with the consent of the issuer, be made publicly available, regardless of whether the Attorney General responds to such a request or the issuer withdraws such request before receiving a response.

(3) Any issuer who has made a request to the Attorney General under paragraph (1) may withdraw such request prior to the time the Attorney General issues an opinion in response to such request. Any request so withdrawn shall have no force or effect.

(4) The Attorney General shall, to the maximum extent practicable, provide timely guidance concerning the Department of Justice's present enforcement policy with respect to the preceding provisions of this section to potential exporters and small businesses that are unable to obtain specialized counsel on issues pertaining to such provisions. Such guidance shall be limited to responses to requests under paragraph (1) concerning conformity of specified prospective conduct with the Department of Justice's present enforcement policy regarding the preceding provisions of this section and general explanations of compliance responsibilities and of potential liabilities under the preceding provisions of this section.

(f) **Definitions**

For purposes of this section:

(1) A) The term "foreign official" means any officer or employee of a foreign government or any department, agency, or instrumentality thereof, or of a public international organization, or any person acting in an official capacity for or on behalf of any such government or department, agency, or instrumentality, or for or on behalf of any such public international organization.

(B) For purposes of subparagraph (A), the term "public international organization" means--

(i) an organization that is designated by Executive Order pursuant to section 1 of the International Organizations Immunities Act (22 U.S.C. § 288); or

(ii) any other international organization that is designated by the President by Executive order for the purposes of this section, effective as of the date of publication of such order in the Federal Register.

(2) (A) A person's state of mind is "knowing" with respect to conduct, a circumstance, or a result if--

(i) such person is aware that such person is engaging in such conduct, that such circumstance exists, or that such result is substantially certain to occur; or

(ii) such person has a firm belief that such circumstance exists or that such result is substantially certain to occur.

(B) When knowledge of the existence of a particular circumstance is required for an offense, such knowledge is established if a person is aware of a high probability of the existence of such circumstance, unless the person actually believes that such circumstance does not exist.

(3) (A) The term "routine governmental action" means only an action which is ordinarily and commonly performed by a foreign official in--

(i) obtaining permits, licenses, or other official documents to qualify a person to do business in a foreign country;

(ii) processing governmental papers, such as visas and work orders;

(iii) providing police protection, mail pick-up and delivery, or scheduling inspections associated with contract performance or inspections related to transit of goods across country;

(iv) providing phone service, power and water supply, loading and unloading cargo, or protecting perishable products or commodities from deterioration; or

(v) actions of a similar nature.

(B) The term "routine governmental action" does not include any decision by a foreign official

whether, or on what terms, to award new business to or to continue business with a particular party, or any action taken by a foreign official involved in the decision-making process to encourage a decision to award new business to or continue business with a particular party.

(g) **Alternative Jurisdiction**

(1) It shall also be unlawful for any issuer organized under the laws of the United States, or a State, territory, possession, or commonwealth of the United States or a political subdivision thereof and which has a class of securities registered pursuant to section 12 of this title or which is required to file reports under section 15(d) of this title, or for any United States person that is an officer, director, employee, or agent of such issuer or a stockholder thereof acting on behalf of such issuer, to corruptly do any act outside the United States in furtherance of an offer, payment, promise to pay, or authorization of the payment of any money, or offer, gift, promise to give, or authorization of the giving of anything of value to any of the persons or entities set forth in paragraphs (1), (2), and (3) of this subsection (a) of this section for the purposes set forth therein, irrespective of whether such issuer or such officer, director, employee, agent, or stockholder makes use of the mails or any means or

instrumentality of interstate commerce in furtherance of such offer, gift, payment, promise, or authorization.

(2) As used in this subsection, the term "United States person" means a national of the United States (as defined in section 101 of the Immigration and Nationality Act (8 U.S.C. § 1101)) or any corporation, partnership, association, joint-stock company, business trust, unincorporated organization, or sole proprietorship organized under the laws of the United States or any State, territory, possession, or commonwealth of the United States, or any political subdivision thereof.

§ 78dd-2. Prohibited Foreign Trade Practices by Domestic Concerns
(a) **Prohibition**

It shall be unlawful for any domestic concern, other than an issuer which is subject to section 78dd-1 of this title, or for any officer, director, employee, or agent of such domestic concern or any stockholder thereof acting on behalf of such domestic concern, to make use of the mails or any means or instrumentality of interstate commerce corruptly in furtherance of an offer, payment, promise to pay, or authorization of the payment of any money, or offer, gift, promise to give, or authorization of the giving of anything of value to--

(1) any foreign official for purposes of--

(A) (i) influencing any act or decision of such foreign official in his official capacity, (ii) inducing such foreign official to do or omit to do any act in violation of the lawful duty of such official, or (iii) securing any improper advantage; or

(B) inducing such foreign official to use his influence with a foreign government or instrumentality thereof to affect or influence any act or decision of such government or instrumentality, in order to assist such domestic concern in obtaining or retaining business for or with, or directing business to, any person;

(2) any foreign political party or official thereof or any candidate for foreign political office for purposes of--

(A) (i) influencing any act or decision of such party, official, or candidate in its or his official capacity,

(ii) inducing such party, official, or candidate to do or omit to do an act in violation of the lawful duty of such party, official, or candidate, or (iii) securing any improper advantage; or

(B) inducing such party, official, or candidate to use its or his influence with a foreign government or instrumentality thereof to affect or influence any act or decision of such government or instrumentality, in order to assist such domestic concern in obtaining or retaining business for or with, or directing business to, any person;

(3) any person, while knowing that all or a portion of such money or thing of value will be offered, given, or promised, directly or indirectly, to any foreign official, to any foreign political party or official thereof, or to any candidate for foreign political office, for purposes of--

(A) (i) influencing any act or decision of such foreign official, political party, party official, or candidate in his or its official capacity, (ii) inducing such foreign official, political party, party official, or candidate to do or omit to do any act in violation of the lawful duty of such foreign official, political party, party official, or candidate, or (iii) securing any improper advantage; or

(B) inducing such foreign official, political party, party official, or candidate to use his or its influence with a foreign government or instrumentality thereof to affect or influence any act or decision of such government or instrumentality, in order to assist such domestic concern in obtaining or retaining business for or with, or directing business to, any person.

(b) **Exception for routine governmental action**

Subsections (a) and (i) of this section shall not apply to any facilitating or expediting payment to a foreign official, political party, or party official the purpose of which is to expedite or to secure the performance of a routine governmental action by a foreign official, political party, or party official.

(c) **Affirmative defenses**

It shall be an affirmative defense to actions under subsection (a) or (i) of this section that--

(1) the payment, gift, offer, or promise of anything of value that was made, was lawful under the written laws and regulations of the foreign official's, political party's, party official's, or candidate's country; or

(2) the payment, gift, offer, or promise of anything of value that was made, was a reasonable and bona fide expenditure, such as travel and lodging expenses, incurred by or on behalf of a foreign official, party, party official, or candidate and was directly related to--

(A) the promotion, demonstration, or explanation of products or services; or

(B) the execution or performance of a contract with a foreign government or agency thereof.

(d) **Injunctive relief**

(1) When it appears to the Attorney General that any domestic concern to which this section applies, or officer, director, employee, agent, or stockholder thereof, is engaged, or about to engage, in any act or practice constituting a violation of subsection (a) or (i) of this section, the Attorney General may, in his discretion, bring a civil action in an appropriate district court of the United States to enjoin such act or practice, and upon a proper showing, a permanent injunction or a temporary restraining order shall be granted without bond.

(2) For the purpose of any civil investigation which, in the opinion of the Attorney General, is necessary and proper to enforce this section, the Attorney General or his designee are empowered to administer oaths and affirmations, subpoena witnesses, take evidence, and require the production of any books, papers, or other documents which the Attorney General deems relevant or material to such investigation. The attendance of witnesses and the production of documentary evidence may be required from any place in the United States, or any territory, possession, or commonwealth of the United States, at any designated place of hearing.

(3) In case of contumacy by, or refusal to obey a subpoena issued to, any person, the Attorney General may invoke the aid of any court of the United States within the jurisdiction of which such investigation or proceeding is carried on, or where such person resides or carries on business, in requiring the attendance and testimony of witnesses and the production of books, papers, or other documents. Any such court may issue an order requiring such person to appear before the Attorney General or his designee, there to produce records, if so ordered, or to give testimony touching the matter under investigation. Any failure to obey such order of the court may be punished by such court as a contempt thereof.

All process in any such case may be served in the judicial district in which such person resides or may be found. The Attorney General may make such rules relating to civil investigations as may be necessary or appropriate to implement the provisions of this subsection.

(e) **Guidelines by Attorney General**

Not later than 6 months after August 23, 1988, the Attorney General, after consultation with the Securities and Exchange Commission, the Secretary of Commerce, the United States Trade Representative, the Secretary of State, and the Secretary of the Treasury, and after obtaining the views of all interested persons through public notice and comment procedures, shall determine to what extent compliance with this section would be enhanced and the business community would be assisted by further clarification of the preceding provisions of this section and may, based on such determination and to the extent necessary and appropriate, issue--

(1) guidelines describing specific types of conduct, associated with common types of export sales arrangements and business contracts, which for purposes of the Department of Justice's present enforcement policy, the Attorney General determines would be in conformance with the preceding provisions of this section; and

(2) general precautionary procedures which domestic concerns may use on a voluntary basis to conform their conduct to the Department of Justice's present enforcement policy regarding the preceding provisions of this section.

The Attorney General shall issue the guidelines and procedures referred to in the preceding sentence in accordance with the provisions of subchapter II of chapter 5 of Title 5 and those guidelines and procedures shall be subject to the provisions of chapter 7 of that title.

(f) **Opinions of Attorney General**

(1) The Attorney General, after consultation with appropriate departments and agencies of the United States and after obtaining the views of all interested persons through public notice and comment procedures, shall establish a procedure to provide responses to specific inquiries by domestic concerns concerning conformance of their conduct with the Department of Justice's present enforcement policy regarding the preceding provisions of this section. The Attorney General shall, within 30 days after receiving such a request, issue an opinion in response to that

request. The opinion shall state whether or not certain specified prospective conduct would, for purposes of the Department of Justice's present enforcement policy, violate the preceding provisions of this section. Additional requests for opinions may be filed with the Attorney General regarding other specified prospective conduct that is beyond the scope of conduct specified in previous requests. In any action brought under the applicable provisions of this section, there shall be a rebuttable presumption that conduct, which is specified in a request by a domestic concern and for which the Attorney General has issued an opinion that such conduct is in conformity with the Department of Justice's present enforcement policy, is in compliance with the preceding provisions of this section. Such a presumption may be rebutted by a preponderance of the evidence. In considering the presumption for purposes of this paragraph, a court shall weigh all relevant factors, including but not limited to whether the information submitted to the Attorney General was accurate and complete and whether it was within the scope of the conduct specified in any request received by the Attorney General. The Attorney General shall establish the procedure required by this paragraph in accordance with the provisions of subchapter II of chapter 5 of Title 5 and that procedure shall be subject to the provisions of chapter 7 of that title.

(2) Any document or other material which is provided to, received by, or prepared in the Department of Justice or any other department or agency of the United States in connection with a request by a domestic concern under the procedure established under paragraph (1), shall be exempt from disclosure under section 552 of Title 5 and shall not, except with the consent of the domestic concern, by made publicly available, regardless of whether the Attorney General response to such a request or the domestic concern withdraws such request before receiving a response.

(3) Any domestic concern who has made a request to the Attorney General under paragraph (1) may withdraw such request prior to the time the Attorney General issues an opinion in response to such request. Any request so withdrawn shall have no force or effect.

(4) The Attorney General shall, to the maximum extent practicable, provide timely guidance concerning the Department of Justice's present enforcement policy with respect to the preceding provisions of this section to potential exporters and small businesses that are unable to obtain specialized counsel on issues pertaining to such provisions. Such guidance shall be limited to responses to requests under paragraph (1) concerning conformity of specified prospective conduct with the Department of Justice's present enforcement policy regarding the preceding provisions of this section and general explanations of compliance responsibilities and of potential liabilities under the preceding provisions of this section.

(g) **Penalties**

(1) (A) Any domestic concern that is not a natural person and that violates subsection (a) or (i) of this section shall be fined not more than $2,000,000.

(B) Any domestic concern that is not a natural person and that violates subsection (a) or (i) of this section shall be subject to a civil penalty of not more than $10,000 imposed in an action brought by the Attorney General.

13.2 US Foreign and Corrupt Practices Act (FCPA)

(2) (A) Any natural person that is an officer, director, employee, or agent of a domestic concern, or stockholder acting on behalf of such domestic concern, who willfully violates subsection (a) or (i) of this section shall be fined not more than $100,000 or imprisoned not more than 5 years, or both.

(B) Any natural person that is an officer, director, employee, or agent of a domestic concern, or stockholder acting on behalf of such domestic concern, who violates subsection (a) or (i) of this section shall be subject to a civil penalty of not more than $10,000 imposed in an action brought by the Attorney General.

(3) Whenever a fine is imposed under paragraph (2) upon any officer, director, employee, agent, or stockholder of a domestic concern, such fine may not be paid, directly or indirectly, by such domestic concern.

(h) **Definitions**

For purposes of this section:
(1) The term "domestic concern" means--
(A) any individual who is a citizen, national, or resident of the United States; and
(B) any corporation, partnership, association, joint-stock company, business trust, unincorporated organization, or sole proprietorship which has its principal place of business in the United States, or which is organized under the laws of a State of the United States or a territory, possession, or commonwealth of the United States.

(2) (A) The term "foreign official" means any officer or employee of a foreign government or any department, agency, or instrumentality thereof, or of a public international organization, or any person acting in an official capacity for or on behalf of any such government or department, agency, or instrumentality, or for or on behalf of any such public international organization.

(B) For purposes of subparagraph (A), the term "public international organization" means --

(i) an organization that has been designated by Executive order pursuant to Section 1 of the International Organizations Immunities Act (22 U.S.C. § 288); or

(ii) any other international organization that is designated by the President by Executive order for the purposes of this section, effective as of the date of publication of such order in the Federal Register.

(3) (A) A person's state of mind is "knowing" with respect to conduct, a circumstance, or a result if--

(i) such person is aware that such person is engaging in such conduct, that such circumstance exists, or that such result is substantially certain to occur; or

(ii) such person has a firm belief that such circumstance exists or that such result is substantially certain to occur.

(B) When knowledge of the existence of a particular circumstance is required for an offense, such knowledge is established if a person is aware of a high probability of the existence of such circumstance, unless the person actually believes that such circumstance does not exist.

(4) (A) The term "routine governmental action" means only an action which is ordinarily and commonly performed by a foreign official in--

(i) obtaining permits, licenses, or other official documents to qualify a person to do business in a foreign country;

(ii) processing governmental papers, such as visas and work orders;

(iii) providing police protection, mail pick-up and delivery, or scheduling inspections associated with contract performance or inspections related to transit of goods across country;

(iv) providing phone service, power and water supply, loading and unloading cargo, or protecting perishable products or commodities from deterioration; or

(v) actions of a similar nature.

(B) The term "routine governmental action" does not include any decision by a foreign official

whether, or on what terms, to award new business to or to continue business with a particular party, or any action taken by a foreign official involved in the decision-making process to encourage a decision to award new business to or continue business with a particular party.

(5) The term "interstate commerce" means trade, commerce, transportation, or communication among the several States, or between any foreign country and any State or between any State and any place or ship outside thereof, and such term includes the intrastate use of--

(A) a telephone or other interstate means of communication, or

(B) any other interstate instrumentality.

(i) **Alternative Jurisdiction**

(1) It shall also be unlawful for any United States person to corruptly do any act outside the United States in furtherance of an offer, payment, promise to pay, or authorization of the payment of any money, or offer, gift, promise to give, or authorization of the giving of anything of value to any of the persons or entities set forth in paragraphs (1), (2), and (3) of subsection (a), for the purposes set forth therein, irrespective of whether such United States person makes use of the mails or any means or instrumentality of interstate commerce in furtherance of such offer, gift, payment, promise, or authorization.

(2) As used in this subsection, a "United States person" means a national of the United States (as defined in section 101 of the Immigration and Nationality Act (8 U.S.C. § 1101)) or any corporation, partnership, association, joint-stock company, business trust, unincorporated organization, or sole proprietorship organized under the laws of the United States or any State, territory, possession, or commonwealth of the United States, or any political subdivision thereof.

§ 78dd-3. Prohibited Foreign Trade Practices by Persons Other than Issuers or Domestic Concerns
(a) **Prohibition**

It shall be unlawful for any person other than an issuer that is subject to section 30A of the Securities Exchange Act of 1934 or a domestic concern, as defined in section 104 of this Act), or for any officer, director, employee, or agent of such person or any stockholder thereof acting on behalf of such person, while in the

13.2 US Foreign and Corrupt Practices Act (FCPA)

territory of the United States, corruptly to make use of the mails or any means or instrumentality of interstate commerce or to do any other act in furtherance of an offer, payment, promise to pay, or authorization of the payment of any money, or offer, gift, promise to give, or authorization of the giving of anything of value to--

(1) any foreign official for purposes of--

(A) (i) influencing any act or decision of such foreign official in his official capacity, (ii) inducing such foreign official to do or omit to do any act in violation of the lawful duty of such official, or (iii) securing any improper advantage; or

(B) inducing such foreign official to use his influence with a foreign government or instrumentality thereof to affect or influence any act or decision of such government or instrumentality, in order to assist such person in obtaining or retaining business for or with, or directing business to, any person;

(2) any foreign political party or official thereof or any candidate for foreign political office for purposes of--

(A) (i) influencing any act or decision of such party, official, or candidate in its or his official capacity,

(ii) inducing such party, official, or candidate to do or omit to do an act in violation of the lawful duty of such party, official, or candidate, or (iii) securing any improper advantage; or

(B) inducing such party, official, or candidate to use its or his influence with a foreign government or instrumentality thereof to affect or influence any act or decision of such government or instrumentality. in order to assist such person in obtaining or retaining business for or with, or directing business to, any person; or

(3) any person, while knowing that all or a portion of such money or thing of value will be offered, given, or promised, directly or indirectly, to any foreign official, to any foreign political party or official thereof, or to any candidate for foreign political office, for purposes of--

(A) (i) influencing any act or decision of such foreign official, political party, party official, or candidate in his or its official capacity, (ii) inducing such foreign official, political party, party official, or candidate to do or omit to do any act in violation of the lawful duty of such foreign official, political party, party official, or candidate, or (iii) securing any improper advantage; or

(B) inducing such foreign official, political party, party official, or candidate to use his or its influence with a foreign government or instrumentality thereof to affect or influence any act or decision of such government or instrumentality, in order to assist such person in obtaining or retaining business for or with, or directing business to, any person.

(b) **Exception for routine governmental action**

Subsection (a) of this section shall not apply to any facilitating or expediting payment to a foreign official, political party, or party official the purpose of which is to expedite or to secure the performance of a routine governmental action by a foreign official, political party, or party official.

(c) **Affirmative defenses**

It shall be an affirmative defense to actions under subsection (a) of this section that--

(1) the payment, gift, offer, or promise of anything of value that was made, was lawful under the written laws and regulations of the foreign official's, political party's, party official's, or candidate's country; or

(2) the payment, gift, offer, or promise of anything of value that was made, was a reasonable and bona fide expenditure, such as travel and lodging expenses, incurred by or on behalf of a foreign official, party, party official, or candidate and was directly related to--

(A) the promotion, demonstration, or explanation of products or services; or

(B) the execution or performance of a contract with a foreign government or agency thereof.

(d) **Injunctive relief**

(1) When it appears to the Attorney General that any person to which this section applies, or officer, director, employee, agent, or stockholder thereof, is engaged, or about to engage, in any act or practice constituting a violation of subsection (a) of this section, the Attorney General may, in his discretion, bring a civil action in an appropriate district court of the United States to enjoin such act or practice, and upon a proper showing, a permanent injunction or a temporary restraining order shall be granted without bond.

(2) For the purpose of any civil investigation which, in the opinion of the Attorney General, is necessary and proper to enforce this section, the Attorney General or his designee are empowered to administer oaths and affirmations, subpoena witnesses, take evidence, and require the production of any books, papers, or other documents which the Attorney General deems relevant or material to such investigation. The attendance of witnesses and the production of documentary evidence may be required from any place in the United States, or any territory, possession, or commonwealth of the United States, at any designated place of hearing.

(3) In case of contumacy by, or refusal to obey a subpoena issued to, any person, the Attorney General may invoke the aid of any court of the United States within the jurisdiction of which such investigation or proceeding is carried on, or where such person resides or carries on business, in requiring the attendance and testimony of witnesses and the production of books, papers, or other documents. Any such court may issue an order requiring such person to appear before the Attorney General or his designee, there to produce records, if so ordered, or to give testimony touching the matter under investigation. Any failure to obey such order of the court may be punished by such court as a contempt thereof.

(4) All process in any such case may be served in the judicial district in which such person resides or may be found. The Attorney General may make such rules relating to civil investigations as may be necessary or appropriate to implement the provisions of this subsection.

(e) Penalties

(1) (A) Any juridical person that violates subsection (a) of this section shall be fined not more than $2,000,000.

(B) Any juridical person that violates subsection (a) of this section shall be subject to a civil penalty of not more than $10,000 imposed in an action brought by the Attorney General.

(2) (A) Any natural person who willfully violates subsection (a) of this section shall be fined not more than $100,000 or imprisoned not more than 5 years, or both.

(B) Any natural person who violates subsection (a) of this section shall be subject to a civil penalty of not more than $10,000 imposed in an action brought by the Attorney General.

(3) Whenever a fine is imposed under paragraph (2) upon any officer, director, employee, agent, or stockholder of a person, such fine may not be paid, directly or indirectly, by such person.

(f) Definitions

For purposes of this section:

(1) The term "person," when referring to an offender, means any natural person other than a national of the United States (as defined in 8 U.S.C. § 1101) or any corporation, partnership, association, joint-stock company, business trust, unincorporated organization, or sole proprietorship organized under the law of a foreign nation or a political subdivision thereof

(2) (A) The term "foreign official" means any officer or employee of a foreign government or any department, agency, or instrumentality thereof, or of a public international organization, or any person acting in an official capacity for or on behalf of any such government or department, agency, or instrumentality, or for or on behalf of any such public international organization.

For purposes of subparagraph (A), the term "public international organization" means --

(i) an organization that has been designated by Executive Order pursuant to Section 1 of the International Organizations Immunities Act (22 U.S.C. § 288); or

(ii) any other international organization that is designated by the President by Executive order for the purposes of this section, effective as of the date of publication of such order in the Federal Register.

(3) (A) A person's state of mind is "knowing" with respect to conduct, a circumstance, or a result if --

(i) such person is aware that such person is engaging in such conduct, that such circumstance exists, or that such result is substantially certain to occur; or

(ii) such person has a firm belief that such circumstance exists or that such result is substantially certain to occur.

(B) When knowledge of the existence of a particular circumstance is required for an offense, such knowledge is established if a person is aware of a high probability of the existence of such circumstance, unless the person actually believes that such circumstance does not exist.

(4) (A) The term "routine governmental action" means only an action which is ordinarily and commonly performed by a foreign official in--

(i) obtaining permits, licenses, or other official documents to qualify a person to do business in a foreign country;

(ii) processing governmental papers, such as visas and work orders;

(iii) providing police protection, mail pick-up and delivery, or scheduling inspections associated with contract performance or inspections related to transit of goods across country;

(iv) providing phone service, power and water supply, loading and unloading cargo, or protecting perishable products or commodities from deterioration; or

(v) actions of a similar nature.

(B) The term "routine governmental action" does not include any decision by a foreign official

whether, or on what terms, to award new business to or to continue business with a particular party, or any action taken by a foreign official involved in the decision-making process to encourage a decision to award new business to or continue business with a particular party.

(5) The term "interstate commerce" means trade, commerce, transportation, or communication among the several States, or between any foreign country and any State or between any State and any place or ship outside thereof, and such term includes the intrastate use of —

(A) a telephone or other interstate means of communication, or

(B) any other interstate instrumentality.

§ 78ff. Penalties
(a) Willful violations; false and misleading statements

Any person who willfully violates any provision of this chapter (other than section 78dd-1 of this title), or any rule or regulation thereunder the violation of which is made unlawful or the observance of which is required under the terms of this chapter, or any person who willfully and knowingly makes, or causes to be made, any statement in any application, report, or document required to be filed under this chapter or any rule or regulation thereunder or any undertaking contained in a registration statement as provided in subsection (d) of section 78o of this title, or by any self-regulatory organization in connection with an application for membership or participation therein or to become associated with a member thereof, which statement was false or misleading with respect to any material fact, shall upon conviction be fined not more than $5,000,000, or imprisoned not more than 20 years, or both, except that when such person is a person other than a natural person, a fine not exceeding $25,000,000 may be imposed; but no person shall be subject to imprisonment under this section for the violation of any rule or regulation if he proves that he had no knowledge of such rule or regulation.

(b) Failure to file information, documents, or reports

Any issuer which fails to file information, documents, or reports required to be filed under subsection (d) of section 78o of this title or any rule or regulation thereunder shall forfeit to the United States the sum of $100 for each and every day such failure to file shall continue. Such forfeiture, which shall be in lieu of any criminal penalty for such failure to file which might be deemed to arise under subsection (a) of this section, shall be payable into the Treasury of the United States and shall be recoverable in a civil suit in the name of the United States.

(c) **Violations by issuers, officers, directors, stockholders, employees, or agents of issuers**

(1) (A) Any issuer that violates subsection (a) or (g) of section 30A of this title [15 U.S.C. § 78dd-1] shall be fined not more than $2,000,000.

(B) Any issuer that violates subsection (a) or (g) of section 30A of this title [15 U.S.C. § 78dd-1] shall be subject to a civil penalty of not more than $10,000 imposed in an action brought by the Commission.

(2) (A) Any officer, director, employee, or agent of an issuer, or stockholder acting on behalf of such issuer, who willfully violates subsection (a) or (g) of section 30A of this title [15 U.S.C. § 78dd-1] shall be fined not more than $100,000, or imprisoned not more than 5 years, or both.

(B) Any officer, director, employee, or agent of an issuer, or stockholder acting on behalf of such issuer, who violates subsection (a) or (g) of section 30A of this title [15 U.S.C. § 78dd-1] shall be subject to a civil penalty of not more than $10,000 imposed in an action brought by the Commission.

(3) Whenever a fine is imposed under paragraph (2) upon any officer, director, employee, agent, or stockholder of an issuer, such fine may not be paid, directly or indirectly, by such issuer.

Chapter 14
Other Integrity Materials

14.1 Corporate Anti-Corruption Policies: FCPA Blog Articles[1]

14.1.1 Benchmarking Alert: Here is 3M's Anti-bribery Policy[2], Harry Cassin, November 1, 2021

Minnesota-based 3M has over 100,000 patents and produces around 60,000 products—including the N95 face mask. Here are five interesting points from its anti-bribery policy.

1. **Local customs aren't a defense.**

   3M employees and any third party to whom this Principle applies, must not provide, offer or accept bribes, kickbacks, corrupt payments, facilitation payments, inappropriate gifts, to or from Government Officials or any commercial person or entity, regardless of local practices or customs.

2. **You're responsible for our business partners' bad acts.**

   3M employees must not allow any Business Partner to provide, offer or accept bribes, kickbacks, corrupt payments, facilitation payments, or inappropriate gifts, or 3M and the employee may be held responsible for the actions of the Business Partner.

3. **Facilitating payments are bribes.**

   Facilitation payments are bribes and are prohibited . . . A facilitation payment or "grease payment" is a small sum of money paid to a Government Official in order to

---

[1] https://fcpablog.com/tag/policy-benchmark/ (reproduced with their kind permission).
[2] https://fcpablog.com/2021/11/01/benchmarking-alert-here-is-3ms-anti-bribery-policy/

expedite routine and nondiscretionary activities, such as obtaining a visa or work order, installing telephone service, or initiating electrical service. 3M prohibits facilitation payments, which can violate the UKBA and other countries' anti-bribery laws.

This is similar to Apple, Novartis, Microsoft, Volkswagen, Airbus, and GM which ban all facilitating payments. Coca-Cola and Tesla might approve some facilitating payments. Walmart doesn't mention facilitating payments at all.

4. **Cups of coffee aren't bribes.**

Small courtesies, such as a cup of coffee, a token gift of nominal value, or a reasonably priced lunch or dinner, are not bribes.

5. **Hiring decisions can be bribes.**

The U.S. Foreign Corrupt Practices Act and other countries' bribery or corruption laws may consider the hiring of a family member of a Government Official as bribery, depending on why the family member was hired, his or her qualifications, and the Government Official's ability to make decisions that could affect 3M business. Relatives of Government Officials may be hired by 3M. However, special care must be taken when an applicant is the close relative (such as a spouse, child, sibling, niece, nephew, aunt or uncle) of a Government Official who is in a position to influence a decision related to the purchase, prescription, or use of a 3M product or 3M service, or to any other governmental action that would benefit 3M's business.

* * *

View more anti-corruption policy benchmarks here.

Here's the full three-page anti-bribery principle: https://fcpablog.com/wp-content/uploads/2021/09/3M_Anti-Bribery-Principle-PDF_FCPABlog.pdf

14.1.2 Benchmarking Alert: Here's General Motor's Full Anti-corruption Policy[3], Harry Cassin, September 1, 2021

Last year, General Motors produced over 6.8 million vehicles and employed over 150,000 people. Here are five interesting points from its global anti-corruption policy.

1. **All bribery is prohibited, even if you don't think it's wrong.**

GM prohibits all bribes, including conduct you may not consider a bribe or even improper, but fits a legal definition of corruption.

---

[3] https://fcpablog.com/2021/09/01/benchmarking-alert-heres-general-motors-full-anti-corruption-policy/

2. **A well defined list of valuables.**

Anything of Value: Anything that might have value to the recipient, including cash or cash equivalents (e.g., gift cards), gifts, gratuities, goods, loans, discounts, cars (including loaner, discounted, and "test drive" vehicles), entertainment or tickets, meals or drinks, travel or lodging, charitable contributions, political contributions, training, services, personal favors, paying bills for others, forbearances, offers of employment, hiring someone's friend or relative, or anything else that is valuable to the receiver, even if it would not be valuable to anyone else.

3. **Figure out if you are dealing with a government official.**

It is your responsibility to understand whether you are interacting with a government official—either a U.S. official or a non-U.S. official—and to comply with applicable law and GM policy.

4. **No facilitating payments, ever.**

A facilitating payment is a payment of small value made to low level government employees to obtain a non-discretionary, routine governmental action to which GM is legally entitled. While permitted under U.S. law in narrow, strictly defined circumstances, even very small facilitating payments may violate the U.K. Bribery Act and local statutes. Accordingly, this Policy strictly prohibits all facilitating payments.

This is similar to Apple, Novartis, Microsoft, Volkswagen, and Airbus which ban all facilitating payments. Coca-Cola and Tesla might approve some facilitating payments. Walmart doesn't mention facilitating payments at all.

5. **Extortion needs to be accurately recorded.**

Extortion payments are payments that are necessary to ensure the health or safety of GM employees or of Third Parties associated with GM, including payments to avoid imminent physical harm or imminent illegitimate detention. Threats of purely economic harm are not extortion. Although extortion payments are permitted by this Policy, this is a very narrow exception that requires legal analysis. You must obtain approval from your RCO or another member of GM Legal before making such a payment, and you must report any extortion demand to your Managing Director immediately, whether or not you seek to make a payment, unless it is not possible to do so. If it is not possible to report the demand and seek approval for any payment as just described, the incident must be reported within one (1) business day, absent physical or technological impossibility. Extortion payments must be accurately recorded in GM's books and records.

Microsoft's anti-corruption policy is the only other one where we've seen extortion mentioned.

* * *

View more anti-corruption policy benchmarks here.
Here's the full thirteen-page anti-bribery policy:

https://fcpablog.com/wp-content/uploads/2021/08/GM_Global_Integrity_Policy_fcpa_blog.pdf

14.1.3 Benchmarking Alert: Here's Coca-Cola's Full Anti-bribery Policy[4], Harry Cassin, July 20, 2021

The Coca-Cola Company, incorporated in 1892, is one of the world's oldest, most well-known, and widely consumed brands. How does it's anti-bribery policy compare?

1. **It takes daily effort.**

It is therefore vital that you not only understand and appreciate the importance of this Policy, but also comply with it in your daily work.

2. **Don't pay bribes, or you might end up in jail.**

Company employees that violate these laws can also face severe civil and criminal penalties, including jail time.

3. **No facilitating payments (except sometimes).**

The Company's prohibition on bribery applies to all improper payments regardless of size or purpose, including "facilitating" (or expediting) payments. Facilitating payments refer to small payments to government officials to expedite or facilitate non-discretionary actions or services, such as obtaining an ordinary license or business permit, processing government papers such as visas, customs clearance, providing telephone, power or water service, or loading or unloading of cargo. Generally, facilitation payments are prohibited by this Policy, except for a very limited set of circumstances for which prior written approval must be obtained from both Company Legal Counsel and E&C.

This is similar to Tesla. In contrast, Apple, Novartis, Microsoft, Volkswagen, and Airbus ban all facilitating payments. Walmart doesn't mention facilitating payments at all.

4. **Never give a public official a gift card.**

It is never permissible to provide gifts, meals, travel, or entertainment to anyone (government officials or commercial partners) in exchange for any improper favor or benefit. In addition, gifts of cash or cash equivalents, such as gift cards, are never permissible.

---

[4] https://fcpablog.com/2021/07/20/benchmarking-alert-heres-coca-colas-full-anti-bribery-policy/

14.1 Corporate Anti-Corruption Policies: FCPA Blog Articles

5. **Some employees must certify compliance.**

Every quarter, in conjunction with the Company's Securities and Exchange Commission ("SEC") Certification process, applicable employees are required to certify the accuracy of several representations related to this Policy.

This is the first time we've seen SEC certification mentioned in an anti-bribery compliance policy.

* * *

View more anti-corruption policy benchmarks here.

Here's the full eight-page anti-bribery policy:

https://fcpablog.com/wp-content/uploads/2021/07/Anti-Bribery-Policy-_-The-Coca-Cola-Company-FCPA-Blog.pdf

14.1.4 Benchmarking Alert: Here is Pfizer's Anti-bribery Policy[5], Harry Cassin, December 20, 2021

The New York-headquartered biopharmaceutical giant paid the DOJ and SEC $60 million in 2012 to settle FCPA offenses in Bulgaria, Croatia, China, Czech Republic, Italy, Kazakhstan, Russia, Serbia, Indonesia, Pakistan, and Saudi Arabia. How does Pfizer's anti-bribery policy compare?

1. **Pharma is a high-risk industry for bribes.**

As a pharmaceutical company, Pfizer must be particularly sensitive to bribery and corruption issues when government officials are involved because governments are often both the regulators of Pfizer products and major customers.

2. **Pay attention to books and records and internal controls.**

No false or artificial entries may be made in the books and records for any reason, and all payments and transactions, regardless of value, must be recorded accurately.

3. **No facilitating payments.**

Under Pfizer policy, a facilitation payment means a nominal, unofficial payment to a Government Official for the purpose of securing or expediting the performance of a routine, non- discretionary governmental action. Such payments are illegal in most countries and Pfizer is committed to eliminating such payments from its business. Pfizer prohibits any Pfizer employee or Business Associate from offering or authorizing the offer of a facilitation payment (directly or indirectly).

This is similar to Apple, Novartis, Microsoft, Volkswagen, Airbus, GM, and 3M which ban all facilitating payments. Coca-Cola and Tesla might approve some facilitating payments. Walmart doesn't mention facilitating payments at all.

---

[5] https://fcpablog.com/2021/12/20/benchmarking-alert-here-is-pfizers-anti-bribery-policy/

4. **No commercial bribery.**

Under Pfizer's anti-bribery and anti-corruption policy, Pfizer's employees and Business Associates must never engage in commercial bribery.

5. **The extortion defense.**

Under Pfizer policy, when a payment is extorted by an imminent threat to the health, safety or welfare of a Pfizer employee, the demanded payment may be made. However, once the immediacy of the situation has been resolved, the payment must be reported to a member of Pfizer's Legal Division, including information on the circumstances and amount of the payment. Any such payment always must be accurately and completely recorded in Pfizer's books and records.

This is similar to GM and Microsoft, the only two other mentions of extortion we've seen.

* * *

View more anti-corruption policy benchmarks here.

Here's the full four-page anti-bribery policy:

https://fcpablog.com/wp-content/uploads/2021/12/Pfizer_Anti-Corruption_Policy.pdf

14.1.5 Benchmarking Alert: Here's Walmart's Full Global Anti-corruption Policy[6], Harry Cassin, May 12, 2021

In June 2019, Walmart paid the DOJ and SEC $282 million to settle allegations that it violated the FCPA by paying an intermediary in Brazil for help obtaining construction permits and having weak anti-corruption internal controls in Brazil, China, India, and Mexico. How does its three-page anti-corruption policy compare?

1. **It's global.**

To effectively implement this policy, Walmart shall maintain an effective risk-based Global Anti-Corruption Program (the "Program") designed to prevent, detect, and remediate bribery and recordkeeping violations. As part of the program, Walmart shall adopt operating procedures specifically targeted to the corruption risks that exist for all of its operations, worldwide.

2. **It's helpful to not report anonymously.**

All reports to Ethics & Compliance are treated as confidentially as possible. It helps with follow-up if you identify yourself. If you are not comfortable identifying

---

[6] https://fcpablog.com/2021/05/12/benchmarking-alert-heres-walmarts-full-global-anti-corruption-policy/

yourself, you can make anonymous reports to the Ethics Helpline to the extent allowed by law.

3. **No (mention) of facilitating payments.**

This policy prohibits corrupt payments in all circumstances, whether in dealings with government officials or individuals in the private sector.

Every company we've benchmarked has explicitly mentioned facilitating payments. Apple, Novartis, Microsoft, Volkswagen, and Airbus ban them. In contrast, Tesla might approve some facilitating payments.

4. **Don't fake it.**

Knowingly reporting false information is contrary to our values and will be subject to disciplinary action. Also, anyone who reports a suspected violation may be subject to disciplinary action to the extent he or she violated any Walmart policy or procedure.

5. **There are incentives.**

Appropriate incentives and punishments for associates, executives and third parties for adherence to or violations of, respectively, the relevant policy and related procedures.

* * *

View more anti-corruption policy benchmarks here.

Here's the full three-page anti-corruption policy:

https://fcpablog.com/wp-content/uploads/2021/04/Walmart_Global_Anticorruption_Policy_FCPA-Blog.pdf

14.1.6 *Benchmarking Alert: Here's the Full Airbus Anti-corruption Policy[7], Harry Cassin, April 28, 2021*

In January 2020, Airbus SE paid $4 billion to settle global bribery and trade charges with French, UK, and U.S. authorities after an eight-year investigation. How does its anti-corruption policy compare?

1. **Tell employees the risks (of policy violations).**

Violations of anti-corruption laws carry significant civil and criminal penalties, and put the reputation, hard work and business of Airbus and its employees at risk. Any employee who fails to comply with this Policy and the Directives referenced below will be subject to appropriate disciplinary action.

---

[7] https://fcpablog.com/2021/04/28/benchmarking-alert-heres-the-full-airbus-anti-corruption-policy/

2. **A valuable list.**

Anti-corruption laws make it illegal to offer, promise, give, solicit or receive "anything of value", in exchange for an "improper advantage". The term "anything of value" is broadly interpreted under the law. In addition of cash or money, which immediately come to mind, a bribe can also take other forms, all of which convey value to the receiver, for example:

- Providing luxurious or overly frequent gifts and hospitality to someone;
- Promising to pay for personal medical, educational or living expenses;
- Making sponsorships or donations to the "pet charity" of a public official;
- Extending employment or an unpaid internship to the relative of a key decision-maker;
- Offering an investment at below market value of a company controlled by a public official who would benefit personally.

3. **No facilitation payments. . . unless you're in danger.**

Consistent with most anti-corruption laws, Airbus prohibits facilitation payments. A narrow exception exists if a facilitation payment is made in the context of avoiding or preventing an imminent threat to the health, safety or welfare of an Airbus employee. In such cases, the employee should immediately inform a member of the Legal & Compliance team.

This policy is similar to Apple, Novartis, Microsoft, and Volkswagen. In contrast, Tesla might approve some facilitating payments.

4. **Get the board involved.**

The Ethics & Compliance Committee of the Board of Directors also plays a key role in the oversight and continued development of Airbus' Ethics & Compliance programme, organisation and framework for the effective governance of ethics and compliance, including all associated internal policies, procedures and controls.

5. **It's gettin' better all the time.**

When misconduct reveals a gap in compliance policies, procedures or tools, Airbus undertakes revisions to its Ethics & Compliance Programme commensurate with the wrongdoing and in light of lessons learned.

* * *

View more anti-corruption policy benchmarks here.

Here's the full nine-page anti-corruption policy:

https://fcpablog.com/wp-content/uploads/2021/04/Airbus-Ethics-and-Compliance-Anti-Corruption-Policy_fcpablog.pdf

14.1.7 Benchmarking Alert: Here's Volkswagen's Full Anti-corruption Policy, Harry Cassin April 8, 2021

Volkswagen left its mark on the history of the world with the love it or hate it Beetle. Is it a similar story with its (incredibly) thorough anti-corruption policy? Let's dive into the Antikorruptionsrichtlinie (my word).

1. **It's 36 pages long.**

The purpose of this Guideline is to raise awareness among all employees* of the dangers of corruption and provide assistance on how to follow internal rules at the workplace.

For comparison, Apple's is four pages. Novartis was the previous longest we'd benchmarked at six pages.

2. **When it comes to public officials, hold the butter.**

Benefits granted to officials and holders of political office are particularly susceptible to being considered a form of corruption. In most countries, more stringent criminal law regulations apply to dealings with officials than with business partners or private persons, mainly to ensure the impartiality of the administration. In some countries, what is known as "buttering up" of officials or holders of political office is punishable as a criminal offense. This refers to the favorable treatment of officials or holders of political office by giving them relatively small favors or benefits. It is therefore advisable to exercise particular caution when dealing with authorities and / or their representatives and to take a very restrictive approach to granting benefits.

3. **Use of examples.**

Favoritism is often linked to corruption. This involves a person using their position of power to obtain an advantage for a family member or an acquaintance.

Example: As an employee of the Volkswagen Group you are negotiating a large sales order from a business partner. One day the business partner's employee responsible for order management asks for a meeting. During the meeting he offers to arrange for the order to be placed with the Volkswagen Group. However, in return he asks you to fix an apprenticeship for his nephew without going through the regular application process.

4. **Facilitating payments? Nein. Nein. Nein.**

Facilitation payments (also called bribes) are relatively small amounts paid to officials in order to accelerate routine official procedures to which citizens are legally entitled. Bribes are a criminal offense in any countries and are therefore prohibited.

The Volkswagen Group expressly prohibits facilitation payments.

This policy is similar to Apple, Novartis, and Microsoft. In contrast, Tesla might approve some facilitating payments.

5. **Donations are important to the Volkswagen brand.**

The Volkswagen Group supports organizations and events worldwide through sponsorship and donations. These strengthen the Volkswagen Group brands. Donations are important measures which express how we perceive our social responsibility.

* * *

View more anti-corruption policy benchmarks here.

Here's the full 36-page anti-corruption policy:

https://fcpablog.com/wp-content/uploads/2021/04/volkwagan-anti-corruption.pdf

14.1.8 Benchmarking Alert: Here's the Full Microsoft Anti-corruption Policy[8], Harry Cassin, March 24, 2021

Microsoft has one of the most interesting anti-corruption policies we've reviewed and the only one to cover two rarely acknowledged topics: extortion and threats.

1. **Why we don't pay bribes.**

As described in our Standards of Business Conduct, Microsoft's business relies on the trust we build with our customers, partners and suppliers. Offering or paying bribes or kickbacks breaks that trust. Bribery influences the decisions made by our customers and is inconsistent with Microsoft's mission to empower every individual and organization on the planet to achieve more.

2. **You won't be punished if Microsoft loses out.**

You will not be punished for refusing to pay or take a bribe or kickback, even if your refusal results in a loss of business to Microsoft.

3. **The extortion defense.**

Imminent Threats: If there is an imminent threat to your health or safety, such as a threat of physical violence, you may provide a payment to avoid immediate harm. Loss of business to Microsoft is not an imminent threat. Whenever possible, you should first consult with and obtain authorization from the Business Conduct and Compliance alias before making the payment. If prior approval is not possible, you must report the payment within 48 hours of its occurrence to the Business Conduct and Compliance alias.

---

[8] https://fcpablog.com/2021/03/24/benchmarking-alert-heres-the-full-microsoft-anti-corruption-policy/

14.1 Corporate Anti-Corruption Policies: FCPA Blog Articles

4. **No facilitating payments, ever.**

Do Not Make Facilitating Payments: A facilitating payment is a payment to secure or expedite a routine government action by an official. Do not make facilitating payments.

This policy is similar to Apple and Novartis. In contrast, Tesla might approve some facilitating payments.

5. **Don't hire princelings or others based on threats against the company.**

Hiring Decisions Must Not Benefit Government Officials: Do not hire an official or someone suggested by, or related to, an official to help Microsoft obtain or keep business, or if the official offers to give a benefit to Microsoft or threatens to act in a way that harms Microsoft if the requested hiring decision is not taken. Always use Microsoft's normal hiring process. Before hiring an official or a candidate suggested by an official, review and comply with the Procedure for Hiring Decisions Involving Government Officials.

* * *

View more anti-corruption policy benchmarks here.

Here's the full five-page anti-corruption policy:

https://fcpablog.com/wp-content/uploads/2021/03/Microsoft-Anti-Corruption-Policy-FCPA-Blog.pdf

14.1.9 Benchmarking Alert: Here's the Full Novartis Anti-bribery Policy[9], Harry Cassin, March 17, 2021

Novartis updated its anti-bribery policy four months after the Swiss pharma paid $346.7 million to resolve FCPA offenses in Greece, Vietnam, and South Korea. Here are some interesting details from the latest version.

1. **No gifts, even culturally-appropriate unbranded ones.**

Gifts of any kind including personal gifts, cultural acknowledgements or promotional aids etc., whether branded or unbranded, must not be provided to Healthcare Professionals (HCPs) or their family members.

2. **Use the "front page" test to avoid embarrassment.**

Before giving a gift or providing hospitality or entertainment to anyone, consider whether the reputation of Novartis, yourself, or the recipient is likely to be damaged if news of the gift, hospitality, or entertainment appeared on the front page of a newspaper. If this would embarrass either Novartis or the recipient, do not proceed.

---

[9] https://fcpablog.com/2021/03/17/benchmarking-alert-heres-the-full-novartis-anti-bribery-policy/

3. **No facilitating payments, even if legal.**

Novartis prohibits facilitation payments, irrespective of whether local law permits facilitation payments.

This policy is similar to Apple. In contrast, Tesla might approve some facilitating payments.

4. **Public vs. Private? Not so different.**

Novartis does not distinguish between public officials and employees of private sector organizations so far as bribery is concerned; however, it is important to recognize that public officials are often subject to rules and restrictions that do not apply to persons who operate in the private sector.

5. **In some places, every healthcare professional is a public official.**

In some countries, doctors, pharmacists, clinical trials investigators, and nurses are public officials irrespective of whether they are working at a government institution.

* * *

View more anti-corruption policy benchmarks here.

Here's the full six-page anti-bribery policy:

https://fcpablog.com/wp-content/uploads/2021/03/novartis-anti-bribery-policy.pdf

14.1.10 Benchmarking Alert: Here's Tesla's Full Anti-corruption Policy[10], Harry Cassin, March 10, 2021

Elon Musk is well known for his brevity on Twitter, and Tesla's worldwide bribery and anti-corruption policy shows the compliance department also likes to keep things simple.

1. **A whole policy in 10 words.**

Boiled down to its essence, our policy is: Don't offer any bribe to anybody, anytime, for any reason.

(And when in doubt, please consult with the General Counsel or the Legal Department.)

---

[10] https://fcpablog.com/2021/03/10/benchmarking-alert-heres-teslas-full-anti-corruption-policy/

2. **Talking about the risk to the brand up front.**

From the "Overview" section: Involvement in bribery or corruption can result in lasting damage to our brand and our reputation. It can also result in multi-million-dollar fines and penalties, plus jail time for participants.

3. **A $50 limit on gifts, meals, and entertainment.**

In the normal course of business and depending upon the circumstances, a non-cash gift, meal or entertainment of USD $50 a person or less would be considered modest and reasonable.

4. **Some facilitating payments might be approved.**

Facilitation payments are not permissible, except in certain limited circumstances. You must obtain express written approval from the General Counsel or the Legal Department prior to making facilitating payments of any kind.

This policy is different from Apple, which doesn't allow any facilitating payments.

5. **No political contributions, even if legal.**

Other than a political contribution specifically approved in writing by the General Counsel or the Legal Department, no political contribution shall be made, directly or indirectly, with corporate funds or assets regardless of whether the contributions are legal under the laws of the country in which they are made.

* * *

Here's the full five-page anti-corruption policy:
https://fcpablog.com/wp-content/uploads/2021/03/tesla-worldwide-bribery-and-anti-corruption-policy_fcpa_blog.pdf

14.1.11 Benchmarking Alert: Here's Apple's Full Anti-corruption Policy[11], Harry Cassin, March 1, 2021

Last week, Apple debuted its new ethics and compliance site containing links to policy documents on a wide range of compliance topics. The company's anti-corruption policy includes some interesting details.

1. **A complete ban on facilitating payments.**

Facilitating payments are a type of bribe generally used to facilitate or expedite the performance of routine, non-discretionary government action. These types of payments are typically demanded by low-level officials in exchange for providing a

---

[11] https://fcpablog.com/2021/03/01/benchmarking-alert-heres-apples-full-anti-corruption-policy/

service that is ordinarily and commonly performed by the official. These payments are not permissible and are strictly prohibited by Apple.

2. **"Rumor has it." Three red flags to look out for when it comes to third parties.**

Be on the lookout for these red flags when dealing with third parties and subcontractors and alert Business Conduct if you become aware of any of the following:

- Rumors of, or a reputation for, bribery;
- Minimal detail on invoices or expense claims involving interactions with public officials or government agencies, including lump sum requests, requests for large commissions or payments, or payments made through a third party or another country;
- A close relationship with a public official or ministry, or insistence on using a specific consultant or one who provides little to no obvious added value.

3. **An expansive view of who is a public official.**

A "public official" is any person who is paid with government funds or serves in a public function. This includes individuals who work for a local, state/provincial or national government, or a public international organization, as well as employees of public (government-owned or operated) schools, hospitals, and state-owned enterprises. Employees at such organizations are considered public officials regardless of title or position.

4. **A country-by-country chart for meal limits for public officials.**

Meals provided to non-U.S. public employees and officials must comply with the posted country-by-country chart of Permissible Limits for Business Meals Provided to Non U.S. Public Officials.

5. **Travel expenses for public officials are allowed, but they all have to be pre-approved.**

If permitted under local law, Apple can pay reasonable travel expenses for public employees or officials that are directly related to the promotion, demonstration, or explanation of products and services. However, all such travel expenses must be pre-approved by Business Conduct or Legal.

* * *

Apple has long been a market leader and innovator in the compliance and sustainability fields, even if we don't always understand its disclosures.

Here's the full four-page anti-corruption policy:

https://fcpablog.com/wp-content/uploads/2021/02/Apple_Anti-Corruption_Policy_FCPA_Blog.pdf

14.2 Lists of Movies

14.2.1 Movies About Fraud and Corruption

To help raise awareness, a list of fraud or corruption-flavoured movies (the description and details of the movies are courtesy of www.IMDB.com):

- **Rogue Trader** (1999)—The story of Nick Leeson, an ambitious investment broker who single-handedly bankrupted one of the oldest and most important banks (Barings Bank) in Britain. Director: James Dearden; Starring: Ewan McGregor, Anna Friel, Yves Beneyton, Betsy Brantle
- **The Wolf of Wall Street** (2013)—Based on the true story of Jordan Belfort, from his rise to a wealthy stockbroker living the high life to his fall involving crime, corruption and the federal government. Director: Martin Scorsese; Starring: Leonardo DiCaprio, Jonah Hill, Margot Robbie, Matthew McConaughey
- **The Wizard of Lies** (2017)—The fall of Bernie Madoff, whose Ponzi scheme robbed $65 billion from unsuspecting victims; the largest fraud in US history. Director: Barry Levinson; Starring: Robert De Niro, Michelle Pfeiffer, Alessandro Nivola
- **The Big Short** (2015)—In 2006–7 a group of investors bet against the US mortgage market. In their research they discover how flawed and corrupt the market is. Director: Adam McKay; Starring: Christian Bale, Steve Carell, Ryan Gosling, Brad Pitt
- **Catch Me If You Can** (2002)—A seasoned FBI agent pursues Frank Abagnale Jr. who, before his 19th birthday, successfully forged millions of dollars' worth of checks while posing as a Pan Am pilot, a doctor, and a legal prosecutor. Director: Steven Spielberg; Starring: Leonardo DiCaprio, Tom Hanks, Christopher Walken, Martin Sheen
- **Margin Call** (2011)—Follows the key people at an investment bank, over a 24-hour period, during the early stages of the 2008 financial crisis. Director: J.C. Chandor; Starring: Zachary Quinto, Stanley Tucci, Kevin Spacey, Paul Bettany
- **Enron: The Smartest Guys in the Room** (2005)—Corporate audio and videotapes tell the inside story of the scandal involving one company's manipulation of California's energy supply and its, and how its executives wrung a billion dollars out of the resulting crisis. Director: Alex Gibney; Starring: Kenneth Lay, Peter Coyote, John Beard
- **Matchstick Men** (2003)—A phobic con artist and his protégé are on the verge of pulling off a lucrative swindle when the former's teenage daughter arrives unexpectedly
- **Wall Street** (1987)—A young and impatient stockbroker is willing to do anything to get to the top, including trading on illegal inside information taken through a ruthless and greedy corporate raider who takes the youth under his wing. Director: Oliver Stone; Starring: Charlie Sheen, Michael Douglas, Tamara Tunie, Franklin Cover

- **Wall Street 2: Money Never Sleeps** (2010)—Now out of prison but still disgraced by his peers, Gordon Gekko works his future son-in-law, an idealistic stock broker, when he sees an opportunity to take down a Wall Street enemy and rebuild his empire. Director: Oliver Stone; Starring: Shia LaBeouf, Michael Douglas, Carey Mulligan, Josh Brolin
- **Too Big To Fail** (2011)—Chronicles the financial meltdown of 2008 and centers on Treasury Secretary Henry Paulson. Director: Curtis Hanson; Starring: James Woods, John Heard, William Hurt, Erin Dilly
- **Working Girl** (1988)—When a secretary's idea is stolen by her boss, she seizes an opportunity to steal it back by pretending she has her boss' job. Director: Mike Nichols; Starring: Melanie Griffith, Harrison Ford, Sigourney Weaver, Alec Baldwin
- **The Bank** (2001)—The Bank is a thriller about banking, corruption and alchemy. Director: Robert Connolly; Starring: David Wenham, Anthony LaPaglia, Sibylla Budd, Steve Rodgers
- **Boiler Room** (2000)—A college dropout, attempting to win back his father's high standards he gets a job as a broker for a suburban investment firm, which puts him on the fast track to success, but the job might not be as legitimate as it once appeared to be. Director: Ben Younger; Starring: Giovanni Ribisi, Vin Diesel, Nia Long, Nicky Katt
- **The Laundromat** (2019)—A widow investigates an insurance fraud chases leads to a pair of Panama City law partners exploiting the world's financial system. Director: Steven Soderbergh; Starring: Meryl Streep, Gary Oldman, Antonio Banderas
- **Betting on Zero** (2016)—Documentary about hedge fund titan Bill Ackman and Herbalife. Writer-Director: Ted Braun
- **L'Argent** (1983)—A forged 500-franc note is passed from person to person until carelessness leads to tragedy. Director: Robert Bresson, Writer: Leo Tolstoy (inspired by "Faux billet"), starring: Christian Patey, Sylvie Van den Elsen, Michel Briguet
- **Inside Job** (2010)—Takes a closer look at what brought about the 2008 financial meltdown. Director: Charles Ferguson, starring: Matt Damon, Gylfi Zoega, Andri Snær Magnason.
- **To Live and Die in LA** (1985)—A fearless Secret Service agent will stop at nothing to bring down the counterfeiter who killed his partner. Director: William Friedkin, starring: William Petersen, Willem Dafoe, John Pankow
- **Floored** (2009)—For some people, risking everything is nothing. Director: James Allen Smith, starring: Bobby Ansani, Jeff Ansani, Ron Beebe
- **The Inventor: Out for Blood in Silicon Valley** (2019)—The story of Theranos, a multi-billion dollar tech company, its founder Elizabeth Holmes, the youngest self-made female billionaire and the massive fraud that collapsed the company. Director: Alex Gibney, starring: Alex Gibney, Elizabeth Holmes, Dan Ariely
- **Panic: The Untold Story of the 2008 Financial Crisis** (2018)—This documentary looks at the factors that led to the 2008 financial crisis and the efforts made by then Treasury Secretary Henry Paulson, Federal Reserve Bank of New York

President Timothy Geithner, and Federal Reserve Chair Ben Bernanke to save the United States from an economic collapse. Director: John Maggio, starring: Gary Ackerman, Ben Bernanke, Jill Biden
- **Michael Clayton** (2007)—A law firm brings in its "fixer" to remedy the situation after a lawyer has a breakdown while representing a chemical company that he knows is guilty in a multibillion-dollar class action suit. Director: Tony Gilroy, starring: George Clooney, Tilda Swinton, Tom Wilkinson
- **American Hustle** (2013)—A con man, Irving Rosenfeld, along with his seductive partner Sydney Prosser, is forced to work for a wild F.B.I. Agent, Richie DiMaso, who pushes them into a world of Jersey powerbrokers and the Mafia. Director: David O. Russell, starring: Christian Bale, Amy Adams, Bradley Cooper
- **Can You Ever Forgive Me?** (2018)—When Lee Israel falls out of step with current tastes, she turns her art form to deception. Director: Marielle Heller, starring: Melissa McCarthy, Richard E. Grant, Dolly Wells
- **Chasing Madoff** (2010)—A look at how one investigator spent ten years trying to expose Bernie Madoff's massive Ponzi scheme that scammed an estimated USD 18 billion from investors. Director: Jeff Prosserman, starring: Bernie Madoff, Frank Casey, Gaytri Kachroo
- **The Insider** (1999)—A research chemist comes under personal and professional attack when he decides to appear in a 60 Minutes exposé on Big Tobacco. Director: Michael Mann, starring: Russell Crowe, Al Pacino, Christopher Plummer
- **Money Monster** (2016)—Financial TV host Lee Gates and his producer Patty are put in an extreme situation when an irate investor takes them and their crew as hostage. Director: Jodie Foster, starring: George Clooney, Julia Roberts, Jack O'Connell
- **Bad Banks** (2018)—TV mini-series (12 episodes). Ambitious Jana is confronted with the unscrupulous machinations of the world of finance. Her working life is determined by egotism, the pressure to succeed and machismo. She soon has to decide how far she is prepared to go for her career. Creator: Oliver Kienle, starring: Paula Beer, Barry Atsma, Désirée Nosbusch
- **Madoff** (2016)—TV mini-series. The rise and fall of Bernie Madoff, whose Ponzi scheme bilked USD 65 billion from unsuspecting victims; the largest fraud in US history. Stars: Drew Gregory, Bruce Altman, Anthony Arkin
- **Rising High** (2020, original German title: Betonrausch)—Charting the rise and fall of three corrupt real estate agents who accumulate absurd wealth in no time but fall into a vortex of fraud, greed and drugs. Director: Cüneyt Kaya, starring: Emily Goss, David Kross, Frederick Lau
- **The China Hustle** (2018)—An unsettling and eye-opening Wall Street horror story about Chinese companies, the American stock market, and the opportunistic greed behind the biggest heist you've never heard of. Director: Jed Rothstein, starring: Soren Aandahl, Carson Block, Dan David
- **Win It All** (2017)—A small-time gambler agrees to stash a bag for an acquaintance who is heading to prison. When he discovers cash in the bag, he can't resist

the urge to dip into the funds. Director: Joe Swanberg, starring: Jake Johnson, Rony Shemon, Morgan Ng
- **Baazaar** (2018)—A wide-eyed graduate learns the ugly side of ambition when he joins in the dubious business practices of his idol, a ruthless Mumbai stock tycoon. Director: Gauravv K. Chawla, starring: Radhika Apte, Saif Ali Khan, Chitrangda Singh

In addition, FCPA Blog carried an article by Richard Cassin (17 March 2020) with the following suggested films (mainly additional but some overlap):

1. The Big Short (2015)
2. Margin Call (2011)
3. The Big Easy (1986)
4. A Most Violent Year (2014)
5. American Hustle (2013)
6. The Wolf of Wall Street (2013)
7. Syriana (2005)

With honorable mentions for the following:

- The Godfather: Part II (1974),
- L.A. Confidential (1997),
- Serpico (1973), and
- The Firm (1993).

14.2.2 Movies about Whistleblowers

Transparency International (the global NGO working to end corruption) prepared and published the following movie list about whistleblowers (there are summaries of the movies on Transparency International's blog[12] or on www.lmbd.com):

- Serpico
- The Laundromat
- Erin Brockovitch
- The Insider
- Snowden
- Crime and Punishment
- The Post
- Silkwood
- The Informant
- All the President's Men
- Official Secrets

---

[12] https://www.transparency.org/en/blog/11-movies-about-whistleblowers-that-you-cannot-miss

14.2 Lists of Movies

TI's announcement resulted in these other movies being mentioned in comments:

- The Constant Gardener
- The Band Played On
- Dark Waters
- The Report
- The Whistleblower
- Mr Smith Goes To Washington
- The Great Hack

Other possible movies include:

- The Clearstream Affair;
- Class Action;
- Two movies on Assange—We Steal Secrets and The Fifth Estate;
- Fair Game;
- North Country; and
- A documentary, Citizenfour

Printed by Printforce, United Kingdom